W9-APO-340

SPORTS

IN

NORTH

AMERICA

DEDICATION

To My Mother and Father,
Iola and Joseph Menna

SPORTS
IN
NORTH AMERICA

A DOCUMENTARY HISTORY

EDITED BY
LARRY K. MENNA

VOLUME 2

THE ORIGINS OF MODERN SPORTS

1820–1840

Academic International Press

1995

SPORTS IN NORTH AMERICA. A DOCUMENTARY HISTORY
VOLUME 2. ORIGINS OF MODERN SPORTS, 1820–1840
Edited by Larry K. Menna

Copyright © 1995 by Academic International Press

ISBN: 0-87569-136-6

Composition by Janice Frye

Printed in the United States of America

By direct subscription with the publisher

A list of Academic International Press publications
is found at the end of this volume

ACADEMIC INTERNATIONAL PRESS
POB 1111 • Gulf Breeze FL 32562–1111 • USA

CONTENTS

Indexes

PREFACE

This volume is a collection of the most important and representative primary documents concerning the transformation of sports in North America from 1821 to 1840. These documents, taken in whole or in part from books, journals, newspapers, and pamphlets of the era, are diverse: rules and regulations of sporting clubs, newspaper reports of local, national and international competitions, accounts of wildlife experiences, reminiscences of sporting events or games, letters, editorials, and other suitable materials. These documents are reprints of the originals, except for excerpted materials where text has been deleted for clarity or to meet space requirements. Otherwise, spellings and other language have remained faithful to the original documents, including errors and illegibilities.

The Introduction summarizes the major developments that transformed sports and pastimes in North America from 1821 to 1840. Industrialization, urbanization, immigration, class disparities, gender and racial issues, and others all played important roles in the evolution of sports during this period. The material in Chapters 1 and 2 establishes the foundation for the remaining chapters. Chapter 1 presents sources that demonstrate many of the ideological shifts and biases toward physical exercise, health, and gambling which often served to hasten as well as hinder the emergence of modern sports. Chapter 2 documents the development of sports journalism and writing. The greater attention given to sports and pastimes both reflected and contributed to the growing role of sports in American and Canadian cultures. The other chapters tell the history of either specific sports, such as horse racing or boating and rowing, or groups of sports and games, such as field sports or animal sports, emphasizing the social, cultural, economic and political forces that shaped the third and fourth decades of the nineteenth century.

The organization of this volume posed several challenges to the historian which require a few methodological explanations. First, the definition of sport itself was problematic, because much of sport in the United States and Canada from 1821 to 1840 possessed a premodern character and thus defied modern definitions, criteria, or characterizations. If sport is defined as organized competition based on physical activity or exertion, then many of the so-called sports in this volume would be excluded. But to dismiss sports because of their premodern character would distort the development and evolution of sport in North America. This volume is intended to present the transformation of sport from its premodern origins to the beginnings of its various modern forms. Accordingly, this volume contains many games, pastimes, or activities vital to North America's early sporting heritage. Many of these activities such as rounders, cricket or football developed into more organized sports later in the nineteenth century. Some did not, eventually disappearing from the sporting scene. At least one, cricket, did both. This volume offers some reasons behind the subsequent success or failure of these pastimes by examining their roots.

The second difficulty, organization of the volume, was a direct offshoot of the first. Because many of these sports were premodern, modern conceptions of organizing and grouping various sports and games into chapters were often irrelevant, inapplicable, or inappropriate. Thus, some chapters in this volume present many sports and other activities in a different organizational context than in subsequent volumes for the sake of clarity and accuracy. For example, baseball and cricket did not deserve chapters of their own in this volume because the former was not more important during this period than many other ball sports and other pastimes such as quoits and fives, while cricket, though showing signs of modernization during the late 1830s, remained an unorganized, informal sport until the following decade. Most of the ball sports and popular premodern amusements are under one chapter heading. The grouping of some sports for later periods under the heading of pub sports failed to have any substantial meaning between 1821–1840. Though some sports were sometimes associated with pubs during the early nineteenth century, many of them, such as billiards, were more accurately identified with the private homes and parlors of the upper classes. Though some historians have preferred to organize sports in categories of strength and skill, I believe they failed to provide adequate differentiation, further confounding matters, as most sports or games during this period could fall easily under such headings.

The final problem was the paucity of documentation, especially for the 1820s. Many of the sports newspapers were established during the 1830s and those founded during the previous decade often relied on English sports journals for information and news. Despite the existence of other daily presses from 1821–1840, few references or accounts detailed many of the pastimes and activities because of the informal, unorganized, and local nature of the competitions and the participatory aspect of sports until the 1830s, when sport and sports reporting made their first moves toward their modern forms. The sources chosen reflect many aspects of the sports, games, and activities of the era, including class, race, ethnicity, gender, geography, and politics. This volume includes several sources that describe the experiences of women, Native Americans, and various ethnic groups. Blacks receive less treatment than other groups owing to the scarcity of resources. While the sources are diverse, they still reflect the athletic and cultural dominance of white middle and upper classes during the period. Despite efforts to include material from diverse geographical areas these documents recount the ascendancy of major urban areas such as New York, Philadelphia, Boston, Toronto and Montreal in the growth, development and coverage of sports in North America.

It is impossible to conduct research for a volume of this nature without the invaluable assistance of librarians and staff, and I would like to express my gratitude and appreciation to all those who helped me at the following institutions: the New York Public Library, the Boston Public Library, the Widener, Houghton, Pusey and Gutman Libraries of Harvard University, the Columbia University Library, the Starr Library of Middlebury College, and the New-York Historical Society. I would particularly like to thank George Kirsch of Manhattan College, who kindly recommended me for this project. His sound scholarly guidance and suggestions improved my work, and his friendship along the way was much appreciated. I also appreciate the efforts of Kris Lauer of Fordham University, whose critical reading of parts of the manuscript improved my prose. I would like to thank Irene Keogh, Bellinda Wise, and Lois Johnson, librarians at Greenley Library, the State University of New York, Farmingdale, for cheerfully processing what must have seemed like an endless stream of requests. I also would like to thank United University Professions for a 1993 Faculty Development Award which helped bring this project to completion. I appreciate the efforts of my student assistants, particularly Catherine Miller, whose last minute assistance was crucial.

I would like to acknowledge a special bond to Joyce Bartle and her eight–year–old son, Matt, whose own love of sports, I hope, will one day lead him to learn their history through this and other volumes in the series. Their support and understanding have been invaluable in the writing, researching, and compiling that went into this work. I have chosen to dedicate this book to my mother and father, who instilled in me at an early age the importance of learning and who made sure, at great sacrifice to themselves, that I received the best opportunities to further my education.

Larry K. Menna

State University of New York, Farmingdale

INTRODUCTION

The period from 1821 to 1840 is crucial to our understanding of the nature and evolution of sports in North America for two reasons. First, during this period sports experienced fundamental, often dramatic change that provided the foundation for the modernization of sports and the growth of spectator sports in the mid- to late nineteenth century. In this twenty-year span the beginning of the transformation of sports from a premodern to a modern activity occurred. This transition to modern sports has been paradoxically understudied by historians, yet overemphasized in the scholarly literature examining this era. More importantly, these changes were so extensive that they deserve scholarly treatment in their own right and not, as often has been the case, as merely preconditions or precursors to the subsequent development of modern sports. Second, the antebellum period experienced tremendous social, economic, cultural, and political changes that directly and indirectly influenced the evolution of sports and, at the same time, were given meaning and expression through sports. This reciprocal relationship, or dynamic, between sports and society must transcend simplistic, vague connections between such forces as urbanization or industrialization and the rise of sports to include the specific ways in which sports became part of the social and cultural fabric.

From 1821 to 1840 sports and pastimes in the United States and Canada reflected the heritage of the various nations that colonized the continent—England, France, Holland, and Spain, but none more so than that of Britain. Most of the colonies in the New World had English origins and those that did not, such as New York, either were influenced strongly by British traditions and customs or, by the late colonial period, came under English control. As a result, the English legacy was evident in the cultural, political, and social practices of Americans and Canadians alike.

Amusements, pastimes, and sports were no exceptions. The extensive development of sports and sport reporting in England exerted a constant influence on North American sports and served as a standard of excellence for which sportsmen on this side of the Atlantic could strive. Foxhunting, boxing, horse racing, and cricket were but a few of the activities that North Americans transported and adapted to their new surroundings. Yet, as late as 1840, sportsmen in North America relied on British book and journal publications for information about horse and dog breeding, rules and regulations, and equipment, even after the establishment of sports journals in the United States. Most of the published material in American journals such as The American Farmer and The Spirit of the Times were drawn from influential British sports publications such as Bell's Life in London and The English Sporting Magazine, and many of the more popular sporting books in Britain found a ready American audience in both English and American editions.

Moreover, American dependence extended to equipment and technology. Most of the guns, ammunition, bows, strings, saddles and bridles, and fishing gear were imported from England, and the horses and dogs used in hunting and racing were either imported from Britain or of British descent. Thus, many sports in North America from 1821 to 1840 reflected their English roots and traditions and owed a tremendous debt to the British sporting scene. Only towards the latter part of this period did North American sportsmen begin to challenge seriously their British counterparts for supremacy in only a few sports and initiate the process of development that would culminate decades later in the ascendancy of such so-called "American" spectator sports as baseball and football.

Although Britain exerted the most influence in the development of sports in North America, by no means was it the only important European influence. Scottish traditions found expressions in curling and athletic games in both Canada and America; Dutch culture and technological innovations contributed to the popularity and development of skating, especially in New York City; and German reformers, after launching the gymnastic movement in their country, introduced the sport and its principles to a receptive American audience.

As much as North American sports were influenced by their European heritages, they were equally shaped by historical developments and changes as well as the landscape and environment of the United States and Canada. One of the most important forces vital to understanding the development of sports and recreation was urbanization. Although the pace of urbanization and industrialization accelerated dramatically after 1840, it had increased significantly in the previous twenty years. As farmers in such areas as New England and the Middle States experienced demographic pressures and economic competition from the West rural family members and farmers themselves moved to the city in search of employment. Technological innovations and improvements in transportation further fueled industrial and commercial expansion and the growth of large and medium-sized cities. Gradually, commercial and industrial subregions and regions emerged, with local farmers supplying the cities with various specialized crops and products, and merchants and manufacturers sending finished goods to the nearby countryside.

The movement from rural to urban areas disrupted previous living patterns, produced different cultural and social attitudes, values and fears, and generated new lifestyles. In particular urbanization, along with manufacturing and commerce, altered the practice of sports and pastimes. Urban growth pushed the hinterlands farther away and created spatial considerations previously absent from rural America. Such frontier and rural sports and activities as hunting and animal baiting became difficult within urban areas and their immediate vicinities; soon sportsmen substituted new sports such as pigeon and target shooting to maintain their skills and to satiate their sporting appetites. Urban growth not only curtailed some of the activities of rural America and Canada but placed greater limits on physical exercise in general within what was considered an unhealthy environment. As a result, professionals such as physicians and health reformers during the early nineteenth century emphasized the connection between physical exercise and health. The subsequent close association of physical exercise with improved health in the public mind became one of the most powerful societal justifications for sports and an important precondition for the emergence of modern sports. Furthermore, this rationale, by asserting its practical benefits, imparted a legitimacy and a value that sports had previously lacked.

Urbanization also affected the development of sports and amusements in other significant ways, not all of them positive. The movement from the countryside to the cities, which particularly involved young, single men and women, undermined traditional patterns of family authority and supervision. Antebellum moralists decried the loss of parental control but they also accepted the demographic shifts from country to city. Consequently, such writers as William Alcott sought to inculcate self-control, character, and moral rectitude in adolescents and young adults as a counterbalance to the social dangers uniquely posed by urban society. Included among the corrupting influences were, of course, the gambling and drinking associated with many urban sports and pastimes such as horse racing, billiards, and boxing. Before many sports could assume their modern form, the widespread public commitment to these moral beliefs would have to be substantially weakened. Not surprisingly, the physical and psychological dimensions of urban life created the need for diversions provided by amusements and sports and hastened the decline of traditional morality.

The impersonal nature of urban life also caused residents to form a variety of associations, based on common or shared interests, backgrounds or experiences. The creation of sports organizations and clubs served many functions but one of the most significant was to establish social bonds and to maintain societal cohesion. These new organizations became attempts to replace traditional forms of authority that were challenged and destroyed by urbanization with newer, more horizontal forms of allegiances. In rowing and yachting, horse racing, rackets, cricket, and quoits, for example, clubs provided their members with a social life by holding informal social gatherings at the conclusion of sporting activities or by sponsoring formal balls and seasonal events.

The increase in sporting clubs was related to another significant development during the antebellum period—the deepening chasm between rich and poor. Although this disparity existed in both city and country in the first half of the nineteenth century, its effects were more visible in urban areas. By about 1830, in New York, Boston and other major cities, 4 or 5 percent of the people owned over half of the wealth and in the decades ahead the gulf between rich and poor would only widen. Very rarely did the lower classes escape the drudgery and poverty of their daily labor and meager existence. Alarmed by the growing inequalities of urban life and the inapplicability of the American Dream to the existence of immigrants, blacks, and the lower classes, the middle classes sought to ameliorate the conditions of the masses and assimilate them in middle class culture by forming a variety of voluntary organizations, especially benevolent associations.

Amidst these socioeconomic disparities the wealthiest classes in urban areas segregated themselves from the masses by residing in exclusive neighborhoods and forming social clubs, including sports organizations. From 1821 to 1840 many sporting clubs were initially the domain of the upper classes, though toward the end of this period some clubs began to attract or allow middle class members. Two of the fastest growing and most popular spectator sports of the era—boat and horse racing—reflected their elitist origins and domination by their wealthy participants. In the early nineteenth century, clubs were social institutions through which the upper and upper-middle classes asserted their social ascendancy. Interclub rowing matches during the 1830s, for example, were less competitive contests than social events among, and for the amusement of, the upper classes. Even pugilism, which later became associated with working classes and foreigners, for a time attracted elite gentlemen to its ranks through the establishment of gymnasiums for sparring.

Despite the association of sport clubs with the wealthy the emerging upper-middle and middle classes played significant roles in their creation, organization, and maintenance. Throughout the second quarter of the century membership in many sports clubs simultaneously served different functions. It offered the middle classes the opportunities both to aspire to greater wealth by mingling with the rich and powerful and to distance themselves from the lower or working classes.

For the most part, however, the working classes lived closer to subsistence level and obviously possessed limited means to participate in many sports and amusements. Yet, within the urban environment, in place of formal organizations and clubs, working men often substituted informal meeting places. In their world the tavern or saloon provided the same social functions as the associations and clubs did for the wealthy. Sports and games such as billiards, shooting, and boxing became important social events and competitive contests at local or neighborhood pubs. The familiar atmosphere of the tavern was a natural choice for working men to conduct these activities and the drinking, gambling, and raucous behavior that became part and parcel of these contests were a byproduct of the location as well as of the values and culture of the clientele.

Within this working class world immigrants played an important role. Although the wave of Irish and German immigrants did not occur until after 1840 immigrants were a crucial element of the working force and in some cities, such as New York, actually formed a majority. They brought to North America their own customs, traditions, values, and habits, and once here, sought to maintain them through a variety of institutions, organizations, and associations. In particular, immigrants practiced the sports and games they had learned in their native country and, as a result, popularized many of them. Well-known English and Irish boxers traveled to North America to give exhibitions and to conduct matches. During the 1820s Germans introduced gymnastics into the United States as part of school reform, initially at the Round Hill School in Northampton, Massachusetts and later at Harvard, Yale, and other colleges and universities. Many other activities such as rackets, rounders, boating, and cricket likewise carried on their foreign heritages in America and Canada through native sons.

The perpetuation of foreign cultures through sports and games in North America acquired deeper social meanings and constituted significant cultural expressions within a rapidly changing antebellum society. Local sports heroes not only unified immigrant neighborhoods and increased national pride within a foreign North America but, more importantly, embodied long-standing ethnic hostilities among the lower classes through their athletic feats and competitions. Thus, boxing matches in which the combatants were often immigrants regularly erupted into street brawls, pitting the ethnic supporters of one fighter against those of another.

Moreover, although the emphasis on sports and physical exercise at times undermined traditional gender roles and concepts of gender within antebellum society, sports as a cultural expression more often than not reflected and preserved existing gender relations. The economic and social independence that young women gained through working in the New England textile mills, for example, would take another generation before reaching cultural expression in the women's movement during the 1840s and several more before effecting many deep political, economic, and cultural changes. From 1821 to 1840 the participation of women in many sports and amusements was limited by society's conception of their proper place and demonstrations of female skill and strength violated societal notions of femininity and beauty during much of the antebellum period. Except for sleighing, horseback riding, and perhaps dancing—activities which allegedly possessed demonstrated health and moral benefits, women were excluded from participation in most sports and games. As a result, sports and pastimes perpetuated male domination within the society and the formation of clubs further increased the activities of the male outside the home. The male atmosphere of the tavern, for example, reinforced the bachelor predilections of its clientele, and even the social events of wealthy sports clubs likewise served to maintain, rather than challenge, the traditional gender roles of both upper class men and women.

Perhaps more than any other development during the second quarter of the nineteenth century, the beginning of the lengthy process of societal ordering and economic and commercial rationalization affected the evolution of sports and pastimes. Although this process culminated at the end of the century its early forms were already beginning to take shape from 1821 to 1840. The transportation revolution, symbolized by the completion of the Erie Canal in 1825, the stirrings of industrialization, and the growth of commerce and the market economy in many areas heralded a new era that would forever change North America. Although the political and social responses to this ordering process would not be resolved during the antebellum period, America and Canada began to debate and confront, sometimes peacefully, sometimes not, the complex issues involved.

Sports and pastimes in North America were affected by these demographic, social, economic, technological, and political changes. They were likewise propelled by the force of their own internal development apart from the environment within which they either thrived or declined. As some sports and games grew in cultural importance, participants kept records, established uniform rules and regulations, created institutions and associations, and initiated formal competitions—all of which produced greater newspaper and magazine coverage. In a sense, then, sports in North America from 1821 to 1840 both moved within the changes of the early to mid-nineteenth century and yet generated their own transformations.

Chapter 1

CHANGING ATTITUDES TOWARD EXERCISE AND SPORT

The period from 1820 to 1840 witnessed an important shift in the attitudes and ideas about exercise, athletics and sport that at once mirrored and influenced the robust expansion of the young republic. The increased interest in health, physical fitness, and sport during early nineteenth-century America signaled the rejection of earlier notions and conceptions of exercise and the convergence of new intellectual currents and historical developments. Although these changes set in motion forces that would not reach full expression or fruition until mid-century, they played an important role in American culture and society during the 1820s and 1830s and constituted a necessary step in the evolution of modern sport, particularly the development of organized athletic competition.

The intellectual and ideological transformation in exercise and sport during the early nineteenth century was dramatic. Prior to 1820, Puritan notions of exercise and leisure still proved remarkably strong in American culture, despite the steady decline of Puritanism since the late 1600s. In the Puritan world, leisure, which included sport and games, weakened society's collective religious commitment and devotion, and corrupted the morals of its members, especially because of the close association of sport with gambling. In addition, the expenditure of energy on frivolous leisure activities reduced the attention and effort devoted to more productive pursuits beneficial to all. In this chapter, the excerpt from William Alcott's A Young Man's Guide discusses the moral dimensions of gambling and demonstrates the persistence of Puritan morality well into the 1830s.

But, after 1820 or so, many influential groups in American society repudiated this legacy and developed different attitudes toward health, exercise and sport. Drawing on ancient and Enlightenment philosophical traditions, educational reformers, health advocates, utopian communities, and physicians emphasized the unity, not the separation, of the mind and the body, and sought to implement this idea in their respective endeavors. According to these groups a healthy body provided the foundation for intellectual achievement, sound morality, and character development. As a result, exercise and sport quickly became the means to attain such health and its formidable intangible benefits. By the late 1800s, sport had been transformed into the proving ground for the assertion of manliness and strength of character, a legacy which remains relevant today. "An Oration Delivered at Middlebury," by an alumnus of that college, and "On Exercise," an article from the American Turf Register, discuss the connection between physical, moral, and intellectual development.

However important ideological developments were to the changing attitudes toward physical fitness and sport from 1820 to 1840, they were of less significance than the spectacular historical developments of the era. Jacksonian America witnessed not only the democratization of politics but also the beginnings of urbanization and industrialization. As a consequence, new problems peculiar to the city emerged as did reform efforts to rectify them. With increasingly large numbers of people concentrated in

smaller areas, such issues as health, education, and poverty became significant to the
overall vitality and quality of city life. Soon, concern over these social ills engendered
a plethora of reform movements in addressing temperance, public schools, asylums and
prisons, and women's rights. And when foreigners, especially the English, criticized
Americans for their physical degeneration and inactivity and their failure to live up to
the physical rigors once demanded by frontier life, Americans, with their pride insulted,
were left with little alternative but to take action.

Within this atmosphere, exercise and sport offered to many reformers a viable solution to urban problems. Educational reformers such as Horace Mann supported the
introduction of playgrounds at elementary schools in order to overcome the intellec-
tually debilitating effects of sedentary instruction and confining schoolrooms on children. The educational movement also advocated the integration of gymnastics into
school curricula. Perhaps the most famous early experiment along these lines was the
founding of the Round Hill School in Northhampton, Massachusetts in 1823 by George
Bancroft and Joseph Cogswell. There, Charles Beck built a gymnasium and taught
gymnastics to the school's students in the hope of ending the neglect of children's
physical, and hence, mental and moral development. Characteristic of the Age of Jackson, the common or public elementary school movement instilled in youth the importance of citizenship to the successful operation of a republic and of self-improvement
as a function of the relationship between mind and body. "The Report of the Secretary
of the Board of Education," by Horace Mann, documents the integration of play-
grounds into public schools in Massachusetts.

Others groups also advocated exercise and sport as an antidote to the social ills of
Jacksonian America. A burgeoning literature by physicians documented the physiologi-
cal foundation to the benefits of exercise on intellectual achievement and moral development. Utopian communities, such as Brook Farm in Massachusetts, New Harmony
in Indiana, and Oneida in New York, propounded the interdependence of the mind and
body and made physical exercise and play a fundamental part of their experiments in
social organization. Health reformers wrote numerous exercise manuals for parents and
teachers, instructing them in the correct and proper form, techniques and movements
of calisthenic exercises. Women in particular were the focus of many of these manuals. Reformers such as Margaret Coxe and Catherine Beecher asserted that exercise was
as crucial to the development of women as it was to that of men and encouraged their
fellow females to exercise, arguing that it enhanced natural feminine grace and beauty.
In this section, "The Female Student" by Almira Phelps and "A Course of Calisthenics" by an anonymous author addresses these gender issues.

The efforts of these groups spurred the development of exercise and sport and a
press that specifically dealt with health, physical exercise, and sport during the 1820s
and 1830s. The press disseminated and popularized these conceptions of mind and
body, albeit with an inconsistency characteristic of such endeavors, and made sport an
increasingly vital and acceptable aspect of American culture. By 1830, horse racing,
pedestrianism, boxing, and yachting and boating had received increased interest from
the public, despite vicissitudes in their appeal and success. During the next several
decades, other sports would generate followings of their own, but by then sport had

become much more organized and competitive, associated with its own set of Victorian values, and leisure, play, and sport had acquired a legitimacy and popularity denied them during the antebellum period.

THE VALUE OF MORAL, INTELLECTUAL AND PHYSICAL DEVELOPMENT

The integration of physical exercise, intellectual development, and moral discipline became a fundamental part of educational reform during the antebellum period. The following address, An Oration Delivered At Middlebury, Before the Associated Alumni of the College, on the Evening of Commencement, August 19, 1829, was delivered by John Frost, a graduate of Middlebury College and a Presbyterian minister, and is a fine example of the thinking behind such reforms. It is reprinted by permission of Middlebury College.

COMMENCEMENT ORATION AT MIDDLEBURY COLLEGE, 1829
by John Frost

MR. PRESIDENT, AND FELLOW ALUMNI,

The place where we have assembled, and the occasion on which we have convened, naturally lead our thoughts to the subject of education. No subject within the reach of human contemplation is more important, and none perhaps excites a deeper and more extended interest at the present day. The whole system of education, from the university, down through every grade, to that of the infant school, is now passing the ordeal of discussion and experiment. Universities and Colleges are changing their courses of study and discipline, and adapting them to the real or imaginary wants of their patrons. Monitorial schools, and high schools, gymnasia, polytechnic, and military schools, are springing up, and offering their peculiar advantages to the youth of our land.

At these various movements, some, too old to change, may be alarmed. Others, visionary in their temperament, or too inexperienced to estimate the danger of innovation, may be inclined to catch at novelties, which experience will prove useless. But those who have marked the improvements, which have been made with a few years, in governments, in the arts, and in almost every department of human action, will believe, that neither themselves nor their fellows are too wise to learn; and while they will not hastily abandon what has become venerable by usage, neither will they, on the other hand, tremble at discussion, nor discountenance experiment. The country in which we live is favourable to improvement. Mind, as well as body, is here *free*. Neither ecclesiastical, political, nor scholastic intolerance prevents men from speaking and publishing their thoughts on any subject. Little tyrants we have, who, if they could, would by authority awe into submission those who have the audacity to differ from them. But such is the extensive and deep-rooted aversion to arbitrary power in every form, that he who dares to tread on his neighbour is sure to rouse a republican spirit, which will soon make him repent of his temerity.

Education comprehends all that discipline and cultivation, bestowed on the powers of man, from the days of infancy and childhood, until he leaves his instructors, and enters upon the great theatre of human life. The *object of education is, or at least, ought to be, to give to all the powers of men their highest possible perfection. In other words, every youth ought to be so educated, as to enable him to answer in the highest degree, the great purposes for which he was created, both in the life that now is, and that which is to come.* This high and holy object has been overlooked or disregarded by many parents and teachers. Their only aim has been to educate those committed to their care, so as to render them conspicuous in society. Had they discovered that death was an eternal sleep, and heaven and hell more phantoms, the discovery would have led to no material change in their plan of education. An education thus conducted may gratify the pride of parents; it may fire the youthful bosom with ambition; it may create distinctions in society, which may produce hauteur and contempt in one class, and servility and envy in another; but it can never receive the approbation of Heaven, nor secure the permanent peace, prosperity and happiness of nations and individuals. As believers in christianity, we are bound to adopt a system of education which accords with the spirit of our holy religion, and which is best adapted to diffuse this spirit through every class of society, and to the remotest habitations of man.

Shall parents, taught by heaven's King, that crowns of glory are prepared for their offspring in heaven, and charged *to train them up in the way they should go,* submit to a system of education calculated to rob them of their birthright? Shall love of money, or of fame, allure them; or shall the scowls and growlings of infidelity frighten from the path of duty? No. If that helpless creature, which now clings to a mother's bosom, is destined by its Father in heaven to immortality; if, within its little heaving breast, is lodged an embryo intellect, which ere long may rank with that of an angel; if that lovely stranger is gifted with a heart, which, rightly directed, may at some future period glow with the intensity of seraphic love, while it gazes on uncreated beauty; shall it be educated not for heaven, but earth? Instead of presenting it the food of angels, shall it be insulted and degraded by feeding it with husks? The heart of christian love answers—No longer let heaven's offspring be thus abused. Give it an education worthy of its royal descent, and its high and holy destination.

But I shall have occasion to enlarge on this branch of the subject in its appropriate place.

Education is naturally divided into three great departments, *intellectual, physical, and moral.*

Intellectual education embraces the culture of the natural faculties of the mind, the understanding, the judgment, the memory, the imagination, and the taste. That system of study best adapted to develope and strengthen all powers, and thus produce what may be denominated a *cultivated* and *well balanced mind,* ought to be selected. Though much fault has been found by some with the course of studies pursued in our colleges, yet it is on the whole as favourable to intellectual improvement, as could reasonably be expected in the present state of our country. If there be any fault generally applicable to our colleges, it is, that more branches are taught than can be thoroughly taught in so short a period. It is an easy task for instructors to swell their catalogue of studies, which, if thoroughly understood, would make an accomplished scholar; but it is not so easy a task to swell four years into eight. The truth is, many branches of study taught in our colleges ought to be previously taught, and others pursued to greater extent. This would give time for the acquisition of important knowledge in our colleges, which cannot be so well acquired elsewhere. The study of languages and mathematics must constitute the basis of a thorough education. The study of ancient languages is useful to all, but is indispensable to students whose profession is to be theology. Those designed for the gospel ministry ought to be thoroughly acquainted with the original languages of the bible. It will be disgraceful to our academies and colleges and theological schools, with the facilities now enjoyed, if they do not furnish such students with sufficient knowledge of the original languages of the bible, to enable them to read it with ease, and pleasure, and profit, through life. But the fact ought not to be concealed, that the knowledge acquired has generally been so limited, that it has been of little practical utility, and by nine-tenths soon neglected and forgotten.

The Hebrew language ought now to be studied in all our colleges. If there is not sufficient time, students looking forward to the ministry ought to be exempted from the study of the Latin and Greek classics, after entering college, and devote the time thus saved to the study of the bible in the Greek and Hebrew languages. So far as intellectual cultivation is concerned, such study would be equally beneficial, and with respect to the moral influence, unspeakable more so. And so important is this study to the profession, that the church has a right to demand it from our colleges. The remarks recently published on this subject, by a professor in one of our theological institutions, claims the immediate attention of the guardians and instructors of our academies and colleges. The writer deserves the thanks of the christian community, for the independent spirit and hallowed zeal which he has manifested in relation to this important study.

Great have been the defects of the higher schools for the education of females. More attention has been paid to ornament than to the solid and useful acquisitions. Judging from their education, one would suppose the great business of their future life was to sing, to paint, and to dance. Several females, however, of great intelligence, in different parts of our country have within a few years past done much to raise the standard of female education, and to give to that portion of our species an intellectual elevation worthy of their sex; and no one perhaps has done more than that enterprising lady with whom the speaker was associated in this place in the instruction of youth, after closing his collegiate studies, and who has, by her unabated zeal and untiring efforts, from that period to the present, acquired a high and deserved reputation.

In intellectual education, the most important end to be attained is the *power* of self-improvement. He who has learned the art of employing to the best advantage the powers which God has given him, has laid the foundation on which he may build the most valuable super-structure in future life.

But it was not my intention to make extended remarks on intellectual education. Had I the ability, to which I lay no claim, to specify defects, and to point out improvements, I should have no great zeal to do this; and the main reason is, that this department of education has received, and will doubtless continue to receive, that attention which its importance merits, while physical and moral education have been shamefully and criminally neglected. Indeed, if important improvements are to be made in a system of education, designed to give the mental powers their greatest vigour and expansion, I apprehend they will principally arise from the adoption of a more thorough and judicious system for the culture of the physical and moral power of our nature. That the blessings of civilisation and christianity have not long since been enjoyed by all nations, has not been owing to the want of sufficient intellectual knowledge. Had all the energies of men of cultivated intellect been steadily directed to the advancement of the temporal and spiritual good of their species, our earth would ere this have been filled with knowledge and righteousness, and we should now have been blessed with, the long predicted, and happy day of Zion's highest glory. But the physical and moral energy, essential to the accomplishment of such a work, have been wanting.

The importance of physical education is, however, beginning to be appreciated by the more intelligent and practical portion of the community. Some, like the speaker, have been taught its importance, by the evils they have personally experienced through its neglect. Had their physical education been conducted in accordance with the laws of Hygeia, their intellectual attainments and their usefulness might have been far greater. The frequent instances of bodily and mental debility and disease occasioned by application to study, without sufficient exercise, have excited alarm, and led to inquiry for a remedy. It is believed that at least one-fourth of those who pass through a course of education for the learned professions, sink into a premature grave, or drag out a miserable and comparatively useless life, under a broken constitution. At sufferings thus produced, humanity weeps. The loss of useful talent, sustained by the community, and especially by the church, is also severe, and calls loudly for reform. Sickness and death will come sooner or later on all: But God forbids both murder and suicide: And teachers should take heed that they are not found guilty of the one, nor their pupils of the other. A reform has commenced. It is witnessed in our infant schools, where, instead of confining children to their seats for hours together, they are permitted to enjoy that freedom of bodily action which nature dictates. Bodily activity is united with mental cultivation. Thus that cheerfulness and innocent pleasure, which are the birthright of children, are secured, and the idea of happiness is associated in the infant mind with that of mental and moral cultivation.

The fact that the body and mind have a powerful influence upon each other, is well known. How often do we see the most vigorous mind rendered incapable of effort, when the body has become enfeebled by disease? And when the mind is borne down under disappointment and suffering, how often does the body become pale and emaciated, till at length it sinks under the oppressive load? These facts being admitted, it is not necessary that we should possess the knowledge of the physician, and be able to describe every part of this complicated machine, and the various effects which may be produced upon its fluids and solids by different causes, in order to appreciate the importance of a system of discipline, which shall give the greatest possible energy to both body and mind.

The Greeks and Romans were not insensible of the importance of physical education. Gymnastic sports of various kinds were connected with their schools, for the purpose of giving the utmost strength, hardihood and activity to the bodies of their youth. Of late years, gymnastic and military exercises have been introduced into seminaries of learning, in Europe and in this country. These facts show that serious evils exist, and that the public mind is waking up to this subject. But it is not yet half awake to its unspeakable importance. As God designed man for great mental as well as bodily effort, it would be a reflection on his wisdom to suppose, that properly regulated, these efforts are injurious to health. There is a fault somewhere. Who dare charge it upon our Maker? It must be sought in ourselves. A proper attention to facts will teach us in what it consists, and suggest the remedy. The time will come, when the most cultivated and vigorous minds will be found connected with the most energetic bodies.

"The languid eye; the cheek
Deserted of it bloom; the flaccid, shrunk,
And wither'd muscle, and the vapid soul,"

ought as rarely to be found in our academic halls, as in the habitations of our hardy yeomanry. "*Sana mens, in corpore sano*," is, with proper management, emphatically the privilege of students. They may enjoy even better health than the most laborious. Alternation of bodily and mental effort will be found more favourable to health, than the long continued muscular action of the farmer and the mechanic. Studious men have more knowledge of the regimen essential to health than others; and their situation for following it is generally more favourable. That "temperance in all things," which God has enjoined, especially in eating and drinking, united with that exercise of the mental and physical powers for which he made us, will be found to insure the most perfect health.

But all the evils experienced from bodily weakness and disease, are not the fault of students, nor of the present generation. Physical debility, and a predisposition to many diseases, are the inheritance left us by our forefathers. Men have not that mental and physical strength and activity which they would have inherited, had their predecessors conformed to the divine will, and strove to be "*temperate in all things.*" We have not that strength of constitution possessed by the ancient Hebrews, or even the Greeks and Romans, with all their vices. Where, in modern times, has a leader in the armies of Israel appeared, who, like Moses, was able, at eighty years of age, to conduct them on to the promised land; and of whom it might be said, at the advanced age of one hundred and twenty, that "*his eye was not dim, nor his natural force abated.*" That Moses had a remarkable constitution for that age, is probable. But it is equally probable, that a departure from the simplicity of nature, and the introduction of luxuries and vices, operating through many successive generations, have produced a deterioration in the human constitution. This may be one way in which God "visits the iniquities of the fathers upon the children, unto the third and fourth generation;" and if so, the combined efforts of three or four generations are necessary to the entire removal of the curse. Let such a system of physical and moral education be universally adopted, as is necessary to make the experiment, and doubtless the human constitution would be highly improved, many diseases banished, and the period of human life lengthened. Then would be witnessed in the church what Isaiah saw in prophetic vision: "There shall no more be seen there an infant of days", nor an old man that hath not filled his days; for the child shall die an hundred years old. For as the days of a *free*, shall be the days of my people; and mine elect shall *long enjoy* the work of their hands."

The manner in which the children, and especially the daughters, of many parents, are educated, tends to produce a delicacy of constitution, which unfits them to meet the unavoidable ills, or to perform the important duties of future life. The daughters of wealthy and fashionable parents are not unfrequently shut up, during their early years, in warm rooms, like exotic plants in a hot house, through fear of exposure. At length they are sent aboard to a boarding school, to obtain what is termed an accomplished education. Having acquired a smattering of literature and science, and attended to painting, and music, and dancing, they return home. Here, instead of becoming acquainted with domestic affairs, under the eye and direction of a mother, and learning what would contribute much both to their usefulness and happiness, amid the sober realities of married life, they are seated most of the day in the parlour, with their needle or their novel, or decked out in all the extravagance of fashion, to attract the attention of the gay and superficial; to please, and be pleased. By management like this, many a fair female, who, with judicious training, might have been an ornament to her sex and a blessing to the world, is rendered vain and trifling. In married life she become the subject of nervous debility and a thousand nameless ills, a source of perpetual anxiety and disappointment to her husband, a burden to herself, a curse to her offspring, and an offence to God.

No greater evil can befal a young man of sense and virtue, than to be united with a female, whose naturally delicate frame has been subjected to all the enervating processes of fashionable life; whose passions have been left without moral restraint, and whose spirit has become proud, capricious and ungovernable, by the habitual indulgence of weak and doting parents. Had we Lycurguses for legislators, such females would be doomed to celibacy, with their dandy suitors, by the laws of the land. They are both unfit to be the parents and guardians of those into whose hands are to be committed the momentous interests of this great and growing republic; and especially are they unfit to be the parents and guardians of those who are to *"endure hardness, as good soldiers of Jesus Christ,"* and to lead on his spiritual forces to the conquest of the world.

It is time that intelligence and virtue gave laws to the customs and fashions of society. Not only the more sober and intelligent part of community, but the church itself, has been too much influenced by the manners, and habits, and practices, of the gay and thoughtless. She has almost lost sight of that holy and dignified simplicity, which adorned her character in primitive days. This disgraceful servility must be exposed and exterminated. The success which has attended the efforts for the promotion of temperance is encouraging. The friends of humanity, of learning, and religion, must take their stand, and by precept and example, give tone to public sentiment and practice. They have the power, under God, to do this. They can redeem a world long enslaved by folly and sin, and render it a habitation of wisdom and righteousness. But how shall this be effected? A momentous question, and one that claims a more profound answer than I have time or ability to give.

The great effects produced on muscular strength, on health, and on the animal spirits, by gymnastic and military exercises, by riding, walking, hunting, sailing, and by that system of training which is practised in Europe to prepare men for boxing, show that much may be done. [The effects ascribed to the training system are almost incredible. The period of daily exercise abroad is at least four hours, and within door at least two hours. A prominent object is, to keep the body and mind constantly occupied through the day. No ardent spirits are allowed. The food is small in quantity, and of easy digestion. Eight hours of sleep are allowed, and temperance in all things strictly enjoined. By these means, it is said, the appetite and digestion become uniformly good, and the mind cheerful, the wind and strength astonishingly increased, and the sleep sound and refreshing. This system is said, also, to be an effectual remedy for bilious complaints. The lungs become strong, the skin smooth and elastic, and the spirits lively. The bones become hard like ivory, not easily broken, and the nerves strengthened. No trained person, it is stated, is subject to palsy or nervous depression. The form is improved, the movements are graceful, and life itself is much prolonged. What a lesson is here for those who profess to believe it their duty *to glorify God in their body and spirit, which are God's!*] Parents may do much. Let them consider it a religious duty, due to their children, to their country, and to God, to do all in their power to give their children such bodily health and vigour, as will enable them to be most useful in future life. Let them commence a rigid system of discipline in early childhood, and persevere in it till their children arrive at manhood. Body and soul are the Lord's, and it is as much our duty to take care of the one as the other. Great responsibility in relation to physical education rests upon physicians. They ought to diffuse through community, a knowledge of those hygeian laws, which the Author of our bodies and minds has ordained, and enforce their importance by the whole weight of their professional influence. They may thus do their fellow men more good by the prevention of disease, than by its cure. Surely the humane physician will not refuse to do this, lest he should diminish his business. [Since this address was delivered, the first number of "The Journal of Health" has appeared, published at Philadelphia, and conducted by an association of physicians. This work is written in familiar style, and adapted to all classes. If the first number be a fair specimen of those which shall succeed, this work will be an invaluable blessing, and ought to be read by every family in the land.]

In all our schools, and especially in our higher seminaries, systematic exercise ought to be introduced. Every student should spend three or four hours daily in such exercise, in order to preserve and increase his physical energy, and enable him to pursue with pleasure and success his studies through life. There are great difficulties in introducing any regular system of exercise into literary institutions. These difficulties are so formidable, that many to whom the instruction of youth is committed are deterred from making any effort. They see the evil, but despair of a remedy. Provisions for riding are too expensive for general use. Walking is beneficial, but is not sufficient. There are serious objections to military exercises. They are necessary in a national institution, like that at West Point, specially designed to prepare youth for the army and the navy. But they are unsuitable for literary institutions in general. To some part of gymnastic exercises, there are objections almost as weighty as those against military, when they become the habitual exercise of a student, from year to year. Those which embrace the various and usual movements of the body, and which may be taken with little or no apparatus, at almost any time and place, are unexceptionable. But many other exercises, such as climbing poles and ropes and ladders, wrestling, hopping, jumping, swinging, vaulting on wooden horses, &c. are not so congenial to the feelings of the pious heart, as the cultivation of the earth and mechanical employments. They are better suited to the playful feelings of children, than to the chastened affections of riper years. And one great objection to all these factitious modes of exercise is, that, aside from health, they have no practical utility. The regulation among the Jews, that every child should be taught some useful trade, was founded in wisdom and common sense. Could a regular system of manual labour, in the agricultural, horticultural, and mechanical arts, be introduced into our higher institutions, it would be an unspeakable blessing. Such a system would be as favourable to health as any artificial plans we can devise. It would be a reflection upon divine wisdom and benevolence, to suppose we could introduce any artificial mode of exercise, for daily use, that would be more conducive to health, than that in which God designed that the greater part of mankind should be employed.

A system of manual labour, while it promoted health, would be attended with many other advantages. It would exclude in a great degree those plans of mischief, which are projected and executed in the hours of relaxation from study. Considerable pecuniary profit would accrue. Allowing that there are two thousand students in a course of education for the learned professions, and that they could earn upon an average one dollar per week, by three hours of profitable exercise, and allowing forty weeks per year for study, and eight years for a course of study, the avails of this exercise would be no less than six hundred and forty thousand dollars. How would such a spectacle of industry and economy among students, in this day of christian enterprise, gladden the heart of piety. And what a salutary influence would such an example of industry, in those who are to move in the higher walks of life, would be diffused by the learned through the lower classes of society. Such knowledge would be useful to every professional man in future life, and especially to ministers of the gospel in our new settlements, and to the missionaries to the heathen. Persons thus educated, if now successful in their profession, would not be helpless. Such a system would enable those who intend to devote their lives to agricultural, mechanical, commercial, or manufacturing pursuits, to acquire an education, and then return to business with their habits of labour unimpaired.

As had been observed, there are difficulties in introducing such a system of exercise into our literary institutions; but none, probably with patience, experience and perseverance will not overcome. Many of the most useful improvements, such as have been made in navigation, in printing, in manufacturing, in steam power, and gas light, have been attended with still greater difficulties. Whether there is yet among students, parents and instructors, sufficient love of industry, sufficient energy and virtue, to sustain such a system, is questionable. But if religion prevails, it will soon become a question of consequence with students, whether it is right for them to spend one fourth part of their time in unproductive exercise. The glory of gymnastic exercises is already departing. If any regular system of exercise is ever to become general and permanent among students, it will be manual labour. Like the simple pleasures, it never tires by repetition. The effects and profit of such exercise secure a permanent interest. But gymnastic and military exercise, required of students from year to year, will become irksome. The ever recurring thought, too, added to the uninteresting nature of the exercise, "*I am doing this merely for my health,*" will increase the aversion.

Yes, working with the hands, at some useful business, are the gymnastics which it is hoped will prevail, ere long, in our literary institutions and theological schools. Let no one call these an innovation. These are the good old gymnastics of the pilgrim fathers of New England. They were practised by Christ and his apostles. They are as old as the human race. They are of divine appointment, and were commenced in Eden by our progenitor, and this too before he transgressed. Such gymnastics will be fashionable in the millennium, when the ropes, and poles, and ladders, and wooden horses, of modern gymnasts, are thrown aside and forgotten; and by them the whole earth shall be converted into the garden of the Lord, a spectacle delightful to angels.

The cultivation of our moral powers is by far the most important part of education. It is comparatively to little purpose, that we give to youth a cultivated intellect and a vigorous arm, if they have not a heart to prompt to beneficent action. Better would it have been for many youth, and for the world, had he never trod on classic ground. Education from the days of infancy, ought to be so conducted as to purify, expand, and elevate the affections of the soul. Infant schools and sabbath schools are setting an example in this respect worthy of universal imitation. This moral discipline must be followed up and perfected in our higher institutions. Every seminary of learning in our land ought to be a school of Christ, in which youth are training up for immortality. A pious parent, when he places his child within the walls of an academy or college, ought to be able to feel that his morals are as safe as while under the paternal roof. It is a fact that ought not to be disguised, that the morals of youth frequently become corrupted in our academies and colleges. Said a man of distinction, whose opportunities for a correct judgment have been surpassed by few in our country, "Could the veil be lifted from some of our higher seminaries, and all the sources of youthful corruption exposed, the better part of community would demand an immediate reform, or withhold their patronage."

Every institution for the education of youth, that does not exert an influence favourable to morality and religion, is unworthy of the patronage of a christian community. There should be no just occasion for theological seminaries to complain that their pupils bring with them *the spirit of college*, which," it is said, *"we all know, is often a sad mixture of vanity, pride, selfishness, and self-dependence!"* Never was there a period in this or any other country, more favourable than the present for the introduction of a healthful moral influence into our higher seminaries of learning. Infant schools, and sabbath schools, and bible classes, are bringing forward a better generation than any preceding one. Those who have thus been taught are becoming themselves parents and teachers and guardians of youth. They will call for a more wholesome moral influence and if God, in awful judgment, does not cloud the brightening prospects of our country and world, this demand will soon be heard and answered. These institutions which exert a good moral influence, will receive their patronage; others will be abandoned as a nuisance.

But how, it may be asked, shall such a moral atmosphere be diffused through our academic institutions? I answer, by the inculcation of the great truths of the bible. All experience proves that there is no substitute. Let its authority be established over the consciences of youth, by a thorough examination of its evidences, under enlightened and virtuous instructors. Let them feel that the great law of love to God and man, which it promulgates, must be their rule of conduct. None but bigots, and infidels, and villains, have any thing to fear from such a use of the bible in the temples of science. The common ground on which evangelical churches stand, is enlarging, and already broad enough for the establishment of such a basis for the moral education of youth. The days of idolatry and superstition are passing away. We must, as a nation, be enlightened Christians or downright infidels; and institutions for training our youth will possess the same character. It is high time, therefore, for every disciple of Jesus to determine, so far as his influence is concerned, what their character shall be. A better system of moral philosophy than we now possess, is greatly needed in our colleges, and it is to be hoped will soon be furnished by some jurist of pre-eminent talents and piety. The sciences, which are only other names for the works of God, furnish much matter for producing religious impressions. Properly taught, they may be made powerful auxiliaries to the bible in the moral education of youth. They are too often taught and studied, as though both teacher and pupil were atheists.

The connexion which exists between the truths of christianity and intellectual improvements, has been traced with a masterly pen, by a fellow alumnus who has preceded me. That the great moral truths of christianity, firmly believed, should have a powerful influence on the intellectual improvement, is manifest from the acknowledged principles of mental philosophy. The motives which these truths present are incomparably more powerful to wake all the energies of the soul, and to keep them in constant action, than can be found in any of the objects of interest which this world presents. So little are the great mass of mankind influenced by worldly considerations, in the acquisition of knowledge, that it is morally certain they never can become greatly enlightened without the aid of moral truth. There are no motives sufficiently powerful to lead the learned to teach them, nor can any considerations be presented to their own minds, sufficiently powerful to induce them to learn. But if, by some unheard of means, all nations were gifted with cultivated minds, still, without the constant influence of moral truth, their evil affections and passions would lead to revolutions in governments, to poverty, and vice, and crime, in neighbourhoods, and families, and individuals, which would cover them with barbarian ignorance. The gospel alone teaches man his true dignity. It unfolds a future world of glory. It teaches him that his present life is but a moment in his eternal duration. It places all on a level, made of *one blood*, children of the same Father, subject to the same laws, and candidates for the same immortal honours. It inculcates a pure and disinterested benevolence. It bids man love his neighbour as himself, and extend to all the means of present and future happiness. This moral system teaches every individual self-government and temperance in all things. Obedience to its rules preserves men from that luxury, and effeminacy, and vice, which, according to the opinion of many able statesmen, will forever render wars and revolutions necessary evils in the human family.

Let the motives here presented be brought to bear on every mind, and intelligence, and virtue, and peace, and prosperity, will universally prevail. Here, in these motives to human action, is to be found the only redeeming spirit, by which our world can ever be blessed with light, and joy, and peace. It should, therefore, be a settled principle with statesmen, and philanthropists, and christians, that if the family of man is ever blessed with a large measure of intellectual cultivation and temporal prosperity, moral truths, and especially those of the bible, will be the honoured instrument of a change so desirable. The bright bow of promise, whose lofty arch shall compass the world, must be formed by the commingled rays of literature, science and religion. Those who would separate them, could they succeed, would doom all nations to a perpetual succession of wars and revolutions, and the great body of the people to an endless night of mental darkness. The interests of the common people, who in all nations constitute the vast majority, have in every age been in a great degree disregarded. Nothing but the doctrines and precepts of the bible will ever lead the higher classes of society to promote the best good of the lower. The bible declares "God is no respecter of persons." It says to all, however exalted their station, "*Mind not high things; but condescend to men of low estate.*" Every child in this republic ought to have a thorough education—intellectual, physical and moral. Every son and daughter of our farmer, our mechanics, and manufacturers, ought to be allowed as much time for the acquisition of useful knowledge, as is required to obtain what is now termed a liberal education. Such an education is indispensable to the highest exercise of religious affections. Great attainments in literature and science are not necessary to the existence of piety. But moral truths can influence the heart only as they are perceived. A knowledge of the character, the government, and providence of God, and a perception of the duties they involve, imply that such a mind is highly cultivated, and stored with knowledge. Though the assertion may to some appear extravagant, I venture to aver, that the time will come, when every child in our land will receive what may be denominated a liberal education. Yes, the time will come, when every child of the great family of men will be blessed with an education truly liberal and christian. To the church is the promise made—"All thy children shall be taught of the Lord. For the earth shall be full of the knowledge of the Lord, as the waters cover the seas." Then the word eternal truth, in the Greek and Hebrew languages, will be as common in bible classes and in the habitations of the righteous, as it now is in our own language. This day of Zion's greatest glory is drawing nigh; and the signs of the times point to America, as a distinguished instrument in ushering in the long wished for morn. Now is the time to expect great things; and now, too, is the time to attempt great things. Our common schools and infant schools, our sabbath schools and bible classes, are laying a foundation for a superior generation; and if our academies and colleges and theological seminaries are moulded to the improving state of society, to the exigencies of the church, wherein dwelleth righteousness." Now, I repeat it—now is the time for laying plans on a grand scale, which shall stand out in actual accomplishment, when our heads lie low in the grave. We have arrived at an interesting era in the history of our country and of our world. This young republic is rising with unexampled rapidity to a commanding eminence among civilised nations. That spirit of liberty, which has here sprung up, is spreading far and wide. It has made our elective franchise almost universal. It has taught our freemen an independence of thought, of speech, and of action, that will combine to form a *public opinion*, as irresistible, right or wrong, as the majestic march of a sun in the heavens. No means should be neglected to give a right direction to mind thus *free* and *independent*, and to form *a virtuous public sentiment*; a better safeguard to the church than her creeds and confessions, and to our country than her fleets and armies. We have an extent of territory capable of supporting a population equal to that now on the globe. In the great valley of our Mississippi, stretching along its course between the Allegany and the Rocky mountains, the population of all Europe might be planted, and find ample sustenance. If no disastrous events occur to impede our progress, some of the present generation will live to see in this favoured land one hundred millions of freemen! Who can contemplate these things without deep emotion? Who dare predict the political and moral influence which this country will exert on human destiny?

The age, too, in which we live, is full of interest. By the improvements in printing, in travelling, and in navigation, together with that spirit of enterprise which springs from commercial competition, and the spirit of benevolence which is sending missionaries to every land, the whole civilised and uncivilised world is brought into close contact. Mind acts upon mind with the rapidity of electricity. Every ingenious thought and sentiment goes out from the press in all directions, like the rays of light from the sun. The certain consequences of this state of things is, that changes will be great and sudden. Revolutions will be effected, not by the slow process of force, but by opinion. If God is soon to appear in his glory, to build up Zion, what great moral revolutions are at hand! If the strong holds of sin and Satan are soon to be demolished, what mighty battles are to be fought, and what powerful forces are to be marshalled for the combat! By whom is this great work, under God, to be effected? By a race of heroes, such as the world never saw; by men gifted with intellects of the first order, braced with nerves no dangers can shake, and prompted to deeds of valour by hearts baptised with fire from above, which the mountain waves of sin's dark ocean cannot quench. And where are they? A few only are in the field. Some may be found in our theological schools, in our colleges and academies. Some are in our sabbath and infant schools. Some are in the humble dwellings of the pious poor, nurtured in a mother's arms, and blessed with a mother's prayers. But most are yet unborn. And now is the time, when our academies and colleges should be purified, and fitted for training these moral heroes, who, led on to battle by the Captain of Salvation, shall ere long give redemption to an enslaved world.

And may we not cherish the fond hope, that the beloved Alma Mater will be among the foremost, in preparing these soldiers of the cross for the service of the mighty Conqueror? Let such be her character, and she shall live till time is no longer; and when these elements shall melt with fervent heat, her name shall be repeated on the hill of Zion, and held in everlasting remembrance. The present century is a new era in this world's history. It has given birth to most of the great plans of moral enterprise, whose object is to restore this revolted province to the favour and protection of her King. And with the commencement of this wondrous century, our Alma Mater dates her birth. Already has her influence been felt in our pulpits, our forums, and our halls of legislation, at home, and our missionary stations, abroad. Her sons have published salvation where David strung his lyre, and where Isaiah saw in prophetic vision these latter days. They have ascended the hills where Jesus bled and died, and rose and ascended, and where apostles first published his resurrection. Located amidst an intelligent and virtuous population, remote from the dissipation of crowded cities, and in a state whose hardy and enterprising sons are formed for deeds of noble daring, may not the friends of learning and religion look to her for some future Luthers, and Calvins, and Whitefields, and Brainerds, and Edwards', and Martyns, who shall be prominent leaders in that "sacramental host of God's elect," by whose prowess the world shall ere long bow in submission at Immanuel's feet? That such glories may adorn her brow, be the prayer of her grateful alumni to the latest generations; and when the archangel's trump shall wake the dead, may they, with all their beloved presidents, and guardians, and teachers, enter that superb temple of science and religion in the heavens; where, associated with angels, they may study with everlasting and increasing delight the wonderful works of that Holy One, who *in wisdom has made them all.*

THE EVILS OF GAMING

During the second quarter of the nineteenth century, traditional patterns of social relationships were destroyed and new ones formed. This was particularly true for family relationships, in which forms of parental control over marriage and courting underwent considerable change. As young men and women exerted more control over the selection of spouses and the terms of engagements they increasingly gained an independence and autonomy over their own affairs that they previously lacked. As a result, many advice books directed at the nation's youth appeared before the Civil War and enjoyed enormous sales. These manuals usually accepted demographic changes of an urbanizing America and preferred to offer moral instruction to youth. One of the most popular of these books was William Alcott's The Young Man's Guide, which went through more than thirty editions between 1833 and 1858. The following excerpt, taken from the 1836 edition of Alcott's famous book, demonstrates public moral disapproval of gambling and its association with some sports.

ON GAMING
by William Alcott

Even Voltaire asserts that 'every gambler is, has been, or will be a robber." Few practices are more ancient, few more general, and few, if any, more pernicious than gaming. An English writer has ingeniously suggested that the Devil himself might have been the first player, and that he contrived the plan of introducing games among men, to afford them temporary amusement, and divert their attention from themselves. 'What numberless disciples,' he adds, 'of his sable majesty, might we not count in our own metropolis!'

Whether his satanic majesty has any very direct agency in this matter or not, one thing is certain;—gaming is opposed to the happiness of mankind, and ought, in every civilized country, to be suppressed by public opinion. By gaming, however, I here refer to those cases only in which property is at stake, to be won or lost....

Gaming is an evil, because, in the first place, it is a practice which **produces** nothing. He who makes two blades of grass grow where but one grew before, has usually been admitted to be a public benefactor; for he is a **producer**. So is he who combines or arranges these productions in a useful manner,—I mean the mechanic, manufacturer, &c. He is equally a public benefactor, too, who produces **mental** or **moral** wealth, as well as physical. In gaming, it is true, property is shifted from one individual to another, and here and there one probably gains more than one loses; but nothing is actually **made**, or **produced**. If the whole human family were all skilful gamesters, and should play constantly for a year, there would not be a dollar more in the world at the end of the year, than there was at its commencement. On the contrary, is it not obvious that there would be much **less**, besides even an immense loss of time? [Every man who enjoys the privileges of civilized society, owes it to that society to earn as much as he can; or, in other words, improve every minute of his time. He who loses an hour, or a minute, is the price of that hour debtor to the community. Moreover, it is a debt which he can never repay.]

But, secondly, gaming favors corruption of manners. It is difficult to trace the progress of the gamester's mind, from the time he commences his downward course, but we know too well the goal at which he is destined to arrive. There may be exceptions, but not many; generally speaking, every gamester, sooner or later, travels the road to perdition, and often adds to his own woe, by dragging others along with him.

Thirdly, it discourages industry. He who is accustomed to receive large sums at once, which bear no sort of proportion to the labor by which they are obtained, will gradually come to regard the moderate but constant and certain rewards of industrious exertion as insipid. He is also in danger of falling into the habit of paying an undue regard to hazard or chance, and of becoming devoted to the doctrine of fatality....

The famous philosopher Locke, in his 'Thoughts on Education,' thus observes: 'It is certain, gaming leaves no satisfaction behind it to those who reflect when it is over; and it no way profits either body or mind. As to their estates, if it strike so deep as to concern them, it is a **trade** then, and not a **recreation**, wherein few thrive; and at best a thriving gamester has but a poor trade of it, who fills his pockets at the price of reputation.'

In regard to the **criminality** of the practice, a late writer has the following striking remarks.

'As to gaming, it is always **criminal**, either in itself or in its tendency. The basis of it is covetousness; a desire to rake from others something for which you have neither given, nor intend to give an equivalent. No gambler was ever yet a happy man, and few gamblers have escaped being positively miserable. Remember, too, that to game for **nothing** is still **gaming**; and naturally leads to gaming for **something**. It is sacrificing time, and that, too, for the worst of purposes....the taste of gaming is always regarded as an indication of a radically bad disposition; and I can truly say that I never in my whole life—and it has been a long and eventful one—knew a man fond of gaming, who was not, in some way or other, unworthy of confidence. This vice creeps on by very slow degrees, till, at last, it becomes an ungovernable passion, swallowing up every good and kind feeling of the heart....'

My life has been chiefly spent in a situation where comparatively little of this vice prevails. Yet I have known one individual who divided his time between hunting and gaming. About four days a week were regularly devoted to the latter practice. From breakfast to dinner, from dinner to tea, from tea to nine o'clock, this was his regular employment, and was pursued incessantly. The man was about seventy years of age. He did not play for very large sums, it is true; seldom more than five to twenty dollars; and it was his uniform practice to retire precisely at nine o'clock without supper.

Generally, however, the night is more especially devoted to this employment. I have occasionally been at public houses, or on board vessels where a company was playing, and have known many hundreds of dollars lost in a single night. In one instance, the most horrid midnight oaths and blasphemy were indulged. Besides, there is an almost direct connection between the gambling table and the brothel; and the one is seldom long unaccompanid by the other.

Scarcely less obvious and direct is the connection between this vice and intemperance. If the drunkard is not always a gamester, the gamester is almost without exception intemperate. The is for the most part a union of the three—horrible as the alliance may be—I mean gambling, intemperance, and debauchery.

There is even a species of intoxication attendant on gambling. **Rede,** in speaking of one form of this vice which prevails in Europe, says; 'It is, in fact, a PROMPT MUR-DERER; irregular as all other games of hazard—rapid as lightning in its movements—its strokes succeed each other with an activity that redoubles the ardor of the player's blood, and often deprives him of the advantage of reflection. In fact, a man after half an hour's play, who for the whole night may not have taken any thing stronger than water, has all the appearance of drunkenness.' And who has not seen the flushed cheek and the red eye, produced simply by the excitement of an ordinary gaming table?

It is an additional proof of the evil of gaming that every person devoted to it, **feels** it to be an evil. Why then does he not refrain? Because he has sold himself a slave to the deadly habit, as effectually as the drunkard to his cups.

Burgh, in his Dignity of Human Nature, sums up the evils of this practice in a single paragraph:

'Gaming is an amusement wholly unworthy of rational beings, having neither the pretence of exercising the body, of exerting ingenuity, or of giving any natural plea-sure, and owing its entertainment wholly to an unnatural and vitiated taste;—the cause of infinite loss of time, of enormous destruction of money, of irritating the passions, of stirring up avarice, of innumerable sneaking tricks and frauds, of encouraging idle-ness, of disgusting people against their proper employments, and of sinking and debaing all that is truly great and valuable in the mind.'

Let me warn you, then, my young readers,—nay, more, let me **urge** you never to enter this dreadful road. Shun it as you would the road to destruction. Take not the first step,—the moment you do, all may be lost. Say not that you can command yourselves, and can stop when approach the confines of danger....

When you are inclined to think yourselves safe, consider the multitudes who once felt themselves equally so, have been corrupted, distressed, and ruined by gaming, both for this world, and that which is to come. Think how many families have been plunged by it in beggary, and overwhelmed by it in vice. Think how many persons have become liars at the gaming table; how many perjured; how many drunkards; how many blas-phemers; how many suicides. 'If Europe,' said Montesquieu, 'is to be ruined, it will be ruined by gaming.' If the United States are to be ruined, gaming in some of its forms will be a very efficient agent in accomplishing the work.

Some of the most common games practised in this country, are cards, dice, billiards, shooting matches, and last, though not **least,** lotteries. Horseracing and cockfighting are still in use in some parts of the United States, though less so than formerly. In addition to the general remarks already made, I now proceed to notice a few of the particular forms of this vice.

1. CARDS, DICE, AND BILLIARDS

The foregoing remarks will be applicable to each of these three modes of gambling. But in regard to cards, there seems to be something peculiarly enticing. It is on this account that youth are required to be doubly cautious on this point. So bewitching were cards and dice regarded in England, that penalties were laid on those who should be found playing with them, as early as the reign of George II. Card playing, however, still prevails in Europe, and to a considerable extent in the United States. There is a very

common impression abroad, that the mere **playing** at cards is in itself innocent: that
the danger consists in the tendency to excess; and against excess most people imagine themselves sufficiently secure. But as 'the best throw at dice, is to throw them
away,' so the best move with cards would be, to commit them to the flames.

2. SHOOTING MATCHES

This is a disgraceful practice, which was formerly in extensive use in these States
at particular seasons, especially on the day preceding the annual Thanksgiving. I am
sorry to say, that there are places where it prevails, even now. Numbers who have
nothing better to do, collect together, near some tavern or grog-shop, for the sole purpose of trying their skill at shooting fowls. Tied to stake at a short distance, a poor
innocent and helpless fowl is set as a mark to furnish sport for the idle men and boys.

Could the creature be put out of its misery by the first discharge of the musket, the
evil would not appear so great. But this is seldom the case. Several discharges are
usually made, and between each, a running, shouting and jumping of the company
takes place, not unfrequently mingled with oaths and curses.

The object of this infernal torture being at length despatched, and suspended on the
muzzle of the gun as a trophy of victory, a rush is made to the bar or counter, and
brandy and rum, accompanied by lewd stories, and perhaps quarrelling and drunkenness, often close the scene.

It rarely fails that a number of children are assembled on such occasions, who listen with high glee to the conversation, whether in the field or at the inn. If it be the
grossest profaneness, or the coarsest obscenity, they will sometimes pride themselves
in imitating it, thinking it to be manly; and in a like spirit will partake of the glass, and
thus commence the drunkard's career.—This practice is conducted somewhat differently in different places, but not essentially so.

It is much to the credit of the citizens of many parts of New England that their good
sense will not, any longer, tolerate a practice so brutal, and scarcely exceeded in this
respect by the cockfights in other parts of the country. As a substitute for this practice
a circle is drawn on a board or post, of a certain size, and he who can hit within the
circle, gains the fowl. This is still a species of **gaming**, but is divested of much of the
ferocity and brutality of the former.

3. HORSERACING AND COCKFIGHTING

It is only in particular sections of the United States that public opinion tolerates
these practices extensively. A horserace, in New England, is a very rare occurrence. A
cockfight, few among us have ever witnessed. Wherever the cruel disposition to indulge in seeing animals fight together is allowed, it is equally degrading to human
nature with that fondness which is manifested in other countries for witnessing a bull
fight. It is indeed the **same** disposition, only existing in a smaller degree in the former
case than in the latter.

Montaigne thinks it a reflection upon human nature itself that few people take delight in seeing beasts caress and play together, while almost every one is pleased to see them lacerate and worry one another.

Should your lot be cast in a region where any of these inhuman practices prevail, let it be your constant and firm endeavor, not merely to keep aloof from them yourselves, but to prevail on all those over whom God may have given you evidence, to avoid them likewise....

I am sorry to have it in my powers to state that in the year 1833 there was a **bull fight** four miles southward of Philadelphia. It was attended by about 1500 persons; mostly of the very lowest classes from the city. It was marked by many of the same evils which attend these cruel sports in other countries, and by the same reckless disregard of mercy towards the poor brutes who suffered in the conflict. It is to be hoped, however, for the honor of human nature, that the good sense of the community will not permit this detestable custom to prevail....

Useful Recreations.

The young, I shall be told, must and will have their recreations; and if they are to be denied every species of gaming, what shall they do? 'You would not, surely, have them spend their leisure hours in gratifying the senses; in eating, drinking, and licentiousness.'

By no means. Recreations they must have; active recreation, too, in the open air. Some of the most appropriate are playing ball, quoits, ninepins, and other athletic exercises; but in no case for money, or any similar consideration. **Skating** is a good exercise in its proper season, if sollowed with great caution. **Dancing**, for those who sit much, such as pupils in school, tailors and shoemakes, would be an appropriate exercise, if it were not perpetually abused. By assembling in large crowds, continuing it late at evening, and then sallying out in a perspiration, into the cold or damp night air, a thousand times more mischief has been done, than all the benefit which it has afforded would balance. It were greatly to be wished that this exercise might be regulated by those rules which human experience has indicated, instead of being subject to the whim and caprice of fashion. It is a great pity an exercise so valuable to the sedentary, and especially those who sit much, of both sexes, should be so managed as to injure half the world, and excite against it the prejudices of the other half.

I have said that the young man must have recreations, and generally in the open air. The reason why they should usually be conducted in the open air, is, that their ordinary occupations too frequently confine them within doors, and of course in an atmosphere more or less vitiated. Farmers, gardeners, rope makers, and persons whose occupations are of an active nature, do not need out-of-door sports at all. Their recreations should be by the fire side. Not with cards or dice, nor in the company of those whose company is not worth having. But the book, the newspaper, conversation, or the lyceum, will be the appropriate recreations for these classes, and will be found in the highest degree satisfactory. For the evening, the lyceum is particularly adapted, because laboring young men are often too much fatigued at night, to think, closely; and the lyceum, or conversation, will be more agreeable, and not less useful. But the family circle may of itself constitute a lyceum, and the book or the newspaper may be made the subject of discussion. I have known the heads of families in one neighborhood greatly improved, and the whole neighborhood derive an impulse, from the practice of meeting one evening in the week, to read the news together, and converse on the more interesting intelligence of the day.

Some strongly recommend 'the sports of the field,' and talk with enthusiasm of 'hunting, coursing, fishing;' and of 'dogs and horses.' But these are no recreations for me. True they are **healthy** to the body; but not to the morals. This I say confidently, although some of my readers may smile, and call it an affectation of sensibility. Yet with Cowper,

'I would not enter on my list of friends

The man who needlessly sets foot upon a worm.'

If the leading objects of field sports were to procure sustenance, I would not say a word. But the very term **sports**, implies something different. And shall we sport with **life**—even that of the inferior animals? That which we cannot give, shall we presumptuously dare to take away, and as our only apology say, 'Am I not in sport?'

Besides, other amusements equally healthy, and if we are accustomed to them, equally pleasant, and much more rational, can be substituted. What they are, I have mentioned, at least in part. How a sensible man, and especially a Christian, can hunt or fish, when he would not do it, were it not for the pleasure he enjoys in the cruelty it involves;—how, above all, a wise father can recommend it to his children, or to others, I am utterly unable to conceive!

PHYSICAL EXERCISE AND FEMALE EDUCATION

Almira Phelps was a prominent figure in female education for much of the nineteenth century. Through numerous textbooks and writings, she championed the cause of physical education and supported the introduction of science into the classroom. Perhaps her most influential work, The Female Student; or Lectures to Young Ladies, published in 1833, focused on the importance of mental as well as physical discipline.

THE FEMALE STUDENT, OR LECTURES TO YOUNG
LADIES ON FEMALE EDUCATION, 1833.
by Almira Phelps

Preliminary Views on Education in General.
LECTURE III.
Nature and Objects of Education

The true end of education is to prepare the young for active duties of life, and to enable them to fill with propriety those stations to which, in the providence of God, they may be called. This includes also a preparation for eternity; for we cannot live well, even in this world, without those dispositions of heart which are necessary to fit us for heaven. To discharge aright the duties of life, requires, not only that the intellect shall be enlightened, but that the heart shall be purified. A mother does not perform her whole duty, even when, in addition to providing for the wants of her children, and improving their understanding, she sets before them an example of justice and benevolence, of moderation in her own desires, and a command over her own passions: this may be all that is required of a heathen mother; but the Christian female must go with her little ones to Jesus of Nazareth, to seek his blessing; she must strive to elevate the minds of her offspring by frequent reference to a future state; she must teach them to hold the world and its pursuits in subserviency to more important interests, and to prize above all things that peace which, as the world giveth not, neither can it take away.

Thus comprehensive, my dear girls, is education; *it consists in training the body to healthful exercises, and elegant accomplishments, in cultivating and developing the mental powers, in regulating the passions, and above all, in forming religious habits. M. Julien, in his 'Essai General d'Education,' says, "Education is an apprenticeship for life; its true end, like that of existence, is well-being or happiness. But although all men either by reflection or instinct seek this end, although all desire to be happy, most are ignorant of what happiness really consists in, what are the elements which compose it, and the means of obtaining it. Reason, observation, and experience appear to point out three essential and necessary elements of happiness—health of body, elevation of soul, and cultivation of intellect....*

PART II.
Physical Education
LECTURE VI.
Health. Neatness.

...The term physical education is used in reference to the improvments which can be effected in the human frame and the senses, by a proper system of discipline. Among the ancients, physical education occupied a large share of attention: it is now becoming a subject of inquiry among those who perceive the evils which have resulted to the body from a disproportionate cultivation of the intellectual powers. *Mind* is ultimately the object to be acted upon, in physical as in other branches of education....

You peceive how early *physical habits* may be formed. Nor are *mental habits* less early or less strong in their growth and development; we shall at present confine ourselves to the former. We have already observed that the term physical, as applied to education, has relation to the body. Not that thy body itself, strictly speaking, can form any habits; this is nothing more than a collection of particles of matter, which have previously existed under the various forms of animal or vegetable substances, and which will again be separated to appear under new aspects, forming parts of organic or inorganic bodies. These material atoms are not subject to any of the laws which govern mind; but while united to the mind they are governed by it. The body is an instrument which the mind directs; and as in this state of existence they must dwell together, it becomes of great importance that they should mutually promote the welfare of each other.

The mind may at times sigh for deliverance from its burthensome companion; it may be conscious that but for this it could range through the infinity of space, visit distant worlds, and exist in an atmosphere untainted by human follies: yet He, who made man, has thought proper to consecrate a union between matter and mind, so that in this life they compose but one individual....

To learn then the best methods of rendering the bodily organs subservient to the good of the mind, is physical education. The body may be considered as a servant which the Creator of the mind has bestowed upon it, or a traveling companion for the journey of life. As we would strive to teach a servant his duty, to render him familiar with the offices which he will be required to perform, so should the body be trained to such exercises and duties, to such privations and efforts as the good of the mind may require. Whether, therefore, we regard the body as an instrument to be wielded by the mind, an humble companion, or a servant, the importance of attention to it, as closely connected with ourselves (for it is the mind which constitutes our identity) need not be urged....

A sound mind in a sound body ("*mens sana in corpore sano*") was an ancient motto, denoting the most perfect state of man as a human being; but as the field of knowledge has been widening by new discoveries, the intellectual part of mankind have fallen into the error of neglecting bodily health in their zeal for mental improvement. As respects our own sex, both fashion and increased attention to the mind have been alike injurious in producing habits tending to physical derangement and debility....

In common with many others who have taken a share in the education of the young, we feel that physical education has been too much neglected. In the mental efforts which the teachers, as well as pupils, of this institution have been obliged to make, in order to attain the desired standard of intellectual improvement, much has been suffered, through a nelgect of exercise.

When the mind is deeply interested in literary and scientific pursuits, it is prone to forget the body; this, by being suffered to remain long inactive, becomes reluctant to move, and visits back such neglect, by headaches, languors, sleeplessness, indigestion, and a thousand other ills, tending to paralyze the mental energies. Aware as we all are of this danger, connected with the pursuits of knowledge, it is be hoped we may profit by past experience, and retrieve, as far as possible, by a systematic course of exercise, the health which has been sacrificed.

Calisthenics, [From two Greek words, signifying grace and strength] or female gymnastics, is very properly becoming a branch of education. I have, however, seen with regret, that many of you appear to engage in physical exercise with reluctance, as if every moment taken from your studies were time lost. With the view already given of the intimate connection between the mind and body, you must be convinced that the latter cannot with impunity be neglected. And yet even our pleasant morning walks seem, by some, to be counted an unnecessary and tedious walk, and youthful limbs are sometimes seen dragged heavily along, as if already touched by age and infirmity. An early walk in a fine summer morning to our classic Mount Ida, will not only afford a needful physical exercise, but presenting you with a lovely picture of the combined beauties of nature and art, tend to raise in your minds cheerful images, and to lead your thoughts to the Author of all good....

As a branch of physical education, dancing is recommended by physicians; when practised merely as a school exercise, it seems not liable to the objections which many urge against promiscuous dancing assemblies....Riding on horseback is a very healthy as well as graceful exercise; yet it is somewhat questionable whether there is not too much the appearance of display in a young lady's prancing through the most public streets of a large city. A rural excursion on horseback is more safe and proper.

THE PSYCHOLOGICAL BENEFITS OF PHYSICAL EXERCISE

Although the anonymous author of the following document was concerned with the benefits of calisthenic exercises, not athletic sports, she, along with many others, helped to provide the ideological foundation for widespread public acceptance of physical exercise and sports. The following excerpt, drawn from A Course of Calisthenics for Young Ladies, In Schools and Families, with some Remarks on Physical Education, published in 1829, promotes the psychological as well as the physical benefits of calisthenic exercises into school curricula and family life through an epistolary format.

EXCERPTS FROM
A COURSE OF CALISTHENICS FOR YOUNG LADIES, 1829

LETTER I

MY DEAR FRIEND,

You have requested of me a plain account of the fashionable exercises called Calisthenics. In complying with this request, I will endeavor to give a full course of these useful exercises adapted to schools or to families. Considering them, as I do, as essential part of the present system of female education, I am anxious that their object should be well understood, and that they should be universally adopted.

It is next to impossible to introduce an improvement in Education, or indeed in anything else without meeting with opposition. Some fearless innovators will propose and attempt anything that suggests itself to their fertile imaginations. Instead of being guided by reason, they launch upon the ocean of improvement, without rudder or compass, and when they think themselves "on the full tide of successful experiment," they are only rapidly driving ashore, where the wrecks of their absurd inventions, serve not only as a warning to the too venturesome, but as a terror and discouragement to the too timorous.

But Calisthenics have stood the test of experiment. If the precepts and examples furnished by antiquity are forgotten, the modern examples of France and England have shown their utility. These exercises have been there introduced into many schools for girls and into private families, and are considered indispensable in the physical education of females. A few schools in our own country are beginning to adopt them, but hitherto, they have had no manual of exercises, and have therefore labored under serious disadvantages. It will not be long, I trust, before the practice of Calisthenics shall be perfectly familiar to every female school in the United States.

Before entering upon the main subject of these letters, I shall make a few remarks on the Physical Education of young children.

"The indolence of mind, which is often the accompaniment of a sweet and easy temper, is, perhaps, a more frequent cause of miscarriage in private education than any other. It is a deceiver which, under the specious appearance of uncommon goodness, produces the most mischievous effects. To a person of principle engaged in education, this easy indolence of temper is the greatest of all misfortunes, because it operates in such a manner as not to alarm the conscience." [Hamilton on Education]

Alas, how many children have been laid in their early graves because this baneful indolence prevented their mothers from knowing their duty! It is not neglect, nor want of affection of which they are accused, but ignorance, which becomes criminal, when it leads to such fearful consequences.

Every mother should be convinced that her *children require a great deal of vigorous exercise*. They are as fond of skipping and bounding about as other young animals. You might as rationally attempt to restrain the sportive gambols of a lamb or a kitten as of a healthy child. Nature has taught those exercises which are most conducive to little children's health and happiness, and there is no need of other teaching. Keep them out of danger and let them choose their own innocent sport. It is delightful to observe the graceful, unstudied movements of the little creatures while they are at play. Their picturesque grouping, and beautiful attitudes, have often called forth the admiration of the painter and taxed his skill in imitation. Unfortunately, the restraints of the school-room soon destroy this charming ease and sweet gracefulness....

LETTER IV.

After candidly considering the evils which I have hastily enumerated, you are doubtless convinced that they call for remedy. I will now attempt to show you how Calisthenics are designed to arrest these evils. I hope to be able to prove to you that they are precisely what we need to meet the necessities of the case. They are recommended by an able writer on curvature of the spine, in the following manner, viz.-"Well-regulated exercises, then, are desirable. Such are the Calisthenics. When first introduced into this country, (England) they were of much too violent and athletic a kind; but through judgment and experience, are now reduced to a series of graceful, dignified and natural movements, admirably adapted to promote an equable development of the physical powers, and to call into action in regular succession, every part of the muscular system." [Duffin on "Deformity of the Spine"....]

The word Calisthenics, as you probably know, is derived from two Greek words, signifying strength and beauty.

1. They bring every part of the system into action.
2. Expand the chest.
3. Bring down the shoulders.
4. Make the form erect.
5. Give grace to motion.
6. Increase muscular strength.
7. Give a light elastic step in walking.
8. Restore the distorted or weakened members of the system.
9. Prevent tight lacing.

10. Promote cheerfulness.

11. Render the mind more active.

12. They are conducive to general health....

LETTER VII.

The 10th reason mentioned favor of Calisthenics, was, that *they promote Cheerfulness.*

"The perpetual restraint under which a girl is kept from the first dawn of intellect, robs her of that exercise to which nature prompts, and fritters down, subdues or destroys her emotions," while it banishes prematurely all the buoyancy and activity of youth.

Unhappily, so confirmed, do inactive habits of body become, that in many cases, the least exertion is fatiguing, and produces bitter complaints, and even anger. A girl who would commit ten pages to memory without murmuring, would not, perhaps, walk twenty rods without fretting and scolding, and actually feeling exhausted by such an enormous exertion of physical power.

Too often the short space of time not devoted to study, is employed in poring over the pages of some old or new sentimental novel, which will almost inevitably produce a sickly sensibility, a morbid delicacy of feeling and taste, destructive to the happiness and usefulness of after life.

The seeds of that discontented, repining, capricious spirit,—the torment of domestic life—are often sown at school. Wearied out with study, and dull for want of exercise, girls often send their thoughts to their distant homes. Memory, aided not a little by imagination, pourtrays that 'sweet home' a perfect paradise. They lament their hard fate in being banished from their Eden, and literally, *making the worst of every thing* about them, they become ill-humored, selfish and unkind—wanting in politeness to their teachers and their companions, and miserably discontented with themselves. This is often, very often, entirely the result of a disordered state of the physical system, produced by want of exercise:—

"The heart a torpid winter leads,

And each clogged function lazily moves on."

"It would afford room for much more interesting speculation, were we to trace the mysterious connexion that exists between corporeal and mental defects; to inquire into the harshness of a Johnson, and the melancholy of a Pascal," the passionate violence of a Queen Elizabeth, and the sweet temper of the actively benevolent Mrs. Fry.

Calisthenics soon overcome reluctance to motion. Vigorous exercise sends the blood bounding through the veins, and produces natural healthful excitement. Activity becomes pleasurable. The dark cloud of sullenness, which has shaded and disfigured the countenance, passes away, leaving it bright and glowing with health and good humor.

A more cheerful group can scarcely be imagined, than a school released for a while to practice Calisthenics. Unless they were really enjoyed, they could not be very beneficial. You have only to see the expression of hilarity on every countenance, and hear the oft-repeated joyous laugh, to give you abundant evidence that there are zest and pleasure in the exercises....

By speaking so often of the school-room, and of the importance of these exercises for schools, I may have unintentionally, led you to suppose that they are only suitable for those institutions. Far from it, my friend, they are equally needed in families. Every mother who has young daughters, should attend to the subject herself; she should, if possible, qualify herself to join in their exercises; it will contribute much to her own health and happiness, thus to join in her children's recreations....

"Exercise is not only useful in adding to the symmetry of the form, but also in lighting up and invigorating the spark by which that form is animated and beautified."

The body is incapable of more than a certain definite proportion of exertion; when this is expended, what becomes of the mind? Can it act without its companion? Can it reason, judge, remember, with full force, when the exhausted frame is unfit to perform its duties? It is very true, that the soundest minds are not always found in the strongest bodies; and equally true, that a mighty, gigantic mind, may dwell in a weakly, care-worn, diseased frame. Not-withstanding, you will allow that a sound, healthful constitution of body, must materially aid mental operations. In order to preserve this, all the means ordained by Nature for its preservation, should be carefully and constantly used.

After an hour or two of intense mental application, fifteen or twenty minutes should be spent in exercise. The greater progress made in study the next hour, will more than redeem the time thus employed.

Those who discover decided genius early in life, sometimes suffer by intensity of application. Stimulated by injudicious praise, and urged on by their parents and teachers, they advance in the outset of their career with more speed than prudence. It is not well in any race to advance too rapidly at first; a gradually-increasing, sure pace, is wisely chosen by those who would first reach the goal; those seldom win, whose bounding coursers start at full speed.

We might often trace to physical causes, those lamentable failures which have occasioned such severe disappointment to parents, where precocity of genius has led them to anticipate the most brilliant career for their gifted offspring. Premature talents are very undesirable. Plants are much more strong and healthy, when they gradually unfold themselves under the natural genial influence of sun, air, and the rains of heaven, than when forced into maturity by the skill of the gardener. Not only the beauty and fragrance of the flower, but the full ripeness and rich flavor of the fruit, depend upon this gradual development....

You would think it a gross absurdity, were I to enter into a labored argument to prove that *women need health*. Yet this plain fact has been questioned, if the old adage be true, that 'actions speak louder than words.'

It has been thought *vulgar*, to possess 'rude health.' The delicate, interesting beings, withering like a rose-bud ere it expands, have called forth not only sympathy, but admiration and affection.

The little attention hitherto bestowed upon physical education has produced this result, namely; to nurture fragile, delicate creatures, who must wither, or be swept away by the first rude blast of real life to which they are exposed. The horror of being *dumpy* and stout, has prevented them, when there was any such alarming tendency, from indulging freely their natural appetite for food. The model of perfection in their minds, has been a shadowy, sylph-like being,

"Of so thin and transparent a hue,

"You might have seen the moon shine through."

If the ruddy glow of health has been wanting, parents and teachers have not been quite as anxious as they should have been to restore it, misled by these erroneous ideas of what constituted female elegance and beauty....

The guardians of youth awfully neglect their duty, when they forget that mind forms only a part of the delicate and beautiful structure committed to their care. It is time they were awake and on the alert; the knell of those who have been hurried by neglect or injudicious management, to their untimely graves, is sounding in their ears—will they not take the alarm?

The *natural constitution of the female sex is delicate, and therefore needs the more care.*—This is wisely ordered. Man, robust and daring, loves to be the protector, the defender of the 'weaker sex.' It inspires him with a tenderness of affection to which he would otherwise be a stranger.

"The bird that we nurse,
Is the bird that we love."

Our Creator has made this physical difference wide enough without any efforts on our part to increase it; on the contrary, it is our duty, religiously, sacredly to preserve our constitutions, and those committed to our care, from injury. We love to depend for support upon others; we rejoice that strength and power are given to man, and shelter ourselves beneath his protecting arm; still we should increase our own firmness and vigor, and during the season of childhood and youth, carefully preserve the health which God has given our daughters.

The *varied and arduous duties which woman is called upon to perform, require vigorous health.* A daughter, a sister, a wife, a mother, how important the station she holds!

It is her high duty and her holy privilege to be 'a ministering angel' to the weak, the sorrowing, the suffering, and the dying. To watch unwearied by the couch of sicknesses; to bear with the infirmities of the aged; to endure with untiring patience the cries of helpless infancy, and the petulance of childhood; to soften the waywardness and turbulence of youth, and to soothe by kindness, minds rendered peevish and irritable by constant intercourse with a hard, unfeeling world.

Often, she is left upon the stormy ocean of life, to buffet the waves alone. Alone, did I say? No; when they roar and rage tumultously, threatening to destroy her, she lifts the eye of faith to "the widow's God and Judge, the Father of the fatherless, in his holy habitation." The ivy which has long fondly clung around the oak, torn from its friendly support when the tree is felled by the resistless stroke, at first, trembles and shrinks from every blast, but at length, it lifts itself heavenward, grows strong and vigorous, even yielding shelter and aid to the fragile little plants that wind around the parent vine.

To woman, the task is mainly committed to mould the plastic mind; to lead by precept and example, into the paths of usefulness and virtue; to stimulate to holy and noble deeds; and, dread responsibility! to secure eternal happiness to her offspring, by forming their characters upon the perfect model of our Blessed Redeemer. Alas! how many can answer from their own sorrowing hearts—'who is sufficient for these things?' Health is gone, and with it all the energies, physical and mental, which are so much needed.

If, then, we would fit our daughters for their high duties and responsibilities, let us pour instruction into the minds like a mighty river; let us polish their manners and refine and elevate their affections, and at the same time, carefully preserve the material of the system.

I will just hint to you, in conclusion, some of the beneficial effects of calisthenics in promoting general health.

The appetite is increased, and the digestive organs strengthened, to perform their office. You will say, perhaps, that I am like some venders of quack medicines, whose nostrums will cure all "the ills that flesh is heir to." Nevertheless, I say unhesitatingly, that nothing has ever been prescribed for our sex, in cases of dyspepsia, so efficacious, "so certain a cure," as calisthenics. The person who was said to have vanquished the monster by some new and wonderful means, when his secret was revealed to the world, candidly confessed, that *diet* and *exercise* were the most sovereign remedies. I have proved by actual experiment, attended with complete success, the remedy which I so confidently prescribe.

As head-achs, weak eyes, and pain in the limbs, often arise from the disordered state of the stomach, occasioned by inactive habits, these will be thrown off. Do you say I have discovered 'the grand panacea'? Try it yourself, try it for your daughters, and may Heaven bless it, as the means of your perfect restoration.

Yours, truly,

M....

LETTER VIII.

In every seminary for young ladies, there should be a teacher of Calisthenics. If the school is too small to support the expense of a separate teacher, it should be joined to some other department, which is filled by an able intructress. To adopt the suitable exercises to each individual; to study their effect, and pursue, or relinquish, as circumstances require, to analyze the causes of distortion, of ungraceful movement, of muscular weakness, of general debility, and judiciously apply the remedy, surely demands no common share of penetration and acquired information. Time, and study, and thought, are necessary. An additional sum paid by each parent to defray the expense of a teacher, who would be constantly devoted to the care of the health and manners and physical habits of his child, would do her more real service than the vast sums which he willingly expends for comparatively useless accomplishments.

The time, I trust, is not far distant, when Calisthenics will be introduced into every female school in the United States.

After reviewing the course of these exercises, which I have given you, I am glad to learn, that, in your opinion, "there is nothing either boisterous, rude, vulgar, or indecorous, in them;" you farther say, that "they are not dangerous." I cannot say as much for all the French and English exercises which I have seen; some of them are improper for girls, and others appear to me dangerous. I am confident that improvements may still be made, and other exercises added. Whenever this is done, I shall communicate them with pleasure.

Do not suppose that in my devotion to the subject, I have forgotten that other exercises are beneficial. Riding on horseback, where it can be practiced, is a very healthful and delightful exercise, too popular and too fashionable to need any labored recommendation. A medical writer of some eminence has, however, given this salutary caution: "When young ladies are educated at home, *horse exercise* is in general very desirable, where it can be attained. It must not, however, be denied, that the propriety of this kind of exercise for delicate females, in whom exists any tendency to distortion of the spine, has been questioned; since from the awkward position in which it obliges them to sit upon the saddle, a disposition to curvature is apt to be induced." A walk in good weather, and a long one, too, is healthful and agreeable. As it is well to have an object in view, when walking, I would, but not on this account alone, strenuously recommend the study of Botany. Rambles in pursuit of plants, over hill and dale, scrambles up the rocks and mountains to gather the delicate flowers concealed among them, afford exhilarating exercise. "Eaton's Manual of Botany," and Mrs. Lincoln's late work, for young botanists, and invaluable walking companions.

Drawing from nature is also an admirable method of increasing the pleasure and profit of a walk. The sketch of a single picturesque old tree, may often be placed in the port-folio, and a walk that would otherwise be tame and tedious, thus becomes interesting in a high degree.

But these exercises do not supersede the necessity for regular ones, which can be practiced at any hour, without asking permission of 'wind or weather.'

Yours, &c.

M...

PHYSICAL EDUCATION AND SCHOOL REFORM

During the antebellum period Massachusetts assumed the lead in public school reform, primarily because of the efforts of Horace Mann. As secretary of the state board of education from 1837 to 1848 Mann implemented a number of reforms, including a minimum school year, specialized teacher training, and secular subjects and applied skills. More importantly, he broadened the public school curriculum to include a variety of subjects beyond the religious and literary training that previously characterized schooling. Part of this broadening was the introduction of exercise as a fundamental feature of public education. The following document is taken from Mann's Report of the Secretary of the Board of Education on the Subject of Schoolhouses, a supplement to his First Annual Report as secretary in 1838.

REPORT OF THE SECRETARY OF THE BOARD OF EDUCATION
ON THE SUBJECT OF SCHOOLHOUSES, 1838
by Horace Mann

SUPPLEMENTARY TO HIS FIRST ANNUAL REPORT.

YARDS OR PLAY-GROUNDS

On the subject, I have never seen, nor am I able to prepare, any thing so judicious, and apposite to the condition of the districts in Massachusetts, as the following paragraphs, taken from a Report, published in 1833, "by order of the Directors of the Essex-County Teachers Association."

"As the situation should be pleasant and healthful, so there should be sufficient space around the building. With the number who ordinarily attend these institutions, not less than a quarter of an acre should ever be thought of as a space for their accommodation; and this should be enclosed from the public highway, so as to secure it from cattle, that the children may have a safe and clean place for exercise at recess and at other times. We believe it no uncommon thing for a district to meet with difficulty in procuring a place for a house; for while most wish it to be near, they are unwilling to have it stand on a notch, taken out of their own field. This reluctance to accommodate the district may have been carried too far; the actual may be less than the imagined evils. Yet it is not without foundation; for in most instances, from the scanty and niggardly provision made by the district, the man knows that his own cultivated fields must and will be made the place of the scholars' recreation. We do not overstate, when we say, that more than half the inconveniences which persons thus experience in their property from the contiguity of a schoolhouse, arises from the insufficient provision made for the children by the district. While all the district may think that a neighbor is unaccommodating, because he is unwilling to let them have just land enough to set their house upon, the real truth is, that the smallness of the lot is the very thing which justifies his reluctance; for whether he theorize or not on the subject, he well understands that he will have to afford accommodations, which the district are unwilling on their part to purchase. Every schoolhouse lot should be large enough for the rational exercise which the children ought to have, and will take. It would be well to have it large enough to contain some ornamental and fruit trees, with flower-borders, which we know children may be taught to cultivate and enjoy; and by an attention to which their ideas of property, and common rights, and obligations, would become more distinct. By attention to what belonged to themselves, they would be kept from many of those wanton injuries too often done to the possessions of those near them.

"In regard to space, no one can be ignorant of the general practice. We believe it would be difficult, in this county, to find a score of these building, where the lot is as large as the most inexperienced on the subject would judge necessary.

"In by far the greater number of instances, there is no more ground than that which is occupied by the building; while many of them actually stand partly or wholly in the highway. The children, therefore, have no resort but to the public highway, or the private property of their neighbors, for amusement. Healthful and vigorous exercise is restrained; the modesty of nature is often outraged; and, not infrequently, a permanent and extensive injury done to the finer and better feelings, which ought, at that age, to be cultivated and confirmed by the most careful attention, not only as a great security from sin, but as a most lovely ornament through life. Besides this, there being no place for pleasant exercise for the boys out of doors, the schoolroom, during the intermission at noon, becomes the place of noise and tumult, where, not from any real intention, but in the forgetfulness of general excitement, gentlemanly and lady-like feelings are turned into ridicule, and an attempt to behave in an orderly and becoming manner subjects the individual to no small degree of persecution. We have often witnessed such instances, and known these who refused to engage in these rude exercises forced out of the room, and kept out during the greater part of an intermission, because their example cast a damp upon a course of rude and boisterous conduct, in which they could not take a part. Whatever others may think, it is our belief, that this noise and tumult are, in a great measure, the natural overflowing of youthful buoyancy, which, were it allowed to spend itself in out-door amusements, would hardly ever betray itself improperly in the house....

Boston, March 27, 1838.   Horac Mann
Secretary of the Board of Education

HEALTH AND EXERCISE

The health benefits gained from physical exercise that were emphasized by reformers and physicians after the 1820s originated partly in the perceived negative effects of urbanization on living and work patterns. Writers especially made the connection between the active labor of preindustrial lifestyles and general fitness. The following document, reprinted from the November 1838 volume of the American Turf Register and Sporting Magazine, discusses this theme.

ON EXERCISE

As we are now obliged to relinquish the more active and exciting sports of the field, and instead of following the gallant pack o'er hill and dale in pursuit of sly reynard, are obliged to rest contented with the recollection of the moving incidents by 'field or flood,' which we have experienced in the course of last season, perhaps a few cursory '*non medical*' observations, as the fashionable term now is, on the advantages of exercise, and its influence on the human frame may not be unacceptable.

Frederick the Great observed, that when he considered the physical structure of the human frame, it appeared to him as if 'nature had formed us rather to be postillions than sedentary men of letters,' which expression, though no doubt strong, is in a great measure borne out by the evident adaptation of our bodies for activity and exertion; and it is a curious remarkable fact, and one that easily can be tested by all who choose to try the experiment, that any particular parts of the body that are made use of more than others, become *by use* more thick, muscular, and more capable of bearing long-continued exertion than they were before—for example, the very powerful arms of our blacksmiths and sailors, and the extraordinary muscular developments in the legs of opera dancers and others who exhibit feats of agility in public, and which I attribute entirely to the constant practice, and severe exercises to which they subject themselves, by which the muscles of the arms of the former, and of the legs of the latter are brought into play. Need I call to mind the difference in muscular power between the human right and left arm in support of my argument? which difference of strength in favour of the right arm is occasioned by the constant use from infancy upwards of the right hand and arm on almost all occasions, in preference to the left: for I consider the su-perior muscular power of the right arm, *to be the result of education*, for when a child is not taught *by his parents or nurse* to use his right hand *always*, in preference to his left, he perchance uses his left hand on most occasions and hence becomes *left-handed*; or perhaps he becomes 'ambidexter' from not using either in preference. These cases appear to prove that in infancy our arms are both equally strong, but that by education and practice either becomes nearly as strong again as the other. On joining a gymnastic class, in the course of the first month's practice the arm between the shoulder and el-bow joints (the place of the biceps muscle,) will increase from three-quarters of an inch to fully an inch above its previous circumference, owing to the muscle being brought into full action; but it will not increase in the same ratio afterwards, as the nearer it approaches its full development the less will be the progressive proportional change *in size*, but it will get much *more firm*. Again, if the usual quantum of exercise be dimin-ished or left wholly off, the decrease in the *firmness* of the muscle will take place in an equal degree, though the size of the arm itself will not be much lessened. When commencing the practice of gymnastics the lungs soon become oppressed, the body perspires violently, unless care is taken to begin with the more gentle kinds; and the muscles over the whole body, for a few days at first, become stiff and sore, especially those of the arms, which are principally brought into play; but after a short period, *if the exercise be persevered in daily*, these symptoms almost entirely disappear, and he, who lately was fatigued with five minutes practice, will, at the end of a month, be able to undergo the most violent kinds of exercise *for hours*; and if close attention to diet be observed at the same time, his skin will become beautifully clear and elastic, and totally free from all pustules or eruptions; and the hand of a man in good condition ad-mits of the light of a candle being seen through it when held up between the eye and the flame; his bones will become more tough and less likely to be injured by violence or accident, his chest will be expanded, and the size of his abdomen reduced, so as very much to improve the appearance and figure; but one of the most important consequences of regular practice at gymnastics, or other systematic exercise, is the improvement of the `wind', as without free respiration neither man, nor any other animal, can make long-continued, and violent exertion, without complete exhaustion.

There is not any nation that is so much addicted to exercise in its various modifi-cations as the British, to which our naturally active dispositions, combined with the variableness of the climate, neither enervating the body by its extreme heat, nor chilling the blood by excess of cold, are chiefly conducive. It is generally observed that in cold climates so long as the people are uncontaminated by luxurious habits, voluntary ex-ercise, even to fatigue, is customary; but when luxury, by enervating the body, renders it less capable of undergoing fatigue, the habit of taking regular exercise is left off, and thus the frame becomes less able to resist the attacks of disease. We are also most partial to exercise *in the open air*, with the healthy winds of heaven playing around, and invigorating us with their genial influence, which of itself I hold to be of infinite importance, as I am of opinion that a man derives more benefit from one hour spent in exercise *in the open air*, than from treble the quantity *under cover*. The various kinds of exercise, too, which are most usually practised in this country are, with very few exceptions, taken 'sub dio'—and those most worthy of mention are: 1. Hunting. 2. Shooting. 3. Fishing. 4. What may be termed simple Equestrian exercise in contradis-tinction to its more violent twin-brother, 'hunting.' 5. Walking. 6. Running. 7. Quoits.

8. Cricket. 9. Golf. 10. Skating. 11. Curling. 12. Rowing. 13. Swimming. I can only call to mind four varieties that are worthy of being practised by *a man in door*, viz: Fencing, Dancing, Gymnastics, and Billiards, which last variety is particularly adapted for persons in delicate health, as it brings into play a large proportion of the muscles of the body, and engages the attention in an agreeable manner, while it does not distress by its violence as many others do. Exercise prevents disease, or rather perhaps fortifies the body against it. If good health were a commodity that could be brought like a box of 'Morrison's pills' or other health-conferring nostrums, who is there that would not hurry to the mart and purchase eagerly, even though they were obliged to swallow the box as well as its contents at one unsavoury mouthful? But exercise, which would *certainly produce the desired result* in many cases, is despised and neglected, and people allow themselves to drag on a comparatively miserable '*vegetable existence*,' and to drop into a premature grave, because they will not *be at the trouble* of taking the exercise that would assuredly lead to the enjoyment of a green old age; for, as Dryden says:

'The wise for health, on exercise depend;

God never made his work for man to mend.

By chase our long-lived fathers earned their food,

Toil strung their nerves and purified their blood.'

A gentleman mentioned to me the other day, that the late celebrated Doctor Gregory, in the course of one of his lectures in the college of Edinburgh, stated, in his presence, 'that a man cannot stand *perfectly motionless*, for half an hour; and that he, (Dr. G.) had once tried it, and had fainted at the end of twenty minutes, for that the blood requires the aid of the motion from the body in order to retain its full circulating power.'

We read occasionally in the public prints of some person or other, who has arrived at a very advanced age, walking a considerable distance or perhaps reading very small print; and most assuredly we are to attribute the power of doing so to the daily systematic exercise, and generally speaking, temperate habits of life to which that person was accustomed, and which had not only enabled him to reach his advanced age, but had preserved to him his faculties, and the power of continuing that exercise from which he derived so much benefit. Old Parr, of Salop, who lived to the great age of 152 years, and Henry Jenkins, of Yorkshire, who lived to the surprising age of 169 years, were, both distinguished for their active and temperate mode of living. We read that in the early history of mankind disease was hardly known. And why was disease and its attendant consequences so little known in those days? Because men were then more dependent on active exertion for their daily bread, and other necessaries of life; the body by labour, i. e. *exercise*, was maintained in a healthy state; the pores were kept free, the proper circulation of the blood was maintained, the body itself was hardened by almost constant exposure to the open air, the digestive powers were strengthened, and all noxious humours dissipated by perspiration, which when retained in the system occasions a large proportion of 'the ills that flesh is heir to.' I shall now hasten to conclude, or you will be thinking that I have no occasion to take exercise to improve *my wind*: take exercise at least once a day, so as to excite the natural heat, and other functions of the body; take that exercise which has the most general effect upon the system, and which induces you to be in the open air; *be regular* in taking exercise; do not take much exercise after a hearty meal; and when you do eat you may be assured that exercise adds more relish to your food than 'the King of Oude's Sauce' or any other condiment of that description that ever was invented.

                                                              A Follower of the Chase.

Chapter 2

THE EMERGENCE OF SPORTS JOURNALISM AND WRITING

Sports journalism and writing emerged during the antebellum period for a variety of social, technological, and political reasons. Riding the wave of nationalism after the War of 1812, the young republic spurned its British origins and attempted to develop its own cultural identity and independence. More importantly, the war had underscored American reliance on English manufacturers and served as a stimulus to the development of domestic industry and the advancement and application of new technologies. The emergence of a Northern, urban middle class and the consolidation of a Southern planter class provided a strong social base for the rise of interest in leisure activities, physical exercise, and sport.

Prior to the antebellum period, and less so during it, the publishing world relied quite heavily upon its British counterpart, as the latter dominated the American market. Because of the absence of adequate copyright protection, writing provided little remuneration for American authors. As a result, American publishing failed to develop in its own right, remaining dependent on the British for much of its material. Thus, many of the works issued in America during the antebellum period were simply reprints of books previously released in England. One of the consequences of such developments was the channeling of American talent into periodical literature, particularly newspapers and magazines. It is little wonder that journalism and such literary expressions as the short story developed in America at the expense of the novel. In America some of this talent was directed into sports writing; soon the appearance of more literary sporting works became a regular feature of many publications. "A Week in the Woodlands" by Frank Forester became a watershed in American sports coverage.

Another important factor in the rise of American publishing was technological innovation. During the early 1830s mechanical improvements in publication such as the introduction of the steam press allowed for much faster printing, increased volume levels, and cheaper costs. The expenses associated with publication also were reduced by the transportation revolution that swept America at the time. The construction of turnpikes, canals, and railroads, along with a much improved postal system, facilitated the distribution of books, magazines, and newspapers to an increasingly interested public and disseminated information and news within a rapidly expanding nation. The common school movement, one of many incarnations of the democratic spirit of the age, led to a more literate public eager to absorb the voluminous journalistic outpouring of the period. Topics of all kinds—economic, religious, cultural, but especially political—were debated in an ever increasing number of journals.

The emergence of sport journalism and writing formed an important aspect of the growth of American publishing and reflected many of the social patterns of the day. In the 1820s and 1830s publications devoted to sport proliferated. The American Turf Register and Sporting Magazine and The Spirit of the Times became the two most important sport publications, though United States Sporting Magazine and New York Sporting Magazine made brief appearances. Other journals such as The American Farmer, The New York Evening Post, and The New York Spectator provided more limited coverage of sporting events and developments but nonetheless played an important part in documenting early forms of sport. Although these sporting journals initially devoted a majority of their space to stories and articles from such British sporting publications as Bell's Life in London, by the late 1830s they had substantially reduced their reliance on British publications and were producing most of their own material. Many of the documents in this chapter, including "Introduction to the American Turf Register," "To Our Friends," and "Prospectus," address the early issues of sports journalism.

The editors of the major sport journals wielded enormous power over the antebellum sporting scene. William T. Porter, editor of The Spirit of the Times, and John Stuart Skinner, editor of American Turf Register and Sporting Magazine, influenced the nature and direction of sport reporting and writing, cultivated a sporting audience, and shaped the development and appeal of sport prior to the Civil War. During the 1830s healthy competition between these two journals sometimes degenerated into bickering and backbiting as the document "Journalistic Competition" illustrates. These two editors recruited correspondents from all regions of the nation—from the North to the South to the West, from the cities to the frontier—to report on a variety of sports and to nurture a truly national following. These editors loaded their publications with all sorts of useful, practical sporting information, particularly about the sports of the turf. Weekly columns such as "Prospects of the Northern Turf Campaign," the "Turf Register," and others, which discussed horse-breeding, horse-racing, and horse-training, became invaluable aids to sportsmen and thereby secured a niche for sporting journals with the American public, a development that by no means guaranteed their financial success.

But the credibility and viability of these sporting journals depended upon the ability of their editors to overcome two difficulties. First, because most of these papers were published in northern cities such as New York and Baltimore, they needed to avoid a strictly regional or sectional bias in tone and coverage. These editors did not lose sight of the fact that early sport was dominated by the turf, which had a strong following in the South and West, and any effort to establish a successful sporting journal required support from these two areas. The Spirit of the Times, for example, made sure to include articles on southern, western and Canadian turf news and racing, hunting, and boating and yachting, and sought to avoid, albeit with limited success, a northeastern urbane tone.

Second, although these journals addressed their appeal to the social and economic elite of all sections, economic fluctuations forced them to widen their audience. The 1837 panic particularly injured the sport of horse racing for some years, resulting in a concomitant decline in coverage and a need for different stories and articles. Sporting journals had always attempted to include some material of interest to the frontiersman and farmer, but the economic downturn and the social changes that accompanied it caused them to devote more space to backwoods existence, livestock, farm implements, county fairs, and local fiction. By 1840, the size and circulation of sporting journals had increased remarkably while maintaining the diversity of their appeal and audience.

THE FOUNDING OF THE AMERICAN TURF REGISTER

After 1829, J.S. Skinner left The American Farmer to start a new publication devoted to sports of the turf—The American Turf Register and Sporting Magazine. He forcefully stated his intentions to keep his journal decidedly American, thus breaking with many of the American sports journals that relied on English sporting newspapers for their material. The following article is reprinted from the September 1829 edition of the American Turf Register and Sporting Magazine.

INTRODUCTION TO THE AMERICAN TURF REGISTER
AND SPORTING MAGAZINE, 1829

"There are intervals when the studious and the grave must suspend their inquiries, and descend from the regions of science; and to excel in those innocent amusements which require our activity, is often one of the best preservatives of health, and no inconsiderable guard against immoral relaxation."

Rev. W.B. Daniel

The want of a repository in this country, like the English Sporting Magazine, to serve as an authentic record of the performances and pedigrees of the *bred* horse, will be admitted by all, whether breeders, owners, or amateurs of that admirable animal. The longer we remain without such a register, the more difficult will it be to trace the pedigrees of existing stock, and the more precarious will its value become. Is it not, in fact, within the knowledge of many readers, that animals known to have descended from ancestry of the highest and purest blood, have been confounded with the vulgar mass of their species, by the loss of an old newspaper or memorandum book, that contained their pedigrees? Sensible for years past of the danger which in this way threatens property of so much value, and persuaded that it is not yet too late to collect and save many precious materials that would soon be otherwise lost, the suscriber hopes to supply the long looked for desideratum, by the establishment of "THE AMERICAN TURF REGISTER." But though an account of the performances on the American turf, and the pedigrees of thorough bred horses, will constitute the *basis* of the work, it is designed, also, as a Magazine of information on veterinary subjects generally; and of various rural sports, as RACING, TROTTING MATCHES, SHOOTING, HUNTING, FISHING, &c. together with original sketches of the *natural history and habits of American game of all kinds*: and hence the title, *The American Turf Register and Sporting Magazine*. It will of course be the aim of the Editor to give to his journal an original *American* cast, conveying at once, to readers of all ages, amusement and instruction, in regard to our own country, its animals, birds, fishes, &c. In the absence of domestic materials, the magazines received from abroad will supply an ample stock of appropriate matter.

Of the Rev. Dr. Parr, a man profoundly learned, and, what might be expected to follow, an exemplary minister, and a liberal christian, we are told that "it was a fixed opinion in his mind that, above all other means, social entertainments are the most effectual for promoting kind feelings and good will among men and neighbors." The physical capacity to cherish and rear our families, and the resolution to peril our lives in defence of political and religious freedom, is as certainly invigorated and heightened by occasional exhilaration of the mind and spirits, as the elasticity of the bow is maintained by frequent relaxation. Hence the wisdom and benevolence of the scriptural warrant, there is "a time to weep, and a time to laugh, a time to mourn, and a time to dance." The knowledge of mankind, so essential in every practical pursuit, nay, the yet more essential knowledge of one's self, is not to be found alone in solitary labour nor in solitary meditation; neither is it in a state of isolation from society that the heart most quickly learns to answer to the calls of benevolence.—Sympathy springs from habits of association and a sense of mutual dependence on each other; and the true estimate of character, and friendly and generous dispositions, are under no circumstances more certainly acquired, nor more assuredly improved and quickened than by often meeting each other in the friendly contentions and rivalries that characterize trials on the turf, or the no less exhilarating but more protracted ecstacies of the chase, or when we to

"——rance the purple heath
Or naked stubble; where from field to field
The sounding coveys urge their labouring flight
Eager amid the rising cloud to pour
The gun's unerring thunder."

In undertaking to get up the Sporting Magazine, the Editor confesses he is urged in some degree by the same sort of humble, and he hopes blameless, ambition that prompted him to commence the American Farmer, without a single subscriber. In this case, as in that, he sees the country without such a work; it is a new field which no one has attempted to occupy—but his reliance too, is now, as then, far less on himself than on gentlemen of talent and spirit, who may be willing to contribute the results of their experience, and the anecdotes and materials within their reach. In a word, on that readiness to aid in the accomplishment of liberal and useful purposes, which, in all countries, distinguishes the true sportsman. Moved by no sordid considerations, we would cheerfully resign the undertaking for the sake of its success, and the pleasure and benefit which such a work, if well executed, will confer on the community, if any one, of whom there are many, with better capacity and more adequate talents will undertake it—but from much observation we are fully persuaded that only on (if one) magazine on these subjects can be supported—rivalry, by dividing the materials, would only fritter away its spirit and impair its value, more especially as a STUD BOOK.

It is confidently anticpated that in the department of original sketches of natural history alone, the subscriber though not a sportsman, will be remunerated for his patronage. Each number will be embellished with a hansome engraving. Finaly, as to the style and execution of the work, the first number may be received as a fair specimen;

entitled to some allowance for the imperfections inseparable from the first essay in a new and somewhat complicated and difficult enterprise.   J.S. Skinner.

INAUGURAL ISSUE OF THE SPIRIT OF THE TIMES

The Spirit of the Times and Life in New York announced its unique intentions, goals, and objectives in its inaugural issue on 10 December 1831, from which the following two documents are reprinted.

PROSPECTUS
OF THE
SPIRIT OF THE TIMES AND LIFE IN
NEW YORK, 1831

In undertaking the publication of a paper, devoted, as this is designed to be, to the pleasures, amusements, fashions and divertisements of life, the subscribers have been animated by the persuasive encouragements and gratuitous promises of support, of many of the most influential, enlightened and respectable members of the New York community. It is, to a certain extent, a field unoccupied by others, and one which is deemed important to be filled. For while the politicains, the theologians and the literati of our country have each their separate oracles which (like that at Delphos) proclaim aloud and defend their several opinions and interests; the cause of fashion, of pleasurable entertainments, of taste and recreation, find but few publications of a periodical kind, appropriated solely to their encouragement and support. To paint "life as it is," without the artificial embellishments of romance; to speak of its propensities for enjoyment, its appetite for pleasure, and indulgence, and its tendency to enter into occasional follies, is to do what many must approve, and no one can condemn. For it is certainly no more improper to *record* the acts of men, than to promulgate them orally to the world. "Pleasure," says a French nobleman, "is the chief busiiness of life;" and however seemingly incorrect the maxim may be in the estimation of some, yet it is literally true: for the devotee certainly takes pleasure in the exercise of his religion, the merchant and mechanic in their several branches of employment, and the man of letters in his books: while the sportsman who chases the hare, or attends the ring or the race, is only pursuing plesures in congeniality with his natural or cultivated taste.

In presenting this new candidate for favor and patronage to the public, it is the intention of the publishers to render it as interesting as possible, and to please all if they can, without wounding the feeling or disturbing the prejudices of *any*.—The language will be always chaste, so that the most delicate may approve. The paper will treat FASHION, TASTE, and SCENES OF REAL LIFE, gathered from the every day exhibitions of the world. THEATRES, MUSEUMS, and other fashionable places of resort, will receive appropriate notices, while the SPORTS OF THE TURF, the RING, the PIT, of the FISHER and the FOWLER, will engross no inconsiderable portion of attention. The proceedings of the COURTS, civil and criminal, will as far as possible be given, when matters of interest occur; and more especially those of the POLICE, where Life in all its forms and coloring is so faithfully portrayed. It is also the intention of the editors to devote a considerable portion of each paper to the compilation and dissemination of the news of the day, in a summarial form, which will serve as a brief and faithful record of all important passing events, condensing a large mass into a comparatively small compass.

With these intentions, fully and fairly proclaimed, and with the most perfect good feelings towards all our co-laborers in the same vocation, we present ourselves before an enlightened community as candidates for their patronage and smiles. Terms,—Three Dollars in advance.

WILLIAM T. PORTER,
JAMES HOWE.

TO OUR FRIENDS

...But instead of presenting our readers with mere description for the end of amusing them, we would emulate a nobler design. Far be it from us to lose sight altogether of *National* objects; *"propatria,"* should be the maxim of every citizen. And as others have taken the department of intellectual repasts under their superintendence, it is our care especially to endeavor to place before the eye of the care-worn and sedentary citizen, *rural pleasures* in all their enticing freshness—to invite him to strengthen his body by periodical healthful exercise—to enable him to boast of the *mens sana in sano corpore.* So that we may be fellow-laborers and co-operators with the liberal-minded physician of the present day, and emulate for our country, the same firmness of nerve and sinew, which gave to the ancient Roman his superiority when combating with the savage, and which conferred upon "the awful fathers of mankind," a great part of their glory and all their power.

In this way, instead of reducing our sheet to the rank of a mere contributor to the momentary appetite of a literary *gourmand,* we should be assisting in the great work of building up a sound physical frame for the Republic, and through the vehicles of games, diversions, and amusements, allure the nervous, the learned, the palsied artizan, and the pale manufacturer, to the practice of those manly exercises which confer the luxury of health upon the individual; and place at the disposal of the nation in the hour of danger, a hardy population and therein, a safe palladium of its rights.

IMPROVEMENTS IN JOURNALISM

The Spirit of the Times experienced many changes during the 1830s. The following announcement, reprinted from the 3 March 1832 issue of the Spirit revealed its objectives and goals as well as its dependency on English sporting journals.

TO OUR FRIENDS AND PATRONS

As we present our paper to our friends today in a different dress, we take advantage of the occasion to say a word in apology for the indifferent figure we made under our old head. We assure our readers, that any opinions they may have formed of our taste, from our supposed satisfaction with the *sorry cut* which has before disfigured the head of the paper, must necessarily be erroneous. We have been aware from the beginning, of its shabby appearance, and we have seriously regretted it. We were much disappointed in it ourselves, having been led by the opinions of Artists to expect quite a different thing. In deciding to commence our publication under a "star of inauspicious," rather than to delay till a new head could be executed, our determination may have been, and we fear was, ill-judged. We now abjure the ill-omened influence, and look for success under a more propitious planet.

To those Editors who have noticed and ventured to encourage our publication thus far, we now offer our acknowledgements, and hazard the expectation that the different garb we have assumed will not dispose them to withdraw their kind offices. To others, who, from a mere glance at our former head, have ranked us with a class of publications which depend for support on their envious scandal or gross indelicacy, (a class which none deprecate more sincerely than ourselves) we have only to name our regret that they did not look further, and our wishes that they may now give us our due, "be it for good or be it for evil."

There are many, we doubt not, who, having chanced to meet with our publication, have conceived a dislike to it from the same fertile source of prejudice, its forbidding head, (we beg pardon for referring so frequently to the poor thing.) This rock of offence has now been removed, and with it, we hope the prepossessions to which it may have given rise in the minds of many; to all such, and the public at large, we beg once more briefly to state the scope of our design. It will be our *principal object* to fill our columns with interesting accounts of the fashionable sports and pastimes of the day.

All manner of Field Sports delight us, and we have a peculiar penchant for Racing. We hold in all becoming reverence the memory of Izaak Walton, and his redoubtable and, in actual service, not unequal follower, Jack Crane, under whose auspices our own piscatory taste and skill were required. And further, (with the reader's leave) we are among the number of those "who lean to the soft side of the heart,"—we take pleasure in the fascination of the song and the dance, and, like a Lady, "at an Opera, we expire." This simple statement of the peculiarities of our taste will enable the reader to make a shrewd guess at the character of our paper. It is modelled, so far as we may be said to have our model, upon Bell's Life in London. But the different degrees of attention given to the sports of the Turf and the Ring &c. in England and in America, will lead to a corresponding departure in us from our great pattern. Our columns will be filled with articles of a more miscellaneous character of *less local* interest; as may be seen at once by a reference to our Prospectus in former papers.—In fine, it may be said that our object is *not only* to give as correct a picture as possible of "Life in New York," but likewise, full and interesting details of the "Spirits of the Times."

It has not escaped us that the greatest obstacle to our undertaking will be the questionable character we are liable to have imputed to us, on the score of good breeding. If, however, the utmost propriety in our selections of the paper,—the most gentlemanly courtesy towards every one,—and unwearying assiduity in the general management of our concern, can remove any such unfavourable impression, we look with perfect confidence for a liberal patronage.

IMPROVING THE BREED

One of the most important steps in the modernization of sports, especially horse racing, was the dissemination of information. Sporting journals served both the lay public as well as professionals in their reporting and in this way contributed to the growth of sports. The document reprinted below first appeared as part of the masthead of The Spirit of the Times on 11 March 1837.

NEW VOLUME OF THE SPIRIT OF THE TIMES FOR 1837

The First volume of the New Series of this journal was completed on the 11th of Feb. last, and the first number of a new column [the Seventh] was issued on the 15th of Feb. 1837, in which was contained, in addition to its usual varieties, an Alphabetical List of AMERICAN WINNING HORSES, Four Mile Heats, for 1836, which in subsequent numbers will be succeeded by Tables of the Winners at 3.2. and 1 miles— a perfect LIST OF STALLIONS for 1837. Table of WINNING TROTTING HORSES—and a complete List of ENGLISH WINNING HORSES, at all distances, during the year 1836. In the Lists of Winning Horses the reader is presented at one view with the age, color, sire, dam, and owner of each horse, with the weight carried, the time, the horses beaten, the date of the race and the course, with the folio of the page specified in which in the paper the detailed report of the race will be found. In the List of Stallions is given the name, color, pedigree, owner or agent's address, and terms, of all the distinguished Stallions in the Union, the whole comprising a mass of intelligence to be found in no other publication in this country, and which combines every leading feature embrace by the Stud Book, the Turf Register, and the Racing Calendar.

The *Sporting Department* of the new volume of the Spirit of the Times, (which commenced on the 15th Feb. last), will be made more interesting and valuable than ever. To this end it will present a complete AMERICAN RACING CALENDAR, complied with the utmost accuracy. The Races over the principal Courses in the Union will be reported by *our Special Correspondents* at the earliest day, and we shall rely upon the courtesy of the Secretaries of Clubs, and sporting friends generally, to furnish us with reports of other meetings. THE ENGLISH TURF will also claim our attention, and everything relating to it will be carefully culled from the British Sporting Magazines and papers, likely to contribute to the interest or information of the American Breeder and Turfman. Trotting Matches—Sales and Importations of Blood Stock at home and abroad—American and English Winning Horses—Reviews of Stallions—Pedigrees and Performances of Distinguished Horses—Essays on Breeding, Training, and racing—Challenges—Field Sports of all descriptions—On Dits in Sporting Circles, etc. etc., all come within the scope of our design, and we all bend every faculty to meet the expectations of those partial friends who desire that THE SPIRIT OF THE TIMES shall be acknowledged as the most authentic, comprehensive, original, and attractive SPORTING CHRONICLE that issues from the press. So far as SPORTING INTELLIGENCE is concerned, the Editor has no hesitation in promising it to his readers *earlier*, and in a *greater variety*, then can be procured through any other channel whatever. In addition to a wider and more intelligent circle of private correspondents than any weekly journal in the whole range of newspaper press, Two Special Correspondents in the remote sections of the Union are constantly and exclusively engaged in furnishing for the Spirit of the Times the Sporting Intelligence and current On Dits of the day. The Editor is also in the regular receipt, by the English packet ships, of *every Sporting Magazine and Paper* published in Great Britain, in addition, to a great variety of literary periodicals....

Such are more prominent features of the plan of the Spirit of the Times, varied as they are by the Current News of the day, Foreign and Domestic, and the thousands of subjects within the scope of metropolitan journal of the largest class. Gentlemen eminent for their talent and standing in society, throughout the country, have contributed to its success, not more by enrolling themselves among its firm friends than by enriching its pages with their communications. The Editor is not at liberty to name his contributors, but is warranted in stating frankly that they comprise a great majority of the leading Breeders and Turfmen in the United States. He has also regular correspondents in most of the large cities and town of the Union, and is also indebted to many American gentlemen abroad for their kindness in forwarding him the earliest Sporting and Green Room Intelligence.

JUSTIFICATIONS FOR SPORTING JOURNALS

The growth of the sporting press was crucial in the development of the sport of horse racing during the second quarter of the nineteenth century. The two major sports journals, The Spirit of the Times and the American Turf Register and Sporting Magazine, provided those connected with horse breeding, training, and racing with invaluable information and knowledge, and as a result, promoted the sport. The following letter is reprinted from the August 1838 edition of the American Turf Register and Sporting Magazine.

PATRONAGE OF SPORTING WORKS

Mr. EDITOR:

Nothing is more fatal to success in life, than a short-lived and ill-judged economy, or what may be more properly termed, parsimony; this thought has been suggested by the perusal of your Register and the Spirit of the Times. I am almost the only *subscriber to both* in the country where I reside, it is large, populous, and wealthy, with a fertile and productive soil, adapted by climate and location to the production of grain and grasses, and in no part of the United States can blood stock be raised to more advantage.

Not in the hills of Arabia does the horse find a climate more congenial, here his health is free from all those diseases incident to the low countries, while the nature of the soil insures firm hoofs, and flinty clean legs to sustain him under the extraordinary performances which the perfection of his form and the development of his powers may promise. Of this they have had the most satisfactory proof, such as no man can question or doubt; few gentlemen in this vicinity have bestowed any attention on blood, yet in some few instances they have bred from the right sort, and in every one they have paid well, a single instance may suffice to shew what can be done. Some few years since, a full bred mare at an advanced age was purchased from the lead of a wagon, where for a long time she had been expected to draw, not only the load, but the wheelers also; this mare, then old, was bought at one hundred and fifty dollars, put to breeding, in a few years, she and her colts sold for six thousand dollars; her owner at no time encountering more than the simple expense of breeding and rearing, had be trained his horses, and availed himself of the best markets, they would have brought him more than double the money: this is, in some degree, though not entirely, wandering from my subject, for I did not intend to write a dissertation on breeding horses, but shew what I deemed the proper course of those already engaged in that business.

Interest is the great balance wheel of society, it moves and controls the whole, and there would be no difficulty in getting men to pursue the proper course, were it not for the blinding influence of avarice, while in looking too intently on small present expenditures, entirely shut out the view of all distant profit. Such is the situation of those in our country, who hold or rear blood stock, and neglect to take both your periodical and the Spirit of the Times; for to the establishment and publication of the Register we owe the first impulse given to the establishment of jockey clubs in our country, and as a consequence, the increased value in all the blood stock, and for some years past you have found an able and indefatigable assistant in the Spirit of the Times.

If any man doubts the influence of the general value which the Turf Register has exerted, let him refer to the price of *racehorses, stallions,* and brood mares, some ten years since and now, and he must be worse than an *infidel* not to believe; in truth at this day, breeding blood horses has become a most important part of our rural economy, and he that shall promote it will deserve well of his country. In my opinion, the annual sales of blood in the United States, nearly equals in amount any of our great staples, cotton alone excepted, and he that shall promote or sustain its value, entitles a man most justly to consideration and respect, and it becomes a public duty to reward such labour—and as it is duty of all so is it likely to be neglected.

By the aid of the papers above named, the value of horses has been increased at least one thousand per cent; their labours benefit many thousands of their fellow citizens, who so far, have not contributed one cent to either the Turf Register or the Spirit of the Times; this is truly, a most short-sighted policy, for every one must see, that those papers have mainly contributed to the establishment of *jockey clubs*, these offer purses, which induce training, remunerate liberally those who win, enable them to buy horses at high prices, and others who wish to share the golden harvest, follow their example, and purchase at corresponding high prices; all this may be said most truly to be the work of two publications, which have each such a patronage as barely sustains them. Now is it proper that a large portion of the community should benefit by the labours of two individuals, and themselves contribute nothing? Would any man of just and honourable feelings be willing that such should be his position toward another? If he would only take the trouble to look into, and think upon the matter, I am certain he would not; and I am persuaded, if this article could be generally read, your subscription list and that of the Spirit of the Times would have a liberal increase of names.

While on the subject of neglect, permit me to notice that of the newspaper editors generally, many of them exchange with the Turf Register and Spirit of the Times, yet we scarcely ever see any notice of, or extract from them: yet are they both of more real service to the country than all the political papers of the day. If they would only now and then treat their subscribers to extracts, it would surely afford a pleasing variety, and like a pinch of cephalic rouse them from the lethargic influence of a dull editorial.

I have been induced to mention in the same paragraph the Register and the Spirit of the Times. No man of spirit, enterprise, or pleasure should be without both of them; in the Spirit of the Times, he will find the earliest intelligence on all subjects connected with the turf, the field, the stage, it is in short, the sheet calendar of taste and fashion.

The Turf Register is a monthly condensation of all deemed most important on matters connected with the turf, and the care and improvement of blood stock, printed in the neatest manner, the selections made with such attention as to divest them of many of those errors incident to more hasty publications; as a register of races and pedigrees, it may be referred to as a text book; for when an error, (sometimes unavoidable,) has crept into one number, it is corrected in the next, so no man need be misinformed. This work if bound and kept, may always be referred to with advantage and convenience, and the breeder who is without it, has little chance to know the real value of his horses, and must at the same time remain ignorant of many things important for him to learn, in the management of what is or may be the most valuable part of his property. [The fact, that the above was intended for the benefit of breeders and stock owners in general, will excuse its appearance in this periodical, more especially, as the writer truly remarks, as the newspaper press of the country pay very little attention to the Turf Register, its contents or its beneficial effects on the interest of the public; one more remark, and we commit the subject to the jury: The article is the spontaneous emanation from the writer's own mind, both in its suggestion and execution, nor did we know of or expect any such article from his pen. If the newspapers generally, would give this article an insertion in their columns, they would doubtless do material service to their readers, besides doing us a favour; which latter consideration, we have no reason to think, will militate against its general republication by them. Now that we publish this article for the benefit of breeders and the Spirit of the Times, may we not ask the latter to republish it for the benefit of whom it may concern?—EDITOR TURF REGISTER.]

A.

THE INCREASE IN SPORTS COVERAGE

With the growing interest in sports, sports journalism responded accordingly by improving its coverage in both quantity and quality. In addition, the introduction of engravings to complement the reporting was introduced to enhance the coverage. The following article, reprinted from the 9 March 1839 edition of The Spirit of the Times, announces changes in the sports reporting of that journal.

TO OLD SUBSCRIBERS

The reader has now before him the "Spirit of the Times" in the enlarged form, which we have often promised him, and in this article it is our purpose to lay before him, as briefly as possible, some of the considerations which have induced us to embellish it with costly Engravings, and to make a change in its size and appearance, and consequently in its price.

Every old reader must have remarked that the limits formerly devoted to the Sporting Department have again and again been too narrow. The Sports of the Turf for the last five years have been, and are still, advancing in popularity beyond precedent; immense capital has been invested in Blood Stock as a matter of business, and still more by gentlemen of wealth, leisure, and spirit, who regard the Turf not only as a National Sport, but as the manliest and most elegant of amusements. New Jockey Clubs are springing up in every section of the Union with a magical rapidity "rather alarming"' to the denizens of the old "race horse regions," and this in the face of general pecuniary embarrassment. To record all the races now run in the United States under the auspices of organized Clubs would require a sheet of no trifling dimensions, but to embrace a more extended plan, and furnish, as we have aimed to do, a comprehensive CHRONICLE OF THE SPORTING WORLD, requires one not inferior in size or appearance to any in the country.

But it is not alone the increase of Sporting in America that demands more space in our columns. The lively interest with which the British Turf has ever been regarded by American gentlemen has recently been enhanced to an immense extent by heavy Importations of Stock from abroad, and by sure indications that these will go on increasing. We have all derived our tastes for Field Sports and Racing from our English ancestry, and the experience of England in Breeding, and Training, and the fact that all our stock trace directly to that country, has ever drawn the attention of our Turfmen to the records of their races;—and the more intimate connections made by recent importation of so many horses to the United States, requires that we should be still more familiar with their entire Turf System.

For these reasons, we long ago resolved upon enlarging the limits devoted to the Turf in our columns, and as this could only be done, without encroachment upon other and favorite departments, by enlarging our whole paper, we have made the change— a great, and we hope a final one.

But the "Spirit of the Times," this week, has not only been increased in size, but improved in every respect. Great expense and infinite labor have been lavishly employed to effect this object, and we hope not without success. It can hardly be necessary to direct attention to each improvement; unless we have entirely failed in our purpose, the reader will detect them himself. It was our resolve to make the paper, in the several departments within its scope, superior to any weekly publication in the country—to gratify our own professional pride, by furnishing a journal IDENTIFIED WITH THE SPORTING INTEREST IN AMERICA, that should be creditable alike to ourselves, and worthy of the cause which it advocated. The ENGRAVINGS on *Steel*, with which we purpose to illustrate the "Spirit of the Times," are an entirely new feature in our plan; we shall publish seven or eight, altogether, in the course of the volume, of which the two accompanying today's paper are fair specimens, save only that they may have been prepared in too short a space of time to justify the outlay which has been made upon them. A very spirited portrait of *John Bascombe*, by TROYE, is already in the hands of the engraver, and will be published at the earliest possible day. Original Paintings of *Mingo* and *Monarch* have also been ordered, to follow in close succession. In addition to these Embellishments, the body of the paper will also be illustrated, on the plan of "Bell's Life in London," by superb Etchings of Horses, Race Caps, Plans of Courses, and similar subjects, engraved on Wood by the most eminent artists.

The improvements that have been noted above, and others, which will be manifest to the reader, it was impossible to make without, at the same time, increasing the price of the paper, which henceforth will be ten dollars per annum. We need not add that we hesitated to make this change, but as all our designs of giving higher value to the paper would otherwise be ruinous to us, we determined to make the alteration, and rely upon those readers to sustain us in it who, we know, prefer a work of a high order of excellence at a fair price, to a less expensive, but inferior publication. Our resolution was not taken without mature reflection, nor unadvisedly. In answer to solicitations for advice from the most distinguished Breeders and Turfmen throughout the Union, before many of whom, as our oldest and best friends, we frankly laid our whole project, we were told, with assurances of their hearty support, to "Go Ahead!" Make the "Spirit of the Times" to the American Sporting World, said they, what "Bell's Life in London" is to the English—flinch at no expense in procuring early information, or in improving its appearance, and the extent and variety of its contents, and you will find that *Brother Jonathan* will not be behind *John Bull* in "backing his friends!" They urged that inasmuch as the "Spirit of the Times" was the accredited organ of an interest embracing only men of literal views, of taste, and of property, it should be complete in its design, and in all its appointments elegant; and they assured us that we had only to make it worthy of them to command their best wishes, and to ensure their cordial support. Gentlemen connected with the Turf, and admirers of Field and Rural Sports generally, whatever may be their particular passion, are proverbially liberal and such mainly constitute the subscribers to this paper. The price of a horse, a gun, a dog, or anything which contributes to their enjoyment, is no object with them, provided it fully meets their views,—and it is believed that they have too much pride to suffer a paper devoted to them and their amusement, to languish for want of that liberality which characterises them in their ordinary pursuits, or to be second to the organ of any other interest, either in its size, appearance, or character.

Nor do we fear to ask him who would consult the closest economy in the support of a periodical, to consider the size of our sheet, the amount of original matter which it contains, the intelligence from so many quarters, gathered at such expense, and the illustrations so costly and appropriate, and then say whether the price be too great! Ask any print-dealer, and he will tell you that six Illustrations, as finished and beautiful as those we give this week, will cost more than double the whole price of subscription. Again, the expense which we incur for Travelling Correspondents and Reporters, (entirely disconnected with any other journal,) and in other arrangements, both in this country and in Europe, to obtain the earliest Sporting Intelligence, exceeds by far what any weekly, nay almost any daily paper in the Union expends in the collection of news.

But we need not argue the matter; readers will form their own estimate of the value of what we give them, and our paper will stand or fall accordingly; we only require to be judged fairly by our merit. That we shall lose a few readers there can be no doubt, but we rely upon those "good men and true" who have thus far manfully stood by us, to "see us out."

RELIABILITY IN SPORTS REPORTING

Improvements in sports reporting were not only introduced by the journals themselves but also demanded by the reading public. In the following article, which is reprinted from the 24 November 1838 issue of The Spirit of the Times, a reader criticizes the accuracy of the reporting of turf races and the unnecessary journalistic embellishments often provided by sports reporters. Such accuracy constituted an important development in the modernization of horse racing.

ON REPORTING RACES "AND SO ON"

To the Editor of the Spirit of Times—The utility and the beauty of the reports of all races is their strict and rigorous accuracy; and rather than have the most humorous and witty account of a race which draws upon the fancy at the expense of truth and the facts of the case, all true sportsmen would prefer the bare statement of facts, without note or comment. Indeed, justice to horses and their owners or breeders demands this, or your records cease to be looked to as the standard of the merits of the horses of the day which they propose to notice, and may loose, if they be allowed to be inaccurate, all the advantages proposed by them, for after, as well as the present, times. One acknowledged inaccurate report, unless it be corrected, may vitiate the credit of a dozen reports from the same source, which may be rigidly correct as to the time made, and other matters.

Under this impression, and with this view of the subject, I consider that the interests of the American Turf demand that every intelligent Turfite should regard it as his bounden duty to have corrected through your paper, any errors that may be officially reported, when there is a certainty that a mistake has been made—else we shall soon have *doubted* the record of a number of extraordinary races which have been made on this side of the water, both as regards quick time and extraordinary durability or bottom. The report of a race should not be regarded as only a newspaper flourish, but a strict record of names and pedigrees, of distance, of time, and of the places of the different horses that run as they come in, if they *can be placed*. And for this purpose the person intending to make the report should hold pencil and paper in hand, and note the facts as they occur, and not depend upon his memory to record the particulars of several races which occur so near together in the same day as to be almost jumbled up together in the memory at its close. Nothing should be said by the *reporter* like these things—that "*Boston*, has he been pressed, could have made his 4 miles in this race in the astonishing time of 7:36"—or that "this heat by *Balie Peyton* and *Duane*—7:42 1/ 2—is the best on record"—or that "in this there were three second rate nags, and three certainly not above third rate." Facts alone should be stated, and these facts left to deduce their own commentaries.

I am induced to indulge in these reflections, after reading a report in your last paper of the 3 mile race at Kendall Course, near Baltimore. In that report it will be found that a horse called *Bustamente* was placed 4th in the 1st heat, 4th in the 2d heat, and distanced in the 3d heat—whilst the facts are that he was 2d in the 1st heat, and ran the 2d and 3d heats through pretty well up, when he was drawn; and never distanced in this, or any other of his numerous races. This horse has good blood in his veins, and although his former owner believed him to have received injuries in two of his legs, which disqualified him as a racer, and his present owner knows nothing about training and conditioning a horse for a race, (as was apparent during the above race,) it is well that every devil have his due, and that this horse should not be declared distanced when he never was distanced, either in this or any other of the numerous races he has run.

In making this correction, I will take leave to say, that Mr. CUSTIS KENDALL is incapable, in my opinion, of making any intentional mis-statements in his report, and that this, if he saw the race, has been the result of neglecting to note the facts as they occur, and depending upon memory, which might easily have brought him into the error of recollection that *Bustamente* was one of the three engaged in the *second* race, whilst it should have been recollected, that he made play all the time among the first set, and kept them if not otherwise inclined, constantly going; for his *reliance* was on his bottom, although in no condition to display either foot or bottom.

VERITAS.

JOURNALISTIC AND SECTIONAL RIVALRIES

In the Fall of 1836, a match horse race pitted a northern horse, Post Boy, against a southern one, Bascomb. Unlike the outcome of the first famous North/South match race between Eclipse and Henry, the southern horse emerged victorious in 1836, creating acrimonious debate between northern and southern sportsmen. This tension was also reflected in the sporting press, as the following article demonstrates. The editorial reprinted below, from the 17 December 1836 issue of The Spirit of the Times, reveals the journalistic competition that developed between the Spirit and the other major sporting journal of the time, the American Turf Register and Sporting Magazine.

THE AMERICAN TURF REGISTER, &C. BALTIMORE

In the number of this Magazine for December, we have found the following remarks which concern ourselves, and upon which in return we purpose saying one word:—

"The *New York Spirit of the Times* is informed, that the article in the October number of the Turf Register, concerning the race between Post Boy and John Bascomb, was furnished by a correspondent; if it had no signature, it was because the writer did not choose to use one. It was sent to us by a private hand, and a respectable gentleman became responsible for its contents. We think proper to enter into this detail, not as an apology for publishing the article, but merely for the purpose of showing that it was not editorial. As to the article itself, it professed to embody the arguments and facts adduced by the friends of Post Boy in his behalf, and as such, were open to refutation, if innocent, by the friends of Bascomb. As the Turf Register takes no partizan interest in any horse or turf question, we could not refuse the article an insertion, even if it had came to us anonymously, without committing ourselves as a partizan of Bascomb. The Spirit of the Times need scarcely trouble itself with our affairs, when informed—which it appears is necessary—that it is quite unlikely that we shall consult its editor as to the propriety or impropriety of publishing any article whatever in the Turf Register.

"We will remark further, that the considerable degree of feeling amongst Southern Turfmen, which the Spirit of the Times says has been caused by the publication of the article alluded to, is confined to the very brief precincts of the editor's own imagination. In all our intercourse with Southern Turfmen, and all our letters since its publication, not one word has been said in allusion to it. We have remarked for some time that the Spirit of the Times is endeavering to injure the Turf Register in the estimation of Southern sportsmen, and its remarks on the publication above alluded to, are intended to have that effect. We are perfectly willing to abide the result, knowing, as well as we do, the character of Southern sportsmen for intelligence and sagacity. The Spirit of the Times must have observed our unwillingness to trouble our subscribers with notice of that paper, or answers to its various attacks; and it will please consider this as the beginning and the end of such matters in the pages of the Turf Register."

However the Editor of the Turf Register may think proper to demean himself towards us, he is most respectfully informed, that as this is not the beginning, so it will not be the end of our notice of him, so long as he may either merit our praise, or deserve our censure. In either case, we shall ever notice the Turf Register, and *hope* to be able to do so for years to come. But we regret that for four or five months past we have had ample reason for censure in our customary remarks upon it. The Editor of that magazine shall not blink the question at issue with us, nor shall he be allowed to stab at us with sly insinuation, and then throw himself upon his dignity, and affect never to have noticed us.

How often we may have been noticed in that publication is immaterial; but that we have been most thoroughly read in that quarter, and fully quoted therein, every reader of the Register knows full well. Yet the Register, disregarding common justice, to say nothing of gratitude, assumed a few months since to caution its readers against "newspaper reports," in a manner that left no doubt as to the identity of the newspaper alluded to, or the motives that prompted the cover attack upon it. This offence against good manners and common honesty was repeated; but that there might be no room for a reader of his to doubt in the premises, that Editor quoted an account of an important race, which reflected severely upon our own report of it, and he accompanied that report with unauthorized imputations upon us. It so happened, however, that the contemporary who originally did us the injustice, having discovered his won error, most fairly and candidly stated the same to his readers. What the Editor of the Turf Register was then bound to do, was plainly to apologize for his own fault, and to publish the retraction of his contemporary. The Turf Register did neither; and if it have a reader who does not see this paper, or Mr. Colden's magazine, that reader must necessarily indulge a prejudice against us as a blundering meddler in the affairs of the Turf, and unworthy of credit.

We remonstrated against these proceedings in plain and mild, though "good set terms." We were determined to make the Register do us justice, or at least, refrain from positive injustice. Nothing was said, however, in reply to us; the Register went on as usual, making up its monthly issues, we had almost said, exclusively from our paper, till our remarks upon his Bascomb article called forth the extract placed at the head of this article. We will not be drawn into a controversy on that subject, inasmuch as the owners of the rival horses, and consequently their feelings and interests, ought not to be touched, merely to put down the Turf Register in an argument. But we may at least say this in reply to the modest assertion in the Register, that "In all our intercourse with Southern Turfmen, and in all our letters since its publication, *not one word has been said in allusion to it*," that one of the best written sporting articles we have read for some months was a forcible exposition of the injustice of the article in the Register. We copied that exposition from the Augusta Constitutionalist, and the Editor of the Register may find it now in our files. That exposition may teach the Register what one Southern turfman thought of the Register article, and we hardly see at this day a Northern turfman who would venture to endorse the claims of Post Boy as having bragged off John Bascomb, and sent him home, "branded with the challenge," &c. &c., or who differs from us in his opinions on the points in dispute.

But farther, the Turf Register is wilfully wrong in saying that we are "endeavoring to injure it in the estimation of Southern sportsmen." The Register knows that we lauded and praised it almost to the extent of puffery, and to the manifest hazard of having our motives suspected by all who *read* the Register. Nor did we cease such a course, till that magazine itself afforded not even an apology for faint praise, but began its reflections on us. We have ever desired, and do still desire, that the Turf Register may flourish. But in all sincerity, were we disposed to aim a blow at its prosperity, we could do it in no way more effectually than by begging all our readers just to read one number of it,—a second dose would be unnecessary, save in the most obstinate cases.

But we repeat, we have no ill will towards the Register; we desire for it success and a large circulation, *and an increase of merit*. And we will go farther, and say, that the last number is an improvement,—that it is the best, on one account, that has been published for months,—it is more original. We have read it all, we believe, with attention,—it has many articles of interest, and some sporting news. We congratulate its readers, and commend it to others.

But let not the Editor imagine that we shall allow him to reflect each month upon us, and then "talk somewhat oddly" of his unwillingness to trouble his readers with notices of this paper. We shall read the Register uniformly and carefully, and continue to advise the Editor "as to the propriety or impropriety of publishing any article whatever;" and we indulge much hope, that with our fostering care, and encouragement, and advice, and a little attention on the part of its Editor, some of our readers may yet live to see the Turf Register an able, interesting, and honest magazine.

THE ART OF JOURNALISM

The following article, reprinted from the 3 March 1832 edition of The Spirit of the Times addresses, in a humorous way, many of the important features of journalistic writing.

WRITING AN ARTICLE

WRITING AN ARTICLE.—Gentle reader, if thou happen to be that sage discreet personage which thy present occupations would seem to indicate, then surely the idea

has never entered thy profound cranium, *of writing an article!* Start not at our positive-
ness—for it may be we are not so dogmatical as might seem at first sight; we only
intended to affirm that thou hast never, in thy moments of sober reason, if not under
the dominion of all-conquering necessity, set thyself quietly down to perpetrate a paragraph, which should please all tastes, from the vinegar palate of the slander-loving
politician, to the licorice tooth of the novel-adoring maiden: to humor all caprices, from
the combativeness of Dick Hardfist, who will peruse nothing but bulletins of boxing
matches, to the more solemn but still one-sided notion of Aunt Dorothy, that nothing
is worth reading but a two-hour's sermon.

We would not advance the idea that there are no materials extant, from which an
interesting essay might be framed,—far from it. There is politics, for instance, upon
which we might write something marvellously agreeable and entertaining—to those
who like it; but the mischief of it is, that to treat of political matters in a manner at all
captivating, we must side with one party; and thus, while we were gracefully cutting
a pigeon wing in the eyes of one subscriber, we should be treading hard upon the corns
of another; and ever and anon, the grating sound of "stop my paper," would salute us,
instead of the "please send me," &c. which now rings so frequently and so musically
in our ears: so it wont answer to meddle with that subject.

Then there is the matter of theology on which we might display our acuteness (or
stupidity, as the case may be,) to the immense edification of some readers, but to the
utter discontent and disgust of others. We might spend an hour in endeavoring to convince our patrons that they were all possessed of souls, and be promptly and positively
refuted by a dozen of them stopping the paper on account of this article, and refusing
to pay for what they had received. We might labor earnestly to convince our readers
that mankind could not deserve damnation and be silenced at once by seeing one of
them steal the very sheet from the files of a free reading-room. So we shall leave
metaphysics entirely in the hands of the reverend Doctors of Divinity, and their com-
peers, the Doctors of the Hall of Science.

We have sometimes fancied that if any class of men in this republican land could
claim an affinity or rather resemblance, to kings, it must undoubtedly be the editors—
and our logic, as usual, shall follow close at the heels of our theory. And so—it must
be confessed, that, in the multiplicity and variety of their *subjects*, there is a striking
resemblance. True, the editor cannot always manage his subjects to please even himself; but then are not kings too, troubled with rebellious and unmanageable ones? Then
the unremitted importunity for office and favor with which a king is assailed—what
is it like but the interminable, unceasing cry for "copy" which haunts the editor even
in his dreams? And, then, is not *he* too beset with importunities for notice and favor?
Not, indeed, in the shape of substantial wealth or office; because the whole world
knows too well that he is the last man of whom to solicit such blessings—but in the
shape of sublimated puffs of nostrums, and glowing descriptions of the unequalled feats
of man-monkeys, and all that sort of thing! But, farther, is not the editor ever busy with
the affairs of nations and cabinets? is it not his province to be most dolefully affected
at the fall of a nation; and to look with alarm upon any event which threatens to over-
turn that vague something, which forms the statesman's watchword, "the balance of
power?" But then we must confess sad difference—the expenditures of the king result
in debts to be sure, but they are the debts of the nation,—while the editor's, we grieve

to say it, are all his own. We had intended that our present writing should be rather humorous than otherwise; and we have unfortunately stumbled upon matters too true to make a joke of—so we drop the subject.

But, what (inquires the reader, who has followed us thus far in our devious rambles,) do you propose to arrive at, in the course of these sage cogitations? Kind sir, we did not intend to inoculate you with any specific dogma, or enlighten you on any matter of history. We have been simply writing an article.

POLITICS AND SPORTS JOURNALISM

For the most part William T. Porter, editor of The Spirit of the Times, did not involve his newspaper in political affairs, confining it to sports and other literary, social, and cultural developments. One of the exceptions to this policy was an article that portrayed the 1836 presidential election as a horse race. The following "account" is reprinted from the 10 December 1836 issue of The Spirit of the Times.

NATIONAL RACE, UNION COURSE, 1836

Presidential Purse of $100,000, given by the People for all American bred horses, with $24,000 added by the Proprietors, to go to the second horse. Four miles out. Entries to carry weight for age. Constitutional rules to govern.

Entries:—

Martin Van Burens' *Kinderhook*	1
Richard M. Johnson's *Tecumseh*	0
Francis Granger's *Anti-Mason*	0
Wm. Henry Harrison's *Tippecanoe*	4
Hugh L. White's *Tennesseean*	5
Daniel Webster's *Federalist*	6
Wm. C. Rives' *Plenipotentiary*	7
Henry Clay's *American System*	dr.
John C. Calhoun's *Nullifier*	dr.

Of the eight that started, Tecumseh, Anti-Mason, and Plenipo' were entered for the second purse only, the most sanguine of their backers not anticipating their taking the first.

THE HORSES. Previous to the start, *Kinderhook* was the favorite against the field. He is a New York bred horse, and for many years was distinguished as a winner at short distances, though addicted to bolting and running against the fence. He was entered under the name of *Magician*, for a National purse some four years since, but went amiss, and would have been withdrawn from the turf, had not the Government bought and placed him under the charge of Old HICKORY, who has been so successful in *training*, as to have acquired the sobriquet of "General." Among the cocktails of the North, Kinderhook was a perfect leviathan, and under Old Hickory's training, even in Missouri, and the extreme South and West, the reputation of his trainer gave him a decided call. Old Hickory's celebrity is based upon solid grounds, though he derives much of it from the circumstance of having distanced a fine field of imported English nags at New Orleans, with *Militia*, that had been in training but a few weeks. Kinderhook is a game looking nag to the eye, though having lost his forelock, and being of small size, he has more than once been started as a "singed cat."

Tippecanoe is a Virginia-bred horse, and broke down in training some years since, previous to which he had never been beaten. His campaigns at the West gave him the call as second favorite for the principal pure, though it was evident his friends was long doubtful whether he was the best horse in the same stable of this race. However, a few private trials decided them to start him, and he was immediately put in training by a clique, well known in sporting circles as the "Opposition." Tippecanoe is by Whig, dam by Constitution, of a grey color, and fine action. His stock is likely to "do the State some service."

Tennesseean has a great reputation at home as an honest running nag, that can be depended upon, though celebrated for neither speed or bottom to an eminent degree. He was entered under the expectation that some of his competitors might go amiss. The odds against him for the race was China to a China orange; but some of his backers were staunch, after it was evident he could not go the pace.

Federalist, by Hamilton's Old Federalist, dam by Hartford Convention, though of undoubted bottom, comes of a stock so unfashionable of late, as to have few backers. He was in hands in which on confidence was placed by the public, having frequently been nominated in sweepstakes, but withdrawn on the day of the race, and some other nag in the same stable named in his place. Under any other circumstances he would have been a favorite. He is a strong outsider, but in a race some years since with Nullifier and American System, he broke down.

The Kentucky champion, *American System*, is one of the best two or three mile horses in the country, but has never been able to go four miles. He was raised in the Old Dominion, so famous for "good ones," but having unfortunately bolted and thrown his rider when contending against a nag called *Military Chieftain* some years since on the National course, his backers have lost confidence in him. When he is right, however, he can cut out the work for the fleetest or stoutest. It was deemed advisable to withdraw him just before the start, in hopes that he may come again at the next meeting in 1840.

Nullifier is a splendid animal, of fine action and appearance, and altogether a good one. He was by Jefferson, the sire of Independence, out of Nullification's dam. He was of uncommon promise, when he first came upon the turf, but such was high spirit and impetuosity, those certain proofs of the purity of his blood, that he unfortunately broke down in training, and afterwards received a kick from *Old Roman* that almost disabled him. Of course he has been withdrawn, to the great disappointment of his friends.

Of the three that started for the 2d purse little need be said. *Tecumseh* was the favorite of the lot and his performance has demonstrated the judgment of the knowing ones. He having run a dead heat with *Anti-Mason*, the matter has been left to the decision of the Club. Tecumseh's pedigree we do not find in the Racing Calendar, but it is notorious that in the West he beat the Indian ponies to sticks. Perhaps his greatest exploit was the carrying of the Sunday Mail Report, when he beat Sanctity, Intolerance, and Bigotry, three noted Yankee horses,—an exploit not excelled by Mr. Osbaldistone, with *Tranby* or *Tom Thumb*.

Anti-Mason, who ran second to Tecumseh, has generally placed himself well, though he has never been entered for a four mile race. A few years since he ran *Marcy*, (by Democrat, dam by St. Tammany, one of the best mile horses on the turf), up to a head, on the New York Course. He is a beautiful horse in shape and size, and had Hickory trained him, there is no doubt he would have given a better account of himself.

Plenipo comes of a good stock, but saw so much hard service when he was running under the name of French Minister, that the "go along" was pretty much taken out of him. His backers, however, were sanguine to the last. Several attempts were made to induce "*Glory*," Mr. Hickory's best rider to mount him, but Hickory swore "by the Eternal" he'd see him hanged first, and then he wouldn't.

THE RACE.—*Kinderhook* had the track, and was under the direction of Old Hickory, his trainer, while Federalist was placed by Bosting on the outer edge to make a straight run for the lead. After the Jockies were up there was so much confusion, and disputing about the positions of the entries among their friends, that several false starts were the result. We had almost forgotten to state that Gen. JACKSON is President of the Club, and officiated on the present occasion.—The Judges of the Supreme Court were appointed timers, and FRANCIS P. BLAIR, Esq., of the Globe, Secretary *pro tem.* The crowd was immense, and so much interest has not been manifested since the day *Washington* challenged the world, and walked over the Course without a competitor.

At length the signal was given, and they were off, Kinderhook leading, Tecumseh well up, and Tippecanoe trailing behind ready for a brush. Tennesseean was badly rode, and the false starts so worried him that he sulked, and when his rider touched his glossy flank with the spur, it was with great difficulty he could be kept in the track. Plenipo after the *first* mile was taken in hand, and Federalist and Anti-Mason took up the running. The pace improved on the second mile, when Federalist declined, and Tippecanoe made play with Kinderhook for the lead, while in their rear, running a dead lock were Anti-Mason, and Tecumseh. Both of them were jockied in masterly style. Anti-Mason, with Morgan on his back is an ugly customer in any field. Tecumseh was bestrode by a half-breed, who having been in Kinderhook's stable, had picked up from Hickory, his trainer, a few hints that were of essential service on the present occasion. On the last quarter of the second mile the tailing commenced. Tennesseean first "shut up " and fell back upon Federalist. Plenipo soon got tired of the pace, although it is said that "Old Virginny never tires," and followed suit by retiring into the ruck, leaving Kinderhook and Tippecanoe first and second, and Tecumseh and Anti-Mason a good third and fourth. We wonder at the conceit of their owners in bringing the former three into the field; they must have been egregiously deceived in their private trials, otherwise their nags are cocktails.

It soon became evident that on the *North* side of the track Kinderhook could outbrush the field, and the same might be said of the long straight sweep from *North* to *South*. In the heavy part of the trace on the West side, Tippecanoe's strength and bottom told fearfully. The shouts sent up by the multitude, "fresh from the people," were deafening, as their several favorites took the lead. The pace gradually improved, until it was too good to last. Kinderhook's backers began, on the 3d mile, to increase the odds on him, while the issue of the contest between Tecumseh and Antimason was so doubtful, that no great sums were laid out about them. As they came down the track on the West side, Tippecanoe went up gallantly, and challenged Kinderhook, and locked him for several hundred yards, when K.'s trainer shouted to his rider to "take the lead and keep it!" After a desperate struggle, Tippecanoe fell back, his rider holding him well together to recover his wind for a final brush on the 1st quarter of the 4th mile. Morgan, on Anti-Mason, was intending to play the same game, but when he took his horse in hand, the game chicken on Tecumseh pulled to him, still keeping the inside of the track and wide awake for a brush. At this point, while the field were going comparatively at their ease, Tennesseean, like another "Monsieur Tonson, came again," as did Plenipo, but after a few jumps, which revived hopes in their backers only to disappoint them, the two were done, Tecumseh and Anti-Mason both going at Plenipo, and giving him the *coup de grace*, while Tennesseean had to contend with the whole field. He soon got in a crowd, and they *do* say there was some foul riding, but where, or by whom, deponent saith not. At any rate he was so effectually done up, that nothing but good management brought him within the distance flag.

Throughout the last mile the interest was most intense, and the running severer than ever. Tippecanoe, who had been going in hand, now let himself out, and his stride was tremendous. Kinderhook's rider, the sly fox, was up to trap, and the bit of blood under him was going steadily, ready to be called upon at the critical moment. Tippecanoe led again down the West side, with Tecumseh and Anti-Mason running a dead lock, with the knees of their jockeys jostling each other. The insider stakes between the two were immense, and though neither was booked for the main purse, the contest between them was hardly less exciting than that between Kinderhook and Tippecanoe. They came in a cluster round the sweep upon the straight run home, and now "the de'il take the hindmost." "Tippecanoe's ahead," was the cry, as they shot round the turn, but here the rider of Kinderhook called upon his horse, who, true as steel, at once "justified his training." "There goes Kinderhook!" "Hurrah for the Magician!" "Don't tell me a Dutchman ever wanted bottom!" "Where's old Tip?" "There's the old veteran—Tip's got him too,—see that, see that! Old Tip-your-canoe-over for ever!" "Go it Kinderhook!" "Only see Tecumseh!—there's foot and bottom for ye!" "Put the screws to him; Morgan." "Give him the steel up to the gaffs!" They came within the gate at a flight of speed, when Kinderhook shied at a *bank*; and Tippecanoe, in endeavoring to take his place, was pulled up so sharply in crossing, as to lose his stride, and never recovered it, while Kinderhook maintained his to the end, by dint of whip and spur, coming in ahead by a length or more. Tecumseh and Anti-Mason, after a brush, unparalleled for severity and continuance, came in neck and neck running a dead heat. Kinderhook was immediately declared the winner, while the Judges have taken time to decide whether Tecumseh or Anti-Mason is entitled to the second purse. Their decision will be declared at Washington on or before the 4th of March next. Thus ended the thirteenth National Jockey Club Meeting on the Union Course.

CULTURAL DIMENSIONS OF SPORTS

As many sports expanded and developed from 1820 to 1840, so did the newspaper industry that chronicled these changes. By the 1830s sports journalism moved beyond the mere reporting of sporting events and began to offer commentary on the social and cultural aspects of sport in North America as well as about sports coverage itself. The following article, originally appearing in the Southern Literary Messenger, is reprinted from the 15 April 1837 issue of The Spirit of the Times.

SPORTS OF THE TURF IN AMERICA

It has been asserted that the national character of a people depends more upon the amusements to which they are addicted, than upon their laws, their literature, or their religious institutions. We think it would be difficult to establish this position by an appeal to the records of history; and yet it well be admitted that amusements exert no inconsiderable influence upon the character of communities. Whether this influence be prejudicial or otherwise, depends of course on the nature of the entertainments to which they devote themselves. In our Southern states, where horsemanship is regarded as a necessary accomplishment for every gentlemen, and ladies esteem an elegant equipage an object even of greater ambition than the expensive decoration of their persons, it is not surprising, that raising fine and beautiful horses should be considered more important than in other parts of the Union. Horse racing, therefore, whose object is to improve the breed of that noble animal by stimulating competition, and offering a reward to the successful competitor, is one of the most popular amusements among us. The passion for this exciting sport is evidently upon the increase in our country. The North, the South, and the West eagerly contend for the mastery, and not a little sectional pride is enlisted upon the issue in every encounter. The celebrated horses, which have been victorious upon the course, are everywhere know, and the pedigree of a blooded steed is traced through a long line of ancestors, whose fine qualities and remarkable achievements are among the most hacknied of topics. The traveller who passes through the Southern and Western states of our country especially, would often be entirely excluded from conversation, if he had not some knowledge of the subject, and it is important, therefore, that he should inform himself upon it. In Carolina, horses are not raised for the market, but no expense is spared in training them for the course. One of our wealthiest and most public spirited citizens has lately imported several fine horses from Europe, with the view of improving the Carolina breed, and had the good fortune to carry off some of the heaviest purses at the recent races. Several journals are already established in our country, whose object is to give an account of the races that occur in different parts of the Union, and even in England; to place before the public the pedigree, history, and peculiar characteristics of the present generation of race-horses, and to keep alive the passion for the pleasures of the turf by sporting anecdotes, and intelligence of a lively description. No magazines are more eagerly sought after, or more diligently read by a large mass of our citizens, and the influence they exert upon the popular feelings and character, is certainly not inconsiderable.

A well written and animated account of the races has appeared in the Charleston Courier, from the practised pen of an eye witness who was every day upon the course, and we shall take the liberty of extracting it nearly entire, as being better and more complete than any thing we could offer to our readers.

"We were greeted on the first day's race, for the Club's purse of $1000, with much of the taste and fashion of the city upon the course. All parts of the State, and the neighboring States, conspired to swell the concourse; and the ladies, by their presence and their smiles, gave a seducing influence to the gay and animated scene. The beautiful and splendid equipages, with rich-liveried coachmen, footmen and out-riders, the skilful and rapid driving, performing involutions and evolutions without accident, whilst the beaux with their gallant steeds kept near the objects of their loves, ready at any moment to play the knight-errant, and to do their fair lady's bidding. In rapid succession the heavy Omnibus and four would be seen wending to the citizens' stand, with its dozen or more passengers. Relieved of its load, with swifter motion it would return again to the city for other passengers, thus continually passing and re-passing each other, like buckets in a well. At the same time crowds of the most promiscuous character would be issuing through the foot-passenger's gate. The sailor, retailer, journeyman, apprentice, fruiterer, confectioner, stable boys, and chimney sweeps, in one dense mass, would gather around the post. In various directions you could see the little urchins playing ground and lofty tumbling over the fence; whilst others, of more grovelling propensities, would make a hole underneath sufficiently large to pass through. The mounted constables were now all employed to keep intruders out, whilst those in the picketed area at the post were constantly in motion to keep it clear of volunteers and the curious. The survey of the whole assembly presented a most variegated view. The eye rested at the same time upon all that was lovely, and interesting, as well as upon that which was loathsome and disgusting. Yet this very variety had its interest. It is by contrast every thing that is lovely is made more enchanting. It is vice that gives lustre to virtue, and avarice clothes charity in its richest drapery. The physical world, with its calms and tempests, its day and night, its winter and summer, spring and autumn, is the grand prototype of the moral world.

Whilst viewing the vast concourse, the martial notes of the bugle burst upon the ear. It was a call for the field that were to contend for the purse. In a short time, the nags appeared clothed and hooded, moving in that slow and sluggish walk for which the racer is remarkable. After promenading the picketed area a few minutes, the bugle sounded the note of preparation. The hood was drawn away, and the clothing removed, and each one stood presented to the crowd in all the courser's symmetry, heightened by his high grooming. Each nag began to enlist friends, according to the respective judgments of the beholders. Bets were now made in various ways; some on the favorite against the field—some on a particular horse for the first heat—some on horse against horse, and in many other shapes. The bugle sounds the order to saddle—all is now anxiety and preparation. It is now that the racer becomes animated—it is now that he realises the fact that a contest is to come, and the eye that was lately so listless, is now all animation and fire. The charge of fair riding, and the distance to be run, are next given; when the tastefully dressed boys, with cap, spurs, and whip, vault into the saddle. The reins are shortened and knotted, and winding them round each hand, they are brought to the post. There is a general anxiety that pervades the bosom of every beholder, whilst they eagerly wait the word "go." At length it breaks upon the general silence, and all are off for victory and fame. The various efforts made by each to out-strip his rival, are extremely interesting. When a favorite takes the lead, smiles of con-gratulation are exchanged between his friends. A deep interest, at all times during the heat, exists, and the conclusion is greeted with hurrahs and cheers by the multitude to the winning horse.

Each nag is now habited again, and walked about for a few minutes. The rubbing and removing the perspiration follows:—each jockey is now on the watch to see which horse cools off best. It is the great criterion by which to determine their fate in the succeeding heat. According to their judgment in this matter, betting is again renewed. After half an hour's delay, all those that were not posted, are again summoned to the contest for the second heat. The same anxiety or greater, is kept up during the second heat, that existed in the first.—The multitude who lately greeted the victor, are now anxious that another should succeed, so that the heats may be broken, and the contest continued. If this event takes place, the sport is redoubled and the joy universal. Again, the jockies watch narrowly the situation of each horse. New opinions are formed, and old ones changed. Betting is resumed, and the wary better sometimes, (discovering the first opinion wrong,) sets about hedging. If successful, he remedies his first error, in no way can he be the loser, if it be a perfect hedge, nor can he win.

If the heats be broken, the contest is renewed, and continued until one horse wins two heats. But four heats can be run, unless there is a dead heat. The rule which ex-cludes all those horses that do not win a heat in three heats, is founded upon principles of sound humanity.

When the race is terminated, many wheel their way to town, and many toward the booths. At the booths, there is an ample provision of eatables and drinkables, with a most awful phalanx of every shade of colour, who are your attendants at the table or the bar. In a population like ours, we probably cannot prevent this, but we would much prefer to see some industrious whites in the same situation. The freedom taken, the coarse joke, are what we complain of. This should be put down by public opinion, and we trust it will be. We are pleased to see that the club is moving in this matter. We also complain of the indiscriminate gaming. We are perfectly certain it is impossible to prevent this vice effectually. It may, however, be greatly circumscribed. We were much pleased at the order and regularity observed at the Citizens' stand. The attendants there were whites. The fare was good, and there was no bustle and confusion. The gaming going on there was much more orderly than that pursued elsewhere. At all events, there was nothing to blame as to the attendants, and the civility of the lessee, or his agents.

The races have passed. For the Club purses there have been twelve different horses in the field. We are not a stickler for the horse's names, but we could have wished that the sponsors of two of them had named them differently. Most frequently the names of our finest country women are given to horses, as well as to ships. But who would not feel offended to see one of Carolina's loveliest daughter's names joined in an en-try with an ill-matched associate. To say the least of it, it is bad taste.

After a retrospect of the past, we cannot but say, taking the good and the bad, the rough and the smooth, we are still an advocate for the sports of the Turf, when regu-lated as they are, by the first and most prominent citizens of our State. The social din-ner, the gay and brilliant ball, are appendages that set off to advantage the sports of the Turf. These were most numerously attended, and the utmost hilarity and good humour crowned each,—and so may it ever be."

There are few persons who visit the course merely to see the race. They go for purposes of social enjoyment,—to meet their friends, to extend their acquaintance, to transact business, and for various other legitimate objects. If the idle and frivolous throng hither, so do persons of the most respectable character. It is a place where society may be seen in every shade of variety, and the world, its follies, its caprices, and its better traits be studied by the curious observer in living examples. Much money is expended, and much foolishly, but it is not lost to the community. The virtuous, honest, and industrious, receive the benefit of it through various channels. If knaves and sharpers get a portion of it, its natural tendency is soon to pass out of their hands into the pockets of those who will make a good use of it. The Races, therefore, have advantages to recommend them. They bring strangers together from all parts of the country; they tend to strengthen the bonds of brotherhood, to create mutual interest, and to bind town and country, and even neighbouring states in more enduring relations of kind feeling and friendly intercourse.

THE EMERGENCE OF LITERARY SPORTS WRITING

Henry William Herbert came from a distinguished British family, but it was in the United States where he made his mark as a writer and sportsman. In America he pursued a life of letters with moderate success at best and in 1839 he reluctantly accepted an assignment from a sporting journal to write a more literary sports piece. Still hopeful of a career as a historical novelist, Herbert initially wanted the piece to be published anonymously and later agreed to have it printed under the pseudonym, Frank Forrester. The assignment turned into a seven-part series and became a watershed in the development of sports writing. The following document, reprinted from the May/June 1839 edition of the American Turf Register was the first installment of the series.

A WEEK IN THE WOODLANDS:
OR SCENES ON THE ROAD, IN THE FIELD, AND ROUND THE FIRE, 1839
by Frank Forester.

DAY THE FIRST.

It was a fine October evening, when I was sitting on the back stoop of his cheerful little bachelor's establishment in _____street, with my old friend and comrade Henry Archer—many a frown of fortune had we two weathered out together, in many of her brightest smiles had we two revelled—never was there a stauncher friend, a merrier companion, a keener sportsman, or a better fellow, than this said Harry; and here had we two met three thousand miles from home, after almost ten years of separation, just the same careless, happy, dare-all do-no-goods as we were when we parted in St. James's street,—he for the West, I for the Eastern World—he to fell trees, and build log huts in the back-woods of Canada,—I to shoot tigers and drink arrack punch in Carnatic. The world had wagged with us as with most others; now up, now down, and brought us up, at last, far enough from the goal for which we started—so that, as I have said already, on landing in New York, having heard nothing of him for ten years, whom the deuce should I tumble on but that same worthy, snuggly housed, with a neat bachelor's menage and every thing ship-shape about him,—and, in the natural course of things, we were at once inseparables.

Well, as I said before, it was a bright October evening, with the clear sky, rich sunshine, and brisk breezy freshness, which indicate that loveliest of the American months,—dinner was over, and with a pitcher of the liquid ruby of Latour, a brace of half-pint beakables, and a score—my contribution—of those most exquisite of smokers, the true old Manilla cheroots, we were consoling the inward man in a way that would have opened the eyes with abhorrent admiration, of any advocate of that coldest of comforts—cold water—who should have got a chance peep at our snuggery.

Suddenly after a long pause, during which he had been stimulating his ideas by assiduous fumigation, blowing off his steam in a long vapory cloud that curled a minute afterward about his temples,—"What say you, Frank, to a start to-morrow?" "Why as for that," said I, "I wish for nothing better—but where the deuce would you go to get shooting?"

"Never fash your beard, man," he replied, "I'll find the ground and the game too, so you'll find share of the shooting!—Holloa! there—Jim, Jim Matlock"—and in brief space that worthy minister of mine host's pleasures made his appearance, smoothing down his short black hair, clipped in the orthodox bowl fashion, over his bluff good natured visage with one hand, while he employed its fellow in hitching up a pair of most voluminous unmentionables, of thick Yorkshire cord. A character was Tim—and now I think of it, worthy of brief description. Born, I believe—bred, certainly, in a hunting stable, far more of his life passed in the saddle than elsewhere, it was not a little characteristic of my friend Harry to have selected this piece of Yorkshire oddity as his especial body servant; but if the choice were queer, it was at least successful, for an honester, more faithful, hard-working—and withal, better hearted, and more humorous varlet never drew curry-comb over horse hide, or clothes-brush over broad-cloth. His visage was, as I have said already, bluff and good-natured, with a pair of black eyes, of the smallest—but at the same time, of the very merriest—twinkling from under the thick black eye-brows, which were the only hairs suffered to grace his clean-shaved countenance,—an indescribable pug nose, and of good clean cut mouth, with a continual dimple at the left corner made up his phiz; for the rest, four feet ten inches did Tim stand in his stockings, about two-ten of which were monopolized by his back, the shoulders of which would have done honor to a six foot pugilist,—his legs, though short and bowed a little outward, by continual horse exercise, were right tough, serviceable, members, and I have seen them bearing their owner on, through mud and mire, when straighter, longer, and more fair proportioned limbs were at an awful discount.

Depositing his hat then on the floor, smoothing his hair, and hitching up his smalls, and striving most laboriously not to grin till he should have cause, stood Tim, like "Giafar awaiting his *master's* award!"

"Tim!" said Harry Archer—

"Sur!" said Tim.

"Tim! Mr. Forester and I are talking of going up to-morrow—what do you say to it?"

"Oop yonner?" queried Tim, in his most extraordinary West-Riding Yorkshire, indicating the direction, by pointing his right thumb over his left shoulder—"Weel, Ay'se nought to say aboot it—not, Ay!"

"Well—then the cattle are all right, and the wagon in good trim, and the dogs in exercise, are they?"

"Ay'se warrant um!"

"Well, then, have all ready for a start at six to-morrow,—put Mr. Forester's Manton alongside my Joe Spurling in the top tray of the gun case, my single, and my double rifle in the lower,—and see the magazine well filled—the glass gunpowder, you know, from Moore and Baker's. You'll put up what Mr. Forester will want, for a week, you know—he does not know the country yet, Tim;—and hark you, what wine have I at Tom Draw's?"

"No but a case o' claret."

I thought so, then away with you! down to the Baron's and get two baskets of the star, and stop at Fulton Market, and get the best half hundred round of spiced beef you can find—and then go up to Starke's at the Octagon, and get a gallon of his old Farentosh—that's all, Tim—off with you!—No! stop a minute!" and he filled up a beaker and handed it to the original who, shutting both his eyes, suffered the fragrant claret to roll down his gullet, in the most scientific fashion, and then, with what he called a bow, turned right about, and exit.

The sun rose bright on the next morning, and half an hour before the appointed time, Tim entered by bed-chamber, with a cup of mocha, and the intelligence that "Measter had been up this hour and better, and did na like to be kept waiting!"—so up I jumped, and scarcely got through the business of rigging myself, before the rattle of wheels announced the arrival of the wagon. And a model was that shooting wagon— a long, light-bodied box, with a low rail—a high seat and dash in front, and a low servant's seat behind, with lots of room for four men and as many dogs, with guns and luggage, and all appliances to boot, enough to last a month, stowed away out of sight, and out of reach of weather; the nags, both nearly thorough-bred, fifteen-two inches high, stout, clean-limbed, active animals; the offside horse a gray, almost snow-white— the near, a dark, nearly black, chesnut, with square docks setting admirably off their beautiful round quarters; high crests, small blood-like heads and long thin manes, spoke volumes for Tim's stable science—for though their ribs were slightly visible, their muscles were well filled, and hard as granite; their coats glanced in the sunshine—the white's like statuary marble; the chesnut's like high polished copper—in short the whole turn out was perfect. The neat black harness; relieved merely by a crest, with every strap that could be needed, in its place, and not one buckle or one thong superfluous; the bright steel curbs, with the chains jingling as the horses tossed and pawed impatient for a start; the tapering holly whip; the bear-skins covering the seats; the top coats spread above them,—every thing, in a word, without bordering on the slang, was perfectly correct and gnostic. Four dogs—a brace of setters of the light active breed, one of which will out-work a brace of the large, lumpy, heavy-headed dogs,—one red, the other white and liver, both with black noses, legs and sterns, beautifully feathered, and their hair glossy and smooth as silk, showing their excellent condition—and a brace of short-legged, bony, liver-colored spaniels—with their heads thrust one above the other, over or through the railings, and their tails waving with impatient joy—occupied the after portion of the wagon. Tim, rigged in plain gray frock, with leathers and white tops, stood, in true tiger fashion, at their heads, with the fore-finger of his right hand resting upon the curb of the gray horse, as with his left he rubbed the nose of the chesnut, while Harry, cigar in mouth, was standing at the wheel, reviewing with a steady and experience eye the gear, which seemed to give him perfect satisfaction. The moment I appeared on the steps, "In with you, Frank—in with you," he exclaimed, disengaging the hand-reins from the territs into which they had been thrust,—"I have been waiting here these five minutes. Jump up, Tim!"—'and gathering the reins up firmly he mounted by the wheel, tucked the top-coat about his legs, shook out the long lash of his tandem whip and lapped it up in good style,—"I always drive with one of these"—he said, half apologetically, as I thought—"they are so handy on the road for the cur dogs, when you have setters with you—they plague your life out else. Have you the pistol-case in, Tim, for I don't see it?" "All roight, Sur," answered he, not over well pleased, as it seemed, that it should even be suspected, that he could have forgotten any thing—"All roight"

"Go along, then," cried Harry, "and at the word the high bred nags went off, and, though my friend was too good and too old a hand to worry his cattle at the beginning of a long day's journey—many minutes had not passed before we found ourselves on board the ferryboat, steaming it merrily towards the Jersey shore!

"A quarter-past six to the minute," said Harry, as we landed at Hoboken.

"Let *Shot* and *Chase* run, Tim, but keep the spaniels in till we pass Hackensack.

"Awa wi ye, ye rascals," exclaimed Tim; and out went the blooded dogs upon the instant, barking and jumping in delight about the horses—and off we went, through the long sandy street of Hoboken, leaving the private race course of that staunch sportsman, Mr. Stevens, on the left, with several powerful horses taking their walking exercise in their neat body clothes.

"That puts me in a mind, Frank," said Harry, as he called my attention to the thorough-breds, "we must be back next Tuesday for the Beacon Races— the new Course up there on the hill; you can see the steps that lead to it from here—and now is not lovely," he continued, as we mounted the first ridge of Weehawken, and looked back over the beautiful broad Hudson, gemmed with a thousand snowy sails of craft or shipping—"Is not this lovely, Frank? and, by the bye, you will say, when we get to our journey's end, you never drove through prettier scenery in your life. Get away Bob, you villain, nibbling, nibbling at your curb! get away lads!" and away we went at a right rattling pace over the hills, and past the cedar swamp; and passing through a toll-gate stopped with a sudden jerk at a long low tavern on the left-hand side.

"We must stop here, Frank; my old friend Engles, a brother trigger too, would think the world was coming to an end if I drove by—twenty-nine minutes these six miles," he added, looking at his watch, "that will do! Now, Tim, look sharp—just a sup of water! Good day, good day to you, Mr. Engles; now for a glass of your milk punch"— and mine host disappeared, and in a moment came forth with two rummers of the delicious compound, big bright lump of ice bobbing about in each, among the nutmeg.

"What, off again for Orange county, Mr. Archer? I was telling the old woman yesterday, that we should have you by before long; well, you'll find cock pretty plenty, I expect; there was a chap by here from Ulster—let me see what day was it—Friday, I guess—with produce, and he was telling they have had no cold snap yet up there! Thank you, sir, good luck to you!" and off we went again, along a level road, crossing the broad slow river from whence it takes its name, into the town of Hackensack. "We breakfast here, Frank"—as he pulled up beneath the low Dutch shed projecting over half the road in front of the neat tavern,—"How are you, Mr. Vanderbeck—we want a beef steak, and a cup of tea, as quick as you can give it us: we'll make the tea ourselves; bring in the black tea, Tim—the nags as usual."

"Aye! aye! sur"—"tak them out—leave t' harness on, all but their bridles"—to an old gray-headed hostler. "Whisp off their legs a bit: I will be oot enoo!"

After as good a breakfast as fresh eggs, good country bread—worth ten times the poor trash of city bakers—prime butter, cream and a fat steak could furnish, at a cheap rate, and with a civil and obliging landlord, away we went again over the red-hills,—an infernal ugly road, sandy, and rough, and stony—for ten miles farther to New Prospect. "Now you shall see some scenery worth looking at," said Harry, as we started again, after watering the horses, and taking in a bag with a peck of oats—"to feed at three o'clock, Frank, when we stop to grub, which must do *al fresco*—my friend explained—"for the landlord, who kept the only tavern on the road, went West this summer, bit by the land mania, and there is now no stopping place 'twixt this and _____," naming the village for which we were bound. "You got that beef boiled, Tim?"

"Ay'd been a fou'il else, and aye so often oop t' road too, answered he with a grin, "and t' moostard is mixed, and t' pilot biscuit in, and a good bit o'Cheshire cheese! wee's doo, Aye reckon.—Ha! ha! ha!"

And now my friend's boast was indeed fulfilled; for when we had driven a few miles farther, the country became undulating with many and bright streams of water; the hill sides clothed with luxuriant woodlands, now in their many colored garb of autumn beauty; the meadow-land rich in unchanged fresh greenery—for the summer had been mild and rainy—with here and there a buck-wheat stubble showing its ruddy face, replete with promise of quail in the present, and of hot cakes in future; and the bold chain of mountains, which, under many names, but always beautiful and wild, sweeps from the highlands of the Hudson, west and southwardly, quite through New Jersey, forming a link between the white and green mountains of New Hampshire and Vermont, and the more famous Alleghanies of the South.

A few miles farther yet, the road wheeled round the base of the Tourne mountain, a magnificent bold hill, with a bare craggy, head, its sides and skirts thick set with cedars and hickory—entering a defile through which the Ramapo, one of the loveliest streams eye ever looked upon, comes rippling with its chrystal waters over bright pebbles on its way to join the two kindred rivulets, which form the fair Passaic! Throughout the whole of that defile, nothing can possibly surpass the loveliness of nature; the road hard, and smooth, and level, winding and wheeling parallel to the gurgling river, crossing it two or three times in each mile, now on one side, and now on the other—the valley now barely broad enough to permit the highway and the stream to pass between the abrupt masses of rock and forest, and now expanding into rich basins of green meadow-land, the deepest and most fertile possible—the hills of every shape and size—here bold, and bare, and rocky—there swelling up in grand round masses, pile above pile of verdure to the blue firmament of autumn. By and bye we drove through a thriving little village, nestling in a hollow of the hills beside a broad bright pond, whose waters keep a dozen manufactories of cotton and of iron—with which mineral these hills abound—in constant operation; and passing by the tavern, the departure of whose owner Harry had so pathetically mourned, we wheeled again round a projecting spur of hill into a narrower defile, and reached another hamlet, but far different in its aspect from the busy bustling place we had left some five miles behind. There were some twenty houses, with two large mills of solid masonry, but of these not one building was now tenanted; the roof-trees broken, the doors and shutters either torn from their hinges, or flapping wildly to and fro; the mill wheels cumbering the stream with masses of decaying timber; and the whole presenting a most desolate and mournful aspect. "Its story is soon told," Harry said, catching my inquiring glance—"a speculating, clever, New York merchant,—a water-power—a failure—and a consequent desertion of the project; but we must find a berth among the ruins!" and as he spoke turning a little off the road, he pulled up on the green sward; "there's an old stable here that has a manager in it yet! now Tim, look sharp!" and in a twinkling the horses were loosed from the wagon, the harness taken off and hanging on the corners of the rumed hovels, and Tim hissing and rubbing away at the gray horse, while Harry did like duty on the chesnut, in a style that would have done no shame to Melton Mowbray!

"Come, Frank, make yourself useful! get out the round of beef, and all the rest of the provant—it's on the rack behind; you'll find all right there. Spread our table-cloth on that flat stone by the waterfall, under the willow; clap a couple of bottles of the Baron's champagne into the pool there underneath the fall; let's see whether your Indian campaigning has taught you any thing worth knowing!"

To work I went at once, and by the time I had gone through, "come, Tim," I heard him say, "I've got the rough dirt off this fellow, you must polish him, while I take a wash, and get a bit of dinner. Holloa! Frank are you ready?" and he came bounding down to the water's edge, with his Newmarket coat in hand, and sleeves rolled up to the elbows, plunged his face into the cool stream, and took a good wash of his soiled hands in the same natural basin. Five minutes afterwards we were employed most pleasantly with the spiced beef, white biscuit, and good wine, which came out of the waterfall as cool as Gunter could have made it with all his icing. When we had pretty well got through, and were engaged with our cheroots, up came Tim Matlock.

T' horses have got through wi' t' corn—they have fed rarely—so I harnessed them, sur, all to the bridles—we can start when you will." "Sit down, and get your dinner then, sir—there's a heel-tap in that bottle we have left for you—and when you have done, put up the things, and we'll be off. I say Frank, let us try a shot with the pistols,—I'll get the case—stick up that fellow-commoner upon the fence there, and mark off a twenty paces."

The marking irons were produced—and loaded—'Fire—one—two—three"—bang! and the shivering of the glass announced that never more would that chap hold the generous liquor—the ball had struck it plump in the centre, and broken off the whole above the shoulder—for it was fixed neck downward on a stake.—"It is my turn now," said I—and more by luck. I fancy, than by skill, I took the neck off, leaving nothing but the thick ring of the mouth still sticking on the summit of the fence—'T'll hold you a dozen of my best regalias against as many of Manillas, that I break the ring."

"Done, Harry!"

"Done!"

Again the pistol cracked, and the unerring ball drove the small fragment into a thousand splinters.

"That's fotched 'um!"—exclaimed Tim, who had come up to announce all ready—"Ecod, measter Frank, you munna wager i' that gate wi' measter, or my name beant Tim, but thou'lt be clean, bamboozled."

Well—not to make a short story long—we got under way again, and with speed unabated, spanked along at full twelve miles an hour, for five miles farther. There, down a wild looking glen, on the left hand, comes brawling, over stump and stone, a tributary streamlet—by the side of which a rough track, made by the charcoal burners and the iron miners, intersects the main road—and up this miserable looking path—for it was little more—Harry wheeled at full trot—"now for twelve miles of mountain, the roughest road and wildest country you ever saw crossed in a phaeton, good master Frank." And wild it was, indeed, and rough enough in all conscience—narrow, unfenced, in many places, winding along the brow of precipices without rail or breastwork, encumbered with huge blocks of stone, and broken by the summer rains—an English stage coachman would have stared aghast at the steep zigzags up the hills—the awkward turns on the descents—the sudden pitches, with now an unsafe bridge, and now a strong ford at the bottom—but through all this, the delicate, quick fingers, keen eye, and cool head of Harry, assisted by the rare mouths of his exquisitely bitted cattle, piloted us at the rate of full ten miles the hour!—the scenery, through which the wild track ran, being entirely of the most grand and savage character of woodland—the bottom filled with gigantic timber trees, cedar, and pine, and hemlock, with a dense undergrowth of rhododendron, calmia, and azalia, which, as my friend informed me made the whole mountains in the summer season one rich bed of bloom. About six miles from the point where we had entered them we scaled the highest ridge of hills, by three almost preciptious zigzags, the topmost one paved by a stratum of broken shaley limestone; and passing at once from the forest into well cultivated fields, came on a new and lovelier prospect—a narrow deep vale scarce a mile in breadth—scooped as it were out of the mighty mountains which embosomed it on every side—in the highest state of culture, with rich orchards, and deep meadows, and brown stubbles, whereon the shocks of maize stood fair and frequent—and eastward of the road—which diving down obliquely to the bottom, loses itself in the woods of the opposite hill-side, and only becomes visible again when it emerges to cross over the next summit—the loveliest sheet of water my eye has ever seen, varying from half a mile to a mile in breadth, and about five miles long, with shores indented deeply with the capes and promontories of the wood-clothed hills, which sink abruptly to its very margin.

"That is the Greenwood Lake, Frank, called by the monsters here Long Pond!—'the fiends receive their souls therefore,' as Walter Scott says,—in any mind prettier than Lake George by far, though known to few except chance sportsmen like myself! Full of fish—pearch of a pound in weight, and yellow bass in the deep waters, and a good sprinkling of trout, toward this end—Ellis Ketchum killed a five-pounder there this spring!—and heaps of summer-duck, the loveliest in plumage of the genus, and the best too *me judice*, excepting only the inimitable canvass-back. There are a few deer, too, in the hills, though they are getting scarce of late years. There, from that headland I killed one, three summers since—I was placed at a stand by the lake's edge, and the dogs drove him right down to me; but I got too eager, and he heard or saw me and so fetched a turn; but they were close upon him, and the day was hot, and he was forced to stet. I never saw him till he was in the act of leaping from a bluff of ten or twelve feet into the deep lake, but I pitched up my rifle at him—a snap shot,—as I would my gun at a cock in a summer brake—and by good luck sent my ball through his heart! There is a finer view yet when we cross this hill—the Bellvale mountain—look out, for we are just upon it—there! now admire!" and on the summit he pulled up, and never did I see a landscape more extensively magnificent—Ridge after ridge the mountain sloped down from our feet into a vast rich basin ten miles at least in breadth, by thirty, if not more, in length, girdled on every side by mountains—the whole diversified with wood and water, meadow and pasture land, and corn-field—studded with small white villages—with more than one bright lakelet glittering like beaten gold in the declining sun, and several isolated hills standing up boldly from the vale!

"Glorious indeed! most glorious!" I exclaimed—

"Right, Frank," he said—"a man may travel many a day and not see any thing to beat the vale of Sugar-loaf—so named from the conelike hill, over the pond there— that peak is eight hundred feet above tide water.—Those blue hills, to the far right, are the Hudson Highlands; that bold bluff is the far-famed Anthony's Nose—that ridge across the vale—the second ridge I mean—are the Shawangunks—and those three rounded summits, farther yet—those are the Kaatskills!—but now a truce with the romantic for there lies _____ and this keen mountain air has found me a fresh appetite!"

Away we went again, rattling down the hills, nothing daunted at their steep pitches, with the nags just as fresh as when they started, champing and snapping at their curbs, till on a table-land above the brook, with the tin steeple of its church peering from out the massy foliage of sycamore and locusts, the haven of our journey lay before us. "Hilloa, hill-oa ho! whoop!—who—whoop!"—and with a cheery shout, as we clattered across the wooden bridge, he roused out half the population of the village.

"Ya ha ha!—ya yah!"—yelled a great woolly-headed coal-black negro—"Here 'm massa Archer back agin—massa ben well, I spect"—

"Well—to be sure I have, Sam—cried Harry—"How's old Poll—bid her come up to Draw's to-morrow night—I've got a red and yellow frock for her—a h__l of a concern!"—

"Yah ha! yah ha ha yaah!" and amidst a most discordant chorus of African merriment, we passed by a neat farm-house shaded by two glorious locusts on the right, and a new red brick mansion, the pride of the village, with a flourishing store on the left— and wheeled up to the famous Tom Draw's tavern—a long white house with a piazza six feet wide, at the top of eight steep steps—with a one story kitchen at the end of it— a pump with a gilt pine-apple at the top if it, and horse-trough—a wagon-shed and stable sixty feet long, a sign-post with an indescribable female figure swinging upon it, and an ice-house over the way!—Such was the house before which we pulled up just as the sun was setting, amongst a gabbling of ducks, a barking of terriers, mixed with the deep bay of two or three large heavy fox-hounds which had been lounging about in the shade, and a peal of joyous welcome from all beings, quadruped or biped, within hearing—"Hulloa! Boys"—walk in! walk in!—What the eternal h—l are you about there?"—Well—we did walk into a large neat bar-room, with a bright hickory log crackling upon the hearth-stone—a large round table in one corner, covered with draught-boards, and old newspapers, among which showed pre-eminent the "Spirit of the Times"—a range of pegs well stored with great-coats, fishing-rods, whips, game-bags, spurs, and every other stray appurtenance of sporting, gracing one end, while the other was more gaily decorted by the well furnished bar, in the right hand angle of which my eye detected in an instant, a handsome nine pound double barrel—an old six foot Queen Ann's tower-musket, and a long smooth-bored rifle—and last, not least, outstretched at easy length upon the counter of his bar, to the left hand of the gang-way—the right side being more suitably decorated with tumblers, and decanters of strange compounds—supine, with fair round belly towering upward, and head volup-tuously pillowed on a heap of wagon cushions—lay in his glory—but no hold! the end of a chapter is no place to introduce—Tom Draw!"

PUBLIC RESPONSES TO SPORTS WRITING

The literary sports writing and chronicles of Frank Forrester, a.k.a. Henry William Herbert, struck a responsive note with many readers who eagerly awaited the appearance of his articles. The following letter, reprinted from the February 1840 volume of the American Turf Register and Sporting Magazine, is testimonial to their appreciation.

COMPLIMENT TO "FRANK FORESTER"

[The following paragraph is extracted from a letter dated Llangollen, Ky., Dec. 23d, written by a fine old gentlemen whose head is silvered o'er by the frosts of sixty win-ters, but whose ardent delight in the sports of the Turf and the Chase is still unsubdued. The graceful compliment to "Frank Forester" is bestowed upon one who will not fail gratefully to appreciate its distinguished source, and who would joy to listen to "the old man eloquent" upon those exciting themes which each describes with such thrill-ing interest and truth.]

By the way, are you not charmed with your correspondent *"Frank Forester"*? So soon as I got a taste of his quality, I sent over to my neighbor, Mr. Burbridge, *to bor-row* (a rascally practice,) the Nos. containing the preceding days of "A Week in the Woodlands," and I have not enjoyed so rich a treat for many a day. There is an ani-mation in the characters that makes them live, and act, and enjoy, in our presence, and with us. The graphic delineations of lake, and wood, and sky—their ever changing variety of aspect—the delightful and memory-treasured associations that must be called up with all who have delighted in Field Sports—the very attitudes of men, and dogs, and horses—the startling whirr of the pheasant and the partridge—the glorious cry of the hounds (the most animating music that my ears ever drank in)—the burst of the antlered buck through the brushwood—the plunge and splash into the lake—the sharp quick crack of the rifle, and the death halloo of the huntsman, are all admirable. While reading them, I forget that I am an old man and that my day is past. But these moments of forgetfulness, are a temporary return to youth and its joyous sports—just so much clear gain—a fair cheating of old father Time! Whoever "Frank Forester" may be, present to him, my dear Sir, the thanks, the hearty thanks of one who almost envies him the power to enjoy "A Week in the Woodlands," and still more the happy talent to impart its pleasures to others.

Very respectfully your obliged friend and humble servant,

J.L.

NATURALIST SPORTS WRITING

In 1837 a group of scientists with the Natural History Survey conducted the first recorded ascent of Mt. Marcy, the highest mountain in New York. One result of this ascent was the publication of a lengthy series of articles by the journalist, poet, and naturalist, Charles Fenno Hoffman, in The New York Mirror during the Fall. The document reprinted below was published on 21 October 1837.

SCENES AT THE SOURCES OF THE HUDSON
by Charles Fenno Hoffman

Mount Mercy—A wolf fight—The wounded huntsman-A generous hound.

The highest peak of the Aganuschion range, or the Black Mountains, as some call them, from the dark aspect which their sombre cedars and frowning cliffs give them at a distance, was measured during the last summer, and found to be nearly six thousand feet in height. Mount Marcy, as it has been christened, not improperly, after the publick functionary who first suggested the survey of this interesting region, presents a perfect pyramidal top, when viewed from Lake Sandford. The sharp cone was sheathed in snow on the day that I took a swim in the lake; the woods around displayed as yet but few autumnal tints, and the deep verdure of the adjacent mountains set off the snowy peak in such high contrast, that soaring as it did far above them, and seeming to pierce, as it were, the blue sky which curtained them, the poetick Indian epithet of TA-HA-WUS, *He splits the sky*, was hardly too extravagant to characterize its peculiar grandeur.

The peculiarities of the ascent of Mount Marcy, and the view from the summit have already been described in the published letters of more than one of the gentleman composing the scientifick party who explored this neighborhood about a month before I arrived here; and I can add but little to what they have already made known. The wild falls of Kas-kong-shadi (*broken water*)—the bright pools of Tu-ne-sas-sah (*a place of pebbles*)—and the tall cascade of She-gwi-en-daukwe, (*the hanging spear,*) will hereafter tempt many to strike over to the eastern branch of the Hudson, and follow it up to Lake Colden; while the echoing glen of Twen-un-ga-sko, (*a raised voice,*) though now as savage as the Indian Pass, which I have already described to you, will reverberate with more musical cries than the howl of the wolf or the panther, whose voices only are now raised to awaken its echoes. The luxurious cit will cool his champagne amid the snows of Mount Marcy; and his botanizing daughter, who has read in Michaux's American Sylva, of pines more than two hundred feet in height, [Michaux, we believe, measured his only specimens of this gigantick growth in the woods of Maine; but Douglass, the English botanist and traveller, states that the pine grows to the height of two hundred and thirty feet on the Columbia River; and Lewis and Clark measured one forty-two feet in circumference, having an estimated height of more than three hundred feet.] will wonder to pluck full-grown trees of the same genus, which she can put into her recticule.

At present, however, the mountain is a desert. Wolverines and wildcats, with a few ravens, who generally follow in the track of beasts of prey, are almost the only living things that have their habitations in these high solitudes; and save when their occasional cry breaks the stillness, the solemn woods are on a calm day as silent as the grave. The absence of game birds, and of the bests of chase, which give his subsistence to the hunter, prevents him from wasting his toil in climbing to the loftiest pinnacles; and so far as I can learn, it is only lately that curiosity has prompted those who have passed a great part of their lives here, to make the ascent. The view, however, when once realized, seems to strike them not less than it does more cultivated minds. "It makes a man feel," said a hunter to me, "what it is to have all creation placed beneath his feet. There are woods there which it would take a life-time to hunt over; mountains that seem shouldering each other, to boost the one whereon you stand up and away, heaven knows where. Thousands of little lakes are let in among them, so bright and clean that you would like to keep a canoe on each of them. Old Champlain, though fifty miles off, glistens below you like a strip of white birch bark, when slicked up by the moon on a frosty night; and the green mountains of Vermont beyond it, fade and fade away, till they disappear as gradually as a cold scent when the dew rises."

Holt, of whom I have before spoken, has had some strange encounters with wild animals among these lonely defiles, which I have attempted to describe; and John Cheney, who has taken the State's bounty for one panther, which he killed with a pistol, had, sometime since, a fight with a wolf, which is almost as well worthy of commemoration as the doughty feat of old Putnam.

It was in winter; the snows were some four or five feet deep upon a level, and the hunter, upon whom a change of seasons seems to produce but little effect, could only pursue his game upon snow-shoes; an ingenious contrivance for walking upon the surface, which, though so much used in our northern counties, is still only manufactured in perfection by the Indians; who drive quite a trade in them along Canada line. Wandering far from the settlements, and making his bed at nightfall in a deep snowbank, Cheney rose one morning to examine his traps, near which he will sometimes lie encamped for weeks in complete solitude; when, hovering round one of them, he discovered a famished wolf, who, unappalled by the presence of the hunter, retired only a few steps, and then turning round, stood watching his movements. "I ought, by rights," quoth John, "to have waited for my two dogs, who could not have been far off, but the cretur looked so sarcy, standing there, that though I had not a bullet to spare, I couldn't help letting into him with rifle." He missed his aim; the animal giving a spring as he was in the act of firing, and then turning instantly upon him before he could reload his piece. So effective was the unexpected attack of the wolf, that his fore-paws were upon Cheney's snow-shoes before he could rally for the fight. The forester became entangled in the deep drift, and sank upon his back, keeping the wolf only at bay by striking at him with his clubbed rifle. The stock was broken to pieces in a few moments, and it would have fared ill with the stark woodsman if the wolf, instead of making at his enemy's throat when he had him thus at disadvantage, had not, with blind fury, seized the barrel of the gun in his jaws. Still the fight was unequal, as John, half buried in the snow, could make use of but one of his hands. He shouted to his dogs; but one of them only, a young untrained hound, made his appearance; emerging from a thicket, he caught sight of his master lying apparently at the mercy of the ravenous beast, uttered a yell of fear, and fled howling to the woods again. "Had I had one shot left," said Cheney, "I would have given it to that dog instead of despatching the wolf with it." In the exasperation of the moment, John might have extended his contempt to the whole canine race, if a stancher friend had not, at the moment, interposed to vindicate their character for courage and fidelity. All this had passed in a moment; the wolf was still grinding the iron gun-barrrel in this teeth: he had even once wrenched it from the hand of the hunter, when, dashing like a thunderbolt between the combat-ants, the other hound sprang over his master's body, and seized the wolf by the throat. "There was no let go about that dog when he once took hold. If the barrel had been red hot, the wolf couldn't have dropped it quicker; and it would have done you good, I tell ye, to see that old dog drag the cretur's head down in the snow, while I, jist at my leisure, drove the iron into his skull. One good, fair blow, though, with a heavy rifle barrel, on the back of the head, finished him. The fellow gave a kind o'quiver, stretched out his hind legs, and then he was done for. I had the rifle stocked afterwards, but she would never shoot straight since that fight; so I got me this pistol, which, being light and handy, enables me more conveniently to carry an axe upon my long tramps, and make myself comfortable in the woods."

Many a deer has John since killed with that pistol. It is curious to see him draw it from the left pocket of his gray shooting-jacket, and bring down a partridge. I have myself witnessed several of his successful shots with this unpretending shooting-iron, and once saw him knock the feathers from a wild duck at fifty yards!

As for the dog who played so gallant a part in this encounter, he met with a sad and ignoble death afterward. You must know that in these woods, where the settlements are a day's journey apart, (for even in reaching McIntyre you travel through twenty-five miles of unbroken forest upon the last stage,) party spirit still finds its way; and those who hound the deer are arrayed against the numerous class of woodsmen, called "still-hunters"—as these last kill the dogs of the former wherever they meet them. Some of the best hounds in the country having been killed by these forest-regulators, Cheney would never allow his favourite dog to wander near the streams most frequented by them; but it chanced one day that the poor fellow met with an accident, which with-drew his care from the dog. The trigger of his pistol caught against the thwart of a boat

while he was in the act of raising it to shoot a deer, and the piece going off in a per-
pendicular direction, sent the whole charge into his leg, tearing off the calf, and driving the ball out through the sole of the foot. With this terrible wound, which, however,
did not prevent him from re-loading and killing the deer before he could swim to the
shore, Cheney dragged himself fifteen miles through the woods, to the nearest log-
cabin. A violent fever, and the threatened loss of the limb, confined him here for
months. But his dog, to whom, while idling in the forest, he had taught a hundred
amusing tricks, was still his company and solace; and though Tray looked wistfully
after each hunter that strayed by the cabin, no eagerness for the chase could impel him
to leave his master's side. At last, however, upon one unfortunate day, poor Cheney
was prevailed upon to indulge a brother huntsman, and let him take the dog out with
him for a few hours. The hunter soon returned, but the hound never came back. Under his master's eye, he had been taught never to follow a deer beyond a certain limit;
but now, long confinement had given him such a zest for the sport, that he crossed the
fatal hounds. The mountain-ridge of a more friendly region was soon placed bewteen
him and his master—the deer took to the treacherous streams haunted by the still-hunters, and the generous hound and his timorous quarry met the same fate from the rifles
of their prowling enemy.

C.F.N.

Chapter 3

ANIMAL SPORTS

Animal or blood sports experienced widespread popularity in the United States and
Canada up to the late nineteenth century. Originally imported from England, such
animal sports as cockfighting and bull and bear baiting originally found a receptive
audience in rural and urban areas but by the early nineteenth century blood sports had
begun to decline in the developing cities for obvious reasons. The sheer physical expansion of the cities destroyed the population and availability of many of the animals
used in these sports in the immediately surrounding areas. Furthermore, the maintenance of the animals themselves posed greater dangers in the more congested and
confined areas of growing cities.

    Urban development was only one threat to the continuation of blood sports in antebellum
America. Beginning in the colonial era, critics of animal sports charged that such contests were
cruel and encouraged the barbaric, dark side of man's nature. By the early 1800s mayors and
city police forces were petitioned by the public to terminate such brutal sports. Moreover,
cockfighting and animal baiting were usually associated with gambling, an activity that elicited strong public outrage and condemnation, strong testimony to the lasting influence of

Puritan attitudes and practices in America. As a result, it is not surprising that cockfighting and animal baiting met with public opprobrium in New England, despite developing their own following in the region, and that these sports found their greatest public acceptance in the South and the West. Regardless of region, American spectators, just like their English counterparts, evinced a deep ambivalence about blood sports. Though captivated by the tenacity, courage, skill, and robustness of the animals, they were often just as repulsed by the viciousness of the matches.

In some areas cockfighting and animal baiting became social events, replete with drinking and gambling, and occasionally intercity or interstate rivalries developed. But, as with many sports during this era, animal competitions occurred primarily on the local level and remained informal contests with locally or regionally drawn rules and regulations. Few newspaper articles or accounts of matches existed, especially in the northeastern or mid-Atlantic states where public disapproval of the sports was more openly expressed. For that reason, most of the documents in this chapter accurately reflect this geographical bias and the premodern character of these sports.

Despite the public pressures against animal sports, they enjoyed a resurgence during the mid-nineteenth century that was to give way, ultimately, to the public's hostility to the sports as cruel to animals. With the founding of the American Society for the Prevention of Cruelty to Animals in 1866 as well as the rise of such spectator sports as baseball and football, the days of animal sports were numbered. By the turn of the century they had virtually become a thing of the past.

COCKFIGHTING IN THE SOUTH

Animal Sports, such as cockfighting and animal baiting, engendered heated opposition as well as strong support during the early part of the nineteenth century. Cocking was enjoyed in the southern United States for the many fine qualities exhibited by the animals—qualities that northerners preferred their fellow humans to have nurtured through healthy, character-building participatory sports. The following letter, reprinted from the August 1831 issue of the American Turf Register and Sporting Magazine, presents both sides of this debate.

COCKING IN VIRGINIA
FROM AMERICAN TURF REGISTER AND SPORTING MAGAZINE, 1831

MR. EDITOR:

To the gentlemen who handed the following account of a main, fought last month in Virginia, I answered that the sport of cocking was not embraced amongst those enumerated in your prospectus. He instanced its great antiquity, and the practice of great Roman generals, who caused the exhibition of game cocks, before battle, to animate their soldiers by examples of courage, as proofs of its *legitimacy*. I told him that its mere antiquity rather proved than relieved it from the charge of barbarity; and maintained that, in the progress of refinement, it must be altogether superseded by sports, better calculated to strengthen the body, to exhilarate the spirits, to soften the temper and *socialize* the heart;—such as hunting, fishing, shooting, racing, quoits, cricket, rowing matches, &c.&c. He replied by giving a list of illustrious *names*, of modern date—grave judges, acute lawyers, profound statesmen, celebrated wits, skilful doctors, and even some sober divines, men of learning, science, patriotism and benevolence, who have attended and now resort to the cockpit, to see those animals, in the highest combination of strength, lightness, action and wind, display those *peculiar qualities*, with which nature endowed *them*, as cockers would fain persuade us, for the amusement of mankind. But to what is it, Mr. Editor, however cruel or absurd, that we cannot be attached by the force of early association?

The main, *he said*, was one of great *interest*. It was fought on the 16th and 17th of last month, at Waterford, Loudon county, Va. between Mr. S. of Harper's ferry, and Mr. H. of Leesburg. Of 17 cooks exhibited, on each side, 14 were matched. Mr. S. beat 8, Mr. H. 5, and 1 was a drawn battle.

The feeders are men of great celebrity for ordering in hot weather. Capt. P. of Martinsburg, was feeder for the winning, Mr. S. of Montgomery, Md. for the losing side.

There were many gentlemen present, but some, as always happens at such places, who should have been placed, according to the English rule, *in a basket, out of reach.*

The birds were vigorous, and in high condition on both sides. Two of the cocks from Jefferson, one called "Blue Bonnets," a sky blue, with a few cloudy feathers; the other, "the Window," a beautiful red, with fine gallant presence, were very superior birds and decided favourites, being conquerors in many a hard fought battle.

RULES OF THE PIT

Cockfighting was an ancient sport whose North American origins were immediately found in the practice of the sport in England. As cocking grew in popularity, Americans relied on British rules and regulations with few modifications. Thus, cockfighting, much like other sports during the antebellum era, organized itself through codified rules and increasingly conducted regional matches along with local contests that were the staple of the sport. The following article, reprinted from the May 1837 volume of the American Turf Register and Sporting Magazine, presents a glimpse into the origins and nature of cockfighting and the changes it experienced before 1840.

RULES OF THE PIT

'The rules of Thomas Turner of Virginia,' have been so frequently inquired for, especially since the challenge of Mr. Edmondson, of Georgia, 'to the Cockers of Hagerstown,' that we have been induced to publish them. They are taken from an old printed copy, furnished by a gentleman, himself an amateur and long conversant with the subject. These rules were extracted from the 'RED LION RULES, by which they used to fight in England, and adopted by a company of gentlemen from Virginia and North Carolina. They merely omitted such of the English rules as did not apply to our mode of fighting; in other respects they are the same as those of Red Lion. Thomas Turner merely had them printed, and hence the term Thomas Turner's rules:—

RULES TO BE OBSERVED IN CONDUCTING A SHOW OF A MAIN OF COCKS

ART. I.—On the morning the main is to commence, the parties decide by lot who shows first. It is to be remembered that the party obtaining choice generally chooses to weigh first, and consequently obliges the adverse party to show first; as the party showing first, weighs last. When the show is made by that party, the door of the cockhouse is to be locked, and the key given to the other party, who immediately repairs to his cockhouse, and prepares for weighing. There ought to be provided a good pair of scales, and weights as low down as half an ounce. One or two judges to be appointed to weigh the cocks. Each party, by weighing the cocks intended for the show a day or two beforehand and having a bill of their respective weights, would greatly facilitate the business of judges. There should be two writers to take down the colours, weights, marks, &c. of each cock. There ought to be no feathers cut or plucked from the cocks before they are brought to the scale, except a few from behind to keep them clean, and their wings and tails clipped a little.

II.—As soon as the cocks are all weighed, the judge, the writers, the principals of each party, and as many besides as the parties may agree on, are to retire for the purpose of matching. They are to make all even matches first, then those within half an ounce, and afterwards those within an ounce; but if more matches can be made, by breaking an even or a half ounce match, it is to be done.

III.—On the day of shewing, only one battle is to be fought. It is to be remembered, that the party winning the show gains also the choice of fighting this first battle with any particular cocks in the match. Afterwards, they begin with the lightest pair first, and so on up to the heaviest; fighting them in rotation as they increase in weight. This first battle too will fix the mode of trimming.

RULES TO BE OBSERVED ON THE PIT

ART 1.—When the cocks are on the pit, the judges are to examine whether they answer the description taken in the match bill, and whether they are fairly trimmed, and have on fair heels. If all be right and fair, the pitters are to deliver their cocks six feet apart (or thereabouts) and retire a step or two back; but if a wrong cock should be produced, the party so offending forfeits that battle.

II.—All heels that are round from the socket to the point are allowed to be fair; any pitter bringing a cock on the pit with any other kind of heels, except by particular agreement, forfeits the battle.

III.—If either cock should be trimmed with a close, unfair hack, the judge shall direct the other to be cut in the same manner; and at that time shall observe to the pitter, that if he brings another cock in the like situation, unless he shall have been previously trimmed, he shall forfeit the battle.

IV.—A pitter when he delivers his cock, shall retire two paces back, and not advance or walk round his cock until a blow has passed.

V.—An interval of————————minutes shall be allowed between the termination of one battle and the commencement of another.

VI.—No pitter shall pull a feather out of a cock's mouth, nor from over his eyes or head, or pluck him by the breast to make him fight, or pinch him for the like purpose, under penalty of forfeiting the battle.

VII.—The pitters are to give their cocks room to fight, and are not to hover or press on them, so as to prevent or retard them from striking.

VIII.—The greasing, peppering, muffing, and soaping a cock, or any other external application, are unfair practices, and by no means admissible in this amusement.

IX.—The judge, when required, may suffer a pitter to call in a few of his friends to assist in catching his cock, who are to retire immediately as soon as the cock is caught; and in no other instance is the judge to suffer the pit to be broken.

X.—All cocks on their backs are to be immediately turned over on their bellies, by their respective pitters at all times.

XI.—A cock when down is to have a wing given him, if he needs it, unless his adversary is on it, but his pitter is to place the wing gently in its proper position, and not to lift the cock. And no wing is to be given except when absolutely necessary.

XII.—If either cock should be hanged in himself, in the pit or canvass, he is to be loosed by his pitter; but if in his adversary, both pitters are immediately to lay hold of their respective cocks, and the pitter whose cock is hung, shall hold him steadily whilst the adverse party draws out the heel and then they shall take their cocks asunder a sufficient distance for them fairly to renew the combat.

XIII.—Should the cocks separate, and the judge be unable to decide which fought last, he shall, at his discretion, direct the pitters to carry their cocks to the middle of the pit, and deliver them beak to beak, unless either of them is blind, in that case they are to be shouldered, that is, delivered with their breast touching, each pitter taking care to deliver his cock at this, as well as at all other times, with one hand.

XIV.—When both cocks cease fighting, it is then in the power of the pitter of the last fighting cock, unless they touch each other, to demand a count of the judge, who shall count forty deliberately, which, when counted out, is not to be counted again during the battle. Then the pitters shall catch their cocks and carry them to the middle of the pit, and deliver them beak to beak, but to be shouldered if either is blind, as before. Then, if either cock refuses or neglects to fight, the judge shall count ten, and shall call out 'once refused,' and shall direct the pitters to bring their cocks again to the middle of the pit, and put to as before; and if the same cock in like manner refuses, he shall count ten again, and call 'twice refused,' and so proceed until one cock thus refuses six times successively. The judge shall then determine the battle against such cock.

XV.—If either cock dies before the judge can finish the counting of the law, the battle is to be given to the living cock; and if both die, the longest liver wins the battle.

XVI.—The pitters are not to touch their cocks whilst the judge is in the act of counting.

XVII.—No pitter is ever to lay hold of his adversary's cock; unless to draw out the heel, and then he must take him below the knee. Then there shall be no second delivery, that is, after he is once delivered he shall not be touched until a blow is struck, unless ordered by the judge.

XVIII.—No pitter shall touch his cock, unless at the times mentioned in the foregoing rules.

XIX.—If any pitter acts contrary to these rules, the judge, if called on at the time, shall give the battle against him.

REGIONAL RIVALRIES

Cockfighting flourished in the southern United States, as regional contests occurred regularly during the 1830s. The following two documents, reprinted from the August 1834 and the November 1836 editions of the American Turf Register and Sporting Magazine respectively, demonstrate the large sums of money involved in cockfighting and the apparent uniformity in the rules observed by sporting enthusiasts in one region of the United States.

GEORGIA AGAINST THE UNITED STATES

Augusta, June 29, 1834

The editor of the Sporting Magazine will please publish the following banter.

I propose to show fifty cocks any time between the second Monday in April, and second Monday in July, 1835. No cock to weigh less than four pounds, nor none heavier than five pounds ten ounces—to fight all that comes within two ounces, for the sum of $2000 or $5000 on the odd one, or $200 a battle, to meet in Charleston, S.C. The banter to be accepted by the 1st of February, 1835, one half of the amount to be deposited in any bank in Charleston, for non-compliance of the same.

Griffin Edmondson.

CHALLENGE TO THE COCKERS OF HAGERSTOWN, MD.

I will meet the cockers of Hagerstown, in June next, at Baltimore; showing thirty-five cocks, within the following weights: from 4 lbs. 8 ozs., to 6 lbs. 8 ozs., for $5,000 on the odd fight, and $100 per battle; to fight agreeably to the Rules of Thomas Turner, of Virginia, provided this challenge be accepted by the 1st day of January, 1837.

If the challenge should be accepted, I propose to deposite, in any named bank in Baltimore, one half of the above amount, as a forfeit.

Griffin Edmondson.

Augusta, Ga. *September* 5, 1836

EARLY COCKFIGHTING

Although many animal sports, particularly cockfighting, was frowned down upon in the northeastern United States, it nonetheless generated much interest among the sporting public. The following article, reprinted from the 3 April 1829 issue of the New York Spectator, documents this enthusiasm for the sport.

COCKFIGHTING

Cock-fighting.—The Journal of Commerce says:—We are told that in a certain steamboat which arrived here not a thousand years since, came passengers 36 game cocks in four boxes, of nine compartments each, for which $360 were paid. They are in fine condition—having had their spurs cut, and ready to be steeled for battle. Their combs, wings and tails, are nicely trimmed and oiled—and in a few days they will be prepared to enter the lists with their fellow combatants.

These characters, we understand, were transported by land, over snow-banks and through mud, from beyond Albany to Poughkeepsie, and thence by water to this city, that their feats might gratify the good people here, and withall—fleece their pockets. At a proper time we may communicate further particulars.

The sporting world will wait with anxiety for the report of the performances of these fathered gladiators.

PUBLIC MORALITY AND ANIMAL SPORTS

Animal baiting produced strong reactions in North America, especially in urban areas where the sport was viewed as posing a threat to public morality and order and as a cruel and vicious activity. The following document, reprinted from The New York Spectator of 7 September 1827 expresses the public revulsion of the practice of bull baiting.

BULL BAITING

Bull Baiting.—The following is the note of "Humanitas," to which we referred yesterday. The author is a gentlemen of respectability, and we therefore call upon the police to interpose and prevent the barbarous spectacle proposed by Mr. Armstrong on Thursday next. One of our friends, in passing
Harlem, at the time, accidentally saw the cruel scene.

Mr. Editor—As a friend of "humanity and correct morals," will you give a hint to the guardians of our city, of a most bloody and cruel Bull Bait, which took place at Armstrong's tavern, at Harlem yesterday afternoon—and also, that notice was given that another "Piece of Sport" of the same kind, would take place next Thursday, at the same place. These exhibitions are scandalous, and with all the vices attending in their train, tend much to paralize every effort that can be made for the increase of morality, and virtue among us.

HUMANITAS

Chapter 4

AQUATICS

As with many of the sports that grew in popularity during the early nineteenth century, aquatic sports, especially rowing, were first developed in England and subsequently transplanted to the United States and Canada. Although rowing captured the public's interest in the 1820s and 1830s, yachting failed to generate the same response. As a result only a few races of this type were reported prior to 1840, though a small number of sailing competitions did occur. Despite this difference, however, neither sport ever involved large numbers of participants. Even the more popular sport of rowing remained primarily a spectator sport during this time, which may have partially accounted for the inability of rowing to sustain its appeal throughout the antebellum period.

During the 1820s the sport of rowing developed as a byproduct of the growth of commerce and trade. In many urban areas such as New York, Boston, New Orleans, and Mobile, rowing contests grew out of the competition by harbormen to sell their services and products to incoming ships. Business success for pilots and salesmen entailed reaching the ships before one's competitor and consequently placed a heavy premium on acquiring the best oarsmen. Private wagering among harbormen became a common feature of daily business and eventually the job-related competition yielded more formally staged races. Thus, the origins of rowing were primarily urban, linked to the lower, working classes as well as to the growth of the cities and the development of commerce.

As an exception to this generalization, in the tidewater plantation areas of the South, rowing often developed out of the necessity to navigate waterways for both travel and trade. As with most other forms of labor in the antebellum South, much of the rowing was conducted by slaves, and as with northern workers, races among crews soon ensued, with each trying to outdo the other in speed and skill. Betting on these races also occurred, with the difference being that in the South, masters, rather than the slaves, wagered with each other and took pride in the accomplishments of their respective crews.

After 1820 popular excitement over rowing increased substantially. Rowing contests attracted huge crowds and offered hefty stakes for the participants as well as the opportunity for observers to win large amounts through side betting. Rules and regulations were established and clubs formed, both of which helped to legitimize the sport. One of the most publicized races of the decade occurred in 1824 between the Whitehallers, one of the best known New York City clubs, and a crew of Englishmen who had just arrived after having saved an American ship in the Caribbean. The English ship traveled with a skull and rowing crew, and during the course of the celebration in honor of the heroic British deed, the captain of the Hussar challenged any American crew to a race of the latter's choosing. The Whitehallers accepted and proceeded to beat the English crew quite handily on a four-mile course off the southern tip of Manhattan. But more important than the outcome was the interest the international race generated. More than 50,000 spectators showed up to watch the race and cheer the Americans to victory, though they must have been disappointed at the lopsidedness of the match. In this chapter, newspaper reports of the contest—"Americans v. the British," "Contest Postscript," and "Summary of the Contest" collectively portray the great excitement generated by international competition.

Although interest in rowing declined in the late 1820s, by the middle of the following decade it had experienced a resurgence but with significant changes. The rowing clubs that were formed were amateur organizations and drew their members from the wealthier classes. The contests among them were less competitive and became more social gatherings than heatedly contested events. The first amateur rowing organization was the Castle Garden Boat Club Association, founded in 1834. Two of the most famous and exclusive were the Wave and Gull Clubs. The creation of the Independent Boat Club Organization soon followed, though it placed more emphasis on competition and less on fashion than did the more elite Castle Garden Association. In the South, especially, rowing challenges were major social events, and balls and banquets honored the occasion.

By the end of the 1830s rowing clubs proliferated, spurred in part by increased press coverage and public approval of the sport as a moral and healthy form of physical exercise. New developments followed such as the nationalization of the sport and the emergence of geographic rivalries. Interest in rowing spread from New York City up the Hudson River to Poughkeepsie and Newburgh, where annual regattas were established and cultivated followings of their own. In addition, by the late 1830s, new forms of rowing competition, such as single sculling, had emerged and contributed to the eventual success of the sport later in the century. The documents in this section describe many of the transformations and developments in aquatic sports.

Rowing contests also assumed geographical and sometimes political dimensions in their brief resurgence. Boston and New York, for example, developed a particularly heated rivalry that mirrored and expressed a deeper, commercial and cultural competition between the two cities. More importantly, southern and northern boat clubs, reflecting the growing sectional animosity over slavery, issued challenges to one another, though few races actually took place. In 1838, after an earlier challenge by a Savannah rowing club was rebuffed by their New York City counterpart, Georgians claimed sectional victory when the Savannah club raced and beat another local club which had used a boat manufactured in the North. "Regional Rivalry," Intersectional Challenge," and "Sectional Response" demonstrate the substance and nature of sectional challenges.

Despite the brief resurgence of rowing in the mid-1830s it suffered a rapid decline during the early forties for reasons that have not been fully explained. The Castle Garden Boat Club Association held its last annual regatta in 1842, a development which reflected the decreasing interest in the sport. Perhaps the sport of rowing had moved too far from its working class origins, or, perhaps the economic downturn of 1837 hindered participation and interest, as it did in horse racing. Regardless of the explanations offered, not until the 1850s did rowing experience another resurgence. By then, yachting, too, had emerged as a major water sport with an appeal and following of its own.

THE PRACTICAL BENEFITS OF SWIMMING

North Americans applauded the health benefits of swimming since Benjamin Franklin first wrote on the subject. Well into the nineteenth century they relied on Franklin's observations about this form of exercise. Although it was not an organized sport between 1820 and 1840, swimming became an increasingly important form of exercise, benefiting from the growing emphasis placed on physical exercise and sound health during the period. This article is taken from The Spirit of the Times, 9 February 1839.

ADVANTAGE OF KNOWING HOW TO SWIM

It has frequently occurred to us that steps should be taken for the encouragement of public Swimming Schools, and we have been pleased to remark that within a few years, several eminent seminaries have, added to their different athletic exercises, taught the practice of swimming. It is remarkable, that an art so readily acquired, so beneficial to health, and one which frequently is so all important, should be so generally neglected; not above ten men in twenty, probably can swim at all, though the art can be acquired in an hour, provided a proper determination accompanies the desire to learn. A spirited boy swims like a duck at ten years old, and yet he cannot explain how or when he struck out fearlessly beyond his depth. Indeed, it is our opinion that a man or boy *can swim* the moment he has confidence enough in himself to *try*. We certainly can learn a boy in half an hour, for we have done so over and over again. As Mr. Weller said when he caught Sam behind the door in amorous dalliance with the housemaid, it is "rayther alarmin'" to them at first, but give a boy a slight support, and *make him believe* that he is really swimming, and without assistance, and in few minutes he gains sufficient confidence to strike out boldly with hands and feet. From this moment he can *swim*, and in three days will most likely offer to make a match with you. Subsequently, practice will make perfect.

It is unnecessary to go into detail of the advantages of acquiring this necessary, healthful, and really elegant art. How often do we read of men falling overboard, and being expert swimmers, maintain themselves above water for almost incredible lengths of time, until assistance reaches them;—of steamboats on fire or blow up, boats upset, and a thousand casualties of the kind, where such and such persons, "being good swimmers, escaped," almost miraculously? A dexterous swimmer, provided he has presence of mind, can readily maintain himself for four to five hours in smooth water. Lord Byron and Mr. Ekenhead were four hours on the water when they swam the "broad Hellespont," from Sestos to Abydos; about two years since a favorite actor, then a member of the stock company at the Park theatre, swam from Castle Garden to the embankment of the Fort on Governor's Island; the distance is not less than a mile and three quarters, as the crow flies, but what with the tide and the variations from a direct line, our friend could not have swam less than three miles. And yet so far from being exhausted was he, that he would have made the effort to return, had not his friends, who accompanied him in a boat, restrained him by main force, for fear of the consequences of over exertion.

A little proficiency in this delightful art—for delightful it really is to every one acquainted with it—is worth all the "Life Preservers" ever manufactured. There is no stopping to "blow up" some *monstrum horrendum* of the India rubber species, and the key of the trunk in which you keep it is never sure to be missing at the precise moment you chance to want it. It is the only genuine Life Preserver after all, and when a man determines to "die game," he can hardly be drowned in fresh water; it is always with you, and as "handy" to "tote" as the hair on your head. An incident occurred the other day to a friend of ours—a distinguished member of the Bar of this city, as eminent for his proficiency in every manly exercise as for his sterling talents and great legal abilities, which affords the most unanswerable testimony of the manifold importance of knowing how to swim. Several versions of the matter having appeared in the columns of our daily contemporaries, we have taken pains to inform ourselves of the facts, which are now subjoined.

Being engaged to appear before the Court of Chancery on the 28th day of January last, at Albany, Mr. J. PRESCOTT HALL left this city for that place on the preceding Saturday, during the violence of the storm. For the purposes of expedition, he travelled alone in an extra stage, with four horses, until he reached Peekskill, about fifty miles on his journey. At this place he found Mr. WILLIAM SILLIMAN, a gentleman of the bar, waiting for an opportunity of proceeding to Albany, and who, by invitation, took a seat in Mr. Hall's coach. An elderly gentleman, of the name of VAN WYCK, of Fishkill, also became a passenger, by his own solicitation; and the party, with four fresh horses, left Peekskill at eight o'clock in the evening, for the purpose of pursuing their journey. When they reached the causeway which leads to Peekskill Creek, they found the road covered with the waters of the Hudson River, which had been driven over it by the strong southerly wind. The driver, being doubtful of a safe passage, paused after he had entered the water, and Mr. Hall ascended to the top of the stage for the purpose of urging him onward. By his solicitation the driver proceeded, but had not advanced far before Mr. Silliman joined his companion on the outside; and then the water deepened so rapidly, that the horses began to swim, and attempted to diverge from the road to the right, but were kept in line by means of the whip and voice. Presently, as the water deepened more rapidly, they diverged again towards the left, and the driver, losing all presence of mind, abandoned his reins, and sprung to the top of the coach. At this moment all were afloat, both horses and stage, and borne away by the force of the current, the horses turned their heads down stream, directly towards the North river. In this condition of things, as the carriage began to settle itself in the water, Mr. Hall bethought him of his companion, General Van Wyck, who, with some exertion, was drawn through a window to the top of the stage.

After floating down about an hundred yards from the shore, the coach, having sunk nearly to its top, struck a sand bar, and there rested; while the poor horses, unable to drag it forward, commenced a struggle for their lives. The off leader was drowned within a few minutes, while the others held out bravely, by swimming and springing from the bottom with their heads erect. In this condition the party remained about half an hour, shouting for assistance, and devising the means of escape. As it was not yet the time of high water, they were fearful of the coming flood, while the struggles of the horses tended constantly to dislodge the coach from its unsteady position, and overwhelm it in the deep water.

After a good deal of anxious consultation, Mr. Hall, against the advice of his companions, (except the poor driver, who being unable to swim, was almost beside himself with alarm,) resolved to make for the shore and procure assistance for the perplexed travellers and their suffering horses. Divesting himself of his boots and coat, he entered the stream, and swam in a direction which gave him the assistance of the current, which he could not easily stem.

After a good deal of suffering from cold, and the rapidity with which he exerted himself, Mr. Hall reached the shore (about one hundred yards from the coach) much exhausted, but able to assure his companions that he was in safety, and able to make another effort for their relief. With "painful steps and slow," he crossed the field where he had landed, and proceeded in the direction of the nearest house. After walking about a quarter of a mile, and suffering severely from his stiffened clothes, and the roughness of the path, without protection for his feet, he encountered a warm-hearted son of Erin, who, after leading him to his hut, and consigning him to the kind cares of his young wife, hastened, by Mr. Hall's request, to procure assistance for the sufferers in the river. His nearest neighbor, Mr. SHERWOOD, when informed of the disaster, with great good sense proceeded at once to Peekskill, village, (distant about two miles from the creek), procured a boat, placed it upon a wagon, carried it to the proper place, and relieved the three persons remaining on the stage from their uncomfortable situation.

Mr. Silliman and his companions remained upon the wreck more than an hour and a half, and three of the horses perished before any assistance could be procured. The fourth being in comparatively shallow water, which enabled him to breathe, escaped death, and was finally brought to the shore.

As for Mr. Hall, he received from the warm-hearted cottagers every kindness his situation required, and Mrs. BRIDGET MAHON, with the aid of her neighbors, soon restored him to life and animation. Her first process was to strip him of his wet clothes, and place him in her own bed; and then by means of camphorated spirits, and hot irons placed to his feet, she restored circulation to his benumbed limbs. To encourage JAMES to great alacrity in his exertions to procure relief, Mr. H. remarked that he had saved his money by placing it in his cap, and that he would reward him for his services. He was checked, however, at once, by these hospital creatures, who both replied—"Don't talk about money—we would do it for the poorest creature in the world, and surely we'll do it for your honor." Kindness and generosity belong to no class exclusively, and when they are found in the bosoms of the poor and lowly, they shine brighter than jewels of rarest price, upon the brows of wealth and ambition. They adorn human nature; they add dignity to our condition, and sooner or later will meet their reward.

INTERNATIONAL CHALLENGE

In late 1824, a British frigate arrived in New York under the command of Captain Harris. The frigate carried its own rowing boat and crew and, upon learning of the accomplishments of New York boatmen, issued an open challenge to the Americans. The Whitehallers, one of the most successful boating clubs since its inception some fifteen years earlier, quickly accepted the challenge and bested their English opponents. The match assumed nationalistic overtones and drew over 20,000 spectators. The following document, which contains the challenge by the British crew, originally appeared in The New York American and was reprinted in the New York Spectator, 7 December 1824.

WHITEHALL AHOY!

Whitehall ahoy!—Capt. Harris, of H.B.M. frigate Hussar, now in our city, having a very fine row boat, is disposed, as will be seen by the following note from him to make a little sport for our Whitehall boys. We are persuaded he will be met, and whichever prevail in the good natured contest much amusement and pleasure will result from it. We will take charge of any communication for Capt. Harris—and as we suspect there will be no backwardness on the part of his officers and crew to back their boat, *our lade of the oar*, who will not want backers either, must stand ready with the mopus.

To the Editors of the American.
NEW-YORK. 3d Dec. 1824.

Gentlemen—The boatmen of this port having learned that I possess a fast row boat, have expressed a desire to try her speed, I therefore beg leave, through the middle of your paper, to state, that on the first fair day after Tuesday next, I will row my boat against any one that can be produced, not excepting the one that I have seen in the Museum. Any communications on the subject may be addressed to me at Park Place House.

I am gentlemen,

Your most obedient servant.

GEORGE HARRIS,

H.M. Ship Hussar.

[We understand that the Whitehall boatmen have accepted the challenge to run for $1000 aside. A note has been addressed to Captain Harris, at Park Place House, agreeably to his invitation.]

The two accounts below are reports of the result of the famous match noted above between the Whitehallers and the British crew from the Hussar frigate. They are reprinted, respectively, from the 9 December and 10 December 1824 issues of The New York Evening Post.

POSTSCRIPT
ONE O'CLOCK, P.M.

Great Boat Race.—The boat race for $1000, between Captain Harris' boat called the *Dart*, and the *American Star* built by Mr. Chambers, and belonging to the Whitehall Boys, took place about half past 12 this day. The *American Star* came of victorious. She beat the English boat about three hundred yards. The concourse of spectators that assembled on the Battery, and lined the wharves on the North River to witness the race, was immense—not less than fifty thousand.—Time of running the four miles, 22 minutes. The White Hallers made 46 strokes the minute, and English rowers only 39. The victors rowed immediately after round Castle Garden, to Whitehall, where the boat was hoisted up, amidst the reiterated cheers of the populace, a band of music all the time playing Yankee Doodle. The American boat was rowed by Cornehus Cammeyer, Alfred Cammeyer, Richard Robbins, and Samuel Beaty; John Magnus, Coxswain. The English boat was rowed by four men from the frigate, capt. Harris steering.

THE BOAT RACE

Boat Race.—We yesterday gave a hasty sketch of the result of the boat race between *Star* and the *Dart*. [This is the real name of the British boat, and not "*Certain Death*," as some of the other papers have it.] The judges of the race were on the part of the American boat, Major Howard, Captain Henry Robinson, and Mr. Richard Sadlier; on the part of the British boat, Mr. Henry Barclay, and two Lieutenants of the Hussar.—Captain Robinson was stationed on board the frigate, and started the boats by firing a signal gun. Mr. Sadlier was stationed in the northern stake-boat off the North Battery, and Mr. Barclay and Major Howard in the southern stake-boat.—On starting, the *Star* took the lead; the *Dart* shortly after came up and lapped her, on which the Whitehall boys applied a little more power to their oars, forced their boat ahead, and maintained the advantage the whole distance. During the race the wind blew fresh from W.N.W. which considerably affected both the boats, and evidently retarded the *Dart*, the smallest of the two, which on coming in was water logged. Both the stake boats had the American and British flag flying, and when the *Star* came in first at the winning point, the crew of the British launch gave her three hearty cheers, and struck their flag.—The distance was four miles, which was performed in the extraordinary short space of 22 minutes, in a heavy swell.

The honorable conduct of Capt. Harris, his officers and crew, is spoken of in the highest terms, and we are pleased to learn that they are fully satisfied with the manner in which the race was conducted. Capt. H. deemed the weather rather unfavorable for his boat, but as public expectation had been greatly excited, he honorably waved all objections on that head. The stakes, $2,000, were presented to the Whitehall Boys in a beautiful purse, accompanied by a sprig of laurel from the English, to be worn by the coxswain of the *Star* as a trophy of victory. In the afternoon, a deputation was sent to invite the crew of the Hussar to an entertainment to be given by the Whitehallers. The whole thing was conducted throughout with propriety and good feelings.

NEW JERSEY BOAT RACING

Although the popularity of boat racing reached new heights during the 1830s there was considerable spectator interest in the 1820s. The following account, reprinted from the 6 July 1825 edition of The New York Evening Post, reveals the early state of the sport.

FOURTH OF JULY RACES

Among the numerous exhibitions and sports of 4th of July, there were few that were better attended, or appeared to give more satisfaction, than the boat race at Hoboken.

The river was covered with row boats, sail boats, and steam boats, filled with spectators, and the walks and lawn in front of the hotel crowded with well-dressed people. Five boats started: the Despatch, Volant, Count Piper, Ella Ruth, and Crawford. The Despatch, from being a new boat, built for the purpose, and much lighter than any of the others, was the favorite, and evidently the fastest; but owing to the superior skill of the oarsmen in the Crawford, who pulled nearly in a direct line from boat to boat, she lost both the first heats, and the prize boat was won by Crawford. Four boats started for the proprietors' purse: this was a single heat, and won with ease by the Despatch. The fourth heat was for the entrance money, and was won, we believe, by the Volant. The boats were all rowed without a coxswain. If either had taken one, she would have probably won, as much time appeared to be lost for want of proper direction, that was gained by the difference of weight. Owing to the number, and admirable arrangement of the boats, on the Hoboken ferry, there was not the slightest confusion or difficulty in crossing or recrossing; and, before sun-down, the thousands who witnessed it, were again in the city, and probably on their way to some of the other numerous amusements of the evening.

INDUSTRIAL REVOLUTION

The introduction of steam technology altered the lives of many Americans before the Civil War by significantly improving transportation and communication in a young and expanding republic. It also influenced the evolution of sports in North America in a number of ways. Steamboats not only transported spectators to sporting events and carried news of the results but began to compete against one another on the nation's waterways, particularly on the Mississippi and Hudson Rivers. Such applications of the new steam technology and the dangers that went along with it created great excitement among the public. The following account, reprinted from the August 18, 1832, issue of The Spirit of the Times, describes an early race along the Hudson River.

THE STEAM BOAT RACE

Nothing the present season has so thoroughly waked up the feelings of those interested in Steamboats, as the race on Saturday last. It is known to all in this community that two very large and splendid boats have just been completed, the Erie and Champlain, but it may not be equally known, that they were expected to surpass in swiftness any boats hitherto on our rivers. The number of boilers, the power of the engines, and their approved model, perhaps justified the expectation to the full extent. The Champlain made her first trip some weeks since, and fully realized by her speed, the hopes of her friends. The Erie was subsequently completed, and after making a few passages to perfect the movement of her machinery, and to get her in trim, it was generally understood that she would on Saturday last, lay herself alongside the lion of the river, the Beautiful North America, and fairly contest the palm of victory.

At the hour of starting, our wharves were crowded by multitudes of interested spectators, all eagerly watching the busy preparation for the coming contest. The North America shot away from the dock first, but being compelled to sweep around a vessel laying in her course, she gave the Erie an opportunity to come along side and thus it is said, they left the city neck and neck. Now came the tug of war, and none could witness the contest between these two perfections of art, without emotions of awe and sublimity.

The tide was favorable and they scud away with almost terrific rapidity—now one and now the other ahead; but at no time was the distance between them sufficient to give alarm or hope to either. Thus, they continued till within a few miles of West Point, when every effort was made by both to contest the passage of the Highlands with their utmost power—The Erie gradually passed her rival, and continued ahead some lengths—shooting up the narrow gorge of the mountains, and touching the landing at Newburgh with triumph in her movements. They left their respective landings at Newburgh at the same instant, the Erie having the advantage in the location of her stopping place. Away they shot, the Erie ahead, and thus continued to Poughkeepsie.

Here the Erie "came to" and while landing her passengers, the North America pushed in ahead, and sent her boat ashore without touching the wharf and was off in a twinkling. Now again commenced a yet severer struggle for the lead. The whip and spur will sometimes effect this object, but here the result was dependant on the exercise of consummate skill and the nicest judgment. The North America held on her way majestically keeping the lead she obtained at the Poughkeepsie landing. Opposite Hudson, the Erie took the Athens channel, and run by Kingston and Hudson landings, while her rival made them both, thereby losing time and making a longer route by a mile. A few short hours decided this closely contested race. The North America arrived at the foot of State street dock eight minutes ahead of the Erie, making the passage from New York to Albany in the extraordinary short time of nine hours and thirty minutes.

The results of this contest ought not to reflect unfavorably on the Erie, for it is no mean praise of a new and untried boat, to say that the very paragon of steamers when put to her utmost mettle, could only gain eight minutes in a race of one hundred and fifty miles. The effect should rather be, to stimulate the exertions of those concerned, to perfect their boat to the utmost limit of human ingenuity, when they may reasonably indulge the hope, of at least equalling every "floating palace" on our waters.

THE ADVANTAGES OF BOAT CLUBS

The growing interest in boat clubs during the 1830s created a social and cultural justification for their existence. Particularly important were the benefits of the sport—increased physical exercise and health, and advances in ship-building technology. Of course, never far from the public's eye was the concern over the morality of its members and spectators alike. The following article, reprinted from The Spirit of the Times, 9 July 1836, discusses these issues.

BOAT CLUBS

We are gratified to discover a feeling of deep interest springing up on all sides in favor of the association of Boat Clubs in our beautiful bay. The young gentlemen composing the different Clubs are among the most respectable and promising in the city, and in their excursions of pleasure to the several points of popular resort adjacent to the harbor, have manifested such a sense of the respect due to themselves as to secure universal good will and good wishes. Early in the season we published the "manifesto" of the Association, containing some most salutary regulations, especially in relation to excursions upon the Sabbath and carousals on any occasion,—both of which are strictly forbidden.

Within a few days we accompanied one of the Clubs to a favorite and delightful resort, and have renewed cause to express our admiration of an amusement so healthful and so useful. It cannot be too strongly impressed upon our community, and especially the commercial part of it, that this amusement is fraught with most important advantages—of greater moment than the mere pleasurable recreation. It must produce a specific and salutary effect upon the science of boat-building and ultimately upon the skill of our ship-carpenters. Nor is this so trifling a consideration as it may at first seem. Our Boat Clubs will inevitably lead to other associations for aquatic amusements, and especially YACHTING.

Already do we see one or two of these most beautiful of vessels upon our waters.— It is not a week since we stood upon the Battery and watched for a long while the movements of one literally darting about the bay with all the fleetness and grace of a thing born upon the deep. It was one of the most beautiful sights imaginable. Now it need not be urged how valuable to a commercial people like ours, is any amusement which tends so directly to elicit skill and science in ship building. The example of England is before us, where *Yachting* is encouraged as of great national importance to the commercial interest of the country.

But without going so far as this, we desire ardently to see our Boat Club Association fostered, if for this reason only; they furnish a healthful and manly recreation to the young men of our city. It is eminently distinguished from those pleasures most sought after in a town like New York, by its tendency to give strength and vigor to the frame and promote cheerfulness and good spirits. We will not stop to dilate upon this point—various weighty moral considerations must suggest themselves to any one who will reflect a moment on the subject, and who is acquainted with the usual course of life of the young men of the city. The utility of the present Association commends it to the *interests* of the merchants, a character of its members must do to their *respect*.

Let then the merchants manifest their regard for this amusement by subscribing liberally for the purpose of giving a cup, to be rowed for by Clubs at the next Regatta. Let is be costly and beautiful and emulation will be excited and new Clubs will start into existence. Let the Boat Clubs of other cities be allowed, nay, *invited* to join in the

Regatta and contend for the honorable prizes.—This, more than any thing would en-
kindle enthusiasm among the members, and give additional interest and respectability
to the amusement. We are persuaded that a vigorous effort to this end, made by some
of the members of the association would result as we have anticipated. The plan is at
least worth the trial and must draw the attention of those more interested,—the merchants—to the character and advantages of Boat Clubs.

THE NEW YORK RACING SCENE

The concerns of many of the early boat clubs and enthusiasts in the mid-1830s were
the techniques, dress, and size and make of oars and boats used in the sport. This
emphasis was part of the ongoing process of transforming the sport from a premodern
to a modern sport. The following article, taken from the 21 May 1836 edition of The
Spirit of the Times, addresses these and other issues.

NEW YORK BOAT CLUBS

There is great note of preparation at Castle Garden among our numerous Boat
Clubs. The season for aquatic recreation is near at hand, and from the demonstrations
in progress we opine the present will altogether surpass any former season for the
variety and beauty of our water craft. Clubs are being organized on every side, among
our intelligent and respectable young men; and though a few members of the old ones
have taken sleeping partners since last year, and left off rowing to rock the cradle, still
there is energy and spirit enough left among the gallants of the town to man a flotilla
that can any day beat the world in general, and Philadelphia in particular.

Among the rumors of the day, we hear that the Whitehallers will get a challenge for
no small amount of the *swag*, to row against one of the crack clubs. The members of
the Jersey Club—an old and popular one—having moored their boat and cut their
sticks, leave the Whitehallers no other competitors. As for the Clubs of Brooklyn—and
clever fellows compose them—they "dont begin" with the Gothamites, though they
undoubtedly will if ever they get as old. They came pretty near it last year, they say;
and they did, about as near as the boy came to getting the pig. "I say father, I came
pretty darn'd nigh getting Deacon Mullikin's pig for mine to day." "You dont say so,
John:how'd ye de that?" "Why, I axed the Deacon if the pig was his'n, and he said it
was his'n, and then I axed him if he'd give him to me, and he said no, he'd see me—
first!—now if he'd only said yes, I'd had him."

In the course of half an hour's troll about Castle Garden the other day, we "snapped
up various unconsidered trifles" in relation to the Boats stowed away there, and their
crews, "all of which, as the Naval Commissioners say, "is respectfully submitted."

THE WAVE.—The members of this club are out and outers, and with their new boat will show the way to anything that walks the water. CROLIUS has built for them recently a nonpareil of water craft, that for delicacy of model rivals the leg of Vestris. She rows eight oars, and is about five feet in length. If we remember aright a portion of her crew manned *The Swan* in 1834.

THE EAGLE is another "fast crab" of six oars, and having been newly painted and fitted up, looks "rather varmint". She was rowed by the Whitehallers last year against the old *Wave*, but lost the match.

THE DOLPHIN was a crack boat last year and looks like nothing but a good once. She rows eight oars and is in fine order.

THE ARIEL has been out repeatedly this season, her crew being in training to cut out work for the fast ones. She is built for seven oars.

THE ATLANTIC also built for seven oars is manned by youngsters. But they are not boys as their rivals will find. They are strong enough for the stout and too swift for the fast.

THE WAKONA has long been noted for the excellence of her crew; she rows four oars and having been afloat but a year is "just as good as new."

THE MINERVA is another four oar'd boat and a good one, we understand, though we did not see her.

THE NEPTUNE which frequently visits the dominions of His Majesty, is a large nine oar'd boat rather calculated for pleasant water parties than the display of aquatic skill.

What has become of THE STAR, manned last year by the histrions of the Park Theatre, we did not learn, though when it is remembered that we were but half an hour in getting at the facts above, it must be conceded we made the most of our time.

At the request of several members of the Boat Club Association we make room for the following article that appeared in this paper some three years since:—

No city in the old world, or the new, is so admirably situated as this for a boat race; no exercise is so conducive to health and strength, as rowing; and no gala so exciting to those who witness or partake it, as a regatta! It is therefore a matter we have often regretted, that though there are now 15 or 20 regular six oar'd cutter clubs belonging to this city, and all composed of most respectable young men, no plan has yet been matured to bring them altogether, so that they may excite emulation among themselves, and impart pleasure to their friends and visitors.

A small subscription from each club would easily purchase a silver oar, or some other appropriate prize, and the vicinity of the battery affords the most picturesque spot in the world to contest the race in. A regatta thus made up among the young men of the city, would establish rowing as a fashionable amusement, and when once the example were set, it would become a regular enjoyment in which hundreds would partake, and those who now become weak for lack of exercise, would speedily acquire increase of strength, improvement in health, and the opportunity of exhibiting their skill and dexterity to admiring crowds. A more animated scene than a regatta cannot be imagined. The shore thronged with the beauty and fashion of the city; the water covered with boats and barges of every imaginable variety; and the excitement of a contest at once healthy and honorable would render such an event the jubilee of a New York summer.

We hope the gentlemen of the boat clubs will take the thing in hand, and not permit so beneficial an exercise to contribute, as at present, only its least possible quantity of good.

We have received many communications on this subject, some of which contain suggestions that may be useful to new beginners, and no way detrimental to older hands. We beg to throw out a few remarks that occur to us at the moment in hopes that they may prove useful.

Boats. Most of the boats now in use are rather too short in the keel. A four oar'd cutter should be at least 30 feet long, and a six oar'd boat should be 6 feet more. Some competent person should be appointed to examine the work before it is paid for, as several clubs have already suffered for want of having the timbers well secured and properly seasoned.

Oars. Oars should not be too elastic. Much of the rower's force is lost in having too springy an oar; each of them should be 13 feet and a half in length, except the bow and stroke oar which should be half a foot shorter.

Rowing. The stroke should be quick and smart. The body should be bent so as to throw the oar as far forward as possible, and the pull be continued fairly up to the chest. Keeping time, (or "the stroke" as it is termed) is of the greatest importance both as to speed and appearance, and which only practice can perfect you in. In raising the oars on comings in, let the actin of each be simultaneous, the slightest difference looking clumsy and irregular. In racing, do not strive too hard at first, it will incapacitate all for an effort at the critical moment, and remember that is an attribute of bravery to bear triumph or defeat with the same equanimity.

Trimming. Though all the crew should be nearly as possible of the same weight, yet if there be any difference the heavier men should be in the middle. The stroke oar should be in the hands of the steadiest man, as all take their time from him. While the bow-man should be equally expert with the oar and the boat-hook.

Dress. Jackets should not be worn, they confine the arms and chest which should be free. Guernsey shirts are better, and woollen are preferable to cotton, both for wear and retention of color. Straw hats, white trowsers, black kerchief, and a broad belt will then complete a good uniform.

Practice. The mornings are better than the evenings for practice, when they can be so used. Every club should row together three times a week, and very little use will render eight or ten miles an easy distance. In the neighborhood of our city there are hundreds of lovely spots, in visiting which, the air and exercise will amply repay the exertion:all the faculty agree in recommending rowing as the most healthful of exercises, for it not only strengthens the arms, but by expanding the chest and circulating the blood, makes you live longer, happier and better.

> The song that lightens the languid way,
>   When brows are glowing,
>   And faint with rowing.
> Is like the spell of hope's fairy lay,
> To those sounds through life we stray,
>   Nothing is lost on him who sees,
>   With an eye that feeling gave;
> To him there's a story in every breeze,
>   And a picture in every wave.

EARLY ROWING MATCHES

During the mid-1830s, coverage of aquatic events by sports journals and other news-papers increased dramatically, mirroring the growth of these two sports. Many of the earlier aquatic contests differed from the regattas that subsequently became popular, usually matching two rowing or sailing boats against each other. The following ac-count, from the 30 July 1836 issue of The Spirit of the Times, describes this type of rowing and sailing race in New Jersey.

AQUATIC SPORTS—ROWING AND SAILING

There was a grand display of water craft at Hoboken last Monday. The Association and private club boats, with those of Whitehall and Jersey City, were out, and presented a very animating sight. The occasion was the match for $500 a side between the Governor's Island boat *Spring*, and the New York boat *Erie*. We hear the Spring took the lead, and was never headed, beating the Erie by over a length. As the distance was nearly five miles, the match was of course well contested. Hoboken was thronged near the starting point with ladies and gentlemen, and the affair went off with great eclat.

On Tuesday evening the *Wave* Club gave a soiree at the Pavillion, Hoboken, which was attended by most of the city boat clubs, with the crews in full uniform. As each club contributed its quota of ladies, there was a superb assemblage of "fine women and brave men." Several invited guests from this city were in attendance, as also a select party of ladies and gentlemen from Philadelphia. Gaiety and Mirth were the presiding deities of the evening, and the song and the toast succeeded each other in joyous suc-cession. After a *dejeuner a la fourchette*, the enlivening story and mazy dance wore away the evening, until "Jocund day stood tiptoe on the misty mountain's top," when the company retired, alike delighted with present, and anticipating the pleasure of a re-union at many a similar festival.

Thursday's "Express" gives the particulars of a sailing match that came off on Wednesday afternoon, between the schooners *Atlas* and *Sarah Adee*. We quote: It will be recollected that a match came off on the 4th of July last, between the schooners Atlas and Sarah Adee, when the former favored by a sudden gust of wind, carried off the prize. As this was attributed to mere accident, and not to the skill of the hands, another match was proposed for $500, which came off yesterday afternoon. They were to start from Whitehall, go round Sandy Hook, and return to the same place. Thousands attended to witness the contest. On the signal being given, both vessels started in fine style. They had not, however, proceeded far, when the superiority of the Sarah Adee was manifest. She rushed like a winged thing through the sparkling waters, leaving the Atlas three quarters of a mile in her wake. On rounding the Hook, however, the latter gained considerably, and eventually came alongside her antagonist. After a desperate struggle, the Sarah Adee succeeded in again taking the lead, and arrived at Whitehall ahead of the Atlas amidst the plaudits of the spectators."

Several racing and sailing matches are on the tapis, that when matured, shall be given to the public through these columns. It is also in contemplation to raise by sub-scription among our citizens a few prizes, to be given at a splendid regatta, at which all the crack clubs in this and the neighboring cities will be invited to participate.

LOCAL CONTESTS

Although rowing races occurred throughout Canada and the United States during the 1830s, the size and nature of the competitions varied. The following account, reprinted from The Spirit of the Times, 25 February 1837, is a good example of the local and informal character of many of these events.

REGATTA AT ST. SIMON'S ISLAND

The Aquatic Club of Georgia met at Frederica, St. Simon's Island, with their race boats, on the 18th instant. The weather was fair and calm, and the following races took place:—

1st. Col. Dubignon's boat *Goddess of Liberty*, against Mr. Demere's *Columbia*, both 6 oared and about the same size; but, by agreement, the Goddess was rowed with 4 oars, and the Columbia with her full complement—and for this advantage in favor of the Columbia, the Goddess was given two lengths (64 feet). The race was against the tide, and the distance half a mile. Won by the Goddess by 8 feet, not including the odds allowed her for giving up 2 oars. Time not reported.

2d. Col. Dubignon's *Goddess of Liberty*, against Capt. Richard Floyd's *Devil's Darning Needle*—each 6 oars. The match produced much excitement, and considerable betting. The boats had contended last year at St. Mary's running with the current, and the Goddess was victorious, but her friends thought that in a race against the tide, she could beat the Goddess.

The "Devil's Darning Needle" was steered by Capt. Richard Floyd, and rowed by Mr. Nightingale's famous oarsmen. The "Goddess" was managed by Capt. Thos. F. Bryan, and rowed by his oarsmen, not less famous than Mr. Nightingale's. A bend in the course of the river concealed the boats from the spectators at starting, but the firing of a gun announced that they were "off" and every eye was eagerly directed to the first point for their appearance. The Goddess was seen first about half a length ahead of the Darning Needle, and she continued to maintain this advantage in their rapid approach to the Judge's stand, while the rival oarsmen put out the utmost skill and strength for victory. On turning a second point, about 150 yards from the Judge's stand, the Goddess being inside, or nearest the point, was approached so near by the Darning Needle, that the forward oars of the latter struck on the larboard quarter of the Goddess, and a small scuffle ensued among the oarsmen, in which the Goddess lost an oar. Capt. Bryan, however, succeeded in extricating her, and she came out alone in the Judge's stand, the Darning Needle having halted after the accident, which was unavoidable, as the boat is extremely long and flat, and was steered by an oar on a pivot, which made the steering difficult even on a straight line—. The race was determined in favor of the Goddess. Distance a little upwards of three quarters of a mile. Time of the Goddess, 5 1/2 minutes, including the *entanglement*, which is extremely good, considering that the race was against a *strong tide*, and the coarse was serpentine....

3d.—Mr. Demere's Columbia, six oars, against Mr. Samuel Floyd's Volant, four oars—won by the former by two lengths—distance about half a mile—time not reported.

HENRY DUBIGNON,
CHARLES R. FLOYD,
Secretaries, A.C.G.

Frederick, Jan. 20th, 1837.

INTERCITY CHALLENGES

The growth of boating and yachting led to greater coverage of these sporting events throughout Canada and the United States and to intercity and regional challenges and races. The following article, from the 16 September 1837 edition of The Spirit of the Times, details an intercity contest.

AQUATIC REGISTER

Boat racing and sailing has become a matter of such general attention and interest, that we shall be obliged to make a distinct department in the Spirit of the Times for the purpose of chronicling the sayings and doings of the different Clubs and Associations throughout the country. We cannot commence this department with a pleasanter affair than

"THE GULL'S" visit to Philadelphia.—The New York Association Club Boat, *The Gull*, reached town on Wednesday evening, from our sister city where they experienced the kindest and most general hospitality. The Philadelphia Gazette of last Monday contains the annexed paragraphs relative to The Gull and her gallant crew:—

Among the interchanges of civility and compliment with which the volunteer and amateur associations of Philadelphia and New York are in the habit of occasionally regaling each other, we have never beheld any more imposing than that embraced in the *fete* given on Saturday last to the Gull boat-club, of the New York Amateur Association, by the united members of a similar body in Philadelphia. A splendid procession came off on the Schuylkill, in honor of the aquatic delegation from the sister metropolis. It was a beautiful sight, as the fairy craft, handsomely manned, left the shore at Belmont, and sped gracefully round the green island which sleeps so sweetly on the bosom of the river, above the rail road bridge—the destination of the party was to the mouth of the romantic Wissahiccon, and the Falls of Schuylkill. At the latter point the New York members were acceptably entertained; and after a sufficient pause, the oars of the whole array of boats were cleaving the wave, southward bound. As they re-approached the bridge, and swept gracefully under its arches, the *huzzas* went up from such a goodly number of throats, that the verdure on the picturesque hills round about, seemed to quiver in the voice of gratulation. The banks of the Schuylkill, during the procession, presented a most animating spectacle—being *decorated*—we may well use the word—with ladies on horseback, accompanied by gentlemen of the city, and in various vehicles, from the humbly rolling gig to the imposing four-in-hand.

Arrived at the Cottage, a sumptuos dinner table awaited both entertainers and guests. It was loaded, we learn, with all the viands and delicacies of the season; no preparations having been neglected to render the affair—the vinous department in particular—and that it should be. The company separated at an early hour, not displeased with themselves, and at peace with the world.

The Gull Club left the city to-day for their home, bearing with them the good wishes of the entertainers, and the best feelings toward the members of the Falcon, Wave, Gipsey, Dart, and Gondolier Clubs. These reciprocal courtesies are calculated to cement friendly attachments; and when conducted as in the present case the most perfect and gentlemanly propriety, reflect honor both upon the hosts and the recipients of their hospitality.

The GULL in returning last Wednesday, rowed round Staten Island, and dined at New Brighton, after rowing 40 miles, where they were most hospitably entertained by MR. MILFORD at the Pavilion. They were escorted up to town by the Boat Club Association after their delightful visit. The Club request us to make their grateful acknowledgments to the Schuylkill Amateur B.C. Association.

QUEBEC REGATTA

Boating and yachting developed significantly in Canada during the 1830s, and, as the following article makes clear, sporting enthusiasts welcomed and encouraged the growth of aquatic competition between clubs of various regions and cities, as had been achieved in other sports such as cricket and curling. This article, which originally appeared in the Quebec Mercury, is reprinted from The Spirit of the Times, 16 September 1837.

REGATTA AT QUEBEC

Regatta at Quebec.—From the "Mercury" of that city, bearing date the 9th instant, we quote the annexed paragraphs:—

"REGATTA."—A meeting of the gentlemen friendly to promoting aquatic sports was held yesterday, when Stewards were named, and other preliminary measures taken necessary for arranging a Regatta, to take place immediately after the Race meeting. We trust it will be liberally supported, for, though friendly to the sports of the turf, and far from regretting the liberal encouragement the race have received, we cannot but view the promotion of those exercises which render men familiar with the water and with vessels, as peculiarly adapted to a nation whose greatness and whose glory has been nurtured by its skill in maritime affairs. In an extensive port like this, visited during the short period of our summer navigation by upwards of 1,200 sail of vessels, there ought to be found sufficient subscribers to raise ample funds for enabling the Stewards to give several handsome prizes to be contended for by the different classes of sailing and rowing boats which will be entered on the occasion. Amongst others, we learn, a prize will be given for six-oared and another for four-oared boats; these, especially the lst class, are expected to afford great sport.—Indeed, there are in this city and at Montreal, no less than four superior four-oared gigs and cutters, all prize boats, nearly equal in length, and built by the first builders in the ports at which they were constructed; it would be a gallant sight to see all these contending in one race. The boats we refer to are—the *Hookey Walker*, built at Liverpool—the *Cherub* and the *Waterwich*, both built in the Clyde—and the *Thames*, built by Searl, of London, for the officers of the 32d Regiment, in whose possession it now remains. We hope that these gentlemen, with the Montreal amateurs of the oar, will be tempted to take a trip to Quebec, and meet the amateurs of this city in friendly competition for the mastery in this race. In Upper Canada, the Cricket Clubs think nothing of travelling an equal distance to play a match at that national game, and the curlers of Quebec and Montreal have, in the depth of winter, met half way, at Three Rivers, to enjoy a morning's sport on the *rink*, and a friendly "*spread*" in the evening after the fatigues of the day. It cannot be imagined that the amateur watermen feel less interest in their favorite pursuit than has been shown by the Cricketers and the Curlers. The spirit of emulation between rowers in England is so strong, that a party of Saltasha men lately came from Plymouth to London, a distance of 220 miles by the turn pike road, to contend with the Thames watermen upon their own stream and test the qualities of a four-oared boat built by Mr. Waterman, of Plymouth, against one of the same force, built by Mr. Searle, of Lambeth."

THE SOCIAL FUNCTION OF BOAT RACES

With the rising popularity of boat races during the late 1830s, the competitive dimension of matches often gave way to their more social function. Much like sleighing, boating events provided a socially acceptable opportunity for men to court women. The following account of a boat race, reprinted from the 19 July 1837 issue of The New York Herald, describes the social nature of one boat race.

BOAT RACE FROM CASTLE GARDEN
"Row, brother, row"

Yesterday afternoon about half past three o'clock, the spacious water off the Castle Garden was thronged with boats to witness the race between Pioneer and Forget-me-Not. A challenge had passed between the bonny boatmen of Whitehall and those of Fulton market. The Whitehall boys put in Pioneer, rather a dark countenanced animal with a fillet of yellow round her brow. She sat prettily on the waters, was light as a feather, and under the direction of a skilful and knowing crew. On the other hand, Forget-me-Not, sable colored and yet of just features, came up to the starting point with all the grace imaginable. Her oarsmen, with check shirts and white caps formed a striking contrast with those of the pioneer in white shirts and black caps.

Hundreds of boats shot here and there—while intermingling with the crowd, was to be seen the Lafitte, the Alert, the Glide, and many of the same class, propelled by brave young men.

"In regular order set."

Every now and then a mischievous sail boat, managed by mischievous boys, would come thundering down upon you, and make you uncertain as to your fate—when on a sudden, up would go the helm, and she would glide away in another direction. It seemed more like the bay of Venice, with its thousand gondolas, than the harbor of New York.

On the battery, hundreds and thousands were waiting, to see the sport, while the trees seemed white with boys in linen dress. Castle Garden was crowded. The *coup d' all* from the harbor was magnificent. It appeared as if the city had poured forth all its inhabitants to witness some great contest on which their existence depended. The greatest interest was manifested. In the distance were two steamboats crowded with spectators, and they lay to, blowing off their steam, thus adding to the interest of the scene. From the mast-heads of vessels in the neighborhood, many a sailer watched with eager gaze.

At 4 o'clock, the drum beat, and the two antagonists came slowly to the starting place. By lot, the Forget-me-Not had the choice of position. She took the right going from the garden. The stake-boat was stationed nearly opposite, at the distance of one mile and a half.

The signal was given. Away over the heaving wave went the Pioneer and the Forget-me-Not. Now the Pioneer marches off with a firm, steady, and swift gait, leading the Forget-me-Not. See, the Forget-me-Not passes her rival. A shout is heard Hah! again the Pioneer is ahead, and she keeps ahead. Now they approach the stake-boat. Look out, my boys. Still onward presses the Whitehaller. With speedy keel, the Forget-me-Not cleaves the brine beneath. Yonder they go. The Pioneer turns the stake-boat full three lengths ahead of her enemy.

Crossing and re-crossing, the accompanying boats kept on continual. A busy scene it was—enlivened by the gleaming of a thousand feathery oars in the setting sun, and their quick plash in the waters of the noble Hudson. Here they come, booming over the wave.—The oars of the Pioneer made a short and high curve, while those of the Forget-me-Not rose just above the surface, to get their dipping-place.

"I must show you the way," said the confident Whitehaller. "These wastes I have trod before—so hurry on, and faint not. I am your pioneer."

"Your kindness I acknowledge," replied the Fulton market boat, "and should you arrive before me, tell them I am coming—that I fear nothing, and am not faint. Go on, but forget-me-not."

The Whitehaller, now surrounded by a hundred boats came rapidly in. Her rival kept a steady pace, but proved unequal to the task; the Pioneer coming in about sixty yards ahead. The whole multuide shouted, and the brave boys of Fulton market, like men bowed their heads in meekness and yielded. [...] is ever the conduct of the conquered brave. The victors too bore themselves with becoming modesty. This strife in boat racing, when conducted by our New York boys, is truly noble. Emulous, but not envious of each others prowess, they strive in contest fair to test their powers. With such a harbor, such boats, and such oarsmen we shall bid fair to rival the world in "speedy keels" and boatmanship. Our young boatmen are true philosophers. They devote a portion of their time to the poetries of life,—and boat racing is one of them.

There was only one thing wanting. And that was the proud gondola, with lovely woman in it. We hope that the next regutten, many a boat will be seen wafting the pretty girls of New York on the bosom of the waters. If properly done, it will become highly fashionable. Our ladies will thank us for the suggestion, for it will put the gallantry of their admirers to the test. What can be more interesting than an elegantly fitted up boat, with half a dozen beautiful women in it rowed by their beaus or lovers? It is romantic. It is far above the fashionable amusements of the day. The lover, too, can show his intended, on an occasion of this kind, whether he possesses those personal qualifications that ought to be the pride and boast of a suitor. Woman forever should preside at a regatta.

And thus ended the affair at Castle Garden. We did not learn the time in which the three miles were made. Everybody went away satisfied. This is however only a "wake up." The summer will be enlivened by many a race yet.

In relation to the Pioneer and Forget-me-Not, we understand that the latter was forty or fifty pounds heavier than the former. It appears to us that there ought to be a rule among the boat clubs in regard to this matter.—The weight of both boats with their crew should be equal, to obtain any-thing like a certain result from the trial of speed.

We return our thanks to the Fulton market boys for their kind invitation, and hope they may be more successful the next time.

SOUTHERN RACING

Although boat racing was a recent development in Alabama in 1830, the early signs of modernization appeared very quickly—times were kept, crews listed, and terms of the race expressed in agreements. The following account, reprinted in the 20 January 1838 issue of The Spirit of the Times, documents the widespread appeal and popularity of the new sport in the South and the rapid development of intersectional rivalries.

MOBILE BOAT RACE

Seadrift vs. *The Wave*—We find the following account of this match in the Mobile Examiner. The sport has been recently introduced into Alabama, and all classes appear to regard it with favor. The match in question was rowed the 8th instant.

Multitudes were assembled—the decks and rigging of every vessel commanding a view of the river for any distance, were crowded by persons anxious to see the sport, discussing the merits of the competitors in the coming contest.—The steamer Jefferson, freighted with the rank and beauty of the city, hauled into the river which was alive with small crafts of every description, careering rapidly over its bosom. Distinguished from all others, in lightness of build, length of keel, and beauty of motion, came the rival boats, balancing over the dancing billows, as if conscious of the admiration they excited, and rejoicing in the embraces of that element they were so well fitted to grace.

The signal is given—they start—and, as the racer, when under whip and spur of the accomplished rider, dashes onward, so they came sweeping past, the Wave in advance, moving steadily on beneath the measured strokes of their practiced crew. Two lengths behind came the Seadrift, imperceptibly gaining the distance lost by accident at the beginning of the race. They are now too far ahead to allow the spectators to see which is foremost. They turn—and again the Wave is seen in advance, which advantage she continues to hold, until opening the line of the bay, she has to contend with an increase of wind and current, which her light frame is not fitted for. Not so the Seadrift. Being the heavier boat, and carrying two oars more than her opponent, she swept onward, apparently regardless of wind and current, depending on her own good qualities and the exertions of her crew, for that success which eventually crowned her efforts. She arrived at the judges boat, in thirty-two minutes and forty seconds, and eight or ten seconds ahead of the Wave. After a friendly greeting, the Seadrift went aboard the Jefferson, where music closed the sports of the evening.

We understand the members of the Wave club, are ready for another trial of skill, at any time according to the terms of the agreement entered into previous to the last race, namely, a four oar boat against a six, or if that wont suit, the Wave against the Seadrift in smooth water.

The boats were manned as follows:—

Seadrift.	Wave.
Jos. P. Armstrong, *Coxswain,*	John B. Todd, *Coxswain.*
1. Wm. Jones	1. H. McGibbon,
2. Wm. Wood,	2. S. Brown,
3. H. Vail,	3. H. Barton,
4. J. Johnson,	4. H.B. Bolston,
5. D. Geary,	5. R.D. Post,
6. H. Jenkins,	6. H.F. Parker,
7. E. Faber—8 R.C. Vandevoot.	

We are informed that the Seadrift ran foul of a snag immediately after the start.— Ep.

SOUTHERN SOCIETY AND SPORTS

Boat races in the southern United States were often accompanied by elaborate social balls and were great contests over honor and pride. In the South, Savannah, Georgia, was one of the earliest and most important sites for boat races, owing to its wealthy elites and its proximity to coastal waterways. But, as this document demonstrates, other groups and classes began to participate in the sport as it grew in popularity. The following account appeared in The Spirit of the Times, 8 February 1840.

A REGATTA AT SAVANNAH

Our readers will perceive that the *"Tallulah Boat Club,"* recently formed in this city, contemplate a Regatta in February.

We anticipate a day of rational enjoyment. In noticing this new club, a few days since in our columns, we could, if our limits had allowed, (contracted as they were by a diminution of our force, beyond our control,) have alluded to the *Lower Creek Boat Club*, which, composed principally of public spirited mechanics of our city, have the credit of entertaining our citizens and transient residents with this athletic and manly sport for the past two years. The first year they were vanquished by General Charles Floyd, whose experience in these matters made him a powerful competitor, and at whose challenge they entered the field.

Gen. F.'s canoe, the *Lizard*, proved too swift for their beautiful model of a clinker-built boat—*the Star*. But, like true game, they bore their reverses as men, and, by their magnanimity and noble deportment, won the admiration of all. The victory, too, was so much pleased with their gentlemanly bearing, under defeat, as to confer on the Club, the victorious *Lizard*.

The second year the *Lower Creeks* came up to the starting point with renovated ardor: bringing forward a new plant boat—*The Floyd*, named after their generous competitor. She distanced three others, of six oars; two of them canoe boats—*"The Goddess of Liberty"* and *"The Caroline King;"* and *"The Saladin,"* a plank boat, (the latter reduced to five oars, halfway in the contest, by the fracture of one of her rullocks.)

In the second race, (all canoe boats and four oars,) with their victorious *Lizard*, THE CREEKS crept ahead of the three gallant competitors—*The Goddess of Liberty, the Snake* and *the Star*; leaving the second boat, *The Goddess of Liberty*, 290 feet astern.

With these results of an honourable perseverance, we were, last May, highly gratified; for it is almost a received maxim, that —"the man rising above misfortunes in this pilgrimage of life, is an object on which angles even might gaze with envy." The Creeks bore, too, their triumphs with as much grace as their previous defeat.

'Tis such men, composed of such manly materials, to whom the Tallulah Boat Club now throw the gauntlet, for this inspiring and beautiful sport. Other powerful competitors, hitherto successful, from the islands of our Coast will, doubtless, brush up for the games, in which they may hereafter be hailed as victors, for a vanquished opponent is not to be despised. We trust to see them all participate, in February, in promoting a manly recreation, and in assembling the beauty of two conterminous States, to witness the soul-stirring Regatta.

We annex a description of the boats held by the Lower Creeks, whose victorious laurels, the Tallulah boats will have to strive to displace, in the contest for supremacy in rowing.

The *Floyd*, of six oars, is 38 feet long and clinker built. She was built in New York, by Shamburg, from a model furnished by the Lower Creek Club.

The Tallulah and *The Ariel*, of the Tallulah Club, or either, will make a race with the Floyd interesting.

The Lizard, of four oars, is in length 29 feet, 6 inches. Gen. Charles Floyd has the credit of building her.

The Savannah, of the Tallulah Club, we hope to see entered, as one of her competitors.

It will be canoe against the clinker built, and will, of course, be exciting sport.

But *The Lizard*, as well as *The Floyd*, merits hosts of competitors. Let them come from St. Marys—and the intermediate islands;—from Augusta and from parts unknown.

The lists are open. Who'll tilt in the presence of the *lovely fair*.

Savannah Georgian, 17th Jan.

THE FORMATION OF ROWING CLUBS

The sport of rowing experienced tremendous growth and rapid modernization during the 1830s. Boat clubs were formed and contests between localities, cities, regions, and nations occurred with increasing regularity. The following article, which appeared in the 15 September 1838 issue of The Spirit of the Times, portrays one such effort to form a rowing club in a Southern state and also reveals the early part of the process through which the sport was modernized.

BOAT CLUB IN LOUISIANA

BAYOU SARA, 8th Aug, 1838.

DEAR SIR,—Aware that you take a lively interest in all and every one of the "spirited" amusements that are daily resorted to to "drive dull care away," and knowing that everything connected with sport or fun, in whatever/shape, meets with a kind reception in your paper, as an assistance in enlivening its "mirth making" pages, I take the greatest pleasure in announcing to you the fact that a Boat Club has recently been organized here, which, from the endeavors that have been made, and are still making, to ensure its permanency and success, bids fair to rival in all points the older and long since established Clubs of your own entry and its neighbors. You know, from having been here among us of the "sunny land," that our boys are all stout and hearty, the very creatures themselves for "a long pull, and a pull all together" of a hot summer's day. Well, 'tis just fifteen such out and outers who compose the *"Eagle Boat Club of Bayou Sara,"* all as clever and as good as ever "trod shoe leather." The boat, now building in Philadelphia, is to be a "bonny thing," built after the latest and most approved model, both for beauty and speed, and is to man six oars. Among the members, there are some from "every land." New York and Philadelphia are well represented, and they who had from beyond the Mountains are no strangers to such sports. As this on the Mississippi River is a new thing, and, so far as I have learnt, an untried experiment, we beg first of all to lay a claim to age, and as for the mere sensation we may create, and the pleasure we may be the means of affording to our "dark eyed maids," as "of a moonlit e'en" they gaze at our "fairy flight," we'll have to risk and run our chance. Our dress is in the true blue sailor fashion, and for elegance and seamanlike appearance, must leave many older contemporaries in the dark. Our boat is expected here by the first of September, and ere three months roll round, mind you, we'll give them something worth talking about. Until, however, emulation becomes sufficiently great as to enable us to see started from among our citizens "an opposition" Club, we cannot expect to have as much fun or to make ourselves as conspicuous as we would like; but as it is, we'll give Time a trial, and as soon as we look at our fairy bark, and ascertain how she "kicks" through the water, we'll stake our reputation as sailors against any given sum of money, to run either with or against the current.

There is an *on dit* that an opposition Club *will* be started, and that its name, it is already ascertained, will be the *"Feliciana Boat Club."* Vested with authority by the members of the "Eagle Club," I challenge the "Feliciana Boat Club" into existence, or any other that may be in contemplation here, and challenge them likewise to a contest for superiority, to the tune of five hundred dollars—the trial to come off at any given time to come. This *banter*, I trust, will excite the energies of the "Feliciana B. Club" to a sudden organization and preparation for victory or defeat. You must know the sailors here are scarce, and rather a *kiriosity*. Well, on last Sunday, the members of the Eagle Club astonished the natives by an elegant display through town of the "wholehouse," as neat and tidy a set of Jack tars as ever an "old salt" would wish to see, all dressed, too, in sailor's rigging from stem to stern.

When the yacht arrives, I hope to be able to write you of some brilliant achievement on the water, which I trust, with this my first sketch of our rise, and yet feeble progress, may prove acceptable to you and the readers of the Spirit of the Times.

Respectfully your FRIEND

FIRST BOAT RACE IN LOUISVILLE

Boat racing became a national phenomenon during the 1830s, spreading to various regions, cities, and localities. As the sport assumed a more modern character intercity rivalries developed along with other prevalent practices of boat racing such as gambling. The following article, an account of the first boat race in Louisville, Kentucky, is reprinted from The Spirit of the Times, 1 December 1838.

BOAT RACE, PITTSBURG vs. LOUISVILLE

To the Editor of the Spirit of the Times.—Having read some time since in your paper a description of our turf races, I thought an attempt to describe a *boat race* might not prove unacceptable; and if it is not what it ought to be, you must take the will for the deed. Some time since a challenge was given by the *Gipsey* barge club of Louisville Ky., to the Glaucus barge club of Pittsburg, Pa., to row at Louisville from 1 to 4 miles, for from $500 to $1000 aside, the *Gipsey* paying $200 for their expenses, which was accepted by the latter club. Last week the sons of "the Iron city" honored us with their appearance with their Glaucus, and finally agreed the race should come off on Monday the 19th inst., at 3 0'clock P.M., for $500 aside, 2 1/4 miles up the river, and 2 1/4 down, making in all 4 1/2 miles.

About 3 o'clock the shores began to be lined with horsemen, footmen, steam boats, keel boats, skiffs, canoes, barges, yauls, and though last not least, the old-fashioned flat boat, all literally covered with people, and on the steamboats and in the carriages might be seen the bright eyes of beauty gracing the scene with their presence.

Bets were greatly in favor of the Glaucus, in consequence of their established fame, having won two or three races, and the acknowledged strength and powers of endurance of the Pittsburgers, though still the *blood* of the untried Gipseys rendered them no contemptible opponents, and their friends backed them freely. At 3 o'clock precisely the boats were at the starting point, the Glaucus having won the track; she lay in her beauty like a sea bird upon the water, waiting for her adversary to take the station assigned her, which was done by the gallant Gipsey on the outside, and consequently more in the current. There was considerable anxiety to see which would get the start, so as to keep the shore all the way up for the benefit of having the eddy—odds were offered that the Glaucus would take it, as she had invariably done so—and the friends of the Gipsey were equally sanguine.

At the top of the steamboat bell they started with the fleetness of the antelope; and it was seen that the Gipsey gained something the first pull—the second, still more, and at the third and fourth, shot ahead of the Glaucus, amid the deafening shouts of the "corn crackers," and took the track; the Glaucus, nothing daunted, following close in her wake. The first mile the Gipsey still kept gaining and increasing the distance, till at the second mile there was three or four lengths difference. It was found the Gipseys would not hold out, as they rowed a quicker stroke than the Glaucus, at the rate of 5 to 3. The buoy being close by, there was a smart brush—the Gipseys endeavoring to turn as quick as possible and take advantage of the current down stream, and the Glaucus to lessen the distance between them. At this time the excitement was intense among the betting gentlemen, aye, and the ladies too. Horsemen were riding up and down, carrying the news to many a fair face. The Gipsey made the buoy about four lengths ahead of the Glaucus, and in turning, the stroke oar of the former came out of its place, and the turn was not made as well as it ought to have been, but the difference was scarcely noticed, when she got round and shot ahead with the speed of thought (almost). The Glaucus coming to the buoy, and turning beautifully, crossed the track of the Gipsey, and taking the outside as they went down, the Gipsey still ahead, and inclining to the shore, while the Glaucus kept (and wisely too) the current, and widened the distance across from one boat to the other. The Pittsburgers, now saw that the Glaucus was getting the advantage, for as the Gipsey kept inclining to the shore, they lost the current, and made the distance longer by going in the bend of the river, so that at the end of the first mile it was very easily to be seen that the Glaucus had gained a length, though the Gipsey was still considerably ahead. The boats continued in this position for the next mile, or nearly so, until the last quarter stretch, when the Gipsey's found the Glaucus had not only gained her distance, but was still gaining, and had got a length ahead; the struggle was now tremendous. The Gipsey sprung like a fiery steed goaded with the spur, and the Glaucus exerted all her energies in the last grand effort, the friends on both sides making the air resound with their cheering, and kerchiefs waving from carriage and steam boat, to encourage either crew, and as the Gipsey kept gaining little by little, her friends were sanguine of winning, but the distance was not sufficiently long, (I mean from the time they got out of the bend,) and the Glaucus, amid the cheers of the Pittsburgers that almost rent the sky, came in ahead, winning by a half a length!

Thus ended the first boat race in Louisville, and it was a splendid one; the match was rowed in 26 minutes precisely. The judges were—GARNETT DUNCAN, ROBT. J. WARD,—PRATHER, Esqrs. and Capt. C.M. STRADER.

It was apparent the crew of the Glaucus was much better disciplined, they having pulled together so frequently in other races; at any rate, they rowed with the precision of a machine. The Gipsey was evidently the fleetest boat, and was rowed the longest distance in the same time, which proved that her crew had as good bottom as blood, and had it not been that their coxswain steered them into the band of the river, they must necessarily have won, for the pilots and all the "river-men," and indeed every one else knows, it makes from 150 to 200 yards difference in distance, besides the loss of current.   W.H.G.

SECTIONAL CHALLENGE

As boat racing became a phenomenon in the United States and Canada during the 1830s, participants in the sport demanded more accurate and precise reporting of race distances and rowing times for comparative value. Such reporting also promoted competition on a regional or national scale as well as uniform rules and regulations—important developments in the evolution of rowing. In the following document, reprinted from the 17 September 1836 edition of The Spirit of the Times, a Georgian boating enthusiast addresses these concerns and, in the process, displays his own section's thirst for intersectional competition.

SPEED OF RACE BOATS

To the Editor of the New York Spirit of the Times

It would be very gratifying to the lovers of boat racing at the South, if the New York Boat Clubs would be more particular in reporting the time and distance of their races, and also the state of the weather, and the rapidity of the current, either against or in favor of their boats. A first rate boat race is quite as interesting as a first rate horse race, and should be as accurately reported. Of the various accounts given by the New York papers of boat races, there is not one that is satisfactory to persons at a distance; nor have I seen one on the authority of the judges of the races. In the race between the *Wave* and *Eagle*, in 1834, one of the New York papers stated the distance "*about* 2 1-2 miles," and the time "17 minutes and 3 seconds." Another paper said of the distance, "*it is called* 3 1-2 miles"—and made the time "17 minutes." Now these statements, differing one mile as to distance, and 3 seconds as to time, besides the uncertainty attending the words "*about*," and "*is called*," give us no correct notion of the speed of the boats.

There are other statements before me published at New York a few years ago. One describes a boat "built by Mr. Joseph Rancis for the Messrs. Perkins," and says, "four pilots rowed her 2 miles in 7 minutes"—3 1-2 *minutes only to each mile!*

In the other, the race at Quebec, between the Scotch boat *Little Cherub*, and the New York boat *Eagle*, both four oared, is described—and it is stated that the distance run was 4 miles—the time 17 minutes 5 seconds:which gives 4 minutes 15 seconds, and *a little more* to each mile—vastly superior to the performance of the Wave in her trial with the Eagle, but how poor when compared with the speed of the boat built for the Messrs. Perkins! These accounts are very wonderful, but nobody can believe them, who has any knowledge of race boats.—There never has been built, and there never can be built, a boat capable of running with four oars, one mile in 4 minutes 15 seconds, assisted by a tide of ordinary rapidity. I do not mean a mile computed by the eye, nor a nautical mile (which is larger than a land mile), but 1760 yards, *accurately measured* in a straight line. A mile in 6 minutes, in *still* or *slack water*, is admirable performance for a 6 oared boat—a performance which has never been excelled, and but rarely equalled.

New York is not the only race boat region in the United States. We have race boats at the South, (each built out of a single tree) ready to contend against any thing, but they cannot run *a mile in* 3 1-2 *minutes*, nor in 4 *minutes* 15 *seconds*, yet we think they can beat any plank boat.

Could any of your New York Clubs be persuaded to visit Savannah next winter, with their boats and oarsmen, for a trial with our Georgia clippers for a thousand or two? We cannot carry our oarsmen to New York as they are our slaves, else we might be tempted to visit your city with our boats for a trial on the fair Hudson.

St. Mary's, Geo., August 25, 1836.   COXSWAIN

SLAVERY AND BOAT RACING

In some sports, especially horse racing, regional contests pitting horses from the North and South against each other created quite a stir during the antebelllum period when sectional hostilities increased dramatically. With the rise of rowing clubs similar sectional challenges occurred. The following article, reprinted from The Spirit of the Times, 16 December 1837, reflects the growing sport rivalry between the sections and contains a brief discussion of slavery as a factor in a proposed rowing match between boat clubs from New York City and Georgia.

BOAT CLUBS

The Aquatic Club of Georgia has not yet withdrawn its challenge to our New York cracks, to row a straight mile, for $10,000 aside, $2000 ft. The Georgia boat is named *The Lizard*, and it will be observed by the following from *The Advocate*, published at Brunswick, Ga., that our Clubs cannot take the exception raised last Fall on account of the color of the crew of the Georgia boat.

But if we mistake not, it is contrary to the rules of our Association, that any of its members should row for money.

"THE AQUATIC CLUB OF GEORGIA.—The challenge which this club published to the New York boatmen has never been noticed in any official manner.A gentleman of this city met some of the Whitehallers during the summer, and learned from them that they would not consent to row against black servants; but if the gentlemen of Georgia would row their boat, the case would be different.The challenge of the Georgia Club says nothing of the rowers, and the New Yorkers would have avoided the injury their reputation has suffered had they made inquiries of the proper persons.We are authorized to say that the Lizard shall be manned by gentlemen, who, we warrant, shall be the equals of the Knickerbockers in bone and muscle, blood and sinew."

SECTIONAL RESPONSE

The following article, which appeared in the 30 June 1838 issue of The Spirit of the Times, indicates that the debate between the Georgia and New York boat clubs over the challenge initially issued by the Southerners had not been resolved over six months later, most likely because of the Georgia Club's desire to prove themselves against a noted northern opponent.

BANTER TO THE NEW YORK BOAT CLUBS

We find the annexed communication in the Boston Morning Herald of the 13th inst. The writer does not appear to be aware that the Club Boats belonging to the New York Association are deterred from making matches for money or any other prize by an express article in their Constitution. The "Member of the Georgia Club" whose challenge is subjoined, does not demonstrate therein the possession, to an unusual degree, of "that fine sense which men of honor pride themselves upon," notwithstanding his gratuitous and vulgar fling at the Members of the N.Y. Association:—

Messrs. Editors,—Some time since, while at the South, I observed a notice in your paper concerning a boat race which took place at Savannah, Ga. between a northern plank boat and southern canoe. The statement made at that time being essentially wrong, and calculated to substantiate the *false idea* of the invincibility of the New York boats, has caused me to ask room for the following true statement of the case:—The two boats were the Lizard (canoe) and Star (plank) four oars each—length about 28 feet six inches—distance run, 1 mile—purse $500, and boat against boat. The Lizard came out 35 yards ahead. The Star was built in New York by celebrated builders of that city, expressly to *beat* the Lizard, which was then up against any four oared boat of the same length. The instructions to the builders of the Star were to make a boat to beat the Lizard, and neither expense nor trouble was spared to make her a first rate four oared boat, and so positive and confident were the builders that they agreed that the Star should cost the club nothing in case she should accidentally be beaten.

The Lizard was built by a gentleman residing in Camden county, Ga. and a member of the Georgia Aquatic Club. The bombast style of a banter issued by a New York club, some two years since, induced the members of the Georgia club to challenge the New Yorkers for a trial of the relative speed of the plank and canoe boats. Knowing it would be too expensive and unjust for one of the clubs to be obliged to remove their boat the entire distance to the waters of the other club, it was proposed to run off Savannah for the sum of $10,000, not so much for absolute gain as an equivalent for the trouble, necessary expense, &c. of the race.

While at the North last summer, I conversed with some of the officers of the New York club respecting the challenge, and they gave, as a reason for not accepting, that the southern boat was pulled by negroes and that they were gentlemen. I then distinctly stated that the southern boat would be manned by gentlemen, fully equal to them in birth, wealth, or any other point they might choose to enumerate. They did not accept the challenge, nor did they treat it in such a manner as to lead any one (but themselves) to think or believe that in their expression of *gentlemen* 'twas anything but a name. I am now authorised to make up a race to come off at Norfolk or Baltimore, between a two, four, or six oared canoe, against any plank boat of the same length of the accepted canoe, the amount of the challenge to be enough to satisfy any of those fastidious gentlemen of the New York Clubs.

Yours, &c.

A MEMBER OF THE GEORGIA CLUB.

THE NEW YORK BOAT CLUB

As the size and scope of boating events increased, public concern and anxiety developed over the real and potential dangers to morality posed by the large gatherings of spectators and the festive nature of the occasions. The following account makes clear that the members of the New York boating association were concerned with preserving the moral integrity of their sport and made sure that the regatta described in the document below was conducted with hospitality and good cheer. This article is reprinted from the 1 July 1837 issue of The Spirit of the Times.

THE GRAND REGATTA

It is not now more than three or four years since, that we indulged ourselves in the pleasure of a sail in one of the three only boats then owned by a New York BOAT CLUB. They were then an entire novelty in our waters, and an invitation to partake in the delights they afforded was inferior but to *the* invitation to dine with the Common Council on a 4th of July. Since then, Club after Club sprung into existence, until they became so numerous that fears were entertained by the more cautious that immoralities might be engendered, unless guarded by some wholesome regulations, in which they might all acquiesce. This led to the New York Associated Boat Clubs, and we fell particularly gratified in saying that in our opinion, there is nowhere to be found an association of young gentlemen of a higher grade of moral feeling, of purer manners, or more courtesy of demeanor.

We are involuntarily led to make these remarks on taking up our pen to notice quite the most *racy* and spirited affair of the week.—We need hardly say we refer to the late REGATTA, which came off in that beautiful expansion of our river opposite Newburgh.

For many a long day that old and celebrated city has not seen her streets and her wharves crowded with such an influx of strangers from town and country. The West Pointers and the Po'keepsians were there *en masse*. All the beauty and chivalry of Orange and old Dutchess were forthcoming, which altogether presented a scene that may well nigh have rivalled a Venetian Regatta "on the blue lagoon of the Adriatic."

The reports differ as to the time, but we have much confidence in our own. We should be unable to prepare a better report of the affair than the one furnished for the Express. We therefore adopt as much of it as we can find room for. We have taken the liberty of correcting the time therein given, but nothing further.

Tuesday morning.—Rather an ominous looking day. Heavy clouds veil the summit of the Beacons, the entrance to the Highlands. A shower or two during the morning give us hopes the evening may be more auspicious.

The boats are launched again into their native element. The clouds unveil the glorious Beacons and the sun lights up a scene which may seldom be equalled, never surpassed. To go into the descriptive would be rather out of my line, yet I hope some of your correspondents may do it justice.

The arrival of the *Erie* with two hundred, and the Superior with I presume three hundred passengers from the city—the Emerald from Poughkeepsie with a full complement, looked like rather a serious invasion upon our landlord of the United States—already full to overflowing. But after two or three hours all were perfectly satisfied that any house backed by two such counties as Orange and Dutchess would never surrender at discretion.

The hour now approached for the great trial. Black Hawk with her streaming signals was moored in the river just above the U.S. Hotel, and the boats one by one assumed their respective positions, which had been decided by ballot. The following is the order of performances:—

Names, &c. of Boats entered.

1. GAZELLE, scarlet, red and white dress, red and white cap—New York.
2. HIGHLAND WAVE, black, white dress, blue and white cap—Newburgh.
3. GULL, blue, blue and white dress, straw hat—New York.
4. WAVE, black, blue and white dress, blue and white cap—New York.
5. HALCYON, green, green and white dress, green and white cap—New York.
6. PEARL, white, blue and white checked dress, straw hat—New York.
7. MINERVA, East India Particular, red and white dress, red and white cap—New York.
8. CORSAIR, black, green and white dress, red cap—Newburgh.

Distance, to be rowed five miles; to start from the Brewery Dock at four o'clock, P.M.

The Prizes will be awarded to the three successful boats on the Highlander's wharf.

There are several free boats, one from the city, the Atalanta—one from Poughkeepsie, the Washington, and the white lady of Newburgh. It was a beautiful start, the Washington taking the lead, followed by the Gull, &c. at a killing pace. Every roof, every window, every boat, was crowded with spectators, besides acres of people in every direction. From the roof of the Hotel the view was superb, and though it commenced raining at the start no one appeared to regard it during the half hour devoted to the race. The distance to the turn, three sloops in a diamond position, was two and a half miles, and accomplished in the following time:—

1.	Wave, (New York)	32:38
2.	Gull, do.	33:58
3.	Corsair, (Newburgh)	35:00
4.	Highlander Wave, do	36:00
5.	Halcyon, (New York)	
6.	Minerva, do.	
7.	Pearl, do.	
8.	Gazelle, do.	

The Wave was the decided favorite at starting, two to one, and often at larger odds. But the Gull was a worthy competitor, and may well be confident of success in any future trial. The Corsair and Highland Wave, belonging to the Newburgh Association, would rank with the first in any club. With somewhat lighter crews, equally skilful and effective, they could not well be surpassed.

It should be observed that the Poughkeepsie kept the lead during the race. The perfect ease with which the Wave approached her whenever they let out was apparent to all; but by the laws of the association no boat is allowed to race with any one not in the lists. The Wave of course reserved herself for any emergency, not knowing what the Gull and Corsair might do upon the last pinch. The good people of Poughkeepsie were highly delighted, and it is gratifying to *us* to say their boat was exceedingly well handled, and if they would like a single handed contest with the Wave, or any other boat, they can doubtless be gratified.

I cannot close without tendering to the good people of Newburgh, the hearty thanks of the writer for the gratification he received, and sure he is no New Yorker was there who will not say amen! To Captain Wardrop and the owners of the Highlander for their kind offer to convey the boats free of any expense—for the admirable preparations made by the Newburgh Association for their visitors—the kindness and hospitality of the people generally to one and all, are due, as they will surely receive, universal approbation.

A delightful place is Newburgh; and as the warm season is daily expected, a more pleasant retreat cannot be mentioned. So easy of access, scenery unsurpassed, beautiful drives, fine fishing, to say nothing of the bread and butter of old Orange! The United States and Orange Hotels answer admirably for the lower part of the village, as they call it—something of the same kind in the upper would be very desirable. Will not some of our friends there bear it in mind?

T.

After the above report was in type, a friend to whom we have been repeatedly obliged for such acts of kindness, brought us a different report. This friend is himself an accurate timer, and we have frequently relied upon him. We regret that in this case he does not confirm the time given above. We annex merely the time given by our friend, but are as much indebted as though we had used his whole report.

1.	Wave	31:11
2.	Gull	33:15
3.	Corsair	34:00
4.	Highland Wave	34:36
5.	Halcyon	35:50
6.	Minerva	36:51
7.	Pearl	37:20
8.	Gazelle	38:40

The Poughkeepsie boat, *Gen. Washington,* black, with red streak all around, and rowed by Jos. Pardy, John Reed, James H. Elton, Robert T. Garrison, Albert March, and William Flint, with John Joyce for Coxswain, accomplished the distance in 30:58, as is said. They must incontinently challenge the Wave, and so end all disputes.

With the aid of a strong tide, the Wave made the distance from the stake in eleven minutes! Not very slow!

CANADIAN ROWING AND YACHTING

During the late 1830s yachting joined rowing as a popular sport and sometimes both types of contests, along with other sports, were held at the same event. The following account of a Canadian regatta originally appeared in the Quebec Mercury and was reprinted in the 7 October 1837 edition of The Spirit of the Times.

THE QUEBEC REGATTA

Took place on the 21st ult. The Quebec Mercury furnishes the following report. The weather was delightful and serene, but there was not sufficient wind for the sail boats to work to advantage.

The Rowing matches came off in the following order:—

Row Boats—First Class—Gentlemen Amateurs; ent. $8, prize $40.

Mr. Allen's *Waterwitch* (White and Red)	1	1
Mr. Vivian's *Hookey Walker*	2	2

A very excellent match, and the first heat won by the Waterwitch by about half a boat's length. The Hookey Walker was rowed by Officers in the Army, under the disadvantage of never having seen in the boat till the morning of the race, and then consenting, for the sake of sport, to row her with sculls which were far too short, rather than the public should be disappointed the expected race. The comparative merits of these boats are well known, and with equal crews the advantage either might gain in a mile, depending on the state of the water, would not be above a boat's length.

The second heat was also closely contested, and the match was one of the closest we have seen in Quebec.

The same boats were afterwards started for a small purse, manned by sailors of the *Champion*, and the Waterwitch had again the advantage.

Row Boats—Second Class.—Four oared Boats, not Prize or Whale Boats, rowed or steered by sailors and others; ent. $2, prize $20.

Capt. King's (R.N.) *Champion*	1	1
Mr. Colmans' *Narcissus*	2	2
Mr. Pemberton's *Mariner*	3	3

This race was easily won by the Champion's boat, but was more nearly contested by the two beaten boats, though it did not excite so much interest as the first race.

A *By-Match* took place between the Champion and a boat belonging to Mr. Usborne, which was won by the latter.

We have now to notice the Sailing Match, which commenced between the rowing matches, but not to render the account confused we have reserved it for the last, as indeed it did not terminate till dark.

First Class—Yachts.—Ent. $5; first boat to receive $35, and entrances; second boat $30; third boat, $15.

Col. Hon. C. Gore's *Red Bird* (Red Flag at the Fore)	1	1
Mr. Dyde's *Young John Bull* (Green Flag and Harp)	2	2
Mr. Hunter's *Lotus* (St. George's Ensign)	4	3
Mr. Sharples' *Crusader* (White Flag—Maltese Cross	3	4

Mr. D. Burnett's *Rattlesnake* (Red Flag at the Main)   0   5
Mr. Gilmour's *Victoria* (Small Red Pendant)   4   0

We have already said that there was but little wind; at the turn of the tide however, a light air from the northeast enabled the boats to beat down with the ebb tide; the *Red Bird* keeping close to the wind made a good stretch on the first tuck and got well ahead of the little squadron, but the *Young John Bull*, by the good management of Captain Vaughant who sailed her, got first round the boat, off Orleans, having gained nearly a mile upon the other boats which stood too close in to the north shore. The whole squadron were again together, the wind not being sufficient to enable them to mare head against the tide; but towards evening it freshened again from the northeast, sufficiently to carry the lighter boats forward on their course, and they rounded the frigate; and having sailed over the course the second time, came in in the order above shown. The larger boats had not a chance—the *Rattle Snake* did not go round the second time, and the *Victoria*, finding the air altogether too light for her, anchored at the lower boat.

It is the great drawback on Regattas that wind and tide cannot be controlled, and with the most beautiful weather, the want of wind destroyed the interest of the sailing match.

There was one part of the day's amusement in which, however, no disappointment occurred, and that was in the hospitable entertainment a very numerous company received on board Her Majesty's Ship *Champion*, from her gallant commander, Captain King, and the Officers of the ship. The handsome little craft was dressed at an early hour of the day, with the flags of different nations, signals, &c., and the boats were in constant attendance, conveying parties on board, where they met with the most courteous reception. The Bands of the 15th and 83d Regiments were on board, and entertained the company with their choicest music, and refreshments were served in abundance, with the genuine hospitality for which the Officers of the British Navy have ever been proverbial.

The sports concluded to-day with a grand Cricket Match on the Plains of Abraham, the weather, after a tempestuous night, having cleared about noon: we have not heard the result of the match.

The whole of the amusements of the three days have passed off in a manner which gave general satisfaction, and though mentioned last, the Race Ball was by no means the least gratifying part of the arrangements, and we may add, that the preparations made by the Host of the Albion, were in a style that did credit to his liberality.

FIRST ANNUAL REGATTA OF NEW YORK AMATEUR BOAT CLUB

The New York Amateur Club was one of the most important boating organizations in the United States during the 1830s and its growth corresponded to the increasing popularity of rowing and racing. The following account, taken from the November 1835 issue of the American Turf Register and Sporting Magazine, was originally published by the New York Mercantile Advertiser. It describes the first annual regatta of the Club and reveals two aspects about the sport and sports reporting. First, the regatta consisted of only one racing event, with four- and six-oar boats competing against each other in the same race. As the sport evolved, more events of different crew sizes would be added. Second, for the most part, the reporting was brief and focused more on the specifics of the race itself than on the pomp accompanying it.

THE REGATTA

The first annual fete of the "New York Amateur Club" took place yesterday afternoon. Long before the hour of starting, Castle Garden was thronged, and the battery promenade, from Marketfield street to Whitehall, was literally alive with spectators, all apparently impatient to witness the sport. The bay was white with sails, and row boats innumerable plied about, seeking for an eligible situation and several steamers, whose decks were filled with passengers, gave additional animation to the scene.

The boats entered for the contest, presented the most beautiful appearance, and were each of them manned by members of their respective clubs, whose neat and appropriate uniforms excited universal admiration.—They took their places, before starting, in the following order, the Wave being inside or next to the Garden.

1st. The Wave—six oars, thirty-four feet long, black with gold band, black oars; dress—broad blue and white striped Guernsey shirts and caps.

2d. The Dolphin—six oars, thirty-seven feet long, bright blue with gold band—narrow blue and white striped gingham shirts and caps.

3d. The Atlantic—six oars, thirty-one feet long, black with gold band—scarlet and white striped Guernsey shirts and caps.

4th. The Wakona—four oars, twenty-eight feet long, black with gold band—white shirts, blue trowsers, and scarlet caps.

5th. The Jersey—four oars, twenty-six feet long, black with gold band—blue checked shirts, and blue handkerchiefs round their necks.

6th. The Neptune—six oars, thirty-five feet long, green with gold band—oar blades green—narrow blue and white striped shirts, white hats.

7th. The Eagle—six oars, thirty-three feet long, white with narrow blue band—blue and white striped silk Guernsey shirts, and blue and white caps.

At the signal for starting, the Wave shot rapidly ahead, being evidently rowed with more firmness and regularity than either of her competitors, two of which the Eagle and Dolphin, came in contact with each other after the first stroke of their oars, in consequence of which accident, all the others led them several yards; it was soon evident, however, that these boats were managed with much skill and dexterity, and the contest between them in rounding Bedlow's island, was, to those who witnessed it, not the least interesting part of the race—they passed each other more than once, and were side and side for two or three minutes, when an accident occurred to the Dolphin, which gave to her competitor the advantage: the lower gudgeon of her rudder gave way, which was greatly detrimental to her speed. During this time the Wave had gained more than two hundred yards on the Eagle, and in coming up, this space was increased to nearly a quarter of a mile—the Wave returning to the judges' stand about one and a half minutes before the Eagle—distance rowed, 5 1/2 miles. The boats arrived at the judges' stand as follows:—

1. Wave—time, (according to report of judges) 31 minutes.
2. Eagle,—time not noted.
3. Dolphin,   do.
4. Neptune,   do.
5. Wakona,   do.   (4 oars.)
6. Atlantic,   do.
7. Jersey,   do.   (4 oars.)

On coming in, the oarsmen of the Wave were apparently as fresh and vigorous as at the start, showing no symptoms of fatigue whatever. They were all, we believe, inexperienced in *racing*, as the oarsmen on a former occasion did not row on this, but they nevertheless exhibited the nerve and skill of veterans.

The Eagle is an excellent boat, and barring accidents, would have given to the victorious one a tight race.

The Atlantic and Jersey were left some distance behind, each having met with an accident; we understand that one lost a thole pin, and the other an oar.

The weather was as clear and as fine as could have been desired; and no accident occurred to mar the sports of the day.

The distance performed was 5 1/2 miles.

Four splendid silver pitchers were presented to the members of the successful clubs by the judges, the senior of whom, John Lang Esq. prefaced his remarks with the following address.

My young friends.—By your kindness and politeness I have been appointed one of the judges of this afternoon's exhibition, the first of the kind ever presented to an American public, for which I beg leave to thank you. To you, gentlemen, belongs the credit of giving origin to such manly exercise; which tends to promote health, strength, and longevity. If it be said that you are imitating the lords and gentlemen of England in their Regattas, the most fastidious moralist cannot complain, while you devote no hours for rational exercise but those on which your various occupations have no claim. Your early rising and a tug at the oar, give a zest to your daily business, and prepare you for the aquatics of the evening, accompanied by your mothers, sisters, and sweethearts, the witnessing of which has often almost induced me to wish that I were young again. Proud as I feel on this occasion, I have yet to perform the most gratifying part of my duty; and now gentlemen of the *Wave*, I feel honored in presenting you a PITCHER composed of one of the most precious metals, as a small tribute of reward for amateur superiority. In doing this, it delights me, and it must be equally gratifying to those around you, to find among your young aquatic companions, that not one evinces an expression of countenance that is not in unison with your own.

You have, gentlemen, this day set a noble example to the young men of this great and growing city—and while you continue to act within the rules of strict propriety, your Regattas will not only not be opposed but patronized by the best members of the community.

May you live long, be prosperous and happy.

The several members of the Clubs replied in an appropriate manner, after which, with a large number of guests, they partook of a repast, appropriate and splendid.

THE SECOND ANNUAL REGATTA

The account of the second annual regatta of the New York Amateur Boat Club provides a striking contrast with the previous document on the first annual event. The following article, taken from the 24 September 1836 issue of The Spirit of the Times, clearly shows the development of the sport of rowing. By this time the race between four-oared boats was held separately from that of the six-oared ones and coverage of the event improved substantially, presenting more details of the races and better descriptions of the various aspects of the event.

REGATTA

The second Annual Regatta of *New York Amateur Boat Club* Association, took place on Monday last. It was the most brilliant aquatic sport we have ever witnessed—not only from the masterly display of rowing and fine show of boats, but also from the concourse of spectators. The whole extent of the Battery was lined with eager visitants, and the immense upper terrace of Castle Garden was densely crowded. In the expectant throng, the ladies mingled with all the panoply of smiles and beauty, and even outnumbering the men. Their gay dresses formed the best relief to the usual monotonous and heavy aspect of a crowd of men; and the busy hum of "their most sweet voices," as they were laying their wagers on their brother's boats and discussing the rival models, enlivened the scene.

The weather on Monday was excessively hot and appressive, which made the sea breeze which you could catch at the Garden, doubly grateful!

The Stake Boat was anchored directly off the front of the Battery (instead of being concealed as usual behind the Garden), and a line extended from [...] Garden wharf, formed the base from which the boats were to start. The Judges, Commodore RIDGLEY and Alderman CLARK, took their stand in the Stake Boat.

At a quarter past three the signal gun was fired, and the four-oared boats took position in the line in the following uniform order, &c.

No.	Names	Color of Boat.	Uniform.
1.	GLEAM,	Red, White Streak.	Red and White Guernseys.
2.	ATLANTIC,	Black, Gold "	" " "
3.	MINERVA.	" " "	Blue and Striped Shirts.

At the third tap of a drum the boats were off, but two of them running foul, they were called back for a new start, when they got off well together, rowing the distance down to Bedlow's Island without our being able to perceive that either boat had acquired an advantage; but upon rounding the Island and pulling home, one of the boats, the Gleam, fell away a little, and the contest was confined to the Atlantic and Minerva. The former gradually gained upon the Goddess, and beat her some thirty seconds in coming out. The time made by these boats, was nearly as follows:—

Atlantic	38:00
Minerva	38:30
Gleam	40:00

The distance rowed, we regret that we cannot give with perfect accuracy.—Some calculate it at five miles and an eighth, and this from a measurement upon the map, would seem nearly right, but we have heard it called a full quarter of a mile less, as four miles and 7-8ths.

We should do injustice to the Gleam, were we to omit stating, that her crew are all young, and apparently all under 15 years of age; and their endurance and strength, which enabled them to make the time they did, were highly thought of on all hands.

We should also state that the race boats were very much beset by all manner of water craft during the row. The bay seemed covered with sloops, schooners, steamers, and mud-scows, and "*water-million*" skiffs, jolly boats, barges, and sail boats, and not all told yet. They crowded in close upon the race boats, and in both the four and six oared match, a desire was apparent on the part of two or three boats, excluded from the Association, to run foul and impede the contending boats. The whole crowd of spectators was indignant at so contemptible tricks.

Now came off the long wished for trial among the larger six oared boats. Speculation was active, and although the odds in favor of the Wave were not readily accepted at the start, yet much was done about the second prize, for which the Ariel and Halcyon were the favorites. Many, indeed, were willing to take the long odds on the Wave, trusting to some accident, for the crew of that boat are famous for breaking oars and pulling away the thole pins. The *Eagle*, which came in second last year, had many friends to back her, and all the Dutch from the Village "went their death" on the Halcyon.

They started from the line in the following positions, the *Dolphin* being withdrawn on account of the absence of some of her crew whose places it was impossible to supply.

No.	Name.	Color of Boat.	Uniform.
1.	HALCYON,	Green, Gold Streak,	Green and Striped Guernseys.
2.	EAGLE,	White, Red "	Black and Red "
3.	WAVE,	Black, Gold "	Blue and White "
4.	WAKONA,	Black, White "	Blue Striped Shirts.
5.	ARIEL.	" " "	White Shirts.

A false start was made in this case from the Wakona and Ariel running foul. A schooner was anchored so close in upon the line, that the Ariel had to swerve from her course somewhat to keep clear, and in so doing the boats clashed together; but before the signal made to return could be understood by the Eagle and Halcyon, they had rowed some hundred yards. No one regretted this false start inasmuch as in a race of the kind, the only opportunity you have for seeing them well together, and under a press of speed, is just at the start. They got off better the second time—the Wave soon leading, thus giving earnest to those who knew, as we did, the endurance of her crew, that the prize would be hers.—The tide was setting strongly athwart the course to be pursued, and the different boats shaped their courses somewhat differently. The Wave held on in a direct line while the Halcyon and Eagle made a wide detour to the South to round some vessel lying at anchor; the Wakona pursued nearly the course of the Wave, while the Ariel was allowed to feel the force of the tide and sweep to the North. The speed was great and the sight most beautiful, as they moved so gracefully down the bay. An intervening vessel prevented us from seeing which boat first rounded the

Island. When we could distinguish them on their return, the Wave was still leading, but the Ariel close at hand. As they came home they had the sun full in their faces for two miles, and we have been assured by many of either crew, that it was excessively annoying, and indeed almost overpowering.

The Wave first reached the goal, not having been headed once. The Ariel next, and won the prize allotted to the second boat. The time made, a friend noted as follows:—

Wave	30:00
Ariel	30:30
Eagle	32:45
Wakona	33:30
Halcyon	35:00

Neither crew manifested great fatigue, and in passing the length of the Battery we thought the Wave showed as much strength and spirit as before the race.

The three several prizes were presented to the coxswains of the respective boats in the Garden by Commodore RIDGLEY, with various addresses which we have not room to give; and we must plead the same excuse for not doing justice to the Collation given in the Saloon of the Garden by the Association. (The arrival of two Liverpool packets in the same week, always crowds our columns). The members of the Association and their guests kept up their spirits and their wit with "wine and wassail" till a late hour. The gallant Commodore shone conspicuously on the occasion, keeping all in hearty roars by his felicitous sallies. If any thing can give additional popularity to our navy, it is the appointment of such officers as RIDGLEY to the choice stations in the service, when they may render both it and themselves favorites by their courtesy and spirit.

In a future article we intend saying something of the models of the boats engaged in the Regattas and their oars, and the boat-builders themselves, who were present, and eager to aid with their advice and experiences. Before another year elapses, we hope some public spirited individual will set on foot a subscription to defray the expenses, at least, of the prizes given in the Regatta. An amusement so eminently appropriate in a commercial city—so invigorating and so innocent—should be encouraged. And even the ladies, whose regards ever encourage the diversion, and whose smiles crown all its triumphs, would give additional interest to these friendly contests, by presenting to the winning boats ensigns wrought by their own fair hands, and then how the breast of each rower would pant to win a prize so sanctified!

REGATTA ANNOUNCEMENT

By the occasion of the third annual regatta of the New York Amateur Boat Club in 1837, the popularity of the sport had grown to the point where a detailed report of the event after its occurrence would fail to satisfy boat racing enthusiasts and participants. In the following article, a member of the Club announces the event and introduces the various judges and participants a week before the regatta took place. The announcement is reprinted from The Spirit of the Times, 23 September 1837.

ANNUAL REGATTA OF 1837
Of the New York AMATEUR BOAT CLUB ASSOCIATION, at Castle Garden.

[COMMUNICATED BY A MEMBER.]

This celebrated annual race of the Association, comes off on Monday, next the 25th inst., and we have collected a few scraps which we string together for the amusement of our aquatic readers.

Imprimis:—This first race will be for *keel boats and skiffs*, to be rowed by watermen.—The prize will be one of SEAMAN'S skiffs. This will be a most interesting race, as each boat contending for the prize will be rowed by two pair of sculls, and no doubt some of our crack Whitehallers will try their best to carry off the palm. The brothers ROBERTS will also contend, and are the favorites at present; should however the SEAMANS man *their* boat, (The Challenge), *we* know who would carry off the skiff—but mum. The race comes off at half past 3, P.M. The distance—one mile down the bay and return.

The *Second Race* takes place at half past 4, P.M. The following boats of the Association will run:—*Pearl*, 37 ft.; *Conover*, 38 ft.; *Minerva*, 36 ft.; *Gazelle*, 35 ft.; *Naiad*, 32 ft.; *Cleopatra*, 33 ft.; and the *Scylla*, 38 ft., from Newburgh. Report speaks highly of the Newburgh boat, and, if she wins the prize, she will have to be rowed rather fastish; she has one foot more in length, than any of the other boats, and six feet longer than the shortest. This is a decided advantage—very much in her favor. The prizes in this race will be, for the first boat, *a model boat*, built by CROLIUS, a superior piece of workmanship, and the second boat will be entitled to a handsome *Silver rudder yoke and ropes*. These boats will all be manned with six oars, and the distance, two and a half miles down the bay and return.

Most of these boats have been built this season. The *Pearl* is a most beautiful boat, fitted up very tastefully, and possessed of every comfort; she is a good model, and we expect her crew to do their duty. The *Conover*, we know little of; they keep their boat up town, and we have not had an opportunity of seeing her in the water; report, however, speaks well of her. The *Minerva* is another fine boat, and her crew are very expert with the oar; they did very well at the Newburgh Regatta last June, far exceeding the most sanguine expectations. The *Gazelle* is also new this season—a good model; she will run pretty well.—The *Naiad* cannot be expected to do much; her crew was only formed this season, and their boat is not quite so light as she might be, but perhaps they will astonish some people. The *Cleopatra* is another new boat, but of her crew we cannot say anything, never having seen her afloat. The *Scylla*, of Newburgh, is spoken well of, and it is expected by persons residing up the river that she will win the prize; she may, but if she does, she must kept moving.

The *Third*, and grand race, will come off at a quarter past 5, P.M. The prizes for the first and second boats are the same as the other race. The following boats will contend:—*Wave*, 36 ft.; *Gull*, 37 ft.; *Ariel*, 36 ft.; *Halcyon*, 36 ft., and the *Corsair*, from

Newburgh, 36 ft. The distance—two and a half miles down the bay and return. This arrangement we think is much better than going round Bedlow's Island, as the boats were lost to view for some time; as it is, we shall see them the whole of the race, and there will be no danger of rubbing a rock, as there will be no Island to share. From the well known good qualities of the above boats, there cannot be a doubt of this being a most splendid race.—The *Wave* stands No.1—her crew nearly the same as last year, and in better order, we should say—two of them having got married; she will stand her ground, and the boat that goes ahead of her must be continually moving. The *Gull* is a very good boat, and speedy; she will come out, no doubt. The *Ariel* won the second prize in the last Regatta, and ran the *Wave* a little closer than they liked; we think between the *Gull* and *Ariel* it will be a most excellent race from the well known qualities of both crews. The *Corsair* won the third prize at Newburgh, and if they have drilled well, may *perhaps* come in a respectable place. The *Halcyon* is a new boat, and built altogether on a new plan; she was enterered at Newburgh, but did not do much, perhaps in consequence of her crew not having practised enough—in the race at the Garden, last year, she was nowhere, *although the Dutch from the village went their death on her*; they have a new boat this year, and we hope will come out well; at all events, we wish good luck to all.

A cannon will be fired from the Garden a quarter of an hour previous to the start—they will then form a line, and leave at the blast of the bugle.

The prizes will be awarded to the successful boats in Castle Garden, by the Judges. The following gentlemen having accepted the invitation from the Association, will act.

CAPT. PERRY, *U.S. Navy.*
CAPT. ROBINSON, *of Newburgh.*
ALD. PATTERSON, *Ald. of 1st Ward.*

THIRD ANNUAL REGATTA

By 1837 the annual regatta of this celebrated boat club had become an enormously popular and well-attended event, with some 35,000 spectators flocking to the southern tip of Manhattan to watch the races and join in the festivities. The regatta itself had grown from a one- to a three-race event, with new categories of competition. The following account is from the 30 September 1837 issue of The Spirit of the Times.

NEW YORK ANNUAL REGATTA

The Third Annual Regatta of the N.Y. AMATEUR BOAT CLUB ASSOCIATION, took place on Monday last, and afforded the most brilliant aquatic display of the season. The whole extent of the Battery was lined with spectators, as was also the parapet and immense terrace of Castle Garden. An amphitheatre of seats extended from the entrance of the embankment round the outer wall of the Fort to the boat houses, which were filled by ladies and other guests of the Association. Not less than *Thirty-five Thousand* spectators graced this annual *fete*. In the expectant throng the ladies mingled in all the panoply of smiles and beauty, and even outnumbering the men. Their gay dresses formed the best relief to the usual monotonous and heavy aspect of a crowd of those "made of sterner stuff," and the busy hum of "their most sweet voices" as they discussed the rival models and laid their wagers on the boats of their sweethearts and brothers, imparted interest to the gay and enlivening scene. The whole extent of the bay appeared alive with every imaginable water craft. Nearly 200 row boats hovered about the Battery, while innumerable sail boats, of all kinds, and steamers, thronged with a dense mass of spectators, were careering about the harbor. The noble bay teeming with life and animation—the hundred beautiful vessels with gay streamers flying—bands of music playing in every direction, with thousands upon thousands of joyous spectators actuated by the same feeling of interest, exhibited a scene that is seldom seen, and cannot be adequately described.

The Judges, Capt. M.C. PERRY, U.S. Navy—M.C. PATTERSON, Esq., Alderman of the First Ward, and Capt. HENRY ROBINSON, of Newburgh, with a band of music, were aboard of a Pilot boat moored opposite Castle Garden, from which the start took place at half-past 3 o'clock, P.M. The stake boats covered with flags of all nations, were moored at their respective distances, in a line down the bay. Throughout the Regatta the course was left clear, the officers of the different vessels in the harbor having, in the most courteous manner, complied with the request of the Association to that effect.

FIRST RACE, (for a *Skiff*, 22 feet long, built by Seaman, of Jersey City), free for Skiffs and Keel Boats not belonging to the Association. Two pair of sculls. Distance, One mile down the bay and return.

The *Ripple*, of Communipaw, N.J.	1
The *Hornet*, of Whitehall, New York City	2
The *Two Brothers*, of Brooklyn, Long Island	3
The *Yankee Doodle*, of Whitehall, New York City	4

Time of the Ripple, 19:11.

Five started for the first prize, but the four above were the only ones placed, the other being distanced. The winning boat, the "Ripple," was rowed by Abraham Simmons and Cornelius Britton. The "Two Brothers" was the favorite 2 to 1 at starting, but shipping a heavy sea soon after, was easily beaten. One of the brothers Roberts only, pulled an oar. It is proper to remark that before she met with the accident referred to, the "Two Brothers" decidedly led the field.

SECOND RACE, open to Club Boats of the Association that never won a prize in any former Regatta, and their Guests. Prize, *a Boat*, 22 feet long, built by Crolius, and to the 2d boat in the race *a Silver Rudder Yoke*, with cords and tassels. Six oars. Distance, Two miles and a half down the bay, round three stake boats, and return.

Entries.	Length.	Station.
Gazelle	35	1
Naiad	31	2
Cleopatra	33	3
Scylla, of Newburgh	38	4

Minerva	35	5
Conover	38	6
Pearl	36	7

Color of Signal.	*Description of Boat.*
Black and White	Red—gilt stripe.
Blue and White	Black—gilt stripe.
Red and Blue	Black—star on bow.
Yellow and Black	Blue—gilt stripe.
Black and Blue	Light Red—gilt stripe.
White and Red	Black—white stripe.
Red and Black	White.

The discharge of a cannon brought the boats into line, and upon a signal from the Judges, they got off together. The Pearl soon took the lead, the Conover second, and the Gazelle last. A "long pull, a strong pull, and a pull altogether," soon brought her up alongside of the Scylla, of Newburgh, who maintained with her a spirited contest of nearly two miles. The Gazelle reached the stake boat first, the Scylla 2d, and the Minerva 3d, the others being beaten off a long way. In coming home the Conover overhauled the Minerva, and was placed 3d at the finish, the Scylla 2d. The Gazelle increased the distance from her competitors at every stroke after passing the stake boat, and came home about 250 yards a-head. The placing and *"official time"* of each boat is annexed:—

The *Gazelle*	1	Time	33:41
The *Scylla*, of Newburgh	2	"	34:00
The *Conover*	3	"	34:20
The *Minerva*	4	"	34:35
The *Cleopatra*	5	"	36:00
The *Pearl*	dis	"	——
The *Naiad*	dr.	"	——

The Naiad was to have taken part in the Regatta, but was prevented by the absence of two of her crew, which arose from a scandalous lack of courtesy on the part of their employer, who exhibited a most contemptible spirit upon the occasion. The Cleopatra and Pearl, as will be seen, were distanced; the crew of the latter rowed for the first time, a new boat, just completed for them by Montaignier, and so strong was the impression that they would cut out the work, that the Pearl, before the race, was the favorite against the field. At starting she took the lead, but soon after shipping a heavy sea, before she reached the stake boat her crew were compelled to cease rowing, and bail her out.

The *Crew* of the *Gazelle* was composed of Alfred Boyd, coxswain, W. Hinchman, F. Dunderdale, J. Stanley Milford, J. Burke, Henry Gammage, and B. Townsend—the youngest crew in the Association. Their boat was built by Crolius, and was the only one of his manufacture in the race. The *"track was heavy"*—that is, very rough, and each boat shipped considerable water. Better time has been made repeatedly by each, in their trials, when the water was smooth, and it should be stated that throughout the Regatta the Wave alone made her usual time.

The *Crew* of the *Scylla*, of Newburgh, left a strong impression of their skill upon the minds of all. Their *names* are unknown to us, but they will be endorsed in this market, and pass current among the Amateur Boat Clubs of this city as clever fellows of the right sort. We give them joy of their prize; it was manfully won, and in its enjoyment they have the best wishes of thousands of "the Yorkers."

THIRD RACE, for Club Boats of the Association and their Guests.

Prize, *a Boat*, 22 feet long, built by Crolius, and *a Silver Rudder Yoke*, with cords and tassels, to the 2d best in the race. Six oars. Distance, Five miles as before.

Entries.	Length.	Station.
Wave	36	1
Corsair, of Newburgh	36	2
Gull	37	3
Ariel	35	4
Halcyon	36	5

Color of Signal.	Description of Boat.
White	Black-gilt stripe.
Red	Black.
Yellow	Light blue—gilt stripe.
Blue	Black—white stripe.
Black	Green—gilt stripe.

This race was the great feature of the Regatta, and immense sums were laid out about it, and 2 and 3 to 1 on the *Wave* against the field. There was a great deal of betting, too, between the Ariel and the Gull, the former being the most in demand. The Wave crew had a new boat built by Crolius, expressly for this occasion, and the practised use of their, "lusty thews and sinews," caused it to skim the water like a seabird.

Everything being right and tight, and nobody overboard, the signal was given, and the set-too commenced. The first ten strokes of the Wave cleared her of the melee, and gave her the lead, which she steadily maintained from first to last, winning by more than a quarter of a mile with ease. Between the Ariel and the Gull, however, the contest was more desperate. Side by side they rowed nearly two miles, with the most determined energy, but the Gull having the inside passed the stake boat first. The Ariel soon regained her place, and another struggle ensued, when she finally passed and came in 2d, winning the second prize, the Corsair and Haleyon being beaten off an immense way. The time and placing is subjoined:—

The *Wave*	1	Time	29:20
The *Ariel*	2	"	31:00
The *Gull*	3	"	31:15
The *Corsair*, of Newburgh	4	"	31:50
The *Halcyon*	5	"	32:17

The *Crew* of the *Wave* have so long maintained her supremacy in our waters, that they would be favorites in a race were they afloat in a clam boat; they change or rather have changed their boat every year, each time improving upon the last. In their present fragile but beautiful craft, they would be [...] for untold thousands against the world.

By the Constitution of the Association, of which one of the Wave crew was founder, and long its respected President, no boat belonging to it can contend for money, or against any boat not governed by its by-laws, otherwise we should see "the conceit taken out" of some of our bantering friends about the country. The crew of "the all conquering Wave" is composed of Alexander Knight, coxswain, William Matthews, Gustavus A. Rollins, John T. Rollins, George B. Rollins, (ex. Pres. Asso.), Richard Richards, and Abraham Knight.

The *Ariel* crew, which carried off the second prize, are rapidly improving and can "set a mighty hard lesson" to "our neighbors over the way," or almost any where else, from Hudson's Bay to the Gulf of Mexico. It is made up of the following gentlemen:— J.C. Baldwin, coxswain, Charles Moran, J. Holmes, M.L. Baker, J.S. Fay, John Faure, and W.E. Stoutenburgh.

We need hardly remark that upon coming in, the winning boats were greeted with the most deafening cheers, while the different bands played appropriate airs. The day was delightful, though the breeze was fresh enough to create a heavy ground swell. Notwithstanding the immense number of people afloat, and the fact that they were "*continually*" falling overboard, nothing occurred to mar the festivities of the day, that will long be remembered by all present for the unbounded and grateful enjoyment of which it was the occasion.

Immediately subsequent to the races a most interesting scene was presented in the vast court of Castle Garden, namely, the presentation of the different prizes, which were respectively delivered to the successful competitors, by Captain PERRY, of the U.S. Navy, accompanied with pertinent and appropriate speeches, which were happily responded to by the coxswains of each winning boat.

The *Regatta* was not yet over. In the spacious saloon of the Garden, Mr. MARSH had a very elegant and tasteful collation spread out for the entertainment of the Association and their guests, to which a great number sat down. We were precluded by previous engagements from participating in the good feeling and general hilarity which prevailed, but understand that the song and the toast went gaily round—that His Honor the Mayor addressed the company in a speech, to which those made during the present session of Congress are "a mere circumstance"—that a deputation of the Schuylkill Amateur B.C. Association were present, and other distinguished guests, including the better half of the Honorable the Common Council of Gotham, with a sprinkling of the editorial fraternity and the grave and reverend Fathers of the City, to say nothing of the Officers of the Army and Navy—that a thousand and one good things were said and sung—that the collation was superb, and that the Association generally covered themselves with immortal honor by *rowing* up Salt Creek every early riser from the table. The assembly broke up at a late hour, alike pleased with one another, and perfectly convinced that if the Amateur Boat Club Association of New York is not invincible on the water, that when wit, wine, hospitality and genuine good feeling, is the play, they are regular out and outers!

QUEBEC RACES

Regattas increasingly became a popular form of boat racing during the 1830s by pitting a number of boats against each other in a series of competitions. These regattas assumed a social significance that far outstripped their competitive importance. This account, reprinted from the 22 September 1838 edition of The Spirit of the Times, provides a good example of the social nature of many boating events.

THE QUEBEC RACES, REGATTA, AND THEATRE

FRIEND PORTER,—Taking for granted that our good old Quebec "Mercury" has before this enlightened you on the subject on our Races, Regattas, &c. after the usual approved and newspaper official fashion, there is little left me to perpetrate for your columns beyond a few touches of the "ornamental," to frame up the affair as prettily as possible. At which end shall I begin, or shall I plunge at once into the thick of the fight? I'll e'en lay about me after my own most favored fashion; and you must take the thing in the medley manner I give it to you.

Well, the weather was delightful as delightful could be, for the "three days." Had the "clerk" been bribed or blarneyed, clearer skies, blander breezes, or better conditioned roads, or "bit of turf" could not have been had. And then, on each of the mornings in question as noon drew near, the driving and striving, and tearing and swearing, helter skelter, go it, you cripples, cram, ham and d—n it, that took place at the St. Louis Gate, our nearest city outlet to the plains of Abraham. "Oh then! bee me sowl! but it would do the heart of your body good, to see Misthress Casey, sure, and the seven dear childer, stowed away in a crazy caleche, and the Masther himself, is it, hitched on behind—the "blessed kit of them" all the way from "Duffer's coort"—the most fashionable nook of that most celebrated and elegant part of the lower city, entitled Champlain Street—and bound to the `coorse.'" As a digression, how is it that you never see Irish women of the lower or middling orders, to plays, fairs, races, dog-fights, or bull-baits, without "their young at the breast"—this is a fact, and possibly, it may be deemed a strange and melancholy one, when newspaper reports from time to time enlighten us as to the number of infants run every, squeezed to death, and the like.

You may (I should say, your readers may) refer to my last year's report for many items and particulars; for as therein described, so again on this occasion, the same "turn out" of jumping shopmen, counting-house dandies, and so forth in their kiddy "tiles" and "flannen" buckskins, took place. As a matter of course, not a few of them were split on the course, but what of that, for what else could you expect from the "Linkum feedles?"

LORD DURHAM did not make his appearance on the course the first day, but her Ladyship and family were there. On the second day, he came to see his cup run for. His equipage and personal appearance exceedingly plain. The first an unostatious barouche and four, with a couple of outsiders, and the second in plain or coloured clothes. A splendid tent was pitched for his accommodation in the centre of the field, and a new and pretty stand also opposite the Grand Stand was erected for his use. To me he did not seem to interest himself much in the running, even for his own cup, and appeared to take more pleasure and be more intently employed in securing to his little daughter a good view of the sport. My eyes! how the eyes of the women-folk glistened, when they saw the proud viceroy, with his numerous feather deck'd and gold covered aide-de-camps and other similar "dons" of courtly appanage around him, and all the pomp and circumstance of that grandeur which hedges in such "little kings."—I say, how the women (I mean the mothers among them) looked upon and blessed his dear good soul! when they saw him repeatedly kiss his pretty child, a little fairy of some seven years growth of beauty, and standing on the seat of the Pavilion, hold her up in his arms to see the race; peering into her lovely face, animated as it was with all the brightness of childish delight; with a father's joyous fondness, and seemingly unmindful of aught else of purpose or impulse at the moment. Friend P., do you deal in "little responsibilities," God bless 'em. If you do, you will understand me, when I assure you I was more pleased at being a witness of this trait of his lordship's kindly heart—for I am also a father—than with all the glare and tinsel of pompous display around, or the rascality and row, trickery of show, and "leather and prunella" sort of enjoyment, with which some people affect to invest such scenes as are usually identified with a race course.

The *Regatta* came off as all such matter do. Some good rowing, better sailing, plenty of blunt on the move, and plenty of young "gennelmen" as Sam Veller calls 'em, left to bewail blistered hands and sore backs, at their leisure.

ABBOT is here with a company, doing pretty fairly; although, had he been here a couple of months sooner, he would have done a snug business, as we had then a large squadron in harbor, and there was much more bustle, afloat and ashore, than is going on at present. However, Miss TREE is filling the house nightly pretty well for him.

This lady played the other night, when the Hunchback was "commanded." The family and suite of the Viceroy were there. It was stylish, I tell you.—What with a Captain's guard of the "Guards" lining the lobbies; and a host of blue-coated police in rank and file about the doors; and managers in full dress dancing backwards and forwards with branch lights, and all this sort of thing, it was quite "Lunnun loike" on a Royal p'ay night.

Yours in haste, MORGAN RATTLER.

Quebec, 8th September, 1838.

REGIONAL RACING

By the late 1830s boat racing had become a popular spectator sport and had moved beyond the confines of major urban areas such as New York and Boston. The races themselves, as the following account demonstrates, became major social events, attracting men, women, and children from all classes and walks of life, although the participants were for the most part drawn from the upper and, to a lesser extent, the middle classes. This account is reprinted from The Spirit of the Times, 13 July 1839.

THE NEWBURGH REGATTA

WM. T. PORTER, Esq.—*Dear Sir*—Wednesday, the 10th of July, being the day appointed for the Regatta at this place, an immense crowd of persons embarked in the morning boats, all eager to witness the exciting spectacle about to be presented for their gratification. On board the *Highlander* might be observed the strangest and most diversified countenances; here the sturdy oarsman intently and anxiously eyeing the several boats destined to take part in the coming contest, while the mingled expression of hope and uncertainty, confidence and doubt, which alternately marked their countenances, afforded a fine study for the physiognomist. Here, dangling his watch-chain, with an air of unconcern, stands a "knowing one," whose bets have been made with judgment, as he thinks, and who feels a perfect confidence in the result. A short distance off, lunges a *green-horn*, the "wooden spoon" of his class, who has been humbugged by his wide-awake friend to "post his pewter" on a boat, whose capabilities were utterly unknown to him, and whose very name was new to him at the time.

The *Highlander* reached Newburgh at 12 o'clock, and the day was as favorable for the sport as could possible have been desired, though the intense heat of a July sun might have been somewhat tempered without detracting from the comfort of the spectators. A gentle ripple was upon the water—so gentle as scarcely to ruffle the smooth and sparkling surface of the Bay, and a light breeze from the westward refreshed us after our sultry trip through the Highlands.

A salute of some 14 guns from the shore greeted the Highlander as she pass along, which was loudly responded to by the hundreds of passengers that thronged her deck.

When the rival boats started in the race, the sight was one of extreme beauty. The innumerable windows of the Warehouses and Factories were crowded with ladies— every piazza and house-top was stirring with "animated beauty"—the docks and steamboats, and the rigging of the sloops and schooners, were all crowded with an indescribable mass of men, women, and children of all ranks and ages. The splendid bands of music, including the celebrated one from West Point, contributed much to the enjoyment of the scene. And now, my dear sir, that I have endeavored to describe to you the scene at starting, let me introduce you to the "bonny boats," and their adieu.

The first race came off at about half past 2 o'clock—two pairs of sculls—for which the following boats were entered: *Ripple, Serf,* and *Jessie,* of New York, and the *Isaac Martling,* of Haverstraw. The distance to be rowed was nearly six miles. In this race the *Isaac M.* came in far ahead of the *Ripple,* but owing to some infringement of the rules, the silver prize cup, valued at $75, was awarded to the latter—time 53 minutes.

The second race was for four oared boats—prize, a silver vase valued at $150— distance, six miles. The following were the entries—The *Victoria, Duane,* and *Ben Hatfield,* of New York, and *Alwilda,* of Poughkeepsie. After a very interesting contest the Duane came in ahead, winning the race easily, the Ben Hatfield 2d, and Alwilda 3d—but where was the *Victoria*? Have patience, and I'll tell you how the Duane came to win so easily. The *Victoria,* after keeping company with the others as far as the stake boat, preserving a few "links" for the last half of the distance, and being on her return, unfortunately received an ugly scratch along her "back bone" from a sand bar, on which she had to remain, much against her will, for at least half an hour, her crew having to push her off. Had it not been for this untoward accident, it would have been *at least* a tie between her and the Duane—Time, 43m. 35s.

And now the "crowning glory" of the day was to be witnessed—the six-oared race was to come off, a match between the best oarsmen of the land—the following named boats were seen waiting in line for the signal to start:—The *Wave*, of New York, the *Corsair*, *Scylla*, and *Galatea*, of Newburg, the *Lafitte*, of Coldspring, and the *Washington*, of Po'keepsie. They were all well off at the signal, the Scylla taking the lead, with the Corsair close up, the Washington following, and the Wave with her long steady pull, working her way upon them slowly but surely. After a smart pull for it, she overhauled them one by one, passing the Washington about half way to the stake-boat, and taking the lead; she rounded the first two, but before she reached the third she shipped a frightful sea, which placed her crew in damp seas, and at once placed her chance of winning without the pale of possibility. The crew therefore threw up their oars, and allowed the Corsair to take the lead, which boat came in 1st, Lafitte 2d, Scylla 3d, Washington 4th, and Galatea 5th. Time, 39m. 30s.

Thus did the favorite Wave encounter an accident which proved fatal to her chance of victory, when bets were running as high as 20 to 1 on her. She was deservedly the favorite from the first, for with but an ordinary "Wave crew" to man her (Mathews and Rollins being on the sick list), she was cutting out the work for her friends in fine style, when the briny flood destroyed the fairy visions of her backers.

The Corsair, having a picked crew, was not allowed to take the 1st prize, and the Lafitte received the splendid silver vase, valued at $225, and the Scylla the 2d prize— a silver goblet, of the value of $75.

Much dissatisfaction was expressed at the management of the whole affair, and no doubt the experience derived from this day's amusement will give rise to many improved regulations in future. The stake boats were misplaced, and too little attention was paid to retaining the men in their respective boats, and they were consequently allowed to stray too far in quest of "best men" to put in their places.

The *Wave* and *Victoria* rowed from New York to Newburg, leaving New York on Monday Evening, and reaching Hastings' Landing, a distance of 22 miles, in two hours! There they took a comfortable night's rest, and resumed their trip early the next morning, breakfasting at Sing Sing, and dining at West Point. From thence they rowed in the cool of the evening to Fishkill, their place of destination, after a pleasant pull of 60 miles.

Your obed't sevr't,   S.

Chapter 5

BALL SPORTS AND GAMES

Prior to 1840, many types of games and amusements, mostly involving the use of balls, had been transplanted to the United States from England. For the most part they remained premodern, failing to move beyond unorganized, informal contests played at the local level. Some of these games, such as rounders, quoits, and football, provided cheap amusement for young boys and adolescents in a rural America with plenty of open space. Others, such as billiards, rackets, bowling, and fives readily found enthusiasts in the parlors, pubs, and streets of the more congested and growing urban areas. Regardless of their context, however, all of these games remained primarily participatory rather than spectator activities, placed heavy emphasis on individual performance and achievement, and conducted few formal, organized or regulated contests. Not surprisingly, newspapers devoted scant attention to the early development of these games and sports.

The sole exception to most of these generalizations was cricket, which by the late 1830s had begun to move beyond its premodern form. With the establishment of the St. George's Cricket Club in New York City and some early clubs in Philadelphia, the heyday of cricket as a popular sport in America had begun. Soon, local and regional interclub matches occurred, as did a number of international competitions between clubs in Canada and the United States. Though cricket was played throughout America, primarily by English immigrants, much of its development occurred in eastern cities such as New York, Philadelphia, Albany, and Boston. In Canada, cricket developed most extensively in Toronto. The more rapid organization and modernization of cricket as a sport in America was facilitated by the popularity and organization of cricket in England. Because rules and regulations had been formulated previously there, when the sport was transplanted to the United States, it won widespread recognition and acceptance. This development was supported by the British immigrants whose national identity was clearly tied to the game. As a consequence, cricket experienced little evolution once it emerged as a popular and organized sport during the middle of the nineteenth century. Ironically, despite its increasing popularity during this period, by 1870 it had suffered a precipitous decline due, in no small measure, to the rising popularity and development of baseball. By 1920 cricket had virtually disappeared from the American sports scene. "Great Cricket Match at Brooklyn," "Toronto v. New York Cricket Match," "Albany v. Schenectady Cricket Match," and the other documents on cricket in this chapter describe many of the early developments of the sport in North America, including the emergence of an international rivalry between clubs from Toronto and New York.

The period from 1820 to 1840 witnessed the early development of two games that later in the century became popular spectator sports—rounders and football. Rounders evolved into a game called town ball, an early form of baseball. As the formation of the Olympic Town Ball Club in 1831 demonstrates, some clubs were organized before 1840. Rounders was played, without any uniform rules and regulations, by two teams on a sixty-foot square field with a base at each corner of the square. Apparently no requirement or limitation existed as to the number of players on each team. The pitcher, located somewhere in the middle of the diamond, threw to the batter, who was positioned between the first and fourth bases. A ball caught on the fly or on the first bounce constituted an out, with only one out allowed per side. The reminiscence on early Canadian baseball by Dr. Adam Ford, which is included in this section, provides important details and insights into the origins and early development of the game. Similarly, football had few rules and even less organization. At this time it basically consisted of kicking an animal bladder encased in leather around an open field. Football developed a following among college students who often held competitions between upper and lower classmen, thereby fueling the flame of interclass rivalry. The reminiscences by Thomas Wentworth Higginson and Robert S. Minot and the poem, "The Battle of the Delta," portray the state of early football at Harvard College.

The only other game that developed some form of organization was quoits. Although quoits is technically not a ball sport it has been included in this section because it essentially demands the same or similar skills as most ball sports and because it most closely resembles them in movement, format, and motion. Originally a Scottish pastime, quoits became a popular game among the colonists and soon acquired an upper class following and association. The game was played by throwing a flat stone or an iron ring to a "meg" or a pin, approximately twenty yards away. Each player on a side received two quoits, with a quoit around the meg earning two points and the closest quoit to the pin earning one point. The team reaching eleven points was declared the victor. Clubs were organized in a number of cities, North and South, such as Baltimore, Philadelphia, Washington, D.C., and Richmond, with each club providing its own regulations, rules, and administration. These organizations also served as social clubs for their members, who came from the respected professions and upper classes of society. For the most part, however, matches were defined by intraclub, rather than interclub, competition, the latter being the norm for some of the other games and sports of the period. The "Washington Social Gymnasium," the "Philadelphia Quoit Club," and the "Richmond Barbacue Club" vividly narrates the activities and festivities of these organizations.

The other games and amusements of the era—rackets, billiards, fives, and bowling—remained informal recreations during the early to mid-nineteenth century, though some of them did increase in popularity. As a result, these games received little newspaper coverage, a situation which has fostered a sketchy understanding of their development. Rackets and billiards primarily attracted, as they had during the colonial period, participants from the wealthier classes and were played in private clubs, or, as was sometimes the case with billiards, in private homes. By 1850 billiards was associated with a lower-class clientele, taverns and saloons, and gamblers and hustlers.

By contrast, bowling, which was of Dutch origin, continued to attract a broad following until 1850 when the rise of billiards seriously cut into its popularity. The game of fives, similar to handball, was played throughout the United States in both urban and rural areas. Undoubtedly the continued popularity of this amusement in the nineteenth

century was due partially to its simplicity and the minimal equipment and space required for a game. Though sometimes played in a closed court, all that was necessary
to play fives was a ball and a high wall, requirements that could be satisfied almost
anywhere in the United States.

INTERCITY CRICKET CONTEST

Cricket was one of the few activities that evolved from a premodern to a modern sport
from 1820 to 1840. An early stage of this development was the formation of cricket
clubs and the initiation of contests between clubs, at first within a given locale and then
gradually moving into the surrounding area. The following two documents report on
the initial and return matches between the Albany and Schenectady clubs. They are
reprinted from the 23 September 1837 edition of The Spirit of the Times and are early
examples of the coverage and development of the sport.

CRICKET MATCH

On Friday last a friendly game was played in the neighborhood of the city, between
two elevens of Schenectady and Albany. In again taking "the bat," the Albanians were
desirous of entering the field against our Trojan neighbors, and challenged them to play.
The challenge was not accepted. Durip, to the astonishment of many, however, sent
them a challenge, which was accepted, and came off as below. The Albanians had the
affair entirely in their hands. The excellent batting of Wybourn, a name that stands
conspicuous in many of the best contested matches played in England, excited universal admiration. The "Duripians" attribute their ill-success to the absence of their best
bowlers; they will have a chance of redeeming themselves on Thursday week, when
the return match is to be played at Schenectady. The Albany players need not fear the
result. The excellent batting and fielding of Wybourn, Small, and others, as will appear
by the score, will secure to them the victory.

If the Schenectady players had followed their innings, Albany would have left them
in a minority upon their first score, with only four wickets down. Darkness put an end
to the game, and the Schenectady players with such odds against them very wisely
concluded to give up the game.

With such players as Albany possesses, she need not fear the result of a contest with
Troy.

1st Innings.	ALBANY	2d Innings.
Russell—bowled by Dean		24
Shearman—run out		5
Burtenshaw—bowled by Jenner		0

Small—run out	22
Wybourn—not out	56
Knight—bowled by Dean	21
Pellett—bowled by Clout	3
Wilcox—bowled by Clout	1
Wood—stumped by Playford	3
Blackman—bowled by Dean	4
Rose—bowled by Dean	0
Byes	8
	-
	147

2d Innings.

caught by Playford	5
caught by Grower	6
bowled by Dean	8
bowled by Dean	36
not out	10
not out	12
Byes	3
	-
	80

SCHENECTADY.	1st Innings.
Ellis—caught by Shearman	7
Seely—hit wicket	7
Gower—caught by Blackman	0
Jenner—bowled by Knight	11
Dean—bowled by Small	1
Playford—caught by Burtenshaw	1
Clout—hit wicket	6
Colebrook—caught by Small	2
Fryar—bowled by Small	0
Wise—run out	4
Sanders—not out	1
Byes	12
	-
	52

RETURN MATCH

The return match between Schenectady and Albany came off on Thursday, the 28th ult. It was a well contested game, and towards the close excited great interest. The bowling of Wickins, on the side of Schenectady, as will be seen by the score, did terrible execution in the first innings with the wickets of his opponents, indeed, until Field went in, very few runs were got from his balls.—The result of the first innings placed Albany but 13 ahead of her opponent. Schenectady soon cleared that off, and through some good batting by Jenner, who scored 27 in seven threes, one two and four ones, Dean left Albany 74 to dispose of. So great was the confidence of all in the batting of Wybourn, whose wicket was lowered to three runs in the first innings, and others that the odds were in favor of Albany. Four wickets, however, including Wybourn's, were lowered to thirteen runs in a very short time. This altered the appearance of things, and bets were freely offered upon Schenectady. Four more wickets were lowered in quick succession, leaving the two remaining ones 38 runs to beat their opponents. All chance of success for Albany seemed now to be beyond hope. The steady batting, however, of Knight and Burtenshaw turned the scale, and the odds were once more in favor of Albany. The 38 runs were speedily diposed of, and Albany won the game with two wickets to go down.

The following is the score obtained by both parties:—

SCHENECTADY.

1st Innings.

Clout—bowled by Small	2
Jenner—caught by Small	0
Ellis—caught by Burtenshaw	8
Seeley—leg bw.	0
Wickins—not out	29
Dean—caught by Knight	8
Bauldehin—bowled by Small	0
Playford—bowled by Small	1
Wise—bowled by Sherman	0
Edmonds—run out	0
Gower—bowled by Small	0
Byes	5
	-
	53

2d Innings.

bowled by Knight	2
bowled by Knight	27
bowled by Knight	6
caught by Wybourn	3
run out	3
run out	17

not out	10
run out	7
bowled by Small	7
bowled by Small	0
bowled by Knight	0
Byes	5
	-
	87

ALBANY

1st Innings.

Russell—bowled by Wickins	12
Wood—caught by Wickins	2
Shearman—bowled by Wickins	7
Wybourn—bowled by Jenner	3
Small—bowled by Wickins	3
Knight—bowled by Wickins	0
Burtenshaw—caught out	1
Pellet—bowled by Wickins	0
Blackman—run out	8
Field—caught by Jenner	16
Clifton—not out	2
Byes	12
	-
	66

2d Innings.

run out	4
bowled by Jenner	6
leg bw	2
caught by Jenner	0
run out	13
not out	22
not out	13
run out	0
run out	9
bowled by Jenner	3
Byes	4
	-
	76

RETURN MATCHES

As interest in cricket increased, cricket clubs began the practice of scheduling return matches following the initial contest between local or area clubs. In some locales it was difficult to maintain an adequate number of good players, owing to a decrease in popularity of the sport before 1830. But during that decade renewed interest in the sport, partially as a result of the public's support for physical exercise, led to its rapid organization. The following article is reprinted from the 25 August 1838 issue of The Spirit of the Times.

THE GREAT CRICKET MATCH AT TROY

The Albany Daily Advertiser furnished us with the following particulars in relation to the late cricket match at Troy, between eleven players of Schenectady and Troy, and the same number of Albanians. We regret this manly and healthful pastime is not more "cottened to" in this country; a few years since there was a famous Cricket Club in this city, which comprised some of our most eminent citizens, and we should be glad to see it revived. We quote:—

We give the score of the match recently played at Troy, between eleven players of Troy and Schenectady, and eleven of Albany. During the season of 1837 the players of Schenectady were considered an equal match for those of Albany; since then, the Schenectady Club having lost some of their best players, declined to enter into the contest with Albany alone. The Albany Club, on learning this, sent them a challenge, with the privilege of choosing as part of the eleven, as many players as they could find in Troy. This challenge was accepted, and came off as below.

The result of the match, we believe, was somewhat unexpected by the Albany players; who, with the chances against them of playing both cities, (The Trojans having brought into the field six of the eleven players) entered the contest with full hopes of success. They were, however, doomed to disappointment.

The grounds selected at Troy was anything but fit to play upon. It was uneven, and covered with long, rank grass, and in every way ill-suited to the game. It is true that this would act equally against both parties. Still, such a ground ought not to have been selected, especially when there was a better one at Schenectady.

The following remarks which appear in the last number of the "Old Countryman," will not be considered out of place:—

"We are sincerely rejoiced to perceive that the manly and thoroughly English game of Cricket is more and more obtaining notice in America. Of all gymnastic exercises perhaps this is the finest. The fine play of the lungs which it affords, the exercise of the muscles and the limbs, the cheerfulness which it diffuses over the spirits, the acute observation which it teaches to the eye, and altogether the general animation of the system and the consciousness of vigorous strength which the player feels, must strongly commend it both as recreation and healthy exercise."

The return match will be played at Albany on Wednesday, 29th inst.

TROY AND SCHENECTADY.

FIRST INNINGS.

Paris, bowled by Hole	1
B. Corps, bowled by Hughes	1
Seely, caught by Hole	4
D. Longley, bowled by Hole	2
Wickins, bowled by Hughes	0
G. Corps, run out	0
Jenner, bowled by Hole	0
Gower, caught by Hole	4
Bumstead, caught by Small	4
Playford, caught by Hughes	0
G. Longley, not out	0
Byes	0
	-
Total	16

SECOND INNINGS.

caught by Pellett	10
not out	33
caught by Ellis	5
stumped by Hughes	1
bowled by Hole	4
caught by Knight	2
bowled by Hughes	1
run out	1
bowled by Hole	3
stumped by Hughes	0
caught by Pellett	0
Byes	3
	-
Total	63

ALBANY.
FIRST INNINGS.

Pellet, run out	3
Russell, bowled by Wickins	3
Ellis, run out	5
Hughes, leg before wicket	4
Hole, caught by Longley	5
Small, bowled by Paris	0
Sherman, stumped by D. Corps	0
Chatfield, bowled by Paris	0
Ballard, bowled by Wickins	1
Knight, not out	2

Blackman, bowled by Paris	2
Byes	7
	-
Total	32

SECOND INNINGS.

run out	0
foot before wicket	10
bowled by Bumsted	1
bowled by Paris	6
bowled by Bumsted	0
caught by Paris	2
bowled by Paris	5
caught by Longley	0
run out	8
caught by B. Corps	0
not out	1
Byes	3
	-
Total	36

IMPROVEMENTS IN CRICKET COVERAGE

During the late 1830s the competition and skill level of the players improved as did the reporting of the matches themselves. The following article, originally published in The Albany Daily Advertiser, was reprinted in the 15 September 1838 edition of The Spirit of the Times.

CRICKET MATCH—ALBANY VS. TROY

On the 25th ult. we published, from the "Albany Daily Advertiser," the participants of the first match between Eleven players of Troy and Schenectady, and Eleven of Albany, in which the latter scored 32—36 and the former 16—63. The return match, from the same source, is now subjoined:—

The return match between eleven players of Troy and Schenectady, and eleven of the Albany Club, was played on Wednesday last on the ground of the Albany Club, and attracted a numerous and respectable body of spectators. The Albany Club commenced batting, Ellis and Russell going in first, the former, after scoring a 2 and a 3, had his wicket lowered by a ball from Paris. Russell, after obtaining two 2's and four 1's, was caught out in good style by Paris, from a ball bowled with good judgment by

Bumstead. Pellet and Hughes followed, but their wickets were quickly lowered. Small was but a short time at the wicket; he had "a short life and a merry one." He was run out after scoring 11 in a 4, a 3, a 2, and two 1's. Sherman then went in, and in a short time scored 18, by a 4, a 3, four 2's and three 1's. Hole run up a score of 9, and the remainder of the wickets were lowered to 73 runs.

The Troy and Schenectady players then commenced batting, after a few minutes allowed for refreshments. Gower and Corps went in first. The batting of the latter was very good, and a score of 21 was rapidly obtained, in which were three 3's, three 2's, and six 1's, when Hughes found an opening to his wicket. Gower, after obtaining 7 runs, retired in favor of Paris, who quickly added 13 to the score, when a well-delivered ball by Hole reversed his wicket. Wickins followed, and after a somewhat lengthy innings, gave way to a ball delivered by Hughes, having scored 11. The remainder wickets were lowered, and a score of 86 in the whole obtained.

Albany then resumed the bat, and with but indifferent success, until Pellet went in, who for some time kept at a distance the well delivered balls of Paris and Wickins. The latter, however, at length found an opening to the wicket, and Pellet retired with 15 runs. Sherman's 2d innings was almost as successful as his first. He added 11 to his former score, among which was a 4 and three 2's.

The entire wickets were put down to 69 runs, which left the Troy and Schenectady players 57 runs to obtain to beat the Albanians.

This was probably the most interesting period of the match, and in view of the batting of the T. and S. players in their first innings, bets were in their favor. Corps and Gower went in first again. Presently, however, the wicket of the former was lowered by a "rattler" from Small without a run. This materially altered the complexion of affairs. Gower was run out, after having scored 3, by a well thrown in ball by Blackman, who was playing second hind stop. This feat of Blackman's was decidedly one of the finest points in the match. We may also add that three catches made by Ballard, who fielded the long hit, elicited great applause, and materially aided in the result of the game. The fielding on behalf of the Albanians in the 2d innings was much admired. In the first it was rather indifferent. The wickets of the T. and S. were lowered to 19 runs off the bat and 9 byes—28 in all; thus leaving the Albanians victors, with 28 runs to spare.

We have no hesitation in saying that this was one of the best contested matches played in this country since the introduction of the game. The Albanians acquitted themselves well, and sustained their character as players. The defeat of the chosen of the two cities is an event upon which they may justly pride themselves.

The following is the score:—

ALBANY.
FIRST INNINGS.

Ellis, bowled by Paris	5
Russell, caught by Paris	8
Pellet, bowled by Paris	2
Hughes, bowled by Wickins	1
Small, run out	11

Sherman, bowled by Wickins	18
Ballard, run out	0
Hole, run out	9
Knight, run out	5
Blackman, bowled by Wickins	3
Burtonshaw, not out	2
Byes.	9
	-
Total	73

SECOND INNINGS.

bowled by Paris	3
bowled by Wickens	0
bowled by Wickens	15
bowled by Paris	3
stumped by Corps	7
stumped by Corps	11
run out	4
run out	1
bowled by Paris	4
not out	5
bowled by Corps	8
Byes	8
	-
Total	88

TROY AND SCHENECTADY.
FIRST INNINGS.

Corps, bowled by Hughes	21
Gower, bowled by Hughes	7
Paris, bowled by Hole	13
Wickins, bowled by Hughes	11
Seeley, bowled by Hole	0
Bumstead, bowled by Hole	8
Jenner, bowled by Hole	8
Rose, caught by Hole	9
Playford, run out	0
Wenman, stumped by Hughes	1
Fuller, not out	0
Byes	8
	-
Total	86

SECOND INNINGS.

bowled by Small	0
run out	3
bowled by Small	7
caught by Ballard	0
bowled by Hole	0
caught by Ballard	4
caught by Ballard	3
leg before wicket	2
bowled by Small	0
not out	0
bowled by Hole	0
Byes	9
	-
Total	28

CRICKET AND BRITISH HERITAGE

Cricket formed an important part of Canadian sporting life during the 1830s and grew along similar lines as those in the United States. But in Canada, more so than in America, the sport was seen as a way to preserve British heritage and promote its allegiance to England. The following article, however brief, shows these sentiments and is reprinted from the 15 September 1838 issue of The Spirit of the Times.

CRICKET MATCH AT TORONTO, U.C.

The match at cricket, which we announced in Tuesday's paper, was played on Wednesday last, and terminated in favor of the Toronto eleven, who won the game, with ten wickets to spare.

The match was made for eleven officers (of the 85th and 43rd Regts., and Royal Artillery), to play against eleven of the Toronto Club. The players on the side of the officers were Messrs. Mundy, Coote, Lambert, Mead, Jones, Oxenden, and Weit, of the 43d Light Infantry, and Messrs. Todd and Colville, 85th Regt., Mr. Wilkins, R. A., and Mr. Farquharson, unattached. Messrs. Marryatt, R. A., and Frazer, Quartermaster-General, were to have played, but could not attend.

The military eleven played remarkably well; the batting of Mr. Lambert quick, sure, and determined; and of Mr. Coote, free, firm, and graceful, were greatly admired. Mr. Coote's bowling was in excellent style, it was a fine high delivery, of a good length, and wants nothing but practice to become very difficult to play to. Their fielding was active under all the disadvantages of not having previously practised in the field together, and the steady and neat play of Mr. Todd at long stops, and a fine catch made by Mr. Jones were deservedly commended.

On the Toronto side, the bowling of Mr. Groom was every thing that could be wished, steady and effective, and to his good delivery much of the successful result of the game must be attributed. Mr. Loring's short slip was very prettily done, and Mr. J. Robinson took a difficult catch in a capital style; but it was generally remarked that the batting of the Toronto men was, on this occasion, decidedly inferior to their usual practice. We saw none of Mr. Buck's fine play to point and slip, nor any of those striking qualities which Messrs. Barron and Harrington are wont to display, and which give such good practice to the long field. There was much ill luck on both sides. On the part of the officers, many players were very unfortunately run out, no doubt for the cause before mentioned—their not having practised much together; while on the Toronto side, many good bats lost their crickets either at the first or the second ball.

The weather was favorable,and the ground well attended, presenting the gratifying spectacle of a large number of ladies, and townsfolk generally; and in closing our remarks, we give it as our decided opinion, that the encouragement of such a truly British and manly game as cricket, will be affording no mean auxiliary in maintaining in this province British feelings and British principles.

The Patriot.

BROOKLYN CRICKET COMPETITION

The emergence of cricket as a modern sport during the 1830s was partially the consequence of British immigration, as immigrants formed a majority of the membership of cricket clubs. Playing the sport was a way to maintain some of the customs and traditions of their native England in a foreign land and it became common for contests to be conducted between groups of players representing various cities or locales in England. The following account is reprinted from the 13 October 1838 edition of The Spirit of the Times.

GREAT CRICKET MATCH AT BROOKLYN

The match at Cricket between Nottingham and Sheffield players for $100, which we noticed in a former paper, came off at Brooklyn on the 20th inst., but the news by the Great Western obliged us to postpone our account of it. The day was more than usually fine, and the lovers of this noble game we venture to say never enjoyed a higher treat on this side the Atlantic. By the score which we subjoin, it will be seen that the Sheffield party proved more than a match for their opponents, although there was some good play on both sides, particularly the fielding on the Nottingham side. We noticed two splendid catches made by Mr. Wm. Wyvil, but the bowling and fielding of the Sheffield party was such, as to keep their opponents' score uncommonly low. The Nottingham party won the toss, and put the Sheffielders in first, who succeeded in making up a score of 78, thirty-six of which were obtained from the bats of Messrs. Berry and Wheatman, both of whom batted remarkably well. On the Nottingham party going in against this score, they felt considerable confidence, but the bowling of Messrs. Wheatman and Gill, soon made an awful gap in their ranks; they having to resign their bats for a total of 21 runs. The Sheiffield party in their second innings scoring 88, left their opponents scarcely a chance of winning, and with the exception of Messrs. Wm. Wyvil and J. Turton they were equally unsuccessful in their second innings, they making only a score of 23. It is but justice to the Nottingham players to say they were very unfortunate in losing some of their best batsmen by being run out. There was a very numerous and respectable assemblage of spectators on the ground, who appeared highly gratified with the day's sport; every thing went off well, with the exception of a slight accident which happened to one of the Sheffield players of the name of Holmes, who in attempting to catch a ball which had been thrown up, had the misfortune to let it go through his hands and it struck him on the face, damaging his nose and eyes considerably. In concluding our remarks we are happy to be able to state that the challenge which has been offered for several weeks past, by the players of Long Island, has taken up by the New Yorkers, and is expected to come off in the course of the present month, when a most interesting match may be anticipated, the time and place of playing which we shall not fail to notify our readers.

SHEFFIELD.
FIRST INNINGS.

J. Wheatman, caught by Parker	12
Dodworth, caught by Sneath	5
Gill, bowled by Hurst	6
Steade, bowled by Taylor	4
Fisher, bowled by Taylor	4
Bradshaw, caught by Turton	8
Berry, caught by W. Wyvil	24
Taylor, bowled by Hurst	0
Ellen, caught by W. Wyvil	6
Pearson, not out	2
Holmes, run out	5
Byes	1
Wide balls	2
	-
Total	78

SECOND INNINGS

caught by H. Wyvil	35
bowled by Hurst	0
bowled by Hurst	14
run out	7
not out	8
bowled by Hurst	1
caught by Sneath	7
run out	12
bowled by Turton	0
bowled by Turton	0
bowled by Turton	2
Byes	2
Wide balls	0
	-
Total	88

FIRST INNINGS.

Taylor, run out	1
Win. Wyvil, run out	3
Parker, bowled by Gill	2
Alvey, caught by Gill	8
H. Wyvil, caught by Wheatman	3
Sneath, run out	1
Shelton, stumped by Dodworth	0
Turton, bowled by Gill	3
Hurst, caught by Steade	0
Beecroft, caught by Steade	0
Dent, not out	0
Byes	0
Wide balls	0
	-
Total	21

SECOND INNINGS.

bowled by Wheatman	0
caught by Taylor	10
bowled by Wheatman	1
not out	0
run out	1
caught by Gill	0
caught by Dodworth	0
caught by Gill	10
caught by Steade	0
caught by Bradshaw	0

bowled by Steade	1
Byes	0
Wide balls	0
	-
Total	23

MATCH BETWEEN ST. GEORGE'S AND TORONTO CRICKET CLUBS

By 1840 cricket matches between clubs from the United States and Canada began to occur regularly—an important development in the evolution of cricket to a modern sport. The following account, published in the 12 September 1840 issue of The Spirit of the Times, gives an account of what apparently is the first meeting between the St. George's Club, perhaps the best known club in New York, and the Toronto Club.

THE RECENT CRICKET MATCH

When last week we published a report of the match between the Toronto and the St. George's Club, we were fully informed of the particulars of an unpleasant misunderstanding in regard to the match which it was supposed had been made as far back as the week ending August 22. But it was thought better that the exposure, if any took place, should come from the other side. In the following extract from the "British Colonist" of the 9th inst., (a paper published at Toronto, U.C.) full particulars are given. Our Canadian friends have thoughout behaved with the greatest delicacy, and now that a friendly communication is established between the Toronto Club and that in our own city, we may look for an annual renewal of friendly competition at this manly sport of cricket.

This highly interesting match having terminated in favor of the New York City, it becomes our province to perpetuate in our columns the proceedings of the meeting of the two clubs; and as there are some extraordinary and curious points in "the history of the rise and progress" of the match, our "round unvarnished tale" will necessarily be somewhat long, though we trust not tedious, in the telling.

In the Spirit of the Times, of the 22nd ult., and which reached us about the 27th, it was mentioned, that a match at Cricket *was made* with the Toronto Club, for five hundred dollars, and that the New York players would arrive in Toronto about the 1st inst.; the attention of our Cricketers was naturally enough excited, but as they were in possession of no official information to corroborate this notice, it was considered as one of those unauthorised articles which often find their way into even respectable newspapers, and the subject became gradually forgotten: great however was the astonishment of our club to learn, on Wednesday last, after returning from their usual practice game, that the said notice was founded on fact, and that eighteen gentlemen of the New York Club had actually arrived here for the express purpose of playing, what they had been led to understand was already arranged, a stake match at Cricket with the Toronto players:—the writer of this article upon hearing this, immediately waited upon the gentlemen, and, together with three or four other members of the club, welcomed the party to Toronto; after the usual interchange of courtesies, a verbal statement was made by the New York gentlemen of the circumstances which had induced them to make so long a journey for such a purpose; after some conversation it was agreed that this statement should be reduced to writing, and submitted to the Toronto Club at a special meeting to be called for the following day.

On Thursday the necessary steps having been taken to convene a full meeting, the Secretary of the Toronto Club waited upon the St. George's Club and received the written statement, at the same time proposing, that three gentlemen of the New York party should, as a committee of conference, meet the same number from the Toronto Club, to temperately discuss the subject, and consider what course should be adopted under existing circumstances, that would be mutually satisfactory to either Club: this proposition having been favorably entertained, the St. George's Club appointed Messrs. Tinson (their President), Green, and Downing, to form such a committee.

At one o'clock, a numerous meeting of the Toronto Club was held, (W. H. Boulton, Esq., in the chair,) the Secretary having first stated the circumstances generally, read the statement handed him by the New York Club, from which it appears that an individual, calling himself a member of the Toronto Club, had visited New York as the Toronto Club's authorised agent, to conclude a match between the respective Clubs;— that a letter was written by the Secretary of the New York Club to a gentleman in Toronto on the subject, but that this individual informed the New York Club that it need not wait for a reply to that letter, as he was fully empowered to arrange the preliminaries of the match, and which he proposed should be as follows; viz:—The match to be played "*Home and Home*," the first match being at Toronto, each Club to pay the other's expenses to their respective grounds; no definite sum was named, but the individual said the Toronto Club would play for any sum from one hundred to five thousand dollars; that this individual on leaving New York (which he did, we understand, about the 15th ult.) said, that he would communicate to his Club the arrangement he had made, that no further correspondence was necessary, and that the New York Club had only to signify to the Toronto Club the time the match was to come off, and the Toronto Club would be in readiness to receive their fellow-cricketers from New York;—that on the 18th ult. another letter was mailed to Toronto, naming the agreement in a general way; and fixing the 29th ult. for the departure of the St. George's Club from New York. It is proper to mention here, that the two letters above referred to were addressed to a gentleman absent from the city, and it having occurred to the writer, that possibly the letters had not been forwarded, he went to the post-office, accompanied by one of the New York gentlemen, and found the two letters lying there; they were taken out, the handwriting of the address identified; they were opened in the presence of the New York gentlemen, and their contents found to correspond exactly with the statement of the St. George's Club; these letters were produced and read at the meeting; the statement then proceeded to say, that this individual have his name, which is that of a highly respectable family, but which at present it is thought inexpedient to publish, and also represented himself to be an officer in her Majesty's service, and that from these causes the New York gentlemen were impressed with the belief that all was right, and therefore started on their pilgrimage, fully satisfied that the Toronto Club would be ready to welcome them on their arrival; these various considerations having been carefully discussed, a committee, consisting of Col. McKenzie Fraser, W. H. Boulton, and John Barwick, Esqrs., was appointed to meet the committee of the St. George's Club, and were instructed on behalf of the Toronto Club:—

1st. To express their entire ignorance of the whole affair beyond the paragraph in the "Spirit of the Times:—to declare that the individual who had represented himself as their agent, had no authority whatever for his proceedings—and that consequently *The Toronto Club* was compelled to disallow, in the most distinct and unequivocal manner, the arrangements made by this individual.

2d. That while required, upon principle, to repudiate the proceedings of this individual, *The Toronto Club* deeply and unfeignedly regret the disappointment which has been thereby produced, and are most anxious to render the visit of the New York gentlemen to Toronto as agreeable as, under the circumstances, may be possible.

3d. That for this purpose the Toronto Club will be happy to play the St. George's Club of New York a friendly game, say for £50 sterling ($250), and request the pleasure of entertaining the St. George's Club to dinner after the game is finished.

The committees met, and the New York Club, before considering the proposal of the Toronto Club, expressed the opinion, that in the event of the individual proving to be the person he represented himself, the Toronto Club should guarantee them their expenses in the offered match, and the New York Club would guarantee the expenses in the offered match, and the New York Club would guarantee the expenses of the Toronto Club for the return match at New York; this proposal was afterwards modified to paying one-half of the expenses reciprocally; these propositions not being agreed to by the Toronto Club, on the principle, that any such arrangement would make them a party to the imposture practised on the New York Club, and the proposals on our part having also been declined by them, there seemed reason to apprehend that the Clubs would part in anything but that friendly spirit which on every account it was desirable to cultivate between them; at a late hour of the evening, however, the St. George's Club accepted the proposals of the Toronto gentlemen and the match was accordingly definitely determined. We have thought it necessary, even at the hazard of being thought *prosy*, to enter thus fully into these details, because, both in justice to these gentlemen, and in vindication of the upright character of our club, it was desirable that the facts of this extraordinary case should go forth faithfully to the world. It is but performing an act of common justice to the St. George's Club to say, that under the trying circumstances into which, by the misrepresentations of this unauthorised individual, they had been deluded, they sustained throughout the bearing of Englishmen and gentlemen. As regards the individual whose actions have caused so much disappointment, a searching investigation will be instituted into his conduct, and until a result has been arrived at we forbear further observation thereupon.

It is somewhat remarkable that while these things were going on in New York a match between the Toronto and Guelph Cricket Clubs was on the tapis, and had not the match been most unexpectedly interrupted, the Toronto players would have met their antagonists at Guelph, on the very day after the New York gentlemen arrived at Toronto.

Then follows a report of the playing, which appeared in these columns last week. The following are the comments of the editor of the "Colonist" upon the match.

The New York Club appeared to be better drilled than the Toronto players, and there was a unity in their play which the other party wanted; the fielding on both sides were good, although the New York men were the steadier, owing, it must be presumed, to their having had constant *practice together*, and without which no eleven, how good so ever it may be in other respects, can hope to distinguish themselves in the cricket field. With regard to batting, we cannot help thinking that the Toronto Club are quite equal to the St. George's, and if they will lend a willing ear to our humble advice, and *practise steadiness* and *unity of action*, we venture to predict that, in the next encounter they have, they will not disappoint the confidence of their friends, even if they should not succeed in recovering their lost laurels. The weather was very fine, and the whole affair went off with eclat. Among the numerous spectators His Excellency the Lientenant Governor honored the game with his presence, and, their bright costumes showing pleasantly through "the bushes and alleys green;" many fair dames graced the adjoining pleasure ground.

EARLY QUOITS

With the growth of urban areas, the public emphasized the need for physical exercise and a concern for health. Sports played an important role in promoting both and was seen by many as a way to counteract the adverse effects of big city environments. Sporting enthusiasts practiced many different types of sports and pastimes, one of which was quoits. As the following article points out, quoit organizations were formed primarily as social clubs and provided their members with camaraderie and companionship. The document below was reprinted from The American Farmer, 5 May 1826.

RULES OF QUOITS

[The season is at hand for making up parties for occassional excursions to the country, "where blooming health exerts her gentle reign." How much better to repair to the fields, the woods, or to the neighbouring streams, at the close of a week of hard study or sedentary labour, and there spend the afternoon in gunning, fishing, swimming, bowling at nine-pins, pitching quoits, &c., according to one's fancy and the season, than to abuse whole days in *militia mustering!* frequenting gaming-houses, whiskey drinking, &c.

The sedentary and oppressive occupations of a city life, which beget
    "_____ the languid eye, the cheek
    Deserted of its bloom; the flaccid, shrunk,
    And withered muscle, and the vapid soul,"
require to be counteracted by refreshing amusements that are only to be found in the country; and for all such healthful and innocent enjoyments, no city possesses greater

facilities in its immediate vicinity, than Baltimore. There is not a road, nor a water course, that does not afford beautiful situations for recreations such as we have mentioned. In other large cities, in summer season especially, on Saturday afternoons the whole population is in motion. We do not recollect ever to have passed a more pleasant day than at a quoit club party in the neighbourhood of Philadelphia. They meet every Saturday, under the following rules of association:]

RULES OF THE PHILADELPHIA QUOIT CLUB.

1. The number of members shall be limited to 20.

2. To become a member, a gentleman must be proposed at a meeting; and in case of a vacancy, be ballotted for on the succeeding club day. Should the number be complete, the Secretary shall keep a list of candidates to be ballotted for when vacancies happen in the order they were proposed.

3. Two black balls shall exclude a candidate, and no ballot shall take place, unless there be at least 18 members present.

4. The meeting shall take place on the first Saturday in May.

5. No member shall accept of any invitation on club day.

6. No invitation to be given to other than strangers, excepting by the President of the day, who shall have the liberty of inviting two friends.

7. The President of the day, or some other member of the club as proxy for him, shall attend the giving out of wine, porter, &c; to have the wine, coits, &c. locked up in the evening, and to deliver the key to the President of the succeeding day.

8. No hot dishes to be allowed on any account, except vegetables. The penalty for infringing the rule shall be 1 dozen of Madeira for the use of the club.

9. A Secretary and Treasurer shall be appointed; the latter the oldest member, and the former the youngest member of the club.

10. The duty of the Secretary shall be, to purchase the wine, &c. and to give his orders upon the Treasurer for the amount.

11. The duty of the Treasurer shall be, to take charge of the subscription money.

12. The accounts of the Secretary and Treasurer to be settled annually on the 31st December.

13. On the first meeting of the club, each member shall pay to the Treasurer 25 dollars, and be liable to be called upon for their proportion of any additional expense.

OLDEST QUOIT CLUB IN AMERICA

As the title of the following piece suggests, many clubs of the antebellum periods had their origin and persistence in the social functions that they served. The following article, drawn from the September 1829 edition of the American Turf Register and Sporting Magazine, nicely details the membership, function, and upper-class attitudes of perhaps the oldest quoit club in America.

THE RICHMOND "BARBACUE (*or Quoit*) CLUB"

During a recent visit to Richmond, in Virginia, I was invited to a "Barbacue Club," held under the shade of some fine oaks, near "Buchanan's Spring," about a mile distant from the town. I there met with about thirty of the respectable inhabitants of Richmond, with a few guests. The day was a fine one, and the free and social intercourse of the members, rendered it peculiarly pleasant.

This Club is probably the most ancient one of the sort in the United States, having existed upwards of forty years. It originated in a meeting every other Saturday, from the first of My until the month of October, of some of the Scotch merchants who were early settlers in that town. They agreed each to take out some cold meats for their repast, and to provide a due quantity of drinkables, and enjoy relaxation in that way after the labors of the week. They occasionally invited some others of the inhabitants, who finding the time passed pleasantly, proposed in the year 1788 to form a regular club, consisting of thirty members, under a written constitution, limiting their expenses each day by a sort of sumptuary law which prohibited the use of wine and porter.

The Virginians, you know, have always been great *limitarians* as to constitutional matters. Whenever a member died or resigned, (but there have been very few resignations,) his place was filled by balloting for a new one, who could not be elected without the concurrence of two-thirds of the club. It is said, that for many years no vacancy occurred, and a sort of superstitious sentiment was prevalent, that to become a member of the club, was to insure longevity. The Arch Destroyer, however, at length appeared in all his strength, and made such havoc, that only one of the original members (the venerable Chief Justice of the United States) is now surviving.

The club consists of judges, lawyers, doctors, and merchants, and the Governor of the Commonwealth has a general invitation when he enters into office. What gave additional interest to this body, some years ago, was the constant attendance (as honorary members,) of two venerable clergymen—one of the Episcopal and the other of the Presbyterian church, who joined in the innocent pastime of the day. They were pious and exemplary men, who discerned no sin in harmless gaiety. Quiots and backgammon are the only games indulged in, and one of the clergymen was for many years "cock of the walk" in throwing the *discus*. They are gone to their account, and have a chasm that has not been filled.

Some years ago, an amendment was made to the constitution, which admits the use of porter. Great opposition was made to this innovation, and the destruction of the club was predicted as the consequence. The oppositionists, however, soon became as great consumers of malt and hops as their associates, and now they even consent to the introduction of wine at the last meeting of every year, provided there be "a shot in the locker." The members each advance ten dollars to the treasurer at the beginning of the season, and every member is entitled to invite any strangers as guests, on paying into the general fund one dollar for each; while the caterers of the day, consisting of two members in rotation, preside, and have the privilege of bringing each a guest (either citizen or non-resident,) at free cost. On the day I was present, dinner was ready at half past three o'clock, and consisted and excellent meats and fish, well prepared and well served, with the vegetables of the season. Your veritable gourmand, never fails to gale himself on his favourite *barbacue*—which is a fine fat pig, called "shoot," cooked on the coals, and highly seasoned with cayenne—a desert of melons and fruits follows, and punch, porter and toddy are the table liquors; but with the fruits comes on the favourite beverage of the Virginians, mint julep, in place of wine. I never witnessed more festivity and good humour than prevails at this club. By the constitution, the subject of politics is forbidden, and each man strives to make the time plesant to his companions. The members think they can offer no higher compliment to a distinguished stranger, than to introduce him to the club, and all feel it a duty to contribute to his entertainment. It was refreshing to see such a man as Chief Justice Marshall, laying aside the reserve of his dignified station, and contending with the young men at a game of quoits, with all the emulation of a youth.

Many anecdotes are told of occurrences at these meetings. Such is the partiality for the Chief Justice, that it is said the greatest anxiety is felt for his success in the game by the by-standers; and on one occasion an old Scotch gentleman was called on to decide between his quoit and that of another member, who after seemingly careful measurement, announced, "Mister Marshall has it a leattle," when it was visible to all that the contrary was the fact. A French gentleman (Baron Quenet,) was at one time a guest, when the Governor, the Chief Justice, and several of the Judges of the high court of appeals, were engaged with others, *with coats off*, in a well contested game. He asked, "if it was possible that the dignitaries of the land, could thus intermix with private citizens," and when assured of the fact, he observed, with true Gallican enthusiasm, that "he had never before seen the real beauty of republicanism."

CLASS AND QUOIT CLUBS

The sports clubs formed between 1820 and 1840 often consisted of members drawn from the upper classes and catered to their tastes and sensibilities. The following article, published in the February 1838 issue of the American Turf Register and Sporting Magazine, describes both the upper class attitudes of the members of a quoit and bowling club and their political interests.

THE WASHINGTON SOCIAL GYMNASIUM
FROM AMERICAN TURF REGISTER AND SPORTING MAGAZINE, 1838

MR. EDITOR: *Washington, December*, 1837.

As your valuable magazine is the appropriate repository for every thing relating to innocent recreation, healthy exercise, manly sports, or good fellowship, permit me to occupy a page of it, with a brief notice of a new association in this city, bearing the above title, and of its first celebration dinner.

At the beginning of the summer, a number of gentlemen, (comprising such of the members of the old Quoit club, as chose to unite,) organized a new quoit and bowling club, under the name of the *Washington Social Gymnasium*. Having obtained a very eligible site for the purpose, they erected an excellent bowling-house, and laid out two good quoit alleys, all well enclosed, and the whole costing about five hundred dollars. The regular meetings have been three a week, (though many members attend every afternoon, to bowl or pitch,) and these meetings have fully realized the objects of the association; namely health-giving exercise, and the cultivation of sociability and good feeling. The last named benefit you will better appreciate, when I inform you that the association is composed of individuals of both—I might say, of all political parties. This circumstance, indeed, so far from engendering any asperity, or even shyness, among the members, appears to be a happy ingredient in the composition of the club, as party allusions are always sportive, and frequently contribute to the gaiety of the moment. I mention this fact, because I conceive that it does honour to the good sense and gentlemanly character of the members. But of the dinner:

The club having determined to celebrate the close of its first season by dining together, arrangments were made for that purpose, with Monsieur Boulanger, of the American and French Restaurant. The dinner came off on Tuesday, the 21st of November, and I undertake to say, that it was one of the most splendid entertainments ever served up at a public house in the United States, and I much doubt whether the London Tavern, the Cafe de Paris, the Rocher de Cancale, or any other restaurant or hotel in Paris or London ever surpassed it, either in the qualities of sumptuous and recherche viands, splendid appurtenances, or fine wines.

After the last of the numerous courses had been removed, and the dessert discussed, the accomplished and veteran bard of 'Betty Martin,' (Mr. P. T. the poet laureat of the old club, whose felicitous odes to the same strain, you have heretofore favoured with a place in your pages,) rose and delighted the company, with his accustomed happy review of the incidents of the season, and the merits and peculiarities of the several members, embodied in verse, and adorned with the graces of wit, humor, and sentiment. For this amusing effusion, we may ask the favour of a place in your magazine hereafter. A few distinguished and agreeable guests added to the pleasure of the evening, which was spent in the interchange of kind feeling, in drinking heart-warming toasts, and listening to excellent songs. The large company separated at a proper hour, pleased with the dinner, the wines, with each other, with themselves and with the complete success of the 'Experiment,' which brought them together.

EARLY CANADIAN BASEBALL

The following letter, originally published in the 5 May 1886 issue of Sporting Life, provides an important glimpse into the transition of early baseball from a local, premodern sport to a regional, modern one in North America. Sporting events and contests became regular features of militia days in both colonial America and Canada, and Militia Muster Day, an Ontario provincial holiday in honor of King George III's birthday, was no exception in 1838. The author of the letter, Dr. Adam Ford, gives his reminiscence of baseball from his days as a young child in Ontario, Canada. In addition to his medical career, Ford, who participated in a number of sports during his childhood, later distinguished himself in sports through his involvement in the creation and operation of curling and baseball clubs, primarily during the 1870s.

EARLY CANADIAN BASEBALL

A Game of Long-ago Which Closely Resembled Our Present National Game.
Denver, Col., April 26. Editor Sporting Life.

The 4th of June, 1838 was a holiday in Canada, for the Rebellion of 1837 had been closed by the victory of the government over the rebels, and the birthday of His Majesty George the Fourth was set apart for general rejoicing. The chief event at the village of Beachville in the County of Oxford, was a baseball match between the Beachville Club and the Zorras, a club hailing from the township of Zorra and North Oxford.

The game was played in a nice smooth pasture field just back of Enoch Burdick's shops; I well remember a company of Scotch volunteers from Zorra halting as they passed the grounds to take a look at the game. I remember seeing Geo. Burdick, Reuben Martin, Adam Karn, Wm. Hutchinson, I. Van Alstine, and I think, Peter Karn and some others. I remember also that there were in the Zorras "Old Ned" Dolson, Nathaniel NcNames, Abel and John Williams, Harry and Daniel Karn, and, I think, Wm. Ford and Willian Dodge. Were it not for taking up too much of your valuable space I could give you the names of many others who were there and incidents to confirm the accuracy of the day and the game. The ball was made of double and twisted woolen yarn, a little smaller than the regulation ball of today and covered with good honest calf skin, sewed with waxed ends by Edward McNames, a shoemaker.

The infield was square, the base lines of which were twenty-four yards long, on which were placed five bags, thus

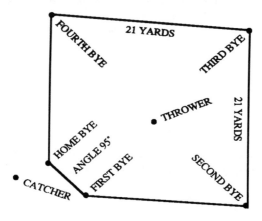

The distance from the thrower to the catcher was eighteen yards; the catcher standing three yards behind the home bye. From the home bye, or "knocker's" stone, to the first bye was six yards. The club (we had bats in cricket but we never used bats in playing base ball) was generally made of the best cedar, blocked out with an ax and finished on a shaving horse with a drawing knife. A Wagon spoke, or any nice straight stick would do.

We had fair and unfair balls. A fair ball was one thrown to the knocker at any height between the bend of his knee and the top of his head, near enough to him to be fairly within reach. All others were unfair. The strategic points for the thrower to aim at was to get near his elbow or between his club and his ear. When a man struck at a ball it was a strike, and if a man struck at the ball three times and missed it he was out if the ball was caught every time either on the fly or on the first bound. If he struck at the ball and it was not so caught by the catcher that strike did not count. If a struck ball went anywhere within lines drawn straight back between home and the fourth bye, and between home and the first bye extended into the field the striker had to run. If it went outside of that he could not, and every man on the byes must stay where he was until the ball was in the thrower's hands. Instead of calling foul the call was "no hit."

There was no rule to compel a man to strike at the ball except the rule of honor, but a man would be despised and guyed unmercifully if he would not hit at a [...] fair ball [...] he was out if the ball was caught either before it struck the ground or on the first bound. Every struck ball that went within the lines mentioned above was a fair hit, every one outside of them no hit, and what you now call a foul tip was called a tick. A tick and a catch will always fetch was the rule given strikers out on foul tips. The same rule applies to forced runs that we have now. The bases were the lines between the byes and a base runner was out if hit by the ball when he was off of his bye. Three men out and the side out. And both sides out constituted a complete inning. The number of innings to be played was always a matter of agreement, but it was generally 6 to 9 innings, 7 being most frequently played and when no number was agreed upon seven was supposed to be the number. The old plan which Silas Williams and Ned Dolson (these were greyheaded men then) said was the only right way to play ball, for it was the way they used to play when they were boys, was to play away until one side made 18, or 21, and the team getting that number first won the game. A tally, of course, was a run. The tallies were always kept by cutting notches on the edge of a stick when the base runners came in. There was no set number of men to be played on each side, but the sides must be equal. The number of men on each side was a matter of agreement when the match was made. I have frequently seen games played with seven men on each side, and I never saw more than 12. They all fetched.

The object in having the first bye so near the home was to get runners on the base lines, so as to have the fun of putting them out or enjoying the mistakes of the fielders when some fleet footed fellow would dodge the ball and come in home. When I got older, I played myself, for the game never died out. I well remember when some fellows down at or near New York got up the game of base ball that had a "pitcher" and "[...]'s" etc., and was played with a ball hard as a stick. India rubber had come into use, and they put so much into the balls to make them lively that when the ball was tossed to you like a girl playing "one-old-cat" you could knock it so far that the fielders would be chasing it yet, like dogs hunting sheep, after you had gone clear around and scored your tally. Neil McTaggert, Henry Cruttenden, Gordon Cook, Henry Taylor, James Piper, Almon Burch, Wm. Harrington and others told me of it when I came home from university. We, with "alot of good fellows more" went out and played it one day. The next day we felt as if we had been on an overland trip to the moon. I could give you pages of incidentals but space forbids. One word as to the prowess in those early days. I heard Silar Williams tell Jonathan Thornton that old Ned Dolson could catch the ball right away from the front of the club if you didn't keep him back so far that he couldn't reach it. I have played from that day to this and I don't intend to quit as long as there is another boy on the ground.

Yours, Dr. Ford

YOUTH SPORTS

Many of the ball games practiced in North America during the early to mid-nineteenth century were played primarily by young boys and adolescents, failing to attract an adult following. The excerpt below, taken from the 1830 American edition of The Boy's Own Book; A Complete Encyclopedia of All the Diversions, Athletic, Scientific, and Recreative, of Boyhood and Youth, was originally published in England and subsequently adapted to the sports and games in America.

FIVES

Fives may be played either single-handed or with partners. A good wall must be selected, with a sound flat piece of ground in front of it; a line must be drawn, about three feet from the ground, on the wall; another on the ground, about two yards from the wall; and a third, describing three sides of a square, of which the wall itself will be a fourth, on the ground from the wall, to mark the bounds. The players toss up for innings; the winner begins by dapping his ball on the ground, and striking it against the wall, above the line, and so that it may rebound far enough to fall outside the line on the ground; the other player then strikes it, in the same manner, either before it has touched the ground, or dapped, (i.e.) hopped from the ground, more than once; the first player then prepares to receive and strike it at its rebound; and thus the game goes on, until one of the players fail to strike the ball in his turn before it has hopped more than once, strike it below the mark, or drive it out of bounds. If the party who is in do neither of these, he loses his innings; if the other, then the in-player reckons one, on each occasion, towards the game, which is fifteen. When partners play, the rules are precisely the same; each side keeping up the ball alternately, and the partners taking turns for innings, as one of the other side gets out. After the ball is first played out, on each occasion, it is not necessary to make it rebound beyond the ground line, which is used only to make the player who is in, give out the ball fairly in the first instance: that is, when he first takes his innings, or when he plays out the ball again, after winning a point....

FOOT-BALL

A match is made between two sets of players of equal numbers; a large ball made of light materials,—a blown bladder, cased with leather, is the best,—is placed between them, and the object of each party is to kick the ball across the goal of the other, and to prevent it from passing their own. The party, across whose goal the ball is kicked, loses the game. The game is commenced between the two goals, which are about a hundred yards asunder.

Foot-ball was formerly much in vogue in England, though, of late years, it seems to have fallen into disrepute, and is but little practised. At what period the game of Foot-ball originated, is uncertain; it does not, however, appear among the popular exercises before the reign of Edward the Third, and then it was prohibited by a public edict; not, perhaps, from any particular objection to the sport itself, but because it co-operated, with other favorite amusements, to impede the progress of Archery.

The rustic boys use a blown bladder, without the covering of leather, for a foot-ball, putting peas and horse-beans inside, which occasion a rattling as it is kicked about....

ROUNDERS

In the west of England this is one of the most famous sports with the bat and ball. In the metropolis, boys play a game very similar to it, called Feeder. In rounders, the players divide into two equal parties, and chance decides which shall have first innings. Four stones or posts are placed from twelve to twenty yards asunder, as *a, b, c, d,* in the margin; another is put at *e*; one of the party which is out, who is called the pecker or feeder, places himself at *e*. He tosses the ball gently toward *a*, on the right of which one of the in-party places himself, and strikes the ball, if possible, with his bat. If he miss three times, or if the ball, when struck, fall behind *a*, or be caught by any of the players, who are all scattered about the field except one who stands behind *a*, he is out, and another takes place. If none of these events take place, on striking the ball he drops the bat, and runs toward *b*, or, if he can, to *e*, *d*, or even to *a* again. If, however, the feeder, or any of the out-players who may happen to have the ball, strike him with it in his progress from *a* to *b*, *b* to *c*, *c* to *d*, or *d* to *a*, he is out. Supposing he can only get to *b*, one of his partners takes the bat, and strikes at the ball in turn; while the ball is passing from the feeder to *a*, if it be missed, or after it is struck, the first player gets to the next or a further goal, if possible, without being struck. If he can only get to *c*, or *d*, the second runs to *b*, only, or *c*, as the case may be, and a third player begins; as they get home, that is, to *a*, they play at the ball in rotation, until they all get out; then, of course, the out-players take their places.

c

b   d

e

a

ANNUAL FRESHMAN V. SOPHOMORE FOOTBALL MATCH

At Harvard College the sport of football dates back to the early 1800s when an annual contest between freshmen and sophomores emerged as a popular event. The following poem, written by a senior named Richmond, was the first recorded account of a football game at Harvard and is reprinted by permission of The Harvard Advocate. The poem originally appeared in the October 1827 issue of The Harvard Register, a short-lived monthly undergraduate journal founded in the same year. The title of the poem refers to the field of the contest—the Delta at that point in time was a triangular area on which the outdoor gymnasium was located.

THE BATTLE OF DELTA
by Rev. James Cook Richmond, Class of 1827

Things unattempted yet in prose or rhyme.
Milton.

THE Freshmen's wrath, to Sophs the direful spring
Of shins unnumbered bruised, great goddess sing;
Let fire and music in my song be mated,
Pure fire and music unsophisticated.

The college clock struck twelve—that awful hour
When Sophs met Fresh, power met opposing power;
To brave the dangers of approached fight,
Each army stood of literary might;
With warlike ardor for a deathless fame
Impatient stood—until the football came;
When lo! appearing at the college gate,
A four-foot hero bears the ball of fate;
His step was majesty, his look was fire—
O how I wish he'd been six inches higher!
His eye around triumphantly he throws,
The battle ground surveys, surveys his foes;
Then with a look—O what a look profound!
The well-blown ball he casts upon the ground;
How stern the hero looked, how high the ball did bound!
"Let none," he says, "my valour tried impeach,
Should I delay the fight—to make a speech"—
"Let it be *warned*," a youthful Stentor cries,
No speeches here,—but let the football rise."
Through warlike crowds a devious way it wins,
And shins advancing meet advancing shins;
"Over the fence!" from rank to rank resounds,
Across the rampart many a hero bounds;

But sing, Apollo! I can sing no more,
For Mars advancing threw the dust before.

   Meantime the Seniors, on the ladder raised,
Upon the strife sublime, ententive gazed;
Secured from blows by elevation high,
The fight they viewed with philosophic eye,
Save here and there a veteran soldier stood,
A noble darer for the Freshmen's good.

   But ah! I vainly strive—I could not tell
What mighty heroes on the greenward fell,
Who lost, who won the honors of that day,
Or limped alas! ingloriously away—
I could not tell—such task might well require
A Milton's grandeur and a Homer's fire;
A realm of foolscap, bunch of goosequills too,
Would scarce suffice to sing the battle through;
How many moons would wax, how many wane,
While still the bard might ply his song in vain;
Yet minstrel's purse and brain but ill affords
Such waste of paper, and such waste of words.

   But see! where yonder Freshman Hector stands,
Fire in his eye, and football in his hands;
Ye muses, tell me who,—and whence he came;
From Stonington—and Peter is his name;
That coat, which erst upon the field he wore,
Was once a coat—but ah! a coat no more;
For coat and cap have joined the days of yore.
So when some tempest rages in the sky,
Shakes the Gymnasium mast, erected high,
That mast so sacred to Alcides' cause,
Which oft has made the country people pause,
Or wonder, as they pass at slower speed,
What can a college of gallows need?
As when the aforesaid storm its tackling rends,
Rope ladders this, and wooden that way, sends;
Still stands the mast majestical in might.
So Peter stood, though coatless in the fight.
At length advancing to the neutral space,
He proudly waved his hand, and wiped his face;
Then with a voice as many waters loud,
He broke the silence, and bespake the crowd.
So oft when stilly, starry eve invites,
To wander forth and taste her fresh delights,

I've heard the *buble* o'er the common sound,
Though all unknown by whom or wherefore wound.
"List to my words; from Stonington I came,
In football matchless, and of peerless fame;
Think ye, fainted-hearted, scientific fools,
That such as Peter waste away in schools?
No, glorious battle called him from afar,
From Stonington, to hear the din of war;
Then if there be a Soph, who boot to boot,
Dares meet the vengeance of a Peter's foot,—
Let him advance, his shin shall feel the woe
That lives, though sleeping, in a Peter's toe."
He said, and ceased,—Jotham stepped forth to view,
A Soph of stature, and of glory too.
"Vain-boasting Peter, dost thou think thy hand
Can Mars and Jotham in the strife withstand?
Minerva aids thee? vaunter, learn to fear,
Mars in the van, and Jotham in the rear!"
He said, and furious rushed upon the foe,
As when two cows to deadly combat go;
Fate interfered, and stopped the impending blow;
For hark! the summons of the Commons-bell,
That music every hero knows so well;
All sympathetic started at the sound,
And ran for dinner from the battle ground.

REMINISCENCE OF FOOTBALL AT HARVARD

Thomas Wentworth Higginson, the author of the following article on football at
Harvard College, was a well-known radical reformer during the nineteenth century. He
distinguished himself in the women's suffrage, temperance, and, particularly, the abo-
litionist movements. Using his position as a Unitarian minister to express his beliefs
on freedom of speech, he put them into action through his involvement in several fu-
gitive slave rescue attempts during the 1850s. He later served as colonel of the 1st
South Carolina Volunteers, the first black regiment in the Union army during the Civil
War. The document that follows first appeared in The Harvard Advocate, Volume 17,
12 June 1874 and is reprinted by permission of that publication.

HARVARD ATHLETIC EXERCISES THIRTY YEARS AGO
by Thomas Wentworth Higginson, Class of 1841

ONE of the most impressive early reminiscences is of a certain moment when I looked out timidly from my father's gateway, on what is now Kirkland Street, in Cambridge, and saw forms of young men climbing, swinging, and twirling aloft in the open playground opposite. It was the triangular field then called the "Delta," where the great "Memorial Hall" now stands. The apparatus on which these youths were exercising was to my childish eyes as inexplicable as if it had been a pillory or a gallows, which indeed it was not so very unlike. It consisted of high uprights and cross-bars, with ladders and swinging ropes, and complications of wood and cordage, whose details war vanished from my memory. Beneath some parts of the apparatus there were pits sunk in the earth, and so well constructed that they remained long after the wood-work had been removed. This early recollection must date back as far as 1830; and by 1835, I suspect, no trace of Dr. Follen's gymnasium remained above the level of the ground....

From that time until 1841, when I graduated, nothing like a gymnasium existed, so far as I know, in Cambridge; that of Belcher Kay being established, I think, in 1844, or thereabouts. The college games of the period were foot-ball, cricket, and, to a limited extent, base-ball. Football was the first game into which undergraduates were initiated, for on the first evening of his college life the Freshman must take part in the defence of his class against the Sophomores. It was then a manly, straightforward game, rough and vigorous, but with none of the unnecessary brutality to which this match-game afterwards descended, and which led to its temporary prohibition. After the first evening match-games ceased, and the sides divided themselves almost at random, the more players the better. It was a much swifter game as we played it than that described in *School Days at Rugby*, and simpler than that now played as the "Harvard Game." But nothing in Tom Hughes's description can exaggerate the fascinations of the sport, to me at least; and I can recall, at this moment, the growing exhilaration as one drew near to the "Delta," on autumn evenings, while the game was in progress,— the joyous shouts, the thud of the ball, the sweet smell of the crushed grass. Then came the taking of sides, the anxious choice of a position, the weary defence, the magnificent "rush." It seemed a game for men and giants, rather than for boys; and yet I remember that it was mainly confined, in those days, to the three lower classes, and that I was more than once reproached for juvenility for being the only member of my class who clung to it through the Senior year; I having then almost attained the age at which students usually enter college,—seventeen. Certainly there are great advantages in the maturer years of undergraduates now-a-days; and the chief benefit is that they are permitted to be "juvenile" a little longer....

THE EARLY GAME OF FOOTBALL

Early collegiate football games often were intramural affairs, pitting upper and lower classes against each other. In the following article Robert S. Minot, a prominent Boston attorney and author of many newspaper articles and translations, reminisces. He was an 1877 graduate of Harvard College and a member of the Football Club. As a sophomore he played football games against both juniors and freshmen, but apparently missed several games because of poor health. The following document describes the primitive state of football during the early nineteenth century and is reprinted by permission of The Harvard Advocate, where it originally appeared in Volume 21, 26 May 1876.

FOOT-BALL FORTY YEARS AGO
by Robert S. Minot, Class of 1877

At this time, when foot-ball playing has become quite the fashion, it may be interesting to know how the game was formerly played; and though most of the readers of the *Advocate* have probably read the first (and best) chapter of *Fair Harvard*, they may not know how much the game has changed. A gentleman, who played on the Delta forty years ago, lately gave me an account of the game as played in his time, which is quite entertaining.

The foot-ball was not of rubber, as might be supposed, but was a bladder in a leather case, like our modern Rugby ball, which we have adopted I believe as an innovation. Finding the Delta too small a confine this bage of wind satisfactorily, they used to take the bladders out of the cases, and replace them by "paper, old rags, dead leaves, or any thing that came to hand." This degraded, soulless mass was the nucleus of a hearty game, however. One can easily suppose there was very little science in it, since a good "warning kick" would scarcely send the ball forty feet. Kicking it being almost impossible, and running with it little or no part of the game after the opening kick, it attracted but little interest except as being an excuse for scrimmages, in which a man showed himself the best player who could kick fastest, and do most hurt to his adversary's shins.

There were two classes of players, "rushers" and "protectors." When the ball came out of a scrimmage, a rusher would try to kick it along in any fashion, and over the enemy's goal-line. The protector on the other side now would pay no attention whatever to the *ball*, except to get between the player and it, and "hack" him or trip him. No handling, however, was allowed, and it was generally answered by a slap in the face. In short, it seems on the whole that the foot-ball was nominal excuse for the pleasant pastime of "shinnying."

Our old "Boston" game must have ben a great and enlightened improvement on this hearty and rough-and-tumble sport; but what an immense stride we have taken, in adopting our present beautiful scientific game!

BOWLING

Although nine- and ten-pin bowling became more popular after 1840, there apparently were serious public objections to it. The following article, reprinted from The American Farmer, 26 June 1829, gives some insight into these objections as well as into the close identification of bowling with the immoral activities of the pub—drinking and gambling.

NINE-PINS

A grave debate has been held in the city council of Albany, upon the question of banishing nine-pins to the suburbs, for the reason among others, that people are disturbed by this amusement in the night. One of the members, Mr. Mather, thought it would not do to *force* morality too much. Mr. Straats did not think playing nine-pins was so great a nuisance as was supposed, and if it were, he had so much regard for the people of the suburbs as for those in the heart of the city. They finally resolved that no minor should be permitted to roll nine-pins in the city, and that the amusement should be prohibited after eight o'clock in the evening.

The citizens of Albany seem to keep very good hours if their dreams would be disturbed by this recreation so early as eight o'clock.

[Quere, is the punishment that prescribed by one of the old blue laws—to stand with his tongue in a split stick? What shall we have next in the way of excessive regulation? as bad in morals as in trade; smuggling is apt to ensue in both cases.—The suppression of one open gentlmanly and manly amusement is sure to give rise to two gross vices—the more vulgar and pernicious for being the more concealed.]

Chapter 6

BOXING

Prior to the early nineteenth century boxing received scant attention in periodical literature, no doubt the reflection of public opprobrium of the sport. The origins of such disapproval lay in the brutal and gruesome nature of boxing during this time, in upper-class hostility toward the working classes, often comprised of immigrants who found boxing attractive, and in the persistence of Puritan values antithetical to what was considered an uncivilized and immoral activity.

From the 1700s to the antebellum period boxing was introduced into the United States by foreigners, primarily of English and Irish descent, who were members of the lower classes in the cities and, as such, evinced the social values and ethnic tensions of their world. In the late 1700s many boxing matches occurred in seaports where British sailors would fight in back rooms, bars, and other sites away from the eyes of the authorities. With the beginnings of industrialization, commercialization, and urbanization after the turn of the century the influx of immigrants and greater disparities in wealth deepened ethnic tensions and hardened class attitudes, both of which found expression through boxing matches.

Before 1838, when the London Prize Ring rules were adopted, boxers generally conformed to the rules established in 1743 by Broughton's Code, which is to say, they followed few regulations at all. Boxers could commit any number of actions that in subsequent decades would be considered illegal, possibly inhumane. Although bare knuckle boxing remained legal until 1892, the practices of choking, biting, kicking and hair pulling were common during the late eighteenth and early nineteenth centuries. In addition, the use of rounds, seconds, and boxing techniques were for the most part absent from the sport during this time. These factors, combined with the lingering moral influence of Puritanism, created an inhospitable climate for the development of boxing as a sport and the growth of an indigenous public following.

By the 1820s, however, boxing had gained a tenuous foothold in America. The emergence of Tom Molineaux, often called the first heavyweight champion, on the international boxing scene sparked American interest in the sport. Molineaux, a former slave, had distinguished himself among his black contemporaries and subsequently fought the British champion. Although he lost, the match caught the public imagination, especially among the urban population. Soon thereafter boxing, as well as the reporting of matches, became more frequent and in 1823 the first known account of a prize fight in America was recorded, replete with round-by-round coverage. This account, by the New York Evening Post, and an article on the public's response to it, by the New York Spectator, are included in this chapter.

Equally important to the introduction of boxing in America was the propagation of sparring, or the science of self-defense, by two recently arrived British immigrants, William Fuller and George Kensett. Both men traveled the Northeast, teaching sparring as a method of gentlemanly self-defense in such cities as New York, Philadelphia, Washington, D.C., Boston, and Baltimore. Fuller established his famous gymnasium in New York, where he taught members of the upper class the skills required to fight off the threatening advances of ruffians and rogues. Though Kensett gave sparring lessons, he also became involved in prize fighting, participating in two of the most important matches between 1820 to 1840. His opponent in these fights was Ned Hammond, an Irishman. Fuller and Kensett won wide reputations for their pedagogical efforts and helped lend credibility to the sport that was sorely lacking. By basing their appeal for the necessity of self-defense on class divisions they played into upper class fears of social change and conflict arising from urbanization and industrialization. More importantly, Fuller and Kensett began to cultivate interest in boxing among a social elite whose support was crucial to the acceptance of the sport in America.

Despite these developments, boxing, for the most part, failed to capture and sustain a national audience as late as the 1840s. The reasons for this failure are many. From 1820 to 1840 the ambivalence with which many Americans greeted the rapid social and economic changes extended to the sport of boxing. The ethnic animosities that many of these boxing matches expressed as well as the disorder, licentiousness, and brawling that often surrounded bouts made the upper classes uneasy. The documents in this section describe the ethnic, social, and class dimensions of the sport for this period.

The sport of boxing would not gain acceptance by the so-called respectable members of society until the dawn of the twentieth century. It is revealing that newspaper editors, whose journals catered to the socially elite, sometimes offered apologetic disclaimers about the nature of the sport even as they continued to report matches. Others such as William T. Porter of the Spirit of the Times refused at certain points to provide coverage of bouts altogether. As "The Spirit of the Times and Public Pressure" demonstrates, Porter, with some misgivings, bowed to public morality in order to protect the respectability of his publication among New York City's social and sporting elite.

Boxing also failed to transcend neighborhood, local, or perhaps regional boundaries before the 1840s because, despite some reforms, it remained a brutal sport both inside and outside the ring. Rules were inconsistently obeyed and bouts informally conducted. Charges of fraud and chicanery invariably called into doubt the outcome of many matches. These accusations, which only inflamed ethnic or social tensions among the audience, often resulted in street brawls and mob scenes. As a result some states, beginning with New Jersey in 1835, passed statutes that outlawed the sport and imposed severe penalties for disobedience. Because most boxers continued to rely on boxing as a short-term remedy for unemployment as they moved about in search of unskilled work, they usually fought only a few fights in their lifetime and could not be considered professionals. With taverns or saloons as the typical location for fights the sport of boxing continued to be associated in the public mind with gamblers and hustlers or, as the upper classes preferred to view them, the very rabble of society.

EARLY BOXING MATCHES

Boxing matches received scant coverage in journals during the second quarter of the nineteenth century because of public disapproval, the local, informal nature of the sport, and the transience of its participants. Although the following excerpt was taken from a document published in 1860, American Fistiana, it nonetheless offers valuable accounts of the major boxing matches from 1821 to 1840. The accounts, however brief, serve to confirm the general chaos, disorder, and violence that accompanied many of the contests during this period.

PUBLIC FIGHTS

The first public ring fight which ever took place in this country was between JACOB HYER AND TOM BEASLEY.—This fight took place as early as the year 1816, and proceeded from a personal quarrel between the men, much of the same character as that which produced the present match between Tom Hyer, the son of the first above named party, and Yankee Sullivan. The fight between Hyer and Beasley, both whom were very large and powerful first class men, lasted through several severe rounds, but was at length decided in favor of the latter by an accident, and Hyer retired from the ring with a broken arm.

JIM. SANFORD AND NED HAMMOND.—The next that we find on record is the prize fight between Jim Sanford, the American Phenomenon, and Ned Hammond, an Englishman. This occurred in 1821, near Belville, New Jersey, but after a period of severe fighting, in which Sanford, though the lightest man, had much the best of it, it was interrupted by the sudden appearance of the Sheriff with his posse comitatus, and was never resumed.

JIM SANFORD AND BILL HATFIELD.-This fight took place in 1824, on this Island, at "Stuyvesant Point," or "Brandy Muley," as the lonely spot, which is now the location of the Dry Dock, was in those days called. Sanford was the victor in this fight against superior weight, in thirty-seven rounds.

NED HAMMOND AND GEROGE KENSETT.—A fight took place between these two men in 1826. It was first pitched at Coney Island, but being driven from there by the Sheriff, the parties retreated to the Union Race Course, where they struck their styles. After some hard fighting Kensett was declared the winner, though the decision was disputed for a long time.

WILLIAM FULLER AND BILL MADDEN, in 1828, fought a match on Long Island. Fuller was the winner after a long contested struggle.

HAMMOND AND KENSETT, in 1829, fought their disputed battle over again for a new purse of $500, but Kensett lost, on having fallen without a blow. The match was subsequently offered to be renewed by Kensett for the same amount, but was not taken up by the other parties.

SANFORD AND ANDY MCLANE.—Elated with his early successes, Sanford had the audacity to match himself, in 1832, against Andy McLane, a first class man of Philadelphia. They fought on the 1st of March of that year near the Bell Tavern, in the vicinity of that city, and McLane was declared the victor, Sanford having lost the use of his right hand during the latter part of the contest. It lasted one hour and twenty minutes, and fifty-four rounds were fought. Sanford, not satisfied to allow McLane to remain a victor, came to this city and induced a sturdy friend of his, Wm. Harrington, of Washington Market, to make a match with McLane. While preliminaries were being arranged for this affair, a fight gotten up between

PAT. O'DONNELL AND JIM O'HAGAN, who fought on the 27th of February, 1832, near Newark, N.J., for $100 a side; but the battle did not come to a definite settlement, as it ended in a general row, in which principals, seconds, spectators all joined.

HARRINGTON AND MCLANE.—In the June following the above, the match, for $500, between Harrington and McLane came off near Baltimore, which was also broken up by a general row. The riot was charged upon the friends of McLane, who were present from Philadelphia in great numbers, and who were determined not to see their champion whipped. Harrington, therefore, claimed the stakes. This kept up a constant feud till 1838, when

HARRINGTON AND JOHN MCLANE, a drover, fought at Hoboken for the fun of the thing, or rather to settle a banter or a grudge. On this occasion Harrington was winner.

JIM REED AND ANDY MCLANE fought near Elizabethtown, in 1834. Reed won by the treachery of McLane to his backers, he having betrayed the fight to one manifestly his inferior, for money. This was the fight at which the Sheriff, who read the riot act, made use of the expression, "Now gentlemen, I've done my duty, and as you don't seem disposed to go, I'll stay and see it out." Reed is the Lieutenant Reed who recently raised a company in New Orleans for the Mexican war, and deserted with the traitor Riley. He was recaptured and sentenced to be shot, but was suffered to escape.

JIM BEVINS AND TOM HUMPHREYS fought in 1835 at Williamsburg, and Bevins won the battle.

ABE VANDERZEE AND JIM PHELAN (the latter of whom had just previously won a battle at White Plains) fought in Rhode Island, this same year, and Phelan lost.

FEARNON AND SPANISH LEW fought the same year, the former, though but an apprentice fresh from his work, cutting the practised pugilist, as the "fancy" term it, "all to pieces."

REED AND BARRETT.—In the same year, Jim Reed and Tom Barrett, alias Long Tom, of Philadelphia, fought at Hart's Island, but after some hard work, the ring was broken in, and a row ensued, which terminated the fight. There was but little difference between them at the close of the fight.

DEAF BURKE AND O'CONNELL fought at Hart's Island on the 21st August, 1838. The fight was won easily by Burke in nine rounds only.

VANDERZEE AND SPEIGHT.—On the 25th of September, of the same year (1838), Abe Vanderzee and Frank Speight fought at Fort Washington Point, up the North River, and Vanderzee won the fight in 14 rounds. Reed and Owens also fought up the North River, and the latter whipped his man.

DEAF BURKE AND O'ROURKE fought in the winter of the same year, at New Orleans but owing to the interference of O'Rourke's friends, Burke was forced to fight his way out of the ring with a bowie knife, and escaped on horseback at full gallop.

OWEN AND REYNOLDS.—During this same winter, George Owens, the Manchester Pet, fought Bill Reynolds, near Cincinnati, for $200, and got whipped in 18 rounds.

O'CONNELL AND O'ROURKE, AND O'ROURKE AND GALLAGHER fought also near New Orleans, but their contests ended in rows, and are undeserving of record among the operations of the ring.

EARLIEST KNOWN ACCOUNT OF AN AMERICAN BOXING CONTEST

Early boxing matches were noted for their unruly crowds, informality, and localism, and often expressed and reflected ethnic animosities. All of these aspects are contained in the following article, the earliest known account of a boxing match in the United States, which appeared in the 10 July 1823 issue of The New York Evening Post.

A BOXING MATCH

The following particulars of a Boxing match which took place last Tuesday, near Corlaers Hook, were furnished us by an eye witness to the brutal scene, and we very much regret that there were no Police Officers at hand to have taken up the principals, their seconds and abettors, and lodged them all in Bridewell. In the name of decency let us not imitate the manners of the old world in the particular.

A Boxing Match—On Tuesday the 8th July, at half past 6 P.M. being near the Ferry at Grand street, I observed a large number of men, women and children collecting, and like others, I followed to Gardner's wharf, at the upper end of Cherry street, where I saw a large ring formed, and on enquiry found, a lad about 18 years old, a butcher, and a man whom they called the Champion of Hickory street, both stripped, and each had a second. After the proper arrangements, the seconds drew back a little, and the word was given for battle.

1st round.—The butcher (whom I shall call the boy,) immediately faced his man with the boldness and courage of a bull-dog. Some good sparring took place, and several blows were exchanged on both sides; but nothing decisive, took place this round.

2nd round.—The butcher drew claret from his opponent's mouth, and had greatly the advantage by a knock down blow.—Two to one on the Boy.

3rd round.—Handsome sparring—the Champion much out of breath—rested on his second's knee, who supplied him with cold water and limes frequently; the Boy at the same time, strutting round the ring like a game-cock—Three to one on the Boy.

4th round.—The Boy, after much play, in which he discovered considerable science, planted a tremendous blow upon the Champion's knob and down he went like a bullock, which occasioned great cheering. Any odds offered, but no takers.

5th round.—The Boy had greatly the advantage, but the seconds would not allow him to follow up his blows when the Champion was retreating. This caused loud murmurs from the spectators, and it was asked why this interference on the part of the Seconds, They answered that it was by agreement, as the battle was for $200.

6th round.—The boy had much the advantage, and appeared to be in high keeping—would take no water, which his opponent was washed and was supported by his second on his knee, and was supplied with lime juice and cold water.

7th round.—This was a short round, in which the Boy had decidedly the advantage.

8th round.—The Champion being decently *milled*, and much fatigued, gave up the fight.—The battle lasted about forty minutes. The challenge, we understand, originated in the following manner:—On the fourth of July, the butcher boy got into a quarrel with a foreigner, whom he beat severely, and who it was alleged he knew was no match for him. This provoked the butcher to offer to fight any man, on one hour's notice being given him, belonging to the same nation as the person he had contended with on the 4th of July, for $200; and he would give them one week to select their man. The offer was accepted, and the result was as above stated.

PUBLIC OUTRAGE OVER BOXING

During the early nineteenth century boxing received strong public opposition because of its supposed threat to societal order, stability, and morality. The brief article below, reprinted from the 15 July 1823 edition of The New York Spectator, appeared shortly after the appearance of the first account of a boxing match and expressed these public fears and concerns.

PUGILISM

Pugilism.—For the first time in our lives, we last evening found in an American paper, (the Evening Post,) a regular scientific account of a boxing match which took place in this city, after the London fashion; and we fully agree with the editor of that paper, that the Police ought to have interfered to prevent the brutal and disgraceful exhibition. We are grieved to find the pernicious customs which disgrace the populace of Europe, creeping in among us. If our civil authorities will permit the torture of wild brutes, or the battles of human ones, the wicked and the curious will attend them. And what will become of the morals of the rising generation—our apprentices, youth from school, servants, male and female, if they have opportunities to mingle in these scenes of riot, brutality, and systematic violations of order and decency, where customs must be acquired which will not bear repetition?

THE BRUTALITY OF BOXING

The brutality and cruelty of boxing evoked public outrage and disgust at the sport. The following document, reprinted from The New York Spectator, 19 October 1824, describes the physical injury and disfiguration experienced by one fighter during one of these early boxing events.

BOXING MATCH

GENTLEMEN:

Passing yesterday from Jamaica to Brooklyn, I was attracted by a cavalcade of carriages going towards the race ground. I soon learned that a boxing match was to take place. On arriving at the ground about half a mile south of the new race course, I found a large company assembled. A ring was already formed of ropes and stakes. In the course of a few minutes the combatants entered the ring, and here commenced one of the most disgusting scenes that ever took place in this country. Figure to yourselves two human beings, (supported to be in their senses,) thumping at each other's heads until they were entirely and tumbling one on the top of the other—then the shouts of *mo-bility*, the seconds washing their mangled faces and bruised bodies. The savage cry of *time* brought the panting men again front to front. "Well done Liverpool:" "Hurra for the Irish," followed every stroke that appeared to do *execution*. Towards the middle of the *game*, a total eclipse of the Irishman's eyes took place. I really cannot describe his appearance. Two arms attached to a mud colored body, appeared to be very active, striking right and left; this was surmounted by what *had appeared* to be a head and face. Where the eyes should have been there were two large colored nobs, with a small red projection for a nose—the rest of the face was quite inexpressible. This figure, however, was the favorite. It seems he had more *pluck* than his fellow sufferer, and a better share of *wind*; at least, it seemed to last longer. After eighteen or twenty rounds, the battle was decided in favor of the Irishman, the Englishman being unable to come to time. It appears, however, that some *foul play* had taken place, and the purse was given to the Englishman. Thus ended this great event, highly to the gratification of the Irish hackney-coachmen, who made the air resound with "*ould* Ireland forever;" and "down with the English."

I saw a number of *worthies* from New-York, variously employed, as *time-keepers, bottle-holders, seconds,* &c. The feeling on the subject, however, by the majority of the company, was not favorable; and it is sincerely to be hoped, that such disgusting scenes, revolting to the feelings and an outrage to society, will never again be attempted in this country. If so, effective measures ought to be adopted to prevent their taking place.

We are led to believe, that the science of boxing is to enable us to "repel the attack of the ruffian." If the men alluded to were "men of science," I can avouch they had no "repelling power." In their fighting, every blow during the battle was on the offensive, with one solitary exception; and this was in consequence of a concussion of two fists, which were intended to reach a very different quarter.

P.

FIGHTING IN NEW JERSEY

As American Fistiana briefly recorded, on 27 February 1832 a fight occurred between Patrick O'Donnell and Jim O'Hegan near Newark, New Jersey. The prize was $100 and the match demonstrated many of the characteristics for which boxing had become notorious—rude behavior, brutality, gambling, and violence. For these reasons, boxing had long suffered under a stigma in North America and the following account, drawn from the 3 March 1832 edition of The Spirit of the Times, illustrates many of the sports early problems.

MILLING MATCH
BETWEEN MCDONNELL AND O'HEGAN

We have been favored with the following account of the meeting of those real lads of the Fancy, McDonnell and O'Hegan, which took on Monday last, for $100 a side. They have before come to the "scratch" and have for some time been in training; both men being backed by the "swells" and "Corinthians" of the first order, whose principal object was to preserve the sports of the Ring, and to give encouragement to athletic exercises.

As we said before, the match was made among the nobs and swells, and gentlemen were appointed to name the place of meeting, whose knowledge of localities, it was thought, would enable them to select a spot free from objection; the place fixed on was Hoboken, that land sacred to "Honorable meetings," but owing to Magisterial interference, they were obliged to give way and break out some other ground. Though the friends of the belligerents used all their eloquence to stall off the traps, it was to no purpose; the persons interfering had their instructions, and expressed their determination to perform their duty. As it was understood that the power of these inexplorables did not extend beyond Hoboken itself, it now became a question for consultation what location was best suited for the display; a fine plot of earth, was agreed on at last, about a mile from the town of Newark, where the stakes and ropes being adjusted, about half past four o'clock the men made their appearance, attended by their seconds, bottle-holders and friends. At this time there was on the ground about 1500, spectators composed mostly of the Fancy and the ground exhibited a...lively appearance.

COMMUNICATION.

McDonnell first appeared in the Ring, and by way of a token threw up his castor, amidst the cheers of his friends. O'Hegan immediately followed him and in turn was loudly greeted; they tossed for choice of ground, which was won by McDonnell, and they immediately commenced the Mill.

Round 1st

Both men came to the scratch, each appeared confident of winning, both cautious for some minutes McDonnell displaying good science and to all appearance the best man; he first broke ground with a faint hit at his opponents breadbasket, who in endeavouring to stop received McDonnell's right on his smeller; both closed and some sharp fibbing followed and claret was observed to flow from Mc's snout: he got away giving his opponent a sharp hit on the pimple which floored him.

Round 2nd.

Both came to the scratch in good style, each displaying great confidence and anxious for the fight; O'Hegan made a straight forward hit at Mc's phiz, but missed and received a muzzler from McDonnell's right, which he immediately gave a receipt for by planting his right on Mc's peeper; some sharp hitting ensued, and this time McDonnell smelt the ground. Here the sons of Greece bellowed aloud for O'Hegan.

Round 3d.

Pretty severe hitting, blows exchanged on both sides for several minutes; in this round they both received severe fibbing, McDonnell evidently appeared to have the best of it, here the ring was broken and the round closed in the greatest confusion; the spectators and fighters being altogether, it was impossible to distinguish what was going on.

Round 4th.

After some delay the ring was again cleared, when both came up fresh, having had time to snort awhile; Mc popped in a right-handed body blow; on retreating O'Hegan followed him up to meet a smashing hit on his countenance which confused his cannister for some moments, but finding there was no time to be lost he plunged in meaning mischief; he this time received a right and left short ribber; Mc got away and again played round his gigantic antagonist for some seconds, when O'Hegan made an attempt to close but met Mc's manly under the left listener, which kept him at a distance, and rather confuted his knowledge box for some moments; he at length came up for something; he attempted a smashing hit at Mc's phiz, but was again disappointed, as in that attempt he received a smart hit which drew his claret profusely; here again the ring was confused and the round closed.

Round 5th.

Mc made play with his left and received a slight hit in return; O'Hegan rattled in for a rally, both receiving punishment; but here Mc peppered him pretty considerably which ended by a muzzler from Mc's right; here the bullying of O'Hegan's party again confused the ring; in this round they were both down, but owing to the confusion we were both down, but owing to the confusion we were not able to see how they came there; (cheers for Mc and loud cries of "Och! and by my soul, Mc's the boy what e'll win the fight, my boys..")

Round 6th.

Both came up with ugly mugs, neither appeared to be pleased with their punishment; Mc played away right and left, missed a left jobber but caught a severe counter hit; a rally, in which slight hits were exchanged; Mc came in with his left, which O'Hegan stopped with his pimple; they then came to a close and went down; (cries of take O'Hegan away, take him away.)

Round 7th.

Both appeared undetermined what to be at for some seconds, each puffing; Mc rushed in with his left giving a heavy snorter; a rally, and both went down; at the end of this round O'Hegan declared he would fight no longer, and both men were taken away by their friends, each claiming the fight. We understand that is left to the Umpires to decide.

Mc appears but little the worse for the fight, with the exception of a dark peeper; we understand that O'Hegan is considerably punished.

BOXING AND JOURNALISM

Public opprobrium of boxing was strong as late as the 1830s. The immorality of the actions associated with boxing—gambling, drinking, and violence—as well as what was perceived to be the sheer cruelty of the sport combined to create vocal public opposition to the practice and, as the following account demonstrates, to the reporting of such contests. Despite respecting the public outcry, sports journals nevertheless expressed their desire to report on the more orderly and respectable demonstrations of boxing. This article is from The Spirit of the Times, 19 May 1832.

THE RING

We have to-day evinced our respect to the "public voice" by expunging the Sports of the Ring from our columns. Yet we reserve the right on any fitting occasion, so far to imitate the example of our contemporaries, as to give now and then a recital of the "feats" of the real fancy—while we shall avoid the disgusting accounts of unscientific cudgel play, that of late has so strikingly adorned the fair sheets of even our friendly admonitors.

Yet we mourn over thee, O! Ring. We wail for thy fallen glories-we lament that no longer we may hang enchanted over the recital of thy matchless sports! Yea, thou arena of bloody-nosed beauty and gladiatorial spirit, thou hast been to us as our first-born. Thy great progenitors "Cain of the bloody mark" gave to thy feats the impress of his nature and sanctifying thy innocent festivities with gore of his brother.

But the Spirit of the Times drives you from our pages. The kind admonitions of our friends instruct us that we may have mistaken "the taste of an American Public." "Genius of the Fancy!"-thy soul-subduing exhibitions has no place in this community! Thou art fled from hence and taken thy abode in the capitol of our country! We deplore thy departure—yet we sympathize in the distresses that drove thee from us! Thou art now amid congenial spirts-the reception thou hast found must delight thee—gratified thou must have been, when at "dewy eve," thou west met and greeted by the champion of thy grouging bonebreaking votaries! Yet we must bid thee a final adieu. To the genius of this people thou art not congenial. Fare thee well, great shade.

BACKCOUNTRY FIGHTING AND GENTLEMANLY SPARRING

The following account, a reprint from The New England Galaxy published in the 12 December 1835 issue of The Spirit of the Times, clearly demonstrates Northern, upper-class attitudes toward boxing and its more vicious offshoots such as gouging and biting. For a time, sparring developed an important following among the gentlemen of Northern society as a part of the gymnasium movement during the late 1820s and 1830s. The following story contrasts the superior athletic skills and morality of a "yankee" gentleman with the brutality and immorality of his Southern opponent. Of course, as if the lesson needed reinforcement, the yankee gentleman triumphed over his crude, drunken Southern rival.

A KENTUCKY FIGHT
"Ay, gouge and bite—pull hair and scratch."

The fight—the fight—oh, yes! I will tell you the story! It was at a small ordinary tavern in ----. I had dined, and was sitting at the fire, toasting my toes, and smoking a segar. A noise attracted my attention, and on turning I found it proceeded from half a dozen burley fellows—beauties, they called themselves—that had come there to wind up their constitutions with potations of rye whiskey. Glass after glass of the *crittur* went down their throats with the accompaniment of oaths and yells, and with each glass they became more and more elated. It was election day, and they were qualifying themselves to give plumpers for their crack candidate, who had just finished a stump speech about half a mile off.

"He's a screamer," said one.

"He's bottom," said another.

"He's grit to the back bone—plenty of liquor," said a third.

"He's real republican—no ruffled shirt or clean hands about him," said a fourth.

"Hurrah! hurrah!" they yelled together, and were just leaving the room when the saw me.

"Aha! a Yankee, by all that's mighty!" cried one of them; "come, stranger, tote out here, and bolt this liquor"—and, as this was said, a tumbler filled to the brim with raw whiskey was put into my hand.

"I'm a temperance man," said I: "it is against my principles."

"D—n your principles!—run the water!" cried one.

"Pour it into his ears!" exclaimed a second.

"Or down his throat with a funnel," said a third.

"Come, stranger," bawled a fourth, approaching and grabbing me by the collar—

"Handle him!" cried another.

"Gentlemen, I—"

"Don't gentlemen us," said the first: "we're no gentlemen, no how you can fix it, we're real wolf-breed, born in a canebrake and suckled by a hippopotamus—real Kentucky from the tips of our noses to the end of our toe-nails."

"But, gentlemen—"

"Come, none of your gumfadgeon to us; down with the liquor at once, or, instead of a gentlemen, we'll make less than a man of you in the twinkling of a thunderclap."

As I finished, I set the glass down. They swore I should drink it. I remonstrated in gentle terms; told them I loathed it; pretended sickness; but they cursed me all round the compass, and calling me a white-livered fool, swore I should drink it.

Gentle words having no effect, I thought to intimidate them by a show of bravery, and to that end took out one of my pistols. They told me they were not to be *skeered* so easy, and only cursed me the more roundly, while one of them again put the glass in my hand. I must confess that I found my courage fast leaving me; and I was in the act of raising my hand to quaff the liquor, thinking it the only way to rid of a bad scrape, when a yell of triumph burst from them, and determined me on a different course. I dashed the vessel into ten thousand atoms.

In a moment a scoundrel had me by the collar; the next I had flung him off, and was standing in the corner with my pistol presented.

"I will shoot the first man that dares to touch me," said I.

"Hurrah, stranger, that's gritty!" shouted one, a giant of a fellow, as he approached.

"I shall fire," said I.

"And be d—d," said he, still advancing.

I took deliberate aim, and, the instant he touched me, I pulled.

The cloth flew from his frock, and, retreating a step or two, he broke into oaths:

"By Gaud, stranger," said he, "do you know me?—do you know what stuff I'm made off? Clear steamboat, seahorse, alligator—run agin me, run agin a snag—jam up—whoop! Got the best jack-knife, smartest wife, blackest child, shaggiest dog, fastest horse, prettiest sister, and biggest whiskers of any man hereabouts—I can lick my weight in wild cats, or any man in all Kentuck!

"Well," said I; and I stood stock still, looking at the fellow, and wondering what he meant.

"Come out here," said he; "come out here, if you're a man—rough and tumble."

"Gouging!" said one of the gang.

"Look ye!" said I, "look ye, scoundrels—I do not well understand you—you are large men, I am small—but let me caution you, that you won't find me so feeble as you think. I can thrash the whole of you, one at a time."

Years before I had practised sparring successfully and upon that ability I was determined to rely.

There was a pause.

"What say you," said I, "are we to quarrel."

They all nodded, and began to rub their hands.

"Well," said I," chose any one of your numbers—promise you will not interfere, any of you, and there is my pistol."

As I said this, I discharged it—the ball rattled against the chimney and rolled back on the floor. One of them picked it up.

"Hellfireation, it was loaded," said he, "it's black with powder, and hot now."

"Loaded," said the fellow I had shot, "to be sure it was—see there!" running his hand into his bosom, and pulling it out covered with blood—"loaded, yes that it was, and we must have it out."

"Then you and I are to fight, hey" said I.

"To be sure—all ready!—cooked and primed—all ready!"

At this there was a general outcry, all present setting up a shout, and shaking their hats.

"Wait a moment," said I, "I'm not ready so fast—I heard you speak of gouging—are we to gouge?"

"Ay, gouge and bite—pull hair and scratch!" was the answer, and again they yelled in chorus.

"And strangle too, I suppose," said I, thinking if any thing would have an effect on them, it would be a show of self confidence and coolness.

As I spoke I tore off my stock with a jerk, and the collar and bosom of my shirt followed—by which means my chest became exposed, and as he caught sight of it, I saw him quail—and well he might, for it is frightful—constant exercise and daily habit of sparring has thrown out the muscles, so that when he saw them they were quivering among the luxuriant black hair with which my breast is covered, like a wounded and exasperated snake.—"Come on," said I, throwing myself into a position to receive him.

He leaped at me—I sprang aside, and he struck the wall with such violence that it stunned him, and he fell at my feet. Impatient I waited his recovery, for I felt that I could easily level him. At length, he gathered himself up, and with curses set upon me—I parried his blows, and gave him two in return—one in the pit of the stomach, and one in the face, that made the blood gush from his nostrils in a steady stream—he staggered against the wall, and stood there retching and panting for more than a minute, with the blood and whiskey running together from his mouth—but the next moment I was under him, as helpless as a babe, stunned and suffocating. Suddenly, I felt his great hand wreathed in my hair, and the thumb approaching my right eye, digging about my temple. I remembered what I had heard—it was gouging!—the thought was madness—with one effort I grappled at his throat—I reached it—I seized the loose flesh, and twisted it—he uttered a shreik of agony—his hold began to loosen—his swollen tongue lolled out of his mouth—his hand fell, and his breath rattled in his throat—I quit my hold, and he rolled from me senseless, black in the face, and apparently dead.

I trembled in every joint, shuddered for fear I was a murderer, and fell senseless at his side.

I revived—opposite was my antagonist, already recovered, and his comrades. He took me by the hand, and acknowledged himself beat. We spent the day together, and they were ready to worship me—to fight for me, for I had conquered their champion.— New England Galaxy

MILLING MATCH IN NEW JERSEY

When the climate in England turned against the sport of boxing in the 1820s and 1830s, English and Irish boxers emigrated to the United States to continue their careers. One of the most famous to do so was James "Deaf" Burke, who had killed a man in the ring in 1833, and who subsequently promoted the sport in America, especially among immigrants. The following article, reprinted from the 21 August 1837 edition of The New York Herald, gives a preview of one of the most important fights during the 1830s, although it mistakenly identified Burke's opponent as O'Conner instead of O'Connell. The fight, unlike most contests during the decade, was an orderly affair with Burke coming away with the victory.

GREAT MILLING MATCH AT ELIZABETH TOWN POINT

GREAT MILLING MATCH AT ELIZABETH TOWN POINT.-A great match of this description outstripping all "Greek, all Roman fame," comes off today, precisely at nine o'clock, between Deaf Burke and O'Conner, the two greatest men, of their age, at this day living in the United States.

Six weeks have been spent in the negotiations, before this great affair terminated satisfactorily to all parties. They fight for $2,000 aside. Deaf Burke is backed by Moccasin Jackson, of this city, and O'Conner by O'Flanagan and McLean, of Philadelphia.—The O'Conner party proposed, at first, a fight for $200—but Jackson, the friend of Burke, considered such an offer as little better than an insult to such a champion as he backed.

"I'll be d----d if I ever let Burke disgrace himself by fighting for such a paltry sum of $200. Nothing less than $2,000 will do for us."

In consequence of this determination, O'Conner had to scour the country in search of friends to increase the stakes. These friends he found in the civilized and refined city of Philadelphia.

For a week past, both champions have been in training, and on diet—roast beef and porter-brown bread—no drink—and plenty of exercise. In fact, they have both, for the present, joined a voluntary Temperance Society.

Yesterday Deaf Burke felt in fine trim, just about the time that the people were going into church. This morning, at six o'clock, each party starts for the scene—each in his own steamboat, engaged for the occasion. The price of tickets in those boats is $2 each passenger—and quite scarce at that. The boats start about the same time, from the North river, and expect to reach the Point below Elizabeth Town by 8 o'clock.

The place selected for the fight is a beautiful field, with a grove near by, at a short distance from the water. Sentries are to be placed around the field, and scouts at short distances, to give warning in case the barbarous officers of justice should seek to interfere with this most elegant and classic sport. The two steamboats will lay at anchor close by, to carry off the combatants in case of accident.

We trust none of the police of New Jersey will have the ignorance and barbarity to prevent those pretty chickens from giving each other a sensible milling. Deaf Burke says, "I'll punish O'Conner for insulting me." A great number of choice sporting characters are here from Philadelphia, Albany, Baltimore, to be present at the exhibition. It will be a great day.

The classic age of Greece is returning. The Olympic games will again set the world on fire—and in a short time it is highly probable that the common era will be abolished, and we shall date every thing from the "New Olympiads" of Elizabeth Town Point. Oh, what a glorious age we live in!

BOXING IN CANADA

Jim Phelan was a prominent American boxer during the 1830s, though he never approached the caliber of Deaf Burke. Like many of his contemporaries Phelan practiced a common trade—he was a grocer—and yet, unlike them, he moved beyond the localism that defined most boxing heroes and contests. During the decade he fought in many regions of the United States and, as the following account documents, in Canada as well. The article is reprinted from the 10 June 1837 issue of The Spirit of the Times.

THE CANADIAN SPORTING WORLD

My Dear Sir—Having at last a leisure moment, I hasten to scribble a line or two to you, in order to prevent your executing your abominable threat of publishing my first scrawl, even though "private," was written most legibly in its heading. You ask me to become a regular correspondent of the Spirit of the Times. I have myself no absolute objection now and then to assist in filling your columns; but how flat and unprofitable my communications would look when in *juxta position* with the interesting correspondence of "B," (who by the bye, writes much in style of NIMROD—don't you think so!) or "N." *cum multis aliis*, who weekly afford your readers a treat as well intellectual as amusing. *Eh bien*, it will be your own fault; however, by way of consolation, I beg to mention that I will always pay postage.

Montreal is, as usual, very dull, particularly in the sporting way, and now, owing to the commercial distress, nothing is to seen but merchants with long faces, duns with still longer phizzes, and lawyers with the longest and most rueful countenances of all. People are really so poor that they absolutely cannot afford even to sue!—awful times amongst the Mackintoshes!! By-the-way, we did have a summut in the sporting way, no less than a real ring fight—to the evil example of the King's lieges, and against the peace of our Lord the King, his crown and dignity. In order to give you some idea of this turn-up between the two gentlemen of the ring, I must mention that one of them, MR. JAMES PHELAN, arrived here about three weeks since, and instantly there appeared several huge placards announcing the arrival of the American pugilist, who had fought numerous battles and had come to Canada to train for a fight with JAMES REID. A few days after, a MR. JOHN BRITTON, from Liverpool, arrived, and in like manner posted up his bills, giving Phelan the *lie* relative to his pretended training for a fight with Reid, and offering to fight him for love or money. This highly gratifying proposal Phelan accepted, and preliminaries being arranged, they met at the Tanneries, about three miles from Montreal, when took place the memorable

FIGHT.

Britton who—*entre parentheses*—is a native of the Green Isle, arrived first on the ground, with Big Charley, (otherwise John Charles), the *big* drummer of the 32d Regt., a bit of a sparring character himself, as his second. Red was his color, and when he threw his castor into the ring he appeared to be pretty confident. Phelan tossed his cap with equal confidence, and was accompanied by Needham, also a pugilistic boy in the small way; he was togged up in green. On entering the ropes Phelan was to all intents and purposes the better man in appearance—his build was good, and I should say that he must have weighed at least two stone heavier than Britton.

First Round.—After much figuring, for I will not call it sparring, Britton succeeded in planting a left-hander on the side of Phelan's neck, which Phelan returned in his adversary's mouth—a close followed, when Britton threw his man, falling with him. First blood (from the mouth) was claimed by Phelan.

Second Round.—Time called; Britton was first up, and both went to work pretty cautiously, Phelan gave first, after a feint, a pretty good blow on his antagonist's neck—a second blow was well stopped by Britton, who returned his adversary's *coup* with interest; they fought to the ropes, and both went down, Britton under.

Third Round.—Britton up first again, and in this round had decidedly the advantage, on elbow on the side evidently sickening Phelan, who fell with him.

Fourth Round—Changed matters wonderfully for the worse for the Patlander, Phelan, though last up from his second's knee, seemed determined to do at once, and put in a tremendous hit on Britton's left temple, which gashed like a razor—here Britton attempted to counter another blow, and bending his head, received two blows on the back part of it, and went down, clinching Phelan however, and most foolishly, as he of course fell heavily on him.

Fifth, 6th, 7th, 8th and 9th Rounds were all alike in favor of Phelan, who had all his own way, and knew it, if one could judge from his manner and monkey gestures and tricks which he played off, as well as from the blows he put in.

Tenth Round.—Britton was here up first, as he was in every round, and at once went in gamely to his man, but his blows, well directed as they were, could not tell, as he was apparently too weak to put in a blow, and was well hit down by a neck blow.

Eleventh Round.—A mere wrestling match—both down—Phelan uppermost.

Twelfth Round.—Britton first up again, and Phelan exposing his face with a most disgusting grimace; Britton stuck him a blow, which had the poor devil been only in strength, would have stopped Master Phelan's mug for some time, as well as won the battle. Phelan here went well up, and struck his man down.

After this round Charley declared that Mr. Britton admitted Phelan was the better man, and Phelan throwing a somerset, which confined me in my previously formed opinion, that he had been brought up in a circus, was declared the winner, and ended his day by saying that he would fight Britton's second on the same ground—an empty boast, as Charley is a man of 43 years of age, and being a soldier could not fight him. Now, with regard to the combatants.—Britton should never enter a ring; he cannot spar, and has not the slightest judgment or science as to sparring. Had my old friend Fuller been present, I verily believe he would have jumped into the ring and thrashed them both out of it. Phelan is a well built, courageous little fellow, and with drilling may become a good boxer, but he must be more cautious; be dressed more tidily, and above all, leave off grimacing and playing antic tricks when he next fights; he hits well, and you might as well beat a barn door as his nob—he never moves a muscle when struck. On the whole it was a poor affair. Phelan can thrash two such men as Britton one after the other before dinner, and then masticate as well as ever. It was however a novelty to the Jean Baptistes, who had never seen the signs of a real set-too before, and to give you an idea of their thoughts on the subject, I was stopped by two in the street, whom I knew, and who thus accosted me—

"Mais, mon Dieu! Mr.   , est ce vrai que deux sacres Anglais veulent se battre aujourd hui pour vien?"

"Oui, et la bataille aura lieu apres midi."

"Yallez vous Jose?" Eh, mon Dieu, il faut y aller; on dit que les Anglais se battent comme des cocquedindes!"

Should Phelan fight with Dragon, a barber here, who I believe is anxious to have a set-to with him, we shall have a better fight than the last....

    I am, dear sir, yours,   A CANADIAN TURFMAN.

THE ART OF SELF-DEFENSE

Although the reputation of the sport of boxing suffered in Canada as well as in England and the United States, it still fascinated sporting enthusiasts in North America and continued to receive newspaper coverage. As the following account makes clear, boxing advocates from the upper classes disassociated themselves from the chaos and brutality of boxing by supporting the more respectable form of pugilism—sparring as the science of self-defense. The following document is an excerpt from an article that appeared in the 14 October 1837 edition of The Spirit of the Times.

SPARRING IN QUEBEC
FROM THE SPIRIT OF THE TIMES, 1837

By the way, while my hand is in, and being a bit in the sporting line, I may as well mention that during the Races the celebrated DEAF BURKE (who had lately reached us,) had a sparring exhibition in the ball-room of the Albion Hotel. There was a numerous and most respectable audience, and the dollars must have counted pretty well in to him. Unfortunately, however, for the expectations of his patrons, little of display was given, as all the Deaf'un's set-tos were with "yokels," or very common-place amateurs, picked up at random from among the spectators, and it was little else than a mere show-up of chicken fighting. He gave, at the conclusion, some representations of ancient statuary, and considering all that should be considered in his attempting a thing of the kind, acquitted himself not badly. Deaf'un, notwithstanding his muscular formation, is lacking the stature necessary to the perfect delineation of such masterpieces of art, being too much of a "King John's man" to very fitly personate an Ajax or an Achilles. Still, Burke, in his own particular department of the fist, gave very conclusive proof, even in his sparring flare-up, that he is a terrible opponent to encounter, and must be a h-ll of a customer to satisfy, to say the best of him.

I do not wish to be invidious in remark, yet while in the sparring room, and a silent looker on at matters as they were conducted, I could not help reverting, in contrast, to the fashion in which these things used to be done in "days of yore" by my worthy friend BILL FULLER, of your city, than whom a more gentlemanly man, in every acceptation of the term, never put glove on hand, or stood up more respectfully and respected in a ring made up of friends and gentlemen around him, either as spectators or pupils. But where do we now see the like of "gentleman Bill" in these times?—Alas! for the respectability of the Ring, where? Is it matter of wonder that the "science" should day after day be losing its votaries and patrons, when we look upon the low vulgarity and arrogant pretensions of so many of its professors? There are other exceptions to its well-doing besides these last mentioned; and the state of the Ring in England for the last ten or fifteen years speaks plainly of all the cause and effect in the history of pugilism, identified with an evident "fall and decline," which, by comparison with the spirit and honesty of other glorious days of the manly art, we need scarcely regret....

MORGAN RATTLER

Quebec (L.C.), Sept. 29, 1837

Chapter 7

EQUESTRIANISM

Horse racing was the most popular sport in North America from 1820 to 1840, thrilling spectators throughout the United States and Canada. The origins of this interest lay both in the immigrants' heritage and their style of life in the New World. Immigrants brought with them their deep interest in horses and horse breeding. They imported horses from Europe, primarily from England, during the formative periods of both America and Canada. Horses also played an integral role in the daily lives of most North Americans, both rural and urban. It is only natural that this familiarity led to competitive equestrian contests among the upper and middle classes. As a result, horse racing developed more quickly, though not always more evenly, than many other sports during this period.

Before 1821 horse racing had been prohibited in some northeastern states in America in order to safeguard public morality. As with many other sports during the antebellum era, most notably boxing, horse racing often attracted undesirables—gamblers, hustlers, and drinkers—to the track. Undoubtedly influenced by the legacy of their Puritan ancestors, opponents of horse racing contended that the prohibition of the sport would help to curb or prevent the growth of this social element.

Despite these prohibitory laws thoroughbred racing flourished in New England and the mid-Atlantic states as it did throughout the continent. In 1820 and during much of the next two decades the sport continued to be premodern, marked by informal rules and regulations, local competitions, and local or regional journalistic coverage. By the 1840s, however, much of this had changed as horse racing assumed a more modern character. The construction of race tracks, the standardization of rules, the dissemination of horse racing schedules and horse breeding information through sports journals and magazines, the publication of stud books, and intersectional and international matches all indicated the growing modernization of horse racing in North America. Many of the documents in this section including "Race Courses, Rules of Racing," "Permanent American Sweepstakes," and Suggestions of a Southern Sportsman," describe these developments.

Horse racing advocates legitimized their sport on utilitarian grounds. They argued that thoroughbred racing improved the breeding of horses and generated significant revenues for communities in which equestrian contests took place. There was much truth to these contentions. During the antebellum period the breeding of horses did indeed improve and became more specialized and expensive, driving horse prices upward. The breeding of horses in the United States, for example, developed on a national level, with the South gradually emerging as dominant. In addition, a number of intersectional contests in America during the 1820s and 1830s became truly national events, undoubtedly increasing spectator interest in horse racing. The Eclipse v. Henry showdown in 1823, an account of which appears in this chapter, inaugurated a series of such matches during which large amounts of money changed hands on and off the track.

Although thoroughbred racing created tremendous excitement among the populace and at the same time modernized itself from 1820 to 1840, it experienced serious growing pains and ultimately failed to sustain its popularity and success throughout the era. Much of the blame for the failures of the sport lay with those most closely associated with it. The unwillingness of the sport's patrons to provide sufficient financial backing and their failure to commercialize placed thoroughbred racing on shaky ground. The Panic of 1837 also played a crucial role in the declining fortunes of horse racing and breeding, particularly in the late 1830s. The consequences of these factors were poorly staged events, dilapidated courses and facilities, inflated stud fees and depressed horse prices, and low attendance. The inability of the patrons to cultivate an appeal that could attract a wide audience beyond the upper classes checked the growth of the sport during these years, though not its modernization. As "The New York Races" and "Communication" demonstrate, the racing community vigorously debated the causes of this decline and entertained countless ways to reverse it.

Like thoroughbred racing, trotting or harness racing was transformed from a premodern to a modern sport from 1820-1840. The construction of race tracks, such as the Centreville, Long Island course, and the formation of clubs such as the New York Trotting Club in 1825 initiated the modernization of the sport. Like other sports of the antebellum era, trotting gained popularity through its affordability, accessibility and participatory nature. Originally, harness racing became a way for urban dwellers to test their skill and mettle against each other along neighborhood city streets. The improvements in roads during the second quarter of the nineteenth century provided an important stimulus to trotting as a sport. Unlike thoroughbred racing, harness racing was conducted with relatively inexpensive common stock breeds, and, with the nearby location of the contests, participants could easily compete after the completion

of the workday and brag about their accomplishments in local saloons before returning home. In the pages that follow, "New York Trotting Club," "Hunting Park (Trotting Club) Association," and "The Trotting Turf in Boston" trace much of the historical
evolution of trotting.

Though trotting played second fiddle to thoroughbred racing for much of the period, it ironically eclipsed the popularity of its more respected rival in the U.S. by the
mid-nineteenth century. The urbanization and the economic expansion of the nation had
contributed to the growth of the sport but, more than anything else, the ability of harness racing to commercialize accounted for its remarkable success. Organizers of trotting made the sport at once affordable to the masses and financially solvent, though less
profitable than thoroughbred racing. They also achieved a broad-based appeal that
resulted in greater sustained success than thoroughbred racing enjoyed, the decline of
which after the 1837 Panic only enhanced the growth of trotting. To be sure, harness
racing suffered from the same allegations that plagued thoroughbred racing, such as
match fixing, and from the incapacity of the sport to police itself. Nonetheless, it provided its fans with several exciting contests that equalled the excitement generated by
many famous thoroughbred matches. In 1838, for example, the celebrated race between
Dutchman and Ratner resembled in mood and substance the historic contest between
Eclipse and Henry some years earlier.

THE FIRST GREAT SECTIONAL HORSE RACE

The revival of horse racing during the 1820s required the emergence of a great horse
to spark spectator interest and to capture the public's imagination. Eclipse became that
horse. After being put out to stud in 1820 by his owner, Cornelius Van Ranst, Eclipse
enjoyed a remarkable resurgence as a racer following the legalization of the horse racing in New York in 1821. For the next couple of years the best interests of Van Ranst
and those of horse racing dovetailed. The excitement generated by Eclipse through his
victories over southern rivals culminated in a contest in 1823 between Eclipse and Sir
Henry for the enormous sum of $20,000 per side. An account of this legendary race,
recorded several years after the event, is given below. It is reprinted from the September 1830 edition of the American Turf Register and Sporting Magazine.

THE GREAT MATCH RACE BETWEEN ECLIPSE AND SIR HENRY—
MINUTELY DESCRIBED BY AN OLD TURFMAN

[It might, at first view, be supposed that the subject of the following communication was already exhausted, but the reader will find in it many minute and interesting

particulars, and will probably agree that the space it occupies, has been well appropriated to the observations of a very critical observer; and the more so, as no race ever run in the United States has attracted as much notice, or had as much influence as that, in promoting attention to the breeding of horses and to the sports of the turf.]

MR. EDITOR: *New York, July 3, 1830.*
As I have never seen in print a full, correct, and impartial account of the following great race, and having, at the time, committed my observations to paper, I now transmit them. As many of your readers may not have witnessed this far-famed performance, to such this relation may be interesting; should you, therefore, deem it worth a place in your entertaining publication, you are at liberty to insert it.

Great match race between American Eclipse and Sir Henry, over the Union course, Long island, May 27th, 1823. Heats four miles, for $20,000. The southern gentlemen to be allowed to name their horse at the starting post.

Doubts were entertained, by some of the New York sportsmen, to the last moment, whether this great match would be contested by the Virginia gentlemen. They, it was perfectly understood, had left Virginia, with five horses, selected from the best racers which North Carolina and Virginia could boast of, and proceeded to the estate of Mr. Bela Badger, adjacent to Bristol, in Pennsylvania, distant from the Union course, about ninety miles, where, having a fine course upon which to exercise and try their horses, they had made a halt.

The horses selected for this great occasion, as also to contend for the three purse races to be run for, on the three days subsequent to the match, heats of four, three, and two miles; were Betsey Richards, five years old, her full brother, John Richards, four years; Sir Henry, four years; Flying Childers, five years, all by Sir Archy; and Washington, four years old, by Timoleon, a son of Sir Archy. With one of the three first named, it was the intention of Mr. William R. Johnston to run the match. Of these, at the time he left home, John Richards was his favorite; his next choice was Sir Henry, and thirdly, the mare; although some of the southern gentlemen (and amongst others Gen. Wynn,) gave their opinion in favour of running the mare, fearing lest Henry might get frightened by so large a crowd of people and swerve from the track.

Unfortunately for the Virginians, their favourite, John Richards, in a trial race, while at Mr. Badger's, met with an accident, by receiving a cut in the heel or frog of one of his fore feet, which rendered it necessary to throw him out of train; Washington also fell amiss, and he and Richards were left behind at Mr. Badger's. With the other three the southern sportsmen proceeded to the Union course, where they arrived five or six days previous to that fixed upon for the match.

The ill-fortune which befel the Virginians by laming their best horse in the onset, seemed to pursue them, for scarcely had they arrived at Long island, and become fixed in their now quarters, when Mr. Johnston, the principal on their part, upon whose management and attention their success in a great measure depended, was seized with indisposition, so sudden and violent, as to confine him not only to his room, but to his bed, which he was unable to leave on the day of the race. Thus the southrons, deprived of their leader, whose skill and judgment, whether in the way of stable preparation, or generalship in the field, could be supplied by none other, had to face their opponents under circumstances thus far disadvantageous and discouraging. Notwithstanding these unexpected and untoward events, they met the coming contest manfully, having full and unimpaired confidence in their two remaining horses, Sir Henry and Betsey Richards, and backed their opinion to the moment of starting.

At length the rising sun gave promise that the eventful day would prove fine and unclouded. I was in the field at the peep of dawn, and observed that the southern horse and mare (led by Harry Curtis in their walk,) were both plated, treated alike, and both in readiness for the approaching contest. It was yet unknown to the northern sportsmen which was to be their competitor.

The road from New York to the course, a distance of eight miles, was covered by horsemen, and a triple line of carriages, in an unbroken chain, from the dawn of day until one o'clock, the appointed hour of starting. The stands on the ground, for the reception of spectators, were crowded to excess at an early hour, and the club house, and balcony extending along its whole front, was filled by ladies; the whole track, or nearly so, for the mile distance in circuit, was lined on the inside by carriages and horsemen, and the throng of pedestrians surpassed all belief—*not less than sixty thousand spectators were computed to be in the field.*

About half past twelve o'clock Sir Henry made his appearance on the course, as the champion of the south, and was soon confronted by his antagonist.

I shall now endeavour to give a brief description of these noted racers.

Sir Henry is a dark sorrel, or chestnut colour, with one hind foot white, and a small star in the forehead; his mane and tail about two shades lighter than that of his body; he has been represented as being fifteen hands and one inch high, but having taken his measure, his exact height is only fourteen hands three and a half inches. His form is compact, bordering upon what is termed pony-built, with a good shoulder, fine clean head, and all those points which constitute a fine forehand; his barrel is strong, and well ribbed up towards the hip; waist rather short; chine bone strong, rising or arched a little over the loin, indicative of ability to carry weight; sway short; the loin full and strong; haunches strong, and well let down; hind quarters somewhat high, and sloping off from the coupling to the croup; thighs full and muscular, without being fleshy; hocks, or houghs, strong, wide, and pretty well let down; legs remarkably fine, with a full proportion of bone; back sinew, or achilles tendon, large, and well detached from the canon bone; stands firm, clear, and even, moves remarkably well, with his feet in line; possesses great action and muscular power, and although rather under size, the exquisite symmetry of his form indicates uncommon strength and hardihood. He was bred by Mr. Lemuel Long, near Halifax, in the state of North Carolina, and foaled on the 17th day of June, 1819. He was sired by Sir Archy, (son of imported chestnut Diomed,) his dam by Diomed, grandam by Belle-air, g.g. dam by Pilgram, g.g.g. dam by Valiant, g.g.g.g. dam by Janus, g.g.g.g.g. dam by Jolly Roger; which four last named are imported horses, and are to be found in the English Stud Book.

Eclipse is a dark sorrel horse, with a star, the near hind foot white, said to be fifteen hands three inches in height, but in fact measures, by the standard, only fifteen hands and two inches. He possesses great power and substance, being well spread and full made throughout his whole frame, his general mould being much heavier than what is commonly met with in the thorough bred blood horses; he is, however, right in the cardinal points, very deep in the girth, with a good length of waist; loin wide and strong; shoulder by no means fine, being somewhat thick and heavy, yet strong and deep; breast wide, and apparently too full, and too much spread for a horse of great speed; arms long, strong, and muscular; head by no means fine; neck somewhat defective, the junction with the head having an awkward appearance, and too fleshy, and bagging too much upon the under side, near the throttle; his fore legs, from the knee downwards, are short and strong, with a large share of bone and sinew; upon the whole his forehand is too heavy. To counterbalance this, his hind quarters are as near perfection as it is possible to imagine. From the hooks, or hip bone, to the extremity of the hind quarter, including the whole sweep from the hip to the hough, he has not an equal; with long and full muscular thighs, let down almost to the houghs, which are also particularly long, and well let down upon the canon bone; legs short, with large bone and strong tendon, well detached, upon which he stands clear and even. Although his form throughout denotes uncommon strength, yet to the extraordinary fine construction of his hind quarters, I conceive him indebted for his great racing powers, continuance, and ability, equal to any weight. I have closely observed him in his gallops; if he has a fault, it is that of falling a little too heavy on his fore feet, and dwelling a little too long on the ground; but then the style and regularity with which he brings up his haunches, and throws his gaskins forward, overbalance other defects.

He was sired by Duroc, a Virginia horse, bred by Wade Moseby, Esq. and got by imported chestnut Diomed, out of Amanda, by Grey Diomed, a son of old Medley. His (Eclipse's) dam was the noted grey mare Miller's Damsel, got by imported Messenger. His grandam an English mare, imported when three years old, in 1795, by William Constable, Esq. of New York, bred by Lord Grosvenor, and sired by Pot8o's, son of English Eclipse. His g.g. dam by Gimcrack, Gimcrack by Cripple, and Cripple by the Godolphin Arabian. He was bred by Gen. Nathaniel Coles, of Queens county, Long island, and foaled on the 25th of May, 1814.

All horses date their age from the 1st of May. Thus a horse foaled any time in the year 1819, would be considered four years old on the 1st of May, 1823. Consequently, Sir Henry, although not four years old complete until the 17th day of June, had, on the 27th of May, to carry the regulated weight (agreeably to the then rules of the course,) for a four year old, viz. 108 lbs. Eclipse, being nine years old, carried weight for an aged horse, 126 lbs.

At length the appointed hour arrived, the word was given to saddle, and immediately afterwards to mount. Eclipse was rode by William Crafts, dressed in a crimson jacket and cap, and Sir Henry by a Virginia boy, of the name of John Walden, dressed in a sky blue jacket, with cap of the same colour. The custom on the Union course is to run to the left about, or with the left hand next to the poles; Eclipse, by lot, had the left, or inside station at the start. Sir Henry took his ground about twenty-five feet wide of him, to the right, with the evident intention of making a run in a straight line for the lead. The preconcerted signal was a single tap of the drum. All was now breathless anxiety; the horses came up evenly; the eventful signal was heard, they went off handsomely together; Henry, apparently quickest, made play from the score, obtained the lead, and then took a hard pull. By the time they had gone the first quarter of a mile, which brought them round the first turn, to the commencement of what is termed the back side of the course, which is a straight run, comprising the second quarter of a mile, he was full three lengths ahead; this distance he with little variation maintained, running steadily, with a hard pull, during the first, second, third, and for about three fourths of the fourth round or mile, the pace, all this time, a killing one. It may be proper to note, that the course is nearly an oval, of one mile, with this small variation, that the back and front are straight lines of about a quarter of a mile each, connected at each extremity by semicircles of also a quarter of a mile each. When the horses were going the last round, being myself well mounted, I took my station at the commencement of the stretch or last quarter, where I expected a violent exertion would be made at this last straight run in, when they left the straight part on the back of the course, and entered upon the last turn. Henry was, as heretofore, not less than three lengths in the clear ahead. They had not proceeded more than twenty rods upon the first part of the sweep, when Eclipse made play, and the spur and whip were both applied freely; when they were at the extreme point or centre of the sweep, I observed the right hand of Crafts disengaged from his bridle, making free use of his whip; when they had swept about three fourths of the way round the turn, and had advanced within twenty-five rods of my station, I clearly saw that Crafts was making every exertion with both spur and whip to get Eclipse forward, and scored him sorely, both before and behind the girths; at this moment Eclipse threw his tail into the air, and flirted it up and down, after the manner of a tired horse, or one in distress and great pain; and John Buckley, the jockey, (and present trainer) who I kept stationed by my side, observed, "Eclipse is done." When they passed me about the commencement of the stretch, seventy to eighty rods from home, the space between them was about sixteen feet, or a full length and a half in the center. Here the rider of Henry, turned his head round, and took a view for an instant of his adversary; Walden used neither whip or spur, but maintained a hard and steady pull, under which his horse appeared accustomed to run. Craft continued to make free use of the whip; his right hand in so doing was necessarily disengaged from the bridle, his arm often raised high in air, his body thrown abroad, and his seat loose and unsteady; not having strength to hold and gather his horse with one hand, and at the same time keep his proper position; in order to acquire a greater purchase, he had thrown his body quite back to the cantle of the saddle, stuck his feet forward by way of bracing himself with the aid of the stirrups, and in this style, he was belaboring his horse, going in the last quarter. Buckley exclaimed, (and well he might) "Good G_d, look at Billy." From this place to the winning post, Eclipse gained but a few feet, Henry coming a head about a length in the clear. The shortest time of this heat, as returned by the judges on the stand, was 7 min. 37 1/2 sec. Many watches, and mine (which was held by a gentleman on the stand) among others, made it 7 min. 40 sec.; and this time the southern gentlemen reported—see Mr. Johnston's letter of the 28th of May, addressed to Mr. Crawford, editor of the Virginia Times.

I pushed immediately up to the winning post, in order to view the situation of the respective horses, after this very trying and severe heat; for it was in fact running the whole four miles. Sir Henry was less distressed than I expected to find him; Eclipse also bore it well, but of the two, he appeared the most jaded; the injudicious manner in which he had been rode, had certainly annoyed, and unnecessarily distressed him; the cause of his throwing out his tail, and flirting it up and down, as already observed, was now apparent; Craft in using his whip wildly, had struck him too far back, and had cut him not only upon his sheath, but had made a deep incision upon his testicles, and it was no doubt the violent pain occasioned thereby, that caused the noble animal to complain, and motion with his tail, indicative of the torture he suffered. The blood flowed profusely from one or both of these foul cuts, and trickling down the inside of his hind legs, appeared conspicuously upon the white hind foot, and gave a more doleful appearance to the discouraging scene of a lost heat.

The incapacity of Craft to manage Eclipse, (who required much urging, and at the same time to be pulled hard) was apparent to all; he being a slender made lad, in body weight about 100 lbs. only. A person interested in the event, seeing Buckley, who had rode the horse on a former occasion, with me, requested that I would keep him within call, and ready to ride in case of an emergency. It was, however, soon settled, and announced, that Mr. Purdy would ride him the second heat, upon which, long faces grew shorter, and northern hope revived.—Six to four was, nevertheless, offered on the southern horse, but no takers.

SECOND HEAT —The horses, after a lapse of 30 minutes, were called up for a second heat. I attentively viewed Eclipse while saddling, and was surprised to find that to appearance he had not only entirely recovered, but seemed full of mettle, lashing and reaching out with his hind feet, anxious and impatient to renew the contest. Mr. Purdy having mounted his favorite, was perfectly at home, and self-confident. The signal being again given, he went off rapidly from the start; Sir Henry being now entitled to the inside, took the track, and kept the lead, followed closely by Eclipse, whom Mr. Purdy at once brought to his work, knowing that game and stoutness was his play, and his only chance of success, that of driving his speedy adversary, up to the top of his rate, without giving him the least respite. Henry went steadily on, nearly at the top of his speed, keeping a gap open between himself and Eclipse, of about 20 feet without much variation, for about two miles and seven-eighths, or until towards the conclusion of the third mile they had arrived nearly opposite the four mile distance post. Here Purdy made his run, and when they had advanced forty rods further, which brought them to the end of the third mile, was close up, say nose and tail. They now entered upon the fourth and last mile, which commences with a turn or sweep the moment you leave the starting post. Here the crowd was immense; I was at this moment, on horseback, stationed down the stretch or straight run, a short distance below the winning post, in company with a friend, and Buckley the jockey, who kept close to me during the whole race. We pushed out into the centre, or open space of the ground, in order to obtain a more distinct view of the struggle, which we saw making for the lead; every thing depended upon this effort of Purdy; well he knew it; his case was a desperate one, and required a desperate attempt; it was to risk all, for all; he did not hesitate. When the horses had got about one third of the way round the sweep, they had so far cleared the crowd as to afford us a distinct view of them a little before they reached the centre of the turn; Eclipse had lapped Henry about head and girth, and appeared evidently in the act of passing. Here Buckley vociferated, see Eclipse! look at Purdy! by heaven on the inside! I was all attention. Purdy was on the left hand or inside of Henry, I felt alarmed for the consequence, satisfied that he had thus hazarded all; I feared that Walden would take advantage of his position, and by reining in, force him against or inside one of the poles; when they had proceeded a little more than half way round the sweep, the horses were a dead lap; when about three fourths round, Eclipse's quarter covered Henry's head and neck, and just as they had finished the bend, and were entering upon the straight run, which extends along the back part of the course, Eclipse for the 1st time was fairly clear, and a head. He now with the help of the persuaders, which were freely bestowed, kept up his run, and continued gradually, though slowly, to gain during the remaining three quarters of a mile, and came in about two lengths a head. As they passed up the stretch or last quarter of a mile, the shouting, clapping of the Eclipse party, exceeded all description; it seemed to roll along the track as the horses advanced, resembling the loud and reiterated shout of contending armies.

I have been thus particular in stating, that Mr. Purdy made his pass on the inside, understanding that many gentlemen, and particularly Mr. Stevens, the principal in the match on the part of Eclipse, (and for aught I know Mr. Purdy himself,) insist that the *go by*, was given on the outside. After the heat was over, I found that my friend Mr. M. Buckley, and myself, were far from the only persons, that had observed the mode in which Mr. Purdy ran up and took the inside track from his adversary. The circumstance was in the mouths of hundreds. In corroboration of which, I will quote a passage from the New York Evening Post, of May 28th, 1823, giving a description of this second heat:—"Henry took the lead as in the first heat, until about two-thirds around on the third mile, when Purdy seized with a quickness and dexterity peculiar to himself, the favorable moment that presented, when appearing to aim at the outside, he might gain the inside, made a dash at him accordingly, and passed him on the *left*."

Here, then, the observations of many, independent of my friend Mr. M. Buckley, or myself, added to the instantaneous and striking remark of B., which did not fail to rivet my peculiar attention, form a wonderful coincidence. Thus circumstanced, and long conversant with turf matters, rules, and practices, and familiar with sights of this kind, it was impossible I could be mistaken. I was not mistaken; the honest belief of some gentlemen to the contrary notwithstanding.

Time, this second heat, 7 minutes, 49 seconds.

THIRD HEAT —It was now given out, that in place of the boy Walden, who had rode Sir Henry the two preceding heats, that Arthur Taylor, a trainer of great experience, and long a rider, equalled by few, and surpassed by none, would ride him this last and decisive heat. At the expiration of 30 minutes the horses were once more summoned to the starting post, and Purdy and Taylor mounted; the word being given, they went off at a quick rate; Purdy now taking the lead, and pushing Eclipse from the score; and indeed, the whole four miles, applying the whip and spur incessantly; evidently resolved to give Sir Henry no respite, but to cause him if determined to trail, to employ all his speed and strength, without keeping any thing in reserve for the run in. Sir Henry continued to trail, apparently under a pull, never attempting to come up, until they had both fairly entered the straight run towards the termination of the last mile, and had advanced within about sixty rods from home. Here Sir Henry being about five yards behind, made a dash, and ran up to Eclipse, so far as to cover his quarter or haunch with his head, and for a moment had the appearance of going past; he made a severe struggle for about two hundred yards, when he again fell in the rear, and gave up the contest.

Thus terminated the most interesting race ever run in the United States. Besides the original stake of $20,000 each, it was judged that upwards of $200,000 changed hands.

In this last heat Sir Henry carried 110 lbs. being two pounds over his proper weight; it not being possible to bring Arthur Taylor to ride less, and although a small horse, and wanting twenty days of being four years old, he made the greatest run ever witnessed in America.

Time, this heat, 8 minutes, 24 seconds.

Thus the three heats, or twelve miles, were run in 23 minutes, 50 1/2 seconds, or an average of 7 minutes, 57 seconds each heat; or 1 minute, 59 seconds per mile.

Notwithstanding this defeat, the southern sportsmen continued to be inspired with so much confidence in their horse, that they offered to renew the contest for a much larger amount, as appears by the following challenge and the answer thereto, which I give as connected with the event.

TO JOHN C. STEVENS, Esq.   *Long island, May* 28, 1823.

Sir—I will run the horse Henry against the horse Eclipse at Washington city, next fall, the day before the jockey club purse is run for, for any sum from twenty to fifty thousand dollars; forfeit ten thousand dollars. The forfeit and stake to be deposited in the Branch bank of the United States at Washington, at any nameable time, to be appointed to you.

Although this is addressed to you individually, it is intended for all the betters on Eclipse, and if agreeable to you and them, you may have the liberty of substituting at the starting post, in the place of Eclipse, any horse, mare, or gelding, foaled and owned on the northern and eastern side of the North river; provided, I have the liberty of substituting in the place of Henry, at the starting post, any horse, mare, or gelding, foaled and owned on the south side of the Potomac. As we propose running at Washington city, the rules of that jockey club must govern of course.

    I am respectfully, yours,   WILLIAM R. JOHNSTON.

(ANSWER.)

Dear Sir—The bet just decided was made under circumstances of excitement, which might in some measure apologize for its rashness, but would scarcely justify it as an example; and I trust the part I took in it, will not be considered as a proof of my intention to become a patron of sporting on so extensive a scale. For myself, then, I must decline the offer. For the gentlemen who with me backed Eclipse, their confidence in his superiority, I may safely say, is not in the least impaired. But even they do not hesitate to believe, that old age and hard service may one day accomplish, what strength and fleetness, directed by consummate skill, has hitherto failed to accomplish.

For Mr. Van Ranst I answer, that he owes it to the association who have so confidently supported him, to the state at large, who have felt and expressed so much interest in his success, and to himself as a man, not totally divested of feeling, never, on any consideration, to risk the life or reputation of the noble animal, whose generous, and almost incredible exertions, have gained for the north so signal a victory, and for himself such well earned and never failing renown.

    I remain, sir, your most obedient servant,

Wm. R. Johnson, Esq.   JOHN C. STEVENS.

SOUTHERN HORSE BREEDING

During the 1820s, gentlemen in the North and the South formed horse breeding organizations. One of these earliest of these societies was the Maryland Association for the
Improvement of the Breed of Horses. The article presented below, reprinted from the
29 April 1825 edition of the American Farmer, attempted to justify the creation of the
association to a skeptical public.

THE MARYLAND ASSOCIATION FOR THE IMPROVEMENT
OF THE BREED OF HORSES

At a meeting of the above named association, held in the city of Baltimore, on the
30th ultimo, it was, on motion of J. S. Skinner, resolved to offer the purses of the association exclusively for horses owned *bona fide* within the state of Maryland; and
President T. Tenant, the hon. John Barney, and J. S. Skinner, were appointed to publish an exposition of the original views of the association, and of the particular considerations under which the above resolution was adopted—in virtue of which
appointment the following views were presented to and approved at a meeting of the
association, on Wednesday, the 27th inst.

—

This society was formed in the year 1823, by many amongst the most public spirited citizens of the state, and the liberality with which it was supported, no less than
the zeal with which it was commenced, promised the most valuable results. Though
these results have been to a certain extent frustrated, or retarded, by some false steps
in the outset, they have not been altogether *defeated*. A number of very promising colts,
as your committee have reason to think, are now coming forward under the influence
of this association; nor have they, from all they can learn, any reason to fear but that,
under its auspices, a general melioration will yet be effected in the stock of that noble
animal, with vast profit to the state at large, and to the great comfort and pleasure of
all those whose pleasures and comforts are connected with his use.

The clear gain that would accrue to Maryland from such improvement as may easily
be made in her stock of horses, would forcibly strike and command the attention of her
landholders, if there were any means of computing and showing to them, the vast
amount of which the state is now annually drained to pay for horses brought from other
states, and which ought, without any additional expense, to go into their own pockets.
A serious, and perhaps yet greater loss, is that which accrues from breeding and using animals of unsightly figure, of...constitution—and of action, both for saddle and
harness, heavy and graceless in itself, as it is uneasy and mortifying to the rider. A true
estimate of the mere aggregate *waste of time*, in a community whose pursuits and
movements are so much associated with, and dependent on the powers of the *horse*,
when the breed in use is cold-blooded and slothful, would excite the surprise and
awaken the anxiety of those who forget not the saying of the wise Franklin, that *time
is money*. Your committee are of opinion, that whether the horse be destined to meet
the shock and mingle in the fray of battle, or whether

"——— in the chase, with emulation fir'd,
He strains to lead the field, top the barr'd gate,
O'er the deep ditch exulting bound, and brush
The thorny-twining hedge,"

for these and all other purposes, his certain improvement and his highest capacities are only to be secured by having recourse to the blood of the thorough bred race horse of Arabian descent. Neither foot nor wind can be relied on but as derivable from that high origin.

The blood horse, says one of the best judges in this country, is originally from a hot climate and arid soil, and where the base-born suffocates with heat, and faints with fatigue, his wind and strength are untouched. His "long slouching walk," says the same accomplished writer and experienced sportsman, "tells on the road and in the plough, especially on a hot sultry summer's day."

With benefits so obvious and valuable, resulting from adherence to the purest stocks, the only thing wanting by the breeders of Maryland horses, was the unerring and indispensable test of a well managed *race course*, to put the genuine stamp on those of highest qualities and greatest power. The great object, therefore, in the view of the Maryland Association was, not so much to stimulate by mere force of *mercenary impulse*, as to open a course for the trial of speed and bottom, under the management of gentlemen whose character would guarantee that these *trials* should be conducted by the strictest rules of honour and propriety, and that every man of unfair repute should be excluded, and every thing of demoralizing tendency banished from the scene of competition. In short, the Canton course is intended to afford a *standard* to measure the powers of the most promising colts which may be reared in this state, and to give to their skilful and enterprising breeders the means of establishing the characters of such as have powers to *excel*. By this means, and by this only, can the least worthy of the race be ascertained, and condemned to the odium of celibacy and hard labour, while the more highly gifted are reserved for the conflicts and triumphs of the turf, and as their last and highest reward, ultimately turned loose to enjoy the pleasures of propagating their like, and the honour of transmiting their names and memories to succeeding ages. To use an illustration familiar to farmers, the standard erected on the turf is as necessary to cleanse, and purify, and perpetuate the breed of fine horses, as is the sieve to winnow and separate the chaff and other offal from sound grain.

The *faux pas* committed by this association, as experience has demonstrated, was in offering at the *onset* their purses to competitors from other states, where the finest horses, the art of training, and the sports of the turf, inseparable from each other, have been sedulously preserved. These horses, preceded by the fame of their wonderful performances, have come from abroad and walked over our course, and borne off rewards which should only be the meed of the highest mettle and the greatest achievement. The breeders of horses in Maryland, comparatively unprepared and inexperienced, have not ventured to enter the lists where certain discomfiture awaited them; and hence the public disappointment in the beneficial...from the measures of this association. Notwithstanding this discouragement, however, your committee are gratified to learn, as before stated, that there are now coming on many thorough bred colts of high promise, which will be ready to take the field and do credit to their owners, under the suitable encouragement and the equal chance of success secured to them by the resolution which restricts the purses to horses *bona fide* owned by citizens of the state of Maryland and the district of Columbia north of the Potomac.

When the sportsmen of Maryland shall have replenished their studs of fine horses, they will be prompt to fling open the gates and challenge competitors from every quarter in the gallant and manly exercises of the course. Finally, your committee solicit with confidence the support of the citizens, and particularly the agriculturists of the state to the further efforts of this association, in the full confidence that it may yet be made to yield all the real profit, and to answer all the valuable purposes for which it was originally designed.

IMPROVEMENT OF THE BREED

During the 1820s and 1830s sportsmen sought to legitimize horse racing by arguing that the sport contributed to the improvement of the breed in the United States and Canada. The following document, reprinted from the 15 February 1828 issue of The American Farmer, presents some guidelines for choosing a race horse.

THE BLOODED HORSE

Most respectfully inscribed to the Amateur, Breeder, Sportman and Trainer of the American Race-Horse.

How to choose a race-horse by his external appearance , and to be a judge of his symmetry by angular demonstration:

Rules

1st. Draw a base line from the stifle joint along the bottom of the chest to the extreme point of the elbow, and to the shoulder blade joint.

2dly. Draw a line from the curb or hock by the hip joint above the back, to an imaginary point.

3dly. Draw another line from the point of the shoulder, ranging with the shoulder and passing above the back, until it intersects the line at the imaginary point.

4thly. Draw a line from the intersecting point of the shoulders, giving the same declension until it intersects the base line.

5thly. From the stifle to the point of the buttock, thence to the hip joint, thence declining to the stifle.

6thly. Draw a line from the hip to the base line, right angular declension, then to the shoulder up to the crest.

7thly. Then draw a straight line, regardless of the curve of the back, to a straight line intersected at the shoulder at the beginning of the crest.

8thly. Then take a line from the point of the shoulder, and angular degree, ranging with the shoulder blade to the top of the breed.

9thly. Then, regardless of the rising of the crest, draw a straight line from the top of the shoulder-blade to intersect with the point of the former line.

Thus, the real symmetry of a grand and beautiful horse, possessed with muscular powers and strength, is formed by a right angled triangle—and the farther from it a race-horse's form is, the less pretensions that horse has to beauty, speed, bottom or lastingness, ability to carry weight, or activity.

A thick upright shoulder, is a very certain mark of a stumbler, and is fit for no use whatever but the slow draught.

A low coupling in the back, is a true mark of weakness; it denotes want of strength, lastingness, ability to carry weight, or speed.

A low loin is a certain mark of weakness, and a weakly and washy constitution.

But a rising loin, of ability to carry weight, speed, activity and lastingness, and a good constitution, symmetry, beauty, and muscular strength.

A race horse's legs cannot be too short.

A great declivity, and thin shoulder, denotes speed.

A narrow breast, weakness.

A horse's breast bone, formed like that of the rabbit, denotes also speed, and is the best form for a race-horse.

A short, broad back, denotes strength; a broad stifle, well let down to the curb or hock, denotes bottom or lastingness, strength and activity.

There are not two race-horses in five hundred, properly formed in the knees; which should be small, divested of superfluous appendages, and strong; they denote activity and strength.

A lax, bending pastern, denotes also speed; a long horse is preferable to a short one, because he can cover a great deal of ground, and can bear pressing better and longer.

The race-horse, upon the whole, whose form in general, is composed of the essential properties of the following, animals, viz. the rabbit, greyhound, and ostrich—is the best.

December 6, 1827.   Gorwood.

RACING IN UPSTATE NEW YORK

The reason for the prohibition of horse racing in many of the states in the northeastern US during the early nineteenth century was that such contests often attracted disreputable societal elements. After the lifting of the prohibition in New York in 1821, those involved in the sport were particularly concerned about demonstrating the benefits of horse racing and the orderly way in which equestrian contests could be conducted if left in the hands of the respectable members of society. The following account, reprinted from the 28 November 1828 edition of The American Farmer, reveals these concerns by the sporting community in upstate New York.

DUTCHESS COUNTY RACES

We are indebted to a friend, who was an eye witness of the different performances of speed at the races at Poughkeepsie last week, for the following particulars. His lively description is worthy a Pierce Egan.

Dutchess County Races—The races over the Dutchess Course terminated on Thursday last, without an accident or occurrence of any kind to mar the pleasures of the thousands who assembled to witness, and were advocates for these periodical and regulated trials of speed, or to excite a felling of disappointment or regret in those who were solicitous to remove the prejudices of such as held racing incompatible with good morals or good order. The first exhibition on the Dutchess Course has gone far to prove the error of the one opinion and the entire fallacy of the other. Their extensive buildings were filled with people of the first standing and respectability from different parts of the state, and the stand appropriated to the ladies crowded with the beauty and fashion of the counties of Dutchess and Columbia. The weather was delightful. The course, one of the most beautiful in the Union, and the strict order and decorum preserved on it, added to the satisfaction of the numbers who witnessed this first attempt in Dutchess to prove the justice and utility of the law, which gives to the farmer (what it is hard to deprive him of) the right as well as the opportunity of trying the speed of his colt, without risking his morals or his limbs. Jeanette, Betsy Ransom, and Rob Roy, were entered for the first day's purse, $500, four miles and repeat. There was but little betting on this race, and little sport expected. Rob Roy was untried for four miles, and Jeanette was known to be lame—Betsy Ramsom was therefore the favorite at three and four to one. The heat was contended for by Betsy Ransom and Jeanette, and contrary (as it often happens) to the general expectation, Jeanette passed her in the last half mile, and won the heat by two or three lengths, and with apparent ease in 7 minutes 53 seconds—Rob Roy just saving his distance. This changed the face of affairs, and even bets were offered by those who argued, that as her leg had stood one trial it might stand another. The second heat proved the fallacy of this hope. Jeanette broke down and came in dead lame, Rob Roy was distanced, and the heat, together with the money, was awarded to the grey mare.

Immediately after the purse race, the ladies' cup, richly chased, and valued at $100, was contended for by Lady Jackson (an Eclipse filly,) Fox and Sportsman, two horses celebrated for their speed—one mile and repeat. It was won by Lady Jackson in two heats—the first in 1 m. 50 s., the second in 1 m. 52 s., and presented to the rider, in the name of the ladies, by Mrs. Livingston.

Splendid, Sir Lovel and Lady Flirt, were enterd for the second day, purse $300, three miles and repeat. This was won in fine time by Flirt in two heats—the first in 5 m. 53 s. the second in 5m. 54 1/2 s. It was a beautiful and well contested race. Splendid passed Flirt in the commencement of the third mile of the second heat, but was unable to maintain his ground; the Lady asserted her right to precedence, and in spite of the strenuous efforts of Splendid and Sir Lovel, regained the lead, and gradually increased the distance between her Ladyship and them, as if afraid of trusting herself longer within the reach of such ungallant competitors. As soon as this race was over, another purse of $50 was given, and run for by Fox, Sportsman, &c. This was won by Fox in two heats—the first in 1 m. 51 s. the second in 1 m. 52 s. Sportsman was very restive, and lost two or three lengths each heat in the start. This day's race was followed by a Ball, numerously and brilliantly attended by much of the beauty and fashion of Dutchess and Columbia counties, got up in good style by the members of the Jockey Club. The room was handsomely decorated by the ladies, and the music and supper such as did credit to the legitimates, Bennett and Samuel, to whom those important departments were confided.

On the third day, purse $200, two mile heats—Trouble, Lady Jackson, Sir Lovel and Hopeless were entered. This was the most interesting race of the three days. Lady Jackson won the first heat in 3 m. 54 1/2 s. beating Hopeless half a length, and was the favourite at three and four to one. Trouble but just saved his distance in this heat, and was supposed (from the shortness of his training and stride,) to be totally unable to cope with so fleet a one as her Ladyship had proved herself to be. But here again they were mistaken; he lengthened his stride and won the 2d heat under a hard pull, in 3 m. 53 s. Hopeless was withdrawn, and the case of the other two evidently as desperate, as the event of the next heat proved. Trouble beat them with ease in 3 m. 54 1/2 s., adding (to the satisfaction of his old friends,) another laurel to his own and his trainers' brows.

The last, though not the least amusing, of the races took place immediately after, for another purse of $50, one mile and repeat. Sportsman, Roman, a colt from Dutchess county, and Dandy Jack contended for it. The first heat was won by Roman in 1 m. 52 s.; the second was a dead heat between Sportsman and Roman; the third heat was won by Sportsman, distancing the Dutchess county colt.—Roman was withdrawn, and it was now 100 to nothing, Sportsman against Dandy, who had contrived, by hook or by crook, to save his distance in each previous heat. They started, and had not gone far before Sportsman bolted, and lost 150 to 200 yards before he could be brought to the track again. Dandy went on his way rejoicing, thinking, no doubt, the gap too wide to be made up; but, alas, poor Dandy (like many of his tribe,) was a rum one to look at and a bad one to go; he was overtaken and beaten almost in the arms of victory. This contest finished the third day, and ended a display as rational as honourable, (when directed by honourable men,) and as useful as most others; at least this is the opinion of a friend to the course and its legitmate objects—amusement, and the improvement of the breed of horse.

NEW YORK TROTTING CLUB

The formation of the New York Trotting Club was an important step in the modernization of harness racing. The following article, reprinted from the 20 May 1825 issue of The New York Evening Post, contains the address justifying the sport's existence by the Club's president on the occasion of its inaugural races.

ADDRESS BY THE PRESIDENT OF THE NEW YORK TROTTING CLUB

New York Trotting Club—The first day's purse was won in handsome style, on Wednesday, by Mr. Clintock's horse *Screws*, beating five others, all under the saddle—2 miles and repeat—decided in two heats. First heat, 5m 57s; second do. 5m 58s. On awarding the plate and purse to the owner of the winning horse, the following address was delivered by the president:-

"Gentlemen—Members of the New York Trotting Club—

"We are convened this day under the most favorable auspices. The infantile state of our company, reduced us to fear for its advancement, and led to the adoption of the most vigorous efforts. All associations, in some part of their history, have been more or less prosperous. In their commencement, the most flattering hopes are entertained of their growth, and even difficulties are overlooked, by reason of the spirit and zeal which characterize their founders. These difficulties, therefore, are usually met with a power proportioned to their number and greatness.

"The association, which I have had the honor of presiding over, has been marked by features the most prominent and expectations the most promising. The number, as well as respectability, of those who compose it, tended to produce these effects, and bid fair to raise it to a conspicuous rank among similar associations of the country. We are further encouraged in the indulgence of this prospect, by the good feelings existing among us, which are concentrated in one and the same end—the welfare and success of our combination. Under the influence of these best of means, (inclination and zeal in acting,) little danger need by apprehended of our success;—oppositions may arise, but they will be as evanecsent as the passing cloud; they arise only to be surmounted.

"In tracing the origin of this association and in considering the motives which induced us to the formation of it, many thoughts suggest themselves, which I shall mention on the present occasion. This association was formed in the course of the last winter, and was soon composed of an adequate number to answer the necessary purpose. An opportunity, however, was given to those who desired to be associated with us, which resulted in the addition of several more to our number. So many advantages have presented themselves since the organization of our association, that those who at first doubted the practicability of effecting this, and were consequently scrupulous about joining us, have subsequently been induced to consider their first impression as weak and superficial, and have overcome the prejudices which formerly swayed them.

"In considering the motives which influenced us in the formation of the association, we need but revert to the utility of the animal whose appearance and speed place him above all other animals. Next to man, the horse is the noblest animal.—The symetry of his features, the just proportions of every part, and, withal, his gay and stately gait, are points which endow him with beauty, nobleness, and strength. Such being the value, a question naturally presents itself: What are the most effectual means of promoting the speed of this animal—so useful to the merchant, the man of pleasure, the agriculturist, and in fact to all mankind? An association has been formed in this city, for a number of years, whose object was to improve the breed of horses, by holding up certain premiums, and awarding them to the owner of the fastest running horse that entered. The success and advantages, which have evidently attended their association, have emboldened us to form one, on a similar plan, for improving the horses of our country in trotting. Hence our association has received the name of the "New York Trotting Club." We have ample means for carrying our plan into execution. All that is required is a determination on our part to do every thing of this nature, every thing depends upon unanimity in action: when discord and prejudice arise, the axe will soon be laid at the root of our Club: let it, therefore, be our especial care to avoid whatever may be prejudicial to the Club, and allow nothing to be paramount to its welfare. "Mr. Clintock,

"Sir,—I have the honor of presenting you the first premium that has been awarded by the New-York Trotting Club. The superiority of your horse, over those with which he contended, establishes his fame on the turf, and clearly indicates the influence of care and proper management in training him. What renders this premium honorable to you, and still more flattering to our Club, is the well contested struggle among so many acknowledged fast horses, and the consequent merit attached to the successful horse.

"It is this emulation which encourages us in our efforts, which fills us with new and promising hopes, which leads us to anticipate the most beneficial consequences from our association. And proud will this association be on subsequent occasions of a similar display of competition and of a like opportunity of rewarding it."

The above association meet every spring and fall. Their trotting course is in a field a little distance off the Jamaica turnpike road, about one mile above the Union race course. Three days in the month of May, and three in September are appointed for trials of speed in trotting. Six horses entered for the first day's premium and yesterday four contended for the purse, in harness, viz—Jersey, entered by White Howard; Hookey-Walker, by M. Clintock; Hercules, by __; Charley, by Mr. Snedeker. Jersey bore off the purse in handsome style—2-mile heats,—1st, 6m 2s; 2d, 6m 5s. Tomorrow concludes the trials for this spring.

EARLY TROTTING

During the 1820s trotting attempted to gain respectability among the public by allaying its concerns over the sport's association with gambling and by rationalizing the need for the sport on the same utilitarian grounds used to lend credibility to thoroughbred racing—the improvement of the breed. The following rules, reprinted from the American Turf Register and Sporting Magazine, October 1829, reveals these aspects of the early growth of trotting.

HUNTING PARK (TROTTING CLUB) ASSOCIATION—PHILADELPHIA

The meeting for the formation of this association was held at the Indian Queen tavern, South 4th street, 8th February, 1828. The object of the association was such as ought to induce similar ones at all the country towns. They would promote a fondness for fine horses, would increase their number, and greatly *augment the value of the capital*, which must always exist in the article of horses. The purpose of the association is clearly explained in the first article, as follows:

ARTICLE 1. For the encouragement of the breed of fine horses, especially that most valuable one known as the *trotter*, whose extraordinary powers cannot be developed, or properly estimated, without trials of speed and bottom, and, in order to prevent those vicious practices which often occur on the *course*, where it is not subject to the government and direction of an association, empowered and resolved to maintain good order—the subscribers agree to associate under the name and title of the *Hunting Park Association*.

It would occupy too much space to copy all the rules, and moreover they are like all others for similar objects—the same offices, duties, &c; we shall only therefore extract some parts which may serve as a sort of guide for other clubs, reserving the printed copy of the rules at length, for the use of any who may desire them.

The government of the association is vested in a president, two vice presidents, a secretary, treasurer and seven managers—to be elected annually.

No new member to be admitted without consent of two-thrids of the board of managers.

Annual subscription ten dollars.

Each rider to be neatly dressed in a fancy silk jacket, jockey cap and boots—and all horses to carry weight according to age, as follows:

An aged horse,	- - 150 pounds.
Six years old,	- - 143
Five years old,	- - 136
Four years old,	- - 129
Three years old,	- - 122

Mares, fillies and geldings allowed three pounds.

Intervals of thirty minutes between heats of four miles—twenty between heats of three miles, and fifteen between every other heat.

All combinations and partnership between horses prohibited, and their owner never again allowed to enter a horse. A horse must win two clear heats, unless he distance all others at one heat—but if three horses win each a heat, then no other horse to start against them.

The *distance* on four mile heats fixed at 320 yards.

On three mile heats at	- 240
On two mile heats at	- 160
On one mile heats at	- 80

ART. 26. All trials for speed shall be under the saddle, unless directed otherwise, by a majority of the members of this association, or two-thirds of the officers belonging to the same; but the first day's and largest purse shall, in all cases, be contended for

under the saddle. When trotting in harness is permitted and authorised, the officers of the association shall give notice of the same, and prescribe the rules, at least one month, before the purse is trotted for.

RULES WITH REGARD TO BETTING.

1. All bets are understood to relate to the purse, if nothing is said to the contrary.
2. Where two horses are bet against each other for the purse, if each win a heat and neither are distanced, they are equal; if neither win a heat, and neither are distanced, they are equal; but, if one win a heat, and the other does not, the winner of the heat is best, unless he shall be distanced; in which case the other,if he saved his distance, shall be considered best; and, when both are distanced, they shall in all cases be deemed equal.
3. When a bet is made upon a heat, the horse that comes first to the ending post shall be considered best; provided no circumstance shall cause him to be deemed distanced.
4. A bet made upon a purse or heat is void, if the horse betted on does not start.
5. All bets made *to play or pay*, except between those who are the bona fide owners of the horses bet on, shall be deemed void, if the contest should not take place.

SOUTHERN RACING ASSOCIATIONS

Thoroughbred racing in Baltimore, as in other cities, was heavily patronized and controlled by the wealthy classes, despite attracting a wide public following. The city served as the headquarters for the influential sporting journal, the American Turf Register and Sporting Magazine. The following document, reprinted from the September 1830 issue of that magazine, demonstrates the concern by horse racing enthusiasts over fair competition and gambling during the early development of the sports of the turf.

MARYLAND JOCKEY CLUB

Rules and orders approved and adopted as the rules and orders of the "MARYLAND JOCKEY CLUB," *to commence and be in force from the third day of June, 1830, and to continue in force until the close of the full meeting in the year 1834, subject to such alterations as may be made from time to time, according to the provisions therein contained.*

1. There shall be two meetings of this Club in each year, and each continue four days, to be called the Spring and Fall meetings. The Spring meeting shall commence on the last Tuesday in May, and the Fall meeting shall commence on the last Tuesday in October.

2. There shall be a President, two Vice-Presidents, a Corresponding Secretary, a Recording Secretary, a Treasurer, and five Stewards, to be appointed by ballot.

3. It shall be the duty of the President to preside in all meetings of the Club, to act as Judge on each day's race, report the result of each day's race, and stand as Judge in all sweepstakes, with such other persons as the parties may appoint.

4. It shall be the duty of the first and second Vice-Presidents to attend all the meetings of the Club, assist the President in the discharge of his duty. In the absence of the President, and in his absence the Second Vice-President, shall act as President *pro tem.*

5. It shall be the duty of the Recording Secretary to attend the Judges in each day's race, assist them with his counsel, keep a book, in which he shall record the members' names, the rules of the Club, and add to them any resolutions which may change the character of either; also, record the proceedings of each meeting, the entries of horses, in which shall be set forth the names of the respective owners, the colour, name, age, and name of sire and dam of each horse, and a description of the rider's dress, and an account of each day's race, including the time of running each heat, and after the races are over, publish the result in the next number of the "AMERICAN TURF REGISTER AND SPORTING MAGAZINE."

6. The Stewards shall serve for one meeting, next succeeding their appointment. They shall wear a white rose, or some other appropriate and distinctive badge. It shall be their duty to attend on the course, preserve order, clear the track, keep off the crowd from horses coming to the stand after the close of a heat. They may employ able-bodied men to assist them, who shall be paid out of any money in the hands of the Treasurer, and they shall be designated.

7. There shall be three Judges in the starting stand, the President and two assistant Judges, and the Timers; the Judges shall keep the stand clear of any intrusion during the pendency of a heat, and also see that the riders are dressed in jockey style.

8. There shall be two distance Judges, and three patrol Judges, who shall repair to the Judge's stand, after each heat, and report the nags that are distanced, and foul riding, if there be any.

9. All disputes shall be decided by the Judges of the day, from whose decision there shall be no appeal, unless at the Judges' discretion, and no evidence shall be received of foul riding, except from the Judges and Patroles.

10. All sweepstakes advertised to be run over the course on any day of the regular meetings of this Club, shall be under the cognizance of this Club, and no change of entries once made, shall be allowed, after closing, unless by the consent of all the parties.

11. The distance stand shall be sixty yards from the Judges' stand for mile heats, and sixty additional yards for every mile in a heat, unless it be the best three in five, when ninety yards to a mile shall be the distance.

12. The time between heats shall be twenty minutes for mile heats, thirty for two mile heats; forty for three mile heats; and forty-five for four mile heats. Some signal shall be sounded from the Judges' stand five minutes before the period of starting, after the lapse of which time the Judges shall give the word, as, "are you ready;" but should any horse be restive in saddling, the Judges may delay the word a short interval, at their own discretion.

13. No person shall start a horse for any purse under the control of this Club, other than a member, he being at least one-third bonafide interested, and producing satisfactory proof of his horse's age, nor shall any member start a horse, if his entrance and subscription be not paid before starting.

14. Any person desirous of becoming a member only for the purpose of starting a horse, may do so, he being approved by the Club, and paying double entrance.

15. All entries of horses to run shall be made in open Club, and in his own hand, on the evening preceding each day's race, by five o'clock, or during the sitting of the Club; and the owner, or person then present, shall give his name, colour, age, and sex, and name of sire and dam of the horse, with the dress of the rider, and no entry made after that time shall be allowed. Provided, if there be no meeting of the Club, then with the Secretary, or Treasurer, by six o'clock.

16. No two riders from the same stable shall be allowed to ride in the same race; nor shall two horses trained in the same stable be allowed to start in the same race.

17. Riders shall not be permitted to race unless well dressed in jockey style; to wit, jockey cap, silk jacket, pantaloons, and half boots.

18. Riders, after a heat is ended, must repair to the Judges' stand; and not dismount till ordered by the Judges, and then with their saddles repair to the scales to be weighed.

19. The horse who has won a heat will be entitled to the track, and the foremost entitled to any part of the track, he leaving sufficient space for a horse to pass him on the outside; but he shall not, when locked by a horse, leave the track he may be running in, to press him to the outside, doing which will be deemed foul riding. A rider may take the track on the inside, but he must do it at his own peril, as should he be poled in making the attempt, it will not be considered foul. Should any rider cross, jostle, or strike an adversary, or his horse, or run on his heels, intentionally, or do any thing else that may impede the progress of his adversary, he will be deemed distanced, though he may come out ahead, and the purse be given to the next best nag, and any rider offending against this rule, shall never be permitted to ride over, or attend any horse on this course again.

20. If any nag shall run on the inside of any poll, they will be deemed distanced, although they may come out ahead, and the purse be awarded to the next best nag; unless he turns round and again enters the course at the point from which he swerved.

21. A nag that does not win a heat out of three, shall be entitled to start for a fourth, although he may have saved his distance.

22. No compromise, or agreement, between any two persons starting horses, or their agents, or grooms, not to oppose each other, upon a promised division of the purse, shall be permitted, or allowed; and no persons shall run their nags in conjunction, that is, with a determination to oppose, jointly, any other horse, or horses, which they may run against. In either case, upon satisfactory evidence produced before the Judges, the purse shall be awarded to the next best nag, and the persons so offending shall never again be permitted to start a horse on this course.

23. All members and their families shall pass the gate free; and all who are not members shall pay the following tolls, viz: For every four wheel carriage, one hundred cents; for every gig, cart, or two wheel carriage, and every man on horseback, seventy-five cents; for every person on foot, twenty-five cents.

24. The age of horses shall be reckoned by the year in which they are foaled; viz:—a horse foaled in the year 1830, shall be considered a yearling during the year 1831, and shall be considered a two year old during the year 1832, and so on.

25. The following weights shall be carried; viz: Two years old, a feather; three years old, 86 lbs.; four years old, 100 lbs.; five years old, 110 lbs.; six years old, 118 lbs.; seven years old, and upwards, 124 lbs.—An allowance of three pounds to mares and geldings. The Judges shall see that each rider has his proper weight before he starts, and that they have within two pounds after each heat.

26. New members can be admitted only upon nomination; there being not less seven members present, always including the President, or one of the Vice-Presidents of the Club; and two black balls will exclude the person nominated.

27. Seven members shall constitute a quorum for business.

28. In betting, when both parties are present, either party has a right to demand that the money be staked before the horses start, and if one refuse, the other may declare the bet void, at his option.

29. If either party be absent on the day of the race, the party present may declare the bet void, in the presence of the Judges, before the race commences; but if any person present offers to stake for the absence for the absentee it is a confirmed bet.

30. A bet made on a heat to come, is no bet, unless all the horses starting in a previous heat start again.

31. A bet made during a heat is not determined until the race is finally decided, unless the heat be particularly mentioned.

32. If an entered horse die, or a subscriber entering him die, no forfeit shall be required.

33. A premium given to another to make a bet, shall not be refunded, although the bet is not run for.

34. All bets made between horses that are distanced the same heat, are considered drawn; and when between two horses, throughout a race, and neither of them wins it, the horse that is best at the termination of the race wins the bet.

35. When a dead heat be run, they may all start again, except the dead heat be between two horses, that if either had been winner, the race would have been over; in which case, they two only shall start again, to decide which shall be entitled to the purse. Such horses as are prevented by this rule from starting again, shall be drawn, and not distanced.

36. When two horses are bet against each other, for the purse, if each win a heat, and neither distanced, they are equal. But, if one win a heat, and the other do not, the winner of the heat is best, unless he afterwards be distanced, in which case, the other, if he shall save his distance, shall be considered best; and both are distanced, they shall be considered equal.

37. Judges may postpone a race, but only in case of rain, or bad weather. No fresh entry of horses will be permitted.

38. No gambling shall be permitted on the grounds under the control of the Club; and a committee shall be designated by the President, for the time being, with authority to employ police officers to aid them, to arrest and bring to punishment, all persons attempting to violate this rule.

39. For the transaction of the ordinary business of the Club, seven members shall be deemed a quorum. But no alteration shall be made in any of the established rules and orders of the Club, except in an open session of a number of members, not less than fifteen.

40. A meeting of the Club may at any time be called by the President, or one of the Vice-Presidents, at the instance of any three members; the notice of said meeting to be given by the Recording Secretary.

41. Gentlemen, residing twenty miles beyond the limits of the city of Baltimore, may be admitted; in the usual way, as members, on paying ten dollars per annum, subscription; except such as may enter horses, who shall pay the full subscription.

The members present proceeded, in conformity with the above rules and orders, to the election of officers of the Club for the ensuing year, and the following persons were unanimously chosen:

Gen. T.M. FORMAN, President.
HENRY THOMPSON, First Vice-President.
S.W. SMITH, Second Vice-President.
B.I. COHEN, Treasurer.
JOHN THOMAS, Recording Secretary.
J.S. SKINNER, Corresponding Secretary.
C.S.W. DORSEY,
J.G. DAVIES,
U.S. HEATH,   Stewards.
W.HINDMAN,
J.D. DONNEL,
JOHN GLENN,
JOHN RIDGELY,   Timers.
LYDE GOODWIN,

[The 16th and 19th rules will be revised, at the suggestion of distant members. We have the prospect of a superb course, and, in other respects, the promise of the most spirited racing in the union.]

UNION COURSE RULES

During the late 1820s horse racing in New York experienced a decline because of the financial insolvency of the New York Association for the Improvement of the Breed, the overall poor condition of the Union Race Track and facilities, and a police force inadequate to the demands placed upon it. These factors combined to prevent New Yorkers from offering substantial purses and from attracting the best horses from around the nation, particularly from the South. As a result, those involved in the sport believed that the best way to provide for the prosperity and growth of the turf was by establishing uniform weights, course lengths, and racing codes. The following document, the rules of the Union Course, is reprinted from the February 1832 edition of the American Turf Register and Sporting Magazine.

RACE COURSES, RULES OF RACING, &c. &c.

[Within the last two years public attention has been turned to the value of the racing stock of horses in our country, and to the best means of keeping it pure and of
improving what we have of it. It is now generally admitted, that for almost every purpose a large proportion of the pure blood is attended with striking advantages—for the
saddle, especially, and for every kind of harness, not excepting the wagon and the
plough. Whilst the pure blood gives more speed every where; it ensures in hot climates
and weather much greater power of endurance. But if it were not for race courses and
the prizes and honours they confer, the pure blood would soon be lost. Indiscriminate
crosses would lead to infinite confusion, and depreciation speedily ensue. Such has
been the effect in Maryland. Where are now to be found any of the valuable stock
which abounded in this state in the day of the Formans, the Ogles, the Ridgelys, the
Spriggs, the Duckets, the Bowies, the Wrights, the Ringolds, the Duvalls, &c. &c. &c?
Scarcely a remnant is to be found, and every remnant is of *precious value*, if its *purity can be established*.

The public appears to be aware of these facts, and accordingly racing is reviving
and new race courses are being established throughout the country.

In many places the subject is new, and those engaged in forming associations are
unacquainted with the rules for their government....we submit the following, which
were prepared by an experienced hand, for the Union Course, at Long Island. Untoward circumstances have, we believe, prevented the reorganization of that Club, and
we submit the rules, which were already in type, for the consideration of those who
may be forming new Clubs, so far as they may be adapted to this particular circumstances. We must take this occasion to add the suggestion, that if it be important to have
all race courses of uniform length, so is it to have UNIFORM WEIGHTS. To establish, as far as possible, an uniform RACING CODE, let each Club give authority to
some one of its members, to meet next spring on the Central Course, there to unite in
a convention for drawing up and promulgating a set of rules, &c. best calculated to
insure honourable management and prosperity to the American turf.]

SECTION 1. That the Proprietor of the course, or other person duly appointed as
Clerk of the course, shall keep a match book, day book, or record of racing transactions or decisions, and book of bettings, at the club house, (so called) on the race
ground, open to the inspection of the subscribers or members of the club, (in case there
should be one;) receive the stakes, collect the entrance money, and be responsible for
all money thus received or collected.

2. That an account of all horses to run each day, for any purse, plate, subscription
or stake, shall be noted in the day book: and all rules or orders, made from time to time,
shall be registered therein, as also all daily occurrences of note.

3. That all matches, subscriptions or sweepstakes, to be run at any future meeting,
or during a present meeting, shall, as soon as made or entered into, be specifically
reported to the keeper of the match book, by one of the parties interested, and thereupon it shall be the duty of the keeper of the match book to enter and register the same;
setting forth the names of the respective parties, the age, description of pedigree, of
each horse, gelding, mare or filly, the amount of each stake or subscription, the amount
of the forfeit, and the conditions fully.

4. That where any match, subscription or sweepstake, is made or entered into, at any period prior to the day on which the same is to be run, each stake or subscription shall be paid to the keeper of the match book, or other person appointed to receive the same, by 6 o'clock in the afternoon of the day previous to such race, who shall immediately mark the payments to the credit of the name or names of the person or persons thus paying; unless the parties, by mutual consent, signify to the keeper of the match book their assent to dispense with making stakes.

But where a match, subscription or sweepstake, happens to be made or entered into on the same day on which it is to be run, the same shall forthwith be reported to the keeper of the match book in such manner and specific form as will enable him to make a full and correct entry thereof; and the respective stakes or subscriptions shall forthwith be paid or deposited, and entered accordingly, unless the parties agree, as aforesaid, to dispense with making stakes.

5. All stakes shall be made in cash or current bank bills, and in no other shape, without the consent of the party or parties concerned, or on whose account such stakes are to be made. And in default thereof, and in default of making good any respective stake, at the time and in the manner set forth in this and the preceding section, the person making default shall forfeit in like manner as if he had not produced his colt, filly, horse, mare or gelding to start; and shall have no claim to the stake or stakes, even though his colt, filly, horse, mare or gelding, should have started and come first. And this to remain as an established rule, unless such person has previously obtained the consent of the party, or of all the parties respectively, with whom he is engaged, to dispense with his making his stake, as aforesaid.

N.B. This rule does not extend to bets, which are to be paid and received as if no such omission had happened.

6. That all forfeits unpaid before starting for any match, subscription or sweepstake, shall be paid to the keeper of the match book, or such other person appointed to receive them, and the same by him duly noted, before 7 o'clock in the evening of the day such forfeits are determined. And that no persons shall be allowed to start any horse, mare or gelding, for any purse, plate, match, subscription or sweepstake, unless he shall have paid all former stakes and forfeits to the keeper of the match book by 7 o'clock of the evening prior to the day of starting.

7. That one meeting at least shall be held in October, and the like in May; that each meeting continue three days, and be held on Tuesday, Wednesday and Thursday; and that the regular purses or prizes, as well as all matches, not exceeding $1000 each stake, subscriptions or sweepstakes, not exceeding $500 each, be run for on those days, unless the consent of the Proprietor of the course be first obtained to the contrary, or unless it should be deemed expedient to postpone the race of any day on account of bad weather.

8. That it shall be the duty of the keeper of the match book to make a list of all matches, subscriptions or sweepstakes, to be run for during each meeting; together with a copy of all stakes to be made, and the day and hour of showing, staking and entering, which shall be fixed up on the Monday immediately previous to the first day of each meeting, in the club room, at the race course, and in the Judges' stand at the starting post, and continue there each day of the meeting, as notice for staking, showing and entering, and no other shall be insisted upon.

9. That the keeper of the match book shall, at 5 o'clock of Monday evening of the week in which each meeting is to be held, and at 5 o'clock each evening during the meeting, read aloud in the club room a list of all the purses, plates, matches, subscriptions or sweepstakes, entered on the match book, or day book, to be run the day following, together with that of the horses entered to run for the same; and the owner of each horse entered to run for any purse, plate, match, subscription or sweepstake, contained in the list, shall then declare whether his horse is intended to run or not, which declaration shall be deemed obligatory, if in the affirmative, unless the horse be taken ill or matched; and if in the negative, his name shall be erased from the list. And after the book of entries for the day is closed, no horse shall be allowed to enter for any purse, plate or prize, upon payment of double entrance money.

10. That the first time any horse, mare, colt, filly or gelding, shall enter for any purse, plate, prize, match, subscription or sweepstake, upon this course, he or she shall show at the club house, or other place appointed as the place of entry; and then and there pass an examination as to age, by the managers or stewards, for that purpose, between the hours of 4 and 5 o'clock of the afternoon of the day previous to that on which he or she is intended to run, at which examination the owner shall deliver a certificate of the age, marks and pedigree, as fully as can be obtained, which shall be duly registered; excepting such horse, mare, colt, filly or gelding, is matched to run on the day of entrance, so as to interfere with the time of entering, in which case he or she shall show and pass an examination, and produce the certificate, within one hour after the engagement is over; and in default of so doing, shall be subject to all the forfeiture which would have incurred for not having brought due weight to the scale, unless an aged horse or have carried weight as such.

11. That the Proprietor of the course, or keeper of the match book or day book, shall fix the hour each day on which any purse, plate, match, subscription or sweepstake, shall be run for.

12. That the ground cannot be engaged for trials more than two days during any one week, and then only for one hour during each day, by the proprietor of any stable of running horses, who must make application to the Proprietor, or Clerk of the course, for the use of the ground for that purpose, who will grant it if not previously engaged. And whenever the ground is thus engaged for a trial, intimation thereof being given by affixing a notice on the gates of the course, or other appropriate places, all owners of horses, grooms, trainers, feeders, stable boys, and all other persons whatever, must withdraw from the ground and the neighbourhood thereof, and in default or neglect of so doing, be subject to the censure and penalties set forth hereafter in the 13th and 14th sections.

13. That any member, or subscriber, who may be discovered watching a private trial, or procuring any person to watch the same, after an application had been made for the use of the ground, and due notice thereof given, as specified in the 12th preceding section, who, upon complaint thereof being made to the Clerk of the course, stewards or managers, and upon an investigation had by them, or by a committee named for that purpose, shall be convicted thereof, shall have his name erased from the list of members or subscribers, and never again be admitted; and no horse in which he shall thereafter be directly or indirectly interested, or owner of, in whole or in part, or concerned in as trainer, or otherwise, be permitted to start for any purse, prize or plate,

or to enter into any match, subscription or sweepstake, to be run over this course. And any person, not a member or subscriber, who, it may be shown to the satisfaction of the Clerk of the course, or the stewards or managers, has been guilty of watching any trial, or procuring any person to watch the same, as aforesaid, subsequent to the adoption of these rules and regulations, shall be debarred of ever becoming a member of this association, or a subscriber to this course.

14. That in case any gentlemen who keeps running horses has cause to complain of any trainer, feeder, rider, groom boy, or other person employed by him, or entrusted with the knowledge of trials, of having discovered them, directly or indirectly, by betting, or wilfully, in any other way, (unless allowed so to do by his employer or master;) or if any person, as aforesaid, living with any gentlemen, shall be discovered in watching any trial himself, or procuring any other person so to do, or by any unfair means whatever, endeavouring to discover any trial or trials, on such complaint being carried to the Clerk of the course, or to any one of the stewards or managers, he is to summon a meeting of not less than six members or subscribers, or gentlemen conversant with turf matters, as soon as convenient, who shall appoint a committee of three to examine into the accusation; and in case they shall be of opinion that the person, or persons, is, or are guilty of it, then the person, or persons, so found guilty, shall be dismissed from the service of his or their employer or master, and shall not be employed by any member of the Jockey Club, or any subscriber to this course, in any capacity whatever. Nor shall any horse, &c. fed or rode by him or them, or in the care or management of which he is, or they are concerned, be suffered to start for purse, plate, match, subscription or sweepstake; and the names of such persons as are found guilty shall be entered on the day book, and made known, by being inserted in a paper for that purpose, to be fixed up in the club room.

15. Whereas, the seducing a trainer, groom or rider, from his employment, or enticing him, or inducing him to leave his employer, more especially during the time of training, may be attended with evil and serious consequences to any gentlemen keeping running horses, any may be the means of deranging his establishment so far even as to prevent his bringing his horses in proper order to the starting post, therefore, it is ordered, that if any member or subscriber, or any trainer, groom or rider, or other person whatever, seduce or entice, any trainer, feeder, groom, rider or stable boy, in the employment of any gentlemen keeping running horses, or before the said trainer, feeder, groom, rider or stable boy, has been duly discharged by his said employer, he shall be deemed guilty of unfair and improper conduct, and shall be subject to be complained of to the Clerk of the course, or to the stewards or managers, in like manner as set forth in the 13th and 14th preceding sections, which complaint shall in like manner be investigated, and if convicted thereof, he or they shall be subject to the like penalties and privations, as set forth in said 13th and 14th sections.

16. That no gentlemen, or his groom or trainer, shall try the horse of any other person, except that of his declared confederate, with any horse of his own, or in his possession; or shall borrow or hire any horse, &c. not belonging to his avowed confederate, to run in any private trial, without giving notice of such trial, before it shall be run, to the Clerk of the course or keeper of the day book, setting forth a description of the horse or horses, or their pedigrees, with the names of their owners, and cause the same to be entered on the day book, or other book kept for that purpose; and

no persons to be deemed confederates who have not declared themselves, by causing their names to be registered as such, by the Clerk of the course, or keeper of the day book.

17. That the course and exercise ground be divided by an actual line of demarkation, so as to afford two distinct tracks. That the part next to the poles or railing be the *race track*, and the other the *exercise ground*. That the race track be kept solely and exclusively for *races* and *actual trials*; the latter to take place only after regular application made to the Clerk of the course, or Proprietor, and permission obtained, according to the rule prescribed in the 12th section. And any member, groom, trainer, or other person, running any race or trial thereon, or exercising any horse thereon, or causing him to be exercised thereon, without permission thus first obtained, shall forfeit and pay, to the Clerk of the course, $20 for each horse, and for each and every offence; and in the event of refusing to pay said forfeit, shall be precluded from ever thereafter bringing any horse on the ground, and no horse in which he is in any way interested, either as owner, trainer, groom or rider, be allowed to exercise or race thereon, until such fine be paid.

18. In the event of a Jockey Club being formed, they shall meet annually at the club house, on the race ground, at 12 o'clock, A.M. on the Monday of the week of the first spring meeting, for the purpose of transacting business, and that they dine together on that day. That three members of the Club be then appointed stewards, or managers, for the ensuing year, to commence their office on the day following. One new steward to be appointed every year on the Monday of the week of the first spring meeting, by the steward who quits on that day, subject to the approbation of the members of the Jockey Club then present. The first and second vacancy of the three stewards first appointed, to be settled by drawing lots, and ever afterwards the senior steward is to quit his office on the Monday of the week of the first spring meeting annually.

19. That all disputes, relative to racing, shall for the future be determined by the three stewards or managers, or by the Clerk of the course and two referees nominated by him, and two referees to be chosen by the parties concerned. If there should be only two stewards present, they are to fix upon a third person, in lieu of the absent steward.

20. Any person conceiving himself aggrieved by any decision of the Clerk of the course, or of the stewards, may appeal to a general meeting of the Jockey Club, (in the event of one sitting,) who, it shall be the duty of the Clerk of the course, or the stewards, or any one of them to convene, upon being requested by the party considering himself so aggrieved; and they shall proceed forthwith to hear and decide upon the matter in appeal. That at least thirteen members be present, a majority of whose votes shall govern. And in case no jockey club exist, then the Proprietor, or Clerk of the course, shall summon six subscribers, or gentlemen or respectability, to hear and decide the appeal.

21. That the members of the Jockey Club shall be elected by ballot, which ballot shall take place at the club room on any day in any meeting. That each candidate be proposed by a member and seconded by a member, and the names put up in the club room and entered on the day book at least one day preceding the ballot, as notice thereof. That nine members at least be present at the ballot, and that two black balls exclude.

22. That each member, or subscriber, subscribe for three years. That the yearly subscription be twenty dollars, payable in equal semi-annual enstalments, on or before the Monday of the week of the first spring and first fall meetings, to the Clerk of the course, or such person as may be appointed to receive the same; and that, in consideration thereof, they shall be allowed to pass the gates of the course, with saddle horse, or carriage, and introduce the ladies and children, which compose their respective families, free of further charge, and have admission to the stand and that part of the course within the picket and draw gates.

23. That in the event of a Club being formed, the Clerk of the course and the stewards produce their accounts annually on the Monday of the first spring meeting, and be accountable to the Club for all the money which may have been received by them in right of the Club.

24. That no person, a resident of the states of New York or New Jersey, who is not a subscriber prior to the meeting then held, shall be allowed to run any trial upon the race track, or make use of the exercise ground, or run for any purse or plate, at said meeting, without first producing a certificate of permission from the stewards, or Clerk of the course, and paying to the Clerk of the course double entrance fees and half a year's subscription.

25. No member or subscriber shall enter the horse of any other person who is not a subscriber; nor any horse of which he is not the owner of, in whole or in part, and of which he has not been the owner of, in whole or in part, for the four months then last past, unless he has trained the said horse, and enters and runs him for his own account.

26. Any person residing beyond the limits of the state of New York or New Jersey, although neither a member of subscriber, may join in any match, subscription or sweepstake, or enter a horse to run for any purse or plate, upon payment of the usual entrance money, and upon obtaining permission from the stewards, or Clerk of the course: Provided, such horse is not owned by an inhabitant of the states of New York or New Jersey, not a member or subscriber, or by some person heretofore excluded from this course.

27. That no persons except subscribers, or such as have tickets of admission, shall be permitted to occupy the stand reserved for subscribers; nor shall any other be permitted to go within that part of the track enclosed by the picket fence and draw gates, except the grooms or trainers, or owners of the horses, actually engaged in the race then going on. And no groom shall be allowed to introduce more than four assistants.

General Rules concerning Horse Racing.

The Clerk of the course, or other competent person, expressly appointed, ought in all cases to start the horses and place them as they come in.

  320 rods are a mile.
    40 rods are a distance when running heats of four miles.
    30 rods are a distance when running heats of three miles.
    20 rods when running heats of two miles.
    10 rods when running heats of one mile.
    15 rods when running heats of one mile, the best three out of five.

4 inches are a hand.

14 lbs. are a stone.

1. Catch weights are, each party to appoint any person to ride without weighing.

2. Give-and-take plates are, fourteen hands to carry a started weight; all above or under to carry extra, or be allowed the proportion of 7 lbs. for an inch.

3. A whip plate is weight for age and weight for inches.

4. A post match is to insert the age of the horse in the articles, and to run any horse of that age, without declaring what horse till you come to the post to start.

5. A handicap match is for A. B. and C. to put an equal sum into a hat. C. is the handicapper—makes a match for A. and B. who, when they have perused it, put their hands into their pockets, and draw them out closed; then they open them together, and if both have money in their hands, the match is confirmed; if neither have money it is no match. In both cases the handicapper draws all the money out of the hat; but if one has money in his hand and the other none, then it is no match, and he that has money in his hand is entitled to the deposit in the hat.

6. The horse that has his head at the ending post first wins the heat.

7. Riders must ride their horses to the weighing post to weigh, and he that dismounts before, or wants weight, is distanced.

8. If a rider fall from his horse, and the horse be rode in by a person that is of sufficient weight, he will take place the same as if it had not happened: Provided, he go back to the place where the rider fell.

9. Horse plates or shoes not allowed in the weight. Horses not entitled to start without producing a proper certificate of their age, if required, at the time appointed in the articles, except where aged horses are included; and in that case, a junior horse may enter without a certificate: Provided, he carry the same weight as the ages.

10. All bets are for the best of the plate, if nothing is said to the contrary.

11. For the best of the plate, where there are three heats run, the horse is second that wins one.

12. For the best of the heats, the horse is second that beats the other twice out of three times, though he does not win a heat.

13. A confirmed bet cannot be off without mutual consent.

14. Either of the betters may demand stakes to be made, and, on refusal, declare the bet void.

15. If a party be absent on the day of running, a public declaration of the bet may be made on the course, and a demand whether any person will make stakes for the absent party. If no person consent to it, the bet may be declared void.

16. Bets agreed to pay or receive in town, or at any other particular place, cannot be declared off on the course.

17. If a match be made for a particular day in any meeting, and the parties agree to change the day, all bets must stand; but if run in a different meeting, the bets made before the alteration are void.

18. The person who lays the odds has a right to choose his horse or the field.

19. When a person has chosen his horse, the field is what starts against him; but there is no field without one starts with him.

20 and 21. If odds are laid without mentioning the horse before it is over, it must be determined as the bets were at the time of making it.

22. Bets made in running are not determined till the plate is won, if that heat is not mentioned at the time of betting.

23. When a plate is won by two heats, the preference of the horses is determined by the places they are in the second heat.

24. Horses running on the wrong side of the post, and not turning back, distanced.

25. Horses drawn before the plate is won, are distanced.

26. Horses distanced, if their riders cross or strike, or use any other foul play, or take the track before he is clear of the other horse, and the next best horse declared winner; and such jockey shall never again be permitted to ride for any purse or plate upon this course.

27. A bet made after the heat is over, if the horse betted on does not start, it is no bet.

28. When three horses have each won a heat, they only must start for a fourth, and the preference between them will be determined by it, there being before no difference between them.

29. No distance in a fourth heat.

30. Bets determined, though the horse does not start, when the words "absolutely", "run or play", are made use of in bettings, viz: "I bet that Mr. A's horse Sampson 'absolutely' wins the king's plate at Newmarket, next meeting;" the bet is lost though he does not start, and won though he goes over the course himself.

31. In running of heats, if it cannot be decided which is first, the heat goes for nothing, and they may all start again, except it be in the last heat, and then it must be between the two horses, that if either had won the race would have been over; but if between two, that the race might have been determined, then it is no heat, and the others may all start again.

32. Horses that forfeit are the beaten horses, where it is "run or pay."

33. Bets made on horses winning any number of plates that year, remain in force until the first day of May.

34. Money given to have a bet laid, not returned if not run.

35. To propose a bet, and say "done" first to it, the person that replies "done" first to it, makes it a confirmed bet.

36. Matches and bets are void on the decrease of either party, before they are determined.

37. No horse shall carry more than five pounds over his stipulated weight without the judges being informed of it.

38. No two or more horses, trained or owned by the same person, either solely or in partnership, shall be permitted to start for the same purse when heats are run.

39. Every horse must be ready to start precisely at the time mentioned in the advertisement of the race, and shall be allowed thirty minutes between every heat, and in weighing shall be allowed one pound for wastage.

40. No combination or partnership in running will be permitted. If, therefore, any horse shall win a purse, and it shall appear to the satisfaction of the judges, before the purse is paid, that such horse did run in partnership with any other horse, the purse shall go to the *fair* winner; and the owner (and rider, if found accessary) of such horse shall thenceforward not be permitted to start a horse on this course.

41. Horses shall take their ages from May-day; that is, a horse foaled any time in the year 1830 will be deemed a year old on the 1st of May, 1831.

The following weights are to be carried over the Union course.

An aged horse,	126 lbs.
Six years old,	121 lbs.
Five years old,	114 lbs.
Four years old,	108 lbs.
Three years old,	90 lbs.
Mares, fillies and geldings, allowed	3 lbs.

The weights carried on the Central Course are:—

Two years old,	a feather.
Three years old,	86 lbs.
Four years old,	100 lbs.
Five years old,	110 lbs.
Six years old,	118 lbs.
Seven years old, and upwards,	124 lbs.

An allowance of 3 lbs. to mares and geldings.

THE MODERNIZATION OF HORSE RACING

During the early to mid-1830s the proliferation of jockey clubs, improvements in breeding, and the construction of race courses reflected the increasing popularity of horse racing. But soon those involved in the sport demanded uniformity of rules—a necessary development in the modernization of the sport. In the following article, reprinted from the May 1834 issue of the American Turf Register and Sporting Magazine, one enthusiast proposes the calling of a national convention for this very purpose.

SPORTING INTELLIGENCE

A CONVENTION PROPOSED—*to establish uniformity of rules appertaining to betting, weights, distance, &c. &c. to be held at the Central Course next autumn.*

MR. EDITOR:

If we may judge from the number of new clubs forming, and the rapid increase in value of thoroughbred stock, it may be presumed that racing, as an amusement with some, and as a profession with others, is claiming an attention, almost as marked and spirited as that which distinguished the old dominion, between the years 1750 and 1790, ere the effects of the Revolutionary war put a stop for a while to the "Virginia Passion."

Under such promising and agreeable auspices, I would suggest to you the propriety of making an effort to put, if possible, the sports of the turf throughout the United States, upon a better footing. I mean that some regular system or set of rules appertaining to weights, betting, &c. should be adopted by a convention, for the government of all clubs throughout the Union, instead of each particular club being left, as now, to its own guidance. The time has arrived, when every horse, whether he run at the north, south, east or west, should be subjected to the same tests; which, we know, is not the case now. At present, the same weights are not carried perhaps, in any two of the states; nay further, *perhaps not at any two places of meeting in the same state.* The courses are not of the same length; many of them of different forms, with various distance posts, some fixed at sixty yards in each mile; others nearer.

Now, as long as this state of things continues, as long as there is not an uniform standard of weights—the only true test of speed and bottom,—I would ask, how are any calculations to be made? How are persons to ascertain any thing approaching to accuracy, with regard to particular horses they may be interested in? How are they to judge of the relative powers of any two horses in the country?—How are they to decide between them, if a selection of a stallion or a mare for a breeder is to be made? Must it be inferred, when a four year old in Kentucky, or any where else where light weights are carried, runs a *four mile heat* in 7m. 58s. *but carrying only 94 lbs.* (which I believe is the rule in Kentucky,) must it be inferred, I say, that he is a very superior nag; or on the other hand, are we to presume, that, as *he did no more than this* with such a light weight, if he had started in some other state where heavier weights are put up, he might not have been any where in the race; as for instance, if this four year old had run in Charleston, South Carolina, he would have been compelled to carry 102 lbs. eight pounds more than he did in Kentucky, equal to several seconds in four miles; which, supposing he did his best in Kentucky, would bring his time in the heat to something a little worse than "*common time*:" a poor business! I mean nothing offensive, but merely use this as one argument, among a hundred I could adduce, in favor of an immediate adoption of a more equal and proper order of things.

But with these few hints let me proceed to the object of this communication, which is to recommend, that *a convention composed of three delegates from all the clubs already organized in the United States,* be holden at Baltimore, at the next fall meeting of the "*Maryland Jockey Club.*" I mention Baltimore because it is a central spot, convenient alike to the Northern and Southern sportsmen. All clubs desirous of being represented, should assemble as early as convenient, and appoint their delegates. The precise time of the Baltimore fall races should be ascertained and announced in your Magazine, so as to give persons at a distance notice, that they may regulate their movements accordingly. I would also recommend that such clubs as may hold meetings, and will in all probability be represented, should from time to time, inform you of the same: and that all secretaries be enjoined to give you such information for publication. It may act as a stimulus to many that may otherwise be lukewarm and indifferent, and perhaps induce such, from the force of good example, "to go and do likewise." I feel no doubt that a full and general attendance will be effected if you interest yourself in this matter. It is unnecessary, therefore, for me to enlarge upon the subject, or to dwell upon the interest, the proceedings of a convention held for the purposes I have stated, would have for breeders, trainers, and indeed for every one impressed with a due sense of the importance of giving value to the racehorse. The advantages to result from a uniformity of weights, and the discussion and arrangement of many *"another matter"* of importance to the welfare of the turf, that would *ex necessitate rei* be settled, are too apparent to need comment: suffice it for the present to say, that such a convention will assuredly be the means, in a few years, of infusing a right spirit within us—of placing the sports of the turf upon a liberal and equitable basis—inducing fair and honorable competition, and restoring that golden age "when races were established at almost every town and considerable place; when the inhabitants almost to a man were devoted to this fascinating and rational amusement; when all ranks and denominations were fond of horses, especially those of the race breed; when gentlemen of fortune expended large sums of their stud, sparing no pains or trouble in importing the best stock, and improving the breed by judicious crossing."

[The proposition so well explained and enforced in the preceding communication, will not fail we apprehend, to meet with general approval. At a meeting of the Maryland Jockey Club, on the 25th of October, some of the most liberal and judicious sportsmen of New York and Virginia being present, a resolution was adopted for such a convention at Washington, but from various causes, the proposition was not carried into execution. We hope to hear from the secretaries of all the clubs, that the plan of our correspondent has been sanctioned, and to be favored with the names of the delegated appointed.]

UNIFORM RULES

By the 1830s many sportsmen advocated the standardization of rules and regulations as one way to guarantee fair competition and to give some legitimacy to horse racing records. Horse racing had become a national phenomenon with interstate and regional matches occurring as a regular feature of most racing calendars. Without uniform rules these types of contests and the records that they generated had little comparative value for horse owners. The following document, reprinted from the 14 May 1836 issue of The Spirit of the Times, demonstrates the increasing desire among horse racing enthusiasts for a uniform method to determine the age of a horse.

SUGGESTIONS OF A SOUTHERN SPORTSMAN

Wm. T. Porter, Esq.   *Plaquemine, LA., April* 16,1836
Dear Sir—You have asked for information as to the rule of calculating the age of horses in the Southern Country. Presuming that the Secretaries of the different Jockey Clubs, can furnish the most certain information upon the subject, I, as one of them, answer this inquiry.

At the organization of the Plaquemine Jockey Club, the rule adopted (rule 30) was, that the age of the horses should be reckoned by the year in which they were foaled— i.e. a horse foaled in 1835, shall be considered a yearling during the year 1836—a two year old during the 1837—and so on. It having been ascertained, however, that all the other Clubs of the State had a different rule, and that under it, horses took their age from the first of May, it became necessary to conform our scale to their's in order to put our track upon an equal footing.

This subject, Sir, is one of great importance; the first rule is the only just one; the practice of reckoning the age of horses from May day, ought to be abolished as deceptive, and unequal in its operation. In England the Horse takes his age as I am informed, from January, the rule being literally the same as that we first adopted.

It seems to me that the proper course would be to adopt for the U. States, some general code of Laws for the regulation of turf matters, which any gentleman can compile by bringing together the various regulations of different Clubs, the rule observed in England, and such improvements as have been suggested at various times in the different Sporting Periodicals. Let this compilation (the manuscript) be submitted to a Committee at Baltimore, New York, Charleston, Natchez, and Nashville. The compilation being approved, it to be printed for the benefit of the compiler (with a view to meet the expense of publication) or otherwise, as may be thought expedient—and let it be adopted throughout the United States, by the different Clubs, as "a rule of conduct." Let some penalty attach to those Clubs which do not adopt—such as a refusal to publish their races, proceedings, &c., in the Turf Register, your paper, or other Sporting Magazines. But they will all adopt, as in case of dispute, the question will certainly be decided, *by Sportsmen*, under the provisions of the new code—and most probably by the Courts.

The hints are thrown out for your consideration.

To resume. The rule appears to be throughout Louisiana, and in the State of Mississippi, to reckon a horse's age from the 1st of May. The Spring races, are I believe without exception in Louisiana or Mississippi, fixed for some day preceding the first of May—and of course, the horses run much under their actual age.

In this State—Bets made on races, are valid agreements and are enforced in the Courts.

Very respectfully your obedient servant,
FREDERICK H. DAVIS.

MONTREAL TURF RACE

By the late 1830s the sports of the turf in the United States and Canada often attracted entrants from both nations. The reporting of these events had become quite detailed as to weight, distances, number of heats, and placing. The following account, reprinted from the 2 September 1837 issue of The Spirit of the Times, is typical of the sports coverage given to equestrian events.

MONTREAL (U.C.) TURF CLUB RACES

Commenced over the *St. Pierre Course* on the 21st ult., and were well attended throughout. Among the spectators our Montreal contemporaries speak in the most glowing and flattering terms of a concourse of the gentler sex. It will be seen from the report annexed, which we have made up from those in the Montreal Daily Herald, that the Long Island stable in attendance "contrived to pay expenses" pretty handsomely. MONDAY. Aug 21, 1837. The *Trial Stakes* of 2*l*. 10s. each. p.p.,to which the Stewards added 20*l*. Mile heats.

Timothy Wynn's b.m. *Silk Stocking*, by Shark, aged, 9st. 4lb	1	1
M.E. Davids' b.c. Vivian, 5 yrs. 8st. 10lb.	2	2
A.P. Hart's b.h. *Young Diamond*, (late *Brilliant*,) by Brilliant, out of Matilda, by Sir Walter, 5 yrs. 8st. 13th		bolt

Time, 2:01-2:10. Young D. bolted in 1st. heat.

SAME DAY—*Second Race*—The *Turf Club* Purse of 50*l*., added to a Sweepstakes of 5*l*. each, p.p. Free for all horses. Three mile heats.

Mr. Kelsey's ch.h. *Mark Moore*, by Eclipse, out of Lalla Rookh. by Oscar, 5 yrs. 8st 4lb	1	1
Mr. Richard's g. *Waverley*, by Duroc, aged, 8st. 11lb	2	2

This race was won easily by Mark Moore, who was ridden by little Barney; time, 6:30. It was anticipated that Mr. Yarker's *Rival* would have been down from Kingston, to contest with Mark Moore and Waverley, and considerable disappointment was felt when it was understood that the alteration in the days of racing prevented his being here in time.

SAME DAY—*Third Race*.—The *Garrison Plate* of 35*l*., ent. 2*l*. 10s, p.p; One mile and a distance, heats; free to all horses; gentlemen riders. Three horses must start or no plate will be given.

Mr. Kelsey's ch. h. *Pyrrhus*, by Adam, out of Cottage Girl, by Eclipse, 5 y. 9st. 6lb.	2	1	1
Mr. Richards' b.m. *Childers*, aged, 9st. 11lb	1	2	2
Dr. Jones' b.m. *Kings Own*, (late *Brunette*,) by Cock of the Rock, out of Noblesse, aged, 9st. 11lb	3	dr	

This race was well contested by Pyrrhus, ridden by Mr. Gibb, and Childers, ridden by Mr. Weir.

TUESDAY, Aug. 22.—The *Tatterrall Purse* of 10*l*. ent. 1*l*. 10s., p.p.; open to all horses; One mile and a distance, heats. The winner to be claimed for 35t.

Mr. Richards' ch. g. *Waverley*, by Duroc, aged, 9st. 4lb	1	1
Mr. Beniot's ch.m. *Queen Victoria*, (late *Princess Victoria*) 6yrs. 9st	2	dr

This race excited but little interest, as Queen Victoria would not start until Waverley had gone a considerable way found the course, although his rider cantered until both horses were neck and neck, when Waverley shot out and gained the race easily, without turning a hair, which he walked the course for the second heat. No betting.

SAME DAY—*Second Race*—The *Proprietor's Purse* of 20*l*., added to a Sweepstakes of 2*l*. 10s. each, p.p.; open to all horses; Mile heats.

Mr. Kelsey's gr.m. *Eliza Derby*, by Imp. Autocrat, dam by Hickory, out of Maid of the Oaks, 3 yrs 6st. 6lb	1	1

Mr. Richards' b.m. *Childers*, aged, 8st. 11lb   2   2
Time, 2:05-2:08

This race exited a great deal of interest, owing to Childers being a former favorite, and the beautiful symmetry of Eliza Derby, whose backers spoke in very high terms of her, although she had never run a race. Before the first heat, bets were about even, but afterwards they rose to 5 to 3 and 2 to 1 in favor of the grey mare. She was universally admired, and we doubt not will, in two years, astonish some of the Long Island sportsmen. Both horses ran in beautiful style, and altogether, this was the best contested race this season.

SAME DAY—*Third Race—Ladies Purse* of 20*l.* added to a Sweepstakes of 2t. each, p.p., for horses bred in the province; Gentlemen riders; One mile and a distance heats.

Mr. Weir's (32 Regt.) b.g. *Shamrock*, by Cock of the Rock, aged, 10st. 11lb   1 4 1
Mr. Timothy Wynn's b.m. *Silk Stocking*, aged, 10st. 11lb   4 1 2
Mr. A. P. Hart's ch. h. *Walterson*, by Sir Walter, aged, 11st   2 2 3
Mr. Richards' ch. g. *Rob Roy* (late Ploughboy, aged, 10st. 11lb   3 3 4
Mr. Benoit's ch. m. *Queen Victoria*, (late Princess Victoria,) 5 yrs. 8st. 10lb dis
Time, 2:08—2:07 1/2—2:07 1/2

In this race Shamrock showed that he was made of good stuff, and disappointed some of the knowing ones, who seemed under the impression that Silk Stocking would be the winner. Bets were freely taken in favor of the latter against the field, and after the second heat, so much was she the favorite that 5 to 1 was offered by her backers. In the third heat Shamrock, who was capitally rode [in fact so were all the horses], won in magnificent style by a brush when round the corner at a moment when Silk Stocking looked like the winner. Queen Victoria was distanced the first heat. Walterson made a good first heat with Shamrock, and brushed in a very good second with Silk Stocking, in the 2d heat. In the 3d heat he made play for a half a mile, but it would not do, the Mare and Shamrock had the foot of him. Capt. Markham, 32d Regt., rode Rob Roy, Mr. A. Farquhar rode Silk Stocking, and the other horses were ridden by the gentlemen whose names appear in the list.

The weather was very unpropitious during the morning, but cleared up about noon, leaving the course in excellent order for racing. The spectators were not so numerous as on Monday, the lowering appearance of the sky preventing many ladies and gentlemen from attending.

There was a race on Wednesday, but, says the Herald, "owing to the brilliant sport expected from the number and variety of the races, the course was crowded on Thursday at an early hour by the beauty and fashion, as well as the *snob*-ility of Montreal. Carriages of all descriptions, from the distingue chariot to the humble cart, were in requisition, and the toddlers also were more numerous than on any former occasion. All the stands were crowded to excess—their inmates, no doubt, envied by the poorer sportsmen who could not muster sufficient rag money to soften the obdurate hearts of the door-keepers."

THURSDAY, Aug 24.—A *Hurdle Race* of 2 sovs. each, for horses that have hunted with the Montreal Fox Hounds; Two mile race. Gentlemen riders; 12st.

This was a splendid race and gallantly was it contested, especially by Der Teutel, Henrietta, and York; so much so, that at the last hurdle but one it was difficult to say which horse had the advantage. Der Teufel gained about a length at that leap, and kept it to the winning post.

SAME DAY—*Second Race*—The *City Purse* of 35*l.* ad led to a Sweepstakes of 3*l.* each, p.p.; open to all horses except the winner of the Turf Club Purse; Two mile heats.

Mr. Kelsey's ch.h. Pyrrhus, 5 yrs. 8st. 4lb   walked over

SAME DAY—*Third Race*—The *Garrison Handicap Race* of 25*l,* ent. 2*l.* 10s. h. ft; free to all horses; Two mile heats. Three horses must start for this race or no money will be given.

Mr. Richards' ch. g. *Waverley,* by Duroe, aged, 10st   1
Mr. Weir's (32d Regt) b.g. *Shamrock,* by Cock of the Rock, aged, 9st   2
Mr. A.P. Hart's b.m *King's Own,* (late Brunette,) aged, 8st, 7lb.   3
Mr. Richards' ch. g. *Rob Roy.* (late Ploughboy,) aged, 8st. 4lb   4

This race was admirably contested by Waverley and Shamrock, the former gaining by a couple of lengths. The rider of Shamrock claimed a cross, but as it could not be substantiated, the Stewards decided that it was all right.

SAME DAY—*Fourth Race*—*Cocked Hat Stakes* of 10*l.* added to a Sweepstakes of 10s each, p.p.; Half mile heats.

This race excited a great deal of interest and good humor, owing to the novelty of the customer, the gentlemen wearing cocked hats, which made them look at a distance like a general's staff. After the 2d heat Captain Bell withdrew Missisquoi.

SAME DAY—*Fifth Race.*—The *Beaten Plate* of 7*l.* 10s., ent. 1*l.* 5s; open to all horses beaten during the meeting: Mile heats.

Mr. Richardson's b.m. *Chalders,* aged, 9st   1   1
Mr. A.P. Hart's ch. h. *Walterson,* by Sir Walter, aged, 8st. 4lb   2   2
Mr. Benoit's ch m. *Queen Victoria,* (late Princess Victoria,) 6 yrs. 7st. 4lb 3 dr

Childers gained this race easily. Queen Victoria would not start when the word was given for the 2d heat, and was withdrawn by her owner.

Between the 1st and 2d heats there was a race run by Mr. A.P. Hart's ch. h. *Young Diamond,* late Brilliant, by Brilliant, out of Matilda, by Sir Walter, 5 yrs., and Mr. M.E. David's b.c. Vivian, 5 yrs. The match was for a mile race, provided Young Diamond did not bolt-the bet twenty pounds. On starting, Diamond took the lead, but Vivian coming up close to his heels caused him to bolt.

Thus ended the Montreal Races for 1837, affording some good sport, and we are happy to say, unaccompanied by anything which could mar the general harmony and good feeling which prevailed. As the exchequer of the Turf Club is not in the most flourishing condition, we hope an accession of new members for next year, will enable us all to enjoy the animating sight of a well contested race.

QUEBEC RACES

Horse races often became great social events attended by all classes and types of people. The following report, reprinted from the 14 October 1837 issue of The Spirit of the Times, is more concerned with the social dynamics and dimensions of the occasion than with the sporting contests themselves. The article raises the issues of the prospect of riotous behavior and the necessary precautions taken to insure tranquility during an event that combined horse racing with other athletic events.

THE QUEBEC RACES AND 'ALL THAT SORT OF THING'
THE RACES-REGATTA-DEAF BURKE

To the Editor of the New York Spirit of the Times.

It is probable you will have received before this time a newspaper account, or sort of "marked race bill" detail of the business doings of our (shall I say "glorious) Three Days" fun and frolic, in the shape of racing and regatta display. I will omit all the usual dry fashion and fact on neck and neck work, whether the grey filly bolted, or the bay favorite broke down-how "*Skyscraper*" stuck in the mud, and the boasted speed of "*Blue Blazes*" ended in smoke—whether "*Fairy Foot*" stumbled through her work like a clumsy cart-horse, and how "*Snuff-the-moon*" made a short job of it by going rump over head at the first start,—all this agreeably diversified with learned strictures on the handsome riding of "*White and pink sleeves*,"—how "Black and all black" sat his horse like a sand-bag, and "Red cap and tartan jacket" gave graceful evidence of being "all giblets and wings" in the style of his jockey horsemanship. I repeat, that impressed with the probability of all this being in advance of the mail by which you will receive this, I will at once drop you a familiar "odd and end' fashion of describing the matters in question.

To commence with the Races, and these races held on the plains of Abraham— the celebrated, and, shall I say, a most classic plains of Abraham, so renowned in the lustrous pages of martial story. True, indeed, that

"On the famed field where heroes fought and died,

Now blacklegs brawl and tricking jockies ride."

However, this last more for the sake of the metre than borne out by fact, as I feel certain there is as little of trickery or the "knowing go-bye" in practice on our course as on any else in the world. But as the moral character of the thing is not exactly the question in hand, why we'll drop the matter here with the mere expression of the belief, that honorable and straight-forward principles ever rule our sporting displays in this quarter, of whatever character they be, and such I trust will ever govern them.

Let us mount up into the Grand Stand for a sort of bird's-eye view of the course, and the multitude crowding it in every direction. The landscape itself is a splendid one, and is well worth a few moments pause and resting on the open staircase to contemplate. Immediately in front, extending to the woody precipices beetling over the noble St. Lawrence, and spreading out on either hand to a considerable extent, are the memorable "plains"—an immense common or field of green sward, slightly undulated. On the one side you have the block-like and lofty grey masses of the citadel defences in the distance, with a massive mantled tower here and there intervening like a grim and

armed giant keeping watch over that wide battle-field: on the other side the far off
green woods of *Carousse* throw into pleasant relief the various tasteful villas, snug
country boxes, &c., built around its borders; while away in the far, far background are
to be seen hill, valley, and mountain, glittering church spires, and scattered white cot
and clustering hamlet—the latter, particularly, as you look over the lovely valley of the
St. Charles, might be well likened to a handful of pearls flung thickly and at random
over a footcloth of green velvet. Then again to revert to the prospect in front, you have
the blue expanse of the mighty river below you, studded with ocean and river craft of
all characters; and beyond these the towering shores of Point Levi, and the beautiful
and cultivated country behind, spreading away to the dimly azure mountains, which
faintly mark to the eye the seeming boundary line between earth and heaven. Well, so
much for the stage and scenery, now for the actors and the "properties." To commence
with the Grand Stand, (which, by the way, is always filled on these occasions with the
fair *elite* of our beauty and fashion, and of a grade and character, too, which makes
them no minor adornments to such assemblages.) Immediately in front is a fine regimental band, in full uniform, enlivening the scene at intervals with its rich and spirit-
stirring music. Mounted officers galloping about, and soldiers of the garrison in little
knots, or strolling in every direction in all the gay variety of their tasteful uniforms. A
number of these are employed in keeping the crowd off the lines of the course near the
winning-post, and they execute their office with the best possible good nature; and
though partially armed, yet such is kindly understanding between the pedestrian mob
and the red-coats, that a flourish of their slight rattans speaks intelligibly enough to the
purpose—and it rarely or ever happens that the white glove significantly laid a moment
on the bright bayonet kilt must hint its authority to some reckless and brawling ruffian,
who will persist in breaking through the ropes. It is surprising to mark how summarily
effective a military police is above all others in instantly suppressing even the disposition to riot or outrage; and it's a pity, for the cause of peace and good order, that they
are not more generally in fashion where promiscuous crowds assemble, even for
amusement. In France they understand these things well, let your advocates of mob law
and civil freedom argue as they will. The peaceable, well-conducted citizen has nothing
to fear from armed guardians of this kind, and everything to hope from the protection
they afford him from the drunken and disorderly ruffian, who otherwise laughs to scorn
generally weak and ineffective display of civil authority. But this is a digression, once
more to the argument. Bands of sailors from the harbor below, for the greater part with
their grog aboard, are cruising about, and cutting all sorts of "go-ashore' capers under
the excitement which internally as externally gives their fitful temperament a lift. See,
they have just had a frolic with some raw *habitants* or peasants, whom the novelty of
the scene has attracted from their homeward course from market. One country fellow,
probably frightened at the rough practical jokes of the fun-loving seamen, has taken
to his heels, and the sailors are in full chase. No pig with his tail greased for the particular occasion ever "pulled foot" with more perplexity of escape than *Johnny
Crapean*, with the tail of his *bonnet bleu* flying in the wind behind him. He is dodged
on every side-the smart young "topman" is close upon him—he makes for the fence
as his last hope—it's a rasping leap—but over he goes in a style that might have
shamed our subsequent hurdle match, and on he keeps over hedge and ditch till out of
sight, such has been the poor devil's fright, leaving behind him his blue head gear in

the clutch of his pursuer, who comes back with the trophy whirling in the air in the excess of his mad jollity....

BRITISH GOVERNMENT PATRONAGE OF CANADIAN HORSE RACING

The patronage of sports by the British government, particularly horse racing, was one way British customs and traditions were preserved in the Canadian provinces during the 1830s and 1840s—a period of Canadian history marked by intense conflict between French Lower Canada and British Upper Canada. The following article, reprinted from the March 1837 edition of the American Turf Register and Sporting Magazine and originally published in a British journal, discusses the importance of British government support in the development of horse racing in Canada.

THE CANADIAN TURF

[We copy from the English New Sporting Magazine for November, 1836, the following article on the turf in Canada. We are sorry that the writer should have found it necessary to make so long a voyage to reach the public eye, and would suggest that he hereafter take passage in our ship.]

MR. EDITOR:

While your excellent and entertaining Magazine has been so long the receptacle of sporting intelligence from the 'far Ind'—and for which your readers in every quarter of the world are deeply your debtors,—it has lately afforded infinite gratification to the lovers of sport in this '*the far west*,' to find that your publication has been opened to some of our humble doings in this remote, but still loyal and attached portion of the empire, by the insertion in your number for June last, of the capital communication of 'Chasseur;' who has made some palpable hits at the enemies of sporting in general, as well as told a true unvarnished tale throughout. I hope that 'Chasseur,' may be induced to renew his correspondence with you; and that the approaching 'season' may be such as to afford him ample space, and verge enough, as well as plenitude of sport to 'the Montreal Hunt.' It is particularly to be hoped that neither the redoubted *Morris*, nor any other sportsman, is destined to experience a renewal of any of those local obstructions and petty political annoyances which have hitherto disgraced the Papineau and Roebuck snarlers in this otherwise most happy country; but on the contrary, that honest `Jean Baptiste,' will soon be made to learn who are the real friends of this distracted province—the Papineau *clique*, or `*les sacres Chasseurs du Roi*.' But a truce to politics: the subject is becoming absolutely stale here; and the only anchor of our hopes of present safety and future peace and prosperity, is his most gracious majesty William IV, who has lately condescended to become the patron of the sports of a portion of his empire with which his majesty has been long and *personally* acquainted, and munificently to confer upon it an annual king's plate of fifty guineas!

How this came about, it is the object of the present communication to inform you, Mr. Editor, and, through the medium of your far-famed Magazine, the sporting world at large. Be pleased to know, then, that for many years, both hunting and racing have been carried on with considerable spirit in this province. How the former was begun and conducted during a long series of years by its respectable father in this part of the world, I again beg leave to refer your readers to the correct and judicious statements of your correspondent 'Chasseur.' And as to the latter, it will only be necessary to observe, that if it received, so it could not but have merited the patronage and support of noblemen—the king's representatives—distinguished for every public and private virtue. These were the late Duke of Richmond, and Lords Dalhousie and Aylmer. But the following documents, which, I trust, are destined to be perused by your readers all over the world, will throw additional light on a subject that has of late become peculiarly interesting from the fact already stated, that our 'sailor king' himself—God bless him!—has condescended to become the royal patron of 'sport' in his Canadian dominions.

On the 29th of July, 1835, being the second and last day of the Three Rivers races for that year; the following address was personally presented by the trustees and stewards to his excellency Lord Aylmer,—his lordship being then on the eve of his departure from the province:—

'*May it please your lordship*,—We, the trustees and stewards, for the time being, of the Three Rivers race course, respectfully beg permission to approach your lordship with the expression of our sincere regret at the annunciation and prospect of your lordship's departure from this province, of whose public counsels and social happiness your lordship has been so long the guardian and ornament.

'We feel it to be a duty especially incumbent upon us, to thank your lordship for the manner in which you have been pleased to distinguish the Three Rivers race course; for having at once patronized the same with a liberality worthy of a true sportsman, and, for three successive years, presented us a handsome silver cup to be run for by horses bred in the province: thus generously promoting innocent amusement in a country as yet but young in the sporting world, and the rural and agricultural interests of one of the most valuable provinces in the British empire.

'And now, my lord, farewell! We beg to assure your lordship, that, in common with all classes of his majesty's loyal subjects in this province, we shall ever entertain a high sense of your lordship's distinguished worth in public, and in private life, as well as a liberal sportsman; and that we shall always rejoice to hear of your lordship's welfare and happiness.

'In conclusion, we beg that your lordship may be pleased to convey to Lady Aylmer the sentiments of our sincere esteem, and of our grateful remembrance of the countenance which her ladyship was so kind as to confer on the Three Rivers race.—July 29, 1835.

To this address his lordship was pleased to reply in terms expressive of thanks and gratified feelings—that it was also satisfactory to him to learn that his attendance at the Three Rivers races had been so favourably considered, and that in doing what had proved to him of so much personal pleasure and satisfaction, his lordship had, at the same time, been so fortunate as in a measure to contribute to the rural and agricultural interests of the province: his lordship then assured the trustees and stewards that he took leave of them with regret, he should never forget their kind attention on every occasion of his attendance at the races; and then concluded by alluding to the kind expressions in their address towards Lady Aylmer, which he should not fail most certainly to communicate to her ladyship.

At the same time the trustees and stewards delivered into the hands of Lord Aylmer the following memorial to the king, with a request that he would be pleased to convey it to the foot of the throne. His lordship kindly replied, that he would comply with the wishes of the memorialists, and gladly embrace a fitting occasion of presenting their address, and, he had no doubt, with success.

'May it please your majesty! That with the view of promoting in this your majesty's province of Lower Canada, those rural sports which have contributed so much to the harmless enjoyment, and manly character of our fellow-subjects in our beloved fatherland, as well as for the purpose of exciting emulation in improving the breed of horses throughout this portion of the British empire, your memorialists obtained ground, and for several years established and maintained a race course, called 'the Three Rivers race course.'

'That your majesty's excellent representative in this province; the Right Honourable Lord Aylmer, has been pleased to patronize this race course, and for three successive years to present to your memorialists and their predecessors, a handsome silver cup to be run and competed for by maiden horses bred in the province.

'That as his lordship is now about to leave the province, to the infinite regret of your memorialists and of every good sportsman; and as, in the humble and respectful opinion of your memorialists, nothing could so much tend to the promotion of their original object, as the royal countenance and patronage of your majesty, they have ventured to place this memorial in the hands of my Lord Aylmer, in the hope that, at his lordship's kind intercession, your majesty will be graciously pleased to confer upon the Three Rivers race course, for the benefit of the province at large, an annual king's plate, of such amount, and under such rules and articles as your majesty, in your royal munificence, may be pleased to determine and command. And your memorialists, as duty bound, shall ever pray for a long and happy reign to your majesty over this great empire. Three Rivers, July 29, 1835.

The following correspondence is a clear and gratifying proof of the readiness and liberality with which his majesty is uniformly disposed to comply with the reasonable wishes of his good and loyal subjects, wherever they may be situated; and also another proof of the determination of his majesty, that Canada *shall* not be given up either to radicals or republicans.

DEAR SIR: *Quebec, June* 8, 1836.

'I have much pleasure in handing you enclosed a letter from Lord Aylmer to me, with an enclosure from Sir Herbert Taylor, by which you will observe that we have succeeded in procuring from his majesty, a 'king's plate,' to be run for in the lower province; and by the enclosed copy of a letter from Mr. Walcott, the governor's secretary, you will perceive that his excellency Lord Gosford has fixed the Three Rivers course to be the one on which the plate is to be run for this season. You will have the goodness to make this communication to the gentlemen of the turf club. The Three Rivers races will, I have reason to believe, take place in the last week of July, and that

the conditions of the race will be the same as those of last year's cup given Lord Aylmer. I am, dear sir, sincerely, your obedient servant,
William Forsyth, Esq. Montreal   MATTHEW BELL.'

'MY DEAR LORD ALYMER: *Windsor Castle, April* 17, 1836.
'I have had the honour to submit your letter of the 10th inst. to the king, who will have great pleasure in giving annually a king's plate of fifty guineas, to be run for in the province as the governor may think proper to indicate in the early part of each year. His majesty desires you will make a communication to the above effect, to the trustees and stewards of the Three Rivers race course, in reply to their memorial, and that you will inform Sir Henry Wheatley, his majesty's privy purse, to whom the fifty guineas should be paid in London. Believe me to be, my dear Lord Aylmer, yours sincerely and faithfully,

(Signed)   H. TAYLOR.'

MY DEAR MR. BELL: *Carleton Hotel, Regent Street, London,*
                                              April 21, 1836.
'I hasten to transmit you a copy of a letter I have received from Sir Herbert Taylor, in answer to the petition addressed to the king by the trustees and stewards of the Three Rivers race course, which was entrusted to me previous to my departure from Lower Canada. In my reply to Sir Herbert Taylor, I have taken upon myself to say that I felt assured that the intelligence of his majesty's gracious intentions to give annually the sum of fifty guineas for a king's plate to be run for at such place in Lower Canada as the governor shall indicate in the early part of each year, would be received with heartfelt gratitude, as an additional proof of the interest which his majesty takes in all matters connected with the welfare of his majesty's faithful subjects in Lower Canada.
'I beg you will do me the favour to communicate his majesty's gracious intentions to the trustees and stewards of the Three Rivers race course, and to the members of the Montreal turf club, and that you will make me acquainted with the names of the persons in England who may be appointed to receive annually his majesty's donation of fifty guineas, in order that I may be enabled to make the necessary communication to Sir Henry Wheatley, as directed in Sir Herbert Taylor's letter. I remain, dear Mr. Bell, with great truth and regard, your very faithful servant,
(Signed)   AYLMER.'

'SIR: *Castle of St. Lewis, Quebec, June* 7, 1836.
'His excellency the governor in chief, having taken communication of the letters which you have transmitted for his perusal, respecting his majesty's gracious intention to give annually the sum of fifty guineas for a king's plate, to be run for at such place in Lower Canada as the governor shall indicate in the early part of the year; I have received his excellency's commands to request you to acquaint the trustees and stewards of the Three Rivers race course, that he has been pleased to name Three Rivers as the place at which the king's plate is to be run for this year; and his lordship desires me to add, that he leaves it to the discretion of the stewards to fix the time when the races shall take place. I have the honour to be, sir, your most obedient humble servant,
(Signed)   S. WALCOTT,
The Hon. M. Bell.   *Civil Secretary.*'

Immediately after the receipt of this communication, a meeting of the trustees and stewards of the Three Rivers race course was convened, when the following resolutions were passed, expressive of their deep sense of gratitude to his majesty for his munificent donation, and indicative of the sincere spirit of duty and loyalty with which they were inspired; a spirit that may be said to prevail throughout the whole of Lower Canada, however adverse the political feelings of parties.

'At a meeting of the trustees and stewards of the Three Rivers race course, holden on the 11th of June 1836, Mr. Dumoulin in the chair. The Honourable Matthew Bell having communicated to the meeting a letter from the right honourable my Lord Aylmer, enclosing copy of a letter to his lordship from Sir Herbert Taylor, intimating that his majesty had been graciously pleased to bestow upon this province a king's plate of fifty guineas, agreeably to the memorial of the said trustees and stewards, to be run for annually over such course as his excellency, the governor, may deem proper to indicate. On the motion of Mr. Chisholme it was

'*Resolved*, That Lord Aylmer be solicited to convey to the foot of the throne the humble and dutiful thanks of the meeting for this gracious token of the king's royal munificence; and respectfully to assure his majesty, our royal benefactor, that this meeting will never cease to be gratefully affected with a due sense of the honour and favour thereby conferred on his majesty's loyal subjects in Lower Canada; being, as this meeting believes, the first instance of a similar royal donation having been conferred on any part of the king's dominions abroad.

'*Resolved*, That the grateful acknowledgments and affectionate remembrances of this meeting be conveyed to Lord Aylmer, the constant and generous patron of the Three Rivers race course, for having laid our memorial before the king, and secured to this province so great and beneficial a mark of the royal bounty as a king's plate of fifty guineas.

'*Resolved*, That Mr. Bell be requested to transmit a copy of these resolutions to my Lord Aylmer, with the most ardent prayers of this meeting for his lordship's health and happiness.'

Thus, sir, you have a sketch of the rise, progress, and complete establishment of the manly and interesting sport of racing in those hyperborean backwoods, to which I trust you will be induced for the future to devote a small portion of your attention and regard. I beg leave to enclose a memorandum of this year's sport at Three Rivers, which I hope may prove gratifying to your readers. The ground there is inferior to none in the world; and for extent and beauty of prospect cannot be surpassed. I always am, dear Mr. Editor, your sincere admirer,

A SUBSCRIBER.'

THREE RIVERS RACES.

First day, Thursday, July—28.—The king's plate of fifty guineas. Entrance five pounds; heats, two miles and a distance, open to all horses bred in the province of Lower Canada, that never won match, plate, or sweepstakes; three year olds, 8st. 2lbs.; four year olds, 9st. 8lbs,; five year olds, 9st.; six year olds, and aged, 10st.

Mr. A.P. Hart's b.m. Brunette, aged, by Cock of the Rock out of Noblesse,	3 1 1
Mr. W. Sharp's b.m. Witch, five years old, by Sir Walter, dam Countess,	1 2 2

Mr. W. M'Grath's b.g. Shellaleh, aged   23 dis.

Mr. M'Donald's c.m. Canada Lass, aged,   4 dis.

Mr. M. David's b.g. Vivian, four years old, by Brilliant, out of the
imported mare, Berwickshire Lass,   5 dis.

Mr. Gibbs' b.f. Victoria, four years old, by Sir Walter, dam Roxana, (bolted.)

St. Maurice stakes of forty dollars, open to all horses, entrance five dollars; heats
one mile and a distance; weights, three year olds, 7st. 7lbs.; four year olds, 9st. 3lbs.;
five year olds, 9st. 9lbs.; six year olds, and aged, 10st.

Mr. Yarker's g.g. five years old,

Mr. Judah's c.h. Walterson, aged, by Sir Walter, out of an imported mare, 2   2

The Ladies' purse of fifty dollars, open to all horses, entrance ten dollars, heats one
mile and a distance; gentlemen riders; weights, 10st.

Mr. Yarker's c.m. Rival, aged,   1   1

Lieut. Weir's (32d Regiment) b.g. Shamrock, aged,   4   2

Mr. A.P. Hart's b.m. Childers, aged,   2

Mr. Provandie's c.m. Juno, six years old,   3

Capt. Smith's b.b. Bessy Bedlam, aged,   5

Friday—The Three Rivers stakes of fifty pounds, open to all horses, entrance five
pounds; heats two miles and a distance; weights, three year olds, 7st. 4lbs.; four year
olds, 9st. 8lbs.; five years old, 9st. 9lbs.; six year olds and aged, 10st.

Mr. Yarker's c.m. Rival, aged,   1   1

Mr. Cuvillier's c.h. Walterson, aged,   2   2

The Produce stakes of twenty pounds, open to all horses bred in the district of Three
Rivers, that never won match, plate, or sweepstakes, entrance five dollars; heats, one
mile and a distance; weights, three year olds, 8st. 2lbs,; four year olds, 9st. 3lbs.; five
year olds, 9st. 9lbs.; six year olds, 9st. 12lbs.; aged 10st.

Mr. J. Bell', b.g. Minatoo, four years old,   1   1

Mr. C. Carter's b.m. Adelaide, aged, (bolted,)

Mr. Judah's b.c. Baptiste, four years old,   2   2

The Farmer's purse of forty dollars, to be run for by Canadian agricultural horses,
bred in the district of Three Rivers, heats one mile and a distance. Weights to be handicapped by the stewards.

Mr. Hart's b.m. Childers,   1   1

Mr. Judah's c.b. Walterson,   2   2

A private match for twenty-five sovereigns. Owners on.

Lieut. Weir's (32d regiment) b.g. Shamrock,   1

Mr. Hart's b.m. King's-Own, late Brunette,   2

A good race.

NEW ORLEANS RACING SCENE

During the antebellum period New Orleans became the racing center in the South and
its upper classes the dominant element in the sport. The following editorial, reprinted
from the 9 June 1838 issue of The Spirit of the Times, provides a good insight into the
mentality, values, and beliefs of the city's wealthy horse patrons.

SOUTHERN RACING

The intelligent editor of the "*Southern Advocate*" published at Huntsville, Alabama,
devotes *eight columns* of that journal of the 15th ult., to reports of the Spring Races
in Mississippi and Louisiana, accompanied with the following sensible remarks:—

HORSE RACING—From the *New York Spirit of the Times*, we have complied,
condensed, and thrown together most of the Spring Racing in Mississippi and Louisiana. The accounts may not be new to many of our readers, but as it is the peculiar
province of that excellent sporting journal, to furnish authentic and accurate reports of
races, we have preferred waiting its receipt and copying from it, to giving the loose and
often inaccurate statement of the papers. There is, however, one improvement which
we would suggest to the Clerks of Jockey Clubs generally, and especially to the reporters for the Spirit of the Times—that is, in giving the races over any course, to state the
exact length of the track, as that is quite as important as the time, the weight, age,
pedigree, and other particulars, which are generally given with sufficient precision.

It appears that there are three distinct race courses in the immediate vicinity of New
Orleans, each supported by a Jockey Club composed of the most honorable, distinguished, and wealthy citizens, who have associated together, lending their names,
employing the influence of their station in life, and contributing their money, most
freely, to the encouragement of these animated sports. Under the auspices of such
names, the owners of good horses have the surest guarantee of fair and honorable
competition, and a certainty of equal justice. With these assurances, both the breeder
of blood stock and the sportsman have the strongest inducement to submit the pretensions of their horses to such a test as the New Orleans race courses afford. An additional inducement is the high premium offered in the rich prizes and purses, contributed
by the different associations, to be run for. These exceed in amount those of any other
place in the world, being more than double the whole sum contributed by the Crown
of Great Britain for the support of the turf. The honorable character of those associations, and the large amount of public money put up to be run for, have been the means
of attracting some of the best horses from New York, to meet and test their powers over
the New Orleans courses. Such actors could not fail to drew immense crowds of gay,
fashionable, and respectable people, who seem to have taken great pleasure in coun-
tenancing and encouraging these sports. Those courses have been laid out, improved,
and fitted up in the very best style, and at so heavy an expense, that they are not likely
to be soon abandoned. The united associations contribute from *fifty to sixty thousand
dollars, annually*, in prizes of $1000 to $3000 each, to the successful competitor, all
of which is a direct premium or bounty to the owner of the best horses. Nothing can
have a better influence upon the breed of this noble animal, then such kind of public

encouragement, and we may add, that there is no branch of agricultural industry which contributes so largely to the pleasures of a country life, as the rearing of superior domestic animals. With such a market as the South finishes, the agriculturalists of North Alabama, Tennessee, &c., have the strongest pecuniary inducement, apart from the pleasure it affords, to engage extensively in breeding fine horses. Farmers more than 1000 miles off, come past our very doors with the products of the breeding studs, in search of the New Orleans market—a market which, with proper exertion on our part, we might all but monopolize, and which would yield us vast sums annually. No country is better situated, as respects its vicinity to good markets, its soil, climate, and agricultural products—the habits and predilections of the people generally, and, above all, the supply of the right sort of stallions. North Alabama and Tennessee, by the spirited exertions of a few individuals, can boats of several which combine the essential requisites of constitution, speed, and stoutness, in a pre-eminent degree. And it may be confidently affirmed that at no distant day, this section of country will be supplied, from its own productions, with as valuable a strain of the blood horse as can be found in any part of the world.

Horse racing itself is far from being profitable to the turfman. It is an expensive amusement, in which the most successful do little more than defray expenses from their winnings. But it is essential—indeed, it is indispensable, in order to a proper comparison of the merits of horses. No other exhibition can infuse into the multitude the same spirit and zeal for the horse as public trials in a fair field; and without this feeling, the value of a superior horse can never be properly appreciated. We are well aware horse racing is sometimes obnoxious to objections, but without pretending to justify any immoral practices of those assemblies, we rejoice exceedingly to see those sports in Louisiana placed under the management of their most influential and distinguished citizens—gentlemen who will not tolorate any irregularity or unsportsmanlike conduct in those who are engaged in the immediate objects of the meeting. In the honor and integrity of those associations, the owners of horses have the surest guarantee that no partiality will be shown, or any thing permitted to injure the character of his horses, or destroy the legitimate pleasures of the sport.

NORTH V. SOUTH CHALLENGE

The sectional horse race between Post Boy and John Bascomb generated almost as much enthusiasm as the heralded contest between Eclipse and Henry many years earlier and served to revive, albeit temporarily, some of the lost excitement over the sport during the late 1830s. Although Bascomb, the southern entry, clearly won the challenge race over his northern rival, members of the sporting press, motivated by sectional feelings, continued to debate the strengths and weaknesses of each horse. The article below appeared in the October 1836 issue of the American Turf Register and Sporting Magazine and formed part of the sectional editorial exchange that followed the race.

POST BOY AND JOHN BASCOMB

In many of the remarks suggested by the late match between Post Boy and Bascomb, made in papers professing to be the annalists of racing, there are many which might have been spared as both inaccurate and illiberal. The character of the match being professedly a question of the relative speed and bottom of northern and southern horses, was calculated to revive much of that ancient excitement that led to the race between Eclipse and Henry; and which it appears, from some southern remarks, has lost but little of its keenness in the recent race between the descendant of the latter and his southern conqueror; for such we may call him, until time and events shall question his right to the title. That the story, as it may be hereafter told, of this match, may be accompanied by the opinions and feelings of the day, it is well that the facts be stated by a person possessed of the power and disposition to be both accurate and candid. In the early part of last year, a post match was made professedly between the north and the south by two individuals of some sporting celebrity. This match came off on Tuesday, the 31st of May last, and at the post John Bascomb and Post Boy were severally named as the champions of the lists. The race terminated in favor of Bascomb, but under circumstances that justified new and distinct propositions for another trial. The friends of Post Boy, therefore, on the day of the race, made a public challenge to run a match race with Bascomb over the Union Course, on any day within thirty days, for $10,000, which was declined. On the ensuing day they again publicly offered to enter both horses on the ensuing four mile day, and to run for an inside stake of $5,000, to this no answer was made. A similar proposition was then made by the friends of Post Boy, to bet the odds of $5,000 to $4,000. At length an individual from the state of Alabama, authorised, as he stated himself to be, by the owner of Bascomb, accepted the offer for the $5,000, with a forfeit of $500. The preliminaries were scarcely settled, when Col. Crowell requested it as a favour from one of the then owners of Post Boy, that his friend might be released from the acceptance of the match, and it be annulled.—This favour was conceded, on a stipulated condition, that the concession should be publicly announced, as a favour desired and requested by the owner of Bascomb. A public challenge was then offered to run Post Boy against Bascomb in the ensuing fall, at the odds of $11,000 to $10,000. This proposition was declined, and at the close of the races, and after every fair proposition had met with a flat refusal, a counter proposition was offered by the owner of Bascomb to this effect: By a fiction, to assume that Bascomb was in Alabama, and to give or take $4,000,—to make a race for $20,000, either on the Union course or on that of Augusta, in Georgia. The fiction, though well enough to justify a proposition, was rather too much of a fiction for its acceptance. The friends of Post Boy had received rather too strong an evidence of the presence of Bascomb on the Union course, to believe that he was then at Augusta, and thought that $4,000 was too much odds to ask from a beaten horse, when both horses were there and could be trained on the spot. A second counter proposition was then made, to run on equal terms in Virginia, or on the Central track, at Baltimore. Both of these counter propositions were declined by the friends of Post Boy, because they designated a place of running different from that on which Post Boy had been beaten, and this defeated the great object of the match, which was to test the character of the two horses on the same track on which he had been beaten, that the variation of the ground and the difference of weights might not hereafter be a subject of controversy. It ought to be borne in mind, that his was a race of a peculiar character, made under the influence of sectional feelings; and if in its termination it has left a doubt in regard to the merit of the winning horse, it is a question for the consideration of southern sportsmen, how highly they will estimate a success, which is alleged to be the consequence of indisposition on the day of the race, and which, whether true or false, still backed as the allegation was by the money of the north, must be presumed to be true. In declining to meet Post Boy has not the south perilled the well earned reputation of their favourite, and though loaded with the spoils of the field have they not surrendered the great trophy, the field itself, and sent back their favourite, John Bascomb, to the plains of Alabama branded high in his forehead with the challenge of Post Boy?

Many in the south may content themselves with the simple event that Bascomb has won the race. This can, however, be little consolation to his spirited owner. In the warmth of his feeling for the fame of the south, he had generously acquiesced in the proposition to send his horse to the north. To him the question must often occur—what did he gain in the race that may not be lost by his refusal of the challenge of Post Boy? Has his horse established an unquestioned supremacy in the opinion of the men of the turf, and whose opinions are hereafter to control the fortunes of his horse? Sedulously sought, and indeed pursued by his beaten antagonist in every field where there was any chance of finding him, and where winners are generally found? Sought on the four mile day on Long Island, and pursued to Trenton, in the vicinity of which he then was—challenged publicly to meet in either field—what, I ask, is to be that opinion? These horses are now, by the retirement of John Bascomb in the south, destined never to meet, their racing career is soon to be closed, public discussion is soon to sit in judgment on their relative merits, and when it does it will refer to the position they relatively occupied before the race—that of Post Boy was one of commanding character. In the space of twelve months he had won four jockey club purses of four mile heats, beating in two heats the best horses of the north, and the then esteemed two best horses of Virginia—I refer to Black Heath and Juliana. He had won two matched races against horses of some celebrity for their speed both from the south. He had won his last four mile race in two heats of 7m. 52s. and 7m. 51-1/2s., hard in hand and without a struggle, over a track by no means good. He had pulled to every field, and under such a pressure as to leave it a question with some whether he could not pole every horse he had beaten. Bascomb, it is true, was a favourite horse of the south, but how had he acquired his fame. He had never won a race of three mile heats in less than six minutes. I now speak from the Turf Register. He had won a single four mile heat in 7m. 44s. over the finest track on the face of the earth, carrying twelve pounds less than his age prescribed in the north.

Post Boy had been trained for the match on Long Island, where the winter had been one of unprecedented severity, and where, up to the 11th of April, the whole face of the country had been covered with snow. Bascomb had been trained in Georgia for his match with Argyle, which came off on the 12th of April, after which he immediately started for the north, over a country well calculated for walking and even galloping exercise. He had had a long and hard training, and required the very relaxation that his journey afforded him to recruit. He arrived on Long Island three weeks prior to the 31st of May. Those who are judges of the process of preparing a horse for a race, will be able to estimate the relative advantages that the southern horse possessed over his northern competitor. On these terms of inequality they met; one indicating a high state of condition, the other remarked by the best sportsmen of the south as the reverse. Their keen glance soon detected that indeed was too perceptible to escape the most inexperienced of those who had on former occasions witnessed the triumphs of Post Boy. Nor were they undeceived by his performance in the race: the first mile was run in 2m. 2sec. Bascomb leading his antagonist by three lengths, and under circumstances that satisfied the friends of Post Boy, that it was out of his power to run his mile in less time, and it is the sincere belief of the writer of these remarks, (notwithstanding the idle opinions and statements that have been offered by journalists to the public,) that no urging could have exacted a greater degree of speed in that mile, as it was apparent the spur was freely used, and only spared when it ceased to produce any effect.

The sporting world had long been familiar with Post Boy's stride and the style in which he had run in former races, and now remarked the change. They had often seen him in his first mile yawing from right to left, his rider swinging to him in all the uncertainty of who was to be master, in less by many seconds than Bascomb ran his first mile. They now saw him for the first time, accomplish his first mile extended in his stride, with his mouth closed and apparently incapable of making an exertion to reach his leading competitor. It may be asked, to what cause is to be attributed this singular change, (for change it must be,) when the same horse that could not reach Bascomb in a first mile of a first heat, while fresh and unexhausted, in 2m. 2s. over the Union Course, runs on the ensuing week his last mile of a four mile heat over the course at Trenton, in 1m. 47s. It may be attributed to his general condition or temporary indisposition—it is sufficient for the fame of Post Boy that it is a fact. It is sufficient that evidence does exist to show either one or the other; and that notwithstanding he was beaten, he will at this moment be backed against any horse in the United States, for as large a sum as ever yet was staked on a match race in this country. That he now stands forth as the acknowledged challenger of Bascomb, and as the winner of two jockey club purses against the best horses of the north and the south since his race. That in eleven days he ran twenty-four miles, winning sixteen—eight of which were fetlock deep in mud. Therefore if the position he occupied before his race be commanding, that which must now be assigned to him since his race with Bascomb is not less so.

It is said, that the position of Bascomb since his race, does not impose upon him any obligation to offer or receive a challenge; that whether he owes his success to what sporting men call luck, or to his greater speed and bottom, is a question that he cannot now be called upon to agitate. That standing, as it is said, at the head of the American turf, he owes no allegiance to the rule that prevails in the ring in England, that no pugilist shall continue to wear the honors of the champion unless prepared to defend them against every challenger. That the law of racing acknowledges no such rule, and that the great horse, whose saddle he now wears as a trophy, did under similar circumstances refuse a similar challenge.

To this it may be replied, that there might be force in the objection had the challenge proceeded from any other horse than Post Boy. But that Post Boy, as the selected champion of the north, has rights against John Bascomb, the selected champion of the south, that could not be claimed or admitted in the person of any other horse; for instance, had the challenge reference to a different horse, it might with propriety be declined, upon the ground that as Bascomb came here to meet but one champion in the lists to be named at the post, he could acknowledge no obligation to meet any other. That the north and the south had put in issue at the post a single fact, which of the horses *named* was the better horse, that the trial of that issue must be limited to them, and that if either through an accident occurring in the race, or from indisposition preceding the race, either one or the other had been incapacitated, it was not in the spirit of racing to refuse to the horse so incapacitated, the opportunity of sustaining the reputation he had nobly won and fairly acquired on the turf. That the challenge of Post Boy, founded upon an alleged indisposition perceptible during his race, and fully developing itself immediately after the race, was a privilege conferred upon the beaten horse by the very character of the match, which in the true spirit of racing he had a right to claim, and which, in the same spirit, the winner had no right to decline, and that admitting that Eclipse did on a former occasion decline the challenge of Henry, still in referring to the history of that match, it is evident that it was under circumstances differing materially from those under which Post Boy and Bascomb met.

That Eclipse had been named against the world. His competitor might have been selected from the north or the south—He might have been taken from the deserts of Arabia, or selected from among the victorious winners of the Doncaster, the Derby, or the Oaks; the terms of the match had no limitation, no reservation. If with these fearful odds against him Eclipse succeeded, with what propriety could the beaten horse, alleging no accident, no indisposition, but, on the contrary, in the finest condition that the art of man could produce, claim the privilege of a challenger. The remarks now submitted to the public are intended to represent with a sufficient degree of accuracy, the terms on which the north and the south have brought, I presume, to a final termination, the controversy in regard to the late race.

It is true the north feels a strong and exciting interest in the fame of Post Boy, and were, and are anxious to remove all uncertainty in regard to the station they have assigned to him in the racing calendar.

The merit of Bascomb they have never questioned, and the higher he stands in their estimation the more gratifying it would be that he should establish beyond all controversy his claims to that rank. They are both the property of the country, and it is matter of little moment to that country on whose brow is fixed the laurel, provided it is rightly placed.

A SOUTHERN RETORT

Taking offense at the northern bias of the article in the American Turf Register and Sporting Magazine, a racing fan from Georgia reminded readers that Bascomb did in fact beat Post Boy and thus was the superior horse. The response, originally published in the Augusta (Ga.) Daily Constitutionalist, was reprinted in the 26 November 1836 edition of The Spirit of the Times.

BASCOMB AND POST BOY

A writer in the American Turf Register and Sporting Magazine for Oct., having attempted to reverse the position of these celebrated horses, in the public estimation, by placing Post Boy first and Bascomb second, it is an act of sheer justice to expose the errors of the writer and the sophistry of his reasoning. "Render unto Cæsar the things which are Cæsar's." Bascomb fairly vanquished the champion of the northern turf, and in doing so, made, as I consider, the best 4 mile race that has ever been run in the United States, not excepting even the great match between Henry and Eclipse. The average time of the two first heats between Eclipse and Henry was 7:43. The average time of Post Boy and Bascomb was 7:50. No one who is a judge of a track will dispute, that a horse could have been run each mile 2-1/2s. quicker, in the condition of the track at the Eclipse and Henry race, than could have been done when Bascomb and Post Boy made their run. Assuming this to be correct, it would bring down the time of Bascomb to 7:40. The weight which Henry carried was heavier than is now carried by horses of the same age, but any difference on that score was more than counterbalanced by a very high wind which prevailed on the day of Bascomb's race. If then I be correct in my calculations, (and I feel very certain that I am) Post Boy has not only transcended the best effort of his celebrated sire, but far surpassed *himself* on any former occasion, and I do believe out-stripped every living horse in America except his conqueror John Bascomb.

The writer also states that Post Boy challenged Bascomb to run on the Island this fall at an odds of $11,000 to $10,000, and that the proposition was declined and met by a counter proposition to this effect: *By a fiction*, to assume that Bascomb was in Alabama, and to give or take 1000 to make a race for $20,000, either on the Union course, or on that of Augusta, Georgia. Now sir, Col. Crowell assumed no such *fiction*. He knew very well that it would suit his business much better to train his horse where he could keep an eye on his affairs at home, at the same time, and for this convenience he was willing to pay a difference of $2000, or bet a difference of $1000. On the other hand, had Post Boy made the match to run on the Island he would have had the sum of $2000 to compensate, in part, the extra expense which he would incur and damage which his business at home might sustain in consequence of his absence. Was this fiction? It is preposterous to call it so. Now, sir, how stands Post Boy's proposition? Why, sir, it was this: Col. Crowell, if you will make a match for $10,000, and give us a change to retrieve the lost reputation of our horse, we will give you $500 to pay your expenses at the Astor House this summer, and as to the injury which your plantation affairs might sustain, why you must settle that in the best way you can. Was this, sir, a fair proposition? Was it such an one as would naturally come from those who were (as they now pretend) *confident* of success on a second trial? How will it compare with Col. Crowell's proposition, to give or take? As the writer says, Bascomb was there at Post Boy's side and that his presence there was no fiction, for they *felt* that he was there. True, sir, and he would have had to take as many steps to get to Georgia as Post Boy, would have to drink the same water, breathe the same air, and in every respect would have been upon an equal footing. Then you may inquire why the friends of Post Boy were willing to match him in New York and not in Georgia? or when they were so eager to bet $11,000 to $10,000, they could not be urged into a bet of $24,000 to $20,000? It may be accounted for in this way, and I can account for it in no other. It was very well understood that the difference between Bascomb and Post Boy was not very great, and that although Bascomb fairly beat him, still there was a chance that Bascomb might break down in his training, and pay forfeit, or he might be out of fix, and be defeated, and thus, by *accident*, yield to Post Boy the trophy which he had won by his *superiority*. You may think that the owners of Post Boy were willing to risk a great deal for the mere *chance* of retrieving a lost reputation. Why, Sir, the owners of Post Boy would not have had to go a dollar in the race. Chagrin would have stimulated some to take a share of the bet, and the interests of the Turf, the Taverns, &c., would have taken the balance. This may account to you for their unwillingness to run for $20,000 at Baltimore, only 200 miles from Post Boy's stable, when it was 800 miles from Bascomb's.

The writer says that "many in the South content themselves with the simple event that Bascomb has won the race." We are not so simple as that either. When we find, sir, that we have eclipsed the greatest effort of the present day, that we have driven the northern champion to make time that his friends themselves had scarcely dared *imagine*, we are assured that we have something more substantial to rest upon than the mere fact of winning the race.—Now, sir, I will show you the inconsistency of the writer: He tells us in one breath that they would not make the match to run over any other ground than the Long Island Course, because they wanted to test the character of the two horses on the *same ground* where they had been defeated, in order that the *variation of the ground*, &c., might not be a subject of controversy. In the next breath he informs us that Post Boy followed Bascomb to Trenton—was here no variation of ground? While he was in pursuit of Bascomb, why did he not follow on as far as Baltimore, where the friends of Bascomb would have backed him to an unlimited extent? Why at Trenton—had Bascomb entered for the purse, Post Boy would have had a *chance* (by catching Bascomb lame, sick, or off his foot) of mending his shattered reputation, and *that chance* would have cost him but $25—whereas, by following on as far as Baltimore, this *chance* might *perchance* have cost them $20,000.

The writer goes on to say that Bascomb had never won a race of three mile heats in less than six minutes. This is an error. He ran it in less time over the La Fayette Course last December. He then goes on to say that he ran a single four mile heat in 7:44, over the finest track on the face of the earth. Now, sir, I say unequivocally, that *it is not so*, and I will put the friends of Post Boy to the test. The writer states that he ran his fourth mile at Trenton in 1:47. Now, sir, I will procure for him a bet of five thousand dollars, that Post Boy cannot run over the La Fayette Course a single turn on any day in May or June next, with his appropriate weights, in the time laid down for his fourth mile, say 1:47. I will pledge myself to procure the sum of $5000 on the issue, and if they desire it, I do not doubt being able to procure the sum of $25,000. In dry weather about two thirds of the ground is very firm, but the balance is rather heavy from having been sanded. The shape of it is unfavorable, some of the turns being short.

Another proof that it is not *very* favorable to *time* is, that no horse has ever yet moved around it in less than 1:50, even with our favorable weights which the writer speaks of. The best time, two miles, that has ever been made, was 3:50, and the best four miles was Bascomb's 7:44, which stands 12s. better than Bay Maria's time the same week, and to have saved her life she could not have made the time which she had made six months previously, in her race with Post Boy on the Island, with only two more pounds weight upon her back. According to the best calculation I can make, a horse is able to make as good time on the Union Course in June, with New York weights, as he can make on the La Fayette Course in April, with our weights. In one breath he wishes us to believe that Bascomb is no great scratch after all; in the next, when he remembers that he cannot lower Bascomb without bringing Post Boy down with him, he wishes us to believe that he is a wonderful animal, but that Post Boy is a little more so. He informs us that Post Boy ran his first mile in 2:2, and under circumstances which induced his friends to believe that he could not have performed it in any quicker time. This is rather too severe a tax upon *our* credulity, though it may be very satisfactory to those who *wish* to believe it. In the first place we are in the habit of believing that *every* horse *can* run his *first* mile quicker than the second, second quicker than the third, and so on. Now, as the first mile took 2:2, and as the whole distance was done in 7:49, it follows that some part of the ground was done in less time. Now, if contrary to all former experience, Post Boy increases his speed with his distance, he had better banter the world for eight mile heats against horse flesh, and if he will continue on to 30 miles, he can banter the very lightning from the heavens. Neither does this writer's statements correspond with the manner of running Post Boy in previous races. He (as I am informed) always ran a waiting pace, and when he ran at the Union Course, made his run from the north corner in the last mile. This was the game he expected to play upon Bascomb, and would have carried it into execution had not the managers of Bascomb (who had suffered before from that north corner) kept Post Boy so busy that when he got there the brush was gone.

I will close this communication already too lengthy, with the declaration, that I have no interest whatever in John Bascomb; that I did not bet a cent on the issue of the race between him and Post Boy; that I have no sectional feeling in the matter, and that I am prompted in my vindication of the former, purely from a love of justice. I *challenge* the writer in the Turf Register to make the same declaration. I hope that I am wrong, but the whole tenor of the article referred to, looks to me like an *interested* attempt to bolster the fallen fortunes of a powerful horse, who stands now on the Turf second only to John Bascomb. There is where he *ought* to stand at present, and there let him remain until *fairly* promoted.

PHILO JUSTICE.

Whenever Post Boy outruns his own and Bascomb's time, he may banter with a show of reason. It will not have so much the appearance of a *chance* game, where there would be great gain and little loss.

Augusta (Ga.) Daily Constitutionalist.

LONG ISLAND TROTTING

By the late 1830s, trotting eclipsed thoroughbred racing in popularity, but the former also began to suffer from many of the same disreputable elements that plagued the latter. The following article, taken from the 21 October 1837 issue of The Spirit of the Times, addresses these issues in a report on a race at one of the most important trotting tracks in the country—the Centreville, Long Island course.

CENTREVILLE (L.I.) TROTTING COURSE

The annual Fall meeting commenced on Tuesday last with prospects of fine sport, that were hardly realized, all things considered. The disappointment arose from the unlooked-for withdrawal of *Andrew Jackson* on the first day, under circumstances that imperatively demand explanation. The entries for the purse were *Daniel D. Tompkins, Andrew Jackson, Fire King,* and *Locomotive.* The day being fine, a large concourse of spectators were assembled, and the betting was heavy. The field against D. D. Tompkins was current early in the morning, but after the horses were brought on the track, 100 to 75 was offered on him. Andrew Jackson was the main dependance of the backers of the field, 100 to 25 being offered vs. Fire King, and 100 to 15 vs. Locomotive. A half hour or more was occupied in endeavoring to get a fair start, during which time the betting was briskly going on; we have no doubt more money was laid out about this single race than there was during the entire Club meeting on the Union Course. At this stage of the matter, Mr. JOHN R. SNEDIKER, one of the Judges, (Mr. Hicks was the associate Judge,) announced that *Andrew Jackson was withdrawn!* That the scandalous character of this circumstance should be fully comprehended, we desire to impress it upon the reader's mind, that it was not done until after a dozen false starts were made, and every inducement given the public to believe that it was the intention of the parties concerned to start him. We will not take it upon us *to assert* that the race was "made safe" by certain parties who had "put their foot in it," but we *believe* one of the owners of Andrew Jackson was paid the amount of the purse and his expences to withdraw him. At any rate, withdrawn he was, and hundreds were "chisseled," and regularly "done" out of their money by this outrageous and barefaced humbug. It was no sooner announced that Jackson was drawn, than 100 to 25 was offered on Daniel D. Tompkins against the field, and no takers. In fact the field had no chance, nor was there any loop-hole of retreat through a "hedge." The fielders were "stuck," bamboozled, and "done brown." It may be as well to hint to owners of trotting horses that scenes like the one just noticed cast a reflection upon themselves, whether obnoxious to censure or not; and if they have any regard for their characters as sportsmen and men of honor, transactions of this sort must be sifted. The occasional occurrence of these scenes, and the suspicion of foul play they have engendered, has driven from the trotting course the great majority of those who are fond of the sport, until it is considered almost disreputable to enter a trotting horse for a public purse, or even own one. We know dozens of gentlemen in this city owning "crack" horses, who on this account would not have publicity given to their names for the price of their nags. The public are beginning to regard a trotting race as a regular "*do*," and unless the men of character who still participate in the sport clear themselves of any imputation, by at once ruling off the course those who disgrace it by attempting or accomplishing anything like foul play, trotting courses, and everything pertaining to them, must "go to pot." As regards the race under discussion, no reflection can rest upon either the proprietor of the course or those interested in the other entries. They had neither lot nor part in the matter. It need not be urged that Andrew Jackson (thank Heaven he was from Philadelphia) was out of condition; if he was, that fact was fully ascertained before a dozen attempts to start were made. No, he was only withdrawn until it was believed he could not win, and until opportunity was given *the sharps* to "come down" on the *flats*. The latter were effectually "cleared out." The half owner of Andrew Jackson, who was present, may claim that as the horse was his property, he had a right to trot or draw him, as he chose. If such a right is acknowledged, then we have only to urge that his horse was brought on the track, and attempts were made to start him with the field, simply with a design to gull the public. He is welcome to choose either horn of the dilemma, and it is only left for us, as the conductor of an honest and impartial sporting press, to warn the public how they risk their money on a horse whose owners will trot him or withdraw him as suits their interests, without any regard to those of the public.

The Trot.—Fire King, who had the track, led off at a rattling pace, with Locomotive well up, while Daniel D. T., well in hand, waited upon them a few lengths in their rear. This relative position was maintained unto the half mile post in the 2d mile, where Daniel D. T. pressed Locomotive, and he broke up. Daniel soon lapped Fire King, and after a severe brush Fire King also broke, and Daniel passed. Locomotive having got his stroke again, also passed Fire King, and came in 2d, Daniel winning the heat by half a dozen lengths. Fire King was now drawn, though his performance thus far had realized the anticipations of his friends. Had Peter Whelan, who rode him, suffered Daniel D. to pass, and then had come again on the last quarter, winning the heat would not have been quite so easy as falling off a log. Fire King should not have led the field: it was not his play. If he could have been well up with Tompkins at the the gate on the last mile, we should probably have had "broken heats" at least. The second heat was pretty well contested by Daniel D. and Locomotive, both of whom broke up, and the latter twice, from which he came in nearly a distance behind. The time was excellent, being made 5.16-1/2—5.11-1/2 by the Judges, though several gentlemen known as accurate timers made the last heat 5:13.

The *Second Race*, in Harness, brought out three very promising goers, in *Unexpected, Lady Hamlet,* and *Polly Ogden*. They went off at a fair rate, and Unexpected led the field nearly the whole first mile; at the stand all three were abreast, and as they passed the gate the hubs of the wheels touched. Before they reached the half mile post, Lady Hamlet bolted into the bushes, and deposited her ... bottom up, and Goodrich upon the top of a shrub oak. He soon reached terra firma—righted his drag, and was once more in motion, when Lady Hamlet frightened again by a "Ghost," once more "upset his apple-cart," and his chance was out. Polly Ogden broke up inside the gate, and Unexpected won the heat unexpectedly by three lengths. The second heat, trotted in half a second less time, resulted in the same way, Unexpected leading from the start to the finish. Report:—

TUESDAY, Oct. 17, 1837.—Proprietor's Purse $200, free for all trotting horses carrying 145 lbs. Two mile heats, under the Saddle.

Jesse Gilbert's s.g. *Daniel D. Tompkins*	George Young	1	1
Albert Conklin's s.g. *Locomotive*	Albert Conklin	2	2
Peter Wheelan's gr. g. *Fire King*	Peter Wheelan	3 dr-	1
John Wraver's Ll. h. *Andrew Jackson*	John Brady	dr	

Time, 5:16—5:11-1/2.

SAME DAY—*Second Race.*—Purse $100, free for all trotting horses that never won a purse over $50. Weight in harness, 145lbs, the same as under the saddle. Two mile heats, in Harness.

Mr. Lewis' b.g. *Unexpected*	Owner.	1	1
G. Edwards' s.m. *Polly Ogden*	Owner.	2	2
Mr. Goodrich's br.m. *Lady Hamlet*	Owner.	bolt.	

Time, 5:48-1/2—5:48.

The attendance on the second day was "very fair," as well as the sport, for "green horses." The report is to the following effect:—

WEDNESDAY, Oct. 18—Purse $100, free for all horses that never trotted for money; wts. as before; Two mile heats, under the Saddle.

F. Goodrich's gr.m. *Emma Wheatley*	Whelpley	1	1
H. Woodruff's b.g. *Patrick Henry*	Hiram Woodruff	2	2
W. Young's bl.m. *Bonny Black*	George Young	3	3
C. Bertine's b.g. *Duming*	C. Bertine	dis	
P. Wheelan's b.g. *Unknown*		dr	

Time, 6:43—6:47.

SAME DAY—*Second Race.*—Purse $100, for "green horses" as before; same weights; Two mile heats, in Harness.

Geo. Spicer's s.g. *Apollo*	George Spicer	1	1
G. Sampson's b.g. *Dandy*		3	2
H. Jones' b.g. *Andrew*		2	3

Time, 6:09—5:48.

The weather on Thursday looked lowering as if determined to *dampen* the spirits of the amateur whips in their drive to the track, but about 12 o'clock it cleared up. A considerable number were in attendance, and the trotting went off in fine style.

THURSDAY, Oct 19.—Purse $200, free for all horses; weights as before. Two mile heats, in Harness.

G. Edwards' s.m. *Polly Ogden*	George Edwards	2	1
... Conklin's b.g. *Emperor*		1	dis

Time, 5:38—6:06.

SAME DAY—*Second Race.*—Purse $50, ent. $10 each, added, free for all, weights as beford: Mile heats, best 3 in 5, under the Saddle.

Albert Conklin's s.g. *Locomotive*	A. Conklin	1	1	1
Hiram Woodruff's b.g. *Pompeii*		3	3	2
Peter Wheelan's gr.g. *Fire King*		2	2	3

Time, 2:36—2:36—2:37.

TROTTING REFORMS

Despite the increased popularity and success of trotting during the 1830s, the sport suffered from some of the same problems and public perceptions that dogged thoroughbred racing. The document below, taken from the 24 November 1838 edition of The Spirit of the Times, discusses many of these concerns and offers some ways to address them.

HINTS TO THE TROTTING GENTRY

In our "business transactions" with the world, whether "fair," like the Colonel's, or more resembling the crooked dealings of certain Auctioneers named by the "Sun," difficulties arising from any cause may be settled at a tribunal governed by certain fixed laws; but not so in the sporting world; there, honor is the only governing principle known or acknowledged, and it stands all in hand who move in that world, to maintain its supremacy. Whether its dictates have been slighted in other sporting circles than trotting, 'tis not my intention to enquire. Trotting is my subject; and on our trotting courses it is to be hoped honor and justice will prevail at all hazard. Let it not be understood that any open violations of right have as yet taken place; but to a careful observer of passing events, should he have been a frequent visitor at our trotting meetings, it will appear evident there has been an increasing disposition in a certain class, to take the right of deciding into their own hands; or, at best, receive the decision of those duly appointed—compare it with their own opinion, and if opposite to their views, raise a tremendous hue and cry—denounce it as unfair, unjust—applying alike to the decision and judges pronouncing it, the foulest epithets which could be raked from a Billingsgate lexicon. Such a scene has been witnessed more than once; and doubtless some of those participating in it, have regretted their conduct when the excitement which occasioned it had passed away, and reason regained possession of their minds. 'Tis impossible calculating the evil which accrues from one such scene; it acts as a precedent, induces a second, more aggravated than the first, and perhaps on slighter grounds—those have mingled in it who might reasonably be expected to act otherwise; and as each individual possesses a personal influence in a greater or less degree, others are induced to follow an example, until the few who commenced a disturbance have increased in numbers, leaving those in the minority, who, uninfluenced by passion or prejudice, were capable of perceiving the justice of the judgment given, by those whose unpleasant duty it may have been to decide:—indeed this brow-beating of Judges seems to be reduced to a perfect system; the noisy and turbulent may be seen, while the Judges are in consultation, collecting a congregation within hearing distance, and at the highest key on which their voices can be pitched, distorting some facts, and placing others in an entirely wrong position, until the merest trifles are raised into matters of importance, and from all statements, it would puzzle a Philadelphia lawyer to discern truth from falsehood—right from wrong:—while others may be heard offering bets to any amount, and at longer than "Poughkeepsie odds," that the decision when given would be thus and so; always, however, in that direction in which their pecuniary interest induces them to content for;—is it unreasonable to suppose there have been Judges sufficiently timid to be influenced by overhearing such remarks and proceedings, and induced to give judgment which they supposed would meet the views of the majority, rather than their own ideas of strict justice.

There appears but one course which the friends of good order can pursue; if Judges are placed in the stand whom those interested may deem unfit, let objections be made; but after permitting horses to start, their decision should be received without a murmur, and supported, "crooked or straight;"—having accepted them as law-givers, right or wrong let their decisions be maintained;—though notwithstanding the frequent threats used during such unpleasant scenes which may have occurred, to the credit of the trotting circle be it said, that few and far between are the instances on record of a refusal to give up money according to decision, or of suits at law to recover it of stakeholders who may have so handed it over to either party.

Is not a degree of censure due to some of our riders and drivers as the cause of these disturbances? do they not consider, or at least, appear to act, from the belief, that excellence in riding and driving does not consist in judgment, coolness, a quick eye and steady hand, but rather in the ability to take little advantages, too insignificent in themselves to distance a horse, yet serve as sparks to be blown into a flame by the partizans of either;—in a desperate contest against a high-strung horse, the "music" which can be struck up by the opposite rider is frequently made the *means* of winning a race, openly avowed and promised before-hand, and if crowned with success, gloried in— yelling and bawling like fiends incarnate, 'tis true is not violating the "Rules;" but 'tis taking a contemptible advantage of the disposition of an opposite horse, instead of relying on the speed and ability of your own to win;—there is none more than our riders and drivers who should feel a high-minded pride, or refined sentiments of honor—'tis as the air they breathe, and it would be well for some, would they but follow the example of one, who justly occupies the first place among them; not more for his abilities, than the detestation of taking other means to win than the powers of his horse, which has marked his course for years, and given him an enviable reputation.

A few words respecting *Matches on the road*—Among the community in which we live there is, and has always been, a large and influential body who are opposed to racing in all its forms; whether that opposition is based on reason or prejudice 'tis needless to enquire, but surely 'tis policy to take any steps in our power to lessen it. With that class nothing has tended more to increase it against trotting, than the frequent races and matches coming off almost daily on the Third Avenue. Not that a dash now and then is to be refrained from on the spur of the moment, when your measure is politely requested, or the speed of your nag implicated; but to enter deliberately into an agreement to perform a match on the road is wrong, if not criminal; it is to be deprecated by the friends of order, and should not be countenanced directly or indirectly, either as Judge, stakeholder, or even witness. Whatever advantages a horse may possess in performing a match on a certain piece of ground over which he may have been accustomed to travel, should not be allowed to outweigh the impropriety of the act; had we no other than the public road, that fact might be urged as some excuse, but with a track like the Beacon, always open gratis to parties matching, nothing can be reasonably advanced in extenuation of road matches. The writer is among those who have thus sinned, but having seen the error of his ways, promises amendment for the future.

To redeem trotting from its degradation, something more is to be done than the mere applying a remedy to some of the evil practices named; it must be made profitable to those who give their time and attention to it, whether as Proprietors of a Course, or owners and trainers of trotting horses; while to the public sufficient amusement must be offered to induce them to come forward in sufficient numbers to defray necessary expenses. The Proprietor of the Centreville has this Fall offered not a single purse;* while the Proprietors of the Beacon, with more liberality than discretion, have given thousands in purses, depending on the public for remuneration. It is possible to pursue a medium course, and by mingling sweepstakes and purses, secure the same number of entries and trots, yielding an equal fund of amusement to visiters, and a more profitable result to the proprietors. There is no lack of materials for sport. When has there been seen a greater number of trotting horses in train, than early this Fall; rising twenty at the Beacon, ten or a dozen at Centreville, and the same number at the Red House and on New York Island, of all grades of speed. Freely did the owners come forward and enter them for the sweepstakes at Centreville, and the purses at the Beacon. As for the *quality* of the materials, let it be asked where, even in its better days, did the annals of Trotting record a performance of a 5 yr. old equal to *Lady Suffolk's*, last Spring at the Beacon, 2 miles in 5:15-1/2—or *Dutchman's* 3 mile 2d heat, over the same course, in 7:50, which had he been pushed the last 150 yards, would certainly have been performed in 7:48, and perhaps less. In "the city of brotherly love," too, our old pet has been showing them by a 2d heat, 2 miles in harness, cut out in 5:13, over a heavy track, that he is not only in the lead among the living, but yet able, at the bidding of his owner, to contend for his long worn title of *Champion* of the Trotting Turf. We have then the materials, lacking neither in quantity or quality, and all that is now wanting to call them into action, is the fostering hand of the public. If with that public, prejudices have grown and strengthened against our favorite sport, let care and perseverance be used, to do away such prejudice. It is an old maxim, that a garment should be cut according to the cloth, and if the receipts will not justify the aggregate amount which has been paid in purses, would it not be better policy, instead of reducing the *amount* of the purses, to reduce the *number* of them; instead of four days trotting, but three. Creating a less number of purses would induce more entries for each, and there would be but little prospect of a horse walking over for a purse, save the nonpareil—*Awful*; and even he only for his own peculiar race of three miles and repeat, in harness.

It has been proposed by several influential individuals, that a Trotting Club be formed; and it would be well, perhaps, that the merits of the proposition be canvassed, and the subject reflected upon by those to whom these few hasty remarks are addressed. Among the many advantages that would accrue from it, a few may be enumerated. A certain fund would be raised, which a proprietor could base the purses on, instead of relying, as now, entirely upon the precarious and uncertain support of the public for remuneration. Under the present system, nine tenths pay their subscription at each meeting, and expect to have furnished them sufficient sport in return, as an equivalent for their money, utterly regardless of the expense or loss which may accrue to the proprietors therefrom, and feel no disposition to use their influence in promoting or seconding the endeavors of the Proprietors. Under the government of a Club, the reverse would be the case; each would feel that he had an interest in its welfare and success—pride would induce all to promote the object for which that Club had been formed; and as any body of individuals, from their concentration and united efforts, possess more power, and acquire greater influence than the same number of individuals would, disunited and separate, we may reasonably look to a regularly formed Club, as the most certain method to give trotting a better representation with the public, and regain the popularity which it once possessed. The plan is a practicable one and though too late in the season to commence this Fall, can be matured through the winter, and go into operation with the Spring meeting. Trotting has its friends and supporters; warm and enthusiastic ones, who wait but to be called together and organized, by some one possessing more experience, years, and influence, than

JEREMIAH Trot.

—————

*Instead of giving purses "out and out," he has added a sum to each sweepstakes, so that he has really put up as much money to be trotted for, as if he had pursued the other course. He is of opinion that the sport has been increased in this way, and there are many who coincide with him in the belief.—*Editor*.

BOSTON TROTTING

Thoroughbred horse racing in New England never achieved the popularity that it did in other parts of the United States and in Canada, primarily because of the lasting influence of Puritan morality. Despite public criticism of the sport, racing did occur for much of the antebellum period in the region for the purpose of improving the breed. New England did, however, make a notable contribution to horse racing through trotting. During the early 1800s, trotters such as Snap, Boston Blue, the first trotter to run in public for a stake, and Albany Pony ran against time. The following article, reprinted from the 27 July 1839 issue of The Spirit of the Times, discusses the state of trotting in Boston from a historical perspective.

THE TROTTING TURF IN BOSTON

Notwithstanding the citizens of Massachusetts have done little or nothing for the Turf, few states in the confederacy have accomplished more in ameliorating the condition and improving the breed of carriage and road horses. The "Old Bay State," too, was among the earliest to introduce a better stock of cattle and sheep, and, at the present moment can boast of some of the finest in the Union. A great number of thorough-bred stallions have been imported into the State designed to improve the breed of carriage horses, while Massachusetts was for many years the market for those thorough-bred colts that were thrown out of training on Long Island. Imported Roman, the sire of Major JONES' fine filly, *Zenobia*, stood for several years in that state; among other English horses that landed there, many of whom never left the state, may be mentioned Barefoot, Serab, Allfours, De Bash, Derby, Figaro, Nicholas, Kilton, Magnum Bonum, and King William. The stages in Massachusetts and Vermont are better horsed than in any other states in the Union, save that of New Jersey; and it is a well established fact that a matched pair of New England horses will command 20 per cent more in a Southern or Western market than any others. They are not only better broke but are handsomer, and go in more style, while they are almost always fine travellers; as for hardiness and endurance, a pair of Northern horses can outwork and outlast two pair of ordinary horses, a fact which we attribute entirely to the infusion of better strains of blood. A country stallion in New England could not pay expenses if he made no pretentions to blood, so strong is the prejudice against a downright cocktail; every man, woman, and child, agrees with FANNY KEMBLE that "nothing but the thorough-bred does it quite well:" therefore, though spurious in a majority of cases, a ten dollar stallion Down East, has a pedigree as long and as rich as Sir Archy himself. Hundreds of colts from New Jersey and Long Island have found their way, however, into New England, including many sons of Messenger, Mambrino, Duroc, Expediton, and Eclipse, and to this circumstance are the Northern states indebted for their present fine breed of road horses.

The establishment of Trotting Courses near this city and Philadelphia, has given a fresh impetus to breeding horses, for the road; and it having become fashionable to drive fast horses the price has advanced beyond precedent, for good performers on the road. Several extensive farmers in Vermont and Massachusetts are now engaged in breeding horses expressly for the Trotting Turf, and one gentleman in the former state, (the owner of *Washington*,) has met with great success. A pair of handsome carriage horses will command in this city, Boston, or Philadelphia, from $650 to $1000, while a pair of very "fast crabs," will command from $1200 to $1800.

For the reasons given in a previous paragraph, a majority of the horses on the Trotting Turf here, as well as in Philadelphia and Baltimore, were bred in New England; to the city of Boston is due the credit of "setting the ball in motion." Some fourteen years since a horse called the *"Old Boston Blue,"* after beating everything in that section was brought onto this city, where he won a heavy match by trotting a mile under three minutes! It was considered at the time an extraordinary performance, and attracted considerable attention. Up to that day very little attention had been paid to the subject of trotting, but public attention being excited it was not long before other horses were found quite equal to the rate of speed, and from that date to the present it has been constantly improving, until there are dozens of horses at our livery stables here, and in Boston, that can trot their mile in harness inside of three minutes. On our Third Avenue, the Boston Mill Dam, or any other fashionable drive, a horse would be termed "slow," and voted of "no account," that could not in harness, get down very close to the forties!

Without making great pretentions to extraordinary speed, the citizens of Boston have an immense number of very fine horses; their carriage horses are equal to any, while those used in the "truck" or dray are immeasurably superior in point of size, strength, and beauty to any in the Union; indeed many of their truck horses are equal to those used on the road, and some of the finest carriage horses we have ever seen were bought out of the truck in Boston. The amateurs in horseflesh, the whips and knowing ones of the Literary Emporium are very much inclined with our friend *"Boots"* to "lie low in the tall grass and pull poke root!" We are not at all sure if they cannot "beat us into fits" now that *Dutchman* has been "sold to the enemy" in Philadelphia; we are confident they have as many horses whose rate is between 2:35 and 2:45, notwithstanding they shake their knowledge-boxes and appear to be looking divers ways for Sunday when the subject is mentioned. At the last match between Dutchman and Awful, one of them having got his Ebenezer up, offered for $1000 each match to produce from Boston a horse that should trot a mile in 2:30, and a mile in 2:28—or he would take $5000 to $1000 the same horse could trot his mile in 2:25!

In 1837, several spirited and wealthy individuals formed an Association, and purchased the site for a handsome trotting course at Cambridgeport, a few miles from Boston, upon which several meetings were held last season. The soil of the track being sandy and deep, it is impossible to make New York time, but the performances on it are such that all the "Bosting Boys" require is "a fair field and no favor." They have a great advantage over us here and in Philadelphia, from the fact that their "Trotting men" are gentlemen, while in the other cities alluded to the term is one of reproach; so much roguery has been practised before now on the Trotting Turf that a *gentleman* is ashamed to acknowledge the ownership of a public trotter. It never will become respectable until half a dozen or more of the "Fergusons" and such scamps are ruled off, and it is incumbent on the great majority of "trotting men" to clear the course of such characters.

It will probably be a matter of surprise to many of our readers to be informed that the "Spirit of the Times" has a circulation in the city of Boston nearly equal to that of any other in the Union in proportion to the number of its population; the list of his subscribers would be considered a very high compliment to the Editor was he at liberty to publish their names; and it is with as much pride as pleasure that he assures his readers generally that while his Boston subscribers are second to none as regards character, intelligence, and wealth, they are behind no others in the readiness and cheerfulness with which they "fork out their tin in advance!" Not long since one of them being "moved by 'the Spirit,'" sent us the name of *Twenty* of his friends, and paid their subscriptions in advance! There's a specimen of our Down East Subscribers, and a "trotting man" too! And here's a letter from the same gentleman, who is engaged up to his neck in business

"In the Cotton trade and Sugar line,"
so that all proper allowances must be made for him. Besides, we happen to know that two or three New Yorkers are enjoying his profuse hospitality, and "pretty hard boys" they are too, each one of them being "a nice man for a small party." The wonder is, how the deuce he ever found leisure to write any sort of a letter, much less one so clever as the following:—

BOSTING, JULY 17, 1839.

Dear P.,—Since the killing time made by *Dutchman* and *Awful*, three miles in sulkies, and *Aaron Burr* and *Columbus* in wagons, (the latter with 400 pounds up), it has waked up the Bosting Boys to try if they can't do something "a small sprinklin' past common;" but we have at length come to the conclusion that our horses will appear first-rate mean without we have something better than a *sand bank* to go upon, and consequently have bound ourselves to make the Cambridge Trotting Park at least a decent Course for time; and as you know nothing about it from personal observation, (the more shame for you for not giving us the pleasure long since of "York's tall son's" presence, opinion, and advice,) I will tell you what it was, and what I think it will be. It *was* an uneven sand-bank, which has been ploughed up and laid out with four straight runs, of nearly equal lengths; with four inclined planes of a descent of 5 inches to the 100 feet to each plane, which makes the course to the eye appear a perfect level. It is just one mile around, measured three feet from the inside fence. The soil of our track being of light yellow sand which will not tread, we are now covering it with a blue clay about four inches thick; on the top of this we are putting 1 1/2 inches of black loam, which is to be harrowed together, and then rolled. I am confident it must make a first-rate track. The Course is also being fenced in, and convenient stands are now building. After this is done, all we want to make fun for the public, and gratification for ourselves is, some 7:41-in-harness-trotting-crab amongst us; and such a one we shall have if you will give us a fair chance and a little time.

Why should we not, Down East, have a good trotting cattle, as you of the great City of Gotham? I think we have here the *material* to make first-raters, and the "Boston Boys" are determined to have some that are not inferior to any of the Nonpareils and out and outers of the city, Philadelphia, or Baltimore. Mind you, we are now in our infancy; the atmosphere, soil, and the "spirit" of our city, is so much in our favour, that the day is not far distant when we will say to you Gothamites, "pick out your best trotting tits and bring them to the Cambridge Trotting Park, and we will 'stake the expenses,' *and* a $2000 *spot*, we can beat them, at your own race!"

But I am letting my pen get the better of my discretion in talking (to a 7:41 community of trotters) in this way. However, I know them all, and feel sure they wont hurt me, without first letting me know they are about giving me a "touch up" that will scare me, if I am not in first-rate condition. Therefore I'll say no more, save to tell you what matches have already been made to come off in August, as soon as the course is finished, which will probably be by the 10th. George Edwards, of Cambridge, names an untried 5 year old sorrel mare *Lady Richmond*, against Henry Jones' (of New York,) sorrel gelding, saddle, carrying 135 lbs., which, if I might be allowed to judge from what I have heard, will be a smartish sort of a match, as the knowing ones offer to bet even, that 2:28 don't win the money.

Also, a match between Mr. Brownell's bay gelding, *Young Buckskin*, and Mr. Walton's sorrel gelding, *Independence*, Mile heats, in saddle, best 3 in 5, carrying 145 lbs., for $500 a side, half forfeit.

Also, a match between Mr.____'s bay colt, *Pescara*, and Mr.____'s chestnut colt, *Pizarro*, Two mile heats in harness, for $200 a side, play or pay, 145 lbs. up.

Also, the following matches between Mr. Brownell's bay gelding, *Young Buckskin*, and Mr.____'s roan mare, *Highflyer*,—Mile heats, to go as each pleases, for $200 a side,-Two mile heats in saddle, and another of Three mile heats in saddle, for $200; 145 lbs., up in each.

I think the above matches will come off between the 10th and 20th of Aug., or as soon as the course gets fine, after which there will probably be purses offered to induce your fast goers to give us a taste of their quality, for a little Boston money, at least, I hope so. In haste, very truly yours.

A CALL FOR CHANGE

Noted sportsman John C. Stevens had played an active and influential role in the evolution of thoroughbred racing in New York since the early 1820s. But by the late 1830s, he and other enthusiasts had witnessed the decline of the sport. In the following letter, which appeared in The Spirit of the Times on 3 December 1836, Stevens suggested that the division of purse money would bring about much needed improvements in the sport.

DIVISION OF PURSES

We are pleased that the columns of this paper have been selected as the medium through which to communicate to the Sporting world the clear and forcible discussion contained in the annexed letter. The question involved in it has frequently been a subject of consideration with ourselves, and as we have ever thought favorably of the proposed division of purses, we are much gratified that it should be thus fairly presented to the consideration of turfmen generally by the gentleman who first conceived it, and whose personal influence as a sportsman "of the right sort," will go far towards bringing into practice the rules at which he arrives by his reasonings.

The change proposed is a radical one, and the adoption of its material points as calculated to revolutionize the whole system of racing in this country. Firmly persuaded that some change in our present system is called for, and feeling much confidence that the scheme now proposed will obviate present difficulties, and alone prevent recourse to the extreme remedy applied to the same evils in England, we invite that attention to the subject which its importance deserves.

Our columns will at all times be open for the use of turfmen on either side of the question, and we beg they would employ them freely.

TO THE EDITOR OF THE SPIRIT OF THE TIMES

Dear Sir,—I have at length found time to fulfil the promise I made some months ago, of putting upon paper the plan I then suggested of improving our horses and increasing our sport. I have long been satisfied, that our present mode of testing the qualities of a horse is far from being a good one. So convinced are they in England that in running heats, the best horse is as likely to lose as to win, that they have (with the exception of a few King's Plates) nearly, if not entirely, abolished them. Still, I should regret to see their method adopted in this country—for although our test is by no means a certain one, theirs, in my judgment, is still less so. We put up light weights and run heats—they put up heavier weights and run a single one. We can test the comparative speed and bottom of our horses—they can test the comparative speed, but not the comparative endurance, of theirs; for there is no more certainty that the winner of a single heat, with 119lbs. on his back, (their weight for a 3 year old), would, in 20-minutes afterwards, be able to win a second, than if he carried 90lbs. And there is perhaps as little risk of injuring our horses in running heats with 90lbs., as there is in running a single one with 119lbs. We have, besides, another very great advantage. Our riders, though far, very far short of theirs in skill and experience, are far less liable to be tampered with. Few men would be bold enough to trust their reputation to the keeping of a boy of 10 or 12 years old, who would be almost sure to tell the story to his cronies, and who, for sixpence worth of gingerbread, would probably break any promise he might make.

Most of the objections to our mode may, I think, be obviated—the alteration of the distance from 240 to 120 yards in four mile heats (for which suggestion I am indebted to my friend Capt. STOCKTON) is admitted to be an improvement. The adoption of the following plan would, in my opinion, be a greater one:—

My proposition is, instead of giving the whole purse to one horse, to divide it. Of eleven hundred dollars, (to which amount no proprietor who now gives $1000 would refuse to raise it), I would give to the winner of the first heat, say $400—to the horse that was second in that heat, $100—to the winner of the second heat, $300—and to the winner of the third heat, $300.

2d. If a horse won the first and second heats, he should be entitled to the whole purse, with the exception of the $100 given to the horse that was second in the first heat.

3d A distance or drawn horse should in no case win anything.

4th. If the horse that won the first heat should be distanced in the second or third, the $400 should go to the horse that was second in the first heat, provided *he* saved his distance in the two lost.

5th. There should in no event be more than three heats.

6th. When a dead heat is made, the amount allotted to that heat to be divided between the horses making such heat.

The great object, it will be perceived, is to induce every horse to run for every heat. It will be admitted that the principal reason for racing the horse is, that we may, by this means, select the fleetest and stoutest. We value highest, and breed from such as have shown more speed and endurance. Is our present method a sure test of either one or the other? Is it not better adapted to, and does it not as often display, the skill of an experienced manager, as the powers of the horse? What would a man of common sense say to me, if I should invite him to witness a trial of three or four horses, that we might select (for a match, or any other purpose,) the best, and he should overhear me giving such directions as these to the riders:—"Now Bill, you must not run a yard for the first heat—go a couple of rounds with them—get them to running and cutting each other's throats, and then pull quietly back, and save your distance—you'll fix them the next heat." "Tom, you must run for the first heat—you have the heels of Jack, so mind and trail him—keep ten or even twenty yards behind him—never lap him until you get to the distance, then give her whip and spur, and win by a brush, the shorter the better for you." He would, I think, be apt to ask me, after the race was over, how much wiser I was for the trial—for that it appeared to him, the simpler and better way would be, to direct them all to do their best in every heat. Would any sane man think, for an instant, of making a private trial in such a way?—if not, why should a public one be so made?

That the best horse does not always win, under the existing regulations, will not be denied; and it may be impossible so to regulate racing, that he *always* shall do so. But the chance of going wrong, and of giving reputation, and the purse, to a horse that has

not deserved it, will not, by the mode I propose, be so great. It would render this ancient and useful sport more interesting and attractive, by making the contest a more
equal one, and by giving the best horses the best chance to win,—it would make it a
fairer one. If, in a match, one horse beats another twice out of three times, the race is
over, and he is declared best. Why should it not be so in a field? What fairer claim has
a horse in a field that has been beaten two or three successive heats, to a fourth or fifth
trial? If he did his best in the two first, and was beaten, it ought to (and in a match it
would) suffice. If he did not do his best, he should, if possible, be made to do so, for
it would be rank injustice to give either credit or money to a horse that had been resting
himself in the race, while others had been running;—yet this frequently occurs; so
frequently, that in my opinion, it is an even chance that in a large field, the best horse
does not win. The others do, and will naturally combine against the horse they deem
most formidable.

Take as an example, the last four mile race over the Union Course. *Bumper,
Atalanta, Post Boy, Gipsey, and Veto*, started for the Jockey Club Purse. Bumper won
the first heat, and it was evident from the running, that neither Post Boy, Atalanta, or
Veto, had a chance with him for it. Gipsey laid up, and saved 100 yards in the heat.
For the second heat, every horse in the field contended—for if Bumper went for it (and
he did do so) and won, the play was over, and their chances out. At the end of three
miles and a half, Atalanta was dead beat by Bumper, and it was so evident that Bumper
or Gipsey would win the heat, that Mr. BRANCH ordered his boy to pull back, and save
his mare. This good judgment left her fresh for another heat, and won him the money—
for Gipsey, who was admirably ridden, and had been watching their struggles, the
moment Atalanta was beaten, came up and collared Bumper, and after one of the severest runs ever witnessed, beat him by a neck to the post—Veto was distanced, and
it was all Post Boy could do to save his. The 3d and 4th heats were won by Atalanta,
stoutly and closely contested by both Bumper and Gipsey.

Now what a comment is this upon our mode of selecting the best horse? *Bumper*
distances *Veto*—beats *Atalanta* the first two heats—beats *Post Boy* all three—and
Gypsey the first and the last, and yet gets not a cent of the money! Is not the injustice
here most glaring? What chance would either of these have had with *Bumper* (on that
day) single handed? If *Gypsey* had not saved 100 yards the first heat she could not have
won the second; and if *Atalanta* had not rested for the last half mile of the second, she
could not have won the third heat.

This is not an unusual or solitary instance, as every man at all acquainted with the
turf will vouch; so far from it, that there is scarcely a meeting that events of a similar
nature do not occur. Ought it to be so? It would not, I think, so have happened if $400
had been allowed to the horse that was first, $100 to him that was second in the first
heat. But if it *had* so occurred, it would have been some consolation to have received
the $400 so fairly and hardly earned.

The only variation from the common custom, that I am aware of, is a *Trenton*; here
$300 out of a thousand is given to the horse that is second in the last heat; this, in my
judgment, is making bad worse. It operates as an inducement *not to run* for the first
heat. The rule that makes the horse that is second best in the last heat, second best in
the race, has always appeared to me objectionable. When in a field, and according to
this rule, a horse is betted against another, it will depend upon the *amount* of the bet

which heat he runs for. If the bet be double the purse, he will probably run for neither—taking care only to be a-head of the horse betted against in the last heat. Of this the public, perhaps, know nothing, and back him, it may be, against the field, supposing, as a matter of course, that he will do his best to win the purse, but which he will be little likely to attempt.—He would scarcely risk $2000 to win one. According to this rule, a horse may win the first heat—be beaten by a head in the second—run a dead heat for the third, and yet have neither name or place in the race, because he was second in the fourth to some horse that had been, perhaps, first or second in neither, and, it may be, had *run* for neither, and one, too, that if compelled to do his best, or keep pace with the others for either of the first three heats, might have been distanced instead of being second in the last. But give a portion of the purse to the winner and to the horse that is second in the first heat, and the inducement to lay up is taken away or lessened according to the amount given for the heat, and there is little doubt that the credit and money they get they will honestly earn.

The rule that makes the winner of a heat better than the horse that is second in the last, is, like most others, not infallible. A horse may contend for the first heat, and be beaten 6 inches by one that can win no other—and he may be second each time to the winner of the last two heats—having contended for all, and beaten the winner of the first heat twice out of three times, he would be entitled to the second place. But how often does this case occur? Does it not oftener, much oftener, happen that the horse that wins, or is second the last heat, has not run for the first? In a field where *all* are doing their best, two may beat the others 100 yards or more in the first heat, and yet neither be first or second in any other heat. But instead of beating the others by 100 yards, suppose they had done so by five only, would not the chance be 4 to 1 that one of these would have enough left in him to win the second heat? It *might*, and perhaps has happened, that a horse has been able to beat another 100 or 120 yards in a first four mile heat, and yet be unable (though restrained to the speed of his antagonist) to win the second. But if it has, or does so happen, it happens so rarely as to make it an exception to the general rule.

It may be objected, that in running three heats only, if three several horses each win one, it will not be decided which is the best: granted; but as, according to the present rule, it frequently happens that the *worst* horse in the race wins, and he is only *made best* by *the rule*. I can see no reason why the rule may not as well make the winner of the first or last heat; or he that wins the first and is second, the last; or he that is second the first, and wins the two last heats, best in the race. In my humble judgment, the chance of selecting the best, in either case, and when every heat would be probably run for, is greater than by the old method.

There is yet another inducement to this change, and though last, it will not be deemed least in the eyes of those who own the horses, or those who witness their exertions—*Humanity*. How few owners are there of good horses, that after seeing them do their utmost for three successive heats, of four miles each, were it not to decide the bets made by others upon a horse, that he has in some measure made public property, by entering for a public purse, but would gladly forego his chance for the money and send his horse to the stable? I sincerely believe that nine out of ten of those who are but lookers-on at a race, would gladly sanction a rule that would render it unnecessary to task so severely, if not uselessly, the powers of so noble and generous an animal.

How many of those who witnessed, in their memorable race, the efforts of *Black Maria* and *Trifle* for three successive heats, and their struggles for a fourth, with a competitor comparatively fresh—who that was present that day and marked the meek expressive glance cast towards the Judges by one of these doomed ones, when brought up to struggle through a fifth, will forget it? I, for one, shall not. If there were no other inducement save only this one to alter the present law, the remembrance of this race and its effects should, with me, suffice. Of the three that started, one was for months but the shadow of herself—one was crippled and laid up for a year, and the other *died* in a few months after. Was the Purse a compensation for a tithe of all this mischief?

And here, too, is another striking illustration of the justice of the present law. *Maria*, after a severe contest, beats *Trifle* the first heat by half a length—the second is a dead heat between the two, and *Trifle* beats *Maria* by a neck for the third. Now, *Lady Relief* was in this race, and was beaten to sticks by both *Maria* and *Trifle* in all three heats. She did not run for the first, and for aught I know, might have run for neither; but she, although beaten in three successive heats, is allowed by the rule to start again, and is placed before *Trifle* because she is ahead of her in the last!

If a trial of skill between the owners, as to who can best manœuvre and direct his horse or his rider in the race, is thought of importance, the rules as they now stand answer the purpose perhaps as well as any we can make; but if a trial between the horses is the object, the sooner, in my humble opinion, they are altered, the better.

The various ways in which this altercation would benefit the proprietor of a race field, are so apparent as scarcely to need mention. It would add to their profits by adding to the interest and attraction of the race. It would induce many a man to train and enter a horse that would not think of doing so under the present rule; for though he might not be able to beat *Post Boy* or *Mingo* the race, he might win a heat and so pay the expense of the trial. It would render racing less of a monopoly, by dividing among a number that which is now given (and often unjustly) to one. In short, were I to enumerate all the advantages of this change, it would occupy more of my time and your paper than either of us could well spare.

Your obt. servt.,   JOHN C. STEVENS.

New York, *Nov. 26th, 1836.*

DECLINE OF THE TURF

Horse racing revived in New York between 1833 and 1837 under the direction of two southerners, Alexander L. Botts and David H. Branch, but as a result of the Panic of 1837 experienced another downturn over the following few years. Despite the national scope of the depression many New Yorkers attributed the origins of the decline to local factors—overexpansion of horse racing in the Northeast, mismanagement of race courses, exorbitant entrance fees, and few format innovations. The following letter from a New York racing insider is reprinted from the 8 December 1838 issue of The Spirit of the Times and gives an insider's view of the decline of the sport.

COMMUNICATION

THE NORTHERN TURF-Its late falling off-Cause thereof-The Union and Beacon Courses, management thereof-Brief history of the origin of the latter-Eagle Course, N J, management thereof, spirited and liberal conduct of its proprietor-Proposed match for $50,000, England vs. America, remarks thereon, &c.

MR. EDITOR,-The racing upon all the courses north of South Carolina for the present year being now over, and the decline in the support of the Turf during 1837 and 1838 being manifest, so far, at least, as a diminution in the usual number of spectators affords evidence, yet more especially evinced by the meagre attendance given to those of New York and New Jersey, and the total omission of the usual Fall meeting upon the Course at Trenton, I ask permission to offer some remarks upon the cause of this falling off, and upon some things in connection therewith, which may have a bearing upon the same, and the reputation of the *Northern Turf*.

Up to 1827, or 1828, we had only one race course to the northward and eastward of Maryland, that of the Union Course upon Long Island, New York, got up by what was termed "The New York Association for the Improvement of the breed of Horses," upon sixty-nine acres of land, which was leased. After the great match between Eclipse and Henry, run upon this course in May, 1823, the spirit of racing gradually subsided, and in 1828 had so far declined, that it was evident that the Club, or Association, could no longer support the course, either from the avails of their own annual subscription, or the contributions levied on spectators, although there were but two meetings held annually, the one in May, and the other in October, at each of which the meagre sum of $1000 only was given, to be run for in paltry purses of $500, $300, and $200, for heats of four, three, and two miles. The race track had become much out of order, the Pavillion, or Club house, required repairs, it had become necessary to erect new Stands for the accommodation of spectators, the present one being so far decayed as to be unsafe, the Association were in debt to the proprietors of the ground for rent, and so far from having any funds in the hands of their Treasurer, were in arrears to him for advances already made. In short, everything indicated a dissolution of the Association, and a termination of the sport. In this state of things, during the October meeting, 1828, Mr. C. R. COLDEN, a member of the Club, submitted to the managers a plan for inclosing the course, and urged upon the Club its adoption, as the only visible means of obtaining the requisite funds, and of reviving the spirit of racing, and the credit and reputation of the course, all of which was then at the lowest ebb, and at the same time proposed that $10,000 be immediately raised for that purpose, by creating stock to that amount. This proposition was generally approved of: nevertheless, the Club did not feel inclined to take up the stock. Upon their declining so to do, Mr. C. offered to carry his design into operation at his own individual charge, provided they would assign to him the leases which they held for the ground, about ten years of the term being then un-expired, and also transfer to him all their right, title, and interest to the premises, and give him the sole and uncontrolled management of the course. Upon this offer a vote was taken and carried in the affirmative. Whereupon Mr. C. purchased the fee simple of the land, and early the ensuing Spring went to work, enclosed the whole ground with a high and strong picket fence, erected now and substantial stands for spectators, built a new Judges' stand, repaired the Pavillion, or Club house, improved the race track, put a railing all round the inside of it, erected a strong and efficient picket along the inside of the straight run home, in order to restrain the too near approach of footmen, about 400 yards in length, with draw-gates at—each extremity, by the closing of which, either prior to the start, or after a heat, the rush of spectators is withheld, and a spacious arena afforded for parading at the start, or rubbing down and breathing the horses, free from the annoyance of the crowd.

In May 1829 Mr. Colden, having completed his arrangements, or nearly so, opened the course, and held two meetings during that month, thus first establishing the two meetings, Spring and Fall, and with the very slender support of a Club of only 49 members, and the lean subscription of ten dollars from each ($490), gave to be run for at each meeting $1250, in purses of $600, $400, and $250, thus paying in prizes during each racing month $2500, where only $1000 had heretofore been given.

The success of the undertaking at once became evident, and in a short time so confirmed, that inclosed courses, similarly arranged, were shortly got up, or revived, at Trenton, New Jersey, (of which I shall presently take more particular notice,) Baltimore, Washington, various places in Virginia, the Carolinas, and, indeed, throughout the States generally, in situations where it was previously deemed futile to make an attempt of the kind. From this period may be dated the revival and more permanent establishment of the Turf. The price of race horses and blood stock advanced beyond all precedent; the certainty of the forthcoming of money or prizes to be run for induced many turfmen, who had been for a long time inactive, to seek for horses and re-commence training; the high prices offered and paid for promising colts of fashionable blood, induced capitalists to make investments, and turn their attention to breeding, and from that period, everything in connection with the turf, and through all its stages, from the breeder to the trainer, racing man or professed turfite and stallion keeper, assumed a steady business-like shape. It so continues in the more southern and western parts of the Union—witness the encouragement given at New Orleans. That there should be a falling off in the more northern and Atlantic States, is to be regretted. To what is this to be attributed? I shall speak only as to New York and New Jersey, and the want of attendance on the courses therein, my more immediate vicinity.

In the Spring of 1833, if my memory serves as to time, MR. ALEX. L. BOTTS, from Virginia, having obtained possession of the Union Course, opened it under his immediate management, as proprietor, with a subscription of $20 each from each member of a Club consisting of something like 200, giving two meetings, (Spring and Fall,) with purses or prizes at each, of $1000, $500, and $300, for heat races of four, three, and two miles. He was subsequently joined by Mr. DAVID H. BRANCH, also from Virginia, and the course continued to be managed by these gentlemen with *great emolument*, no doubt, up to the Fall of 1837, when the falling off in the attendance began to be visible, and during the whole of the last season very great, so much so, indeed, that I am given to understand the proprietors declare, that if no change for the better takes place, it will be impossible for them to offer prizes to the same extent as heretofore. It must be borne in mind, that during the period that the Union Course afforded such handsome receipts, that, with the exception of the Eagle Course at Trenton, there were was none to interfere with it, or to intercept its usual frequenters, north of Baltimore. In 1834 or 1835, the Legislature of New Jersey repealed the law prohibiting horse racing in that State, and the restriction being thus removed, the Eagle Course was, consequently, not only better, and with more confidence, attended, but a new Jockey Club was formed, chiefly from the gentlemen residing in Philadelphia, under the appellation of the Philadelphia and Camden Jockey Club, and in the Fall of 1836 another course was laid out and opened, opposite that city, on the Jersey side of the Delaware, and that, too, under the management, countenance, and ownership of influential turfmen; here, then, many from Philadelphia and its neighborhood, who were disposed to visit a race meeting once or twice a year, and who otherwise would have been present at the Union Course, made a halt. But this was far from all.

Since the possession of the Union Course passed from Mr. Colden, in 1832, he had ever been on the look out for a more appropriate location upon which to establish another, and out of this has grown the more lately got up Beacon Course, (as it is named,) laid out upon Bergen heights, in New Jersey, about one and a half mile distant from Hoboken ferry, and as the origin of this course is not generally known, a brief account of it may be acceptable. Mr. Colden pitched upon the northernmost part of the Hoboken embanked meadow land, owned by SAMUEL SWARTWOUT, Esq., as suitable for this project, and entered into a partial arrangement with Mr. Swartwout for the establishment of a race course thereon, but was induced by Mr. Browning to relinquish it for the ground where the Beacon Course has since been laid out.

A bargain was struck between Mr. B. and Mr. C., and Mr. Browning accordingly went to work, Mr. Colden giving, occasionally, instructions furnishing the plan, &c. The parties acted under a confidential verbal or parole agreement, until the latter part of the ensuing month of August (1837), when Mr. Browning gave to Mr. Colden a stipulation, or agreement, in writing, engaging to give him a lease of the premises for the annual rent of $6000; but Mr. Browning finding that he could make a more advantageous bargain with Mr. Botts, he did so, in violation of his contract with Mr. C., retaining one equal half interest in the Course, with an understanding that he would convey a quarter to Mr. David H. Branch, provided Mr. Branch, then in Virginia, should wish to take it. Thus Mr. Colden, notwithstanding he had been the sole planner and promoter of this establishment, and had given something like six months' attention to getting it forward, was left without the slightest acknowledgement or recompense, to seek his redress at law. Mr. Branch subsequently took the quarter interest reserved for him, as before said, and in the early part of November following, (although the contemplated improvements were far from completed, and to this day remain so,) the Course was opened, and races took place as advertised, under the joint direction of Alex. L. Botts, David H. Branch, and Cyrus S Browning, proprietors! Here, then, under the direction of these gentlemen, we have, in place of one course, as formerly, two, one on the Long Island side of the city, eight miles distant, and the other on the Jersey side of the Hudson river, only a mile and a half inland, with two race meetings held on each, both Spring and Fall, making eight, with about as many trotting meetings. Two racing meetings are also held during the year at Camden, three generally at the Eagle Course at Trenton, one or two on the Hunting Park Trotting Course, near Philadelphia, making in all sixteen or seventeen racing meetings, the farthest off less than 100 miles from New York, and all these to be supported by the same spectators, or nearly so, the same turfmen, the same race horses, and, I may say, with the same means, or by the purses of the same men!

Is it then to be wondered that the proprietors of these courses (considering this constant repetition) should discover a diminution in the heretofore number of both amateur spectators and practical turfmen? to go these continual rounds would be to many a labor in place of pleasure! In England, at Newmarket, the emporium of their turf, they hold seven meetings annually at New York, as has just been shewn, we have eight upon the two courses, besides those incessant trots, week after week, and day after day. Is it, then, that the spirit of racing has so far declined as to refuse to support the turf, or that the turf has rode the spirit to death? Let which of the two may be the primary cause, I am of opinion that upon investigation, a reciprocity of those evils will be found to exist, and in no small degree kept by injudicious management, and the extortionate prices exacted for admission. Prior to the management of the Union Course devolving upon Mr. Botts, or upon Messrs. Botts and Branch, the annual subscription of members was $10; since the occupancy of these gentlemen it has been $20. Formerly, for permission to pass through the outside gate, the price was 25 cents, and the like sum for a place on the common stand; thus spectators had a full view and comfortable place for the charge of 50 cents. Messrs. B. and B. charged, as of old, 25 cents for passing the gate, but enhanced the price of tickets to the stand 100 per cent, the charge for saddle horses and carriages passing the gate raised, I think, but little. By the new regulation made this last Fall, and henceforth to be enforced, the charge for each individual passing through the outside gate, other than members of the Club, is also increased 100 per cent. Thus 50 cents for passing through the gate, and 50 cents more for a place upon the common stand, levies a contribution of one dollar each daily upon all who obtain a full view of the sport; that this exaction will remedy the want of attendance at present complained of, or eventuate to the interest of the proprietors, I very much doubt. At the Beacon Course the charges have been about the same as those last named, no beneficial effect, I will venture to say, has in consequence been manifest; so far from giving general satisfaction, they have been loudly remonstrated against by the populace, and of the dissatisfaction thereby created, the want of attendance complained of may be taken as evidence. Add to this, there have been some things connected with the management of this last named course, and allowed thereon, far from calculated to give it that character of vital importance to a place of the kind. The first was that catch-penny affair called a "Match against time," got up late in the Fall, or early in the winter, of 1837, the history of which may amuse.

It was given out that a man, for a large bet, the amount of which was set forth in the advertisements, was to ride 300 miles in 24 hours, when the fact was, that no such bet was pending, or such match made, not a horse trained for the purpose, and scarcely a single one provided until within two or three days of that on which the start was to take place, and then some hacks, picked up here and there, or any place at which they could be hired. At length the appointed day came; at one o'clock P.M. this fellow started, and kept going round and round at a hand gallop, until sometime in the night when all was quiet, and the word was given that the course was deserted (as it has since been discovered), he dismounted, and for several hours went to rest. Before daylight, however, he was again in motion, and numbers repaired to the ground to witness the latter part of the performance and learn the result. By way of keeping up the farce, and decoying as many as possible into this money-trap, he continued to ride until about 12 o'clock the following day, when having only one hour of the stipulated time left, and judging that all who intended being present were already on the ground, he stopped, declaring with the most unblushing assurance, that he gave up the bet, it being impossible to win, as he was then something like three hours behind time! I do not charge all the proprietors with being privy to this shameful affair, but that it was sanctioned, if not got up by one of them, *Mr. Browning*, will not, I believe, be denied. Next came *Jack Ass* races, Foot races, Athletic exercises (as the buffoonery there exhibited was dubbed), and trot, trot, trot after trot innumerable. The net was no sooner set and sprung, than it was set with intent to be sprung again, thus converting the course into a money-trap; baits of this kind may do to catch rowdies, noddies, and boobies, but are little calculated to give reputation, or keep up the credit, honor, or dignity of the turf, much less to render it the resort of the elite or fashionable, or ensure the patronage of *gentlemen* turfites.

I have now to make some observations relative to the management and spirited conduct of Mr. ELIJAH BROWN; junr., proprietor of the Eagle Course at Trenton, N.J.

It would appear that Mr. Brown had selected the 30th of last October as the day on which the Fall meeting upon this course should commence, and had so caused notice to be inserted in the "Spirit of the Times." That subsequent thereto, Messrs. Botts and Branch, regardless of this, advertised the Second Fall meeting upon the Union Course to take place on the same day. Of this Mr. Brown, by a communication in your paper of September the 29th, complains, as by referring thereto it will be seen, and rather than enter into an unprofitable contest with them or be driven to alter his day, revolves for the time being to shut up the course. It will be recollected that previous to the year 1834 or 1835, the laws of New Jersey prohibited horse racing, notwithstanding which, as far back as 1827 or 1828, if my memory serves, Mr. Brown established his course at Trenton, and such was the police fair management, and orderly conduct there observed, that though under the very eyes of the Legislature, chief magistrate, and Grand Jury of the county, that no measures were taken to restrain him or break the course up—on the contrary, he met with tacit encouragement, purposely held a race meeting at the time the Legislature was in session, presented the members with tickets of admission, and invited their attendance, with intent to show the innocent and inoffensive manner in which the sport was conducted, and thus, beyond doubt, went far to bring over many to vote in favor of a repeal of the then existing restraining law. Thus the Eagle Course and its proprietor have certainly been the pioneers of free racing in New Jersey, and any attempt at this day to squeeze it out of existence, between the Beacon or Union Courses, in the hands of gentlemen from the South, can not be deemed generous, nor will it, I trust, be tolerated by the sporting public—

"Render unto Caesar the things that are Caesar's."

Mark the more recent arrangements of Mr. Brown for the ensuing season!! At this time, while the proprietors of the Union and Beacon Courses complain so piteously, talk of retrenchment as to the amount of purses to be given in future on the Union Course, and have already done so on the Beacon, while they at the same time add to the prices of admission—the proprietor of the Eagle Courses comes out in the most spirited manner to offer purses at the next Spring meeting, far exceeding any as yet given upon any course in the Union, north of Louisiana! $3,100 to be paid as follows— four mile heats, $1500; three miles, $700; two miles, $400, with a second race on the third and fourth days, one mile heats, for $100! Here, then, we have the spirited proprietor of this establishment, which, in comparison with the Union, Beacon or Camden, may be considered an outside or country course, and by their proprietors no doubt considered secondary, setting them an example of generosity, furnishing a pattern of good management, and in point of liberality taking the lead. I observe that the advertisement of the next Spring races above alluded to, which appeared in your paper of the 1st December inst. terminates with the following notice—"The time of the meeting will not again be altered under any consideration." This unquestionably has reference to the clashing as to time occasioned last Fall by the proprietors of the Union Course, in their advertisement, inserted subsequent to that of the Eagle Course, having selected the same week for their second meeting; and being now again first in the field, the proprietor of the Eagle Course seems to have taken up the gauntlet with a determination to sustain his ground. It is to be regretted that any thing like jarring or untoward feeling should exist, between the proprietors of race grounds—it can neither redound to their advantage, or that of those by whom they are supported; yet if such a disposition is allowed to exist, Sportsmen, one and all, and the turf-going public in general, especially those of New Jersey, are in honor and by a reciprocity, bound to support the Eagle Course, in acknowledgment of the spirited manner in which its proprietor has come out, undaunted either by the pressure of the times, or the clashing of interest. He says in language not to be misunderstood, that *racing shall not go down*— let turfmen respond to it.

RACING REFORMS

Although the economic downturn in 1837 contributed mightily to the decline in thoroughbred racing, most racing supporters blamed proprietors and turfmen for the problems with their sport. In this letter, reprinted from the 8 June 1839 issue of The Spirit of the Times, the author calls for improved facilities and better organization as keys to reviving racing in the North.

HINTS TO THE TURFMEN AND PROPRIETORS OF COURSES

NEAR NASHVILLE, May 15, 1839.

Dear Spirit,—Sporting gentlemen at the South and South-west are highly pleased at the spirited measures taken by their brethren in New York, to revive the state of the Northern Turf, and we would be glad to fall upon some plan that would add a fresh impulse to those manly sports in this great region. When one reflects on our insulated situation—the difficulties, expense, and delays of travelling—the paucity of public amusements—the domestic occupation and the rural propensities of our inhabitants— and contemplates the general salubrity of our climate, and the amazing productiveness of our soil, he would naturally conclude that nothing was wanted, except the will and the spirit, to render this fine country unrivalled in the whole world for the Sports of the

Field and the Turf. So far as I know, there is no positive want of good feeling, and certainly but little open hostility to the Turf, but there seems rather to be a want of system, and harmony, and union among the friends of the Turf, whose exertions, instead of being concentrated, are frittered away and enfeebled by a diversity of objects and individual interests.

In illustration of the idea intended to be conveyed, I will instance the multiplicity of race tracks and Jockey Clubs in the immediate vicinity of each other: although they prove a lively interest in the cause, and a liberal support from the public, yet these praiseworthy efforts are not productive of those beneficial results that might have been attained under a more perfect organization of the entire materials. It appears to me that sporting gentlemen are too often inclined to consult their individual interest or convenience rather than the general prosperity of the Turf; and farmers are apt to lose sight of the improvement of the stock—the legitimate end of racing—by withholding their contributions, unless the races are to be held at their very door, as it were. Now it is well known that numerous requisites are indispensable to constitute an eligible sire for public racing, many of which never enter the head of the spirited projectors of a new course, and for the want of which their best efforts often result in disheartening failures. They seem to forget that money does not always make the mare go.

1st. The soil should be of the proper consistence for training, and also favorable for running upon without endangering the horses' legs. It is a great desideratum to obtain the *right sort of ground* for hard work, and of vastly more importance than evenness of surface—a matter of secondary consideration. We are not quite sure that a gently undulating surface is unfavorable to quick time—but whether or not, naked tracks are liable to such frequent changes from the influence of the elements, that *time* ought not properly to be considered as conclusive evidence of a horse's merits; indeed, we are inclined to the opinion that entirely too much stress is laid upon it in estimating his performances.

2d. *The water* should be abundant at all seasons, of good quality, and convenient to the stables.

3d. The adjoining country should be capable of supplying, abundantly and cheaply, every article required for the sustenance of horses, all of the very best quality; and in addition, the surrounding farmers and mechanics should feel deeply interested in advancing the welfare of the Turf.

4th. The fixtures and all the appointments should be of a *permanent* character, safe and convenient in themselves, and adequate to the reasonable wants of trainers, grooms, and servants, as well as horses. In short, it should be a desirable and a comfortable home for all who are in any wise connected with the stables.

5th. If in the vicinity of large towns the course might be inclosed, and a reasonable charge made for admission; but if near any country town, the race course should be open to all pedestrians.

6th. The sports should be so arranged as to *consume the greater part of the day*, and each day should present an agreeable variety, not only to suit the tastes of all, but to suit the capacities of all descriptions of race horses. This thing of ordering one race per day, and all of heats, to the end of the chapter, to be repeated at every course in the country, week after week, and year after year presents a listless monotony to all except those who are immediately interested in the result, and goes far to disgust the public with these frequent repetitions of familiar scenes. To make racing popular, there should be an attractive variety in each day's sport, like theatrical entertainments, and enough of it to occupy the attention of the audience, and keep them from the gambling booths and doggeries, which are a curse upon the land, and the bane of all rationa amusements.

These and numerous other requisites are quite important, if not absolutely necessary to the prosperity of the Turf at any place, yet how few of these essential elements of prosperity are found concentrated at any of our country places of sport? There are within an easy day's ride of Nashville some four or five Jockey Clubs, and as many race tracks. Each meeting consumes a week or more of every season, though the whole racing at all the meetings would not afford more than one good week's sport. This is an illustration of what was meant by the remark, "that the efforts of the friends of the turf were frittered away and enfeebled by a diversity of objects and interests," instead of being concentrated, and consequently strengthened, by a union of exertions. The evils resulting from this state of things are abundantly apparent to all who are practically acquainted with the affairs of the Turf, and nothing more is wanting but concert and harmony to effect a most salutary reform. There is not money enough offered at any one track to induce enough horses to make the racing interesting. For the want of horses, but insufficient stabling, and other accommodations, are provided at each track. Subscribers to the Jockey Club, disappointed in the sport, gradually drop off, and not only withdraw their patronage, but cease to attend, and thus, step by step, the whole thing dwindles away, and finally expires. You may remember that in this, the very heart of the Western race-horse region, there was not last Fall a single well-contested race over any of the surrounding tracks, and in more than one instance, one stable won every race at the meeting, and generally without a contest. The Nashville Club has itself expired by its own limitation, and as yet a new one has not been formed. The most important stake (in amount) ever made, is to be run over the Nashville Course four years hence, to be governed by the rules of a Club not in existence.

These matters are suggested for the consideration of those whom it most concerns, that, in the formation of a new Club, they may obviate as far as practicable the objections here alluded to. We should remember that A NEW ERA in the affairs of the Turf has recently commenced; that the metropolis has been transferred to New Orleans, which has become the great point of attraction for all the crack horses of the country; that all turf engagements in this quarter should be so arranged as not to interfere with the races there; indeed, all breeders and owners should have an eye to that place for the destination and ultimate sale of their horses.

I perceive one of your correspondents objects to the number of rival tracks near New Orleans, and very justly remarks that people get tired of three weeks' racing. One principal reason of that is, the want of variety, and the absence of open days. If all the racing over the three courses were confined to one half of the number of days, with suitable intervals, they would all be better patronised. The race courses there are splendid amphitheatres, established at vast expense, and a profusion of money sent forth to attract the best performers; and, as in all other rival public amusements, the most attractive bill of fare will ensure the best audience. But the citizens of New Orleans, whose countenance and support are of the greatest value, are actively engaged in business, and are loth to devote an entire day to witness a *single race*. If they devote an entire day they should have a full and a good day's sport, of a pleasing variety, and then to ensure a full attendance, some small interval be allowed. With such changes in the arrangements, and the introduction of a variety of sweepstakes, all the courses near New Orleans will doubtless continue to receive ample encouragement, more especially if the times should be prosperous again, and trade flourishing.

AN OBSERVER.

NEW YORK RACING

By the late 1830s horse racing in New York had declined for a number of reasons, many of which had to do with the management of the sport by its patrons, organizers, promoters, and enthusiasts. The poor condition of race tracks, the lack of a broad appeal to the masses, and insufficient financial support all put horse racing in a sad state. The following letter, reprinted from the 26 January 1839 edition of The Spirit of the Times, outlines many of these problems and some solutions proposed by New Yorkers.

THE NEW YORK RACES

In the absence of themes of more immediate interest, the prominent topic of discussion in our sporting circles for the last weeks has been the proposed National March between *John Bull* and *Brother Jonathan*; and this has eventually led to an enquiry into the causes of the apparent decline of Racing at the North, and to the proposition of various schemes, having for their object its establishment upon a better footing. The fact that three or four influential Northern turfmen have retired within the last year, has excited the fears of many of its staunchest supporters here and elsewhere, that either our races have been have been sadly mismanaged, or that they are about sinking into a galloping consumption. The circumstance of a string of twelve horses, including several tried good ones, having left Long Island within a few days, under charge of a popular trainer, to be run and sold at the South, has very naturally excited a considerable degree of feeling in the public mind. Several communications have been addressed to us on the subject, and as it is one of paramount importance, we have no hesitation in devoting to it all space at our command. We are pleased to find that a very general and earnest sentiment pervades the community in favor of establishing the whole system of racing upon a firmer basis, and of extending to it a prompt and generous support. As an illustration of the feeling existing, the proprietors of one of our prinicpal hotels express their readiness to give a Plate of the value of $500 for the encouragement of the Turf on Long Island, and we have no doubt, if the Union Course was properly fitted up for the convenience of the public, and a little more enterprise and spirit infused into the management, the racing season of 1839 would prove to the proprietors of the Course the most prosperous they have ever experienced.

To revive the Northern Turf generally, and especially that of Long Island, it is proposed to offer such inducements to our present breeders and turfmen as will not only
tend to encourage them to persevere, but enlist an addition to the number;—to add to
the attractiveness of the races by giving such brilliant purses as will command the attendance of distinguished horses from distant States, and thereby ensure sport of the
highest order; and to make such perfect arrangements at the Course for the comfort and
enjoyment of spectators, with particular reference to ladies, as will merit their approval,
and induce their attendance.

Without reflecting upon the causes which have led to the gradual decline of the
interest in regard to racing in this city, we directly proceed to introduce several communications on the subject of its revival. It must suffice to say, that our last few meetings were "stale, flat, and unprofitable" to all concerned, and without stopping to
inquire into the cause, it becomes the imperious duty of all having the prosperity of the
Turf at heart, to concert measures for giving increased popularity to this manly pastime—to afford additional encouragement to breeders and turfmen, and by remodel-
ling our present system of racing, to make it more profitable to the proprietors of
courses, and more worthy of the fostering patronage of an enlightened community.

The following Proposition has been handed to us by one of the most staunch and
influential supporters of the Northern Turf as the *Basis of a Constitution* for a New
Jockey Club. It is the fruit of many years practical experience, and much calm reflection, and were we permitted to name the writer, no observations on our part could add
to the weight of the expression of his sentiments on the subject.

It is proposed that the New York Jockey Club shall be composed of twenty-five
members, who shall be associated for five years—the number not be increased—and
in case of vacancy, such vacancy shall be filled by a majority of the whole member
consenting, by ballot, to the admission of any person proposed by a member. Each
member shall contribute the sum of $200 per annum for the whole term—to wit, $100
payable the first day of April, and $100 payable the first day of September of each year,
for which they shall give their promissory notes.

The Club shall lease from the proprietors, the Union Course and its appendages, for
the term of five years, the whole to be under the control of the Club. The gate money,
stands, admission to the enclosure, etc. shall be paid to the proprietors of the Course,
as compensation for such use, but the Club shall fix the rates of charges. From these
receipts the proprietors shall furnish and pay all the civil officers, gate keepers, and
attendants necessary during the several meetings, and furnish the Club with dinners,
or other refreshments during the meeting, free of charge.

The meetings shall commence on the 2d Tuesday in May, and 1st Tuesday of October, of each year.

The amount of subscription shall be applied to the Jockey Club Purses and the
salary of a Clerk.

For Four mile heats	$1000
Three " "	800
Two " "	500
Clerk	150
	———
Making, each meeting	$2450

All Sweepstakes, or Matches, or any race whatever, run on the Course during the regular meetings, to be under the direction and cognizance of the Club.

All forfeits shall be paid into the hands of the Clerk of the Club on, or before, the day the race comes off, and any defaulter to be precluded from running a horse on the Course on a regular meeting.

No horse shall be entered for a purse but by a member of the Club, who shall be held responsible for the entry and management of the same.

The President shall be appointed from the number of 25 by a majority of the whole. He shall hold his office during the term of five years; and in case of death or resignation, his place shall be filled by another election, in like manner; but only the residue of the term; and in case of his absence from a regular meeting, he shall give thirty days previous notice to the Executive Committee, who shall call a meeting of the Club ten days previous to that on which the races commence, at which meeting a President pro. tem. shall be appointed.

On the last day of the regular meeting in the Spring of each year, an Executive Committee of three members, elected by ballot, shall be appointed to manage the affairs of the Club for one year from that day.

Proceed we now to a second Proposition, of which we give the bare outline, not having room this week for details:—

Twenty gentlemen shall constitute the Club, subscribing $300 each per annum, for a term of 3 to 5 years. They shall lease and have entire control of the Course, appoint their own officers, and pay their purses.

They should admit Honorary Members of the Club on payment of $20 each per annum, which should entitle them only to the freedom of the Course.

Members of respectable Clubs in other States, distinguished strangers, and gentlemen accompanying Ladies, should be admitted free, by invitation of the President.

Strangers' tickets for each meeting should be $5, giving them all the privileges of Honorary Members of the Club.

The charge of admission to the Grand Stand should be 50 cents—to the Public Stand 25 cents, and to the Field Stand (placed opposite the Club, Ladies', and Grand Stands), 12 1/2 cents.

The managers of the Course, under the Club direction, should provide a dinner for the Club, to which none should be admitted, except by invitation of the President.

The Club should have erected spacious and handsome Stands, fitted up with especial regard to the comfort and convenience of the visitors.

As inducements to Turfmen of sister States to bring their horses to Long Island, and for the encouragement of our own, they should offer, in Purses, $5000 at each meeting, in the following order: a purse of $2000 for 4 mile heats—$1000 for 3 mile heats—$700 for 2 mile heats, and $300 for Mile heats, and appropriate the remaining $800 in such contributions to Plates, Marches, or Stakes, as they may deem most likely to conduce to the increase of sport. From each Club purse the sum of 20 per cent, shall be deducted, and given to the 2d best horse.

After paying the purses, the balance of the receipts from the Stands, entrance money, gate fees, etc., should be paid over to the proprietors of the Course.

Here's a third Proposition, that we "cotton to amazingly," as its practicability has been tested for many years abroad with signal success, and as we happen to know that the requisite means could be readily obtained to carry out the plan to its fullest extent "both here and elsewhere." It is, in brief, to the following effect:—

Let ten Gentlemen of spirit and wealth form an Association, or Joint Stock Company, contributing $5000 each, and more if required, for the purpose of either leasing and improving the Union Course, or establishing a new one in the immediate vicinity of the City of New York, on a scale of splendor, taste, and liberality unknown on this side of the Atlantic.

The Purses to amount to not less than $6000 each meeting, and the number of races to fall short of not less than three per day.

The price of admission to the common Stands to be less than half the customary rates, with free admission to the field and view of the course. The price of admission to the Grand Stand for Ladies and Gentlemen, $1 per day. Honorary members of the Club to pay $20 per annum—Strangers, with like privileges, $5 per meeting—Gentlemen accompanying Ladies, free.

The business of the Association to be conducted on the plan of the Doncaster, Epsom, and Newmarket Courses, in England,—the dutes devolving upon three Stewards, who are responsible to the Association and the public for the faithful performance of their duties.

We have room for one more Proposition, and a very sensible and straighforward one it is, characterized by the writer's acknowledged good sense and business tact. If we only had him at the head of affairs, we migh expect Lord CHESTERFIELD here with *Don John*, Lord BENTINCK with *Harkaway*, and Col. PEEL with *Ion*, and other good men and true with their formidable strings to meet Boston, Monarch, Maria Black, Wagner, Duane, Omega, Vashti, Balie Peyton, and enough more to make up "a nice party" for their reception. But to his Proposition—thus it is:—

To the Editor of the Spirit of the Times: DEAR SIR,—As racing in this section of the country appears to be on the decline, and our Long Island meetings to have lost their interest, in a great degree, it becomes the imperative duty of all supporters and friends of the Turf among us to concert measures for the revival of this national and truly manly pastime. I will not detain you with a detail of the causes which, in my opinion, have led to this sad falling off in the interest and excitement with which the public formerly regarded the races of the Union Course; but, if you will afford me an opportunity of expressing my views, I think I can suggest a plan which would not only place the Northern Turf upon a firm basis, but render it more than ever popular with the community at large.

In the first place, Sir, inducements must be offered to people of all grades to attend the races. Build an addition to the Public Stand, and cover it; also build an addition to the Ladies' Stand, and under it have two or three parlors for their accommodation, and one for Ladies exclusively; to that apartment attach water closets, and every convenience found in a well ordered hotel; during the late Fall meetings these rooms should be warmed, and at all times particular attention paid by the proprietors to the comfort and enjoyment of the ladies who graced the course with their presence. On no other ground can ladies be induced to visit the course, and without their attendance, racing here cannot be made, to any considerable degree, either fashionable, popular, or profitable.

In the second place, open a Subscription List for a certain number of subscribers, and invite the patronage of our most influential, intelligent, and wealthy citizens for the encouragement of racing; let these subscribers constitute the Club, on paying $100 or $200 each, as may be deemed proper. I think from one hundred to two hundred gentlemen can readily be found in this community, who would do so with pleasure. Then open another Subscription List for citizens of New York, at $10 per annum, with the privilege of inviting one, two, or three of their friends within the enclosed space, and upon the Members' Stand, on payment of the price of a ticket to the Public Stand.

Put the price of the Public Stand at a low sum, say 50 cents, and build an Uncovered Stand in a suitable place, removed from the others, for a Field Stand, and make the price to it 25 cents. You may also build your public stand so strong, that you can admit an equal number upon the top of it, and if you please, make that the Field Stand at 25 cents. Make the price of admission to the Field at one shilling each person—25 cents for a waggon, with one or two persons—a sulky at 18 pence—saddle horse one shilling—waggons, with four persons, 50 cents—back, with four persons, 50 cents, not including driver—an omnibus at one shilling each passenger. Let the drivers in all cases enter free, and every gentleman's servant enter free. Have a suitable number of Stewards appointed to receive gentlemen with their ladies Stand at 50 cents each; have one stand for the ladies of gentlemen belonging to the Club, and another for a public stand for ladies, and make the two Ladies' Stands exclusive for the ladies and the gentlemen accompanying them, and allow no gentlemen to enter either, unless requested by the ladies, or the gentlemen so accompanying them. Have an apartment to each of those stands appropriated for a refreshment room, with suitable refreshments for the ladies, etc. There should also be a sufficient number of posts set out upon different parts of the Field, with a single chain to each, for the accommodation of gentlemen with horses, etc. Also have water closets attached to each stand upon the ground.

The reason of my fixing the prices so low is in order to induce people to go there, for it will make no difference to you in expense whether there are on the ground 1000 persons or 100,000, and you must be aware that nine-tenths of the people who attend races can all afford to pay more money than the rate I have put down. It will be necessary, also, for you to make an arrangement with the Rail Road Company to run a train of cars to the course in time for the races and one back after they are over, and have the price fixed at 25 cents each way, which they can afford to run and make money.

And then you must offer such purses to be run for as will be sure to afford amusements and sport—such purses as will pay stables from all parts of the country to come expressly to Long Island. Give every man who has a stable free admission; if you lose money the first year, you can afford it; make it fashionable for people of all classes to attend the races, and you will be repaid ten fold. Appoint your meeting so that they will not interfere with other tracks, and be sure to have from two to three races each day. Not only make your purses large enough to induce stables from a distance to come here, but divide them so that the 2d and 3d horses may receive a proportion. You will find in such cases that you will have a greater number of entries, for many stables may have put their horses in training, and feeling confident that they stand no chance of winning the purse, they will not incur the expense of an entry, when, if they were to receive a proportion, they would be induced to enter, and thereby insure sport. A considerable number of purses may be made up aside from those given by the Club, or the Proprietors, and if there is sufficient inducement offered to distant stables to visit us, a variety of sweepstakes and matches might be got up to increase the attraction of the meetings.

You must be liberal, in order to make others liberal; and you will find, by giving $10 subscribers the privilege of introducing friends at something like 50 cents or a dollar, that there will be a great number of strangers from all sections of the Union, and you might have boxes in different parts of the course, where strangers may deposit such sums as they may feel disposed, and thereby create a "Strangers' Purse." Give a Proprietor's Purse of $2500, for four mile heats, and from that give the 2d horse $500, the 3d $200, the 4th $100, and the 5th his entrance back. You will in that case insure a field which must give sport, and repay many for training horses that if not able to beat such cracks as Boston, their owners think "no small beer" of; you are well aware that all cannot own first rate nags, but many may own good 2ds, 3ds, and 4ths. Then give a Members' Purse of from $500 to $1000, which can be very readily made up, giving a proportion to 2d and 3d horses—then a Subscribers' Purse of 4 to 5 or $600, also proportions for 2d and 3ds—then a Merchants' Purse—then a Hotel Purse—a Rail Road Purse—a Ferry Boat Purse—Steamboat Purse, and a variety of other purses, that may be made up by a little exertion, for every person a resident of the city knows that any excitement or amusement that may be got up to induce strangers to visit us must be an advantage to all, for every extra dollar expended by a stranger is a benefit to all.

But the most important part of all, after furnishing accommodations at the Course, is, to make your prices for admission, and the means of getting to the Course, such that every peson can attend the races without feeling the expense and you will find they will all go, men, women, and children. *But remember, you must make them comfortable when there.* Place an amusement so popular as racing within the reach of the community, and you will find thousands to patronise it; but you must afford them amusement when they visit the arena of your sports, or they will not attend a second time.

"Common sense and a little cyphering," as Sam Slick would say, must convince you that the above suggestions will bring profitable results, for we are emphatically a sight-seeing people, and are willing to pay to see sights; but we are not willing to pay so exorbitantly as to take our last dollar, nor will we pay even, a small price, unless you let us see something for it.

A MEMBER OF THE NY JOCKEY CLUB.

Readers at a distance must not suppose from the tenor of the above communications that Racing is going down with us. Far from it; there is no lack of good will towards our only national sport, nor is there wanting the spirit and determination to support it. The large purses given by Clubs in other cities of less pretensions, and the eclat with which their meetings go off, has excited a commendable feeling of emulation among our citizens. Possessing, as they do, all the elements which contribute to the successful prosecution of the sport—the finest course in the Union, crack horses, spirited turf-men, experienced breeders, and an immense population, notoriously fond of the sports of the turf, they are determined the Metropolis of America shall not be outdone in a matter in which they take a very correct and natural pride. From the days of old

Eclipse, she has occupied in racing annals a proud pre-eminence, and her Road horses, like her "high mettled coursers," have acquired a reputation for high breeding, speed, and stamina, of which she is proud to boast, and equally determined to maintain. She only desires that those immediately interested should commence the ensuing campaign with increased spirit, and stands ready to co-operate with them in their exertions, by a prompt, a steady, and a generous patronage.

NATIONAL SWEEPSTAKES

The growth of sports journalism during the 1830s led to an increase in the dissemination of information about horse racing and breeding throughout North America. Racing advocates supported the systemization of rules, regulations and standards, and the initiation of regular national contests in order to improve the breed and the sport. The following letter, taken from the September 1839 edition of the American Turf Register and Sporting Magazine, documents many of these concerns.

PERMANENT AMERICAN SWEEPSTAKES

The suggestions made by the Editor and several correspondents of the "Spirit of the Times," of establishing permanent sweepstakes, after the manner of the Derby, St. Leger, and others in England, having received the favorable consideration of the racing public, one prinicipal object of calling their attention to the subject, has been obtained. If intelligent and honorable gentlemen (such as the great body of the Breeders of blood stock and Turfmen in the United States unquestionably are) will give themselves the trouble to examine any new project, and reflect attentively upon the probably consequences of its adoption, they will be most certain to arrive at the correct conclusion, and then, if they can be brought to act in concert, the result must be beneficial. It is possible I may attach too much importance to the plan of establishing fixed annual sweepstakes, and I may have anticipated from them greater advantages than are likely to ensue; or I may have mistaken the proper mode of effecting the object, by means of a *National Convention.* Some of your correspondents, evidently entertaining the best feelings towards the advancement of the cause, seem to think the plan of any thing like a *National Stake* impracticable, from the great territorial extent of the confederacy, and the difficulty of transporting horses from the extremities to the centre. Others have doubts whether a convention of Turfmen can be obtained at all, to deliberate on the affairs of the Turf. However variant opinions may be upon these points, no one questions the advantages which would result from placing the condition of the Turf upon a more fixed and permanent basis; and with your permission, I will now proceed somewhat in detail, to present the subject in a more practical and tangible form.

The United States, as it respects the breeding of blood horses for the Turf, may properly be divided into two grand divisions, viz, the Eastern and Western. These are so entirely separated by natural boundaries, and so far asunder, that it has seldom if ever happened that a three-year-old race-horse has performed in both divisions. The distance, therefore, would present an insuperable obstacle to a national stake for *colts of that age*; but when this difficulty (which at first view appears so formidable) comes to be more closely analyzed, in connection with the Turf statistics of the country, and the geographical position of those States where breeding and racing most abound, it will not appear of such appalling magnitude, as to deter zealous sportsmen from the attempt to establish one place of meeting for four-year-olds and upwards, where all may stand nearly upon an equality, and where the best of his year may (barring unavoidable casualties) receive a just reward for his superior merits.

RACING STATISTICS.—One of the signal advantages of your invaluable sporting journal, and for which alone it deserves the patronage of every farmer who breeds a colt, is the accurate statistical intelligence it furnishes of all Turf transactions, condenses and arranged in tabular form, for the more convenient reference. I am sensible that the mass of your readers can scarcely appreciate the incessant vigilance and the immense labor of collecting this information, and arranging it in a manner to present the whole at a glance, but all are ready to bear witness to their great value. From these tables it appears there are ONE HUNDRED AND SEVEN known and ascertained places of sport, or race-tracks, in the United States, each of which is under the jurisdiction of its own Joceky Club, and subject to its laws: at most of these courses there are two meetings annually, continuing from four to six days each, and races of heats are invariably run, generally from one to four miles each, the purses being graduated to the length of the race. Of these, forty-four may be said to belong to the Eastern division, and sixty-three to the Western. Of the former, Virginia is about the centre, and Tennessee in the West.

Eastern Division.

Virginia has . . . . 13 race courses.

North of Virginia.		*South of Virginia.*	
District of Columbia	1	North Carolina	6
Maryland	3	South Carolina	10
New Jersey	4	Georgia	5
New York	1		—
Pennsylvania	1	Total 21	
10			

Recapitulation:

Virginia	13
North of Virginia	10
South of Virginia	21-44

Western Division.

Tennessee 10

North of Tennessee.		*South of Tennessee.*	
Kentucky	17	Alabama	10
Missouri, Illinois,		Mississippi	8
Indiana, and Ohio	6	Louisiana	8
	___	Arkansas	4
			___
Total 23		Total 30	

Recapitulation:

Tennessee	10
North of Tennessee	23
South of Tennessee	30-63

Although, as above remarked, it has seldom or never happened that a colt in his three-year-old form has shown in both these districts, yet from the greater number of race-courses in the Western Division, and the proportionally increased value of the public purses, some of the veterans of the East have been attracted to the South-West, where they have invariably received a most hospitable welcome and a fair field.

BREEDING STATISTICS.—From another highly interesting table, in the first number of the New Series of the "American Turf Register and Sproting Magazine," (a work which, for variety and extent of useful information, and elegance of execution, is not surpassed by any other of the kind in the world,) we learn that there are in the United States *one hundred and sixty-two* public stallions, thoroughbred, and their pedigrees given. Of these forty-six are in the Eastern Division, and *one hundred and sixteen* in the Western. The States which have the greatest number are—

Tennessee	37	Arkansas	7
Kentucky	36	Georgia	6
Virginia	23	North Carolina	5
Alabama	17		

By reference to the map it will be seen that Virginia is near the centre of the race-horse region in the Eastern Division, and that Tennessee bears the same relative position in the Western; and further, that Georgia occupies a middle position between the two.

Now in view of all these facts, and considering the rapidity with which race-horses and race-courses are multiplied, and the irregular manner in which the sports are got up and conducted, it early occurred to me that the interests of all concerned in breeding and racing, would be promoted by the establishment of annual sweepstakes at convenient points in each division, for three-year-old colts, and fixing upon some middle ground for four-year-olds from all parts of the country. Hence the orignial suggestion of three sweepstakes, one of which for three-year-olds in the Eastern Division, another for the same age in the Western, and a third on middle ground for four-year-olds and more advanced horses.

But this could not be carried out without the concert and union of the leading Turfmen throughout the country, and there seemed no better way, than to get them together to agree upon time and place; and while together, it occurred to me that such a body, so conversant with the condition of the turf, might form a separate Club and adopt rules and regulations which would exert a salutary influence on the whole country.

Gentlemen are no wise backward in subscribing for stakes, and those, too, for the largest sums. The moment one is proposed, it is carefully scrutinized, and if the conditions are not highly objectionable, or the place extremely inconvenient, they are not deterred by the amount. On the other hand, if the conditions, time and place are not to the fancy of a gentleman, he rallies his friends and proposes another at a different place, which in some respects would conflict with the former, and which might result in producing ambitious and excited feelings. Both these parties we may suppose are zealous supporters of the Turf, and if the opportunity had presented of comparing opinions, the objectionable features in the conditions of the stakes might have been so altered as to suit the views of both.

One man, with a long purse and a numerous stud, and perhaps several confederates, may prefer stakes for a large sum, with very disproportiate forfeits, while another in moderate circumstances and a limited stud, wishing to make but a single entry, would choose a lower entry and a higher forfeit. Such diversity of views and interests, of course, will always exist, but the most injurious consequence might in a great degree be obviated, by fixing upon certain places, and establishing thereat, annually, such stakes as would accommodate the greatest numbers. And this highly desirable object, it appears to me, can never be affected except by the concerted action of the leading gentlemen connected with the Turf. When it is known that certain events will take place periodically, it will be an additional inducement to engage in breeding and racing, especially to all who are not too remote from the place of meeting; and what is of vast importance, it will induce those having charge of the course and its appurtenances, to make ample preparations for an increased attendance of men and horses, and to provide every necesssary accommodation both for training and racing.

Now suppose some forty or fifty gentlemen obligate themselves to each other to run three sweepstakes annually for three years, (and there are doubtless a hundred or more gentlemen who would be willing to enter into such engagements, if the time, place and conditions, were first settled to their satisfaction,) they would be enabled to fix upon places most convenient to the majority, and establish such regulations as would obviate existing evils and abuses of all kinds, which have gradually crept into use, and caused discontent among the votaries of the Turf themselves, and rendered the sport obnoxious in a certain degree, to the public. The Turf in the United States is yet in its infancy and although grown to be a leading feature of our national recreations, a great and flourishing national interest, yet no attempt has been made to systemise its operations, to improve and elevate its condition, and to correct irregularities. The longer things remain in their present disjointed condition, the difficulty of any thorough reform will be commensurate with the rapid increase of race courses and race-horses in all parts of the country. Although the public, with unbounded liberality, contribute two or three hundred thousand dollars annually, in purses and prizes, (which are, and of right ought to be, awarded as the respective Jockey Clubs deem fit, and with which we have not desire to interfere,) yet it is evident that sweepstakes are increasing in favor, both with Turfmen and the public, and it may not be hazarding too much to predict, that at no distant day they (sweepstakes) will be the most attracitve events of every meeting. In amount, they will be as thousands to tens, compared with the Jockey Club purses; and a corresponding improvement of the laws of racing, regulations of the course, appointments, and other preparations for training—in short, a better organization of the entire *materiel* in its present increased and yet increasing state, will become necessary to ensure the permanent prosperity of the turf. Suppose these forty or fifty, or, mayhap, one hundred gentlemen, should select *three* places of sport, one (say) within fifty miles of Petersburg, Va., for the Eastern division, one within fifty miles of Nashville, Tenn., for the Western, and a third within fifty miles of Augusta, Ga., and agree to run their sweepstakes both Spring and Fall at the two former, and about the month of February or March, at the latter (Georgia). Petersburg and Augusta are easily reached by steamers and railways (those admirable contrivances for annihilating space and time,) and these improvements are stretching out their arms to the West and South-West, and are prosecuted with so much energy, that at no distant day the whole country will be intersected with them. Nashville is conveniently situated to the great breeding States, Kentucky, Tennessee, and Alabama, which have within their limits not less than ninety, out of one hundred and sixty-two thorough-bred stallions in the United States; and the approaches to it, by means of MacAdamized roads in every direction, are every day becoming more expeditious.

Whatever places this association of gentlemen should select would at once become the Metropolis of the Turf in their respecitve divisions, and they would assume the same promincence in this country, that Newmarket, Epson and Doncaster hold in England. And what would racing in England (that paradise of the blood horse) be without her Newmarket, to train, educate and try the young things—Epsom for the annual festival of the Derby and Oaks, and Doncaster for the St. Leger?

The advantages which would enevitably result from such a union of interest, such a concentration of the energies of all in anywise connected with the Turf, are too obvious to require specification; and it is greatly to be desired that those gentlemen who are favorable to the proposition, will at once come forward and give it their cordial support, and lend to the cause the influence of their names. If any better plan can be devised for attaining the same object, gentlemen should speak out and let the public have the benefit of their reflections...

A SUBSCRIBER TO THE PEYTON STAKES.

P.S. It may not be remembered by all, that the original proposition contemplated *three* stakes annually, $1000 each, $250 forfeit, for three years; but for permanent stakes, I would recommend a much lower entry, to render them acceptable to every breeder, upon something like the following plan:—For the three-year-old stake let the entry be made and the stake closed on the 1st of January, when the colt comes two years old—that is, let the stake to be run in 1841 close in January 1840—the entry about $400 each, half forfeit, or only $100 forfeit if declared and paid 1st January previous to the race; if more than forty remain in, divide the entries into two classes, if more than sixty into three, &c. Give the second horse $——, and let the winners of the different classes run for the declared forfeits. Such a low entry would induce a numerous subscription, and the division into classes would increase the chances of winning, would increase the sport and provide a good field for each class. By this arrangement the best of the year would be brought together, and the comparative merits of each ascertained by repeated trials over the same course at the same meeting.

Other sweepstakes would be started for various amounts and distances, and occasionally a heavy match; all of which would render these meetings both important to those connected with the Turf, and highly interesting to the whole community. Preparations would be made upon a scale corresponding with the public wants, and if these places should become what they ought to be, eligible for training, large numbers of horses might be expected to reamin there the year round, which would be an immense advantage to the surrounding country.

Again—By a number of such sweepstakes at the *same* meeting, a better opportunity than often occurs would be afforded of testing the merits of a horse by the time. The length, form and condition of courses are so variant, (to say nothing about watches), that little can be known of the powers of a horse(except relatively with his competitors in the race) from the time, as reported at most of the Jockey Club races. It is true that would be the case any where, but when there are large entries and numerous races at the same meeting, the result would be more satisfactory, than an isolated event over another course.

NEW YORK RACING

Thoroughbred horse racing experienced tremendous growth and popularity by the mid-1830s. One of the oldest and most influential jockey clubs in the nation was the New-York Jockey Club which through its leadership, contributed to the professionalization of the sport. The following rules, reprinted from the February 1840 volume of the American Turf Register and Sporting Magazine, demonstrate the precision that clubs used in drafting their own regulations and their concerns about the evolution of the sport.

RULES AND REGULATIONS
ADOPTED BY THE NEW-YORK JOCKEY CLUB,
APRIL 9, 1836

1st.—THERE shall be two regular meetings of the NEW-YORK JOCKEY CLUB, at the Union Course, in each year, to be called *Spring and Fall Meetings*. The *Spring* meeting to take place the *first Tuesday in May*; the *Fall* meeting, the *first Tuesday in October*.

2d.—There shall be a President, Vice-President, Secretary, Treasurer, and four Stewards, appointed annually, by ballot.

3d.—It shall be the duty of the President to preside at all meetings of the Club.

4th.—It shall be the duty of the Vice-President also, to attend all meetings of the Club, to assist the President in the discharge of his duty, and to act as President, *pro tem.*, in the absence of the President.

5th.—It shall be the duty of the Secretary to attend the Judges on each day's race, assist them with his counsel, keep a book in which he shall enter the Rules of the Club, and add to them any Resolutions which may change the character of either; shall keep also a book to record the proceedings of the meeting, the entries of horses, matches and sweepstakes, an account of each day's race including the time of running each heat, publish the Races, and after they are over publish the result.

6th.—The Stewards shall serve for one meeting next succeeding their appointment. It shall be their duty to attend on the Course, preserve order, clear the track, keep off the crowd from the horses coming to the stand after the close of a heat—may employ able-bodied men to assist them, who shall be paid out of any monies in the hands of the Treasurer.

7th.—There shall be three Judges in the starting stand, whose duty it shall be to keep the stand clear of intrusion during the pendency of a heat, and also to see that the riders are dressed in Jockey style.

8th.—All disputes shall be decided by the Judges of the day, from whose decision there shall be no appeal, unless at the Judges' discretion. They shall have power to appoint distance Judges, and three Inspectors to be placed at each quarter stake, whose report alone, when so appointed, shall be received of any alleged foul riding.

9th.—The distance to be run—for the Proprietor's Purse, shall be Two Mile Heats—for the Jockey Club Purse, Four Mile Heats; and a Purse shall be put up, Three Mile Heats. Entrance money to be 5 per cent. on the amount put up.

10th.—Every horse shall carry weight according to age, as follows:

An aged horse	126	pounds.
Six years old	121	"
Five years old	114	"
Four years old	104	"
Three years old	90	"
Mares, fillies and geldings, allowed	3	"

11th.—When in running a distance is

In four miles,	120	yards.
In three miles,	90	"
In two miles,	70	"
In one mile,	45	"

12th.—The time between heats shall be as follows:

For four mile heats	35	minutes.
For three mile heats	30	"
For two mile heats	25	"
For mile heats	20	"

13th.—All sweepstakes and matches advertised to be run over the Union Course on any day of a meeting, shall be under the cognizance of this Club; and whenever a subscriber makes a nomination, he may change it at any time before the stakes close.

14th.—No person shall enter a horse for any Purse under the control of this Club, unless he produces, if required, proof of his horse's age; nor shall he enter a horse unless he be at least one-fifth interested in such horse or purse, and unless his entrance and subscription be paid.

15th.—All entries of horses shall be made under seal, addressed to the Secretary, enclosing the entrance money, specifying the name, sex, age, pedigree, name of person entering, and dress of the rider; which entries shall be made on each day, preceding a race, and shall be opened by the Secretary on that day at 5 P.M., and declared by the President, or the person so officiating; after which time no further entries shall be received: but the President, or person so officiating, may, for good cause, postpone the time of entering for a period not exceeding two hours from 5 P.M.

16th.—Any person desirous of becoming a Member for the purpose of entering a horse, may do so, he being approved by the Club, and paying double entrance; but none but a Member can enter a horse for a Club Purse.

17th.—The winning horse of the Jockey Club Purse or Purses, shall not be permitted to enter for the Proprietors' Purse or Purses, nor the winning horse of the Proprietor's Purse or Purses, for the Jockey Club Purse or Purses, during the same meeting.

18th.—No compromise or agreement between any two persons entering horses, or their agents and grooms, not to oppose each other, upon a promised division of the Purse, or any other motive, shall be permitted or allowed; and no persons shall run their horses in conjunction, that is, with a determination to oppose jointly any other horse or horses which may run against them. In either case, upon satisfactory evidence produced before the Judges, the Purse shall be awarded to the next best horse, and the persons so offending shall never again be permitted to enter a horse on the Union Course.

19th.—No two riders from the same stable, shall be permitted to ride in the same race. No two horses from the same stable, or owned in whole or in part by the same person, shall be allowed to enter in the same race for any Jockey Club or Proprietors' Purse; and in the event of such double entry being made, both shall be void.

20th.—Riders shall not be permitted to ride, unless dressed in Jockey style—liveries to be recorded in the Secretary's book, and not permitted to be assumed by others.

21st.—Riders, after a heat is ended, must repair to the Judges' stand, and not dismount until ordered by the Judges, and then carry themselves their saddles to the scales to be weighed; nor shall any groom or other person approach or touch any horse until after his rider shall have dismounted and removed his saddle, except by order of the Judges. A rider dismounting without such permission, or wanting more than one pound of his weight, shall be considered distanced.

22d.—The rider who has won a heat, shall be entitled to the track, and the foremost be entitled to any part of the track, he [leaving?] a sufficient space for a horse to pass him on the outside; but shall not, when locked by another horse, leave the track he may be running on, to press him to the inside or outside; doing which shall be deemed foul riding. Should any rider intentionally cross, jostle, or strike his adversary's horse or rider, or run on his heels, or do any thing else that may impede the progress of his adversary, he will be deemed distanced, though he come out ahead, and the Purse will be given to the next best horse; and any rider offending against this rule, shall never again be permitted to ride over, or attend any horse on this Course.

23d.—Every horse that shall fail to run outside of every pole, shall be deemed distance, although he come out first; and the Purse shall be awarded to the next best horse.

24th.—Horses shall take their ages from the first of January; that is, a horse foaled in 1835, will be considered a year old first of January 1836.

25th.—A signal shall be given from the Judges' stand five minutes before the time of starting, after the lapse of which time, the Judge shall give the word to such riders as are ready; but should any horse prove restive in bringing up or starting, the Judges may delay the word a short interval, at their discretion.

26th.—All Members, and such of their families as reside with them, shall pass the gates free; and the Members themselves have free admission to the Members' stand. All who are not Members, shall pay the following tolls at the gates, viz.:

For every four horse carriage with not more than four persons (if more, 25 cents for each over four),

$2 00

Every four wheel carriage, with two horses and not more than four persons (each over four, 25 cents,)

1 00

Every four wheel carriage with one horse and two persons,

75

Every two wheel carriage with one horse and two persons,

50

Every person on horseback,

50

Every foot passenger, or person in a Member's carriage, not a Member,

25

27th.—New Members can only be admitted on recommendation. Any person wishing to become a Member, must be so for the unexpired term of the Club, and must be balloted for. Three black balls shall reject. A non-resident of the State of New-York introduced by a Member, can have the privilege of the enclosed space and Members' stand, by paying $3 for the meeting.

28th.—Ten Members of the Club shall be deemed a quorum for the transaction of ordinary business and admission of Members; but not less than twenty to alter a fundamental rule, unless public notice shall have been given ten days of such contemplated meeting. The President or Secretary may call a meeting; and the President and Vice-President failing to attend, a Chairman may be selected. Members of the Club privileged to invite their friends to the Jockey Club Dinners, by paying for the same. No ladies admitted to the Ladies' Pavilion, unless introduced by a member. No citizen of the State of New-York can be admitted to the privileges of the enclosed space, Members' Stand, or Ladies' Pavilion, unless he be a Member.

29th.—A distanced horse in a dead heat, shall not be permitted to start for another heat in that race; but when a dead heat is made, all the horses not distanced may start again, unless the dead heat be made between two horses that if either had been winner the race would have been decided; in which case, the two only must start to decide which shall be entitled to the Purse. Such horses as are prevented from starting by this rule, shall be considered drawn; and all bets made on them against each other, shall be drawn, excepting those put behind the post.

30th.—If a rider fall from his horse, and another person of sufficient weight rides him in, he shall be considered as though the rider had not fallen, provided he returns to the place where the rider fell.

31st.—When in the opinion of a majority of the Officers of the Club, the weather, or any other good cause shall require it, they may postpone any Purse Race; but in case of such postponement, no new entries shall be received if any had been made; but such postponement of a Purse Race, shall give no authority to postpone any sweepstakes or machines made or advertised to be run on that day.

32d.—When the tap of the drum is once given by the starting Judge, there shall be no calling back, unless the signal flag shall be hoisted for that purpose; and when so hoisted, it shall be no start. To remedy the inconvenience of false starts, there shall be a signal flag placed at a point which can be readily seen by the riders, at from one to three hundred yards from the Judges' stand. When a start is given and recalled, a flag from the Judges' stand shall displayed, and the person having in charge the signal flag shall hoist the same as a notice to pull up. It shall be the duty of the starting Judge to give this rule in charge to the riders.

33d.—A bet made after the heat is over, if the horse betted up does not start again, is no bet. A confirmed bet cannot be off without mutual consent.

34th.—If either party be absent on the day of a race, and the money be not staked, the party present may declare the bet void in the presence of the Judges before the race commences; but if any person present offer to stake for the absentee, it is a confirmed bet.

36th.—No horse shall carry more than five pounds over his stipulated weight, without the Judges being informed of it, which shall be declared by them, whereupon all bets shall be void, except those made between the owners of such running horses. Every rider shall declare to the Judge that weighs him, when and how his extra weight, if any, is carried. The owner is held responsible for putting up and bringing out the proper weight. He shall also be bound before starting to weigh his rider in the presence of the Judges.

37th.—The person who bets the odds, has a right to choose the horse or the field. When he has chosen his horse, the field is what starts against him, but there is no field unless one starts with him. If odds are bet without naming the horses before the race is over, it must be determined as the odds were at the time of making it. Bets made in running are not determined till the Purse is won, if the heat is not specified at the time of betting. Bets made between particular horses, are void if neither of them be winner, unless specified to the contrary. Horses that forfeit, are the beaten horses where it is play or pay. All bets, matches, and engagements, are void on the decrease of either party before determined. Horses drawn before the Purse is won, are distanced. A bet made on a Purse or horse, is void if the horse betted on does not start. When a bet is made upon a heat, the horse that comes first to the ending post is best, provided no circumstance shall cause him to be deemed distanced. All bets are understood to relate to the Purse, if nothing is said to the contrary. A horse not winning a heat in three, shall not start for a fourth.

38th.—When two horses are betted against each other for the Purse, if each win a heat, and neither are distanced, they are equal; if neither win a heat, and neither distanced, they are equal; but if one wins a heat and the other does not, the winner of the

heat is best, unless he shall be distanced, in which case the other, if he save his distance, shall be considered best. If a horse wins a heat and is distanced—so, too, if one
be distanced the 2d heat, he shall be better than one distanced the first heat, &c.

39th.—Any person entering a horse younger than he really is, shall forfeit his entrance money; and if the horse wins a heat of race, the heat or Purse shall be given to
the next best horse. If the objection be made to the age of the horse *after* the heat or
race is run, the disqualification must be proved by the person making the objection.

40th.—If a horse be entered without being properly identified, he shall not be allowed to start, but liable for forfeit, or the whole if play or pay-all bets on a horse so
disqualified, void.

41st.—Where more than one nomination has been made by the same individual in
any *sweepstakes* to be run over the Union Course, and it shall appear to the satisfaction of the Club that all interest in such nomination has *bona fide* been disposed of
before the time of starting, and that they have not been trained together, or in the same
stable, both may start, although standing in the same name.

42d.—No conditional nomination or entry shall be received.

43d.—Should any person entering a horse, formally declare to the Judges that his
horse is drawn, he shall not be permitted to start.

44th.—In the event of the Club postponing a regular meeting, it shall have no
power to postpone any Matches or Sweepstakes made for that meeting.

45th.—In Sweepstakes and Matches made to run at a particular meeting, without
the parties specifying the days; the Proprietor must give ten days notice of what days
they will be run on, during that meeting.

46th.—The words *absolutely or play or pay*, necessary to be used to make a bet
play or pay—done and done, also necessary to confirm a bet. If a bet shall stand; but
if the owner dies, the bet is void. If a bet be made using the expression play or pay,
and the horse dies, the bet be made without using the expression play or pay, and the
horse or owner dies, it is no bet.

47th.—In Sweepstakes and Matches, the Judges shall draw for the track. In Purse
Races, they shall take their places as drawn the preceding evening by the Secretary.

48th.—Catch weights are each person to appoint a rider without weighing—Feather
weight signifies the same. A Post stake, is to name at the starting post. Handicap
weights, are weights according to the supposed ability of the horses. An untried stallion or mare, is one whose get or produce never started in public. A maiden horse or
mare, is one that never run.

49th.—A horse receiving forfeit, or walking over, shall not be deemed a winner.

50th.—In a Match Race of *heats*, there shall be a distance, but none in a *single* heat.

51st.—Any Trainer, Rider, or Rubber, going into a stable without a certificate of
good character from his last employer, if such employer be a Member of this Club, may
upon specification of any improper act or deportment of such Trainer, Rider, or Rubber, at the discretion of the Judges of the day, be excluded from the Union Course—
provided such complaint be made to the President, or officer so officiating, before the
signal to saddle for the first heat be given. It is further provided, that any Trainer, Rider,
or Rubber, that may be so employed, with or without certificate of good character, may

be objected to in like manner, for good cause shewn to the Judges of the day—provided the offence specified shall have occurred subsequent to the last semi-annual meeting.

52d.—No person shall be permitted to pass into the enclosed *space* on the Union Course, without shewing his ticket at the gate; nor shall any person be permitted to remain within the enclosure, or Members' stand, unless he wears a badge, that the officers on duty may be enabled to distinguish those privileged. Officers who shall permit the infraction of this rule, shall forfeit all claim to compensation, and must be employed on this express condition.

53d.—Membership of the New-York Jockey Club, shall be for Three years, commencing Spring 1836—subscription Twenty Dollars per annum, payable each Spring—subscription to be paid, by original signature, or on nomination, will be bound for the unexpired term of the Club from the period of joining.

54th.—In all cases where any act or thing is prohibited by these Rules, without any penalty being attached to a violation of such prohibition, the Judges shall have power to impose such penalty as they deem proper.

Upon the expiration of the Club of 1838, a new Club was formed, adopting the preceding Rules and Regulations, with the following Resolution:—

New-York, April 24th, 1839.—RESOLVED—That a Club be established for Three Years. No subscription less than $20, or more than $50 per annum, payable annually whether present or absent. Extra meetings, if given by the Proprietors, to entitle them to make a separate charge for admission to the privileges of the Course. For the present subscription, the Proprietors to give Two meetings, the one Spring, the other Fall; and to put up, under the control of the Club, the amount thus raised, in Purses, during the two meetings; and are not expected to put up a larger amount than paid in by subscription. Members paying $50 per annum, have the privilege to invite a friend (being a non-resident of the State of New York) to the two meetings. Gentlemen joining the Club on nomination, after its organization, will be held liable for the unexpired term of the Club, from the period of joining.

THE FIRST STEEPLE CHASE IN NORTH AMERICA

The infusion of British miliary regiments into the Canadian provinces during the unification struggles in the 1840s had a direct impact on equestrian sports in the country. Not only did many of the troops encourage sports of the turf but many of their officers had distinguished themselves in British racing circles. One of the benefits of their presence was the running of what the Montreal Herald claimed was the first steeple chase in North America. Note the prominent role of military personnel in the following account, a reprint from the 31 October 1840 issue of The Spirit of the Times.

FIRST STEEPLE CHASE IN CANADA

The Montreal "Gazette" furnishes the following spirited account of a brilliant Steeple Chase which came off on the 15th inst. near that city. The "Gazette," by-the-bye, is edited with a great degree of ability, and we are frequently indebted to it for interesting Canadian Sporting Intelligence:—

We mentioned, on Thursday, that the first steeple chase ever run in "British North America," took place that day in the neighborhood of this city. The day was very fine, and, at an early hour, all parts of the course were crowded with spectators in carriages, on horseback, and on foot, to-witness one of the most exciting sports of the Turf. His Excellency of the Governor General and suite were present; and also, Major General Clitherow and lady, Mr. Murdoch, Chief Secretary, and lady, the Attorney General, Colonels Gore, Campbell, Love, Young, &c. &c.

The course was in the form of a circle, of three miles in length, intersected by upwards of twenty fences and ditches, to be cleared in course of the race. At about three o'clock the following horses started for the prize, which, we learn, amounted to ninety pounds.

Lieut. Col. Whyte's (7th Hussars) b.h. *Heretic*
Mr. H.G. Jones' b.h. *Barbeau*
Lieut. Col. Whyte's (7th Hussars) b.h. *Guardsman*
Capt. Scott's (K.D.G.) b.h. *Tearing Dog*
Mr. Douglas Jones' (73rd Regt.) b.h. *Angelo*
Mr. Richards' ch.g. *Waverley*
Capt. Jones' (Q.I.D.) b.g. *Prince Charlie*
Mr. J.F. M'Donald's b.m. *Nancy*
Mr. Cleaver's (K.D.G.) b.m. *Duvernay*

Owner	1
Owner	2
Capt. Sutton, 7th Hussars	3
Mr. Newgill, R.A.	dist.
Mr. Umacke, 71st Regt.	dist.
Mr. Cotton, 7th Hussars	dist.
Mr. Duchesnay, 1st P.M.	dist.
Owner	dist.
Mr. Hillier, 7th Hussars	dist.

At starting, Col. Whyte took the lead, and gallantly maintained it during the whole race, displaying a skill in horsemanship, and an ease and grace in riding, which at once surprised and delighted the spectators. He was followed, in excellent style by the rest of the field, all of whom richly deserve the most unqualified praise for the art which they displayed in the management of their horses, and the bold and fearless style of their riding. The first obstruction consisting of a fence and a ditch, was gallantly cleared by all, with the exception of Waverley, who, it was regretted, declined to have any thing more to do in the affair. For some time similar obstructions were got over in the same style, until Prince Charlie deemed it advisable to decline any more *fencing*. Barbeau then took the lead of Nancy, which before was second; the rest of the field falling gradually in rear of the first three. The race now became doubly interesting, on account of the increasing height and length of the fences and ditches, but the riders and their cattle were up to almost every difficulty of the kind. Heretic led in, as he commenced, in gallant style, closely followed by Barbeau and Guardsman; the remaining five being distanced, but getting over their work in a creditable manner. Colonel Whyte won the race by about twenty lengths. It is impossible for us to convey any adequate idea of the exciting nature of the whole affair, nor of the dauntless bearing of all concerned in it. We congratulate them on their escape from any serious hurt and injury; and trust that the Montreal Steeple Race, of the 15th inst., will not be the first and last of its kind. Those who, on this occasion, exhibited so excellent and gratifying a specimen of the noble field sports of England, are entitled to the best thanks of the public here; and we assure ourselves that it will be long before it can be forgotten to our fellow-citizens who were spectators on the occasion.

The "Daily Herald," of Montreal, gives the following account of this sporting affair:—

The first Steeple Chase in British America came off yesterday (Oct. 15), on a farm about two miles distant from the city, situated near the St. Michel road, and owned by Mr. O'Flaherty. The novelty of the chase brought great crowds to the field, among whom we observed His Excellency the Governor General and suite. The course was three miles long, in the form of a circle, and we understand there were twenty-six fences and ditches to be leaped over by the riders. The following are the names of the horses entered for the race, with those of their riders and owners:—

Capt. Scott's (K.D.G.) b.h. *Tearing Dog*, ridden by Mr. Heugill, R.A.

Lieut. Col Whyte's (7th Hussars) b.h. *Heretic*,—Owner.

Lieut Col. Whyte's (7th Hussars) b.h. *Guardsman*,—Captain Sutton, 7th Hussars.

Captain Jones' (Q.L.D.) b.g. *Prince Charlie*,—Mr. Duchesnay, 1st P.M.

D. Jones', Esq., (73rd Regt.) b.g. *Angelo*,—Mr. Roebuck,-Regt.

H.G. Jones', Esq., b.h. *Barbeau*,—Owner.

J.F. McDonald's, Esq., b.m. *Nancy*,—Owner.

Mr. Richards' ch.g. *Waverley*,—Mr. Cotton, 7th Hussars.

S. Cheaver's, Esq., (K.D.G.) b.m. *Duvernay*,—Mr. Hillier, 7th Hussars.

Some time elapsed before the horses came to the starting post; on the word being given Col. Whyte led off at a very fast pace and cleared the first leap of fence and ditch gallantly, as did all who followed save Waverly, who shirked the leap and absolutely refused the next leap which terminated his race much to the disappointment of many, and notwithstanding the exertions of his rider who repeatedly endeavoured to "make him up." The other leaps were beautifully taken until Prince Charlie swerved and refused to leap. The race for two miles continued, Nancy being at first second, but giving way to Barbeau, whose rider rode his horse with the utmost skill notwithstanding an accident which happened to the girths of the saddle. At the round turn a rasping leap was taken by Colonel Whyte in beautiful style although Heretic did not half like it. At the coming in Heretic came over in game style, taking a magnificent last leap, winning the race by about twenty lengths. Barbeau was brought in, in capital style by his owner, and cleared his last leap as if he had not half run his race. Guardsman, who was third, fell short in the last leap, but was crammed out of the ditch by his rider, who was determined not to be fourth. The rest were no-where in the race, but came over as follows:—Duvernay, 4th, clearing the ditch well, as did Tearing Dog, 5th, and Angelo 6th; Nancy, 7th, came gamely up to the leap, but was completely *used up*, falling on the other side of the ditch with her rider, who was not at all injured. Thus ended the first Steeple Chase in Canada, much to the satisfaction of every one, the race being most gallantly ridden by all, and won in the best style, and not one accident occurring.

The "first Steeple Chase in North America" went off with so much spirit and satisfaction that a second one was immediately projected. The "Morning Courier" of the 22d inst. announces it in the following terms:-

STEEPLE CHASE THIS DAY.—Owing to the pleasure derived from the sport of the other day, and the anxiety expressed to witness a renewal, a second Steeple Chase has been resolved upon, and appointed, as our readers have been already apprised by advertisement, for this day. The horses were handicapped yesterday, as follows:—

	stone.	lbs.
Col. Whyte's *Heretic*	13	7
Mr. Jones' *Barbeau*	12	7
Col. Whyte's *Guardsman*	12	4
Mr. Cleaver's, (K.D.G.) *Duvernay*	11	4
Mr. Bamford's *Lady Emily*	11	4
Mr. Jones (73rd Regt.) *Angelo*	10	7
Mr. Smith's *Charley*	10	7
Mr. Cotton's mare	10	0
Captain Sandiman's *Scurry*	10	0
Mr. McDonald's *Nancy*	10	0
Mr. Paynter's *Henrietta*	with'd	

The ground to be run over is two miles in length over Mr. O'Flaherty's grounds, who by his spirit of accommodation in this matter, proves himself to be a keen sportsman and a very obliging neighbor to the good people of Montreal. The start will take place, we understand, at one precisely, or as near as possible to that hour, as the same causes of delay will not exist as upon occasion. We recommend, therefore, early attendance....

Chapter 8

FIELD SPORTS

The popularity of field sports in America and Canada was a natural byproduct of the lengthy process of settlement and colonization. Because the isolation of the frontier left settlers to provide for their own sustenance and protection against native Americans and frontier marauders, the prevalence of guns and ammunition became a distinguishing feature of the colonies in the New World. From the very beginning, the widespread ownership of guns and an abundance of land encouraged settlers, particularly the British, to hunt many different types of game for profit, food, and amusement. The presence of deer, bear, rabbits, fox, wild turkeys, and a long list of various fowl in the United States and Canada offered hunters a rich array of game from which to choose. For those suited to more peaceful outdoor pursuits, the numerous streams, rivers, and lakes provided plenty of opportunity to hone their angling skills. Fishing allowed individuals, or sometimes groups, to combine healthy exercise with character development, as many believed angling cultivated such virtues as patience, kindness, and tenacity.

By the early nineteenth century the development of some areas of America and Canada, especially the expansion of the cities, fundamentally altered the relationship between people and the land and the nature and practice of recreation. Although this transformation was not fully complete until after mid-century the process had begun much earlier. The growth of cities and the introduction of regimented industrial work patterns hampered the ability of urban residents to hunt. The geographical expansion of the cities and the concomitant depopulation of animals in surrounding areas restricted the availability of good hunting grounds within the immediate vicinity and hunters were required to travel longer distances in order to pursue their sport. Their concern for the preservation of game is presented in "Shooting Game Out of Season," "Game Laws of Massachusetts," and other chapter documents.

Although the conditions of city life limited the sport of hunting, sportsmen soon developed adequate substitutes that still preserved many of the features that attracted them to the sport in the first place. Shooting and, to a lesser extent, archery soon emerged as worthy replacements for hunting and, as with many other sports of the era, participants organized themselves into clubs and standardized rules and regulations to promote competition, both important steps in the modernization of these sports. In this period shooting and archery matches were more social than competitive events, with the amount of drinking and betting far exceeding the quality of competition.

Two different types of shooting were practiced from 1821-1840, pigeon and target. The former usually took place in taverns and involved the killing of pigeons at distances of about one hundred yards. This activity was popular among many classes and in many areas of the United States and Canada. The latter owed its existence to the influence of military practices and skills, and target clubs, especially after 1850, often maintained connections to militia companies. Like pigeon shooting, target shooting usually occurred at taverns. The private individuals involved often wagered considerable sums of money. As both types of shooting grew in popularity, sportsmen kept track of what took place through journals that reported precise descriptions of the numerous aspects of contests. Such precision became necessary in order for sportsmen to evaluate and compare their skills in sports without standardized rules and regulations. "Rifle Shooting in New York," "Sweepstakes Shooting Match," "Target Shooting in Gotham," and other documents in this chapter testify to the popularity and evolution of target and pigeon shooting.

In a similar vein archery clubs were formed, the most famous of which was the United Bowman of Philadelphia, founded in 1828. For the most part archery had been relegated to a limited pastime before the 1830s but with the constraints placed on urban sportsmen archery became an enjoyable club sport. The United Bowmen drew up a constitution and rules and regularly held contests. They even added to the sport by developing their own target, which has become standard today. The history and contributions of the United Bowmen were detailed in their own publication, "The Archer's Manual," an excerpt of which appears in this section, along with an article from the American Turf Register covering their seventh anniversary.

For other areas, such as the more rural, agrarian southern United States or the western frontier of Canada and America, the relationship between people and the land remained for the most part unchanged and sport remained more premodern in character. In these areas the hunting of fox, deer, bear, and fowl remained common pursuits. Game hunts provided rural participants with a comaraderie sorely lacking on the frontier and usually concluded with lengthy celebrations. In most game hunting sportsmen relied on various breeds of dogs who aided in the tracking and retrieving of prey. In turn, the popularity of hunting contributed to improving canine and horse breeding as well as to leading to technological innovations in guns and ammunition. "Game and Sports of the West," "Fort Gibson Hunting Club," and other documents in this chapter describe some of these frontier and rural field sports.

THE PRACTICAL GUIDE TO GAME SHOOTING

In America between 1820 and 1840, game shooting became more regulated and dog breeding and technology more advanced. The American Shooter's Manual, the first detailed treatment on the subject in the United States, appeared in 1827. The virtual absence of game laws, the prevalence of poaching and trapping, and the lack of knowledge about gun maintenance gave rise to the manual. It dealt with a variety of topics such as the breeding of game dogs, types of game, proper methods of game shooting, and gun care and technical innovations. The following excerpt from the manual is from a 1928 reprint of the book.

PREFACE

THE present publication has been undertaken, at the solicitation of several friends of the writer, who, with himself, are anxious to have a treatise on the subject, better adapted to our own country, and at a more reasonable charge, than the British publication which are occasionally imported.

It is proper to premise, that the writer makes no presentations to originality, as to the entire work, but merely wishes the credit of having made a judicious compilation: in doing this, he has consulted the best standard sporting books, as well as the experience of several intelligent sportsmen.

Living in a country destitute of game laws, and almost without any legal restrictions, in regard to its destruction, every man, whose leisure, or circumstances will permit, may become a shooter. But of the multitude who shoot, few indeed, will be found entitled to the appellation of sportsmen; they are very generally game killers, and nothing more.

As soon as a boy arrives at the age of twelve, if he can buy, or borrow a gun, he commences shooting, in company with others, who, like himself, have neither system, nor example. Some of them, no doubt, become expert shots, but it is very rare they can manage dogs, or are safe companions; a majority of the accidents from fire arms, occurring, indeed, among these stripling sportsmen.

One great object of the present undertaking, is then, to diffuse throughout the community, a taste for genteel and sportsman-like shooting, and to abolish that abominable poaching, game destroying habit of ground shooting, trapping, and snaring, which prevails throughout our country, in the neighborhood of all cities and large towns.

It is true, that the art of shooting on the wing, it progressing very rapidly, but the science of dog breaking, is, comparatively, but little understood, and the proper information on this subject, limited to a very few. Though we may boast of many capital shots, yet, it must be acknowledged, that it is rather uncommon to meet with a well broken dog, and this not because our dogs are inferior in docility and intelligence to the European, but, because the same care in breaking and training them has not been observed.

The writer is well aware, that many subjects have been omitted in the present work, which in the opinion of some ought to have been noticed, and that more room has been occupied by others than their importance would appear to deserve. The English books contain more minute details on some of the points, than the size of the present work would admit, and many of them, in our opinion, almost foreign to the subject; for instance, long essays on hydrophobia, the history of powder, and the method of its manufacture; the making of gun barrels, guns, &c., all of which, useless to the shooter, excepting as matters of curiosity, and can be readily found in the different scientific works, from which these accounts are, in general, literally copied, and without the slightest acknowledgment. The writer does not conceive any apology to be necessary for the length of two of the articles, namely, breaking and training of dogs, and shooting; he indeed regrets that the limited size of the work would not permit their more minute consideration. It has been his desire to notice everything, that he considered important to the shooter, and avoid anything like affected minuteness. He has endeavoured to give a reason for every principle advanced, and where there is a difference of opinion among sportsmen to decide, with caution and impartiality. It is hoped that the work will be received by those for whom it is intended, with many grains of allowance, and that a due consideration will be had for the difficulties attending a first attempt on any science or subject....

THE AMERICAN
SHOOTER'S MANUAL

THE art of shooting flying has not been practised in this country, excepting by a few individuals, for more than forty years, and in England for not much more than double that length of time. The greatest improvements in the science, and in the fowling-piece itself, have, however, been made within but a few years; and since its adaption to the percussion powder, it would seem that the gun is capable of little or no important improvement; all that now remains, is for the shooter to acquire a knowledge of the proper use of it.

Many rules are laid down for the young shooter, all of them important, but the most perfect knowledge of them will avail but little, without frequent practice, strictly regulated by those rules.

The first and most important lesson to be acquired, is a habitual coolness and self possession: not to be agitated when the dog is at a stand, nor flurried when the birds are flushed. In fact, it is the want of deliberation that makes all our bad shots. The Juvenile or unpractised sportsman ought, for the first season at least, always to accompany some experienced shooter, attend to his instructions, and closely observe his actions.

Some persons have, injudiciously, recommended swallow shooting as an incipient lesson; but experience has fully proved the fallacy of this practice. Without giving a host of reasons against it, let it suffice to say, that in most instances, when a shooter undertakes to learn by that method, although he may become very expert in destroying those useful, amusing and agreeable little creatures, he never acquires any other character, as a sportsman, than that of a skilful swallow shooter.

The Rail affords beginners in this country advantages of practising on the wing, over those in England, as it is a bird heavy and slow on the wing, flies very fair, and is withal easily killed. In rising it generally makes some noise, by splashing in the water and reeds, by which it will, in some degree, prepare the shooter for its flight. As this bird is so very abundant, at the season immediately antecedent to that of the partridge, we would recommend those who have the opportunity, to practise on it, as a species of game apparently designed for that and no other purpose, in preference to the cruel and unmanly destruction of the pleasant and useful little swallow. Shooting at pigeons flushed by a spring- box or trap, is perhaps as good a method as any other for a somewhat practised shot, to acquire coolness, quickness and deliberation in shooting, as it comes nearest to the most trying of all situations for a juvenile shooter, viz. by a steady dog at a firm stand; he will by this practice, become somewhat prepared for those peculiar feelings which every shooter must, for some time, experience.

A beginner will generally fire too soon, and as a necessary result from this circumstance, too low; this is caused by the apprehension that the birds, from the rapid manner in which they rise, will get out of this reach; Experience, however, will prove to him, that he is under a delusion, as abundant time is always given to single out a bird, bring the gun down, cock and fire.

A gentlemen of my acquaintance informed me, that when young, he was frequently guilty of shooting too soon; and was effectually corrected by an old French gentleman, who, to exemplify his precepts, would take out his snuff box, after the bird has risen, take a pinch, cock his gun, and deliberately kill his bird. It is indeed astonishing, how quickly every necessary preparation for firing can be made.

Another and very important difficulty every beginner has to contend with, is the trepidation and anxiety, he will for some time experience, when the dog comes to a stand; none but those who have felt the sensation, can imagine the reality. I have observed men, and men too who had some experience, on coming up to the dog, show evident symptoms of the horrors; this is only to be got over by coolness, and resolution. Thomas says (and that with much truth) "there is no pursuit or amusement, in which a steady hand, a cool head, and philosophical patience, are more required, than in shooting." How it is, that a dog with a partridge before his nose, will make a man feel so very queer, we are not exactly able to say, further than to attribute it to the novelty of the sight, and the ambition of the shooter to be successful: the latter I think is the principal reason; for we often find shooters, who use the long bow, as well as the gun; and will not hesitate to make up an astonishing nominal account of game they have been so lucky as to kill. Others, to make up a good report, and at the same time to back it with proof, will sometimes purchase, at high prices too, from men who make game killing their business, and then have a grand display for the hall, of their skill and success. Every gentleman can judge of the propriety, or impropriety, of these artifices to establish a character for keen shooting; and can reject, or adopt them at pleasure. My object in introducing the matter, is merely to show, that my reason for attributing in part the strange nervous affection, just mentioned, to the cause alluded to, may be correct.

If notwithstanding the observance of the foregoing rules, the shooter still fins his trepidation, or anxiety unconquered; let him, says the gentleman of Suffolk, "set forth with every appendage but (but what he thinks hard should be left behind) powder and shot. A stiff piece of sole leather may represent the flint, to spare the face of the hammer. When a bird gets up he is certain he cannot kill it; therefore, he can wait to any length, until he gets it at the end of his gun; he must never draw unless positive of seeing the bird in that very point of situation. Let it go; every fresh spring of a bird will make him more composed; and as this tremor wears off, he will grow more uniform in his manner of getting to it, until at last he will cover it, almost to a certainty, at or very near the same distance. Let him accustom himself also never to take his gun from his arm, until the bird is on the wing; and never to vary his eye, from the very one he has fixed upon. Three words should be mentally used, with a pause between, before he brings his piece to the shoulder: this will keep him, as it were, in awe of himself; and as there is no charm in any particular combination of letters, Hold! Halt! Now! may serve as well as any. A day thus spent, he may put some powder into the pan, and flash away, in that manner, the next; pursuing the former directions, until he can stare with steadfastness, and pull without a wink. The day following, load with powder only;and continue this lesson, more or less, until he is calm, as if the leather were yet in the chops. Now the grand and last trial, complete loading. If he feel the least flutter or anxiety on his advance to the point, let him draw his shot at once, and powder also, before he goes up to his dog; and repeat this *toties quoties* until he has whipped himself into a good temper, and disappointed himself in the accomplishment of his wishes."

Although it is impossible to lay down any number of rules, by which a man will infallibly become a good shot; still many important hints may be given, which will much facilitate the undertaking; and at the same time, render him safe to himself and his companions. And here by the by, a word on that rascally practice, of carrying a gun cocked; a practice which cannot be too much reprobated, as a very great portion of the fatal accidents which have occurred in shooting, can be traced to this cause. If there were the slightest necessity, or convenience resulting from it, there would be some palliation for the wilful commission of, what I consider, a grievous crime; but we have before shown, there can be none; as abundant time is always had, to cock the gun, and shoot the bird. This practice is seldom heard of in England, and never tolerated among gentlemen; but it is too shockingly prevalent in this country. One man will tell you that he always carries his thumb on the cock; very true, but his fore finger is against the trigger; so that still there is an equal chance of an involuntary discharge, and though neither the cock nor trigger were touched; besides, a party carrying his gun in that situation, is apt to shoot too quick, or in fact before he is at all prepared; as the very act of taking the thumb off the cock, naturally presses the finger against the trigger. I had the misfortune to witness the death of a man, caused in this very manner: and a friend of mine, a few days since, had part of the brim of his hat shot away, by a fellow, who was, unknown to him, in his rear; and who accounted for the accident, in the same way. Others will say they always carry the nuzzle of the gun up; they only mean, they do so when it is convenient; and when they think of it; besides, it is impossible to carry the gun in that way, in a cripple, or cover. Without entering into a detail of how, and why accidents may, and do result, from this infamous practice, I would advise any gentlemen, who shall be so unfortunate as to be in the field with a companion, who will persist in such improper conduct, to leave him without ceremony, return home, or shoot alone, in another direction. This may savour of incivility; but a man's politeness, should never jeopardize his life, or limbs. If after cocking the gun, the shooter should be disappointed in getting a shot, he should immediately uncock, and in so doing keep the muzzle up, and be careful to let the cock down beyond the half cock notch, and then bring it up again to the half cock; he will ascertain this by hearing and feeling the tell, when the dog goes into the proper niche of the tumbler. After firing one barrel, and designing to reload, be careful to see that the other lock be not cocked: after you have put in the powder, and rammed home the wad properly, instead of putting the rod under your arm, or between your teeth, insert it into the loaded barrel, and give that a smart stroke or two; you will be very apt to find that the wadding has raised in the barrel by the concussion, or recoil of the gun: this practice serves important purposes: in the first place, it prevents you from losing the shot of the loaded barrel; in the second, it prevents any mistake in charging; and the third, and most important is, that all danger of bursting, from the wad rising in the barrel, is obviated.

I saw, a few weeks since, a valuable gun, the left hand barrel of which was very considerably affected, from this cause, a ring, or swell, was formed around the barrel, eight or ten inches from the breech, and in the opinion of the gunsmith, would have bursted, had it not been an excellent twisted barrel.

When in the act of shooting, grasp the gun, with the left hand, near the guard, so that the hand will come partly under the lock; this is much safer in case of bursting, than the more common method, of holding the gun nearer the tail pipe; as it is found that guns more commonly burst about ten or twelve inches from the breech: it is besides, equally convenient to the shooter, unless he has a very heavy piece.

As to the best method of carrying the gun, this is a mere matter of fancy, and convenience; of no consequence, except that the muzzle should be upwards; and never pointed towards your companion: Perhaps the most convenient method is, to carry the piece diagonally across the breast, the barrels resting in the left hand.

Before entering a house, always discharge your gun, or draw the load; especially if you intend to remain in it for hours; if for a shorter time, and you have percussion locks, to take off the caps or primers, may suffice; but with flint locks, nothing but an empty gun ought to be introduced into your own or a friend's house, so many dreadful accidents have occurred from a want of this precaution, that no gentleman who wished to be considered a real sportsman ought to neglect it. Guns are dangerous articles, and should be handled with great caution. On no account, nor under any circumstance, point a gun at another, unless you intend to take his life. In fact, a gun should always be considered as charged.

Some persons have a habit of striking bushes with the gun: this is a bad and dangerous practice, independent of the chance of having an involuntary discharge, the shot is apt to force the wad out, especially if the barrel be smooth, thus making the piece liable to burst, or at least to disappoint the shooter of his bird.

When shooting with a companion, in a cripple or thicket; if necessary for both to go along the same path, the foremost of the party should carry his gun with the muzzle forward, and elevated, as much as circumstances will permit; and the one behind, should carry his piece in the same manner, only pointing to the rear. I have known several accidents to occur, for want of this trifling precaution.

These cautionary rules to the imprudent or careless shooter, may appear womanish; but let him once suffer for their infraction; and he will no doubt be fully convinced of their importance. For my own part, I do consider a careless shooter worse than a Highwayman; the latter will take your property, but the former may deprive you of life.

Daniels, in his "Rural Sports," advises also "not to display your skill by firing close to the head of either man or beast, whether a companion, or a favorite pointer." A story is told of two persons shooting together, when one of them, on exhibiting in this way, put several shots in his friend's arm, who made suitable outcries. In the course of the day the compliment was returned, with interest, by the wounded man:—"You're a pretty fellow," exclaimed the man last hit, "to be so vociferous about my shooting you this morning; why d—n me, I have half your charge now in my leg";—"very likely," replied the other, coolly, "but I killed my hare and your bird was missed."

When a bird has flushed, the shooter should keep his eye on it, cock his gun, and bring her up, at the very moment he intends to shoot, and the instant the bird is in a line with the barrel, provided the bird flies from him, draw the trigger. If there be more than one, he should immediately bring his gun down, and cock, but after having singled out his bird, should never take his eye off the object until he has fired; and not then, if he has reason to think the bird is struck. This he will know, by the feathers parting, or by the bird dropping its legs, or by towering: in the two last cases, he may be pretty confident that the bird is mortally wounded; although it may fly more than the fourth of a mile. Towering is when the bird raises up to an unusual height; and is caused by a wound in his head, or spine. For these reasons it is very important to be a good marker. This faculty is acquired in a wonderful degree, by those men, who push the boats for gentlemen in the rail season. I have known four, or five rail, to be killed in different directions, among high reed, at one time; and all out of view, the shooter perhaps unable to tell, in which direction any, but the last bird shot, might lie: nevertheless the experienced pusher will move the boat, and without any difficulty pick them all up, one by one.

If the wood grouse, (or pheasant, as it is very improperly called in Pennsylvania) after being shot at, twitches up his wing, and turns his body to one side, you may rely on it he is mortally hit: the direction of his flight ought then to be carefully observed, as he will most likely be found dead, though perhaps at a great distance.

If a bird be winged, or wounded so slightly, that it can still run, the shooter should not go after it, until he has reloaded; nor permit his dogs to move, even though the loss of the bird be certain. A contrary practice will teach the dogs bad habits, and make them apt to flush game. It is however, very seldom that a wounded bird, will escape from a good dog.

Much is said in the books on the subject of cross shots; recommending the shooter to aim before, and above the bird &c: of the necessity of this, I am not aware, with a percussion lock, unless at game a long distance off. It has been my practice, always to cover the bird, and all the good shots I have conversed with, say they do the same: I think there is more theory than necessity, for any other method; in fact I think it almost impossible for the shooter to aim (at what cannot be seen) some two, or three feet a-head and at the same time have a sight on the bird: it may perhaps be done by a cross-eyed man, who keeps both eyes open; one to watch the motion of the bird, and the other the sight. An objection also arises to this practice, in as much as some birds will occasionally make a short turn, and then there will be a great chance for a miss. One thing, however, must be observed: and that is, to keep the gun fully bearing on the bird until you have shot; not to suspend this motion when the trigger is drawn, but to traverse the gun until explosion has taken place; unless this be done, no bird flying in a transverse direction will be hit, except by a scattering shot. The easiest shot is at a bird flying directly from the shooter, but the difference between this and a transverse shot, is very trifling. Most persons prefer a left hand shot, but some the right. Some shooters recommend firing with both your eyes open, but for what reason, unless for its novelty, I cannot conceive; there is neither convenience nor advantage in the practice, and besides, I have some doubts as to its feasibility; I have heard, it is true, of individuals who do shoot in this manner, but have never met with them, nor do I know any person who has. The ingenious author of "Rural Sports" says, very properly; "In sporting, it is to be ever remembered that the hand is to obey the eye, and not the eye be subservient to the hand:" and further, that "The object should be fixed, the instant the muzzle of the gun is brought up and fairly bears upon it; the sight becomes weakened by a protracted look along the barrel at a bird, and it is for this reason, that birds, which spring at the marksman's feet and fly off horizontally, are frequently missed; his keeping the aim so long upon them, fatigues the sight and the finger does not obey the sight so readily, as when employed at a first glance. It is not here meant, that a bird is to be blown to atoms as soon as it tops the stubble but that a marksman is, first, to make himself a thorough judge of distance: With that knowledge, in open shooting, he will never put the gun to his shoulder until the bird has flown a proper length, and then fire the instant the sight of it is caught."

To wad a gun properly, the shooter should be well acquainted with the quantity of powder and shot with which his gun will shoot best, and to be careful not to overload; independently of the recoil, which sometimes produces painful effects, the gun is always more or less injured, by cracking the stock; and the chance of killing is much less, than when the piece is properly charged. Guns of the same length and caliber require different loads, some shooting much heavier charges than others. The best method of ascertaining what ought to be the charge is, to take a number of sheets of writing, or wrapping paper, say thirty or forty; and shoot at them the same number of yards: beginning with a small load, and increasing it, until that portion of powder and shot is ascertained, which drives the shot through the greatest number of sheets, with the least scattering. Too great a charge of powder will cause the gun to throw the shot widely, while too heavy a portion of shot will produce a recoil, and weaken the effect. As to the size of the shot, that must depend upon the kind of game you intend to shoot, and the season. During the month of October, in this country, numbers 6 or 7 will be found to answer, and in December, as the birds have acquired more strength and thicker plumage, coarser shot will be required; besides, in partridge shooting, we very frequently find the ruffed grouse or Pheasant which, from its shyness and great strength, is not easily stopped with fine shot. With coarse shot, the shooter is not so likely to hit, but he is more certain of killing than with fine: I believe the higher numbers of shot are too generally used in this Country, at least they are much more so than in England; this arises, I presume, from our having with us, a greater number and variety of small birds, killed merely for the pot, than they have; small shot being found to answer as well for the Rail, Reed bird and Snipe, the season for which is so nearly connected with that for Partridge, that many of our shooters do not think of changing their shot, and continue on with numbers 7 or 8 during the whole season. In England it would seem that some of their shooters carry this matter to the other extreme and shoot with shot entirely too coarse according to our notions of propriety; General Hanger for instance, recommends number 2 for the entire season: it must, however, be remembered, that their partridge is a much larger and stronger bird than ours, but the difference is not so great as to justify such a wonderful disparity in the size of the shot.

In loading, the shooter should keep his gun as far from his body as convenient, and on no account hold it with the muzzle to his face, and he should be very careful that the loaded barrel be not cocked. The percussion lock has, it is true, lessened, in some degree, the danger in charging; as it is not usual to put the prime on the tube before loading; but the danger of charging with one barrel uncocked still remains, and the possibility of an accidental discharge, from fire remaining in the piece, is not diminished. I have known, personally, of an accident of this kind, although in that instance, the party had, fortunately, a long gun, by which very probably he escaped without injury.

But the infrequency of an accident, from any particular cause should not make the shooter less careful to guard against is occurrence, because "what has once happened may again occur."

I may here repeat the trite, but highly important cautionary observation, that in the best of hands guns are dangerous articles, and should be handled with the greatest circumspection and care. It is not prudent for more than two to shoot in company, and when the party is larger, the better plan is to divide, and to shoot by couples, in different directions. When two are shooting in company, it should always be understood, that a bird rising and flying to the right is to be shot by the right hand shooter, and by the left hand man, when the bird flies in that direction. This practice will prevent the occurrence of drawn shots, or any unpleasant feelings between the parties....

On arriving at the field the shooter should be the first to enter—his dogs following, and on no account should he permit them to go out of one field into another, until he is prepared to follow. If he find them disposed to break fence, he should call out ware (pronounced war) fence and not allow them to leave the field until he comes up. He should not, if circumstances will permit, go straight through a field unless he expects to find no game in it, but he should walk in zig zag directions at the same time giving his dogs the wind as much as possible; that is, hunting them against and across the wind. Birds very frequently, when running, go down the wind, and if the dog foots them, on his coming close upon them, they will generally flush; when therefore the shooter finds his dog to be trailing, unless he be an extremely cautious animal, he should call to him hold up, and hunt him to the windward of the direction in which the birds are supposed to be running. When the dog is close upon game, which will be easily discovered by his actions, the shooter should caution him to take heed, to prevent his flushing them, which frequently happens with careless dogs. When there is reason to believe that there may be game in the field or cover, the shooter should not be satisfied with traversing but once, let his dogs be ever so good:—on some days the scent will not lay, and on others, the birds will lie so close as not to be easily found by the dog.

Johnson in his very excellent treatise says, "suppose the young shooter in the field with two dogs; he perceives one drawing on the scent and settling to a point—let him call out to-ho! holding up his hand at the same time: the word will induce greater care in the first dog; and if the other should not be aware of the game, he will immediately look about him, and seeing his master's hand, will keep his position (no matter what his situation may be, either before or behind the shooter) or to speak as sportsmen, will back. I will suppose both the dogs perfectly steady—let the sportsman advance deliberately up to the setting dog, and if the game should not spring, let him go before the dog;—if the birds should run instead of taking wing, he will be aware of the circumstance by the dog following, but if the dog follow or foot too eagerly he should be checked, by the word, take heed! These are anxious moments, but the sportsman must nevertheless, summon all his fortitude, and continue as calm as possible, with his thumb on the cock: when the game springs, pull up the cock, select an individual object; if the bird fly straight forward it is a very easy shot; let the sportsman direct his eye down the barrel and the instant he perceives the bird on a line with the muzzle pull the trigger; in levelling, however, the aim should be directed rather above than below the object; for the shot if correctly thrown will form its centre from the centre of the muzzle of the fowling-piece: nevertheless, in this respect allowance must be made for the trim of the gun, or for the manner in which it throws shot; with which I am supposing the sportsman perfectly acquainted."

Many other remarks and directions might have been given, but I cannot conceive they would have any other tendency than to increase the size of this book, and to confuse the recollection of the reader. It will happen with some persons, that although these instructions may be by them rigidly obeyed, nevertheless they can never become good shots, for this simple reason, that nature never intended they should be. It will also sometimes happen, that the best shots, on particular occasions, may make bad shooting, without being able to account for the cause—when this occurs, I would recommend the shooter to stop shooting and to take his seat by the side of a bank, or at the foot of a tree, and then, by completely abstracting his mind from the object of pursuit, in a short time, get the better of his evil genius: if he can find nothing better (as books are out of the question) let him be diverted by counting once or twice the number of pellets contained in his shot charger. This project I have tried under similar circumstances and with unifrom success....

RECEIPTS

SCABBY EARS
Mercurial ointment, rubbed in a few times, will remove the disease.

CANKER IN THE LIPS
Rub the parts affectd with alum water, two or three times a day, or rub with bole armoniac and burnt alum occasionally.

FILMS IN THE EYE
Bathe the eye frequently, with the solution of blue vitrol of the size of a large bean, in a pint of rain, or spring water, or take of verdigries, one scruple, water, four ounces.

SHOT WOUNDS
Get out the shot, if possible, and rub the parts with mercurial ointment.

SORE FEET
Wash the dog's feet every day, morning and evening with salt and water. In warm weather, warm water and salt.

TECHNICAL TERMS
A brace of pointers, or setters.
A leash of pointers, or setters.
A couple of spaniels.
A couple and a half of spaniels.
A brace of grouse.
A leash of grouse.

A pack of grouse.
To raise grouse.
A brace of partridges.
A brace and a half of partridges.
A covey of partridges.
To raise, or spring partridges.
A brace of pheasants.
A pack of phesants.
A couple of woodcocks.
To flush a woodcock.
A couple of snipes.
To spring a snipe.
A wing of plover.

A pair,—a couple,—a brace.—A pair is two united by nature, e.g., a pair of rabbits. A couple by an occasional chain, as a couple of hounds. A brace by a noose or tie, as a brace of partridges. A pair is male and female; a couple, two incidental companions; a brace, is two tied together by the sportsman.

FORM OF A SPORTSMAN'S JOURNAL

Where Killed	When	Black Game	Grouse	Partridge	Pheasant	Woodcock	Snipe	Duck or Wild Fowl	Hare	Rabbit	Total Each Day	Shots Missed	Remarks on Each Day

General Observations:

FRONTIER HUNTING

During the 1830s hunting clubs were organized throughout America and Canada. The document below is a reprint of the founding and initial proceedings of the Fort Gibson Hunting Club, located in what is today Arkansas. Hunting, and for that matter target shooting, clubs often had close connections with the military and the Fort Gibson Club typified such an association. Club leadership and, by implication, membership was exclusive—it apparently was confined to officers or those with important positions within the miliary post and served the sporting and social needs of its members. The proceedings are reprinted from the June 1835 volume of the American Turf Register and Sporting Magazine.

FORT GIBSON HUNTING CLUB

GENTLEMEN: *Fort Gibson, March 7*, 1835.

Having duly considered the subject for which we, at our last meeting, were appointed a committee, beg leave to offer the following as a Constitution for the government of the Club.

ARTICLE 1. The Club shall be called the Fort Gibson Hunting Club.

ART 2. The officers shall be a President, a Vice President, and a Secretary who shall also act as Treasurer.

ART 3. It shall be the duty of the President to attend all meetings of the Club and preside in all business transactions. He shall call a meeting of the Club whenever requested to do so by three or more members, and order the Secretary to give notice of such meeting the day previous thereto. In the absence of the President, the Vice President shall act as President. A majority of the members present at the post shall constitute a quorum to transact business.

ART 4. The officers of the Club shall be elected annually; those elected at this meeting shall serve until 31st Dec. 1835.

ART 5. It shall be the duty of the Secretary to keep a book in which he shall make a fair record of all the transactions of the Club, and furnish for publication, in the American Turf Register and Sporting Magainze, such accounts of all the interesting hunts, &c. as the Club may think proper from time to time to publish.

ART 6. There shall be a Committee of three appointed by ballot, who shall assess all fines under such By-Laws as may hereafter be adopted.

ART 7. The dogs shall be under the exclusive management of the President, who shall employ a suitable person to take charge of the kennel, and perform such duty in relation thereto as the President may, from time to time, assign him. The kennel shall contain bear, wolf, deer, and fox dogs.

ART 8. All necessary expenses for the purchasing and feeding of the dogs, building kennel, hiring keeper, &c. &c. shall be borne at the joint expense of the Club, the Treasurer shall, on the order of the President, pay the accounts, and is authorized to draw upon the sutler for the necessary funds, for which the Club are pledged.

ART 9. On the withdrawing of a member from the Club, all his right, title, and interest in the dogs, kennel, &c. shall be vested in the Club, and no member shall, in any way, dispose of or transfer his interest to any person whatever.

ART 10. Members admitted to the Club, previous to the 1st January, 1836, shall pay their proportion of all expenses previously incurred; members admitted after that time shall upon admission pay —.

ART 11. All persons wishing to become members shall be proposed by a member in proper person, or in writing addressed to the President, and the member proposed shall be balloted for at the next meeting of the Club; two black balls shall exclude him.

ART 12. Each member shall sign this Constitution and be governed by it and such By-Laws as may, from time to time, be adopted by the Club. This Constitution shall not be altered but by a majority of two-thirds of the members belonging to the post.

Major R.B. MASON, of *Dragoons, President.*

Lieut. F. BRITTON, *7th Infantry, Secretary.*

Members.

S.G.J. De Camp, *Surgeon*	George Birch, *Major.*
W. Seawell, *Lieut. 7th.*	A. Harris, *Lieut. 7th.*
E.W.B. Nowland, *Post Sutler.*	Jno. Dillard, *Major.*
Wm. Eustis, *Lieut. Dragoons.*	A. Montgomery, *Lieut. 7th.*
M. Arbuckle, *Brev. Brig. Gen'l.*	

Resolved, That this Club subscribe for the American Turf Register and Sporting Magazine from its commencement, and its Editor be elected an honorary member.

Resolved further, That the formation of this Club, and the proceedings thus far be published in the American Turf Register and Sporting Magazine.

SOCIAL CLASS AND HUNTING CLUBS

The following account shows clearly the upper class membership and appeal of hunting clubs formed during the 1820s and 1830s. In this particular deer hunt the members donned their club uniforms and pursued their prey in orderly and grand style. Throughout they adhered to club rules, which required a heightened sense of honor, and thereby evinced the behavior and demeanor of the gentlemen they were. In the process of these sporting events, as well as during the celebration afterwards, members enjoyed the commaradarie and brotherhood that became an important facet of clubs of this sort. The following article is reprinted from the March 1838 issue of the American Turf Register and Sporting Magazine.

DEER HUNT

MR. EDITOR: *Camden Co. Geo December* 1, 1837.

The Camden Hunting Club is a society of gentlemen formed in 1827, and is one of the best regulated clubs of the kind in the United States. The following is a description of one of their delightful hunts, from the start to the conclusion of which there was unremitted excitement and action, the game being in view nearly all the time.

We took the field on a fair brilliant morning in summer, with a fine pack of hounds, and selected a drive [Any swamp or thick place in which dogs are entered to start deer, is called on the sea-coast of Georgia, a *drive*—and the manager of dogs is called *"The Driver."*] which was famous as the residence of noble bucks grown fat in our fields. The drive was finely situated for sport. Two roads corssed it about a mile apart, and running obliquely about a mile and a quarter united—so that the drive and the two roads formed a triangle, the interior of which was on open pine barren. To give a correct idea of our position and the course of the chase, I shall designate the left hand road, (viewed from the junction of the roads, as No. 1, and the right as No. 2. Beyond the first, pine barrens and thick forests extended for many miles. Outisde of the second, and not far from it, ran a narrow creek, with a high bluff, and on the borders of the creek was a thick hammock, or forest of beautiful and stately trees.

The stands [The positions occupied by the sportsmen to intercept the game.] on both roads were good, particularly on No. 1. Three sportsmen (Mr. R., the secretary of the Camden club, and myself) were stationed on that road about two hundred yards apart,—and two sportsmen on No. 2. The rest guarded more distant passes. Thus situated we listened impatiently for the signal of the hounds, and kept 'wide awake' towards the drive, lest the bucks, for they are cunning fellows, might *sneak off* unperceived before the hounds began to '*give tongue.*' We had not waited long before we heard a few fine tones, like the distant echoes of a flute, which an unpractised ear would not have heeded. They were the notes of Vixen, a lovely little slut, the first to find and the last to abandon the game. Soon afterwards at intervals, we could distinguish the sweet voices of other favourites of the pack, and they became louder and more frequent, until blended together, they broke upon our hearing in full chorus, that Handel himself, had he been present would have admitted was music.

The game, for which we eagerly looked with our thumbs on the cocks of our guns, and bridle reins gathered up, ready to fire or pursue—or do both, soon appeared. A magnificient buck, sleek as a racehorse, and bounding high over the palmettoes directly towards the stand of Mr. H. The secretary and myself remained motionless, for it is a rule among the memberrs of the Camden club, (although not written) and indeed with all other gentlemen who understand deer hunting, and who deem 'fair play a jewel,' never to intrude on another's stand, or balk him of a shot.

The buck approached within 100 yards and halted,—scenting his enemies on the breeze, and turning his head back to listen for the dogs. While thus engaged, Mr. H. who had dismounted from his horse, crept forward cautiously a few paces, and 'drew a bead' [Language of riflemen for *took aim.*] but both of his barrels *failed*, although the caps exploded. The noise of the caps alarmed the buck—hesitating no longer, he dashed off with an extensive leap, and directed his course parallel to the road, and rather towards the stand occupied by the secretary and myself. Discovering us, however, before he came within the range of our guns, he passed on with increased velocity, and we put our hunters to their best speed to intercept him should he attempt to cross the road on which we were, and to force him if possible into the hammock on the creek. The sportsmen on No. 2, perceiving the buck by our movement, put their horses also at speed, to turn him to us, or to get a shot, should he attempt to cross their road.

At that time the sport was exciting in the highest degree, and the sight was truly beautiful. Five horsemen, conspicuous by their scarlet jackets, [Uniform of the cold.] and their arms glistening in the sun, approaching a given point (the junction of the roads) at full speed, and the buck between, stretched like a line by his exertions to escape while behind him arose his death song from the tongues of a dozen hounds in hot pursuit.

He was surrounded by his enemies, and there was no room for strategem. Nothing but his heels could save him, and he seemed to know that, for never did an animal strive more to gain a place of refuge. Just before him was the hammock with its deep green mantle, which seemed to promise the shelter he so much needed, and towards it he fled like a streak of lightning.

In gaining that shelter he was compelled to cross road No.2, which he cleared at a single bound, passing within a few feet of the foremost sportsman's horse, then at full career. The sportsman, disregarding all danger in his eagerness to shoot, waited not to rein up, but *jumped off*, slighting on his head instead on his feet. Being young and agile, and too much of a man to be hurt by a *topsy-turvey* position, he was on his feet in a moment, and fired at the buck as he entered the hammock, but without effect— his *eyes being too full of sand to take good aim.* The hammock in extent was about 30 acres. On one side near the creek, was an excellent stand, to which I hastened, *by right of original position.* Had the buck leaped into the creek and swam across, as several of his tribe had done under similar circumstances, he would have been safe—but his time had come to die.

I had scarcely reined up my horse before I heard him approaching and saw his tall horns over the tops of the bushes. A few more jumps, and he was in my presence, panting from the severity of the chase. As I levelled my gun he discovered me and made a desperate effort to pass, about 40 yards distant. I fired one barrel with excellent aim, but he did not fall. The other was quickly discharged, yet he kept on, seemingly unhurt. I gave one hasty thought to the 16th rule [16th Rule.—Any member who shall fire at a deer less than 40 yards distant, and not *hit* or *kill*, when the *opportunity is fair*, shall be fined.—No deer shall be considered hit unless *killed*, or unless *blood is seen.*] of the club, then plied the rowels to my horse and gave chase. In a very short time I was near enough to see the blood trickling from several wounds in his side, and when within a few feet of him he rolled over, to rise no more. My couteau de chasse was instantly in his throat, and the sound of the merry horn (the signal of success) gathered the straggling huntsmen and hounds, and in triumph we retired with the buck to our club house, where we enjoyed until a late hour the feast and the wine cup.

GREENWOOD.

CANADIAN GAME HUNT

Sportsmen in both Canada and the United States particularly enjoyed hunting deer, bear, and other large game, activities that increasingly became more difficult to pursue in expanding urban areas. The following account, drawn from the December 1836 edition of the American Turf Register and Sporting Magazine, is a fine example of a literary account of a sporting activity, in this case a bear hunt.

BEAR HUNTING IN UPPER CANADA

We are indebted to our esteeemed friend 'Laddie,' for the following extract from a letter received by him from a friend in Upper Canada.

'You have seen many snowy days, and we have often together admired the elegant and dazzling festoons formed by the pendant arms of some moss-covered larch, heavily weighed down by its burthen of new fallen snow; and snugly ensconced, beneath the protecting canopy of some 'dark boughed fir,' watched with delight the feathery messengers of Father Frost, as they gracefully eddied about in mid air, a few seconds before they added their mite to the trackless waste before us. But L, beautiful as we though all this, you would think it 'poor, indeed,' could you see our snow-storms—the gigantic children of our primeval forests, loaded to breaking, with such rich and fanciful robes that queens might envy!—their immensity and wavy indistinctness fills the mind with such a feeling of awe, as cannot be conveyed in language, it must be felt to be understood,—from such a scene I have but now come; and 'ere proceeding to give you an account of a day's sport I yesterday enjoyed, I must pause to let the sublimity of the scene pass from my yet aching eye-balls.

'About an hour after day-break I was listlessly lounging, not on a Turkisb Ottoman, nor even in an easy chair, but on a wooden settle covered with bear's skin, the trophy of a hazardous engagement and brilliant victory, achieved by my brother John some three moons ago, and which, by the way, makes a very pleasant seat when drawn near the crackling pine logs, as they split and blaze cheerily in the wide fire place; for I have such a thing, seeing that I eschew a dark dingy stove, however warm, with as much abhorrence as I would an empty larder after a severe day's toil. This is a somewaht long digression, but you know I was ever given to be prosy; well, in came John, a look of joyous import in his bright black eye, his step hurried yet firm, his right hand clutching with starting veins his faithful rifle:—before I had time to make any inquiries as

to the cause of his energetic appearance, he burst out with 'Come, sluggard, he cannot be far off; his trail is quite fresh, and you may depend on't he's one of the villains
that stole our lambs in summer.' Now, how my wise frater jumped to this conclusion
does not appear, for he would answer no questions, and I wan e'en left to vague con-
jectures, yet I at once knew it must be a bear he alluded to; so, hastily pulling on my
boots, and catching down my rifle, powder, &c. I was ready for a start. He led me
about a quarter of a mile, by a near cut, to the spot where he had left the trail, and there,
plain enough, I saw the foot-marks of a very large bear. We had two dogs, Old Blucher,
a corss between a famous setter bitch that you wot of, and a New Forest blood-hound.
He is a splendid animal, and as good as he looks; the other we could place no dependence on, as he is young, and had never been tried with any high game. He is also a
cross between a mastiff and greyhound, yeleped 'Bravo.' The snow was some eight
inches deep and very dry, affording no scent, and in many places so powdery that the
trail was almost lost, and always very indistinct: but John is no chicken at this work,
and on he posted, myself and the dogs close at his heels; in about half an hour we came
to a thicket where Bruin had entered; it was of no great extent, and we hastened round
to see if he had gone through, and there we again found the trail but evidently much
fresher: so much so, that old Blucher began to feather, and once or twice threw his
tongue; 'that will do,' was John's first word since leaving the house; on we went. 'Take
time, Blucher; let us all go together.' 'Back, Bravo, you young fool, you will be shy
enough when we want you.' In a few minutes more we came in sight of a scaur with
a block of limestone lying to the day, and beneath this, half concealed by a luxuriant
wild vine, we could observe a narrow slit, just wide enough to admit the lord of the
waste. This den must, in summer, be perfectly hid from the prying gaze, as it was
scarcely visible even in the now naked state of the vine. We now held a council of war,
and, at last, it was resolved to let the dogs try their teeth, and see if we could get a shot
when his highness was engaged by old Blucher, for we did not reckon (as the yankees
say) much upon Bravo. Having looked to our flints and priming, we advanced to the
bottom of the scaur; the mouth of the den was some four or five feet higher, and we
encourage old Blucher to spring up, but to our astonishment the young one, with a
bound, went right into the hole; and then the snort of passion from old rough jacket was
heard, followed by a fierce growl from Bravo, who, with his tail and haunches half
hanging over the tangled-mouth, refused to back out from the monster. Old Blucher
was not trying to get in, but the orifice was too small, and we remained quiet to see
what the young hero would make of it. In a minute or two we gave him a cheer, and
then he suddenly disappeared, and we could hear a desperate and deadly struggle; Old
Blucher now sprung in, and we were left in the greatest anxiety for our poor favourites,
well knowing the powers of a large and savage bear, when confined in such close
quarters, to defend himself. With tight-drawn respiration we waited a few seconds: the
deep fierce rage of the gallant hounds was mingled with the savage snort of the old
bruin, and we scarcely dared hope for both our dogs escaping with life. The next
moment a piercing yell, followed by a desperate rush to the mouth of the cave, filled
us with dismay; but, 'ere an exclamation could escape us, the foaming bloody visage
of the shaggy brute was protruded from the mouth, and we could see that his exit was
effectually prevented by both brave dogs hanging at his neck; it was a moment to remember! I lifted my rifle, intending to plant my ball right through the monster's brain,

but John's hand restrained me; he was apprehensive that the ball might glance and lame, if not kill, one of our fine assistants. Suddenly we saw Old Blucher's hold give way, and the huge grizly savage came rolling down to our very feet, but not alone: the glorious young Bravo held fast by his huge neck, and they rolled over and over writhing amid the blood-stained snow. A short 'now' was ejaculated by my brother, and the next, instant the savage child of the forest rolled lifeless on the earth, his upturned eyes and open jaw telling that the mysterious principle had left his still quivering limbs for ever. My ball had entered behind the shoulder, and passed right through his heart. Poor Blucher was still in the cave, stiff and bloody, and fangs of the ruthless beast had penetrated far into his neck, and he had fainted from loss of blood—We carried him home, and with good nursing and care, I think he will recover. The bear, when measured, was the largest I had ever seen killed. Farewell.

Yours ever,   F.M.'

FOX HUNTING IN CANADA

Fox hunting never achieved the popularity of many other sports during the second quarter of the nineteenth century in Canada and the United States. But, as the following account makes clear, the sport of fox hunting was, among other things, a way to preserve English traditions in a new land—an effort that assumed a different meaning amidst the ethnic competition between English and French in Canada. The following article is taken from the 23 July 1836 issue of The Spirit of the Times.

FOX-HUNTING IN CANADA

DEAR MR. EDITOR,—A voice afar! and far-fetched, perhaps, it will be thought by most of your readers, when they find an attempt is made to give an account of hunting in such a Back-woods place as Canada is generally thought to be.—A pack of fox-hounds, however, there is in Montreal, which, considering the very short season they can hunt, and the many difficulties and disadvantages they have to contend with in a new country work wonders. With them are generally ten or twelve men, whose "Bits of Pink" and other etceteras, would not disgrace a Melton field, and who, in their gallant manner of charging the snake and cedar fences, might almost pose even a crack across the Quorn country,—these fences, with yawners on each side, being ugly things to look at.

There had been a pack of hounds kept, and most excellent sport shown, in Lower Canada for several years, by a gentleman, whose high standing, extreme popularity, and fondness of the noblest sport of his native land calculated him, of all others, to be the founder of fox-hunting (in the English style) in this valuable part of our British possessions. It may be more convincing than the assertions of Mr. Roebuck, to show what evils the Demon of Agitation, which hates every thing English, is at present working (and encouraged by him to do so) with peaceful and happy people of these provinces, when I state, that one of his tail assailed in the House of Assembly the character of the gentleman in question in the most violent manner, merely because he kept a pack of hounds. It was their thrilling notes and the heart-stirring view-holloa of their brave old English gentleman master, that caused fear and trembling in their souls.—But hark back! I am running political riot. These hounds I am sorry to say have been given up; the Montreal hunt got a valuable addition to their force at the time, but unfortunately lost a great part of them by a kind of madness that got into the kennel. The Montreal hunt owe, I believe, their first start to a sporting English butcher, who brought out with him two or three couple of hounds. This hero of the cleaver, with some addition to the strength of these, was mounted, dressed, and became huntsman, supported by the present able master of the hunt, and a few thorough going ones like himself, and I am told, a more indefatigable fellow-to find a fox, and keep his small numbers on him, never existed; and his voice with hounds and view-hilloa will long be remembered by the select few that heard him. The year following a club was formed, and a very fair subscription raised, by which, with several couple of hounds got out from England, and other chance additions, a pack was established. Morris, the present huntsman, succeeded "Marrow-Bones," and a better hand to get away with hounds and live with them never wore a cap. His nerve is astonishing, and he rides a horse well calculated to indulge his rasping propensities. Set Morris on York, and what will stop them? No man as yet was ever born perfect, and it would be better if Morris had some of his predecessors' old Smithfield qualities in cover, and in seeing more of his hounds, and keeping a keener eye to them when going from, and coming to home; and taking a little more pains in staying longer to get them out of large covers at the end of the day. But he has many redeeming virtues. They hunted until the present season, the immediate neighborhood of Montreal, and a country about eighteen miles from home, called "Point Clair." The former was heavy work, large covers, and large swamps: and "Jean Baptiste," harked on by Mons. Papineau, occasionally turned out with pitch-forks, and even guns, to stop "les sacres chasseurs du roi," as they termed the lads in scarlet. And here a very good story of Morris will not be out of place. Wishing to go the nearest way from one cover to another, the field, early last season, took a road leading through the farm of "un Habitant," and passing close to his dwelling; but on approaching the *maison*, they were met by the whole force thereof,—"le pere de famille" armed with a gun, his sons with pitch-forks, whilst the women screamed sacre on the red-coated riders. Not wishing to raise a whole village by showing fight, they turned their horses' heads to the regular road. Morris, however, liking no such trouble, cleared a five railed fence, and was making his way at a canter, with the pack at his heels, when he was brought up by something or other, I believe some late standing oats, and was surrounded by the owners of the soil. Sadly beset by three or four of the pitch fork armed, he, either to give the field notice of his danger, or by chance, pulled out his horn, when to his astonishment, down on their marrow-bones dropt his formidable foes, crying out most lustily, "O, mon Dieu, ne tirez pas"—Morris taking advantage of their, to him, glorious mistake, nearly frightened them to death, and then rode off to tell the field so good a joke.—The Point Clair country is the Oxfordshire of Lower Canada—nothing but stone walls, and very little cover, but plenty of foxes. Many were the brilliant runs they had in it, and long will be cherished its recollection, by those who have seen the flying performances of Dertueffel, the Doctor, Caraskeen, and Jinnums, and though last, not least, that straight goer of the neighborhood on his roan son of old imported Bedford. The dinners, too, the flow of soul and song, the ebullition of honest English feeling, true to church and state, the sporting toasts, and more sporting men who surrounded the mahogany, told that England's sons were there. The distance, however, to Point Clair was so great, and the hunt had the pleasure of seeing a prohibitory threat in a newspaper advertisement, at the commencement of last season, signed by the influentials of the parish, warning them to hunt there no more.—Mons. Papineau again. A proposal was made to try the other side of the river, where large traverse-boats cross every half hour, nearly opposite the town. Their first day in this country proved its merit, for the one or two members who had gone to report, had run of an hour and a kill in a complete open country, and the only fault was too many foxes, the country being for many miles a common intersected with only ditches, and with occasional knolls and stripes of low brushwood. It would have done the hearts good of those who have to complain of blank days, to have witnessed the first two or three times some of the small covers were drawn. Away they trotted out, black, silvery, and the old color, and as they had got on their winter jackets the white tag showed well, (the quantity of fur a fox carries in Canada makes his brush twice the size of English foxes.) Here began a series of such brilliant work, that the two days a week they had hunted this country told at the end of the season a heavy tale of blood; and desperate was the struggle, and long the run that Reynard made to rid himself of his deadly pursuers in most of these. In fact, they had some as clipping runs as any "Chasseur du Roi" needs wish for; and their last day for the season will give a pretty fair idea of how "the trick" can be done in this out of the way place.

Strong was the muster at the traverse-boat in the morning, and ominously joyful looked the face of each man as he rode into the boat. "A southerly wind and a cloud sky proclaim it a hunting morning," and many a joking prognostication was made as to what was to take place, until landed on the opposite shore. They begun by trying some small covers about four miles from the place of landing, which were drawn blank. They, then headed towards "Laprairie," trying several likely bits of brush and fern on the way, and it was not long before was heard Morris' welcome sound of "Hark to music! hark!" He had gone off in great haste, and it was some time before the pack got away to the leading hounds. Together, however, they got with a burning scent, and there they went, tongue that was maddening. His line was evidently to a large cover not a great distance off; this, however, he merely skirted, and now they gallantly headed to the common country before described, with a scent breast high, and the pace racing; he went straight for about four miles, when he was headed back by some people ploughing, and made again for the small covers where he was found; these he run through going his best for a large one, but instead of ringing or staying in this piece of old cover, he went through it like a line. And now the pack dished into view, fast and direct from Chumbly River, which they soon reached—and now they stem the running stream. Water was something new to two of the field now leading, who pulled rein and cast many a wistful look at the gallant pack as they shot away over the Laprairie common, whilst a table cloth might have covered them. Morris, however, at the moment came up, and went at it as he goes at every thing, jumping down a bank into the river. Old York disappeared, and the only thing to be seen was the cap of his rider; duck-like, however, they rose again, and in a few seconds every scarlet coat was breast high in the Chumbly's then turbed waters. Forward, was the cry! His line was now evidently right across the Laprairie common; and across it he did go, and those after him that would not leave him, crossing the new line of rail-road, between that and St. John's, and was run in about a mile further on. Most of the field were up to see the worry. The distance gone over without a check must have been something like fourteen miles.

The long and dreary winter of Canada set in the day following, and the hounds were soon after distributed to their winter quarters—I cannot conclude without paying that tribute which is so due to the present master of the hunt. His exertions last season to ensure a good subscription had its reward; his extreme good management whilst the hounds are in the kennel, and his other arrangements, deserves the thanks of all true lovers of the sport; and his attention to sporting strangers in getting them mounted, generally from his own stable, is a proof that they have the right sort of person at their head. No distance or weather ever finds him wanting. It would be well if those who talk so much about supporting every thing that is English, (and many of them "big wigs" of Montreal), would put their hands in their pockets in support of England's noblest sport, and which has been the cradle to many of the feats of her most daring sons. I will venture it were worth all their "beef-steak clubs" put together.

Go on and prosper! and may I have next season an opportunity of singing, in the works of that crack fellow, Mr. Campbell, of Glen Saddel,

"We have had a run together,
"We have ridden side by side,
We are wedded to each other,
Like a lover to his bride!"

CHASSEUR

WESTERN FIELD SPORTS

Field sports on the western frontier varied somewhat from sports and pastimes elsewhere owing to the different types of game and to the rugged terrain and lifestyle found there. In the following description, two of the sports of the West are discussed—the chasing of wild horses and buffalo in the Arkansas Territory. The article is reprinted from the American Turf Register and Sporting Magazine, October 1833.

WILD HORSES—THE GAME AND THE SPORTS OF THE WEST

MR. EDITOR: *Fort Gibson, Aug.* 1, 1838.

Although the "blind goddess," in her capricious dispensations, has not deemed me worhty a high place among that spirited and jovial fraternity ycleped "sportsmen of the turf," an inherent fondness for the horse, and the interest awakened by a recital of his gallant achievements, have made me a regular reader of your excellent work.

I have observed the polite reception given by you, to all sporting notices and papers, contributed by different gentlemen, on the subject of hunting and the various animals with which they have come in contact.

Having very recently visited the Grand Prairie, southwest of us, where the lovers of genuine field sports will find an inexhaustible source of amusement, among game of almost every variety and of the noblest species, I have employed a leisure hour in embodying a brief relation of the tour, which is submitted to your descretion, as the proper depository of sporting intelligence.

A detachment of infantry and rangers, amounting to about three hundred and eighty men, left this post on the 6th May last, charged with the duty of scouring the Indian country to the southwest, with the double object of preserving the friendly relations existing between the tribes in alliance with the United States and of preventing the hostile incursions of their enemies, the Pawnees.

On the 7th of May we left the bank of the Arkansas, and advanced on our line of march, in a southwest direction, across the northern branches of the Canadian river.

The season of the year was most propitious to the purposes of hunting, as well as of military operation. Nature had fairly unfolded her vernal beauties, and we were traversing a lovely region of undulating prairie, mantled with green, and diversified by "hill and dale, copse, grove and mound:" its deep solitudes occasionally enlivened by herds of deer, whose timid glance and airy bound, as the stirring notes of the bugle fell on their ear, bespoke fear and distrust of their civilized visiters.

It was not until we had advanced some ninety or one hundred miles from Fort Gibson that we fairly reached the game country. As we were not on a neutral ground, between the Pawnees and the tribes friendly to the United States, and as the danger of hunting operates in some measure as a check on all parties, in resorting there, it results that the game (particularly the deer) is more plentiful in that section than it otherwise would be. The buffalo was here first encountered—a striking proof of the rapidity with which this animal recedes before the advances of civilization. Ten years since they abounded in the vicinity of Fort Gibson; and in the summer of 1822, the writer of this, with Major Mason of the army, and a party of keen sportsmen, killed a considerable number of them near Fort Smith, about forty miles east of us. They have receded, it would seem, one hundred miles westward in the last ten years; and it may be safely assumed, that thirty or forty years hence, they will not be found nearer to us than the spurs of the Rocky mountains, unless the numerous bands of hunters of the Choctaw, Chickasaw, Cherokee and Creek tribes, established in this country, should relinquish the chase for the arts of civilized life. On the 26th May we reached the main Canadian river, near the point where it enters the timber bordering the eastern verge of the Grand Prairie, in its flow from the west.

The Grand Prairie extends to the Rocky mountains, and presents to the eye a boundless extent of rolling champaign country, occasinally intersected by small streams, thinly bordered by dwarfish timber. A formidable herd of about one hundred buffaloes was here discovered; and, as the command needed fresh meat, a halt was ordered, and forty horsemen detached to attack them. They gaily moved off in a gallop, armed with rifles. As they neared the herd they quickend their pace to half speed, when they were discovered by the graceless buffaloes, who started off as fast as they could scamper, with their peculiar hobbling, bouncing gait. The hunters now pressed them closely, and penetrated the moving mass at full speed; when each man selected his victim. The sharp, quick report of the rifle was not heard in rapid succession; while the rush of the horses and buffaloes, the shouts of the party on the heights, and the flashes and smoke of the guns, presented altogether one of the most animated spectacles I had ever witnessed.

The whole chase was visible for a long distance to the command, halted on the eminence; and so great was the interest it excited, that numbers were unable to resist it, and dashed off at full speed, to join in the work of destruction. The pursuit terminated in the death of a large number of the buffaloes, whose huge unwieldy carcasses lay strewed over the plain, like heroes on the battle field.

The buffaloe is, when wounded and excited, a very dangerous animal; and there are many instances related of hunters, who, realying too far on their seeming stupidity and unwieldiness, have fallen victims to their ferocity. On one occasion, during our trip, two rangers, in the impetuosity of pursuit, drove a buffalo into a narrow pass; where, finding himself closely pressed, he made battle, goring one of the horses in the thigh and overturning him and his rider. The horse of the other ranger stumbled during the conflict, and threw his rider on the back of the buffalo; which, becoming alarmed at this new mode of attack, now set off at full speed, carrying the ranger with him about twenty yards, until the latter finding the gait not very easy, and likely to continue some time, rolled off the buffalo into the dust—each party mutually willing to dissolve the connection.

This reminds me of an anecdote related to me by Col. A.S.C. of St. Louis, a gentlemen of veracity. While on a trading expedition to Mexico, he had in his employ a motley, but daring set of fellows, consisting of Frenchmen, Spaniards, half breeds and Indians, who were in the habit of bantering each other and boasting of their individual feats of prowess. On one occasion a Spaniard boldly wagered that he would *ride a buffalo*; which being taken up by one of the party, a suitable place for mounting was accordingly found, on an old trail that had become deeply worn by the buffalo; and having secreted himself, a fine old bull of "gentle mien" was encircled and driven into this passage; and, as he passed slowly through the defile, the Don made a spring and lit on his hump, clinging with both hands to the hair of the shoulders, and pressing his knees to the sides in true jockey style. The old bull soon got into open ground, and commenced a series of curvets and caracoles, such as man never saw before, to the great edification of the spectators and trepidation of the rider. The Don, for a little while, kept his seat like a knight of the olden time; but finding that bully possessed both wind and bottom, and that he was getting *a little "tired of the sport*," called out to his tickled companions to shoot the buffalo. They replied, they were afraid of breaking his leg. "Break the leg and be damned," cried the impatient Don, when a volley brought down bully and his rider together; the latter resolving that it should be his last attempt to ride a buffalo.

Progressing southeast from the Canadian river, we reached the head waters of the Blue water river—a beautiful limestone region of elevated prairie, abounding in game of all kinds. Buffaloes were astonishingly numerous here; and I shall not fear contradiction in saying that I saw, in one view, as many as two thousand head. The country lying between the head of the Blue Water and False Onachita rivers is particularly noted for the abundance and excellence of the wild horses which roam in its fertile prairies.

In one drove I estimated as many as one hundred and twenty head, most of them large and well formed. What struck me as peculiarly remarkable was the predominance of the gray color; by which I mean to say, there were more, as I thought, of that color than of any other single color. The same observation has been made, by oriental travelers, of the far famed stock of Arabia. Several horses were caught by rangers; but they were not of course of the best class, which is seldom, if ever overtaken; it being a natural impossibility that jaded horses, on a journey, can carry one hundred and sixty or one hundred and eighty pounds weight, and outstrip a naked and untired animal of the same species with itself.

At our encampment on the Canadian, an incident occurred which very fairly tested the enduring qualities of the wild horse, and will enable us to form a pretty correct estimate of his general powers. There was a fine looking animal discovered near the camp by a party of rangers, and several of them gave pursuit. They run him alternately a distance of about two miles, when they relinquished the pursuit. A third horseman then gave chase on a fresh horse, noted for speed and bottom in a company of one hundred men. The issue proved the vast superiority of the prairie horse, which at first ran before his pursuer at his ease; but, being at length pushed for the distance a quarter of a mile, evinced such prodigious speed and wind, that, in the words of the ranger, he "just stood still and looked at him."

The wild horses and mares taken by the rangers, though small, were remarkable for deep, hard, black hoofs, flat sinewy limbs, full fine eyes, and large nostrils—four of the cardinal attributes of the courser.

Of all the varities of sporting in which I have participated, I have certainly found none so animating as the chase of the wild horse. There are two modes of taking them; one by throwing a running noose around the neck, from a coil held in the hand; and the other by fastening one end of the cord to the pommel of the saddle, and the other to a stick about eight feet long, such a manner that the noose is always open and ready to put over the horse's head. The first mode requires great practice and address. It is employed by the Spaniards of Mexico and South America, who can, it is said; catch a horse by any foot which may be named.

On the head of Blue Water a party of four of us determined to take a run after wild horses. Having equipped ourselves with a noose and stick, tightened our girths, and tied up our heads, we rode forth into the prairie, and soon discovered a large herd of about one hundred head, quietly grazing and unaware of our approach. As soon as we approached near enough to be seen by them, and were gradually recognized, the whole body began to nicker, and was soon in commotion, stamping the ground with their fore feet; while a few of the bolder spirits moved up towards us, slowly and doubtingly, eager to ascertain our character. Each rider now stooped on his horse, laying his head close to his horse's neck; and in this manner we silently advanced, watching closely the movements of the herd, and making each a selection of such an animal as pleased his fancy. This part of the sport was very fine; and, in, the present instance, so many elegant forms of both sexes, and all colors and sizes, presented themselves, that it required not a little promptitude to form a decision. We had not long to deliberate; for, by the time we were within one hundred yards, the increased nickering and confusion showed they had winded us; and the whole herd suddenly wheeled round, and dashed off over the plain, closely pressed by their eager pursuers. We ran them about two miles; but the rocky nature of the country, and the number of deep ravines crossing our track in every direction, prevented our coming up with such as were desirable. Could we have had a clear run the whole distance, we should doubtless have secured some fine animals; as their numbers prevented their running to advantage—caused them to crowd and impede the progress of each other, by which the disparity as to weight, previously referred to, would have been neutralized. On our return towards the main body of the troops, we saw a large stallion, whose fore leg had been broken in the chase; yet, in spite of this, he managed to hobble off on the remaining three very cleverly.

Nothing in natual scenery can surpass the beauty of the prairie when we visited it; and it may be imagined with what delight we stood on a mound, on one occasion, and took into one view the wild horse, the buffalo, the elk, the deer and the antelope, in their native strength and beauty, roving free and untrameled as the air they inhaled. Of each of these different species, with the exception of the elk, a number were killed and taken by the party; in addition to bears, wild turkeys, one wild hare, and numbers of prairie dogs.

From this point we made a short detour southwest, and thence turned northeast, on our return route, as our provisions of every kind were nearly exhausted; and we were, a short time afterwards, compelled to subsist on wild meats,—part of the time without salt,—for the period of thirty-five days.

With what a prurient fancy did we conjure up in our minds the delicate viands, rich sauces, and ruby wines of your northern Barnums and Niblos. In our reveries by day, and dreams by night, we invoked the spirit of the immortal Ude, to gift us with the art of transmitting the odious buffalo jerk into something palatable and digestible.

Long privation had, by the time we reached the point of departure, sensibly affected our rotundity. Our clothes hung in graceless folds on our gaunt and famished limbs, and we were nearly circumstanced like Falstaff's troop—almost without a shirt among us; the "cankers of a calm world and a long peace."

A READER.

THE PROTECTION OF GAME

The depletion of game in urban areas pushed the hunting sportsmen to pass game laws in order to preserve and protect the very sport that they valued so dearly. Only by establishing game seasons, sportsmen believed, would the growth, or at least the maintenance, of game populations be guaranteed. The following discussion, taken from the April 1830 issue of the American Turf Register and Sporting Magazine, addresses the reasons for the persistence of shooting game out of season by some hunters.

SHOOTING GAME OUT OF SEASON

MR. EDITOR: *Philadelphia, February* 27, 1830.

It has been a subject of much regret and mortification with real sportsmen, that so little attention has been given in this country to some of the most important matters connected with the existence of the game, which afford us most of our field sports; and it is much to be feared that many species of it shall have become extinct ere we will be better convinced of the propriety of their better observance. I allude particularly to the detestable practice of shooting out of season, which so unfortunately prevails in most parts of the country. I have just heard of a fellow killing a brace of cocks on the 25th instant, and what is still more disgraceful, boasting that he had killed the first birds, both this and the last *season*, as he called it. I am, Mr. Editor, by no means an advocate for European game laws; but do think that some legislative restrictions more than we have at present, are absolutely necessary to prevent the total annihilation of every variety of game in the settled part of our states, and that at no distant period. By restrictions, I do not wish to be understood as desiring that any *exclusive* privileges should be allowed, or qualifications obtained by ownership of real estate, or pecuniary purchase from government; but that the time and season of shooting each particular bird, or quadruped, should be established by law, with heavy penalties for its infraction. Regulations of this kind would be advantageous, as well to the game eater as to the game shooter, as they would be at least in some degree conducive to its preservation. The only enactment we have on this subject in Pennsylvania, relates to the killing of deer, which makes the season commence on the first of August, and expire on the last day of December. Yet, notwithstanding the liberality of this law; which embraces five months in the year, some gentlemen of our legislature was unreasonable enough at the last session to endeavour to procure a bill to be passed diminishing this partial restraint, or in fact, I believe to abolish it altogether; but for the honour of the state, and espcially of the committee to whom it was referred, it was reported against, accompanied with a recommendation that the season should be reduced and a greater penalty for violating the law be imposed. In the city of Philadelphia, there are some municipal regulations as to selling or exposing game in the *market*; but that is easily evaded by selling it in the liberties, or by carrying it to the eating or private houses of those who disregard every legal or moral consideration which interferes with their pockets or depraved palates. What a delightful morsel must be a woodcock, shot on the nest, or killed with the ramrod; or a partridge, murdered in the months of February or March; as tough, stringy, and ill-flavoured as an ancient goose; nevertheless these birds find their way under these disgusting circumstances to the tables of food so unnatural and unwholesome. The misfortune is, that so long as purchasers can be had, there are persons to be found, base enough to furnish the market. I am well aware that legislative interference in this matter cannot entirely destroy this disgraceful practice; but it may do much to diminish it, especially if the consumer or purchaser is made equally punishable with the poacher. Public opinion is generally in unison with our laws, and he who is base enough to violate the least of them, although perhaps, otherwise unpunished, is far from being considered a worthy or honest citizen. The object in troubling you with this hasty communication, is to institute an inquiry into the extent of the grievance complained of in other states, and to receive the suggestions of some of your intelligent correspondents, as to the most probable means of producing its remedy.

I shall in the next No. if this be acceptable, presume to give my own opinion and that of more experienced sportsmen, on the commencement and duration of the proper seasons for shooting the different game birds in this state; and trust, in the mean time, you will receive the opinions of gentlemen in other states, on the same subject; by which means, it is hoped that a uniformity of practice and sentiment may be established throughout the country.

PUBLIC AWARENESS OF SHOOTING GAME OUT OF SEASON

The following article, when taken with the previous document, provides a good discussion of the concerns that sportsmen expressed over the threat to their sport by disobedient hunters and demonstrates the politicization of sportsmen over this issue. The article is reprinted from the July 1830 edition of the American Turf Register and Sporting Magazine.

AGAINST SHOOTING GAME OUT OF SEASON

MR. EDITOR: West Point, April 24, 1830.

I have read with much pleasure your Turf Register and Sporting Magazine. In your eighth number...I perceive a paragraph, dated Philadelphia, February 27, 1830, on the subject of shooting game out of season. This practice has become intolerable, and should be held in contempt by every true sportsman. In no part of the country is it so prevalent as with those in and about the city of Philadelphia, and in the county of Gloucester and Burlington, in New Jersey. It is now thirty-five years since I first commenced shooting on the grouse plains in New Jersey. I have been a constant attender during that time, with the exception of three or four years that I was out of the country. When I commenced upon them, the birds were numerous. A party of three or four could kill as many as they could wish; (say fifty, sixty, eighty birds,) and more if they wished, in three or four days shooting; but we then never thought of shooting them before the month of October. This bird is almost annihilated, in consequence of those who call themselves sportsmen, commencing the murder of the young birds about the first of August. The young birds are hatched in all the month of June, and, consequently, are about six weeks old in August, when those barbarous *soi disant* sportsmen sally forth and commence their slaughter upon them most unmercifully. I have heard of one company, in the month of August, killing upwards of ninety grouse in one day, and before they left the ground, the birds were spoiled, so that they placed them on trees, and left the greater part of them as unfit for use, being so offensive that they were not worth taking home. One other instance: a gentleman of my acquaintance told me, that he happened at the house of one of them, and saw eight birds strung up, and that they were offered him as a present; they were in that state that he would not accept of them. I know them well, and could name them. Their object is to boast of having killed so many birds. They conceal their being young birds that could not fly, or get out of the way, and, as your correspondent justly terms it, "might have been killed with the ramrod." In the fall of 1820 I applied to the legislature of New Jersey for a law for the preservation of game. The object was to preserve the grouse and deer from being killed out of proper season. The law was passed, for the commencement of the shooting of grouse and deer on the first of September, and to end with deer on the first of January, and with grouse on the first of February; the penalty for deer twenty dollars, that for grouse, (out of season) two dollars. This law appears to have brought the game into notice; and so far from having the desired effect, I am of the opinion, that there are ten where there were formerly not more than one, who pursue the game out of season. From the city of Philadelphia they will take a carriage, and sneak down to the hunting grounds in the night, shoot (or catch, for they cannot fly,) as many of the unfledged birds as they may find in the course of the day, and sneak home again, like sheep stealers, the next night. In 1822, two gentlemen took a carriage at Camden, opposite to Philadelphia, in August, and travelled all night, shot twenty-seven young birds, and returned in the course of the next night. Some honourable sportsmen, who I am acquainted with, hearing of their having gone down, applied for warrants for them, and, with a peace officer, waited for their return. About one or two o'clock in the morning the sportsmen drove up to the tavern, in high glee. After the common salutations, the officer served warrants upon them for the penalty for killing game out of season. They were much surprised indeed, that sportsmen should be thus treated, and, at first, were disposed to be obstreperous; but, on more mature reflection, and finding the Jerseymen resolute and determined, they became composed, and a compromise took place, they agreeing to pay twenty dollars, with a promise never to be guilty of the like offence again; which promise, I have reason to believe, they strictly adhered to as long as they lived. They were gentlemen, and, I am sorry to say, are now no more; they both died about four or five years since. The twenty dollars was given to the overseer of the poor, for the benefit of the poor of the township. In the fall of 1822, I again applied to the legislature, and procured an amendment of the game law, altering the time of commencing shooting from the first of September to the first of October, and the penalty from two to ten dollars, for killing grouse out of season, for every bird found in possession of the delinquent; but all to no purpose. If this law could be put in force, in a very few years this valuable game would become abundant, otherwise, in a few years, it will become extinct.

RANGER.

MASSACHUSETTS GAME LAWS

As hunters depleted the game contained in various regions of the United States and
Canada game laws furnished a way to protect the diversity of game found in North
America. The following article, from the September 1838 issue of the American Turf
Register and Sporting Magazine, gives some of the game laws of the state of
Masschusetts from an article that originally appeared in a Boston newspaper.

GAME LAWS

The editor of the Turf Register requests his friends in the different states where there
are game laws, to furnish him with them for publication in the Turf Register. A brief
abstract of their provisions will be sufficient. It cannot have escaped the notice of
observing men, that all kinds of game are rapidly disappearing from the Atlantic states;
and that unless the game laws, where there are such, be enforced, we shall soon have
none. In those states where there are no game laws, it is respectfully suggested, that
means be promptly taken to lay the subject before the legislatures at their ensuing
sessions. All that is necessary to the preservation of game, is to pass laws and enforce
them rigidly, for the prevention of taking game of all kinds during their respective
breeding seasons, and until the young are full grown; and this will be no hardship to
the people, for during those times no kind of game is fit for use. It is however, at these
particular seasons that more game is destroyed than during the whole of the legitimate
game season; for it is then the birds, &c. are most easily taken, and the taking of a
single bird then, causes the destruction of whole broods of young. The Boston Atlas
furnishes the following condensed view of the

GAME LAWS OF MASSACHUSETTS.

'Between March and the 1st of September, no partridge or quail, and between
March and July 4th, no woodcock, snipe, lark, or robin shall be killed, taken, sold, or
bought under forfeiture of two dollars for every partridge or quail, and one dollar for
every snipe, robin, woodcock, or lark, Ten dollars for every grouse or heath-hen, between the 1st of January and 1st of November. (These birds are only found in Martha's
Vineyard.)

'*Salt Marshes*—No person shall take, kill, or destroy any birds on any salt marshes
between 1st of March and 1st of September; and if any person within the limits of any
town, to which the provisions of this section shall extend, shall shoot, take, kill, or sell
any of the birds therein mentioned within such time, he shall forfeit the sum of two
dollars for every offence.

'Killing or taking plover, curlew, dough-bird, or chicken-bird in the night, forfeits
one dollar for each bird. The same forfeiture for destroying birds except in the usual
mode of fowling.

Deer not to be killed from the 1st of January to 1st of August on $20 forfeiture.'

VIRGINIA ANGLING CLUB

Angling was but one of many field sports and pastimes enjoyed by North Americans from 1820 to 1840 and, like many others of the period, was organized through clubs and associations. The following playful article, written by a member of an angling club in Virginia, describes in great detail and hyperbole the physical and social aspects of the club as well as the benefits accrued from such a peaceful and healthy activity as fishing. This document is reprinted from the May 1833 edition of the American Turf Register and Sporting Magazine.

ICTHYOPHAGI

MR. EDITOR: *Occoquan, Va.* April 5, 1833.

In the lower part of that peninsula formed by the waters of the magnificent Potomac and the Rappahannock, called the northern neck of Virginia, far famed for chivalry, beauty and hospitality; and whose streams abound in the finest flavoured oysters, the largest frogs, the fattest soft crabs and terrapins, and other delicious inhabitants of the deep, dwell the society of Icthyophagi; who on festival days, dress in garments made of fish skins, eat nothing but fish, drink like fish and tell fish stories; somewhat like our pious brethren, the yankees, on fast days. Every member of the association is obliged to call his dog, his horse and at least one of his children after some particular fish, and during the meetings of the society to assume the name of some fish. THe Honorable Preserved Fish, of New York, was elected an honorary member, nemine contradicente; *Tench* Ringgold has also been admitted after some debate on his christian name; Mr. Price *Roach* also; as independent of his piscatory cognomen, his physiognomy has much resemblance to that of a certain fish, being somewhat wide between the eyes, and having a huge expanse of mouth. I intend at some leisure time to give you the very interesting debates on the admission of these honorary members, which I took down in short hand. Each member is obliged to appear in his fish skin garment on festival day, equpped as the law directs, with line of fish gut, hook of fish bone and rod of whale bone. Details are dull; they admit neither the graces of ornament, the wisdom of sentiment, nor sallies of a lviely and luxuriant imagination; let it therefore be sufficient that the truth is narrated, and that the style is perspicuous. The temple built by this society is more beautiful than the palace of the Sun, erected by the poetic imagination of Ovid; fact outruns fancy, and exceeds all description; it is constructed of the larger bones of whales, and ornamented with those of smaller fish and curious shells and skins. The door is adorned with four columns, entablature and triangular pediment of the Doric order, all composed of the bones and scales of large and small fish; ornamental windows, adorned with columns, entablature, and pediment; the coilings are so artfully covered with fish scales, representing the waves of the sea, as to deceive the eye. Four wreathed columns of bones, shells and scales, in the centre of the room, seem to support the roof. Suns, circles, half moons, dolphins, flying fish, whales spouting water, sturgeons leaping from the element, pelicans and fish hawks, are curiously formed of bones, fins, and scales and inlaid in the walls and ceiling. Neptune and Amphitrite, sea nymphs, mermaids, &c., besides the world resting on the back of a terrapin, which rests on nothing; and in the center of the ceiling is a large splendid lantern covered with transparent fish skin, adorned with columns of Corinthian order, and a ball and fish on top. Over the door in the interior of this beautiful edifice are the American arms curiously wrought in tortoise shell. The floor is an elegant Mosaic pavement of shells of different and brilliant colors. The whole temple is in its construction a miracle of art, and is one of the finest specimens of novelty, taste and splendor ever beheld by the enraptured eye of man. Fish apears, bone hooks, gut lines and other piscatory curiosities from the Pacific ocean decorate the interior of this splendid temple. A reverend clergyman presides over this society, and the standing toast is, fish for the table, and flesh for the bed, on the day of the last festival, the posteriors of an hundred frogs were consumed; God knows how many soft crabs and terrapins, besides fat oysters and the finny tribe innumerable. Several of the society have large conservatories for frogs and terrapins; one member thinks he has among his eels, the Murena of the ancients. The reverend president has capon carp in his pond; though I believe this was first practised by Tull. And one gentlemen since Billy Pope's tame fish...and dancing terrapins...contemplates having a choice band of singing frogs in his conservatory. I am credibly informed that some of them already perform surprisingly well, and "discourse most excellent music." I would recommend him to teach them the Gymnastic exercises; certain I am they would succeed at "leap frog." But I have already consumed too much time, and must conclued with the following apostrophe. Happy country! where the sea furnishes abundance of luxurious repast, and the fresh waters an innocent and delightful pastime; where ther angler in cheerful solitude, strolls by the edge of the stream and fears neither the coiled snake, nor the lurking alligator; where he can retire at night with his few trouts, to borrow a pretty description of old Isaac Walton, to some friendly cottage, where the landlady is good and the daughter innocent and beautiful, where the room is cleanly lavender in the sheets, and twenty ballads stuck upon the wall. There he can enjoy the company of a talkative brother sportsman, have his trouts dressed for supper, tell tales and sing old songs; there he can talk of the wonders of nature with learned admiration, or find some harmless sport to content him and pass away a little time without offence to God or injury to man.

M.G.

URBAN ANGLERS

Many of the sports and pastimes practiced in the Midwest retained much of their outdoor spirit during the antebellum period despite the development of many cities as commercial centers. In these urban areas outdoorsmen often formed various clubs to practice their sports, to maintain their skills, and to enjoy the camaraderie from such shared experiences. The following document, reprinted from the March 1832 volume of the American Turf Register and Sporting Magazine, describes the organization of one such club and its achievements in a developing commercial center.

THE CINCINNATI ANGLING CLUB

Mr. Editor: *Cincinnati, Ohio, Jan. 30*, 1832.

This club is composed of twenty-five members, associated, as their constitution expresses it, to "enjoy, in harmony and good fellowship, the delightful and healthy amusement of angling, and to improve themselves in the *science* of that innocent sport."

The club was organized on the 25th of August, 1830, under suitable regulations for its government. The best fishing is in the Great and Little Miami rivers;—the first about fifteen miles west, and the latter seven miles east of Cincinnati. The fish considered game by the club, are the pike, salmon, and bass;—the latter taken in great abundance, from half a pound to five pounds in weight—the first but seldom—salmon frequently.

From March to November is the fishing season; but September and October are by far the best months. In October the anniversary dinner takes place, and on that occasion there is generally a great turn out of the members, and a fine display of fish. At the first dinner, near the Great Miami, 353 fish were brought in, one of which, (a noble 5 lb. bass, caught by the president,) graced the head of the table.

The whole number of fish taken that year, as reported by the secretary, was 1337; viz:—1 pike, 54 salmon, 1266 bass, and 16 catfish. The latter were caught *accidentally*; for "accidents *will* happen, even in the best regulated" clubs.

Considering that this was the sport of little more than two months, and that several of the members did not partake in it, (business, or absence from the city, preventing them,) it may be called good angling.

The weather during the last year was exceedingly unfavourable for the sports of the "honest angler,"—wet, cool, and changeable. Neither fish nor their admirers had fair play.

Few excursions were made with fair prospects for the angler; but when he did succeed, it was generally with large fish. More heavy fish were taken this year than was ever known before. The anniversary dinner was held in town; but, owing to the very inclement weather, not more than 200 fish were brought in.

The secretary reports for 1831, 1588 fish, viz:—1 pike, (weighing 4 1/2 lbs.) 88 salmon, (the largest 5 1/4 lbs.) and 1477 bass, among which were many weighing from 2 lbs. to 5 lbs. The "brag fish," this year, was taken by Maj. G.—a beautiful bass, weighing 5 1/2 lbs.—the largest bass ever taken in the club.—22 catfish were also returned, and reluctantly entered on record. Although many consider the "cat" a palatable fish, yet his habits are so filthy, and his appearance so uncouth, that he is not held in much esteem by the club. Some of the members, disdaining even to touch him, cut him loose when caught, and kick him back into the water.

Many new and ingenious inventions in angling apparatus have been produced by the club;—evincing that this interesting amusement exercises the mind as well as the body.

Of all primitive sports in pursuit of game, angling admits of more recreation for the mind, more leisure for calm and quiet contemplation, than any other. The exercise may be made easy or laborious, as the angler chooses; but there is little to interrupt his peaceful reflections, or ruffle the serenity of his temper. Seated at a favourite spot, on the banks of the clear stream, if the fish bite, there is no man more happy. But if they don't, which often happens, (for they are an *uncertain* tribe,) even then, the very hope that they will, aided by the soft music of the running stream and the rural scenery around, so completely soothe and engage the mind of the "honest angler," that he is the very model of untiring patience "which endureth unto the end."

The journey itself, to the Great Miami, (the principal fishing stream of the club,) in escaping from the din and bustle of the city, is always interesting, but at times peculiarly so. The scenery, over a gently undulating country, is not bold or sublime, but it is rich and picturesque. In the spring, when the black locust is in full bloom, the sides of the distant hills, which are covered with it, appear like snow banks; and, contrasted with the lively green of the surrounding foliage, are extremely beautiful. In the fall season, more particularly in the "Indian summer," the mellow and silvery light of the sun through the hazy atmosphere—the varied hues of the "falling leaf"—the enlarged prospect opened by the trees, disrobed in part of their foliage, and the cheerful society of three or four brother anglers, who generally make up the party on these little excursions, form such irresistible attractions to the lovers of nature and the "brethren of the rod," that no man who "has music in his soul," or possesses the least portion of the "milk of human kindness," can be dead to their beauties.

AN ANGLER

THE FIRST ARCHERY CLUB IN THE UNITED STATES

In 1828 the United Bowmen of Philadelphia formed the first archery club in the United States. For the most part it followed the rules and regulations established in England but the club did introduce some innovations of its own such as the development of a new type of silk bow string and a slightly different scoring system. In 1830 the United Bowmen issued a small book, The Archer's Manual: or The Art of Shooting with the Long Bow, as Practiced by the United Bowmen of Philadelphia. In it they discussed the history of the sport, archery equipment, drills, and archery sports. The following document is an excerpt from that manual.

INTRODUCTION TO THE ARCHER'S MANUAL, 1830

The bow, as an implement of the chase, is of indefinite antiquity. In the most ancient written production, the book of Genesis, the bow and quiver of Esau are spoken of as things well known. The mythology of the Greks ascribed its invention to Apollo; and Hercules, in the well known fable, killed the centaur with an arrow.

But however early the bow may have been known to the various nations of the earth, it is difficult to believe that their knowledge of it was derived from the same discovery. It is a characteristic of savage tribes, to adhere closely to the habits of their ancestors. The Indian nations who harassed the retreat of Xenophon, retain, to the present hour, the long bows and arrows of reed which that author has described. When, therefore, we discover that the bows and arrows of different districts differ very much in size, form and materials, and in the modes of using them, we are justified in the opinion, that they are of various origin,—and that their resemblance in a few particulars, has been altogether accidental. We cannot connect the history of Italy with that of our own country, merely because vases of the same beautiful proportions are found among the ruins of Herculaneum, and in the graves of the aboriginial Mexicans.

We know nothing of the form of the Jewish bow. That of Greece was nearly in the shape of the letter Sigma, and was strung with sinew. The Roman bow, as we find it on antique medals, resembled the Greek in its general character, but its angles were modified into graceful curves. The bow of the Centaurs is represented, among the sculptures of the Parthenon, as forming, when strung, about the fifth or sixth of a circle, like the bows of the modern English archers; but the ends, or nocks as we should term them, were bent backwards, so that the string when loosed, sprung only against a curved surface. The Parthians used short bows, which they discharged over the shoulder while retreating. The Chinese bow is of horn, of nearly the same form as the Greek: while that of Hindostan, of thick, strong reed, is, when unstrung, nearly straight. The Sough Sea Islanders, and many of the African tribes, use a bow of very hard wood, about five feet in length, and entirely similar in form to the English bow, but strung with sinew.

The materials, of which bows are made, are almost equally various. The bow of one nation is of horn, united by firm ligatures:—that of another, using the same material, has the handle of wood:—a third is of wood altogether:—while many among the rudest, as among the most refined nations, employ two materials, one to give elasticity, and the other toughness.

The arrows are diversified in like manner. Some, as the African and those of the Sandwich Islanders, are short, heavily armed with barbed heads, and without feathering:—those of the East Indies generally are made of cane or reed, very long, and profusely feathered:—and we have ourselves seen, in the wigwam of a Tuscarora chief of our own country, arrows formed according to the fasion of his tribe, which were as accurately proportioned, and as neatly trimmed, as any that could be found among the quivers of our clubs.

Columbus found the bow in use among the American Islanders, and was struck with the address and power with which they applied it to purposes of offence. He mentions that, on his second voyage, a female Indian shot an arrow through the target of a Spanish soldier, and that one of her companions, while endeavouring to escape by swimming, still continued to use his bow with much effect.

The natives of Brazil, when discovered by the Portuguese, used bows of an ell in length; and of such power, that their arrows, which were armed with fish bones, would pierce the hardest boards.

The Indians residing west of the Mississippi, as we learn from a member of our club, who is entirely familiar with their habits, use bows made of the yellow or "bow" wood, Maclura aurantiaca, of Nuttall. This wood grows only on the Red river and the southern tributaries of the Arkansas; whence it is carried to all the nations residing on the tributaries of the Mississippi.

These bows are comparatively short, seldom measuring more than three feet six inches, and are always backed with tendon, taken from the buffalo, and secured on the bow by glue, made from the feet of the same animal. Slips of the same tendon, nicely twisted, form the string. Their size renders them convenient for using on horesback, and their power is such as to drive an arrow completely through the body of the buffalo.

An esteemed bow, but not so frequently used, is made of elk horn, backed in the same manner as those described above.

The arrows are about twenty-six inches long, and are tri-feathered in an indifferent manner. The heads are made, by those who can procure it, of iron: a piece of old hoop is the usual substance, ground into a triangular form, and placed in a slit in the end of the arrow, where it is firmly secured by a lapping of tendon. Those used in war are so constructed as to remain in the wound when the shaft if withdrawn: those used in hunting are attached fimrly, but their shafts are grooved so as to permit the flow of blood along them.

The bow is usually carried in a case attached to the quiver, both made of the skin of the American panther, or cougar, the tail of which remains attached as an ornamental appendage.

The nations which reside very far west, and have comparatively little intercourse with the whites, still use the stone heads, which are found so abundantly throughout the country, and in the immediate vicinity of Philadelphia. They are made of various hard stones, such as chalcedony, hornstone, flint, jasper, agate, or quartz, and with such remarkable neatness, that the most ingenious mechanic, with the aid of tools, would find much difficulty in imitating them. The number of these heads, and their general distribution over the surface of this country, furnish evidence of the existence, at a former period, of a numerous race of Indians, whose hunting grounds extended over the vast tract of country, now the home of the American people.

The application of the bow to purposes of war, was introduced into England by the Normans, who owed their success at the battle of Hastings, to the efficiency of their archers. The hero of Sherwood Forest, the renowned Robin Hood, flourished rather more than a century after this,—and still two centuries later, the victories of Crecy, Poictiers, adn Agincourt, bore testimony to the prowess of the English archery.

The first recognised society of archers, The Fraternity of St. George, was incorporated by Henry VIII, with many privileges, about the year 1540; and at the same time, an act of parliament was passed, requiring every man to arm himself with bow and arrows, and all but judges and ecclesiastics to practise at the butts.

Renewed efforts were made in the reign of Queen Elizabeth, to carry this statute into effect. Roger Ascham, who had been charged with the direction of her early studies, and who afterwards filled the station of her Latin secretary, had written an admirable treatise on archery, and was withal an expert in the art. Under his influence, as it is supposed, commissioners were appointed to promote the use of the long bow throughout the realm, and they were directed to return the names and residence of all delinquents to the Queen. But, as the invention of gunpowder became generally known, the bow naturally fell into disuse; and the laws in favour of archery and archers, though now and then recalled to public notice by the favour of some royal patron of woodsport, were neglected or repealed.

The London archers, however, seem to have retained many of their rights to a late day. The city was bound to provide them with butts and shooting ground; and till after the death of Charles I. this obligation was not unfrequently enforced by judicial decrees, and sometimes by popular violence.

After the restoration, Charles II. made efforts to reinstate the bow in the favour of the people. He was a frequent attendant on the performance of archers, and actually knighted Sir William Wood for his skill in wood-craft. But the civil wars had made men familiar with the use of more powerful weapons,—the cavaliers prided themselves specially in those amusements, of which the vulgar could not partake,—and the stern spirit of the Puritans tolerated no mere pastimes. Archery, as a matter of course, declined in England; and when the Toxophilite Society was formed in the last century, by the exertions of Sir Ashton Lever, the bow and sheaf of shafts had almost passed away into the cabinet of antiquary.

The establishment of this society may be regarded as an era in the history of the bow. It no longer claimed the dignity of a weapon for the national defence; but it resumed its preeminence among invigorating and graceful recreations. Clubs of archers were immediately collected in different parts of the kingdom,—trials of skill were renewed between the champions of different shooting grounds,—and the feats of the gallant outlaw and his merry men, were acted over again on the green sward, under the patronage of noblemen, and in the presence of the fair. The spirit of these institutions has not since declined, and they have greatly increased in number.

THE UNITED BOWMEN OF PHILADELPHIA are, it is believed, the only club which has yet been orgainized in the United States, for the practice of archery. It dates from the spring of 1828.

The want of a manual for the instruction of the members of this club, led them to charge a committee with the preparation of the following little work. Most of its materials have been derived from a treatise by Mr. Waring, the modern English bowyer, or from Ascham's "Toxophilus,"—somewhat modified and explained perhaps, by reference to the limited experience of the committee. It has of course little pretension to originality, or to literary character. More than the object of its authors will have been attained, if it contributes in any degree to introduce among our countrymen a fondness for the sports of archery, the best probably of the gymnastic exercises.

Philadelphia, May 1830

THE ARCHER'S EQUIPMENT.

THE LONG BOW should be of a length equal to the height of the archer who uses it: and its strength should be sufficient to throw the arrow at least one third further than the object against which it is directed.

BOWS are made of various materials. *Self bows,* as they are termed, are formed from a single piece of tough but elastic wood. Such were the bows of the merry archers of old England, of which the material was the yew tree. But the long known difficulty of procuring wood at once tough and elastic has compelled bow makers to combine two or more substances which possess these qualities separately. Thus, it is common to find bows, of which the body is of lemon, cedar, or some scarcely flexible wood, plated or backed, as the phrase is, by a thin slip of tough ash, glued to it firmly. These are called *backed bows*. One of the best used by the United Bowmen, is of the American locust, and is backed with macerated sinew: it has great power, and restores itself perfectly when unstrung. Backed bows, when not in use, require to be carefully protected from moisture, and from excessive dryness; either of which, by impairing the tenacity of the glue, destroys the bow. If it is kept in a proper situation, a bow will require no oiling or other preservative.

The proper form of a bow, when unstrung, is perfectly straight: though bows, when first manufactured, are sometimes made to bend a little backwards, with a view to give them a greater degree of elastic force. The back or outer part of the bow is always made flat, and square with the sides: the inner is generally round.

The extremities of the bow are protected by tips made of horn, of unequal lengths, in which is formed the nock for receiving the string. The lower end of the bow is indicated by the shorter horn.

THE HANDLE should not be in the centre of the bow, but under it: thus the lower limb is shorter than the upper one by the depth of the handle, and is therefore made the stronger of the two. If the centre of the bow was in the centre of the handle, both limbs, being of the same length, should be equal in strength, and should, when strung, approach the form of a sixth of a circle. But the position of the hand, while grasping the bow, would in such case render it impossible to send an arrow from the centre, and in fact would make it necessary to raise it about two and a half inches higher, so as to clear the handle. The upper limb consequently would be more bent than the lower in the act of shooting; and the effect would be irregularity in the range of the arrow, and considerable risk of breaking the upper limb of the bow. As it is important that the arrow should go from the center of the bow, the handle is placed immediately below it; and as, by this means, the lower limb is shortened, and the stress upon it increased, it is made stronger in proportion; so that when drawn by the strong the bow retains a regular curve, and both limbs exert an equal force.

THE FORCE OF A BOW is estimated by the number of pounds weight, which, when suspended from the string, will draw it down to the length of an arrow. This is generally marked immediately above the handle. Fifty pounds is standard weight; and he is a strong man who can draw one of sixty with ease, as his regular shooting bow. Some few however can use a bow of seventy or even eighty pounds.

Ladies' bows, it is said, are from twenty-four to thirty-four pounds.

It may be remarked that the archer exerts a degree of force equal to double the weight of the bow; for if he draws one of fifty pounds with his right hand, the left must have the same strength to resist that pull. But the force of his bow is an imperfect criterion of the strength of the person who uses it; for an experienced archer will bend a bow without effort, which, in the hands of an unpractised stranger, of much greater strength, would be entirely unmanageable.

THE BOW STRING is made of catgut, hemp or silk. The English archers generally use one of hemp, bound or whipped with stout sewing silk, for an inch or two directly opposite the upper end of the handle, where the arrow sets upon it, to protect it from wearing away. As the breaking of a string not unfrequently shivers the bow, such an accident cannot be too carefully guarded against. It is therefore the practice of many archers, to secure the ends of the string in the same manner.

The United Bowmen have substituted a silk string, made of a number of threads of sewing silk, firmly lashed, or whipped together with the same material. Although rather thick, it is perhaps preferable to that used in England, as it is not sensibly affected by moisture.

Whatever the string be made of, it should not be permitted to untwist, or become loose and uneven. This is prevented by waxing it.

The string, when the bow is not in use, should be attached, by a timber noose or knot, (Vide Plate) to the lower end, and should be looped loosely, at the eye or noose, to the notch at the top of the bow.

ARROWS are made of wood selected for its tenacity and lightness. The English use the linden; but the linden of America is of too soft a texture for this purpose. The United Bowmen prefer the white holly, which is rather more dense, and permits the arrow to be made thinner.

The head or pile of the arrow is guarded by a small ferule or ring of metal, which is sometimes slightly pointed. The notch at the smaller end, which receives the string, is called the *nock*. It is generally made of horn, neatly inlaid and secured in the wood. The nock should be exactly as wide as the string of the bow: not so large as to permit the arrow to play loosely, nor so small as to require force to push it on; but just wide enough to press slightly on the string.

The length of the arrow is determined by that of the bow. The arrows of ladies' bows, or of bows five feet long, are twenty-four inches. Bows, under five feet nine inches, have arrows of twenty-seven inches; and for those above five feet nine inches, we use arrows of twenty-eight, twenty-nine, and even thirty inches. But arrows of thirty inches can be used to advantage only with very long bows, and by persons who have a great length of arm. There is, besides, something of risk to the bow in drawing so long an arrow to the head;—indeed few bows are safe, when drawn to the distance even of twenty-nine inches. With bows therefore not exceeding five feet ten inches, it is recommended that no arrows be used above twenty-eight inches long.

Arrows that are intended for very long flights, may perhaps be considered an exception. These, which are called *flight arrows*, are longer and lighter than those that are used in ordinary shooting; but they ought not to be used unless with bows of more than common toughness.

Arrows are of different shapes. Some are thick at the head or pile, and gradually decrease to the nock; others are thickest near the middle; and some again are stoutest close under the feathers, and taper off to the head.

An advantage attending the blunt head it, that when shot into the target frame or any other wood work, it does not enter so far as the sharp, and is therefore more easily extracted. But archers have various opinions on this point; and their differences may be pardoned, inasmuch as arrows of any shape, if they are only straight, will fly well at almost any distance within the range of the bow.

The arrow is feathered near the nock in three equidistant lines; two of which are generally of one colour, and the third different. The odd feather is placed in a line with one projection of the nock, and is called the cock feather:—in preparing to shoot, it is always placed uppermost on the bow. The feathers should be stiff and regularly trimmed. The English archers use those of the goose or turkey; but the quill feathers of the eagle, the swan, or the blue heron are preferable.

The weight of the arrow which should be used must depend in a great measure on the power of the bow. The English archers express it in terms of the coin of the realm, valued at its standard weight. Thus, it is said that arrows vary in weight from three to twenty shillings. Mr. Roberts, in his English Bowman, page 153, gives the following table for selecting arrows.

For shots of 30 yards, weight from 4s. to 6s.

For shots of 60 yards, weight from 3s. 6d. to 5s. 6d.

For shots of 90 to 120 yards, weight from 3s. to 4s. 6d.

But all this is of little practical value. Bows may be equally well calculated for either of these distances, and yet require different arrows; and it is not common to find two archers who select the same arrows, even for the same bow. The strength of the bow is of course to be considered, and whether it has a sharp or dull loose; or in other words, whether it cast quickly, or the reverse: for two bows of the same weight will differ much in the quickness of their motion, and consequently in the distance to which they send the arrow. And then, peculiarities may, and in fact almost always do exist, in the archer's manner of drawing his bow, of loosing the string, of elevating at the mark: all of which should have their influence in determining the selection of his arrows. Attentive practice will decide best in matters of this kind. The arrows of the United Bowmen vary in weight from three quarters to one ounce avoirdupois.

The archer's arrows, that are intended for the same distance, should have the same form and weight: a change in either of these particulars will have the effect of varying the line of flight, and of course will destroy the accuracy of the shot.

The London Toxophilite Society, though they shoot with two arrows only, have always a third of the same kind in their pouch for use, in case either of the others is accidentally broken or deranged. Thus they denominate three arrows a pair: accordingly the expression is sometimes found to have this sense in treatises on archery. The more common term however is a *pouch* of *arrows*.

The United Bowmen's pouch contains three arrows.

THE BRACE is a small shield of smooth stout leather, which is buckled on the inner part of the left forearm in shooting, to prevent its being injured by the stroke of the string. In former times, many archers did not wear anything to protect the arm, but braced the string so high from the bow, that when loosed it could not reach the arm. But this would seem to be a bad arrangement, and must often endanger the bow. Besides, a bow has less play, when overstrung, and of course cannot give an arrow its greatest range. For these two reasons, modern archers generally wear the brace.

A gentleman's bow is said, by Mr. Waring, to be overstrung, when the middle of the string measures from the handle of the bow more than six inches; and a lady's bow, when more than five.

THE SHOOTING GLOVE is intended to save the fingers from being hurt by the friction of the string as it passes over them. It consists of three fingerstalls of stout leather, sewed to three thongs, which unite at the back of the hand in a strap that extends to the wrist, where it is sewed to another that buttons round the wrist. Some archers use only two fingers; but this is not generally practicable, except with weak bows, or in short shooting. To a strong bow, at the full range, the third finger is an important aid. The stalls should not project more over the fingers than is necessary for their protection as the string glides by.

The BELT buckles round the waist; from which on the right side is suspended the pouch or bucket to receive the arrows intended for present use. This is a necesary appendage; as for the want of it the archer must lay his arrows on the ground, and risk their being trod upon and broken.

The TASSEL is suspended from the left side of the belt; and is used to cleanse the arrow, as it is drawn from the ground, before it is placed in the pouch.

The GREASE BOX is suspended from the middle of the belt; and contains a composition for anointing occasionally the fingers of the shooting glove, that the string may pass off the more readily.

The QUIVER is never worn but is roving. In shooting at targets or butts, it is placed by the side of them, a few yards distance, to contain a reserve of arrows.

Quivers were formely made of wood, and afterwards of leather; but, for some years past, tin quivers have been generally substituted, as being lighter, more secure, and less expensive.

The ASCHAM is a long upright case, used by the English archers, for the purpose of containing the whole of their accoutrements. It is not properly a part of the archer's equipment.

The SHOOTING DRESS adopted by the United Bowmen is at once convenient and economical. It consists of a light sporting cap of black bombazet, an iron grey jacket bound with black braid, and a corresponding under dress. It is undoubtedly better suited to our climate in the shooting season, than the green broad-cloth coat and slouched hat with plumes, by which the English clubs are distinguished.

The SACK is large enough to hold the shooting dress; and it contains, in addition, a small flat file for widening or repairing arrow nocks, an additional bow string, a spare ferule or two, a bunch of stout sewing silk, and a wax ball. These complete the equipment of the archer.

By the rules of the United Bowmen, the property of each member is distinguished by some simple badge, as the circle, an arrowhead, the triangle, &c. which is marked upon his bow near the handle, upon his arrows above the feathers, upon his brace, belt, quiver, and generally on all his accoutrements. It is also the mark, by which his shots are indicated on the target, and on the record card....

SPORTS OF ARCHERY.

TARGET SHOOTING. The target generally employed in this amusement is circular, about four feet in diameter, formed of painted canvass or oil-cloth, fastened on a bass of straw, which is wrought together into a flattened mat, resembling the texture of a beehive. It is supported by a frame of soft wood, made light...and so arranged as to present the smallest possible surface in the direction of the arrow.

The target is painted in concentric circles. The centre is gold, of the diameter of about nine inches and a half. This is surrounded by a red ring, four and three quarter inches broad; and this again by a white, a black, and a light blue or outer white ring, each of the same width. The remaining space is painted dark green, and is called the petticoat or curtain.

An arrow in the gold counts nine,—in the red, seven,—in the white, five,—in the black, three,—in the blue, one,—in the curtain, nothing. An arrow on the edge of a circle, or not completely within it, according to the United Bowmen, counts as if it were entirely without it: a different rule is however admitted among many of the English archers.

Two targets are used. They are placed, facing each other, at the distance of eighty, a hundred, or a hundred and twenty yards. The ordinary range of the arrow flight, at the practice meetings of the United Bowmen, is a hundred measured yards.

The archers of the Scotch Guard, it is said, are in the habit of shooting at the distance of a hundred and fifty yards; and it is well known that the old English archers were not permitted to practise at butts which were closer than two hundred and twenty yards. This however is a much greater range, than consists with accurate shooting; and if the information which we have received is to be relied on, the body of the modern Scotch archery are more distingushed for the length, than for the certainty of their shots. Some among them have doubtless been known to place their shafts in a mark of thirty inches square, from a distance of two hundred yards; but such instances cannot be common. The willow wand, that Sir Walter Scott chooses for Robin Hood's mark in the sports at Ashby, was placed at but five score yards,—and even at that distance, his success is sufficiently incredible.

In his earlier practice, the young archer may very well test his strength for a while at a target of seventy or eighty yards.

Ladies' targets are said to be considerably smaller than those for gentlemen, and they are placed at distances of fifty to sixty yards.

By the regulations of the United Bowmen, each member in succession acts on practice days as captain of the target. He calls the roll of the club at the hour of meeting, details the members who are to mark distances and to fix the targets, and throughout the sports of the day is the absolute commander and umpire.

The ground being measured and marked, the targets are placed in such a line as that the sun shall not be in the eyes of the archers at the stands; and the members take stations in a line at the left of one of the targets. At a signal, they advance successively in divisions of two to the front of the target:—the members of the division shoot alternatively, the right first; each taking care to nock, while the other is shooting, so as to save time:—and immediately after shooting the third arrow of the pouch, the division draws off to the right of the target.

As soon as the last division has left the stand, the divisions move regularly across the field to the other target,—taking care, as they approach it, to avoid treading upon the arrows. The captain marks each hit on the target with the appropriate sign of the archer, and makes a corresponding note on the record card. The members collect their arrows, and again take places at the left of the target.

The captain shoots either alone, or as a member of the first division.

No one is allowed to place himself in advance of an archer at the stand, and no speaking is permitted at the moment of shooting.

An arrow, which falls from the string, may be taken up if the archer can reach it with his bow: otherwide, it is reckoned as a shot.

An arrow which passes through the target, or falls to the ground after striking it, counts as a hit, if the archer can show the mark.

The RECORD CARD will be fully understood by examining the...Plate. It is a card, ruled in squares, with the marks of the several archers in the line at the left, and the names of the circles in the line at the top. At the conclusion of each day's sport, the number and value of each archer's hits are marked by the captain in the two columns at the right. The record card given in the plate shows that A. has placed two arrows in the gold, six in the red, &c. &c. numbering in all twenty-eight, of the value of one hundred and eighteen. B. has twenty-nine hits, counting one hundred and twenty-one, and C. twenty-three, counting one hundred and one. A pin is attached to the record card for convenience of notation; the mark of a pencil would be liable to be effaced in the course of the shooting.

As a principal object of the sport is exercise, each archer should collect his own arrows, and shoot alternately from each target. The number of arrows should not exceed three, as it increases the chances of losing them, and the fingers of a person, who is not accustomed to labour, are apt to be chaffed by the bowstring, if too constantly employed.

The grass should be kept very short in the neighbourhood of the targets; and it is generally best to shoot with a little elevation, lest the arrow should be lost, or injured in its feathering: in point-blank shooting, it will often completely bury itself in the ground.

Archers in selecting their shooting-grounds are very properly careful to avoid the vicinity of public roads, and, in fact, every situation in which persons may incautiously approach their targets. He is a weak bowman, whose arrow would not be dangerous after a flight of even a hundred and fifty yards.

PRIZE SHOOTING. The archery clubs have occasional meetings for prize shooting. The Toxophilites of England, the Scotch archers, and our United Bowmen, have two prizes: the first of which is awarded to him, whose whole number of hits counts the highest; the other to the arrow nearest the centre of the gold. Our first prize has been a cup, a silver arrow, or a bugle,—the second, a dozen of arrows or a bow. The former is of course worn by the best marksman of the day,—the latter is often the encouraging reward of a happy shot by an unpractised archer.

Mr. Roberts, in his English Bowman, tells us that a member of the Toxophilite society won the first prize in 1795, by placing four arrows in the gold, seventeen in the red, nineteen in the white, twenty-four in the black, and twenty-six in the outer white; in all, ninety hits, counting three hundred and forty-eight. This was probably excellent shooting, for there are fine marksmen among the Toxophilites; but we should estimate its excellence more fully, if we were told the distnace of the targets, and the time occupied in the contest. At a prize meeting of our own club, after a single season's practice, five arrows were in two hours placed in the gold, nine in the red, ten in the white, fifteen in the black, and twenty-three in the blue; sixty-two hits, counting two hundred and twenty-six:—this is not a great day's work, but it was a creditable performance for young archers.

BUTT SHOOTING. Butts are structures of turf, about seven feet high, and eight feet wide at the base, narrowing towards the top. They are generally from three to four feet in thickness. A set of butts consists of four, so placed as that one shall not intercept the view of another from either of the stands.

The greatest distance between them is from one hundred and twenty to two hundred feet; but two of the butts are so situated as to give marks at one fourth, one half, and three fourths of that distance....

The mark is a round piece of pasteboard, fastened by a peg in its centre to the butt. Its size is proportioned to the distance from the shooting stand,—the mark at two hundred yards being thirty inches square,—at one hundred and fifty yards, twenty-two and a half inches,—at one hundred yards, fifteen inches,—at fifty yards, seven inches and a half. If the greatest distance is but on hundred and twenty yards, the largest mark is sixteen inches.

No arrow is counted, that strikes outside of the pasteboard. The greatest number of hits decides the winner; or if two have the same number, the victory is with the arrow which has struck nearest the peg. If this cnanot be determined, a single arrow is shot by each of the claimants, and he who hits nearest the peg, or the mark, or even the butt itself, gains the day.

The expression, a single end, is applied to shooting at a single mark: a double end is shot, when the arrows are shot back again at the same distance.

As few archers shoot equally well at different distances, it is common, with the view of giving to each the same chance of winning, to shoot an equal number of ends at each of the butts.

The prize shooting of the Scotch Guard is sometimes at butts. Anciently, a goose was enclosed in turf, with only a small part of the head exposed, and the prize was won by him who pierced it with an arrow. The modern practice is to shoot at a small glass globe, fixed in the centre of the mark on the butt; and the successful archer, after receiving his medal, carves a goose at the dinner table. But the sport is still called shooting for the goose.

ROVERS. Archers, who shoot from field to field as they walk, selecting as their marks trees and other conspicuous natural objects, are called a roving party, and their sport a match at rovers. The distance of course depends on circumstances; but the spirit of the amusement requires that the marks should never be closer than a hundred and fifty yards.

No arrow counts, unless it strikes within five bow lengths of the mark. With this qualification, the nearest arrow counts one; and if the same archer has two or three or more arrows nearer than any of those of his ocmpanions, he counts accordingly.

In measuring the distance of an arrow from the mark, and in comparing the positions of two arrows, the centre of the mark is understood to be at the height of a foot from the ground. Where a tree is the mark, therefore, an arrow in a branch is less valuable than an arrow on the ground, which happens to be nearer the mark of a foot from the base; and an arrow that has even struck the trunk of the tree, if more than five bow lengths above the true mark, will count nothing, though it be the nearest.

In measurements to ascertain whether his arrow is within five bow-lengths, each archer uses his own bow, and measures to the nearest part of the arrow:—but when the question is between two arrows, the same bow must be used in measuring the distances of both, and the measurement is to the part of the arrow, which is visible, nearest the pile.

The archer, who counts by a shot at a roving mark, selects the mark for the next shot, and continues to select the marks for the company, till some other counts.

If an archer supposes that the mark chosen is beyond the range of his arrow, he may claim to walk in closer before shooting;—but in such case, he is bound to use a flight arrow, and to elevate to an angle of forty-five degrees.

The game of single bows is seven; but where two shoot against two, as partners, the game is thirteen. If three shoot against two, the game of the larger party is thirteen, and of the smaller, nine. Inequality of skill among the competitors is compensated, as at other games, by an allowance of odds in favour of the weaker.

The quiver is worn in roving; and it should be well filled, as arrows are not unfrequently lost.

A party should not consist of more than six:—if the number in company is greater than this, it should form two parties, which may follow each other. But care should be taken, that they do not come within bow-shot of each other, for fear of accidents.

CLOUT SHOOTING. Clouts are marks, about twelve inches in diameter, generally made of pasteboard, and secured immediately above the ground by a cleft stick, at distances of one hundred and fifty to two hundred yards.

The order of shooting in this sport is the same as in target shooting: but the manner and rules of counting are the same as in shooting at butts; the only difference being that, as the distance in this case is uniform, no arrow counts unless within three bow lengths of the clout.

Sometimes the clouts are made of cloth, secured at each side to a stick. In this form, they can be rolled up, and very portable; and they are in consequence much used by archers, who have not convenient grounds in the neighbourhood for the erection of butts or targets.

The game is the same as in butt shooting.

FLIGHT SHOOTING. This is merely a trial between archers, which can throw his arrow to the greatest distance. The longest and lightest arrows are used for this purpose. But a careful archer is rarely tempted to engage in this sport, as he jeopards his bow, and almost certainly loses some of his arrows. Those who practise it count seven as the game.

SEVENTH ANNIVERSARY OF THE UNITED BOWMEN

The United Bowmen of Philadelphia were the most celebrated archery club in the United States during the 1830s. As with other anniversary sporting occasions, this event combined pagentry and pomp with competition and honors. The report reprinted below is from the American Turf Register and Sporting Magazine, October 1835.

ARCHERY

On Wednesday, September 9th, the company of "United Bowmen" celebrated their anniversary, near Philadelphia. According to the United States Gazette, this association holds its charter from the ancient company in England, that traces its line of existence almost to the merry days of the hero of Sherwood forest. Cards of invitation having been issued to numerous persons, between three and four o'clock the guests assembled, to the number of about twelve hundred, at the elegant seat of Mr. Norris, on Turner's Lane. The United States Gazette thus describes the scene:-

Nearly two hundred carriages were ranged along the lane, and in the extensive avenue to the mansion. From the east side of the extensive lawn in front of the house, was separated by extended lines, an area about fifty yards wide by one hundred and twenty long, for the exercises of the Bowmen. Midway on the east side of the area, was erected a very handsome marquee, in which was Johnson's admirable band of music. Opposite that tent, on the west side of the area, was a table most tastefully decorated, upon which were placed the premiums; and without the line, on the north and west side; were seats for the ladies, who watched with earnestness the movements of the archers. Among the company were representations of all the liberal professions, and all classes of citizens who had lesiure and taste for such enjoyment. Some of the young ladies and gentlemen kindly gave up their places of advantage to their seniors, and we wished them pleasant strolls as they paired off along the delightful walks of the place. How thoughtful thus to give place to the old.

The gentlemen of the Company wore their uniform, which consisted of green frock coats, trimmed with gold, with an arrow on their collars, white pantaloons and green caps; pendant to a black leathern girdle were the appliances of their craft. Their bows were truly beautiful, and the arrows were of the most approved shape and finish. The targets were placed near each extremity of the area, the sporting distance being eighty yards. The company was divided into two classes—each class was ranged near its own traget, and one member of each stepped forward, and both discharged their arrows at the opposite targets; these then stepped aside and another two came forward—and thus till all had discharged their arrows. Near each target shot at, stood a neatly dressed lad with silk flags in his hat, and as an arrow struck the target, he waved a flag of the colour of the circle hit. The bowmen would march, to the sound of music, in file to the opposite extremity, gather up their arrows, and the captain of the target, Mr. Krumbhaar, mark upon a card the number which the members had gained. The centre, or gold spot, counting nine, and each ring counting two less, as one receded from the centre. The two lads, with their flags, moved always towards the target opposite the bowmen. Whenever an arrow struck the centre or gold spot, the band gave a flourish with their trumpets. As time for closing the contest drew near, it was evident that the ladies had taken an interest in the proceedings, and they were anxious to learn the result—to know who were to receive the splendid premiums. The contest was close, and the difference between the few who gained, and the many who missed, was very small. The first premium was the company's "bowl,"—a massive silver vessel, weighing one hundred and fifty ounces, bearing various devices and inscriptions, and receiving from each yearly holder some additional ornament. This is held for one year only. The other premiums are retained by winners. The second premium was a handsone silver arrow, to bear the winner's name, date, and the inscription, SECUNDUS HOC CONTENTUS ABITO. The third premium was a handome silver wassail cup, the stem representing a quiver. When the tally card was reckoned up, the premiums were thus awarded by the captain of the target, with a suitable address:—

FIRST PREMIUM, the Company's bow, to FRANKLIN PEALE—thirty-seven shots, counting one hundred and forty-four.

SECOND PREMIUM to S.P. GRIFFITTS, JR.—thirty-three shots, counting one hundred and twenty-nine.

THIRD PREMIUM to W.H.W. DARLEY. This premium is given for the arrow placed nearest to the centre of the target, without any reference to the number previously gained. It was obtained by Mr. D. at the last shot in the afternoon.

The company was delighted with the place and the means of enjoyment; and when some observed, that in a single round there had been several misses, we heard a young lady archly observe, that there were more *"misses"* than hits. She did less than hustice to the fair part of the company. We are too old to talk about such things, but we have good reason to believe that the *united* company were not the only bowmen of the afternoon.

We are sure that we express the feelings of the very numerous and highly respectable guests, when we refer with grateful pleasure to the liberal courtesy of the United Bowmen, and to their arrangements for the entire accommodation of those who witnessed their elegant and healthful exercise.

A NATIONAL PIGEON SHOOTING SWEEPSTAKES

Pigeon shooting became a popular sport during the 1830s, for both participants and spectators. In the following article a southern sportsman who served as a correspondent to The Spirit of the Times proposes a sweepstakes shooting match whose sizeable purse and entrance fee would simultaneously attract participants from all parts of the nation and exclude those not belonging to the ranks of gentlemen. The writer argues that a sweepstakes contest of this nature would command a national as well as an international audience and suggests that only a large venue, such as the Union course, a horse racing track on Long Island, New York, would be appropriate for an event of this magnitude. The document reprinted below is from the 26 May 1838 edition of The Spirit of the Times.

SWEEPSTAKES SHOOTING MATCH

COLUMBUS (Ga.) May 14, 1838.

W.T. PORTER, Esq.—*Dear Sir,*—It has been my intention for a long time to contribute somewhat to the columns of your interesting and valuable magazine. My anticipation had rested on a period of time somewhere about the first of this month, when I should have an opportunity of furnishing you with the "start," the "go," the "brush," and the "come out" of some of our "swift ones," as the races over our course were advertised to come off at that time. But we were all sadly disappointed. Hammond didn't make his *stately* appearance, and consequently there was *"no* go." Again, I have said to myself, "I'll go out with the boys and take a hunt—chase the Deer and follow the Roe, and then sit down the tell Porter how swift an old Buck can run in Georgia; how lofty he throws his head; how he makes twice the "stride" of Bascombe, and "picks up" quicker than Miss Medley, and how our old men, and even young boys, can give him the "lofty fall," at the distance of one hundred yeards, and that, too, when he is bounding and tumbling like the waters of Niagara." But in this, too, I have failed. Time and tide, which wait for no man, neither for the race horse, nor the swift running deer, have swept by, leaving me in the midst of a variety of occupations, which have altogether engrossed my attention, and in truth, obliged me for a little reason to forget my friends.

I have alluded slightly to shooting, and while it is in my head permit me to offer you a few suggestions to this beautiful branch of sporting. We do not shoot as well, or as much, in this country as they do in England, we we, Sir? And why not? We are centainly not deficient in eye-sight—for what nation under heaven are quicker or keener sighted than the Yankees! We surely do not lack *the nerve* to pull a trigger!

"We are the sons of William Tell,
And shoot to hit the apple."

To what, then, can we attribute our lack of science in shooting! I will venture to put it down to the want of practice; and we shall never practice enough to make ourselves skilful without stronger incentive than mere amusement. I have said that the Yankees are a quick, keen-sighted sort of folks; aye, they ar all that, as I presume you have long since learned. There is no doubt in my mind but that a Bostonian, a Georgian, or a Tennesseean, would shoot much closer to a silver dollar, (i.e. what we call a *speeler* in this country), at the distance of one hundred yards, than he would at a potatoe at the distance of fifty yards. "Money makes the mare go," was an old copy which I have written a thousand and one times in a Connecticut School House; yes, money will make a man "look sharp" and "pull steady," and practise perseveringly until he is perfect. I propose, then, to the sporting world, a great *Sweepstake Shooting Match*, to come off on the Beacon or Union Course; the book for entries to be opened in New York, free for as many as choose to enter, at from *one* to *two thousand dollars* entrance. This scheme you may view as novel, and perhaps somewhat chimerical; but in my humble judgment nothing is more feasible, and believe me, Sir, it can be accomplished without the slighest difficulty, if the ice once be broken.

Sweepstakes naturally draw together a large crowd of people, on account of the variety of interests, and the numerous friends of the contending parties; added to this, gentlemen of a sporting disposition are ready to risk a *little* where there is prospect of winning much. These are my reasons for proposing a Sweepstake.

As to the entrance, I have proposed to make it large, the better to induce gentlemen to enter, and also to justify their travelling from remote parts of the Union. Those gentlemen who practice with a gun, are scattered over various parts of the country, but would doubtless be willing to take chances in a *National Shooting Sweepstakes*, if the purse to be shot for was sufficiently large and inviting; and if the books were to be opened immediately, I have no doubt there would be five hundred entries by the first of October next. Many gentlemen in this State are extremely anxious for the meeting, and ready to subscribe the moment the books are opened.

Pigeon-shooting has long been ranked amongst the choicest of amusements, and specially so, I believe, in New York and New Jersey. There could be no doubt, then, I think, in relation to getting up this match, and the propriety of making Pigeons the game, and of shooting the match at or near New York, will readily occur to every mind. New York would certainly be the most prominent and advantageous ground for such shooting; and principally for the reason, that birds could be more readily obtained there than in any other place, by means of rivers, canals, rail-roads, etc. And besides this, from the immense size of your city, and the great number of fine shots to be found there, the entry would doubtless be larger than at any other place. Suppose a match should be made involving some hundred thousand dollars, what an immense concourse of people would be drawn together! And would not the owner of the Union Course, for instance, be willing to use some extra exertions in procuring birds, when he must know that it would put money in his purse by thousands, which would flow from the gate, stand and bar?

In the event of such a match being made—and should it strike you as feasible, I do not for a moment doubt of its success—I would here suggest that each man should shoot at a given number of birds per day, with a view to place each shooter on an equal footing, as in case of rain or wind, a superior shot might be beaten by an inferior; and besides, it would serve well to keep up the excitement, as it would be impossible to tell who would win until towards the close of the last day's shooting; the result being rendered thus uncertain, it would swell the multitude who would attend,—for every man's friend would be on the spot, anxious for his success.

Such a match would, I think, call a representation from every State in the Union, and since the ocean can be crossed in a fortnight by Steam vessels, who will doubt but that a large number of chances would be taken in Europe, and particularly in England,—for the English boys are crack shots, and passionately fond of the sport.

We know not how others may feel, but we are anxious for the "tilt," and believe that we can beat any body's man;—so strong do we believe this, that in the event of the shooting, a favorite shot in this section of the State will be willingly backed for from one to five thousand dollars as an inside stake.

Thus, then, you have the plan which I have long been anxious to propound, and why should not the match be made? Neither the North nor the South has at this time a "crack nag," and the prospect is indeed remote, of bringing them together again, as in the case of Bascombe and Post Boy, where the strain will be hard, the excitement high, and the betting heavy. But there are lots of men who are not engaged in any particular kind of business, and who have sufficient leisure to practice and make perfect in the science of shooting, and thus to render the game of which I have been speaking, one of great interest, and which would assemble on Long Island a crow, which, for numbers, fashion, and wealth, has not even witnessed since the days of Eclipse and Henry.

Yours, &c.,   CHATTAHOOCHEE.

A RESPONSE TO THE PROPOSAL

The following article is a New York sportsman's response to the proposal contained in the previous document for a national sweepstakes shooting match. The author argues that an entrance fee of one or two thousand dollars would prove too onerous for most interested shooters and thus cause far fewer entrants and a less lively and interesting contest. In short, a gentleman's fee would injure, rather than further, the sport of shooting. The following response is taken from the 30 June 1838 issue of The Spirit of the Times.

THE SHOOTING SWEEPSTAKES

Mr. Editor,—Your correspondent Chattahoochee suggests a Shooting Sweepstakes, but of such an amount that it would be impossible to bring many shooters together;—the interest in such an affair would be in bringing from fifty to an hundred of the best shots in the U.S. to contend for an amount of some consideration, which with an entrance of one hundred dollars would be obtained, for if the regulation was not to close with less than fifty, that would give $5000, and then if it should bring together an hundred, ten thousand would be a pretty sum to docket, besides the glory of beating ninety-nine crack shooters, for no man without some pretention to the like, would think of entering.

It has been mentioned among the N.Y. shooters, and at least thirty are ready to put their names down to the following: If the proprietors of the Beacon Course will enter into it with spirit, it will be an unparalleled affair in the shooting world, and put more money in their pockets than any other sporting transaction. The idea is this—to form a sweepstake of $100, not to close with less than fifty, and as many more as could be brought together by a specified date; twenty dollars to be put down at the time of subscribing, and the balance the day before commencing shooting; to shoot fifty birds each, 25 yards from the trap; limited to *one and a half ounce of shot*, and all to shoot with the same size; the size to be decided by ballot; the proprietors to find the birds, gratis, and give a dinner each day (making 4 or 5 days shooting) to the subscribers. It has been suggested that the proprietors should add a thousand dollars to the Sweepstakes, but the above would be less expense, and give greater satisfaction.

Truly yours,   "SNOOKS"

P.S. The above is a rough outline; and of course is open to any improvement, only taking one thing into consideration—what is to be done, let it be done quickly. S.

THE DEBATE CONTINUES

The following document is the final installment of the exchange between the sportsmen from Georgia and New York. This reply by the author, "Chattahoochee," of the original proposal to the response of the New York correspondent, "Snooks," continues the debate over various conditions and rules of the proposed shooting match. It is reprinted from the 7 July 1838 issue of The Spirit of the Times.

THE SHOOTING SWEEPSTAKES—REPLY

COLUMBUS, (Ga) June 13, 1838.

W.T. PORTER, ESQR.—Sir,—I will not disguise the feeling of gratification which I experienced on noticing so prompt an answer to my communication on the subject of a Shooting Sweepstake; and I am now perfectly confident of the success of the project, knowing that Boston, Philadelphia, and Baltimore, as well as many other cities in the Union not yet heard from, were never found wanting in any matter where sectional pride and feeling were involved.

I am surprised that your correspondent "*Snooks*" should contend that the amount of entrance proposed is too large. I cannot think with him, and I will give my reasons. It will not be denied that a heavy amount of entrance would be required to induce gentlemen to enter whose residence might chance to be from 500 to 2000 miles distant from New York; and should we embrace Europe, from whence we may confidently anticipate entries, provided the affair is got up respectably, and confided solely to the management of gentlemen—then shooters would have to travel from 3 to 4000 miles, and this they could not be expected to do unless the amount to be gained was of great magnitude; besides, some gentlemen not disposed to risk as much as $1000 for $100,000, could get as many of their friends to join them as they might please, and divide the profits in case of either winning.

From my knowledge upon this subject, I conceive it but a fair supposition that there are more spirited sportsmen with the gun in the cities of New York and Philadelphia, and their vicinities, than there are horse racers in America; and it is no unusual thing amongst the latter class of gentlemen to get up sweepstakes for an entrance of from $500 to $1000. In fact, it would, I think, be impracticable to get up a sweepstake of the sort with an entrance of only $100; even gentlemen who are fond of shooting, and who would be strongly disposed to go into a match of the kind, would not feel inclined to leave home, and be absent from their business &c. for perhaps two months, or more, when the entire amount of stakes should they win, would not much exceed, if at all, the amount of their necessary expenses.

"Snooks" proposes that the distance should be 25 yards from the trap, and that the quantity of shot should be 1 1/2 oz. and all of the same size. To this plan I have partial objections, and will offer my reasons. With regard to the distance, I will not stop to raise an objection, although it strikes me that it would be but fair and right to leave that point to be decided by ballot—20 or 25 yards, the two ordinary distances, being proposed. I must, however, enter my protest against confining a man to 1 1/2 oz. of shot, or to a certain size; this I think would be highly improper, first, because my gun might require over 1 1/2 oz. of shot to shoot at all, or at least, such might be my opinion; secondly, it might shoot coarse shot better than fine, or *vice versa*. I would, however, suggest that no man be permitted to shoot with a gun the barrel of which would

chamber a ten cent piece, or in other words, that is over three-fourths of an inch calibre. When I once belonged to a club, such was the rule adopted and adhered to, and
as far as I know, the rule of all other clubs.

As I previously remarked, there is no doubt on my mind that this great shooting
match will be got up, and I am truly rejoiced, inasmuch as when at first I harbored the
idea, my mind often misgave me, and it was not without a great struggle that I
"screw'd my courage up to the sticking point" sufficiently to address you on the subject.

One or two small suggestions and I am done. In case of a large entry, I would hint
the propriety of dividing the purse, as follows:—Give to the second best shot one-tenth,
and to the third one-twentieth, provided the first does not best the second five birds in
fifty (should that be the number of birds thought most suitable), in which event the first
to take the whole amount of stakes, the field being considered distanced. I would further suggest the propriety of allowing each man to take as many chances as he pleases
at the beginning, but no person to shoot or buy another's chance after the match has
commenced. Should the books be opened, of which I conceive there can be no doubt,
I will try to send on eight or ten entries, two thirds of whom never shot at a pigeon in
all their lives!

The spirit manifested by your correspondent "Snooks" argues most favorably for
the match, and leads me in fond anticipation already to sketch the gay, the lively, the
gorgeous, the immense scene when the great empire city and its environment would
display on such an occasion.   Yours, &c.,   CHATTAHOOCHEE.

PIGEON SHOOTING CLUBS

Pigeon shooting emerged as an important field sport in the 1830s in many areas of
North America and consequently clubs were organized to conduct shooting competitions. As the following article demonstrates, sizeable purses were put up, specific rules,
though not uniform, were established for individual matches, and open challenges were
issued. The article is a letter written to the editor of The Spirit of the Times, 21 July
1838.

SHOOTING SWEEPSTAKES—BANTER FROM THE BUCKEYE CLUB!

To the Editor of the Spirit of the Times,—Sir,—Having seen a banter in your paper
a few weeks since, for a *Pigeon Shooting Match* on a large scale, and having talked
the thing over, among some of our would be *shots* in this city, they have authorized me
to say, that if a purse of $500 aside, (say $1000,) be made up, it will be shot for, by
five members of the *Cincinnati Shooting Club*, against any five *Gentlemen Sportsmen*
of any other town or city in the United States, at Pigeons, to be let off from a trap at

20 or 21 yards distance, to fall within 190 yards of the trap, or subject to such other regulations as usually govern Matches of this sort. And further, they they will go from 50 to 100 miles to meet, and accommodate, their brother sportsmen in a trial of skill in the above line.

The Cincinnati stake will be forthcoming at a day's notice, and every exertion will be made to procure birds, for the occasion. Letters addressed to the Presidents of the Cincinnati Shooting Clubs will meet attention, and correspondence opened with competitors, with much pleasure. AN OLD SPORTSMAN.

Cincinnati, June 28, 1838.

RIFLE SHOOTING

With the pace of urbanization quickening in the early to mid-nineteenth century, city dwellers turned to rifle or target shooting as a popular substitute for hunting. The following account, from the March/April 1839 issue of the American Turf Register and Sporting Magazine, demonstrates the growth of shooting clubs throughout the United States and the early signs of the sport's modernization through the reporting of precise measurements and distances involved in shooting matches.

RIFLE SHOOTING

RIFLE SHOOTING.—There are two well organized Associations in this city, the members of which devote considerable time and attention in acquiring a proficiency in the use of the Rifle, and few pastimes are more interesting or manly. Of the "N.Y. Off-Hand Rifle Club" we have the honor to be a member "in regular standing," save that we find small leisure for practice; and we are glad to see that the tragets of our up-town friends, under the designation of the "North River Rifle Society," are reflecting no small credit on "the crack shots of Gotham." A prize of a silver Powder-flask was recently won by Mr. Henry Dibdin, who, at a distance of 50 yards, off-hand, made two shots measuring 1 1/4 inches. Mr. W.L. Davis, at the same time and distance, off-hand, won another prize, two shots in three, measuring 1 3/8 inches.

A few weeks before the organizatoin of the "Off-hnad Club,"... four gentlemen, now enrolled as members, had a trial of skill at Hoboken, near the Beacon Course; three practise rest shooting, while the fourth shoots, off-hand. The distance agreed upon was 110 yards or 20 rods. Each put up his target, and commenced shooting in turn, ten shots each. The shortest string measured 10 1/2 inches. The off-hand shooter, at the same time and distance, made the best 9 in 17 shots, placing nine balls in his bull's eye of 3 1/2 inches diameter. It was then proposed that the off-hand shooter should contend with the three, ten shots each, string measure, the latter still shooting at a rest. The second match resulted in the off-hand shooter's making a string measuring 19 3/4 inches, and the gentleman who made the best target on the first trial reduced his string to seven inches; eight of his shots would have hit a dollar!

On the 13th of the last month, the "Off-Hand Club" held its first monthly meeting for practice, at the Thatched Cottage Garden, Jersey City; although there was a general turn out, six members only engaged. The distance first appointed was 60 yards—ten shots each; the best target measured (string measure) 13 3/8 inches. The second distance appointed was 100 yards—10 shots each; the best target measured 26 3/8 inches. The third distance was 120 yards—10 shots each; the best target measured 26 3/4 inches.

On the 10th instant, the Club met again at Williamsburg; the best target made was by Mr. William Watts, whose 10 shots, at 100 yards, measured 22 7/8 inches.

Mr. W.L. Hudson, rifle-gun maker, 467 Greenwich street, has sent us several targets, made with new rifles from his manufactory, that not only speak well for the excellence of his workmanship, but for his proficiency in the use of these beautiful weapons. Three successive shots off-hand, at 110 yards, with one of them, measures but 1 1/2 inches. This target was made with a rifle weighing 14 1/4 lbs.; length of barrel 2 ft. 10 in.; calibre 60; patent breech; the sights are very fine, as in addition to the front, there is a very slight ball placed in the centre of the tube shade, and a centre shaded crotch on a spring, graduated by a screw; the false breech, or break-off, runs parallel with the barrel, on which rests a springs with a convex perforation for sight; this sighting is unusually distinct. With a rifle of a different pattern, on the 29th ult., Mr. H. made 10 shots at 110 yards, off-hand, which measured 25 inches.

A member of the Savannah (Ga.) Rifle Club, lately made 10 shots Off-hand, at 120 yards, measuring 27 5/8 inches, and 20 shots at the same distance off-hand, measuring 61 5/8 inches. Of course, in all the targets adverted to the shots were successive.

TARGET SHOOTING

The following brief article and the diagrams that accompany it together provide a good example of the attempts by rifle clubs to popularize and modernize their sport. The article and diagrams appeared in the 12 March 1836 issue of The Spirit of the Times under the heading "RECENT RIFLE PRACTICE OF A FEW "CRACK SHOTS OF GOTHAM.""

TARGET SHOOTING

We have great pleasure in having before our friends of the rifle, throughout the country, a few targets recently made by three gentlemen of this city, members of the New York Rifle Club. It is due to the skill of Mr. Harrington to remark that seven out of the ten targets here exhibited were made with rifles of his manufacture, and that his proficiency in their use is only equalled by the high state of perfection to which he has brought them. The targets are facsimiles with the exception of the three first which are not so large as the originals by half an inch each; the marks of the balls are not quite so large although the strike of each as it appears in the original, has been strictly preserved.

Would it not lead to increased proficiency in the use of the rifle, if clubs and amateurs generally should occasionally furnish well-authenticated targets for public examination—thereby exciting a feeling of honorable emulation? Our columns are open to any fair discussion of the subject.

I. Ten successive Shots, At Rest, Fifty-
five Yards,
By Col. H.A. Simons, Feb. 10, 1836.

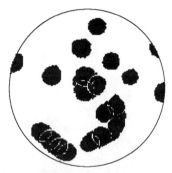

II. Twenty successive Shots, At Rest,
One Hundred Yards,
By A. A. Harrington, Feb. 5, 1836.

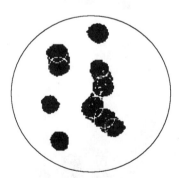

III. Ten successive Shots, Off-hand. One
hundred and Thirty-five Yards,
By Col. H.A. Simons, Dec. 31, 1835.

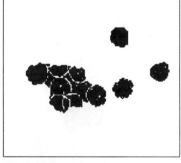

IV. Ten successive Shots, Off-hand,
Forty Yards,
By A.A. Harrington, Christmas Day,
1835.

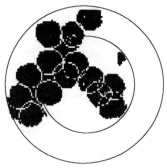

V. Fourteen successive Shots, At Rest,
Fifty-six Yards,
By Capt. S. Lloyd, Dec. 1835.

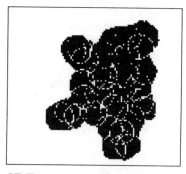

VI. Thirty-two successive Shots, At
Rest, Forty Yards,
By A.A. Harrington, Feb. 25, 1836.

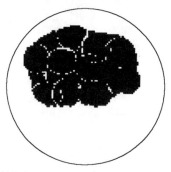

VII. Ten successive Shots, At Rest,
Forty Yards,
By Col. H.A. Simons, jan. 5, 1836.

VIII. Eight successive Shots, Off-hand,
Thirty Yards,
By A.A. Harrington, Oct. 6, 1835.

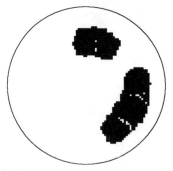

IX. Five successive Shots, Off-hand,
Fifty-five Yards,
By Capt. S. Lloyd, Dec. 9, 1835.

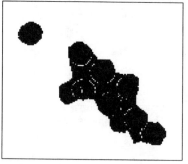

X. Ten successive Shots. Off-hand,
Forty Yards,
By A.A. Harrington, Christmas Day,
1835.

Chapter 9

GYMNASTICS

Between 1820 and 1840, gymnasiums were established in major American cities such as New York and Philadelphia for the practice of various sports, including sparring, fencing, and wrestling, but primarily gymnastics. The founding of these establishments grew out of a public concern for the health of city residents, whose cramped living quarters and sedentary pursuits sharply diverged from the healthy daily routines and occupations of rural life. The first document in this chapter, an excerpt from William Fuller's *The Elements of Gymnastics*, addresses these concerns.

Gymnastics as a formal system of calisthenics and exercises was introduced into the United States during the 1820s by German immigrants, who also formed the bulk of the sport's participants. Three men, all disciples of the founder of German gymnastics, Frederick L. Jahn, were primarily responsible for the early development of the sport in America: Carl Beck, Carl Follen and Francis Lieber. Fleeing to the United States because of political persecution in their native land, these men brought with them Jahn's system of training that combined physical conditioning and mental discipline.

Once here they successfully established gymnasiums modeled on their German counterparts and introduced gymnastic training as part of the daily school curriculum at all levels of the educational system. In 1825 Carl Beck joined the faculty at the new, experimental Round Hill School in Northampton, Massachusetts and soon thereafter built the first gymnasium in the United States based on Jahn's plan. Two years earlier, Joseph Green Cogswell, a noted scholar, and George Bancroft, the famous historian, had founded the school with the expressed purpose of improving the moral, physical, and mental qualities of its students through physical education. While at the school Beck translated his mentor's book, *Deutsche Turnkunst*, or German Gymnastics, into English as *Treatise on Gymnasticks, Taken Chiefly from the German of F.L. Jahn*, an excerpt from which appears in this chapter.

The Round Hill experiment with gymnastics proved highly influential in the subsequent development of the sport in America. In 1825 another disciple of Jahn, Round Hill School teacher Carl Follen, became a professor of church history at Harvard University, where a year later he helped establish the second gymnasium in the United States. Very quickly other universities and colleges, such as Yale and Amherst, followed suit by constructing their own gymnastic facilities. In addition, Follen became the superintendent of the first public gymnasium in America, the need for which both educational and health reformers in Boston had argued was crucial to the maintenance of their city's public health. Follen remained in this position until 1827 when another follower of Jahn, Francis Lieber, arrived from Europe and assumed the directorship of the Boston Gymnasium. Despite the construction of a swimming pool, interest in gymnastics soon declined, resulting in the closing of the city's gymnasium in 1828.

Despite these early efforts to link gymnastics with education it was not until mid-century that German immigrants founded *turnvereins*, or gymnastic societies, in many cities throughout the country such as New York and Cincinnati. By the early 1850s, seventy *turnvereins* had been established in the United States and the American *Turnerbund*, or national union, had brought delegates together from various clubs. The growth of the sport continued during the 1850s but ultimately suffered from the increasing nativism prevalent in the North and Midwest and the controversial antislavery stance adopted by the American *Turnerbund*. After the Civil War expansion again took place, no doubt the result of the demise of the Nativist party, the abolition of slavery, and the support by German clubs of the Union war effort.

THE PHYSICAL AND MORAL BENEFITS OF GYMNASTICS

William Fuller, a British immigrant, had built a reputation in the United States primarily as a teacher of the gentlemanly art of sparring. In New York he established a gymnasium where he instructed members of the upper classes in the science of self-defense. Before 1840, privately owned gymnasiums such as the one owned by Fuller catered to a wealthy clientele, who alone could afford the subscription rates that proved prohibitive for the working classes. In 1830 Fuller revised for an American audience a work on gymnastics originally published in England. The excerpt that follows reflects the strongly held belief in Europe and America in the use of gymnastic exercises as an antidote to the debilitating physical, intellectual, and moral effects of a sedentary, urban existence.

EXCERPTS FROM ELEMENTS OF GYMNASTICS, 1830
by William Fuller

PREFACE
The following pages first made their appearance in London, and with some trifling omissions and alterations, are presented to the public here, with the hope that they may be the means of attracting that share of attention to the subject of Gymnastics, which all, who have given it the smallest portion of their consideration, are pretty unanimous in declaring it to be entitled to.

The Gymnastic exercises may be considered a refinement upon the classic games of antiquity, possessing their advantages without their objections; in fact, suited to a more civilized state of society.

In this improved condition, it has, of late years, awakened a high degree of interest, and has been greatly patronized in the different cities of the old world, as affording all the means necessary to insure a full and healthy development of our physical powers, to which many of the occupations and the confinement of a crowded population, are well known to be so unfriendly. The examples which might be adduced of its wonderful influence in restoring health to the sick, and strength to the weak, are numerous and conclusive; but our limits will only permit us to introduce the following practical and satisfactory elucidations, taken from a work of Captain P.H. Clias, lately issued from the London press, page 11, line 6.

"A student in medicine, attacked with a cerebral affection which kept him in a sleepless state, owed his complete cure to the movements of the superior extremities, practised twice a day until he was fatigued. A man of fifty, attacked by a complete sciatica, did not receive any relief from the most appropriate medicines which had been administered unto him, nor even from blisters; by means of a series of movements, executed in his room, he regained in three days his pliability; he was able to go out, to walk, and to arrange his affairs, in a fortnight. Mr. Clias communicated to us a known fact, which deserves to be related to you. A child, aged three years, could scarcely stand; at five, only after dentition, at seven years old, that he could walk without assistance, but he fell frequently, and could not rise again. Given up by the physicians, he continued in this state till the age of seventeen, when the loins and lower extremities could scarcely support the upper part of his body; the arms were extremely weak and contracted, the approximation of the shoulders contracted the chest, and impeded respiration; the moral faculties were quite torpid; in short, nature was at a stand still. In the month of November, 1815, this unfortunate youth was presented to Mr. Clias, by several students, who intreated him to receive him into his academy; on admission, his strength was tried, that of pressure by the dynamometer was only equal to that of children of seven or eight years. The strength of pulling, ascending, and of jumping, was completely void.

He ran over the space of an hundred feet, with great difficulty, in a minute and two seconds, and could not stand when he had finished.

Carrying a weight of fifteen pounds, made him totter, and a child, of seven years old, threw him with the greatest facility. Five months after he had been submitted to the Gymnastic regimen, he could press fifty degrees in the dynamometer; by the strength of his arms, he raised himself three inches from the ground, and remained thus suspended for three seconds; he leapt a distance of three feet, ran 163 yards in a minute, and carried on his shoulders, in the same space of time, a weight of thirty-five pounds. Finally, in 1817, in the presence of several thousand spectators, he climbed to the top of a single rope, twenty-five feet high; he did the same exercise on the climbing pole, jumped, with a run, six feet, and ran over five hundred feet in two minutes and a half. Now that he is a clergyman, in a village near Berne' he can walk twenty-four miles on foot, without incommoding himself, and the exercises, which he has always continued, have occasioned, instead of a valetudinary state, a vigorous constitution."

These are strong cases, but all who practice its amusements, will quickly be convinced that they cannot be singular ones.

It is in a moral sense, however, that the matter of this pamphlet most powerfully claims our consideration; and viewing it in this light, there can be no doubt, but that the good sense of the community will give to it every possible countenance and support.

To the thousands in this city, whose vocations preclude the possibility of their taking sufficient exercise, in the ordinary way, to ensure a state of health, this presents the strongest claims to their support; as it combines economy of money and time, with results more certain, as well as more beneficial, than from the exercise of walking or riding; as its amusements are not interfered with by the vicissitudes of the weather, or the changes in the seasons.

There can be no good reason why what has been found so useful abroad, should not be introduced amongst us at home; indeed, it has been so in some of our neighboring cities, and with what advantage, the encouragement it has met with, fully testifies. In this city, where the population is so much more numerous and dense, an institution of this nature is still more earnestly called for, and it is to be hoped that in this instance, as in others, public spirit will keep pace with the public wants.

By the annexed proposals, it will be seen how moderate is the sum and few the number, necessary to establish a permanent Gymnasium, to which those who support it, can resort at whatever hours may be most convenient.

THE ORIGIN
OF
GYMNASTICS

GYMNASTICS, comprehends, in signification, all exercises relating to, or producing strength. Although they have so recently been introduced into this country, they were practised by the ancients, particularly the Greeks. The earliest accounts which we have of Gymnastics among them, are in Homer's Iliad, Book 23rd. From Greece, these exercises spread into the Roman Empire. With the extinction of that empire fell these exercises, and it is only within the last few years that they have been revived, first in Germany, and afterwards in other countries of Europe.

The ancients, by the exercises of the Gymnasium, acquired a firm and vigorous state of health; but this, though an incidental consequence, does not seem to have been a primary object; a love of war and a hardiness of frame seem to have been considered, by them, as necessarily co-existent qualities. Even in the tilts and tournaments, which succeeded in the middle ages, manly exercises were cultivated, not so much for restoring or improving the invaluable blessing of health, as to render men more efficient to decide the quarrels of ambition and revenge. It was reserved for several enlightened physicians among the moderns, more particularly to discover and promulgate the knowledge of the sanative powers of Gymnastics; and yet their opinions, though expressed with all the eloquence of language, and enforced by the most accurate deductions of reasoning, made but a very slow and gradual impression.

We come now to consider those objections which the want of experience, and ignorance of the true principles of Gymnastics, with the love of indolence, the attachment to the intense, though illusory pleasure of vice, and that dislike which many people at a late period of life entertain to every thing novel, have raised against an art which is so eminently calculated to produce a sound mind and a vigorous body.

The greatest danger, to which we would fain arouse the public attention, is, the danger arising from inaction—the danger of sitting still. Ask the martyrs to the gout and rheumatism, whether the severest accident which could occur in the Gymnasium, would be the cause of greater suffering than has been inflicted on them by inaction. In

a well regulated Gymnasium, accidents can but rarely occur, and never to a well practised and properly taught Gymnast. So far from his art being peculiarly dangerous, *it
secures him from danger.* Let the Gymnast find himself in a house on fire, let his horse
turn restive, or his vehicle be overturned, we would, in these accidents, insure his life
for a quarter of the sum we should require for that of a stiff and unpractised man. In
such cases, the Gymnast, from the acute perception of his eye, the flexibility of his
joints, and superior strength of his muscles, would have greatly the advantage.

We must acknowledge, that as the means of preserving health, the laborious stand
much less in need of Gymnastic exercises than the studious and sedentary. A sailor, for
instance, may be said to be by profession a Gymnast; but let the reader only reflect how
much the number of sedentary employments have increased amongst us. This is the
natural consequence of a high state of refinement and civilization, and strongly points
out the necessity of exercises adapted to obviate the debilitating effects of such employments. Besides, of many which may be truly said to be laborious, let it be observed,
that only one particular set of muscles is called into action. The blacksmith is only
strong in his arms, while his legs are not superior in strength to those of a haberdasher.
See the agility that the weakest tailors acquire in the right shoulder and elbow; one hour
of their work would tire out the stoutest man who had been unaccustomed to it. The
ploughman will, with ordinary fatigue, guide the plough all day through the hardest
furrows, but might be unable to leap a hedge to save his life. There is hardly any
employment, indeed, which calls for the exertion of all the muscles. To effect this,
recourse must be had to Gymnastics alone. Besides, many professions are carried on
in positions which, however convenient for the purpose, are yet highly inimical to
health. The shoemaker stoops his shoulders, the tailor sits cross legged, the smith raises
his right shoulder and depresses his left; the position of almost all sedentary artists in
worse than any of these, the sternum being bent towards the bowels, and the stomach
pushed backwards.

Having thus answered the objections which have been raised to the study of Gymnastics, it may be allowed us to state its advantages.—Let any one witness the exercises of the Gymnasts, and he will be struck with the glowing excitement which these
exercises inspire. The whole group seems to be engaged in enjoyment, in the most
heartcheering amusement; care, anxiety, and despondency seem to have been left outside the ground. Those even who are past the middle of life seem to feel a re-juvenality.
What effect all this must have upon the health it is easy to perceive; it is evinced by
the tinge of red it gives to the palest cheek, by the animation which at the time sparkles
in the most sunken eye. Even the spectators are not free from its influence. We see that
the graceful and easy performance of the most common action of life, walking, depends
upon a well managed practice. It requires a nicely-regulated poise of the body, we are
persuaded rather more difficult to acquire than many of the positions of the Gymnasium. The human body is easy capable of performing these, but the power lies dormant
until called into action by the Gymnastic exercise. In the moment of peril, when unusual exertions are called for, the unpractised man, in many cases, finds himself as
helpless as a child, or if despair force him to untutored attempts, they are frequently
attended with worse, or at least as fatal consequences as those he wishes to avoid.

Courage is generated by confidence, and confidence is acquired by practice. A
hazardous undertaking, which we have often achieved, ceases to be considered as any

further dangerous than affording us an occasion to call forth all our energies. The well taught Gymnast would, in a case of necessity, take a leap which few could perform, if any would venture. Leaps of great distances and heights he has often attempted with success. By him the length, the height, and the intervening obstacles, could be measured in a moment. Rehearsals of such situations and circumstances have been his daily amusement. He cannot be dismayed at danger who has often played with it, and the principles of his art have supplied him with means to disarm it of half its power.

The want of agility is a common defect amongst almost all classes of people in this country. This arises from our plodding, money-getting habits. A man, whom a certain train of circumstances has enabled to get money, while at the same time he lives luxuriously and *sits at ease*, becomes the envy of all around him. He is supposed to have arrived at the summit of sublunary felicity. Heaven, in composing the human skeleton, formed it with all the joints necessary for performing its natural actions, but man seems to have neglected the gift; his object seems to be to acquire property—never to enjoy it. His wish is to possess gardens, lawns, meadows, and parks, delightful to walk in, but he loses the use of his limbs in procuring money to purchase them. Such a man, by neglecting the use of virtuous corporeal exercise, has mistaken the road to health and happiness. Physic cannot restore him to the former, nor wealth to the latter. He takes but partial glimpses of the fair face of nature; he never threads the mazes of the wood, leaps the brook, nor climbs the mountain. These exercises the habits of his life have long renounced, and he fancies this is in accordance with his years. Indolence has rendered him stiff and inexpert, and he lays the blame on Time. His pains and his inability are, however, the punishment inflicted upon him by outraged nature.

Would the indolent and listless fly to cheerful and invigorating exercise, he would find his spirits enlivened and his mind recover its tone at the price of no self reproach. The exercises of the Gymnasium have enough of difficulty in them to operate, in the aggregate, as a stimulant to the mind, while they invigorate the body. This cannot be said of sedentary amusements, the best of which, though they may be untainted with vice, are yet neither profitable to the soul or the body. The labour of thinking, the deep calculation, the extensive forethought, and indeed the intense application of all the powers of the mind, requisite to play with success a game at chess against a skilful opponent, might, had they been applied to objects of utility, have merited the applause and gratitude of mankind. None but the temperate, none but they whose passions are well regulated by the precepts of prudence and virtue, can ever hope to excel in these exercises; the purer the mind of the Gymnast and the more free from the debilitating effects of vicious habits, the more vigorous will be his arm, the more dauntless his courage....

The Gymnasium is a place sacred to health, temperance, and virtuous perseverance; into it the scarcely awakened midnight debauchee may casually enter, but he cannot profit. He must first renounce the deceitful allurements of vice in the garb of pleasure. He cannot serve the principles of good and evil at the same time; his nerves cannot be rendered tremulously sensitive by immoral indulgence, and his courage steeled to bold exertion; his eye cannot be expected to possess the necessary accuracy of perception, while it is dimmed by the vapours of indigestion; nor his arm exert the required vigor, with its muscles robbed of their moisture by the inordinate indulgence of desires, which, if not restrained by virtue and prudence, like the malicious spell of a wicked enchanter, transform the natural agility of youth into the decrepitude of old age. A well disciplined Gymnast must not, cannot be an intemperate man. The corporeal powers of some iron constitutions may, indeed for a very brief period, imagine their vigour but little impaired by vicious propensities; and others may find in exercise a temporary antidote to debauchery, but they will at last discover that as serenity of mind can only be preserved by an union of knowledge and virtue, so the strength of the body can only be confirmed and improved by temperance and exercise.

Let us hope that the important, though long neglected, branch of education we have been recommending, will now occupy the attention of those real philanthropists who are anxious that even unborn posterity may feel a much more improved state of existence than they themselves ever enjoyed. There cannot be a more noble spectacle than to see individuals, nearly approaching to the end of life, uninfluenced by the love of power, or the desire of gain, and even unstimulated by the voice of extensive fame, actively engaged in promoting the best interests of those with whom, in the ordinary course of nature, they can never associate; sowing the seeds of a happiness of which they can hope only to see the earliest blossoms; and pointing the way to a promised land of delightful fertility which they themselves can never inhabit. It is impossible that the well-merited reward of their exertions can be circumscribed by the brief period of existence, end with the last sigh of nature, and be forever buried in the deep silence of the grave.

We think that we cannot strengthen our foregoing remarks more than by laying before our readers the opinions of several of the most eminent physicians who have written on the subject.

FROM DR. CHEYNE.

"If much study be joined to the want of exercise, it becomes then *doubly* prejudicial, and will, if long pursued, ruin the strongest constitutions.

"Hard study never fails to destroy the appetite, and produce all the symptoms already enumerated, with *headachs, vertigoes, costiveness, wind, crudities, apoploxies, and palsy.*

"Diseases, produced by sedentary life, must be cured by their contraries, namely, the action of the muscular system.

"All nervous disorders seem to be but one continued disorder, arising from the relaxation of the solids. From this arises the want of sufficient force to carry on the circulation, remove obstruction, carry off recrements, and make the secretions.

"In treating of nervous disorders, the solids are chiefly to be regarded.

"The true acquired nervous disorders are produced by intemperance and want of exercise; the juices thereby have been made sizy or corrosive, and the due tone and elasticity of the nerves and solids relaxed and broken.

"If inactivity and want of exercise are joined with luxury, the solids become relaxed and weakened, and the acrimony of the salts and humours gradually increase, then chronical disorders are produced, such as gout, erysipelas, rheumatisms, with all the pains, miseries, and torments arising in this low sunk state of the constitution.

"The joint power of warm air and light food cannot supply the place of exercise in keeping the joints pliable and moveable, and preserving them from growing rusty and stiff: light food may, in some measure, prevent the thickening of the fluids, but cannot do it sufficiently without aid of exercise, nor can it all keep the fibres in due tension, for to that purpose exercise is absolutely necessary."

FROM STROTHER

"The advantages we reap by exercise are numerous; life itself consists in the circular and intestine motions of our fluids, and their uninterrupted passages through canals truly framed.

"Exercise also serves at once as an evacuant and a diversion, by which the humours are put into the condition of flying off without the danger of bringing on spasms. It opens the pores, softens the fibres, and unbends their contractions, and prevents that plenitude, or rarefaction, from whence those pains originally sprang."

"Exercise is recommended in nervous rheumatisms, and more especially in scorbutic ones. In the scorbutic rheumatism, the pain shifts from place to place without any swelling, and they are increased by night; but in the nervous, however so wandering the pains, they are accompanied with convulsions in the tendons." It may easily be seen from what has been previously advanced, how repeated the exercise operates as a cure for such painful disorders.

The famous Van Swreten relates, that a certain priest possessing a rich living, but a martyr to the gout, happened to be taken by the pirates of Barbary, and was detained there a slave for the space of two years, and kept *constantly* at work, which had the following good effect: when he was ransomed from captivity, (having lost all his troublesome and monstrous fatness) he never after had a fit of the gout, though he lived several years after the event.

The exercises of the Gymnasium are so arranged as to bring into the action all the muscles of the body, and not to promote the vigor of one at the expense of the rest, as is generally done by many who imagine they exercise themselves sufficiently. Even riding, which is one of the most salutary exercises, loses its beneficial effects by being made use of *alone*. It strengthens only one half of the body. The lower limbs of those persons who are long on horseback lose a portion of their vigor, by the muscles being compressed, and the full crural arteries somewhat impeded; consequently, the circulation of the fluids rendered more languid.

One and the same exercise for various local debilities, can no more be effectual, than one medicine in various acute complaints.

Surely four hundred and seventy-four muscles, and two hundred and forty-seven bones, which the human body consists of, require both partial and universal action; nor is it to be supposed that such a groupe of muscles and number of joints can remain in right order without being duly exercised.

FROM CAVERHILL

"Exercise ought to be continued daily and regularly. If a person takes violent exercise now and then, or only for a few days in the course of a month, and imagines by that to counteract all the bad effects of the sedentary life he may have led during the rest of the month, he will be much mistaken.

"When the causes of relaxation prevail, it demonstrates the absolute necessity of persevering in proper exercise.

"Nothing so certainly lays a foundation for perpetual fits of the gout than exercise discontinued."

"Whatever assists nature in daily performing her offices by assimilating the chyle brought into the stomach, is properly called digestive, whether it be a rule of diet or exercise; the latter strengthens the blood and renders it brisk, and does most good in chronic cases, such as the gout, which ought to be imputed to the indigestion of the humours.

"The truth of what is said concerning the cause of chronic disorders will manifest itself by the incredible relief derived from exercise."

Our readers may think we multiply examples to prove a truth, of which unbiassed and natural experience carries the conviction. But really, an aversion to exercise has become so habitual among those of our countrymen who can afford to be idle, that we think we cannot do enough to convince them of the injury they are doing to themselves, by sloth and intemperance. A mistake is too prevalent, that a man of fifty or sixty ought to take what is falsely termed his *ease*; that exercise is unbecoming his age; that we have seen elderly persons to whom God has graciously granted a continuance of strength, blush as it were for their power of exerting it, awed by the sneer of ridicule, as if health and agility were indecorous accompaniments to maturity of years and discretion. We are convinced that when a proper physical education, conducted upon truly philosophical principles, shall become universal, the age of fifty may be accounted rather the middle of life than its decline.

We now come to a few general rules, which must be particularly attended to by those who are teachers or directors of Gymnastic institutions. They are mostly extracted from the work of Salzmann:

The pupils ought only to be exercised early in the morning before breakfast, or at least three hours after eating. No person in health is injured by being overheated, but drinking when extremely hot, or being cooled too quickly, in whatever manner it happens, may prove highly pernicious. It is proper, therefore, to take off what clothing can be decently spared, before beginning to exercise, and put them on again immediately after. Lying down upon the cold ground must not be allowed.

On commencing any exercise, begin, not with its most violent degrees, but with the more gentle, and leave off in the same manner. Sudden transitions are always dangerous.

Never let bodily exertion, or your attempts to harden the frame, be carried to excess; let your object be to strengthen the feeble body, not to exhaust and render it languid.

In all exercises attention should be paid to such a position of all the parts of the body, that none may be exposed to injury—For example, the tongue must never be suffered to remain between the teeth, the legs must not be separated too far.

It is necessary, and very advantageous, particularly where the pupils are numerous, to keep up a certain degree of military regularity and obedience to command.

Distinguish the feeble from the athletic, attempt not to make the weak hardy and strong at once, but take time and proceed gradually. The best standard for the feeble at first is their own desire—their own inclination.

Observe what limbs of each Gymnast are the feeblest, and let these be particularly exercised. The left hand and arm are commonly weaker than the right; let them be frequently exercised, therefore, by lifting, carrying, and supporting the weight of the body by suspension, till they become as strong as the others.

The teaching Gymnast must bear in mind, as much as possible, the degree attained by each of his pupils in every exercise, that he may not set them above their ability. This is an important rule for avoiding danger.

In the foregoing pages, we have thus far endeavored to attract public attention to this most important branch of public education. Its utility has, in some degree, attracted the attention of the British government. It has been introduced into the army, and forms an essential part of the training at the Royal Military and Naval Schools, and we have no doubt will be adopted in every private academy in the kingdom.

An account of the introduction of Gymnastics into England, as a branch of Public Education.

Early in the spring of the year 1826, a few individuals who had observed, with what success Gymnastics had been established in many towns in Germany and Switzerland, and how much all young men, who had cultivated those exercises, were acknowledged to have improved in health and morals, they resolved to establish a

LONDON GYMNASTIC SOCIETY,

and for this purpose issued a sensible and well written prospectus of their intentions. A meeting, open to all was appointed to be held at the Mechanics' Theatre, Southampton Buildings. This meeting was numerously attended, when that distinguished oriental scholar, Dr. Gilchrist, was unanimously called to the chair. Professor Voelker, of Germany, who had been for some time in England, as a private teacher of Gymnasatics, benevolently and generously came forward to offer his valuable instructions gratuitously, that the expense attending the undertaking might be the smallest possible to each individual. The attention of the provisional committee, which was then constituted, was directed to procure a fit exercise ground. This was a matter of some difficulty, but after some time they succeeded in negociating for the rental of one of the gardens on the higher part of Spa Fields, near Pentonville. This spot, we believe, has the advantage of the purest air about London. From its elevation and gradual slope, it is consequently dry, and capacious enough, we suppose, to accommodate three hundred Gymnasts. These are arranged in classes, according to their size in graduation, from the tiny-boy, little above the age of childhood, to the tall strapping grenadier-form of the muscular and hardy man. The height and breadth of the bars, and the elevation of the horizontal poles are likewise adapted to these different sizes, and the whole exercises proceed regularly and orderly under the superintendance of leaders to each class, who are chosen from the most proficient pupils, and receive extra instructions from professor Voelker himself.

At the ringing of a bell, each class changes the exercise in which it had been previously engaged, and takes to a new one, prescribed by the plan laid out in writing and fixed up in a conspicuous place of the ground by the director. The hour of meeting, it is to be observed, is six in the morning, as being the best time for exercise, and inducing the salutary habit of early rising. A race, or simply running, commonly concludes what may be truly called the Entertainment, and the whole has hitherto been conducted with that good humoured innocent hilarity, and that friendly attention to each other which the business of the Gymnasium was previously supposed to be so powerfully capable of effecting. The success of the undertaking has, we think, exceeded even the expectation of its most sanguine projectors. Since its commencement, upwards of one thousand pupils have been admitted, and as they cannot all be accommodated at once, two other mornings and two evenings in the week have necessarily been made use of beyond the times originally proposed.

GYMNASTIC EXERCISES

Full Directions for Practising the Whole of the Various Gymnastic Exercises, Selected
    From the Works of the Most Celebrated Gymnasts.

Walking, running and jumping, brought to a certain degreee of perfection, must be the means of our overcoming many obstacles; and in every situation of life produce great advantages to those who can perform them well. Taking these effects into consideration, I have resolved to give this exercise the first place.

It might be inferred, that every body knows how to walk, when not hindered by accidental misfortunes; but experience will convince us to the contrary, and if we give attention we shall not hestitate in remarking, that we see very few persons, however well formed, who, in walking, preserve a really erect position and an air of becoming confidence and dignity.

Force and agility, being the principal qualities from which all our mechanical actions proceed, their development must have a powerful influence on our daily exercises, and communicate, at the same time, the power of executing with facility and velocity, all sorts of movements, in different directions. It is only by possessing these qualities in a certain degree of perfection, that we can acquire an easy, light, and confident gait, be able to support fatigue for a long time, and travel a great distance without suffering any material injury or inconvenience. It will be very advantageous to instruct young persons in a great variety of elementary exercises, in order to destroy the bad habits which they are inclined to contract, and to prevent, at the same time, many corporeal defects.

Walking on the points of the feet, may be considered as preparatory to running and jumping, as it greatly developes the interior muscles of the legs and thighs, and particularly strengthens the joints of the toes; besides contributing to make the walk erect and elegant, it has the advantage of habituating those who practice it, to preserve their equilibrium on the narrowest bases.

Walking on the heels has also the advantage of strengthening the lower extremities, and may be performed either advancing or retreating. During this exercise the knees must be kept straight and the breast forward.

From the description of these exercises it is easy to perceive how much they contribute to develope the force, the agility, and the suppleness of the lower extremities; the hip, the knee, and the muscles of the thigh, which make the movement, are the parts which are the most fatigued.

Walking on the beam, is a repetition of the former exercise; it serves particularly to increase the strength and elasticity of the muscles and joints of the lower extremities. The tiresome position, which the pupil is obliged to keep, during the movement, has the advantage of preparing him for exercises still more difficult.

Being placed on the beam, as on horseback, he raises his right foot which he places flat on the beam, the heel as near the upper part of the thigh as possible; he then raises himself on the point of the foot: in carrying the weight of the body before him, without touching the beam with his hands, the left leg ought to hang perpendicularly, the point of the toe towards the ground. In this position he must keep the balance for some minutes, after which he must stretch his leg out before him, place the heal on the middle of the beam, carry with the assistance of the point of the right foot, the whole weight of the body on the other leg, observing still the same position, and this alternately till he comes to the end of the beam.

As soon as he can thus, with ease, go forward on the beam without the assistance of the master, the pupil should try to go backward, keeping the same balance as in the preceding exercise. Going forward it was the point of the heel which acted, now he is supported by the toes, the leg which hangs is stretched backwards till the toes are placed on the middle of the beam, that he can carry the whole weight of his body.

To execute this movement well, and to act so that the toes can easily find the middle of the beam, it is indispensable to observe, that the hip, and the heel forming a right angle, the point of the toe will infallibly find the middle of the beam, if the body be well placed, and a just balance be kept.

Running only differs from walking by the rapidity of the movements: it might seem by that how useful it is to man: the advantages which this exercise produces are incalculable: its salutary effect operates in a very visible manner on the individual who pratices it; and are reproduced in all the circumstances of his life. Running favours the development of the chest, dilates the lungs, and when moderate, it preserves this most precious organ from the most dangerous and inveterate diseases.

This exercise, in contributing much to render us healthy, may also enable us to avoid innumerable dangers; how many persons have been victims to their incapacity in this exercise? How many unhappy soldiers would have escaped a hard captivity, and even a cruel death, had they been accustomed in their youth to run fast for a long time? Often do unforseen circumstances oblige us to hold our breath for a long time, and to run with the greatest possible rapidity; when our dearest interests force us to the rescue of those we most dearly cherish, and our own preservation may frequently depend on the celerity with which we pass over any given distance. What are the consequences of an exercise so violent when we have not been previously prepared for it? Sometimes the most serious diseases, and the vexation to see an enterprise fail, on which our welfare depended. Or what is still more cruel to us to see the persons the most dear to us perish before our eyes, whom we might have saved had we arrived a few minutes sooner.

If we see very few persons run with grace and agility, we see still fewer run fast for a long time. There are many who can scarcely run a few hundred paces without being out of breath, and unable to go farther; because they perform their movements under a real disadvantage; some by swinging their arms with too much violence, agitate the muscles of the breast, and thereby compress the movement of resparation: others, by bending their knees and throwing them forward, and by making too long paces, fatigue themselves very soon, and also lose a great deal of time. Those who throw their legs too high behind, advance but slowly, though they labour very much.

It is very disadvantageous, whilst running, to throw the upper part of the body backwards, to take too long strides, to press too hard upon the ground, and to breathe too fast.

To run fast and gracefully, the feet should only, as it were, graze the ground, and keep the legs as straight as possible while throwing them forwards....

GERMAN INFLUENCE ON AMERICAN GYMNASTICS

The influence of Carl Beck on the inclusion of gymnastics into the daily curriculum of public schools in the United States was enormous. Following the teachings and methods of his mentor, Frederick L. Jahn, the father of public gymnastics in Germany, Beck and his fellow German immigrants sought to integrate intellectual and moral training with physical education for the public. Consequently they emphasized the egalitarian nature of gymnastic exercise: people from all ranks and walks of life should have equal access to gyms and mix freely within them. The following excerpt, published in 1828, is taken from Beck's translation of Jahn's seminal work on gymnastics.

EXCERPTS FROM A TREATISE ON GYMNASTICS, 1828
by F.L. Jahn, translated by Carl Beck

PREFACE

In bringing before the public a work on a subject which has, of late, attracted deserved attention, I consider it proper to give a brief account of its origin, peculiarity, and use.

The same causes which occasioned the publication of the original, in Germany, about twelve years ago, render a translation desirable in this country. F.L. Jahn was the first in Germany who established a gymnasium on a scale, appropriated for the use of the community at large. Attempts of a more limited nature had been made before, but without ever extending beyond the bounds of their birth-place. It is, by no means, my intention to depreciate the value of these attempts; on the contrary, I believe that those who take an interest in the cause of physical education, would be pleased to become acquainted with the exertions of *Gutsmuths*, and several other men, years before *Jahn* came forward. Gymnasticks were known and practised in various places, but *Jahn* was the author of them as a national institution. How well he understood the deficiency of our education in this respect, and how successful he was in discovering and applying the remedies, is proved, beyond any reasonable doubt, by the establishment of gymnasiums, after his model, in almost every town of Germany, in the course of six or seven years. There is no exaggeration in asserting, that all the youth of Germany, and probably of many other countries, in a few years would have practised gymnasticks as an established part of regular education, had not several of the arbitrary governments of Germany at once put a stop to them, considering them, and rightly, a powerful engine of political freedom.

The applications made to *Jahn* from all parts of the country, for advice and information in establishing gymnasiums, and directing the exercises, were so frequent that they induced him to render his experience more accessible to the public by publishing a treatise on Gymnasticks, which has become the standard not only of most gymnasiums in Germany, but also in France and England.

The school of Messrs. COGSWELL & BANCROFT, in Northampton, Mass. was the first institution in this country, that introduced gymnastick exercises as a part of the regular instruction, in the spring of 1825. Since that time, the interest for this branch of education has been rapidly increasing, and frequent inquiries have been made respecting a subject much esteemed for its expected salutary effects, but little known as to its particulars. Besides this proof of the want of a work accessible to the consultations of every one, more distinct wishes were expressed to me, by several of the most zealous and able friends and advocates of physical education, to translate a work which would be suitable for this purpose, or compile one from the rich existing materials. Although I delayed, for a considerable time, entering upon the undertaking, in the hope that another, more able, might deliver me from the task, I did not doubt to which of the two ways proposed to give the preference. I fixed upon the treatise of *Jahn*, from reasons contained in the preceding lines.

My principal object in executing the translation, has been to exclude whatever is extraneous to a systematical illustration of gymnastick exercises, and to copy the accuracy and brevity of the original in describing the single exercises, as much as possible. There are several subjects closely connected with gymnasticks as a branch of education, highly interesting, which will present themselves to the mind of every reflecting examiner of Gymnasticks, and a few of which I will mention, with the wish that they might become the subjects of impartial and thorough investigation: The effect of the single exercises upon the constitution, and the particular members of the body.—The practical application of the single exercises for particular pursuits and occupations.—The advantages, derived by a republic from gymnastick exercises, uniting in one occupation all the different classes of the people, and thus forming a new tie for those who, for the most part, are widely separated by their different education and pursuits of life.—Of the connexion of instruction in gymnasticks with that of the other branches in institutions for educating instructers for their profession. However useful, and I would say necessary, a thorough examination of these and several other subjects might be, they have been excluded from this work as not strictly belonging to a system of gymnasticks.

As to the description of the exercises themselves, I was aware that a profusion of words, not only does not accomplish what is intended, to convey a clear and correct idea, but, on the contrary, occasions misunderstanding and confusion. Only the essential parts, and the distinguishing peculiarities of each exercise, ought to be enumerated in due succession, and I have endeavored to accomplish this end, by following closely the original which is really distinguished by the plastic power with which it describes the exercises.

This was by no means an easy task. The first difficulty lies in the thing itself, the subject being a new one. We are not accustomed to observe bodily movements with such accuracy, as to retain in our memory with ease, their single parts in their succession. Hence the difficulty for a writer to give, and for a reader to receive, a distinct idea of a given movement, through the medium of a description; and this will be the case, until, by general practice, we shall be enabled to discover the essential parts in every movement, whether we see it performed, or read a description of it.

Although I had a most excellent prototype in the original, yet the genius of both languages is so different, and the German of Jahn so peculiar that I could not make use of all which I found in the original. It is a well known fact that a subject, whether it be entirely new, or only more attended to, will exercise an influence upon the language, in proportion to its importance; it will either coin new words, or transplant them from other languages, or impart a new shade or greater distinctness of meaning to some already existing. This, I have no doubt, will be the case respecting gymnastick exercises, in however a limited extent, if the practice of them should be continued and propagated in this country and England. But, at present, there arises from this very circumstance, a difficulty which would have checked and fettered one whose vernacular tongue is the English, much more a foreigner, and one who has, but for a short time, been acquainted with the language of his adopted country. He is not the person calculated to make any of the changes mentioned; it would be presumption, to treat thus a language which is not his own; he would be subject to the grossest mistakes against the genius of the language.

I endeavored, through the whole work, to avoid this fault, though I frequently felt the want of a word—climbing with hands and feet, and with hands alone (klettern and klimmen)—or of an accurate distinction between synonymous words—leaping, jumping, bounding, springing....

I cannot leave this subject without expressing the wish, that one possessing an equally thorough knowledge of the language, and of gymnastick exercises, might give his attention to this subject. If he should succeed in removing the most obnoxious difficulties, according to a principle easily perceived and obeyed, much trouble and confusion would be saved in future.

This work, both the original and the translation, is intended to guide the practice of gymnastick exercises. No one, therefore, should expect to receive a correct idea of gymnasticks through this work, unless he joins practical exercises to the perusal of it. Gymnasticks are an art, and theory and practice should never be separated. The work is a systematical series of exercises, calculated to call forth the hidden, and to cultivate and increase the rude and infant strength; not a collection of single feats, which is a thing altogether foreign to our present object, and to Gymnasticks in general.

The original appeared without engravings or drawings, except those of the instruments. After Jahn had established his gymnasium in Berlin, the interest for gymnastick exercises was raised to such a height that, during the summer season, usually several individuals, from different parts of the country, spent some weeks or months in Berlin, to become familiarly acquainted with, and to propagate in their respective towns, gymnastick exercises. A treatise was necessary on a subject which spread so rapidly over the whole country, in order to direct, and prevent any extravagance or abuse of, the exercises; but drawings could be dispensed with, where the exercises were introduced into most places by those who had seen and exercised themselves. Not so here. The interest is neither so lively, nor the personal intercourse so easy, in a country of so great an extent. For this reason I resolved to aid the descriptions by a collection of engravings, drawn and engraved by Mr. Francis Graeter, a gentleman not only possessed of great skill in his art, but also familiarly acquainted with Gymnasticks. In order not to confound, rather than assist, and in order not to increase the expense to a degree, which would have rendered the work inaccessible to a large portion of the public, I confined myself, in each exercise to the fundamental, as it were, postures and movements.

Several important exercises are omitted, by no means from an idea that they may be neglected, but because they can be easily acquired, or are so extensive and complicated that a satisfactory treatment would exceed the limits of this treatise. To this description belong expecially Fencing, Riding, Swimming, and military Exercises.

If the present work facilitates the introduction and management of gymnastick exercises, my wish is fulfilled, and I shall consider myself richly rewarded for the trouble which the execution of it occasioned.

CHARLES BECK.

Northampton, Mass. January, 1828.

MANAGEMENT OF A GYMNASIUM

Gymnastick exercises are intended to restore the just proportion of the two principal parts of human education, moral and physical, the latter of which had been neglected for the space of several ages. As long as man has a body, it is his duty to take care of, to cultivate it, as well as his mind, and consequently gymnastick exercises should form an essential part of education. Where man exists, there gymnastick exercises have, or at least ought to have, a place; they are the property of mankind, not confined to any one nation, or part of a nation. It is true, this art, as well as all other institutions belonging to mankind, will assume a different form in different regions; climate, locality, state of civilization, manners in general, form of government, religion will exercise their influence in producing a different form, but the essence remains the same, culture of the body.

It is not our object to stand up as advocates for gymnastick exercises; we take it for granted, that they are not only a useful, but necessary part of education. Every village, however insignificant, ought to, and could, have a gymnasium, as well as institutions for mental education. One completely furnished gymnasium, at least, ought to be in every county. National days might be proper occasions for the youth of the country to shew to their parents the progress they have made in dexterity and strength. The day when the counsellors of the country declared its independence, the days, when the defenders of the country bought that blessing with their heart's blood, might be proper occasions to shew to the nation that her sons are able to preserve what their fathers have obtained.

In order to illustrate the subject for which this section is destined, management of a gymnasium, we shall treat of the following parts separately.

I. OF THE INSTRUCTOR IN GYMNASTICKS

The instructor in gymnasticks has, of all instructors, the most difficult situation. The business of other teachers, is to teach a certain science, in which they, by their daily occupation, almost necessarily advance. The instructor in gymnasticks ought not only to know but also to perform what he teaches. The teacher of a science will always be in advance of his scholars, but the instructor of gymnasticks will soon be equalled by most, and surpassed by some of his pupils. He ought, nevertheless, to be always intent on obtaining as much dexterity in the different exercises, as his bodily constitution allows. Self practice and experience alone afford a clear and distinct idea of every movement and exercise, and of the effects which each one produces. He should carefully avoid becoming ridiculous to the younger boys on account of striking awkwardness and indexterity: The older pupils, for the most part, are satisfied with good intention, and laborious experiment. Even if he is wanting in dexterity in single exercises, yet he should be perfectly acquainted with all parts of gymnasticks, and be familiar with the principles of all. The pupils must be enabled to respect him as a man of education; else he appears, in spite of all dexterity and skill, as a mere juggler.

An instructor in gymnasticks ought strictly to observe the following laws:

1. not to give a bad example, either in, or out of the gymnasium:

2. to refrain, during the time destined for exercises, from all those enjoyments and gratifications which are improper for youth, as smoking or chewing tobacco, drinking spirits, etc.;

3. not to appear too late in the gymnasium, but to be there with the first;

4. to observe himself all laws which have been found necessary, most strictly, and to be the severest judge against himself;

5. not to endeavor to outdo his pupils, but to practise quietly and modestly, without any noise and ostentation.

6. to direct the conversation of the pupils so that it
may be instructive and entertaining, and not offensive in word
or thought;

7. to avoid all stiffness and pedantry, and to be friendly and kind, without surrendering the necessary respect;

8. to prove clearly that he is impressed with the importance of the subject, and not induced by mercenary motives, and vanity;

9. to understand how to deal with his pupils, that they may love and respect him as a man;

10. to act as an elder friend, adviser, and warner among his pupils.

II. OF THE EXERCISES

All exercise has its law and rule, method and discipline, measure and end. In gymnastick exercises one thing follows from the other; the single exercises supply and complete each other, and must be practised by turns. While some members rest after labor, others may exercise; no partiality should be allowed as to right and left. The object is to exercise the limbs, not to perform a feat.

There are, indeed, exercises which must be necessarily practised one after the other; but many must be practised at the same time, else the sameness, even of the most useful exercise, will injure the formation and culture of the body in general. If the greatest perfection in one exercise should be obtained before commencing another, the whole period of youth would not suffice to become perfect only in a few exercises.

Although a pupil should not be occupied constantly with the same exercise, yet there are some, with which the beginning should be made, and which form the introduction and preparation, as it were, for the whole of gymnastick exercises. Every boy, or youth, who has not exercised before, is either entirely stiff, or if he possesses some limberness, he rarely understands to execute a regular movement. The *preparatory exercises*...remove these deficiencies most effectually. They must be practised by every new comer first and considerably, and afterwards frequently repeated. After this introduction the simplest part of every exercise should be commenced, viz : of *running...*, *leaping...*, *climbing...*, *drawing...*, *moving the body, resting on, or suspended by, the arms*, along the *single bar...*, *moving the body, resting on the arms*, along the *parallel bars...*, and *balancing....* In this way the strength of each one is easily ascertained, and how the deficiencies may be remedied.

In the beginning, especially when a new gymnasium is at once completely furnished, it is well to establish as a rule, that the gymnicks practice only such exercises, as have been particularly shewn to them. Being unexperienced, they might easily injure themselves, if, left to themselves, they would try new exercises.

As soon as some progress has been made in a gymnasium, the instructor should choose, or cause to be chosen, monitors from the most sensible and dexterous. The monitors should instruct the new comers in the preparatory exercises, and perform themselves, whenever it is necessary. They must understand how to assist in performing a movement, be especially attentive to avoid an injury, where sliding or falling is possible. They must be able to make a judicious selection from the single parts of a compound exercise. In inspecting the younger and weaker, they should consider that the object is general preparation for gymnastick exercises, not performing particular exercises or feats.

III. OF THE TIME FOR EXERCISES

The problem, to occupy many gymnicks at the same time, is to be solved in a gymnasium. The time, allotted to exercises, should not be too short. Two afternoons, or the larger part of them, in a week, would certainly not be too much to spend in this important part of education. If the time is too short, many are apt to exert themselves too much, and thus to injure, rather than benefit themselves.

The whole time is divided into two portions, the first of which is destined for exercises which each one selects according to his inclination; the second for the regular instruction. During the former, every one chooses his occupation, and practises those exercises, which he likes best, or in which he percieves himself deficient, or which he wishes particularly to cultivate. But both, the instructor and monitors, should be always about, to preserve order, or to direct now this one, now that one. During this voluntary occupation, the instructor has the best opportunity to observe the inclination, talents, exertions, development, progress, and dexterity of every one.

At the expiration of this time, the gymnicks assemble, and, after some rest, satisfy their hunger and thirst with some bread and water. All the pupils are, once for all, distributed into classes, according to age or size. If there should be some considerably stronger or weaker, so as to create inconvenience in exercising with those of the same size or age, they should be put in the next older or younger class.

Here we should advise to keep the most accurate account of each individual as to his frequenting the gymnasium, and industry while there. Since the introduction of gymnastick exercises is so new, and by no means tested so much as might be desirable, it is well that the inferences, drawn from observation, should be founded upon certain facts, not vague suppositions. The duty towards the public, and the cause of physical education, demands such an accuracy, and it occasions but little trouble.

All the exercises are divided into as many classes as there are classes of gymnicks, and are shifted every day, so that in a series of days every pupil passes through all classes of exercises. A monitor is appointed for every class.

IV. OF THE DRESS

A dress for gymnastick exercises should be durable, cheap, and fit for all movements. Linen, not yet bleached, is the best material; and a jacket, or round-about, and pantaloons, the best form. If the changing dresses of fashion are worn, they will affect the exercises, and then these must be divided into exercises for rich, and poor.

All exercises are performed with head and hands bare.

Cravats and neckcloths of all descriptions, but especially those which prevent the free movements of the head and neck, are not only inconvenient, but injurious.

Suspenders should not impede the expansion of the chest, therefore never have any cross-pieces passing, in any direction, over the breast. Boots should not be too high and heavy, but allow a free use of the joints of the foot.

Pantaloons ought to be made so that they allow a free use of the lower extremities; it is injurious both to health and freedom of motion, to have them fastened, around the waist, with a girdle or belt; they should hang merely by the suspenders. Equally inconvenient, if not injurious, are straps, fastening the pantaloons around the feet.

During exercising, the dress can scarcely be too light and cool; after exercising, a coat is of service to prevent taking cold. On this account, a frock-coat is better that any other, because it defends not only the back, but the front, most susceptible of cold.

V. OF THE RESTING-PLACE

During exercising nothing should be spoken, except what concerns the exercise. But, then, there should be a place for rest and conversation. This place should be shaded by trees, and provided with benches, and a black board for the necessary advertisements and communications.

VI. OF THE SPECTATORS

A gymnasium is no theatre, and no one has a right to expect a spectacle. But on the other hand a gymnasium is no secret abode, though it must have its fixed precincts separating the gymnick from the mere spectator. The places for the single exercises should be arranged in such a manner as to afford a perfect view for those without the precincts. Thus every man has an opportunity to obtain a correct idea of the character and value of gymnastick exercises.

The parents, instructors, and guardians of the children, have a good opportunity to observe their children, pupils, and wards, left to themselves among their equals. In this way they are enabled to look deeper into the dispositions and peculiarities of their young friends, than if they kept them constantly by themselves. Thus the whole publick discharges the office of overseers of morals.

VII. OF THE LAWS

Good manners and morals must rule in a gymnasium with a more powerful sway, then elsewhere strict laws. The greatest punishment which can be inflicted, is exclusion from the gymnastick community.

A. *General laws.*

1. Every one who desires to become a pupil in a gymnasium, must promise that he will observe the necessary laws and arrangements.

2. No one shall show a sentiment of hostility which he may entertain against any one of the gymnicks, during the season of exercise, but each shall exercise in peace and cheerfulness.

3. Every gymnick shall exercise only with coat, hat, and neckcloth laid aside.

4. Every gymnick shall exercise in his turn, as he arrives at the place of a single exercise.

5. The gymnicks divide themselves into parties for the single exercises.

6. The number, fixed for each party, shall not be exceeded.

7. No one shall go from one party to another, except the exercises of the former should be too difficult.

8. No one shall intrude into a party when complete, but wait, till one resigns his place, or the whole party stops.

9. The number for the single parties is as follows:

In throwing, not over 12.

In leaping without a pole, not over 12.

In leaping with a pole, not over 8.

In leaping over the ditch without a pole, not over 20.

In leaping over a ditch with a pole, not over 12.

In vaulting, not over 10.

On the single bar, not over 8.

On the parallel bars, not over 8.

In balancing, not over 12.

In skipping with the long rope, not over 12.

10. Every one shall keep from that side near an instrument, from which the start is made.

11. Every one shall make use only of the instruments and utensils in exercises for which each is destined, and on the place appropriate for each exercise. All moveable

instruments (as lances, poles for leaping, etc.) must be returned to their place, after they have been used.

12. During exercising nothing shall be spoken, except what concerns the exercise.

13. He who wishes to look at some exercise, can stand, sit, or lie at a proper distance from the instrument.

14. The exercise should never be covered, or concealed towards the bounds by persons standing before.

B. *Special laws*

a. *For running.*

15. There shall be no talking during running, especially during the racing of many.

16. After running none shall stand still, or sit, or lie, but walk about, in order to cool, and refresh himself by degrees.

b. *For leaping.*

17. The stands for leaping with and without a pole, as well as the strings and pegs belonging to each stand, shall not be confounded.

18. There shall be no pulling, pushing, or climbing up the posts or stands. Two persons shall raise the pegs, improving one or two steps, fixed to the stands for this purpose.

19. The poles to be used are of a length from 7 to 11 feet, and of a proportionate thickness. If any one keeps his own pole, he shall conform with these measures, and mark the pole with his name. Other poles shall be removed.

20. No one shall make use of poles not his own. He who has none of his own, shall use those belonging to the gymnasium.

21. He is not yet qualified for leaping with a pole, to whom a pole of seven feet, and a proportionate thickness, is too heavy.

c. *For vaulting.*

22. No one shall practise vaults, before he has attained some dexterity in the preparatory exercises.

23. Those who wish to join particular classes for vaulting, shall be able to fulfil the following conditions:

   a. to climb up a rope to the height of 40 feet;

   b. to perform the principal exercises on the single bar;

   c. to perform the principal exercises on the parallel bars;

   d. to leap without a pole to the height of his own hips;

   e. to perform all the preparatory exercises with considerable dexterity.

d. *For balancing.*

24. The balancing-pole shall be ascended only on the thick end.

25. In a balancing-combat, only three shall be standing on the balancing-pole, the two engaged in the middle, a third waiting on the thick end.

26. In balancing, only three shall be on the pole; two balancing, and one waiting. As soon as the first draws near the thin end, the second shall stand still.

27. As each one alights from the balancing-pole, he must stop its vibrations.

28. All joggling and tossing on the balancing-pole, is forbidden; nor shall any one pass beneath the balancing pole, while any person is exercising.

e. *For the single bar.*

29. No one shall exercise at a bar, which he is unable to reach standing, or by means of a jump.

f. For the parallel bars.

30. No one shall exercise on bars on which he cannot come to rest upon his arms, by means of hopping.

31. All standers by shall keep at some distance from the bars on all sides.

g. For climbing.

32. The ropes shall not be used for any kind of swinging.

33. When some one is climbing, no one shall hinder him, whether by following, or stretching the rope, unless the climber desire it.

34. No one is allowed to ascend the ladder of a climbing-instrument, unless he is able to climb up the rope belonging to the same instrument.

35. Only on a very high rope the climber is allowed to descend on the ladder; on other ropes he shall descend by the rope, or climbing-pole.

36. Only two are allowed to be on the top of a climbing-instrument, and the first must come down as soon as a third begins to climb up.

37. Only one shall sit upon the cross of the climbing-poles, and only so long, as is necessary to gain strength.

38. No one shall practise on a rope, if he cannot climb up the next lowest one.

39. No one shall be standing within the climbing-instruments.

h. For throwing with lances.

40. Every one shall use the lances, belonging to the gymnasium, or his own, marked with his name, not those of others.

41. The measures for lances are: six, seven, or eight feet long, 1, 1 1-4, or 1 1-2 inches thick. No lance of a different measure shall be used.

i. For throwing with balls.

42. No one shall leave a ball on the ground, but put it in the box.

43. The ground destined for this exercise shall not be approached by lookers on, or at least only from the back of those exercising.

j. For wrestling.

44. No one shall refuse a challenge for wrestling, unless when unwell, tired, or prevented by some evil; dress shall not be an excuse.

k. For games.

45. All who are too small or weak, or have not yet passed through the preparatory exercises, shall be excluded from the gynmastick plays.

46. No one shall join a party of players, unless he was present at the distribution.

47. A general agreement of the party playing, can make an exception from the established rules of a play.

Chapter 10

PEDESTRIANISM

Prior to 1820 pedestrianism, or professional foot racing, attracted few spectators and generated little interest in North America. After that date, it became something of a sports phenonmenon. By the late 1830s pedestrianism, greatly assisted by the change in public attitudes towards physical exercise, was second only to horse racing as a spectator sport. Drawn from all classes and occupations of society, fans marveled at the athletic strength, endurance, and skill of foot racers and welcomed the opportunities to make considerable money through side bets and wagering. As the documents in this chapter illustrate, neighborhoods and larger communities initially championed their pedestrian heroes in local contests, but increasingly these competitions assumed a regional and sometimes an international character, with national pride, bragging rights, and prize money the spoils of victory. In remote areas different types of pedestrianism developed out of native American traditions and customs and the demands and rigors of frontier life. "Frontier Pedestrianism" and "Osage Indians" depict the origins of these early forms of foot racing.

From 1820 to 1840 track and field consisted almost exclusively of foot races. The Caledonian Games, which included a diversity of track and field events, became annual competitions beginning in the 1850s, though some track and field games did occur prior to mid-century. Pedestrian contests were usually held on horse race courses but by the late 1830s, in response to the growing popularity of the sport, courses specifically designed for pedestrianism were constructed at such places as Philadelphia and Hoboken, New Jersey. The distances of the races varied, typically between ten to fifteen miles, but races of fifty miles did occur, however infrequently. In many races runners competed against each other for victory as well as against the clock, or both. At the height of the sport's popularity prize purses, usually put up by promoters, sometimes were in the thousands of dollars, which, when combined with side betting, provided an important incentive for runners and created additional excitement for spectators. Several of the documents included in this section such as "The Great Walk at Philadelphia," "Fraud and a Foot Race," and "Pedestrian Match at Philadelphia," illustrate the diversity in the types of pedestrian contests that occurred during the period.

Without a doubt the most significant event in promoting pedestrianism during this period was the 1835 race that resulted from a wager between John Cox Stevens and Samuel Gouveneur. Stevens, a noted yachtsman and horse owner in New York City, bet that a competitor could run a ten-mile race in one hour. He gladly offered a $1,000 prize money to the victor, with $100 going to the second and third place finishers if they could also finish in one hour or less. If only one runner finished the race in the agreed upon time he would receive all of the prize money.

"The Great Race," as it was called, was held at the Union Race Course on Long Island, and crowd estimates ranged between 20,000 to 30,000 spectators. Not since the great horse race between Eclipse and Henry had a sporting event produced so much excitement and interest. Fans attending the event were lined up for miles on the road to the course, stacked up all the way back to Brooklyn, and they were not disappointed by the outcome. Of the nine runners that entered the race, only one completed the distance in one hour or less—Henry Stannard, a farmer from Connecticut who was sponsored by none other than John Stevens himself. With the race assuming nationalistic dimensions (an Irishman and a Prussian had entered the race), the American crowd, desirous of an American victory, cheered Stannard's achievement. For his victory he received all $1,300.

The race won by Stannard raised the sport of pedestrianism to new heights. Soon different types of pedestrian races were held regularly; steeplechase, sprinting, or walking events. By the mid-1840s numerous contests captured the public's imagination, aided partially by the precipitous decline of horse racing in the late 1830s, the rise of the Caledonian games, the nationalist overtones to pedestrian competition, and the amount of money to be won through purses and gambling. The heyday of pedestrianism proved to be short-lived, however, as the rise of spectator team sports such as football and baseball after the Civil War signaled the sport's downfall.

EARLY FOOT RACING

During the 1820s pedestrianism was much more informal than during the following decade when more regulations were introduced and greater prize money put up. The following document, reprinted from the 2 July 1824 issue of The New York Evening Post, is an example of the type of race that was conducted prior to the sport's popularity in the 1830s.

RACES AT HOBOKEN

For the Encouragement of Athletic Exercises,
FOOT RACES FOR 50 AND 100 DOLLARS,
AT HOBOKEN

The proprietors of the Hoboken Ferry will give $50 to the winner of a foot race, to take place on the 5th of July at 12 o'clock in the orchard at Hoboken; the distance to be 220 yards and repeat—entrance $3. And $100 to the winner of a foot race, to take place at 6 o'clock P.M.—entrance $5, which will be added to the purse; the distance, half a mile and repeat. The winner of the 50 dollars to be excluded from entering for the 100 dollar purse.

P.S. The entrance will be received by Mr. Abram Van Boskerck, at Hoboken, at any time prior to 10 o'clock on the day of the races, and who will also inform the competitors of the rules to be observed. Should the weather prove unfavorable, they will be postponed to some future day. The course is in order for those who wish to train on it.   jy 1

EARLY SPORTS COVERAGE

The following account, reprinted from the 6 July 1824 issue of The New York Evening Post, reports the results from the race discussed in the previous document.

RESULTS OF THE RACES AT HOBOKEN

Races at Hoboken.-The purses were run for yesterday as advertised in the papers, and won as follows. The first of $50, a distance of 220 yards and repeat, was won by a young man from Long Island, by the name of Newton, who took the two first heats after a severe contest, beating four competitors. The second purse of $100, half a mile and repeat was taken by a French gentleman, who entered by the name of Warren, and won by distancing his competitor, the 2d heat, the first being won by a young man celebrated in this part of the world for his swiftness of foot, by the name of Lawrence, and who distanced with ease all his competitors except Warren—time of running 2m. 10 sec. and the course very heavy and newly made so that the performance may be considered unprecedented. Before they started for the 2d heat, bets were 5 to 1 on Lawrence. The runners were tastefully dressed, and the race created much interest, amidst a large concourse of spectators; being conducted in a very proper, sportsmanlike manner. Lawrence is better known under the name of Clam boy, and is considered one of the fastest runners in the United States, having tried his speed in several places and was never beat before.

We understand that Newton the winner of the first purse, has offered to run the half mile heats against either Warren or Lawrence, and that it is probable a match will be made; of which we shall give due notice.

PEDESTRIANISM IN TRANSITION

Many of the early pedestrian matches, like those of other sports, were informal, usually pitting local contestants against one another in front of a small but familiar crowd of spectators. The following account, taken from the October 1829 edition of the American Turf Register and Sporting Magazine, demonstrates both the premodern and modern character of these contests.

PEDESTRIANISM

A match race for $100, was run some time back in Pittsylvania county, VA. by Owen Atkins and John B. Boling, ten miles distance. The greatest anxiety was manifested by the friends of the parties. Boling is a tall, trim looking young man, about twenty-one years of age, and was the favourite courser, though a few knowing ones, who had been engaged with Atkins, (a man about thirty-six years of age,) in hunting parties, and who were fully acquainted with his speed and bottom, predicted a quite different result. When the time of starting had nearly arrived, the friends of the parties, who were fearful of disagreeable consequences, endeavoured to have the race drawn, to which Atkins showed some degree of willingness, while the other, who before had been quiet, now became restless, and appeared anxious for the word to be given, which was accordingly done. The coursers put off briskly, and were followed by thirty persons on horseback. The first several hundred yards they run nearly locked; after which Atkins took the lead, and kept it during the whole course, which he, as near as could be ascertained, ran in about *forty minutes!*

Boling, after running about seven miles, gave up the race. Atkins and his party were so far ahead, that they could not be overtaken by those who were on horseback, until he had run the ten miles. By the best judges it is believed that no man in Virginia is able to run ten miles with Atkins. Neither of the parties sustained any injury from the race.

[*Lynch. Virginian.*]

FRONTIER PEDESTRIANISM

Pedestrianism assumed different forms on the frontier and, as the following account documents, these were quite different from those usually reported in sporting journals. These feats, though hardly of a sporting nature, were typical of frontier sports. The article reprinted below is from the April 1835 issue of the American Turf Register and Sporting Magazine.

PEDESTRIAN FEATS

I have noticed an account of some extraordinary pedestrian feats in the Turf Register,—I give you the following on the same subject, which you may rest assured is correct, as one of the parties is still alive and I believe known to you. Major D. was some years since connected with some of the Missouri Fur Companies, and hearing that one of their trading posts was about to be attacked by a party of hostile Indians, he started at day-light with his pack and rifle, and reached the post before dark, a distance of full eighty miles, and saved the lives of all the post.

While on the Arkansas a few years ago, Col. C. told me that an Osage Indian was started from his post at day-break with a bar of lead weighing sixty pounds, and ordered to reach his brother's post before night, (to anticipate an attack of hostile Indians,) a distance termed one hundred miles, but I believe at least one hundred and twenty. The Indian performed the distance without difficulty. On the way he attempted to divide the lead, in order to lighten his burden, but did not succeed. While I was there, a party of Osage Indians came in with *fresh* scalps, such as hands, feet, ears, &c. of a party of Pawnees, whom they had started in pursuit of between eleven and twelve o'clock that day, and I was told had gone at least fifteen miles, before they overtook them, and killed some fourteen or fifteen, and returned fifteen miles; in all they traversed (*on foot*) thirty miles in that time.

A.

NATIVE AMERICAN FOOT RACING

Pedestrianism was practiced and enjoyed by many cultures in North America, including those of Native Americans. The following document, reprinted from the May 1835 volume of the American Turf Register and Sporting Magazine, is a fascinating discussion of the role of pedestrianism within the culture of one particular Native American nation.

OSAGE INDIANS

Mr. Editor: *Fort Gibson, March,* 1835.

A recent residence of a few weeks at the Osage Agency enabled me to procure some information relative to the manners and customs of the Osages; and I transmit for publication, should you deem the subject likely to interest your readers, some notes made at the time....

To beg, is no disgrace; to be a dextrous thief is an honour....

Their appreciation of theft, arises from the danger incurred and bravery displayed in stealing horses from their enemies. Two warriors once lurked about a town until they ascertained where the horses were kept, and selecting thirty or forty of the best, escaped with their prize. Horses are stolen by night, as their loss is always known at dawn of day, if not earlier, a few hours start only is obtained; and pursuit is made in great force for several days, until the property is recovered, or the pursuers approach so near the towns of their enemies, that they abandon it. A party may only capture horses enough to mount a portion of its members, for their expeditions are usually undertaken on foot, and then is evinced the extraordinary speed and endurance of the Osages; for knowing that pursuit will be made in overwhelming numbers, the cry is *sauve qui peut*, and those who have been so fortunate as to secure horses, think not of waiting for the pedestrians. These last, aware that if overtaken their doom is death, run until late at night, when exhausted nature requiring repose, they snatch three or four hours sleep, but start before day, and run until night again affords them a short and perilous slumber, and the parties (mounted and pedestrian) pass and repass each other until in safety. To run sixty miles between sunrise and sunset is not an uncommon performance; and four men are known, on one occasion, to have run seventy-five. Messieurs A.P. & P.L. Chonteau, in February 1832, when the nation was in council at the Saline, the residence of A.P.C. Esq., offered a wager to the Indian Commissioners, who had expressed some doubts of the relations of their performances, the losers to provide a feast for those Osages present, that they could produce a runner, who should start from that place at sunrise with a letter, proceed to Fort Gibson—the distance estimated between forty and forty-five miles—and return with an answer before night. To attain this degree of speed, great practice is necessary, and in addition to the efforts made on their war, horse stealing, and hunting expeditions, they are frequently running with each other when in their towns, the distance about four miles. When different towns meet on their hunts, it is common for a match to be made between the best runner of each, a prize being offered and a day appointed, to allow time for preparation, the distance from four to ten miles. Great ambition is felt to be acknowledged the best runner of the town and nation; and no exertion spared to attain the distinction. At these meetings, the sports commence with the boys and girls of one town competing with their own sex in the other; and as the excitement increases, the men and women contend in the lists respectively, and the chiefs proclaim a day when each town will start its champion, and offer a prize as already mentioned. Each village supports its champion, and all bet; guns, horses, blankets, ornaments are staked, and not unfrequently, the breech-cloth of the man and the petticoat of the woman, are deposited, and the bettors await the result in a state of *nudity*. Horse races are also run, the distance from three to fifteen miles; and it has been remarked, that the band or town of White-hair, has generally proved victor, when the men contended; but the Big Hill band when horses were run. This system establishing beyond cavil, who are the best runners; these are selected to act as scouts and spies, and upon their reporting the vicinity of an enemy, their position and numbers, if the latter justify the attempt, the runners are sent as a decoy, to hover within two or three miles of the foe, until the latter give chase, when an ambush near their own camp having been formed, some eight or ten miles from that of the enemy, it being supposed that with such an advantage in the start, their runners can run that distance before being overtaken, even by horsemen; they surprise and slaughter the unsuspecting pursuers, if to save their runners they are not obliged to forego the surprise, and to hasten to their relief....

A WALKING RACE AGAINST TIME

Pedestrianism assumed many forms during the antebellum period and, as the following account makes clear, one of those involved walking races. Walking contests themselves varied in their format, as participants either competed against each other or against time or both. The following document, reprinted from the November 1830 volume of the American Turf Register and Sporting Magazine, describes one of the more remarkable pedestrian feats of the era.

THE GREAT WALK AT PHILADELPHIA

A considerable degree of interest has been excited in Philadelphia, by a man undertaking to walk a thousand miles in eighteen days, for a bet of $1000. The performance of this task was commenced by Joshua Newsam, a Yorkshireman, on Thursday, the 30th of September, in the grounds belonging to the Labyrinth Garden, in Arch street, west of Broad. The garden is kept by Thomas Smith, also an Englishman, who, having been a great sporting character at home, took this opportunity to revive one of the manly exercises of England. Smith had seen much genuine enjoyment in various places; was a body servant to Sir Robert Wilson, accompanied him on his adventurous and sometimes dangerous expeditions in Europe, and had shared with him the rich luxuries of metropolitan amusements. Among other things, he related to me his recollections of Captain Barclay's celebrated walk of a thousand miles in as many hours, which he had witnessed. He stated one or two facts in connection with that performance, which I do not remember to have seen in print; namely, that so overpowering was the drowsiness which affected Barclay during the last days of the walk, that he could be kept awake only sticking needles into him, and by firing pistols close to his ears. His legs also swelled prodigiously.

I will now give the result of Newsam's performance during each of the eighteen days.

1. Thursday,	49 miles.	10. Monday,	70 miles.
2. Friday,	46	11. Tuesday,	66
3. Saturday,	63	12. Wednesday,	49
4. Monday,	59	13. Thursday,	62
5. Tuesday,	59	14. Friday,	61
6. Wednesday,	59	15. Saturday,	66
7. Thursday,	57 1/2	16. Monday,	60
8. Friday,	57	17. Tuesday,	40
9. Saturday,	30	18. Wednesday,	46 1/2

1000 miles.

Newsam is a small, slight built man, rather thin than otherwise, and wore a common roundabout jacket, light nankeen pantaloons, woollen stockings, with a pair of common buckskin lace boots, not made to perform this walk in, but such as he had worn during the preceding summer. He walked over a smooth, but not soft path, six lengths of which are equal to a mile. It was formed of earth, rolled hard with a heavy roller, without any gravel. His feet were sore for the first day or two only, after which they became comfortable to him. He moved on at a rate which surprised the crowds who thronged to visit him, carrying a small stick in his hand for the sake of company, as it was too short to use as a cane. He generally started at six in the morning, though on the tenth day, when he walked the astonishing distance of *seventy miles*, he walked two hours before daylight. This was done to make up for the bad work of the ninth day, during which he walked but thirty miles, in consequence of a heavy and continued rain. On that occasion he carried no umbrella, but walked in his wet clothes; and as one part of the path was so low as to form a reservoir for all the rain which fell in the garden, he walked at least ten miles in mud and water over his ankles. The succedding day was also unfavourable, as the mud had dried away but little; yet he walked through all until he had completed seventy miles.

A sprain in the tendons of the leg, which Newsam received about the tenth day, afflicted him considerably for about a week. He complained much of the frequent *turns* he was obliged to make in a single mile—the whole ground being in fact, full of angles; and to this he attributed the sprain in his leg. He said the ground should be as *straight* as possible. As regards the *training* previous to commencing this walk, he had but little, not more than a week; and it consisted in simply practising himself in long walks. His *diet*, however, was peculiar. It consisted of two or three par-boiled eggs, taken the first thing in the morning; breakfast of oatmeal gruel and eggs, with dinner and supper of beef steaks cooked very rare. He drank but small quantities of strong liquors.

The sprain in the ankle affected his spirits considerably, and occasioned a hitch in his gait which made it painful to witness his efforts to get along. He did not complain of being fatigued after the first three or four days, and enjoyed as good health during the whole time as at any period of his life, though the loss in flesh which he sustained amounted to fifteen pounds. His legs were carefully bathed and rubbed every night with warm whiskey—an excellent remedy in all cases where pains and aches occur in the legs or arms, especially after exposure in cold wet weather.

Newsam is about twenty-seven years of age, and until now, has never performed any remarkable pedestrian feat, except indeed, that he once walked 66 miles a day for six days in succession, for a purse of fifty guineas, and won. On the eighteenth day of his late walk, he completed his task about six in the afternoon, having performed the whole in good time; though there is no doubt he would have come in a full day ahead, had the weather been favourable the whole time. Crowds of persons went out to see the *coming in*, among whom were hundreds of ladies; and when the task was announced as done, three hearty cheers were given to the hero. One thing, however, struck me as suspicious—Newsam was to receive $500, of the bet, win who might; yet he was unable to tell the names of those who made the bet! Very few bets, if any, were made upon the walk; and a report which crept into print, that a wager of $10,000, was to be decided by another walk, was probably premature, as nothing has since been heard of it.

M.

Philadelphia, Oct, 25th

PEDESTRIANISM AND SCHEMING

Although pedestrianism developed into a modern sport during the 1830s contests still retained much of their premodern character. A prominent feature of many of these matches was betting, which sometimes involved large amounts of money. The following account, taken from the 13 May 1837 issue of The Spirit of the Times, demonstrates the kind of scheming that existed at the time.

FRAUD AND A FOOT RACE
[From the Charlestown (Va.) Free Press].

The statements contained in the following communication are, we believe, strictly correct. One of the parties engaged in the disgraceful transaction was arrested a few days since, on a charge of defrauding Lang of his money. We were present at the examining Court, and listened to the details of the means employed to effect the scheme of the parties to the race, with an astonishment which staggered our power of belief.

FOOT RACE.—THE OLD FURNACE AGAINST THE WORLD!
Harper's Ferry, April 23, 1837.

Messrs. Editors.—A foot-race which took place on Monday of last week, between John Peacher, jun., and William Howington, citizens of this neighborhood, upon which an individual bet and lost eight thousand dollars in cash, has been an all-engrossing subject of conversation in this community ever since the race, the developments in relation to which are so astounding and extraordinary, that I cannot refrain from communicating some of the particulars. It appears that some time in February last, the match- race was agreed upon between Peacher and Howington, to run form the Old Furnace to Georgetown on the tow-path of the canal, a distance of sixty-two miles. This being made known to an old gentleman in the neighborhood, named James Lang, who had always maintained a fair character for honesty and industry, and who, by a long life of toil and care, had accumulated ten or twelve thousand dollars worth of worldly treasure, he was induced by the persuasions of Peacher, it is said, to make a bet of a few hundred dollars on Howington, the competitor in the race, and placed the stakes in the hands of his friend Peacher, who assured him that he would double his money, as he Peacher, intended to run "booty," and let Howington win the race. Soon came another offer of a bet of several hundred dollars on Peacher, which Lang promptly met by an equal sum on Howington, the stakes again being place in the hands of Peacher. Another and another bet was offered on Peacher by different individuals, and again and again did Lang meet them, until he had the enormous sum of eight thousand dollars staked upon this petty race; the stakes in every instance being place in the hands of Peacher. And the sequel proves, too, that the whole of the betting was carried on by the funds of Lang; Peacher handing over the stakes, as fast as they came into his hands, to his cronies, in order that they might draw further bets from Lang.

The day of the race arrived, and the parties started; Howington, a Vermonter by birth, aged about 55 years, and Peacher, a native of this county, aged about 25 years; the former having been an old soldier, and famous for his long matches and good bottom; the young nag never having been tried for bottom, but known to be as fleet as a greyhound, and wind most excellent. The old nag did his best, but all would not do; he soon lamed, and finally let down at the distance of forty-eight miles; the young nag eight miles ahead, and still "going it" under a heavy pull, accomplishing the whole distance in about twelve hours, and distancing his competitor. And thus poor Lang, instead of realizing a gain of eight thousand dollars, and coming in possession of six- teen thousand dollars, realized a loss of eight thousand dollars! This race may fairly be considered a counterpoise to the celebrated Long Island race, between the noted horses Henry and Eclipse. As a pedestrian, Mr. Peacher may now be fairly considered without a rival.

The sympathy of the community is strong for Lang, (if sympathy can properly be said to exist for either), and nothing but indignation felt towards Peacher. It is believed that Lang was induced by the persuasions of Peacher, who had deliberately formed the plan to deprive him of his money, to fall from his high estate and enter into a scheme calculated to defraud a whole community. The result proves that "honesty is the best policy," for while Lang has lost his money, Peacher has become as "gilded loam or painted clay."

A Friend of the Turf

THE MOST FAMOUS ANTEBELLUM FOOT RACE

The most celebrated pedestrian race of the antebellum era occurred in 1835 at the Union Course on Long Island, New York. It stimulated the growth of the sport during the 1830s by stirring nationalistic feelings, offering considerable prize money, and presenting a novel format. The following account, reprinted from the June 1835 edi- tion of the American Turf Register and Sporting Magazine, reveals the ways in which pedestrianism was modernized in less than a decade.

THE GREAT FOOT RACE

The great trial of human capabilities, in going ten miles within the hour, for $1,000, to which $300 was added, took place on Friday, on the Union Course, Long Island; and we are pleased to state, that the feat was accomplished twelve seconds within the time, by a native born and bred American farmer, Henry Stannard, of Killingworth, Con- necticut. Two others went the ten miles—one a Prussian, in a half a minute over; the other an Irishman, in one minute and three quarters over the time.

As early as nine o'clock, many hundreds had crossed the river to witness the race, and from that time until near two, the road between Brooklyn, and the course presented a continuous line; (and in many places a double line) of carriages of all descriptions, from the humble sand cart to the splendid barouche and four; and by two o'clock, it is computed that there were at least from sixteen to twenty persons on the course. The day, though fine, being windy, delayed the start until nineteen minutes before two, when nine candidates appeared in front of the stand, dressed in various colors, and started at the sound of a drum.

The following are the names, &c. of the competitors, in the order in which they entered themselves:

Henry Stannard, a farmer, aged twenty-four years, born in Killingworth, Connecticut. He is six feet one inch in height, and weighed one hundred and sixty-five pounds. He was dressed in black silk pantaloons, white shirt, no jacket, vest, or cap, black leather belt and flesh colored slippers.

Charles R. Wall, a brewer, aged eighteen years, born in Brooklyn. His height was five feet ten and a half inches, and he weighed one hundred and forty-nine pounds.

Henry Sutton, a house painter, aged twenty-three years, born in Rahway, New Jersey. Height five feet seven inches; weight one hundred and thirty-three pounds. He wore a yellow skirt and cap, buff breeches, white stockings and red slippers.

George W. Glauer, rope-maker, aged twenty-seven, born in Elberfeldt, Prussia. Height five feet six and a half inches; weight one hundred and forty-five pounds. He had on an elegant dress of white silk, with a pink stripe and cap to match; pink slippers and red belt.

Isaac S. Downes, a basket-maker, aged twenty-seven, born at Brookhaven, Suffolk county. Height five feet five and a half inches; weight one hundred and fifty pounds. He was dressed in a white shirt, white pantaloons, blue stripe, blue belt, no shoes or stockings.

John Mallard, a farmer, aged thirty-three, born at Exeter, Otsego Co. New York. Height five feet seven and a half inches; weight one hundred and thirty pounds. Dress, blue calico, no cap, shoes or stockings.

William Vermilyea, shoemaker, aged twenty-two years, born in New York. Height five feet ten and a half inches; weight one hundred and fifty pounds. Dressed in green calico, with black belt; no shoes or stockings.

Patrick Mahony, a porter, aged thirty-three, born in Kenmar county, Kerry, Ireland. Height five feet six inches. Weight one hundred and thirty pounds. Dress, a green gauze shirt, blue stripe calico breeches, blue belt, white stockings and black slippers.

John M'Cargy, a butcher, aged twenty-six, born at Harlaem. Height five feet ten inches. Weight one hundred and sixty pounds. Dressed in shirt, pink stripe calico trowsers, no shoes or stockings.

There was a tenth candidate, a black man, named Francis Smith, aged twenty-five, born in Manchester, Virginia. Mr. Stevens was willing that this man should run; but as he had not complied with the regulation requiring his name to be entered by a certain day, he was excluded from contesting the race.

The men all started well, and kept together for the first mile, except Mahony, who headed the others several yards, and Mallard, who fell behind after the first half mile. At the end of the second mile, one gave in; at the end of the fourth mile, two more gave up; in the fifth, a fourth man fell; at the end of the fifth mile, a fifth man gave in; during the eighth mile, Downes, one of the fastest, and decidedly the handsomest runner, hurt his foot, and gave in at the termination of that mile, leaving but three competitors, who all held out the distance.

The following is the order in which each man came up to the judges stand at the close of each mile.

MILES.

	1st.	2d.	3d.	4th.	5th.	6th.	7th.	8th.	9th.	10th.
Stannard,	3	4	3	3	3	2	2	1	1	1
Glauer,	2	2	1	1	2	3	3	3	2	2
Mahony	1	1	5	5	5	4	4	4	3	3
Downes,	5	3	2	2	1	1	1	2 gave in.		
McGargy,	6	7	7	7	4 gave in.					
Wall,	4	5	4	4 gave in.						
Sutton,	8	8	6	6 gave in.						
Mallard,	9	9	8	8 fell and gave in.						
Vermilyea	7	6 gave in.								

The following is the time in which each mile was performed by Stannard, the winner. Mahony, the Irishman, did the first mile in five minutes twenty-four seconds.

	Min.	Sec.
1st mile,	5	36
2d "	5	45
3d "	5	58
4th "	6	25
5th "	6	2
6th "	6	3
7th "	6	1
8th "	6	3
9th "	5	57
10th"	5	54
	59	44

The betting on the ground both before and after starting, was pretty even, and large sums were staked both for and against time. Downes was undoubtedly the general favorite; and was well known in the neighborhood; he did the eight miles in forty-eight and a half minutes; he had been well trained under his father, who in his thirty-ninth year, performed seventeen miles in one hour and forty-five minutes; accomplishing the first twelve and a half miles in one hour and fifteen minutes.

Mallard was known to be an excellent runner; he had performed sixteen miles in one hour and forty-nine minutes, stopping during the time to change his shoes. He was not sober when he started, and he fell in the fifth mile.

The German had performed the distance between New York and Harlaem, and returned thence (twelve miles) in seventy minutes; his friends were very sanguine of his success. He betted nearly $300 that he would win the prize. He was within the time until the sixth mile, and he performed the ten miles in one hour and twenty-seven seconds. He was four seconds behind time in the eighth mile. Part of the distance he carried a pocket handkerchief in his mouth.

Mahony, the Irishman, had undergone no training whatever; he left his porter's cart in Water street, went over to the course, ran the first mile in less than five and a half minutes; at the end of the sixth mile he was one minute and a quarter behind; at the end of the eighth mile two minutes behind; at the ninth he was three minutes behind, and he performed the ten miles in sixty-one and three quarter minutes. On the 25th of last month, this man ran eight miles in forty-one minutes fifty-six seconds. M'Gargy was out of condition; but he did the five miles in thirty-two and a half minutes. Vermilyea was very thin and in a wretched state of health; he travelled thirty-eight miles on foot, on Tuesday last, to be here in time to enter, and the next day performed eight miles in forty-six minutes; he is an excellent runner, but gave in at the end of the second mile from a pain in the side; he was also thrown down by a man crossing the course in the first mile. Wall and Sutton ran remarkably well, but gave in at the end of the fourth mile for want of training.

Stannard, the winner, we understand, has been in good training for a month. He is a powerful stalwart young man, and did not seem at all fatigued at the termination of the race. He was greatly indebted to Mr. Stevens, for his success; Mr. S. rode round the course with him the whole distance, and kept cheering him on, and cautioning him against over-exertion in the early part of the race; at the end of the sixth mile, he made him stop and take a little brandy and water, after which his foot was on the mile mark just as the thirty-six minutes were expired; and as the trumpet sounded he jumped forward gracefully, and cheerfully exclaimed. "Here am I to time;" and he was within the time every mile. After the race was over, he mounted a horse and rode round the course in search of Mr. Richard Jackson, who held his overcoat. He was called up to the stand and his success (and the reward of $1,300) was announced to him, and he was invited to dine with the Club; to which he replied in a short speech thanking Mr. Stevens, and the gentlemen of the Club for the attention shewn to the runners generally throughout the task. After this, it was announced by Mr. King, the President of the Jockey Club, that the German and the Irishman, who had both performed the ten miles, though not within the time, would receive $200 each.

We are happy to state that none of the men seemed to feel any inconvenience from their exertions; every thing went off remarkably satisfactory, nor did we hear of the slightest accident the whole day. After the foot race was over, a purse of $300, two mile heats, for all ages, was run for by the following horses, and decided as under:

	1st.	2d.		1st.	2d.
Tarquin,	1	1	Rival,	4	2
Post Boy,	2	3	Ajax,	5	dist.
Columbia Taylor,	3	dist.	Sir Alfred	6	d'm.

The first heat was performed in three minutes forty-seven seconds—the second in three minutes fifty seconds.

During the running of this match, a written paper was handed to Mr. King, stating that two native Americans were willing to attempt to walk five hundred miles without eating or drinking, as soon as the purse of $500 should be made up.

The day was remarkably fine, but the wind blew very strongly on the course, and considering the vast amount of money (in bets, &c.) at stake, Mr. Stevens felt uncertain at first how to act, and decided to postpone the race; but the general opinion and desire seem to be against any postponement, and he yielded to this. The result on this account was most fortunate. The race was won handsomely; although when it wanted but twenty eight seconds to the hour, bets at five to three were offered, and taken, that the task would not be accomplished. It is certain that if the wind had not been so high, Stannard would have performed the ten miles in fifty-seven minutes.

SOUTHERN PEDESTRIANISM

As in horse racing, the sport of pedestrianism during the 1830s witnessed several interstate challenges for considerable prize money. The following account, reprinted from the 31 December 1836 issue of The Spirit of the Times, reveals the sport's widespread appeal and popularity.

THE FOOT RACE AT AUGUSTA FOR $3000 A-SIDE

Again our prediction is verified! Perritt beat Day on the 17th, at Augusta, 6 1/2 feet in the 50 yards. We predicted last week Perritt would win the match by a toe-nail, and offered to back him to the amount of his subscription to the Spirit of the Times. We could have been accommodated at the South, for it seems Day was the favorite, and the result "let in" the knowing ones. We *might* have whispered a word in their ears that would have saved them their pocket change, but "bought wit is the best in the world," and we "kept dark" until the expression of our humble opinion could not reach Augusta before the match was decided.

A few hours after our paper had gone to press last Friday, we received from an attentive and obliging correspondent the following letter by the *Express Mail:*—

Augusta, Ga. Dec. 17, 1836,

Dear Sir,—I presume that the earliest intelligence of the result of the *Great Foot Race* on the Lafayette Course, which came off to-day, between Perritt of this State, and Day, of Kentucky, will be worth the postage.

The match was for $3000 a-side. The Kentuckian is a fine figure, and was so much the favorite, that there was very little bye-betting. The knowing ones, however, were taken in, for Perritt won the race easily, beating Day 6 1/2 feet in 50 yards....

Yours, &c.,   A.B.C.

THE EVOLUTION OF PEDESTRIANISM

By the late 1830s pedestrianism had generated enormous public interest and excitement and had made significant strides towards becoming a more organized, formal sport. Some runners such as Henry Stannard had become sports heroes and developed followings of their own. Pedestrian contests began to resemble those of other sports such as boat racing, with races of differing lengths and types as part of the same event. Sometimes these competitions became an early form of modern athletic games. The following report, published in the 8 September 1838 issue of The Spirit of the Times, details these important changes in the sport.

FOOT RACING, ETC. AT HOBOKEN

The first exhibition of Athletic Exercises, commenced on the Beacon Course, opposite this city of Wednesday last, but owing to the illness of STANNARD, who was not in attendance, the interest of the PEDESTRIANISM was in a great measure destroyed. Stannard's celebrity, and the fact that he had been in training for some time for the purses of $500, for three mile heats, and $250 for two miles, prevented any entries for those purses; as he "went amiss" while on a visit, he failed to make an entry himself, and thus the two principal purses were not contended for. The proprietor, however, gave an extra purse of $50 for three mile heats, to which there were three entries. The attendance from town was not so numerous as might have been anticipated, owing, principally, to the want of sufficient publicity given of the purses and sport to be expected. The sport commenced at 3 o'clock, with

A Foot Race of 200 Yards, purse $50-$5 to the 2d in the race.

Peter Van Pelt, of New York City	1
Wm. Van Buren, of Hackensack, N.J.	2
Wm. Vermilyea, of Hallett's Cove, L.I.	3
Jeremiah Ryan, of Croton Water Works, N.Y.	4

Time, 22 1/2 seconds.

Van Buren was the favorite with the Jerseymen, having beaten Stannard in a trial of 200 yards some ten days since. The winner is a public baggage carrier. Ryan is a Patlander employed on the Croton Water Works; he is six feet high, and a heavy built man of about 38; though beaten off three rods, he would have been backed to win had the race been repeated at 400 yards.

Walking Match—Purse $50—$10 to the 2d in the race, for the greatest distance walked in one hour, fair toe and heel.

Wm. Vermilyea, of Hallett's Cove	1
Peter Miller	2
Jeremiah Ryan	0
John Van Ostrand	0

Vermilyea walked 5 miles and 1540 yards.

Foot Race, Three mile heats—Purse $50.

Samuel Clemens, half bred Indian, from Oneida County, N.Y.	1	1
John Van Ostrand	3	2
Robert McGinn	2	3

Time, 16:35-16:54

Won easy; Clemons might have doubly distanced his competitors. He is a cross of the Mulatto and Indian, and an out and outer. A party will back him, we hear, against Stannard; he was loudly cheered on coming in the 2d heat.

SECOND DAY.

Foot Race, Mile heats—Purse $50.

"Samuel Clemsen, "pedigree above!"	1	2	1
Mr _____	2	1	2

Two "others started, but were not placed"

Time, 5:37-6:03-5:52.

Clemens "broke down" in his "fore foot" on the last quarter of the 3d heat, and was obliged to walk in.

Foot Race, Quarter of a mile—Purse $40-$10 to the 2d in the race.

Peter Van Pelt, of New York	1
Pete Whetstone, Jr., of Communipaw	2

Three others started, but were "no where" at the finish.

Time, 1 minute.

Next came off a Jumping Match, for a purse of $25, $5 to the second best; the purse was given to Mr. BROWN, as having covered the greatest distance in three standing jumps. There were five entires; they jumped with weights; Brown cleared thirty-three feet.

To this succeeded a match at Sledge Throwing, for a purse of $10; there were six entries; the purse was won by J. Ryan, (mentioned before) who threw the Sledge, weighing 13 lbs. sixty-five feet.

On the whole, the Exercises went off very cleverly, when we consider that this was the first attempt to get up an exhibition of the kind. Well managed, we have no doubt the sport would be well patronized, and give general satisfaction.

CANADIAN ATHLETIC GAMES

During the late 1830s Scottish Highlander Clubs organized themselves and conducted their first athletic games in the tradition of the Caledonian Games, first developed in

Scotland. Though the first newspaper coverage of the Caledonian Games in the United States appeared in the early 1840s the following account, reprinted from the 2 November 1839 issue of The Spirit of the Times, describes the first anniversary of the Toronto Athletic Games.

THE GATHERING—TORONTO ATHLETIC GAMES

Patrons—His Excellency Lieutenant Governor, aid Major General Sir Geo. Arthur, K.C.H.

Umpire—Colonel Mackenzie Frazer. Q.M.G.

Stewards—The Mayor of the City. MacNab of that Ilk. the Hon William Allan. Hon. Mr. Justice McLean, Hon. Sir Allan N. MacNab, the Sheriff of the Home District, Col Cox. K.H. & P.S. Col. Spark. 93d Highlanders. Col. Wingfield, 32d Regt., Col Bullock, A.G.M. C.A. Hagerman Esq., Attorney Genera, W.H. Draper. Esq. Solicitor General, Major Arthur. 93d Highlanders, Major Reid, 32d Regt. Major Magrath, 1st I.D., Capt F. Markham, 32d Regt., Capt. Sands, K.D.G., Capt. Arthur, A.D.C., Lieut. Domville A.D.C., Lieut. Marriott, Royal Artillery, C.C. Small, Esq., Clerk of the Crown, George Monro. Esq., Peter Buchanan, Esq., T.D. Harris, Esq., Archibald Macdonnell, Esq., C.W. Heath, Esq., John Maitland, Secretary.

FIRST DAY

Wednesday, 11th Sept.

The slumbers of the inhabitants were disturbed at an early hour this morning by "Hey Johnie Cope are ye Wauken yet," and the "Gathering o' the Clans," played through the City, by four Pipers from the gallant 93d, fully attired to the garb of Clan Gregor, reminding us that the Gathering had begun.—At nine o'clock, crowds of spectators and competitors, from all quarters, moved towards Caer Howell, and soon amounted to several thousands, for whose accommodation a convenient stand was erected, capable of holding 500 people, in front of which an extensive space was strongly posted and roped.

In consequence of the necessary absence on a departmental tour of our able Umpire, Capt. F. Markham, of the 32d, was chosen to "reign in his stead."—and then the Games commenced with

Quoiting (22 yards) for a silver jug, value £5, won by Captain John Terrance (from Lanarkshire, Scotland), Farmer, Scarboro'.

Running hop, step, and leap—medal, £2, 40 feet 2 inches. John Overland (from Upwell, Cambridgeshire, England), Tailor, Toronto.

Standing hop, step, and leap—medal, £1 10s., 28 feet 7 inches. John Overland, do.

Running high leap—piece of plate, £3 5s., 5 feet 6 inches. John Overland, do.

Standing high leap—medal, £1 10s., 4 feet 3 inches. John Overland, do.

Throwing light hammer, weight 10 lbs.—medal, £1 10s., 110 feet, Michael Kennedy (from Herbeth Town, County Limerick, Ireland), Toronto.

Putting light ball, weight 18 lbs.—medal, £2 10s., 35 feet 9 inches, Thomas Carradice, (from Jedburgh, Roxburghshire, Scotland), Esquesing.

First sack race, (50 yards)—medal, 15s., James Stanton, son of Robert Stanton, Esquire, Toronto.

Second sack race—medal, 15s, John Monro, son of George Monro, Esquire, Toronto.
Third sack race—medal, 15s, Private Mackay Monro (from Tongue, Sutherlandshire, Scotland), 93d Highlanders.
First short foot race, (120 yards)—medal, £2, Corporal Farquhar Macgilvery, 93d Highlanders, from Campbelltown, County of Inverness, Scotland.

In the evening, at seven o'clock, the Stewards and their friends, sat down to an excellent dinner, which did great credit to the proprietors of the Ontario House, the duties of the chair were ably discharged by His Worship the Mayor, supported by Captains Arthur and Markham; Mr. Secretary Maitland officiated as croupier, supported by P. Buchanan and Thos. Gurley, Esqrs. Many loyal toasts and sentiments proceeded from the chair, which met with ardent and enthusiastic responses from the company, who seemed all equally wrapt in perfect enjoyment. The healths of His Excellency, Sir George Arthur and Sir Francis Head, were drank amid thunders of applause, as was also the health of Captain Markham; a striking proof that the citizens of Toronto equally appreciate wisdom in council, and valor in the field. On the whole, we despair of ever again passing so pleasant an evening.

SECOND DAY

Putting heavy ball, [24 lbs]—piece of plate, £3 5s., 28 feet 3 inches. Thos. Carradice.
Throwing heavy hammer, [16 lbs]—piece of plate, £3 15s., 80 feet 8 inches, Thomas Carradice.
First hurdle race, [120 yards]—medal, £2. Mr. Friend Wilcox, Farmer, Etobicoke.
Wrestling, collar and elbow—medal, £2. Private John Pepper, 32d Regt., from Dublin, Ireland.
Wrestling, collar and elbow, trippers—medal, £2. Private Joseph Rose, 32d Regt., from Nottingham, England.
Wrestling, back-hold—medal, £2, Mr. Charles Hodgson, from Cumberland, England; Farmer, Markham.
First long foot race, [440 yards]—medal, £2 10s., Private David Macleod, 93d Highlanders, from Thurso, Caithness-shire, Scotland.
Second long foot race—medal, £2, Private James Monro, 93d Highlanders, From Tain, Ross-shire, Scotland.
First boys' short foot race—blue bonnet, James Cuthbert, Toronto.
Second boys' short foot race—blue bonnet, Dugald McDougall, Toronto.

There was a concert by the St. Luke family, in the City Hall, in the evening, under the patronage of the Stewards, which gave very great satisfaction, particularly the performance of the young Paganini.

THIRD DAY.

Second Hurdle Race—handsome blue bonnet, Lieutenant Campbell, 32d Regt.
Third boys' short foot race—blue bonnet, Peter McArthur, Toronto.
Second short foot race—blue bonnet, George Williams, a colored man, from the Southern States.
Third hurdle race—handsome blue bonnet, George Graham.
Two bell races, for blue bonnets.

Rifle shooting [120 yards]—medal, £3 5s., C.C. Small, Esquire, Toronto.
Bowling—medal, £3 5s., Robert McClure, Esq, from Ayr, Scotland, Toronto.

FOURTH DAY.

First sweepstakes for rifle shooting—Messrs, Small, Powell, Reid, Fairbanks, Craig, Magrath, Sherwood, Ketchum, Wakefield, and Copland, won by Mr. Fairbanks, Mr. T. Magrath, second.

Second sweepstakes for rifle shooting—the above gentlemen and Messrs. Blevins and Ashfield, won by Mr. C. Small, Mr. Fairbanks, second.

Third sweepstakes for rifle shooting—Messrs. Small, Magrath, Powell, Copland, Reid, and Fairbanks, won by Mr. Fairbanks, Mr. Small, second.

Thus has finished (with the exception of archery and cricket, which it has yet been impossible to bring off) the first anniversary of The Gathering for our Athletic Games, and for which at least six hundred competitors of all classes of the community, and from the five divisions of the earth, have entered the lists and contended for the different prizes with the most perfect good humor, at the same time struggling with the keenest determination to carry off the laurels of the day. The ground was visited from time to time by our universally esteemed Lieutenant Governor, his lady and family, by many officers and gentlemen from distant parts of this and the other provinces, and all the beauty and fashion of the city and vicinity.

Considering the immense concourse of people collected together, it is highly creditable to the stewards, that by their arrangements not the least disorder of any kind has taken place, and it is no presumption to affirm, that this Gathering has rarely been surpassed even at home; the thanks of the community are justly due to Colonel Wingfield and others of the 32d, and Major Arthur and officers of the 93d, who have so much added to the pleasures of the Gathering, by lending the regimental hands, and handsomely contributing to Captain Sands and the officers of the K.D.G. at Niagara, and also the "The Macnab," who has come upwards of 450 miles, having started from Macnab with six of his Highlanders to compete, but owing to the disarrangement of the steamers, from the boisterous state of the weather, he was obliged reluctantly to leave them half way, and only succeeded through great perseverance in reaching Toronto himself on the evening of the second day. "Better luck next time."

We ought not to omit making our distant readers acquainted with the beauties of Caer Howell, where these games took place, and where there is concentrated more material and opportunity for such out-door manly amusements than at any place we remember to have visited. It is situated one mile north of the city, and was some years ago taken on a long lease, by its present spirited proprietor, Mr. Erskine, who maintains there, in good olden style, a capital establishment where the most fastidious gourmand can have, suited to his taste, fish, flesh, fowl, and fruits; and the connoisseur in "liqueur guid" can be abundantly supplied, of which we had ample proof these few days past. It is approachable to pedestrians by a walk tastefully laid out at considerable expense, lined on each side by stripes of young plantation, known as the College Avenue; at the lower, or city end, are posted two very handsome lodges and gates, leading into an open space of many acres, neatly studded with small clumps of trees where it is intended to erect the college of U.C. Before reaching the extremity by fifty yards, strikes off by an almost unseen path, the way through the belt on the west, unto the Caer Howell grounds, and the instant you escape from the thicket, you are taken with surprise by the number of horses tied to the posts and fences, and led about by soldiers and retainers, in and out of livery, mounted and on foot, and by vehicles of every description. The surprise is only begun when up plays a band of music, belonging to one of the regiments, delighting a large concourse of ladies and gentlemen, who are reclining on the rustic seats, or strolling about the grounds; next out bellows some one running at half speed across a green after a black ball, in a flannel jacket, and not the best straw tile in the world, "kissed jack," and then follows a short; these are bowlers, playing on a very neat green formed in the glen, through which meanders a small stream, over which is thrown a covering, and thus between the banks is the bowling green.

Bang goes a shot,—"hit the bull's eye," cries a dozen voices at once. This is another party of gentlemen who have a sweepstakes at rifle shooting, in the hollow above the green, across which is a dam; and here during winter, amateurs at curling enjoy themselves. One may think he is now up to all the secrets,—but no,—the band has stopped, and louder shouts than ever are heard from behind. On looking round, he is struck with an immense, dark-looking, ungainly strong frame building, amongst the trees, (how it got there's a puzzler.) and be at once pronounces it "a mad-House." Silence for a moment, and out bounces six or eight of its inmates, at first sight seemingly quite raised, and all in a precious stew, with clubs in their hands, to attack the quiet unsuspecting spectators of the bowling and rifle shooting, perceives next moment this is a racket court, said to be the best this side the Atlantic; the gentlemen who have been playing have now their rackets in their hands, and drying their brows, complain of thirst, they dive into the saloon to mend that matter. Satisfied of knowing all now, and with half a mind to follow the example of the racketers,—when lo! another great noise gets up,—sure it's some of the horses bolted with a carriage,—no,—all looks quiet in that direction,—but , I soon find I'm standing close to a ten pin alley, (which I before thought was a long stable,) where another large party are busily employed rolling. Determined at last to find out all by taking a wander round,—tried the landlord's punch,—and resolved to explore a little further, by winding our way along the bridge which is here thrown across the ravine, but this was found no easy matter, it being quite crowded by the before mentioned spectators, and by a number of persons supposed by us to be the peace keepers; having accomplished this, and following the current through another plantation, the ear was saluted by the music from the bagpipes playing the finishing tune to that day's Athletic Games—"Guid nicht an' joy be wi' ye a'." On our return we learned that the supposed peace-keepers were no less than members of the cricket club, with their bats, who had been disappointed of their play that day, their ground being still occupied by the Gathering. We reached home highly pleased with our rambles through the Caer Howell grounds, and delighted that our capital can boast of encouraging, so extensively, such national pastimes.

Chapter 11

WINTER GAMES AND SPORTS

Curling, ice skating and sleigh riding were the primary winter games and sports practiced from 1821 to 1840 in Canada and the northern parts of the United States. Of the three activities only curling had assumed some of the characteristics of modern sport by 1840. Curling clubs had been formed in both the United States and Canada and matches between private clubs of both countries had been initiated before 1840 and continued thereafter on a regular basis, particularly between clubs in New York City and those in Toronto. In the decades to come clubs would be formed in other important Canadian cities such as Montreal, Quebec City, and Halifax and in other American cities such as Boston. Newspapers, especially sports journals such as The Spirit of the Times, began to devote space to the reporting of these local, regional, and international contests during the 1830s. Soon rules and regulations were codified and the introduction of terminology helped to standardize the sport.

A legacy of Dutch settlement and Scottish influence, ice skating in the early nineteenth century was purely a pastime, though by the 1850s a skating boom would lead to the formation of skating clubs, sponsored competitions, and formal events. Ice skating remained primarily a participatory activity for boys and young men; only after the Civil War did the activity receive public approval as a suitable, healthy exercise for women. Unlike curling, which attracted the upper classes, ice skating appealed to a broad slice of society. The relatively low cost of equipment, most of which had been developed and constructed in Holland, tended to reduce class discrimination and allowed the participation of working classes in this enjoyable and growing pastime prior to 1840. Only after 1850 did the wealthy attempt to separate themselves from the masses by introducing private skating clubs.

Though some sleigh contests did occur, for the most part sleigh riding remained an informal, unorganized outdoor activity in the early nineteenth century. Unlike other winter games and sports, sleigh riding was enjoyed by both young men and women. The distance of sleigh rides varied from ten to twenty miles and often consumed almost an entire day, lasting well into the evening hours. As with many other amusements of the period, the nature of sleigh riding was social, with the participants usually enjoying music, drink, and dancing at the conclusion of the excursion. The social function of sleigh riding extended to courting, as young men often courted young women through this pastime, an activity undoubtedly facilitated by societal acceptance of this recreation as simple, pleasant, and healthy fun and amusement.

SLEIGHING IN NEW YORK CITY

The social nature of sleighing accounted for its increasing popularity during the antebellum era in North America. Sleighing served an important social function by allowing young men to court young women through an activity that received public
approval. The following article, reprinted from the 28 January 1837 issue of The Spirit
of the Times, describes the social dimensions of sleighing in New York City immediately after a snowfall.

THE SLEIGHING

"First it blew—then it snew—then it thew, and then it friz, horrid."

Tom Hood

This has been an all sorts of a week. On Saturday last it began to "blew"—on Sunday it "snew", on Tuesday and Wednesday it "threw," and on Thursday night, may be
it didn't "friz horrid." We didn't sleep on the Battery to ascertain the fact, nor can we
say with that man of the world, Adonis Church, that "a friend of mine did, and I'll
swear to it."

If the snow had fallen in real, right-down earnest style, all Sunday night, we should
have had capital sleighing; instead of which we have only had a *slaying* of horses. The
late five inches of snow that concealed the beauties of chaste mother Earth, as with a
chemise, as Bennett would say, did-up more horses than even Sampson slew of the
Philistines in three days with the jaw bone of an ass, in the vallies of Gilgal or Zig-
zag, we forget which. Some one has prettily remarked that "snow falls gently, because
it is pushed from Heaven while sleeping." Such was the case last Sunday, in contra-
distinction to the usual practice of snowing in New-York, where, when it snows at all,
it goes the entire swine, like a good Tammany democrat. There is not hook-'em-
snivy—no cut and come again about it. It downs with its dust in big flecks like the
buckwheat cakes at a Dutch farmer's breakfast—solid enough, and heavy enough to
knock a small boy into next Fourth of July—it falls as if kicked from "cloud capp'd
towers" to cover our "gorgeous palaces," and woe be to horses in those days.

The morning after a heavy fall of snow affords a thousand themes for the industrious penny-a-liners of the daily press. They pick up materials for "unfortunate accidents" at every turn, and it is not an uncommon thing for them to meet with
"distressing casualties" in propria personae; such a godsend lasts them a week.

By the time the sun is wide awake, and begins to "draw it mild" on the snow, the
sidewalks are cleared of the upper crust, leaving only enough to serve the science of
Phrenology, which soon becomes so slippery, that bumps and palpable developments
become as plenty on a man's head as eyes in an Irish potatoe. By noon the sun begins
to "cut in fat," and our beautiful Broadway is soon metamorphosed into a precious
horse-pond. In the narrow streets the snow is piled up into miniature peaks of Teneriffe;
and when the sun, as with a long pole, begins to stir up that on the house-tops, without shouting "stand from under," then you see fun. A diorama of the famous "slide"

of the White Hills of New Hampshire, or that the other day at Troy, may be seen every ten minutes, not only free, gratis, but whether you will or no. Avalanches come rushing down from the tops of six storied houses, with Alpine sublimity, and wo betide the unlucky he, or she, on whose devoted head they fall. People get knocked down without a chance of striking back; you can't say to it—"take a man of your size." And then when the thaw spirit is abroad, in what a pickle are the streets. Crossing Broadway is an achievement to be "spoken of the same day" with Leander's swimming the Hellespont. "Adam's Fall," in the garden of Eden, where Eve made a shift to do without dress, and Adam had no tailor, is emulated apparently by his *immediate descendants* of 1837; and what will be a puzzler to future Almanac-makers, the "last *Fall* season" was not over until after the 26th of January.

To return to the sleighing. It was very fair in town, while on the roads radiating from the city it was capital, and the ancient "Passover" was revived by hundreds of green horns, who in their hired sleighs run over one another, and pretty much every thing else. New-Yorkers are tickled to death with the prospect of a sleigh ride, and no sooner is there snow enough to "put your foot in it," than each man, woman and child, seems "possessed with a familiar spirit," while the veritable descendants of the bygone Dutch burgomasters of Niew-Amsterdam are almost raving distressed with delight. In some instances the passion for sleigh-riding is indulged in to an inconceivable and ludicrous extent. It is not to this day an isolated case, to find on a man's door a pencilled notice to the effect that his office or store is "closed in consequence of sickness (or death) in the family." A sleigh-ride, however, is a more effectual remedy than Brandreth's Pills for this prevalent epidemic, peculiar only to New-Yorkers.

Throughout the week the whole city has rung while the lively crash of ten thousand strings of bells. We cannot "begin" to do justice to the varieties of splended and *outre* turn-outs, that like Leigh Hunt's pig, have had a strange propensity to "go up all manner of streets." Every imaginable conveyance has been put in requisition, from the luxurious and fur-lined equipage of old campaigners, to a ricketty crockey crate attached to two long poles. Yea, verily, do not the ancient chronicles of the Spirit of the Times inform us how the milkmen whistled through the streets with the speed of swift sped arrows, and how the sooty coal-man cried forth his *melancholy notes* from a graceless box, perched on reeling runners? How the hearty carman fastened his sleek nag to some lonely wood sled, and emulously put "Bob" to his mettle alongside a lumbering omnibus. But all omnibi were not lumbering. Here and there the haughty Jehus were standing erect in might, wielding aloft their lusty whips, fashioned as it to lash the Hellespont into peace, which ever and anon they cracked in the ears of their prancing studs, that pricked on to the music of their own bells, regardless of the shouts of the loitering, would-be passengers, and throwing up at every fling of their iron-bound hoofs, snow mingled with dirt (which no "dasher" could resist) into the countenances of a mixed-up mass of clerks and smiling masters, promiscuously packed together in the cavernous recesses of a gaudy omnibus, each heart devoutly thankful that in the dispositions which had been made to improve the snowy gifts of father Jove, opportunity was afforded for "modest merit" to take a shilling out.

The most out-and-out affair, was a superb barouche sleigh, drawn by six fiery grey horses, that were driven up and down Broadway at a rate of sixteen miles an hour, crowded full of ladies, the radiant beauty of whose eyes caused thousands to break that commandment which forbids our "coveting any thing that is our neighbor's."

The four-in-hand turn-outs of several whips and bloods about town, were *recherche* in the extreme, and among the knowing ones, Brower's "swell dragman" shone conspicuous, with his *eight* long-tailed greys. Boats placed upon runners, and crowded with jovial crews, occasionally dashed through Broadway, and sporting sleighs drawn by six prancing horses were too common to excite but a passing remark. A very neat and elegant Russian sleigh, singly horsed, excited particular attention. The harness was wound with silver wire, with the wood-work of the haimes projecting a foot and a half above the horse's shoulder, like an inverted ox-yoke, and hung with silver bells. The owner was snugly ensconced in his sleigh beneath "a wilderness" of rich skins, while his tiger, with his feet encased in shoes fastened upon the runners, sat upright upon a high seat secured behind it, and tooled his master's bit of blood with the grace of a Harry Stevenson.

One aspiring phaeton we marked, whose zeal and "excellent ambition" rather out went his ability. Why should ambroisal curls and face divinely formed, persist to brave the terrors of the wintry tempest in the guise of a postillion? And why be vexed that thy knees did quake in spite of thee, and that the speed of thy Pegasus came not up to that of the true blood? Thou wast not formed to thrive in "camps or tented fields," nor yet at Tattersalls. *There* thou must of course be baffled. Recall how haughty Diomede once spared not the snowy hand of even soft Aphrodite, when fleeing to the succour of the son of "deeply blessed Anchises," and how old Jove kissed his beauteous daughter's pouting lips, and chid her for mingling in the affairs of bloody Mars, and bade her concern herself with her own sweet arts of love, and the rights of decorous wedlock. Oh, be the advised, and waste not again thy "sweetness on the desert air," nor think to usurp the right of "swells" of less melting aspect.

As the thaw was progressing, and the snow fast renewing its original shape, an omnibus, "o'ercrowded with her crew"—a domestic circle of mothers, daughters, cousins, aunts, and "babies ten," made a crash, "gave a heel, and then a lurch to port, and going down head foremost, sunk in short;" when at the moment a passing Jehu locked the off corner of the vehicle, instantly emptying the precious casket splash into the black conglomerated mass of mud and snow. Then went up a yell "louder than the loud ocean," and there all was bushed, save the babies and the "remorseless dash" of mud; "but at intervals there gushed, accompanied with a convulsive splash—a solitary shriek—the bubbling cry" of one old maid in her "last agony" for her hat and feathers. The babies were saved—all, save one—"of a soft cheek, and aspect delicate." The boy bore up long, but the heavy crash of his lusty aunt sunk him too deep "within the greedy wave" for breath or utterance. The rest arose, begrimmed with villainous drippings of the inky *brine*, if salt it was; then looked into each other's eye—for eyes none had; then meekly shook themselves—then boo-hoo-ed out a crying.

The road to the Union Course, near which "uncle John R." Snediker dispenses whiskey punch, and the good things of this life, after a style that deserves to immortalize him in this world, to say nothing of the next, has been literally alive all the week. Give Snediker a day's notice, and he will give you a better dinner than money can command at any house short of Cozzens' at West Point, within a hundred miles of Gotham. At Burnam's, Cato's, and Nowland's, too, the crowd has been immense. Not a man, woman, or child has slept a wink at Harlem since the sleighing commenced, and they begin to think with poor Monsieur Morbleu, "By Gar, I shall get some sleeps nevare!" The place is filled with sleighs, crowded to repletion with motley crews, that remind one of Power's famous statues in the Groves of Blarney:—

"Alexander, Confucius, and Sergeant Kittle,
Venus, and Bacchus, and Phillis the fair,
Homer, Plutarch, and Nebuchadnezzar,
All standing out in the open air."

The sleighing on the Avenues is first rate, and advantage has been taken of it by the owners of the crack trotting nags. It is a singular fact, that some of our fastest trotting horses *on the course* are easily beaten by third or fourth rate ones *on the snow*, and vice versa. The private matches in harness are innumerable. Two or three pairs of "fast crabs" are out each afternoon, and the way they slide past everything on the road is rather a caution. Fire-King, Lady Slipper, Modesty, John, and others, have a knack of cutting off a mile on the snow in about 2:50, and there are two pairs of blood mares that are equally fine.

It would occupy more room than we can well spare to describe the scenes of our New York Carnival. How fathers improved the opportunity to display their elegant turnouts, and boys to slide down hill, build castles, snowball servant maids at home, and canary birds through the neighboring windows. We could recount many a laughter-moving tale of brillant belles and bashful beaux—how the former contrived to "do" the latter out of a ride, which joke they afterwards played off at second hand on the livery stable men—how the bucks drove their fours-in-hand before landaus on runners, and how "small deer" were squatted in crockery crates nailed to couples of bean poles—how wood sleds and omnibus-ters choked up Broadway, and ran over or under coal carts and draymen—how ladies fainted and Jehus swore—how boys laughed and babies cut their teeth—how Jemmy Jessamy's were run away with, and how the more they tried to stop their steeds, the more they wouldn't, so they would—how female women got upset—how the sleighs shrieked and streaked it over the cold paving-stones—how bachelors grew amorous, and maidens less shy—how the latter caught beauxs and colds together—how people rode who never rode before—how dabblers in the waters of Helicon forsook the crystal fount to drink whiskey punch at Snediker's—how belles at the theatres were left for bells on the road, and how, finally, the sleighing, like this article, came to an end.

CANADIAN SLEIGH RACES

Sleigh racing was a popular pastime in Canada and the United States, and, as the document that follows illustrates, often occurred spontaneously among the sleigh drivers while waiting for clients. These contests, though informal, created much excitement and afforded drivers the opportunity to test their horsemanship and mettle against one

another. The following article, taken from the 3 February 1838 issue of The Spirit of
the Times, is a lively account of one spirited race in Canada.

CANADIAN SLEIGH-DRIVERS—A CARIOLE RACE
A WINTER SKETCH ON THE ICE-BRIDGE, QUEBEC*

"At once the coursers from the barrier bound;
The lifted scourges all at once resound:
Their heart, their eyes , their voice, they send before;
And up the champaign thunder from the shore!"
"Perchance the reins forsook the driver's hand,
And, turned too short, be tumbled on the strand.

Pope's Homer.

We next come upon a groupe, near that green booth with, the flaming yellow pen-
non, which may well match aught of the picturesque in animated effect to be found in
other climes; and so indeed thinks that busy artist near them, with his little table, and
camera lucida at work, and making the most of the scene around. A number of cart-
ers, or, perhaps, more properly to be termed, in unison with the season, sleigh-drivers,
are congregated together, and with noisy, but good-humored vociferation, descanting
on the merits, and speed in particular, of their several horses. They have come upon
the ice with their carioles to ply for hire; and in the meantime, while waiting for fares,
are ready to test comparative swiftness of their hardy Norman steeds. A race will certainly be the result of all this gaseonading before many minutes have passed over.

Their grotesquely painted leather coats, and gaudy ceintures, or girdles, hairy caps,
russet-looking moccasin-boots, and never-forgotten bauble-decked pipe. All are in
strange keeping with their peculiar vocation, and the constant companionship they hold
with their rough-coated and mettlesome horses, now standing so quietly near. These
last, with the white frost-flakes speckling their shaggy breasts and hides, long icicles
pendant from their shaggy breasts and hides, long icicles pendant from their muzzles,
their harness covered with rows of bells, and party colored ribbons flying in gay *bou-
quets*, or flashing top-knots from their thick plated bridles,—the carioles behind, with
their shining paint and bright fantastic bordering, half filled with the warm ample roles
of brown buffalo hide, altogether add to the novelty of the strange picture, and in which
they seem to be grouped in skilful position too for effect, though all an accident. And
then the varied action of those saucy, smart looking fellows: some seated on the side
of their sleighs, carelessly smoking their short pipes, others in violent gesticulation,
arguing some matter of horse-flesh with a brother *chartier*, brandishing and cracking
their thick whips;—one stooping fellow is continually examining his horse's sharpening
shoeing,—another fixing his steed's bridle more carefully on, or altering the position
of his collar of bells, or perhaps tickling and teasing the vicious animal into tricks of
grimace, and to snap or kick at all near him. Farther on, you may also observe two
knowing fellows at work with the restless muzzle of a venerable poney, whose mouth-
mark seems to be of doubtful or dishonest origin.

A sudden bustle agitates the throng, and as we predicted, a race is about to take place between two rival hereos of the whip, and who also farther bear the additional distinction in the city of being the two most consummate rascals of their fraternity. One will not doubt this latter fact when the eye dwells a moment on the little, crook-backed fellow with the leering grin and sinister physiognomy, as he nimbly jumps upon the front seat of his vehicle, gathers up the reins, and flourishes the whip over his now prancing iron-grey. His opponent, that lean, lank-sided ruffian, with but one eye in his frontis piece, and that eternally winking, the peek of his wolf-skin cap knowingly turned to the back of his head, and the bowl of his pipe downward, all adding to the vile humor of the scoundrel's features; he, too, is mounted in similar position to the other, and ready for the starting word. A moment's pause—the expected "ho!" is bellowed forth, and away they go, with a chorus of wild shouting hurras behind them. They recklessly dash into the crowd, which, well used to such "devil-may-care" kind of intrusions, opens on the instant a ready course for them, and as quickly closes again when they are past. And the ringing of their harness-bells—the hollow thunder of their steel-shed carioles speeding over the shouting ice—the grating swing of the shafts—the sharp clicking noise of the well-armed hoof in its quick bounding—the shrill, screaming halloo, and the loud cracking of the ceaseless whip, intermingled with the yelping howl of some hapless dog they have run over—alike attract the car as well as the eye to the furious course of the fearless competitors. They are to turn in wheeling circuit round that far marquee, and retrace their tract to the place of starting ere the victory is decided. Lee, the cripple, is first to that turn, and with a bound the horse is round the tent; but treacherous glare ice is there, and the swing of the cariole has proved too powerful for the good animal to master in that jerking sweep—he is carried off his legs, and man, steed, and vehicle, in one confused heap, slide sideling on the slippery course for yards. But the hunchback is real game—he recovers himself in an instant; and applying the lash well into his floundering and kicking horse, the "gallant grey" springs up with a desperate bound on his legs, and dashes off on his return. "Richard's himself again;" he thunders back over the icy plain, amid the cheering and deafening plaudits of the thousands witnessing the feat, and comes "handsomely in" to the winning-post, cutting no triffle of a figure that same crook backed dwarf, with his elf-locks streaming in the wind (having lost his cap in the fall at a turn), and his mis-shapen carcase perched up so oddly on the seat of his sleigh. His antagonist has had scarcely better luck than himself at the wheeling point; for his cariole caught the gear of an apple-stall on his blind side, causing his horse to shy through the ring formed around a cock-fight, and thus putting a summary stopper on the battle and sport. The abettors and participators in this last—at least, the effective survivors of the outrage—in revenge, have so severely pelted with frozen lumps of snow that one-eyed vagabond, as to bung up his "best and only" orb of vision, and demolish his pipe, even to the stump clenched fast in his teeth; and it is this mishap which has given his rival the means and time of successful recovery from the fall. As he comes in at dogged canter, he is saluted with a burst on all sides of wild yells and contemptuous hooting; and see, to complete his discomfiture, just as he opens his mouth in attempted and angry vindication of his misfortune, some arch erchin in the deriding crowd dexterously fills it with a well-directed snow-ball, which drives the fragment of the pipe-shank down his throat, and tumbles him over from his roost on the cariole front upon the top of a savage Newfoundlander, who with a fellow is tackled tandem fashion to a juvenile "drag." Both the dogs fail to work at once upon the poor wretch, fastening fiercely upon both scalp and cars; and it is only after a furious onset from the bystanders of scrambling, kicking, and dragging, that he is extricated in a most dilapidated state of body from the clutches of those Labrador-bred devils, and borne off to some near "refuge for the destitute," in the shape of a rum-selling booth, where "mine host" plays the good Samaritan, not by pouring oil into his wounds, but whiskey down his throat, and with such proper effect, than an hour after finds the half-blind scoundrel the "gayest of the gay" among his fellows on the icy course, and rife and ready for any and everything in the shape of merriment or rascality.

Quebec, Jan., 1838.   J.H.W.

*As it appeared in the winter of 1837.

CURLING MATCH IN TORONTO

Although curling did not become a dominant sport in Canada until after the 1850s it did begin to show signs of modernization prior to that date. Curling clubs were formed at least by the late 1830s and competed against one another in local competitions before spectators who had only begun to develop an interest in the sport. The following article, reprinted from the 16 February 1839 issue of The Spirit of the Times, describes an early curling match in Canada.

CURLING MATCH IN UPPER CANADA

An unknown correspondent has kindly furnished us with the details of a Great Curling Match between the Curlers of *Scarboro'* and *Toronto*, which was played on Toronto Bay on the 30th ult., ending in the defeat of the Toronto Club, Scarboro' gaining 48 shotts and Toronto 45. It is believed this was the most interesting Bonspeil that has ever come off in the Province. The "British Colonist" furnishes the annexed report.—

The game was played by 16 players of each party, on two rinks, with one stone each, or eight Scarboro' players against eight Toronto players, on each rink. The party first winning 62 shotts on the two rinks, were to be the victors, and should neither party count that number at half-past four o'clock, the party having the greatest number of shotts at that time, were to be declared the winners.

The players were opposed to each other in the following order:—

RINK NO. 1.

Scarboro'.	*Toronto*.
Mr. J. Findlay	Mr. R. Creighton,
T. Brown,	Spreull,
Glendinning,	Ross,
Wilson,	Leys,
J. Brown,	J. Dick,
Fleming,	Morrison,
Ab'm Torrance,	Denholm,
Capt. Torrance, *Skip*.	Becket, *Skip*.
31 shotts.	15 shotts.

Scarboro' winning on this rink by 16 shotts.

RINK NO. 2.

Scarboro'.	*Toronto*.
Mr. Purdy,	Mr. Creighton, Sen.
W. Findlay,	M'Clure,
Stabe,	M'Donnell,
M'Cowan,	Brent,
Muir,	Capt. Dick.
Gibson,	Mr. Struthers,
Clarke,	Murehieson,
Scott, *Skip*.	Rowan, *Skip*.

Toronto winning on this rink by 13 shotts.

Scarboro' winning on the two rinks collectively by three shots.

The above being the state of the game at half-past four, the victory was claimed by Scarboro'.

That the future Curlers of the rival localities may know how their fathers play in the year 1839, we will also record the number and result of the various Heads, viz:—

RINK NO. 1.

	Heads.	*Single.*	*Double.*	*Triple.*	*Quad.*	*Quin.*	*Total.*
Scarboro' gained	13	5	2	4	0	2	31
Toronto gained	11	7	4	0	0	0	15
Total	24	12	6	4	0	2	46

RINK NO. 2.

Scarboro' gained	7	2	2	2	0	1	17
Toronto gained	21	16	2	2	1	0	30
Total	28	18	4	4	1	1	47

From this statement it will be seen that Toronto gained 32 heads and Scarboro' only 20; and the fact of Scarboro' winning the match notwithstanding, ought to prevail with the Toronto players of Rink No. 1, to use greater caution in their future practice, and to attend more to drawing and guarding than to riding. It may, however, be only justice to them to say, that the playing of the Scarboro' Curlers, on this Rink, was most admirable, both as regards the direction of the Skip and the delivery of the players. They all appeared to be the descendants of those Curlers mentioned in history, who could "throw their stones in within an hair's breadth." Mr. Findlay, the Scarboro' player, who led on this Rink, reminded the spectators of the Discobolus of Myron, or rather of Hercules himself. When he got his foot on the hack and prepared to throw, he was worthy of being studied by Duscrow for his "tableaux vivants."—He hurled along, generally to some spot within the "brough," and straight before the 'tee,' a vast fragment of a mountain, hewn into the shape of a Curling-stone, which has for years been the dread of the Toronto players, and known to them by the designation of "London Hill," and on which the light weights of the Toronto stones could hardly make an impression. The precise play of Capt. Torrance, and of Mr. Abraham Torrance, the seventh player, also powerfully influenced the game. On the side of Toronto Mr. Angus Morrison called forth universal admiration, as well from his correct delivery as from his being with one exception the youngest player on the Rink.

From the match being played near the shore, crowds of spectators were attracted, to most of whom the game was new. On the ice, between the two rinks, a pole was raised, on which the British ensign was hoisted. A third rink was also prepared, and stones and brooms furnished by the Toronto Club, for the accomedation of strangers and others who understood the game, but could not participate in the contest.

At the conclusion of the game, the victors and the vanquished partook a slight refreshment under the flag, in the course of which Mr. Becket, the Secretary of the Club, (in the absence of the President,) took occasion to thank the Scarboro' players for their ready acceptance of their invitation to play with the Toronto Club, thus affording the Curlers of Toronto an opportunity of measuring their strength with such respectable antagonists,—he trusted that they would yet have many similar contests, conducted in the same friendly manner; and although he wished that next winter the odds might be in favor of Toronto, he would now propose the health of the Scarboro' Curlers.

Capt. Torrance, on behalf of the Scarboro' Curlers, said, that they duly appreciated an opportunity of playing with the Toronto Club, as they always would do, whether on the winning or on the losing side,—that they had come to play because they expected, as they had reason to expect, and as they had found—*good playing*—and not for any gambling purpose—*for Curlers never bet or gamble*; and although he was on the winning side on this occasion, and would confess that he always liked to be on the winning side, yet he thought from the playing he had seen to-day we might meet again....

He concluded by proposing "health and prosperity to the Curlers of Toronto," which was drunk by the Scarboro' Curlers with the usual honours; and after three cheers for the Newmarket Curlers being given, the parties left the ice.

SKATING

Skating was enjoyed by many North Americans during the second quarter of the nineteenth century. In the United States large skating followings developed in Philadelphia and New York, partly owing to the easy access to rivers provided by their locations. In New York the lasting influence of Dutch culture also contributed to the popularity and the evolution of the sport. During the 1830s improvements in skating equipment and techniques paved the way for the enormous growth that the sport experienced in the 1850s. The following document, reprinted from the February 1833 edition of the American Turf Register and Sporting Magazine, discusses the origins, practice and development of the sport in America.

SKATING

This is both a manly and innocent amusement; it recommends itself in such a variety of pleasing shapes as to be diligently pursued by the young, and much talked of by the old; its reminiscences are of a character every way agreeable to the mind, and gratifying to the heart, and it may well be ranked among the noblest of pastimes.

The art of skating is of comparatively modern introducion. It can only be traced to Holland, and seems to have been entirely unknown to the ancients. Some traces of the exercise in England are to be found in the thirteenth century, at which period, according to Fitz-Steven, it was customary, in the winter when the ice would bear them, for the citizens of London to fasten the leg bones of animals under the soles of their feet, and then by poles push themselves along upon the ice. The wooden skates, shod with iron or steel, were brought into England from the low countries. With the Hollanders, skating is more a matter of business than pleasure; for it is said that the produce of their farms is carried upon the heads of their men and women, to the towns and cities upon the borders of the canals, there to be sold, and articles of convenience and luxury purchased, and taken back in like manner to the country. Less attention is therefore paid by them to graceful and elegant movements, than to the acquirement of that speed which is necessary to what is termed journey skating, as long and rapid excursions are frequently made upon the ice, when the streams, natural and artificial, by which their country is intersected, are frozen over.

Great improvement in the style of skating has taken place within a few years past, and various figures practised, to which the earliest skaters were strangers. The forward and backward movements, commonly, but, as it is thought, improperly, called High Dutch, show more ease and grace than any others within the range of the skates. They require very little exertion, and, if rightly performed, carry the skater over the ice with amazing rapidity. In the former, the lower limbs should not be permitted to stride much; the swinging foot should always be brought down nearly parallel with the other, when about to receive the weight of the body, and at the same time the body should incline to that side a little to the front, making an angle of about seventy degrees. In this position, the foot having hold of the ice will aid the inclination of the body in making a bold an lengthy curve, as also, a handsome sweeping motion. In the latter, or backward High Dutch, the swinging limb must always act as a balance to the body, and by it a perfect command of the necessary motions acquired; the limb should move in a line with the body kept nearly straight; and the toes pointed downward. In all forward, circular, and sweeping movements, the body should be kept as erect as possible, and stooping of the neck, head and shoulders, avoided. The skater should never look at his feet, and seldom throw out his arms.

In graceful skating, very little muscular exertion is required. The impelling motion should proceed from the mechanical impulse of the body, thrown into such a position as to regulate the stroke. Chasing, running, and jumping, tend to give an imperfect idea of the art, and produce habits that are excessively difficult to break. Both feet should be used alike—when a movement is performed by the one, it should be tried by the other. Too much skating on the inside of the skate prevents the acquirement of the more beautiful part of the art, resulting from the frequent and alternate use of the outer edge of each iron. Skating on the outer edge, being the most graceful action, is the most difficult to perform, and requires much practice and great skill. The beautiful attitudes in which the body may be placed where the skater has a perfect command of his balance, will amply repay him for any care he may have bestowed on the acquirement of this most fascinating part of the exercising. It is scarcely possible, however, to reduce the art to any thing like a system. The best way to acquire a knowledge of it, is to begin when young, and select some good skater as a pattern.

Although it is asserted, by some modern writers, that the metropolis of Scotland has produced more instances of elegant skaters than any other city whatever, the opinion seems to be, that Philadelphia, in this particular, stands unrivalled. The frequent facilities offered by the freezing of her noble rivers, must be borne in mind. There is scarcely a winter in which skating is not practised by a large portion of her population for weeks together, and the climate is of so fluctuating a character, as to prevent any very long interruption of the amusement during the cold season. Many gentlemen, well known to the community, have displayed considerable skill and uncommon grace in the art, and caused this interesting pastime to be generally noticed. It is recommended by its excellent effects upon the body and mind; and perhaps, of all the amusements resorted to, is productive of the least inconvenience, and may be enjoyed at trifling risk. Accidents upon the ice are rare; they are generally the result of great carelessness, and in skating are not more to be dreaded than those met with in the common amusements of youth.

An entire abandonment of the old fashioned skates, commonly known by the name of gutters, dumps, rockers, &c. is strongly recommended. A proper skate iron is in shape very much like the runner of a sleigh, the curvature in it being very slight. The American skates, after an improved plan, are now manufactured by Mr. Thomas W. Newton, No. 60 Dock street, and will in the course of time come into general use, and entirely supersede the foreign article. They are formed altogether of iron, the foot piece being a thin plate of that metal, and the runner fastened to it, by having several projecting points passed through holes drilled in the foot piece, and rivetted, forming a strong and immovable union—a point in which the common kind is very deficient.

The principal advantages consist in the breadth of the foot plate, and the foot being brought *much nearer the ice*. The plate being made right and left, gives the entire breadth of the sole of the boot. It is also a little hollowed and turned upwards in front, fitting the shape of the sole exactly, and so pleasantly that a slight strapping suffices to hold it firm. Instead of being strapped from toes to heel, as in the common way, the strap forms a bracing across the foot, with four attachments on each side. The pressure is thus so equalized as to make it very comfortable. Upon taking off these skates, after hours of use, no cramping of the foot is felt. The great advantage in having so many bearings of the straps is, that the pressure of the large and continually moving tendons of the instep is avoided.

The runners are brought up in front till they turn over and touch the top of the foot, and being rounded on the edges and highly burnished, the appearance is light and handsome. This form is not given merely to please the eye; for, if every skater used this shape, those accidents which sometimes happen, by two persons hooking the points of their skates together, would never occur. The best improvement, lately discovered, consists in making the runner the entire length of the foot, letting it come back to the extremity of the heel.

That great desideratum, the firm fixture of the skate to the heel, has, by a very simple plan, been perfected in the new kind. It is a small catch at the extreme end of the heel, which is with great facility attached to a screw head that is fixed and remains in the boot heel.

The iron soled skate is not a new invention; it was used in the family of the late Mr. Peale more than thirty years back.

In the compilation of this article, we are indebted to one or two friends, adepts in the art of skating, for their ideas upon the subject, and have also derived some assistance from a piece under that head, to be found in Nicholson's Encyclopedia. Should what we have written tend to bring this delightful pastime into general practice in the winter season, we shall be more than repaid for any little trouble its preparation may have occasioned.   P.

SELECTED BIBLIOGRAPHY

PRIMARY SOURCES

NEWSPAPERS AND MAGAZINES
The American Farmer, 1820-1829.

American Turf Register and Sporting Magazine, 1829-1840.

The New York Herald, 1835-1840.

The New York Mirror, 1837-1840.

The New York Post, 1820-1840.

The New York Spectator, 1821-1829.

The Spirit of the Times, 1831-33, 1835-40.

BOOKS AND PAMPHLETS
HEALTH, EXERCISE AND PHYSICAL EDUCATION
William Alcott, *The Young Man's Guide* (1836).

Dr. Charles Caldwell, *Thoughts on Physical Education. Being a Discourse Delivered to a Convention of Teachers in Lexington, Kentucky on the Sixth and Seventh of November, 1833* (1834).

Lydia Maria Child, *The Girl's Own Book of Amusements* (1833).

Joseph G. Cogswell and George Bancroft, *Prospectus of a School to be Established at Round Hill, Northampton, Massachusetts* (1823).

Margaret Coxe, *Young Ladies Companion* (1839).

Dr. Philip Lindsley, *The Cause of Education in Tennessee* (1833).

Horace Mann, *Common School Journal for the Year 1839* (1839).

Almira Phelps, *The Female Student, or Lectures to Young Ladies on Female Education* (1836).

William Channing Woodbridge, ed., *American Annals of Education and Instruction.*

BOXING
American Fistiana, Containing All the Fights in the United States from 1816 to 1860 (1860).

The Diary of Philip Hone, 1828-1851, 2 vols. (1970).

EQUESTRIAN
Cadwallader R. Colden, *An Exposé of the Measures Which Caused a Suspension of the Races on the Union Course in October, 1830* (1831).

The South Carolina Jockey Club (1836).

FIELD SPORTS
American Shooters Manual (1830).

The Archer's Manual. or The Art of Shooting With the Long Bow, as Practiced by The United Bowmen of Philadelphia (1830).

Memoirs of the Gloucester Fox Hunting Club (1830).

GYMNASTICS
William Fuller, *The Elements of Gymnastics* (1830).

Charles Beck, *Treatise on Gymnastics Taken Chiefly from the German of F.L. Jahn* (1828).

SPORTS JOURNALISM AND WRITING
Robin Carver, *The Book of Sport* (1834).

Augustus B. Longstreet, *Georgia Scenes* (1831).

Horace Smith, *Festivals, Games and Amusements* (1831).

SECONDARY SOURCES

HISTORIOGRAPHY
Melvin L. Adelman, "Academicians and Athletics. Historians' Views of American Sport," *Maryland Historian*, 4 (Fall 1973); 123-142, and by the same author, "Academicians and American Athletics. A Decade of Progress," *Journal of Sport History* 10 (Spring 1983), 80-106.

D.L. LeMahieu, "The History of British and American Sport. A Review Article," *Comparative Studies in Society and History*, 32 (October 1990), 838-844.

Robert M. Lewis, "American Sport History. A Bibliographical Guide," *American Studies International*, 29 (April 1991), 35-59.

Roberta J. Park, "Research and Scholarship in the History of Physical Education and Sport. The Current State of Affairs," *Research Quarterly for Exercise and Sport*, 54 (1983), 93-103.

Steven A. Reiss, "The Historiography of American Sport," *Magazine of History*, 7 (Summer, 1992), 10-14.

Nancy Struna, "In Glorious Disarray. The Literature of Sport History," *Research Quarterly for Exercise and Sport*, 56 (1985), 151-160.

GENERAL WORKS
Melvin L. Adelman, *A Sporting Time. New York City and the Rise of Modern Athletics, 1820-1870* (Urbana, Illinois, 1986).

John A. Blanchard, '91, *The H Book of Harvard Athletics, 1852-1922* (Cambridge, Mass., 1923).

Soeren Stewart Brynn, "Some Sports in Pittsburgh During the National Period, 1775-1860," *Western Pennsylvania Historical Magazine,* 51 (1968), 345-363; 52 (1969), 57-79.

Gorton Carruth and Eugene Ehrlich, *Facts and Dates of American Sports from Colonial Days to the Present* (New York, 1988).

John Dizikes, *Sportsmen and Gamesmen* (Boston, 1981).

Foster Rhea Dulles, *A History of Recreation. America Learns to Play,* rev. ed. (New York, 1965).

Allen Guttmann, *From Ritual to Record. The Nature of Modern Sports* (New York, 1978).

Stephen Hardy, "The City and the Rise of American Sport, 1820-1920," *Exercise and Sport Science Review,* 9 (1981), 183-219.

Robert Henderson, *Ball, Bat and Bishop* (New York, 1947), and by the same author, *Early American Sport. A Chronological Checklist of Books Published Prior to 1860 Based on an Exhibition Held at the Grolier Club* (New York, 1937).

Jennie Holliman, *American Sports, 1785-1835* (Durham, N.C., 1931).

Nancy Howell and Maxwell Howell, *Sports and Games in Canadian Life. 1700 to the Present* (Toronto, 1969).

George B. Kirsch, "New Jersey and the Rise of Modern Sports, 1820-1870," *Journal of Regional Cultures,* 4 and 5 (1984-1985), 41-57.

John A. Krout, *Annals of American Sport* (New Haven, Conn., 1929).

Peter Levine, "The Promise of Sport in Antebellum America," *Journal of American Culture,* 2 (Winter 1980), 623-634.

Peter Lindsay, "A History of Sport in Canada, 1807-1867," (Unpublished Ph.D. dissertation, University of Alberta, 1969).

John A. Lucas and Ronald A. Smith, *Saga of American Sport* (Philadelphia, 1978).

Herbert Manchester, *Four Centuries of American Sport, 1490-1890* (New York, 1931).

Alan Metcalfe, *Canada Learns to Play. The Emergence of Organized Sport, 1807-1914* (Toronto, 1987).

Frederick L. Paxson, "The Rise of Sport," *Mississippi Valley Historical Review,* 4 (1917), 143-168.

Benjamin G. Rader, *American Sports,* second edition (Englewood Cliffs, N.J., 1990), and by the same author, "The Quest for Subcommunities and the Rise of American Sport," *American Quarterly,* 29 (Fall 1977), 355-369.

Gerald Redmond, *The Sporting Scots of Nineteenth Century Canada* (Rutherford, N.J., 1982), and by the same author, *The Caledonian Games in Nineteenth Century America* (Cranbury, N.J., 1971).

Henry Roxborough, *One Hundred—Not Out—The Story of Nineteenth Century Canadian Sport* (Toronto, 1966).

Dale A. Somers, *The Rise of Sports in New Orleans, 1850-1900* (Baton Rouge, La., 1972), and by the same author, "The Leisure Revolution. Recreation in the American City, 1820-1920," *Journal of Popular Culture,* 5 (Summer 1971), 125-147.

David K. Wiggins, "The Play of Children in the Plantation Communities of the Old South," *Journal of Sport History,* 7 (Summer 1978), 21-39.

ANIMAL SPORTS
Gerald Carson, *Men, Beast and Gods. A History of Cruelty and Kindness to Animals* (New York, 1972).

AQUATICS
E. Merton Coulter, "Boating as a Sport in the Old South," *Georgia Historical Society,* 27 (1943), 231-247.

Robert F. Kelley, *American Rowing. Its Background and Traditions* (New York, 1932).

Douglas Phillips-Birt, *The History of Yachting* (New York, 1974).

BOXING
Nat Fleischer, *Heavyweight Championship. An Informal History of Heavyweight Boxing from 1719 to the Present Day* (New York, 1961).

Elliot J. Gorn, *The Manly Art. Bare-Knuckle Prize Fighting in America* (Ithaca, N.Y., 1986), and by the same author, "'Gouge and Bite, Pull Hair and Scratch,' The Social Significance of Fighting in the Southern Backcountry," *American Historical Review,* 90 (1985), 18-43.

BALL SPORTS AND GAMES
Louise Belden, "Billiards in America Before 1830," *Antiques,* 87 (January 1965), 99-101.

Warren Goldstein, *Playing for Keeps. A History of Early Baseball* (Ithaca, N.Y., 1989).

Robert H. Henderson, "How Baseball Began," *New York Public Library Bulletin,* 41 (April 1937), 287-291, and by the same author, "Baseball and Rounders," *New York Public Library Bulletin,* 43 (April 1939), 303-314.

George B. Kirsch, *The Creation of American Team Sports. Baseball and Cricket, 1838-72* (Urbana, Illinois, 1989).

Harold Seymour, *Baseball. The Early Years* (New York, 1960), and by the same author, "How Baseball Began," *New-York Historical Society Quarterly,* 40 (October 1956), 369-385.

David Quentin Voigt, *American Baseball. From Gentleman's Sport to the Commissioner System* (Norman, Okla., 1966).

EQUESTRIANISM

Dwight Akers, *Drivers Up. The Story of American Harness Racing* (New York, 1938).

Elizabeth Eliot, *Portrait of a Sport. The Study of Steeplechasing in Great Britain and the United States* (Woodstock, Vt., 1957).

John Hervey, *Racing in America, 1666-1866,* 2 vols. (New York, 1944), and by the same author, *The American Trotter* (New York, 1947).

William H.P. Robertson, *The History of Thoroughbred Racing in America* (Englewood Cliffs, N.J., 1964).

Randy J. Sparks, "Gentleman's Sport. Horse Racing in Antebellum Charleston," *South Carolina History Magazine,* 93 (January 1992), 15-30.

Nancy Struna, "The North-South Races. American Thoroughbred Racing in Transition, 1823-1850," *Journal of Sport History,* 8 (Summer 1981), 28-57.

John H. Wallace, *The Horse of America, in His Derivation, History and Development* (New York, 1897).

Peter G. Welsh, *Track and Road. The American Trotting Horse. A Visual Record 1820 to 1900 from Harry T. Peters "American on Stone" Lithography Collection* (Washington, D.C., 1967).

Hiram Woodruff, *The Trotting Horse of America* (New York, 1868).

FIELD SPORTS

Robert Davidson, *History of the United Bowmen of Philadelphia* (Philadelphia, 1888).

J. Brian Van Urk, *The Story of American Foxhunting. From Challenge to Full American Cry,* 2 vol. (New York, 1940-1941).

GYMNASTICS

Erich Geldbach, "The Beginnings of German Gymnastics in America," *Journal of Sport History,* 3 (Winter 1976), 237-272.

Henry Metzner, *A Brief History of the American Turnerbund,* rev. ed. (Pittsburgh, 1924).

HEALTH, EXERCISE AND PHYSICAL EDUCATION

Jack W. Berryman, "The Tradition of the 'Six Things Non-Natural'. Exercise and Medicine from Hippocrates through Ante-Bellum America," *Exercise and Sports Sciences Reviews,* 17 (1989), 515-559.

John R. Betts, "American Medical Thought on Exercise as the Road to Health, 1820-1860," *Bulletin of the History of Medicine,* 45 (1971), 138-145, and by the same author, "Mind and Body in Early American Thought," *Journal of American History,* 54 (March 1968), 787-805.

Frances B. Cogan, *All-American Girl. The Ideal of Real Womanhood in Mid Nineteenth-Century America* (Athens, Ga., 1989).

Kathryn Grover, ed., *Fitness in American Culture. Images of Health, Sport, and the Body, 1830-1940* (Amherst, Mass., 1989).

John A. Lucas, "Thomas Wentworth Higginson. Early Apostle of Health and Fitness," *Journal of Health, Physical Education and Recreation*, 42 (February 1971), 30-33.

Roberta Park, "The Attitudes of Leading New England Transcendentalists towards Healthful Exercise, Active Recreations and Proper Care of the Body. 1830-1860," *Journal of Sport History*, 4 (Spring 1977), 34-50, and by the same author, "'Embodied Selves', The Rise and Development of Concern for Physical Education, Active Games and Recreation among American Women, 1776-1865," *Journal of Sport History*, 5 (Summer 1978), 5-41.

James C. Whorton, *Crusaders for Fitness. The History of American Health Reformers* (Princeton, N.J., 1982).

SPORTS JOURNALISM AND WRITING

John R. Betts, "Sporting Journalism in Nineteenth-Century America," *American Quarterly*, 5 (1953), 39-64.

Jack W. Berryman, "The Tenuous Attempts of Americans to Catch Up with *John Bull*. Specialty Magazines and Sporting Journalism, 1800-1835," *Canadian Journal of the History of Sport and Physical Education*, 10 (May 1979), 40-61.

Luke White, *Henry William Herbert and the American Publishing Scene, 1831-1858* (Newark, N.J., 1943).

Philip G. Terrie, "Urban Man Confronts the Wilderness. The Nineteenth-Century Sportsman in the Adirondacks," *Journal of Sport History*, 5 (Winter 1978), 7-20.

Norris W. Yates, *William T. Porter and the Spirit of the Times. A Study of the Big Bear School of Humor* (Baton Rouge, La., 1957).

TRACK AND FIELD

John Cumming, *Runners and Walkers. A Nineteenth Century Sports Chronicle* (Chicago, 1981).

George Moss, "The Long Distance Runners in Ante-Bellum America," *Journal of Popular Culture*, 8 (1974), 370-382.

WINTER SPORTS

Sylvie Dufresne, "The Winter Carnival of Montreal, 1803-1889," *Urban History Review*, 11 (February 1983), 25-45.

INDEXES

INDEX OF NAMES

INDEX OF SUBJECTS

INDEX OF INSTITUTIONS

INDEX OF GEOGRAPHIC AND PLACE NAMES

FROM ACADEMIC INTERNATIONAL PRESS*